Advance Praise for *Standing Strong*

"A stirring story of how Grove City College refused to succumb to the spirit of the age and stood firm aided in large measure under God by men of convinced Christian conviction like Charles McKenzie and Paul McNulty."

Alistair Begg, Truth for Life Radio Ministry

"Grove City College stands as a beacon of truth and integrity in the troubled world of higher education. Throughout its 150-year history, the college has offered students a Christ-centered, academically excellent, conservative, and remarkably affordable education that has prepared generations of young people to live with godly purpose and wisdom. An exemplary professor and meticulous historian, Gary Scott Smith has produced a comprehensive and compelling story of an extraordinary institution. Read *Standing Strong* and you will be encouraged about what a college can achieve when it embraces faith, freedom, and excellence, all for the glory of God."

Vice President Mike Pence

"Within these pages lies the story of Grove City College, a remarkable institution that I have visited often and has championed the ideals of faith and freedom for 150 years. Founded in 1876 in my home state, the Commonwealth of Pennsylvania, Grove City College has built its educational mission on two foundational principles: faith in the divine origin of individual natural rights and freedom as envisioned by our nation's founders in the Declaration of Independence and Constitution. For a century and a half, Grove City College has prepared its students not merely to earn degrees, but to emerge as truly educated citizens."

United States Senator David McCormick

"Gary Scott Smith unveils the remarkable 150-year journey of a college that dared to defy secular tides. With vivid storytelling, Smith chronicles how Grove City's Christ-centered mission, bold 1984 Supreme Court stand, and commitment to affordable education have shaped principled leaders. From triumphs over global crises to its unwavering embrace of biblical values and American ideals, this book celebrates a unique institution helping to forge a just, compassionate world."

United States Senator Jim DeMint

STANDING STRONG:

Grove City College's 150-Year Journey in Faith, Freedom, and the Pursuit of Excellence

BY GARY SCOTT SMITH

A POST HILL PRESS BOOK
ISBN: 979-8-89565-486-6
ISBN (eBook): 979-8-89565-487-3

Standing Strong:
Grove City College's 150-Year Journey in Faith, Freedom, and the Pursuit of Excellence

Cover design by Cody Corcoran

Post Hill Press
New York • Nashville
posthillpress.com

Published in the United States of America
1 2 3 4 5 6 7 8 9 10

To David Rathburn '79,
president of the board of trustees, 2003-2020,
Visionary Leader and Generous Benefactor

CONTENTS

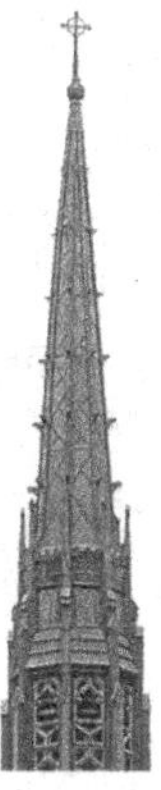

Preface

Let's begin with the elephant in the room. Should Grove City College be celebrating its 150th anniversary in 2026? Grove City officially became a college in 1884, eight years after Isaac Ketler established an academy in the town of Pine Grove, which was renamed Grove City in 1883. The academy's mission was primarily to prepare students for college. However, the academy did offer some college-level courses from its inception, and April 11, 1876, has long been regarded as the starting date for Grove City College. Hundreds of other colleges with similar beginnings use the date when they first offered instruction as their founding year. Thus, it is appropriate to celebrate the 150th anniversary of the founding of Grove City College in 2026.[1]

Some disclaimers and explanations are also necessary. Despite the length of this history, I had to be quite selective in what I included. Distilling 150 years of the college's history, involving forty-three thousand students/alumni and several thousand trustees, administrators, faculty, and staff is very challenging. Many important aspects of Grove City's history had to be omitted. This history highlights key people and the college's mission, policies, strategic plans, capital campaigns, academic life, and extracurricular activities. It seeks to provide a flavor of campus life by discussing many organizations, events, and activities. Athletics, drama, debate, music and the arts, and Greek life are all featured.

Student achievements that occurred in competitions with peers at other institutions in sports and debate are accentuated, as are academic, journalistic, and musical attainments. Impressive accomplishments by faculty, alumni, and trustees are also discussed. In addition, substantive changes in administrative policies, curricula, and rules and regulations as well as turning points and significant controversies, challenges, and shifts in student culture are detailed. To add flavor, profiles of key administrators, faculty, and students/alumni, sometimes based on interviews, are included. Hopefully, this history will help alumni readers relive their college years.

I reviewed all *Collegians* issued in Grove City's history, all presidents' reports to the trustees, and all the trustee minutes. I skimmed many *Ouijas*, *Bridges*, college catalogs, *GēDUNK* magazines, and other alumni publications. Two student assistants helped with this process—Anna Agresti, '24, and Gabriela Gimenez, '25. I benefited from reading three earlier histories of Grove City College—Marietta Dietrich's "The History of Grove City College," an MA thesis at the University of Pittsburgh (1933), David Dayton's *'Mid the Pines* (1971), and Lee Edwards's *Freedom's College* (2001), as well as from the memoirs of Fred Kring and Hans Sennholz. Several interviews conducted with Charles MacKenzie shed light on his presidency and pivotal developments in the 1970s and 1980s. Numerous interviews college archivist Hilary Walczak conducted provide helpful information. My biggest debt by far is to Hilary, who helped identify, find, and scan numerous sources and verify many facts. I interviewed the following individuals: Lee Kessler, Bradley Scott, Jeff Claypool, Brian Leftow, John Sparks, James Bibza, John Moore, Richard Jewell, and Paul McNulty. I thank Paul Kemeny, Gillis Harp, James Evans, Neil Smith, Mary Sue Smith, Richard Jewell, Paul McNulty, and Brad Lingo for providing feedback on my manuscript. Theater director James Dixon provided an assessment of his favorite shows and the college's best actors during his tenure. Debate team coaches Jason Edwards, Andrew Harvey, and Michael Coulter supplied an evaluation of the college's greatest debaters. Music professors Ed Arnold, Doug Browne, Richard Konzen, Joseph Pisano, and Jeff Tedford furnished an appraisal of Grove City's most gifted musicians. Because these lists go back to only 1976 in theater, 1978 in music, and 2008 in debate, I used *Collegians* and college yearbooks to identify exceptional actors, debaters, and musicians from earlier eras. Although intramural sports have been very popular throughout the college's history, and some basketball contests drew hundreds of spectators, I rarely cover them. Swimmers, divers, track and cross-country runners, and field performers set college, pool records, and track records at such a rapid pace that most cannot be mentioned.

I am very grateful to Aleigha Koss, my editor at Post Hill Press, who shepherded this project in a winsome, timely, and effective manner. I also want to thank Kate Post for her skillful, meticulous copy editing and thorough fact-checking that prevented numerous errors.

I spent parts of seven decades associated with Grove City College as a student and professor, and more than thirty members of my family have graduated from the college. During my thirty-nine years on the faculty, I had the privilege of teaching about twelve thousand students and leading six travel interims to Europe, Israel, and China. I began watching college football games in junior high school with my father, a 1942 graduate. My wife is a great-great-granddaughter of Isaac Ketler's wife. Consequently, I am a consummate insider, and I echo Isaac Ketler final words spoken to dean Alva Calderwood: This work has been "a labor of love." Nevertheless, as a professionally trained historian who has spent almost fifty years practicing my craft, I have tried to produce an "objective," accurate history of Grove City College.

Vision and Values

In 1876, twenty-two-year-old schoolteacher Isaac Ketler dreamed of creating an institution to educate and prepare youth for Christian service in the small community of Pine Grove, Pennsylvania. By his death in 1913, Ketler had established and for thirty-seven years shepherded a college that stands out in the annals of American higher education for its diligent efforts to base all its activities on a biblical worldview, pursuit of academic excellence, and focus on free-market economics, Christian formation, and preparing students to be winsome ambassadors of Jesus Christ in all areas of life. Shortly after Ketler died, Oxford University professor Sir William Ramsay asserted that "no other person was so crazy as to imagine that a College" could be created "in the small village where he settled, uninvited and without encouragement."[2] Possessing few material resources, Ketler, by dogged determinism, personal charisma, and trust in God, founded a college that has educated and equipped more than forty thousand men and women to preach, teach, heal, create and operate businesses, care for the least of these, raise children, and serve their families, churches, and communities throughout the world.

Led by Isaac Ketler's son, Weir, who served as president from 1916 to 1956, and Sun Oil executive J. Howard Pew, the president of the board of trustees from 1931 to 1971, the college remained faithful to the founder's vision through two world wars, a global economic collapse, and a public health crisis. The forces of modernism and secularism assaulted and significantly altered traditional cultural values and institutions in the 1960s and pressured Grove City to abandon its historic Christian commitment and distinctive mission. Under the leadership of Charles MacKenzie, president from 1971 to 1991, and Albert Hopeman, board president from 1971 to 1998, the college rekindled and fortified its commitment to faith and freedom, as its administrators and faculty worked unremittingly to integrate faith and learning. Under presidents John Moore (1996–2003) and Richard Jewell (2003–2014), the college strove to enhance its academic program, upgrade its facilities, and strengthen its finances. Paul McNulty, president from 2014 to 2025, spearheaded a campaign to reaffirm Grove City College's Christian identity and commitment to promoting the traditional, conservative values undergirding a free society.

Several foundational principles have guided Grove City College throughout its history. First and foremost has been its commitment to teach and model basic Christian tenets and values and to provide a biblically based perspective of all areas of life. As this history illustrates, this aim has been fulfilled better in some eras than others. Second, the college's holistic approach to education has emphasized students' intellectual, spiritual, social, emotional, and physical development. Third, Grove City has advocated fundamental American principles, especially liberty, democracy, free enterprise, limited government, and the advancement of science. Fourth, the college has encouraged inquisitiveness, critical thinking, and the pursuit of truth. Fifth, Grove City has sought to prepare students not just to do a job but to undertake a God-given calling. Sixth, the college has promoted responsible citizenship and lifelong service to the community, church, nation, and world. Seventh, inspired by their quest to advance the kingdom of God on earth, Grove City constituencies have worked to create a more compassionate, just, and prosperous global order. Eighth, the college has sought to provide an affordable education for families of modest means. Finally, Grove City has provided first-rate facilities located in a beautiful, bucolic setting to help administrators, faculty, staff, and students pursue their common goals and develop a caring community. For roughly the first half of Grove City's history, many of the college's values were mainstream American ones, but since the 1960s, they have become countercultural.

For 150 years, the institution's trustees, administrators, faculty, students, staff, and friends have pursued excellence. Those who have led, taught and studied at, and graduated from Grove City College have much with which to be pleased. As this account highlights, the achievements of Grove City's various constituencies are impressive. For most of its history, Grove City has faithfully fulfilled its founding mission of furnishing a Christian-centered education and graduating men and women of sterling character and strong conviction who strive to serve God and other people. Like every other institution in a fallen world, Grove City has had its foibles, flaws, and failures. In some ways, the college capitulated to societal pressures and trends and sometimes drifted from its historic commitments. Overall, though, for fifteen decades, Grove City has been one of the nation's leading Christian, politically conservative colleges. Throughout its history, the college has confronted and overcome many significant challenges—two world wars, a major economic depression, the pressures of anti-Christian philosophies and secularization, a battle with the federal government, the declining number of college-age students in the Northeast, a global pandemic, and a controversy over critical race theory—to remain a vibrant, highly respected, Christ-centered institution of higher education.

This is a story of triumph and tragedy, hope and heartache, action and apathy, and laughter and lament. But most of all, it is a tale of trustees, administrators, faculty, students, and alumni who demonstrated and fostered Christian commitment, Christlikeness, character, and compassion. Its leaders from presidents Isaac Ketler to Paul McNulty and from board of trustee presidents Frederick Raymond Babcock to Ed Breen all attributed the college's success to God's blessing as they and thousands of other administrators, trustees, and faculty strove to provide an exceptional education at the lowest possible cost in a picturesque environment. With one voice, they would declare: "To God be the glory."

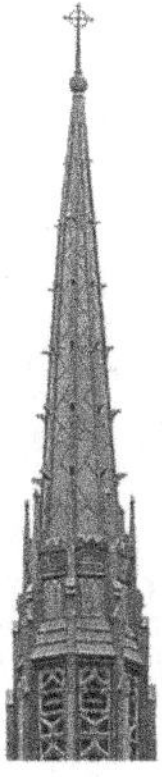

A School Amid the Pines:

Isaac Ketler Fulfills His Dream,

1876–1913

Pine Grove Normal Academy, 1876–1884

In 1876, the United States celebrated its centennial with a magnificent exposition in Philadelphia. That year, more than a quarter of Americans journeyed to the city to visit this showcase of American achievements, which featured an astonishing display of inventions including Alexander Graham Bell's telephone, Thomas Edison's mimeograph machine, and the Corliss steam engine. Meanwhile, the United States was dramatically changing. Millions of immigrants, primarily from southern Europe, were arriving, and cities were growing rapidly. Aided by the completion of the transcontinental railroad, countless Americans were moving to the West.

The centennial year was momentous for other reasons. After a heated dispute, Republican Rutherford B. Hayes was declared to have won the 1876 presidential election over Democrat Samuel Tilden. The "bargain" that made Hayes president effectively ended Reconstruction, an eleven-year campaign to reintegrate Southern states into the Union and to incorporate former slaves into the nation's political, economic, and social life. At the Battle of the

Little Bighorn in Montana territory, about five thousand Lakota, Cheyenne, and Arapaho, led by Sitting Bull and Crazy Horse, killed all three hundred men of Lieutenant Colonel George Armstrong Custer's US 7th Cavalry Regiment. The predecessor to Major League Baseball was formed. Librarian Melvil Dewey invented the Dewey Decimal Classification system. Mark Twain published *The Adventures of Tom Sawyer*.

Education, especially the expansion of high schools and colleges, played a very important role in the United States' progress during the Gilded Age. Prior to the Civil War, more than five hundred colleges were founded, almost all of them by religious groups. After the war, many new state universities were created, including Texas A&M, which opened in 1876. That same year, Johns Hopkins was established in Baltimore as the nation's first graduate university, modeled on European institutions that focused on research. The social sciences emerged as academic disciplines, and the college curriculum expanded. College enrollment would increase substantially during the last quarter of the nineteenth century. Meanwhile, in the rolling hills of western Pennsylvania, an academy was founded in Pine Grove that soon became Grove City College.[1]

In 1798, Valentine and Margaret Glenn Cunningham built a grist mill and a sawmill beside Wolf Creek. Two years later, Mercer County, populated primarily by Scots-Irish Presbyterians, was established. The village the Cunninghams established was incorporated as Pine Grove in 1844. Its principal business in 1876 was the McKay Carriage Works, but coal mining was the region's major industry. Trains running from Pittsburgh to Erie stopped daily in Pine Grove.

Academies began in the eastern United States in the 1750s. Serving as the nation's principal secondary schools, they offered courses in English, arithmetic, logic, geography, history, and bookkeeping to prepare students for the business world and college. Between 1802 and 1870, Presbyterians established fourteen academies in western Pennsylvania and Ohio, several of which evolved into colleges, as well as Western Theological Seminary in Allegheny (adjacent to Pittsburgh) in 1825.[2] Free common schools began in the region in the 1830s, and public high schools soon started, which competed for students with tuition-based academies.

In 1858, a privately-supported school opened in Pine Grove to train pupils for colleges and businesses. In 1876, the school hired Isaac Ketler as its principal. Ketler was born in Northumberland County, Pennsylvania, in 1853 and grew up in a family with twelve children. His family moved to Blacktown, near Pine Grove, and he attended Blacktown's elementary school, where his teachers included Joseph Newton Pew. Ketler left home at age sixteen to work in lumber camps and brickyards in central Pennsylvania to earn enough money to attend college. After two years at Edinboro Normal School, he received a teaching degree in 1875. Ketler taught briefly at Blacktown and nearby Crawford's Corner and then studied Greek and Latin at National University in Lebanon, Ohio.

Because he believed that the school at Pine Grove could become a college, Ketler agreed to take charge of an institution with only fifteen students that guaranteed him no income and required him to supply much of the equipment.[3] Despite having no wealthy friends, family, or benefactors, Ketler was convinced God was calling him to establish a Christian college. Ketler had not crossed the Rubicon, but he had undertaken a daunting venture.

In undertaking his work at Pine Grove Normal Academy in April 1876, Ketler declared that his "select school" strove to "fit young men and women for College, and to prepare those who desire to teach."[4] He sought to provide a rudimentary education for younger children who did not plan to attend college, prepare youth for college, and train elementary school teachers. During this first term, twenty-six pupils attended. Ketler recruited students, inspected boarding houses, oversaw all school operations, managed its finances, and conducted fourteen recitations each day. The 1878–1879 catalog stated that Pine Grove sought to give students "a thirst for knowledge," help them behave properly, and "incite love for the true, the beautiful, and the good."[5]

As the nation experienced an economic recession, Ketler traversed the countryside in a horse and buggy, handing out fliers to attract students. One brochure declared that "Education is power, capital, wealth." All those who resolved to gain an education would "find means by which to obtain it."[6] Ketler doggedly persevered, and enrollment increased from 115 at the end of the academy's first year to 201 in 1877, 313 in 1880, and more than five hundred in 1883. Ketler's teaching ability and personal charm as well as its low tuition (eight dollars—$253 today—for each of the three terms) helped the school grow rapidly. His earnest, diligent, thorough instruction stimulated students to want to learn. The sale of stocks and bonds to Pine Grove residents helped finance the academy.

As noted, the academy had three categories of students. Eight- to twelve-year-old boys and girls in the primary department took classes in spelling, reading, grammar, geography, arithmetic, and vocal music. "School of pedagogy" students prepared to become elementary school teachers; Ketler claimed that they spent twice as much time as their peers in other institutions studying "the common branches of knowledge" they would teach. These students were required to master these subjects completely and to learn the theories and methods of classroom instruction. A third group of pupils took classes to prepare for college. The 1877–1878 catalog boasted that because of its students' "exceptionally fine character and academic achievement," Pine Grove was the only Pennsylvania academy that colleges formally recognized. Its preparatory course fully met or exceeded the requirements of the state's best colleges. Consequently, colleges did not require Pine Grove graduates to take their entrance examinations. During its second year, the academy had nine faculty, including James McClelland and John Courtney, who both taught at the institution for many years. Weir Ketler argued that the early faculty were "almost fanatically devoted" to each other, the institution, and his father.[7]

The school day began for all students with devotions in the chapel. After scripture readings, singing, and prayer, Ketler and other professors spent half an hour discussing the factors that contributed to success, historical developments, and current events. Students were expected to attend worship services every Sunday at a local Presbyterian or Methodist church and were encouraged to attend at least one of their weekly prayer meetings. Ketler assigned impromptu speeches to college preparatory students, and they could choose to give declamations and orations and receive "friendly criticism."[8] By 1878–1879, the academy had four debating clubs, and membership was considered a high honor.

In 1878, Ketler married Matilda Gilson, whose father taught at a local common school and operated a farm. Bright, resolute, and level-headed, she shared her husband's "dreams and aspirations" and selflessly supported him and his educational endeavors. Their son Weir praised her loyalty, wisdom, courage, and prudent counsel to her husband and himself.[9] When she died in 1940, a student described her as "vital force in the development of the college," while a professor argued that Matilda, who had a great faith in God and a fervent belief in Grove City's destiny, had "exerted an important influence in the building of Grove City College."[10]

By 1878–1879, to be admitted to the academy's preparatory course, students had to pass an examination to demonstrate that they grasped the basic subjects high school freshmen were expected to know. Admitted students could take one of two four-year courses—the philosophical or the scientific. They were quite similar, but the philosophical course, designed to prepare pupils to attend college, included more Latin and Greek, whereas the scientific course was devised to train students to teach in high schools.[11] Both programs included classes in geography; political economy; music; US, English, ancient, and world history; algebra; geometry; trigonometry; grammar; composition; elocution; spelling; rhetoric; literature; Latin; physics; botany; chemistry; geology; astronomy; logic; psychology; philosophy; and ethics. All students were required to write an essay at least every three weeks in a history or literature course.[12] Surprisingly, the program included no classes in the Bible or religion.

In April 1879, the academy was granted a charter, which required fifteen trustees to be elected in January 1880. Five men were elected to serve three-, two-, or one-year terms, and thereafter five trustees were to be elected each year. All the trustees lived in the Pine Grove area. Every year, the trustees, faculty, and two college graduates were charged with examining all students and awarding diplomas to those whom a majority of examiners deemed worthy.[13]

The 1879–1880 catalog specified that faculty expected students to use their time wisely, obey school rules, promote the academy's best interests, be teachable, "earnest, honest, energetic and truthful," and avoid profanity. In return, students could expect faculty to "labor zealously" to enhance their "moral, intellectual and physical welfare"; "teach with patience and care"; insist on punctuality, good conduct, and thorough work; closely monitor their behavior; encourage "right living and right thinking"; give students "an exalted idea" of the aims of life; and lead them "to the Lamb of God."[14]

The 1880–1881 catalog explained further that students must possess substantial ability, energy, and common sense, be eager to perform "life's duties," and earnestly strive "to make the most of their time and opportunities." The catalog also highlighted the academy's advantages: it was in a town with a strong Christian environment and had "new, large and handsome" buildings, "earnest and efficient" teachers, and a low cost. Moreover, the academy accepted students at various levels of proficiency.[15] By this date, students could live in two rooming houses on campus—one for men and one for women—or could board in homes in the community.

As Americans mourned President James Garfield's death by assassination in 1881, strove to end "the spoils system" and institute civil service, and heard protests of farmers and laborers about their working conditions, the academy flourished. The 1881–1882 catalog contended that the school was effectively preparing men and women to teach, work in the business world, or attend college. Colleges often gave the latter group advanced standing and required them to take fewer courses to graduate. By this date, the academy also had a department of music that provided organ and piano instruction.[16] In fall 1883, a large, beautifully crafted music hall containing twelve rooms with organs and pianos opened.

The 1882–1883 catalog asserted that the academy gave greater attention to elocution than any other subject. Both faculty and students looked forward to the daily chapel services, which students valued so highly that "no effort is needed to secure prompt attendance."[17]

In loco parentis was a powerful force in the collegiate world during the last quarter of the nineteenth century, and the academy's faculty, driven by their desire to shape students' character and conduct, carefully monitored their behavior. They strove diligently to help students develop both keen minds and sterling character. Students were forbidden to frequent places where bad influences abounded. Happily, there were "no licensed hotels or saloons" within nine miles of town.[18] Catalogs continued to emphasize other advantages of attending the academy: its Christian environment, modern facilities, low cost, practical courses of study, and skilled teachers and the closeness of faculty and students.[19]

While overseeing all aspects of the academy's life and teaching numerous courses, Ketler continued his own education. In 1882, he finished an MA at nearby Allegheny College and two years later completed a nonresident doctor of philosophy degree at the College of Wooster in Ohio. Throughout his life, Ketler read extensively to equip him to teach a wide variety of subjects. In 1883, the trustees adopted a complete classic course of study that served as the basis for the academy transitioning to a college the next year. It was very similar to the philosophical course, but it also included classes in survey, navigation, metaphysics, and political science.

Grove City College: Conducting "the King's Business," 1884–1900

In the 1880s and 1890s, a modern industrial economy emerged in the United States fueled by the development of a national transportation and communication network, the rise of corporations, and a managerial revolution that transformed commercial operations. Amid these changes, on November 21, 1884, a Mercer County court granted a charter and approved changing the school's name from the Pine Grove Normal Academy to Grove City College. The institution took its name from the town, which had adopted this appellation the previous year. The catalog declared that the college "is a Christian but undenominational institution of learning." The college devised a seal with an open Bible at its center; across the Bible is written *Lux Mea,* Latin for "my light," based on Psalm 119:105: "Thy word is a lamp unto my feet, and a light unto my path" (KJV). Although no denomination legally controlled the college, it was de facto a Presbyterian institution, as will be explained later. The charter mandated that all trustees be members of a "Christian sect or creed," but no more than one-third of them could be ministers. The charter also stated that students would be admitted and faculty would be hired "without regard to religious test or belief." Professors were not required to subscribe to a confessional statement, but Ketler appointed only faculty who affirmed basic evangelical tenets.[20] Ketler had realized a significant part of his dream: He had established a Christian college. But even harder work remained to ensure that the institution remained faithful to his original vision and pursued excellence.

"Will anyone deny the providence of God?" Grove City's leaders asked regarding its founding. The college would enable students to "drink at a veritable fountain of living waters." A board of trustees, not to exceed thirty members, was charged with directing the college. The trustees established four committees to oversee their work: executive, finance, instruction, and library.[21]

The new college had three departments: preparatory (to equip younger students to attend college), music, and collegiate. Those who completed the collegiate department's classical course received a bachelor of arts (AB) degree, while those who finished its scientific course, which had been introduced in 1878 to educate teachers and businesspersons, received a bachelor of science (BS) degree. Preparing teachers was an important part of the college's mission. In 1889, only eighty-seven teachers in western Pennsylvania's primary and secondary schools were college graduates.[22] Graduates of the music program received a diploma attesting to their degree of skill and proficiency.[23] Depending on their previous knowledge, natural ability, and work ethic, music students required one to three years to finish their degrees. Twelve professors, including Ketler, provided instruction in these three programs. Half of them were Presbyterian ministers. Two instructors had no college degrees, six held only AB or BS degrees, three had MAs, and only Ketler had a doctor of philosophy degree. As at many other Christian colleges, the president taught the institution's capstone course in metaphysics (philosophy and ethics). Ketler used the era's standard texts written by Princeton's Lyman Atwater, Brown's Francis Wayland, Yale's Noah Porter, and the University of Tübingen's Albert Schwegler. "Students are constantly urged to think for themselves," the catalog declared. This would continue to be a hallmark of the college. All students who passed an examination covering their programs' forty courses, possessed "a good moral character," and seemed likely "to maintain the reputation of the school" were granted AB and BS degrees.[24]

From its founding, the college thrived. Its second year, Grove City had 556 different students and 810 total students attended its four terms—September to December, January to March, April to June, and summer school. To raise the standards of teachers, Grove City began offering a six-week summer school in 1888 for its own students and current teachers. In 1893, the summer term was extended to twelve weeks. The catalog emphasized that college students received "careful and thorough" instruction in Latin and Greek.[25] The college strove to increase the library's collection and quality, which would be an ongoing struggle.

In the late 1880s, many students met for a prayer meeting every Thursday night. Faculty and students created a missionary society to increase interest in missions, financially support alumni missionaries, and promote "the evangelization of the world." Their belief that "the King's business" was urgent prompted college leaders to produce graduates whose hearts burned for reaching the unsaved around the globe. A college temperance union was established to educate students about "the evil effects of intemperance" and to train them to end the "rum traffic." The Christian union was formed to support men who planned to become ministers. Its members assisted churches in the Grove City vicinity with their worship services, youth ministries, Sunday schools, and prayer meetings. They also met weekly to pray, discuss scripture, and plan their work.[26] By the early 1890s, Grove City, like hundreds of other American colleges, created chapters of the YMCA and YWCA. Their participants focused on Bible study and evangelism. "Christ is made the central figure in every college enterprise," the 1891–1892 catalog declared. [27]

In 1888, the New College Building (later called Founders Hall) opened. The four-story structure had science laboratories with "first-class equipment," an auditorium, three large lecture halls, classrooms, a museum, the president's office, and gyms for men and women. By this date, the college also included the academic building (Recitation Hall), erected in 1879, which housed the chapel, classrooms, the library, and a reading room; Music Hall, which was completed in 1879; and Physics Hall, which opened in 1883 and contained twelve classrooms. The college, which consisted of twenty acres, was valued at $100,000 ($3.4 million today).

In 1888, Ketler finished his BD (equivalent to today's MDiv) degree at Western Theological Seminary in Allegheny, across the river from Pittsburgh. After being ordained as a minister in the Presbyterian Church USA (PCUSA), he frequently preached at area churches on Sundays. While Ketler was away working on his degree, professor James McClelland and pastor William McConkey did much of the administrative work. McConkey is arguably the second most important figure in the college's early years. From 1875 to 1888, he simultaneously pastored Center Presbyterian Church and Grove City Presbyterian Church, and then only the latter congregation from 1888 to 1910, which grew from 130 to 861 members. McConkey was a college trustee from 1888 to 1913, served on the board's executive and instruction committees, and helped arrange summer school. Before being ordained, Ketler was a ruling elder in McConkey's church.

In 1889, the college created a business department, which offered courses in bookkeeping, banking, manufacturing, mining, real estate, insurance, and retail and wholesale merchandising. The catalog announced that the program could be pursued "under the best Christian influences"; its cost was low; students could take courses in many other subjects to supplement their business courses; some of Grove City's best professors taught these business courses; and students would be safe from "the vices and allurements of a large city."[28] The next year, the faculty numbered eighteen and Grove City began offering a nonresident, three-year doctor of philosophy degree. Participants in the program read books by Noah Porter, Lyman Atwater, Albert Schweiger, Princeton's president James McCosh, Aristotle, German philosopher Immanuel Kant, and Boston University professor Borden Bowne on psychology, philosophy, apologetics, metaphysics, ethics, and other subjects.

In 1890, Macalester College in St. Paul, Minnesota, tried to lure Isaac Ketler to accept its presidency by offering him triple his Grove City salary, but despite this monetary incentive and Macalester's attractive physical plant and strategic location, he declined. His visit to Macalester convinced Ketler that to thrive, Grove City needed financial support from a broader area. As a result, he solicited the help of several Pittsburgh businessmen. He arranged to meet with his former teacher Joseph Newton Pew, who had become an oil tycoon. Pew had earlier asked the educator to go into business with him. "Now," Ketler declared, "I have come to ask you to go into business with me."[29] Pew agreed to help and suggested that Ketler also talk with Samuel Harbison, a manufacturer of refractory products; Major A. P. Burchfield, president of the Joseph Horne Company; banker W. A. Shaw; and two prominent Pittsburgh religious leaders—Joseph Gibson and William McMillan. Pew was born in 1848, seven miles from Grove City, to strong abolitionist parents who had operated a station on the Underground Railroad. After graduating from Edinboro Normal School, teaching for a few years, and operating real estate businesses, Pew organized the Penn Fuel Company to pipe natural gas to Pittsburgh, which became the nation's first major city to use natural gas in its industries and homes. In 1884, he established Peoples Natural Gas Company and invested in oil wells near Lima, Ohio, which led him to create the Sun Oil Company.[30] Pew served as Ketler's guide, coworker, and principal benefactor.[31] Thus began a partnership between Grove

City College and the Pew family that would powerfully shape the institution.

By 1890, the United States had the world's largest economy, twice the size of Britain, its closest competitor. As America's trade with other nations increased dramatically and European countries competed to establish colonies around the world, the United States felt compelled to join the scramble for territory, build a stronger navy, and enhance its global influence. As these developments occurred, *The Collegian,* the college newspaper, published its first issue in February 1891. The editors warned students to "Keep off the Grass!" a plea repeated often throughout most of college history.[32] The newspaper was published most months until 1914 when it switched to weekly issues. Over the years, *The Collegian*'s topics, format, length, and quality varied, but it has always focused on student life while paying differing degrees of attention to the world beyond the campus. The newspaper has been financed by commercial advertisements, student subscriptions, and student activities fees.

In late March 1891, Grove City created a military department, one of only three in Pennsylvania, to provide exercise for and improve the discipline of male students. "Soon the firing of muskets and booming of cannon will be as common as coming late to class," *The Collegian* editors joked.[33] All physically capable men were required to enroll as cadets. Army First Lieutenant Charles Rowell commanded a battalion of two hundred male students who drilled for an hour a week and had three years of classroom instruction. College leaders praised the program for strengthening participants physically and improving their self-control. Thus began Grove City's long relationship with the United States military that would intensify during World War I and World War II and continue through air force ROTC from 1953 until 1989. Rowell also provided physical training for women.[34] Meanwhile, admission to the college became more difficult as prospective students had to pass examinations in English grammar, practical arithmetic, political geography, US history, Latin and Greek grammar, algebra, and geometry.[35]

In 1892, the college offered several programs of study: a college preparatory course, an ancient and modern classical course, Greek philosophical and Latin philosophical programs, a scientific course, instrumental music (piano and organ) and voice culture degrees, a business program, courses in telegraphy, stenography, and typewriting, and a Doctor of Philosophy degree. The college's four literary societies—Webster and Shakespeare for men and Speedwell and Philokalian for women—remained very important for more than fifty years. Their libraries were often as large as the college's. Their members delivered speeches, read expository essays and poetry, engaged in literary criticism, and debated various topics within their own societies and against each other. For example, one year, the Philokalians debated whether large colleges were preferable to small colleges, while Speedwell debated whether "devotion to fashion is a greater evil than the tobacco habit."[36]

The catalog continued to proclaim the advantages of Grove City College: its beneficial moral and religious tone, low cost, enthusiastic students, "thoroughly competent" professors, superb science laboratories, modern equipment, and military department. No other college its size, Grove City claimed, had "such a wide scope of programs."[37] In 1893, the Grove City School of Art began under the direction of Margaret Williams, a graduate of the Philadelphia School of Design who had done graduate study in New York City and Italy. The 1893, *The Collegian* called students' interest in spiritual matters "intense." It boasted that the college's outstanding stenography and typewriting courses gave graduates very good job prospects.[38] That year, a financial panic struck the United States; by 1895, 642 banks had failed, one-quarter of industrial plants had closed, and millions were unemployed. Nevertheless, the college continued to prosper. Ketler exhorted graduates to have faith in God and depend on the Holy Spirit, who would guide them to truth and strengthen them in "the battle of life."[39]

As advocates of higher criticism attacked the Bible's divine inspiration, Ketler staunchly defended its infallibility and authority.[40] The 1893–1894 catalog declared that Grove City was "first and foremost, a Christian College" which gave "a central place to Christ and Christian learning."[41] The next catalog asserted that "college has become widely known for its Christian influences, thoroughness of instruction, and the opportunity it affords young men and women of limited means to secure an education." It added that its various degree programs compared favorably with "the very best ones" at other colleges and that alumni appreciated the personal interest instructors took in them.[42] The four leading faculty in the 1890s were James McClelland (Greek), John Courtney (mathematics and Latin), Frank Hays (history and political science), and Samuel Dodds (Bible, English, psychology, chemistry) who were all "men of superior abilities and character."[43]

Influenced by Harvard president Charles Eliot, numerous colleges after 1875 adopted an elective system that allowed students to choose many of their courses. Believing that the elective system inhibited student development, Ketler instead followed the example of James McCosh, who prescribed a carefully regimented set of courses. Grove City first offered electives in 1888–1889, and students were increasingly given opportunities to select more specialized courses within their majors.[44] During the Gilded Age, many American colleges, elevated human reason over divine revelation and exalted searching for scientific truths above accepting revealed transcendent truths, a trend that Grove City strongly resisted as evident in its courses called Natural Theology and the Evidences of Christianity.[45]

As debate raged in Christian circles over evolution in the late nineteenth century, Ketler and the Grove City science faculty forthrightly embraced theistic evolution. Ketler insisted that "Whether God by successive acts of His creative might called into being each and every form in which life manifests itself" or whether people's "complex intellectual and spiritual life" evolved "through long ages of physical and spiritual environment" "is a question for speculation, but not for dogmatic statement. God in His written Word has given us the fact, but not the method of His creative power."[46] Science professors assigned books by Yale geologist James Dana and University of California geologist Joseph LeConte, two committed Christians who defended theistic evolution.[47] Meanwhile, maintaining "a high state of religious life" became increasingly difficult as more Grove City students came from public high schools, which offered no religious classes.[48]

The college's first intercollegiate contest was a baseball game against Westminster College in 1884. The 1895–1896 catalog asserted that the faculty had "the right to control, direct, and at will restrain the athletic association of the college."[49] Baseball was Grove City's most popular sport before 1900; the college played about eighteen games a season against West Virginia University, Waynesburg, Indiana Normal School, and other colleges. Grove City played its first football game in 1892, and during the 1890s, competed against colleges, athletic clubs, and industrial teams. From 1893 to 1896, the team's record was 29–7 (.806). In 1896, Grove City finished 8–1, shutting out Pitt and six other opponents. The 1896–1897 catalog praised the college's "commendable" athletic record.[50] Alva Calderwood, '96, who later served for thirty-five years as the college's dean, was a star halfback during these years, and he pitched and played outfield for the baseball team. Another standout was center William Ralph Cunningham, '97, who was named to Walter Camp's All-American team in 1898 and 1899 while attending medical school at the University of Michigan. A basketball team, formed in 1898, played its games by the illumination of oil lamps. Ketler required that all Grove City varsity athletes be amateurs. Only men who affirmed that they had not received any direct or indirect financial aid because of their athletic ability were allowed to play.[51] Grove City won its augural track meet in 1900 against the Erie YMCA 36–0. Because Ketler valued physical as well as intellectual and spiritual development, a professor was hired in 1897 to increase opportunities for students to exercise indoors and outdoors.

As noted, the college was initially funded in part by selling stock to community residents. All 250 stockholders, who owned between one and twenty ten-dollar shares agreed in 1894 to surrender their stock to enable Grove City College to become a charitable institution. Fifteen additional members were elected to the board of trustees for three-year terms, increasing its size to thirty.[52]

Joseph Newton Pew was chosen as president of the board. The four trustee committees continued: The executive managed all expenditures and salaries; instruction oversaw academic departments, visited classes, and hired faculty; finance managed investments and sought to procure a larger endowment; and the library supervised its operations and strove to expand its materials.[53]

In 1896, three of the college programs—the ancient and modern classical, the philosophical, and the scientific courses—included one Bible course, whereas the college preparatory course did not require any. That year, the Schubert Club, the first of the college's many departmental clubs, was established to foster musical appreciation and interest. In addition, the board decided to hold a ten-day summer Bible school. Modeled on the program at Northfield, Massachusetts, created by evangelists Dwight L. Moody and R. A. Torrey, the school, for the next forty-five years, brought scores of prominent pastors and professors to Grove City to teach thousands of ministers and laypeople about numerous biblical and theological topics. Three thousand people attended at least one session of the first Bible school in August 1897, which featured Borden Bowne, the leading proponent of a philosophy called personalism that emphasized God created human beings with moral, religious, emotional, and logical dimensions, reflecting his own attributes.[54] Bowne commended Ketler for making "the new leaven of reverent and progressive scholarship" central at Bible school meetings.[55]

In 1897, the music department was named the Grove City Conservatory of Music. Hermann Poehlman, who had taught piano at the Dresden Royal Conservatory, served as the conservatory's director of music. He also taught music courses and conducted the college's orchestra from 1893 to 1935. His wife Johanna, an opera singer, joined the faculty in 1893 to teach voice. Lois Cory, later the college's dean of women, came from the Royal Conservatory to teach voice in early 1890s. Another renowned musician, Gustav Mehner, joined the faculty in 1900.

During the college's first fifteen years, Ketler wore an amazing number of hats. He supervised the college facilities, safeguarded its financial solvency, interacted with the college's various constituencies, taught ethics and philosophy, served as a counselor and spiritual guide for students, enforced the college's regulations, and was the final court of appeal for many matters. He also preached in churches many Sundays and spoke to countless church and community groups during the week. Ketler was also a husband and the father of three sons. It is truly a wonder that he slept at night.

The Final Years of Isaac Ketler's Presidency: "Sound Scholarship and Christian Character," 1901–1913[56]

As the new century dawned, the Progressive Era began in the United States. Dozens of reformers sought to remedy the problems produced by rapid industrialization and urbanization, massive immigration, political malfeasance, monopolies, poverty, and unsafe labor conditions. Meanwhile, Grove City College seemed poised for a bright future. Attracted by the college's improving academic program and vibrant spiritual life, 623 students enrolled in 1900–1901. In 1900, Andrew Carnegie gave the Borough of Grove City and the college trustees $30,000 to build a free library. Completed in 1902, the building contained a large gymnasium, a library, and a large auditorium. After the borough defaulted on its pledge to provide $1,800 annually for maintenance, Carnegie declared in 1906 that the edifice belonged exclusively to the college; at that point, the library had 5,677 books.

In 1900, the Bessemer Gas Engine Company was founded. By 1926, the company employed almost one thousand five hundred Grove City area residents; in 1929, it merged with the C. and C. Cooper Company of Mt. Vernon, Ohio, to become Cooper-Bessemer. Until the 1970s, the company remained the largest employer in Grove City. In June 1900, Grove City College awarded eleven AB, twenty-three bachelor of philosophy, and six BS degrees, including one to J. Howard Pew; ten music diplomas; and one doctor of philosophy degree. Aided by a $20,000 grant from the Pennsylvania legislature, the college added majors in civil and mechanical engineering in 1901. This was one of the few times that Grove City received direct aid from the state or federal government. The

1902 Bible school included a separate conference for young people sponsored by the YMCA, YWCA, and Christian Endeavor. That year, *The Collegian* expressed hope that Grove City College would become "a thoroughly first-class Christian institution with a faculty of scholarly men and women with high ideals" who prepared students for business and professional careers.[57]

By fall 1903, all campus buildings had electric lights. The next fall, Grove City opened its first dormitory—Colonial Hall—which housed sixty women; its rooms offered "every convenience of a first class college hostel."[58] Room and board was sixty dollars per term ($2,180 today). Fearing that its regulations would curtail their freedom, many women were reluctant to live in Colonial. To help convince them, Colonial initially had no rules. The college insisted in 1905 that young women had the same amenities as exclusively female colleges and that it supplied "every comfort and safeguard which parents desire for their daughters."[59] Grove City offered courses in cooking, home sanitation, home nursing, home management, dietary, and household accounts to equip women who were studying a broad liberal arts curriculum to also be the "Mistress of the home."[60] Lillian Kemp, a graduate of the Drexel School of Domestic Science, oversaw both the college's domestic science courses and Colonial Hall. In 1908, the town's United Presbyterian Church sold its building to the college; renamed Ivy Chapel, it served as a classroom building until the 1950s.

During the Progressive years, in loco parentis continued to prevail. Ketler established rules for studying, courting, athletics, and entertainment. The apparel and moral standards of Grove City students during the late nineteenth and early twentieth century were distinctively Victorian, and students were not permitted to dance or play cards. Grove City refused to admit or retain students who were "addicted to cigarettes," and using tobacco on campus was prohibited.[61] Ketler expected all faculty and staff to abstain totally from alcohol.[62] Students were required to be in their rooms studying by 7 p.m. each night. Some enterprising men used ropes to climb to the windows of women to talk with them. The men arranged signals to avoid being caught by Ketler when he made his nightly rounds, but after apprehending some men one evening, the president had heavy screens nailed to the windows to impede conversing.[63]

In 1906, Herbert Harmon began teaching at Grove City. For the next forty years, he taught physics and engineering courses, coached baseball and football, installed and directed the campus radio station, and created a complete radio-phone outfit, which won first prize in a national contest for its efficient operation. Tragedy struck the Grove City community in 1906. After teaching voice at the college for seven years, Johanna Poehlmann became a featured soloist at the Metropolitan Opera in New York City. In 1906, she was touring in San Francisco with the renowned Italian tenor Enrico Caruso when a massive earthquake struck the city. While helping save a panic-stricken fellow singer who was threatening to jump from a window, Poehlmann was seriously injured by a sliding piano. When she died three years later, of cancer at age forty, *The Collegian* praised her "marvelous accomplishments" and incredible "mental tours de force."[64]

While many faculty at numerous colleges and universities, influenced by John Dewey and other pragmatic and secular philosophers, taught that all truth is relative and that ideas should be judged exclusively by whether they had beneficial consequences, Grove City continued to be faithful to its founding Christian principles. The college gave the Bible central place in its curriculum, Ketler argued.[65] He always strove to ensure that the "ethical and theistic principles" promoted in college philosophy courses harmonized with "the great doctrines of Evangelical Christianity."[66] The 1905 graduating class was the largest in college history—forty-eight men and nineteen women; twelve men planned to become either ministers or missionaries.[67] The June 1905 *Bulletin* claimed that more Grove City alumni had become pastors than those of any other Pennsylvania college.[68] Ketler rejoiced in 1909 that about fifty Grove City graduates were or would soon be serving as missionaries and that "a great revival" was presently occurring on campus.[69]

During the Progressive years, the college provided forty-six weeks of instruction—three twelve-week terms and a ten-week summer term; students needed 180 credits to graduate with either an AB or a BS degree; students were expected to take fifteen credits a term or forty-five per year. Ketler constantly sought to upgrade the quality of instruction, and the credentials of the faculty improved substantially during his presidency. The 1912–1913 faculty held degrees from Harvard, Princeton, Yale, Johns Hopkins, Cornell, Northwestern, Bonn, and the Royal Conservatory of Dresden; seven had PhDs, three had master's degrees, and five had only bachelor's degrees. Professors generally worked ten hours per day six days per week to provide high-quality instruction.[70] The college recruited some distinguished guest professors to teach summer school courses including Borden Bowne and professors from Manchester University in England, William & Mary, and Western Theological Seminary. The 1908 summer school enrolled 208 students, including more candidates for permanent teaching certificates in Pennsylvania public schools than the summer program of any other college in the state.

The Grove City Conservatory of Music was a vital part of the institution; in 1909, it had 254 students, thirty-five more than that of the college. It awarded diplomas for many different proficiencies—teaching piano, vocal music, violin, or music theory; playing piano or violin; and concert or opera singing.[71] The number of students in Grove City's preparatory program declined dramatically in the 1900s as more youths graduated from high schools. In 1909–1910, the college began admitting only students who had four years of high school course work.[72] The 1911 *Alumni Quarterly* claimed that more Grove City graduates were teaching in Pennsylvania than the alumni of any other college.[73]

Despite its growth, Grove City struggled financially in the early twentieth century, prompting Ketler to repeatedly implore the trustees to raise a larger endowment. The college's meager endowment would continue to be a major concern and inhibited paying higher faculty and staff salaries, providing scholarships, erecting buildings, hiring and retaining faculty, and supplying more amenities for students.

The military department remained very important until 1911. Male students were required to buy West Point–style uniforms and to take military courses all four years. Cadets participated in the inaugural ceremonies of William McKinley in 1901, Theodore Roosevelt in 1905, and William Howard Taft in 1909. The 1900 catalog lauded members of the department for increasing their physical strength and fortifying their discipline.[74] The June 1905 *Bulletin* claimed that military training was the "very best form of physical training" and inculcated "the moral virtue of obedience." Moreover, cadets were taught the foundational principles of "good conduct and good citizenship."[75] One cadet claimed in 1903: "We are strong advocates of military drill and discipline."[76] Consistent with national trends, however, interest in the military waned at Grove City, and military training was discontinued in 1911. After war erupted in Europe in 1914, faculty and students reorganized a military company.

All four literary societies had their own well-furnished and equipped club rooms and sponsored many orations, debates, impromptu speeches, and musical activities.[77] In the 1900s, these literary societies were as popular as athletics teams. Extracurricular activities, whether focusing on recreation, self-improvement, or community service, took more of students' time.[78] In 1905, students organized the Prohibition League, which met biweekly to discuss the nation's liquor problem.

The May 1906 bulletin reaffirmed that Grove City "strictly enforces an amateur basis of eligibility."[79] By then, the college had seven buildings valued at $400,000 ($14.2 million today) and baseball and football fields, a one-third-mile track, and a half-mile boating course on Wolf Creek. Soon thereafter, tennis courts were constructed. The 1911–1912 catalog reiterated that "professionalism in all forms is discouraged in athletics." To play on varsity teams, students had to take a full course load and do "fair quality" work.[80] The next catalog insisted that athletic participation must not interfere with academic work.[81]

Despite the college's emphasis on amateurism and academics, its sports teams excelled. Grove City participated in both the National Intercollegiate Association (the predecessor to the NCAA) and the League of Colleges. The 1901 baseball squad finished 14–6, the 1911 team was 17–5, and the 1912 team went 16–1–1. The football team's best years were 1909 (6–2), 1910 (7–1–1) and 1911 (8–0–1). The basketball squad's record was 14–3 in 1901–1902, 13–1 in 1902–1903 (including wins over Penn State, Penn, and Syracuse), 16–3 in 1904–1905 (with victories over Pitt 25–8 and WVU 36–9), and 12–0 in 1911–1912 (defeating Pitt twice and winning the western Pennsylvania basketball championship). Remarkably, Grove City did not lose a single contest in baseball, football, or basketball or any track meets during a fifty-three-week period in 1911–1912. Weir Ketler, '08, was a superb athlete who lettered in football, basketball, tennis, and track and field. A guard with blazing speed, Ketler was a leading scorer in basketball.[82] He was a defensive end in football. The college organized a tennis team in 1908, and Ketler was one of the college's best tennis players ever. His senior year, he also ran the half mile and the mile in track.[83] After returning to the college to teach mathematics, Ketler coached basketball from 1910 to 1913, compiling a 32–7 record. Herbert Harmon coached baseball and football. His 1910, 1911, and 1912 football teams won the collegiate championship of Pennsylvania, compiling a combined record of 21–3–3. The 1911 team outscored its opponent 134–3. He was Grove City's "Knute Rockne," *The Collegian*'s sports editor effused.[84]

Howard Acher, '13, excelled in football, basketball and tennis in the early twentieth century. He played quarterback and fullback for the superlative 1910–1912 football teams and as a forward, helped lead the 1911–1912 championship basketball team. From 1915 to 1919, Acher coached football, basketball, and tennis at Grove City.

During the first years of the twentieth century, Grove City produced five men who played in Major League Baseball. The most impressive was Frank Elmer Smith. After playing at Grove City from 1896 to 1901, he pitched for five MLB teams from 1904 to 1915, going 139–111 with an outstanding 2.59 earned run average (ERA). Had there been a Cy Young Award at the time, Smith would have been a top candidate to win it in 1907, when he posted a

23–10 record with a 2.47 ERA and twenty-nine complete games, and in 1909, when he was 25–17 with a dazzling 1.80 ERA and thirty-seven complete games.[85]

In 1911, some men formed a College Glee Club while others preparing to be pastors, aided by Ketler, created the Ministerial Students' League. Members of the college's YMCA ministered at George Junior Republic, a school for juvenile delinquent males founded two years earlier.[86] In 1911, the college first recognized magna cum laude or cum laude graduates. That year, the college established four $160 ($5,400 today) merit scholarships. All male freshmen were required to take classes in blacksmithing, boxing, and football. That year, college leaders debated whether to build a men's dormitory or a gymnasium. The low ceiling in the gym in the basement of Carnegie Library made shooting baskets extremely difficult. The college decided to construct both buildings, spending $30,000 ($970,000 today) on the gymnasium (dedicated in February 1913) and $85,000 ($2.7 million) on the men's dormitory (dedicated in November 1914). In 1912, the junior class decided to produce a yearbook called the *Ouija*. The newspaper again urged students to stay off the grass. Members of the Shakespeare and Webster Clubs formed the Intercollegiate Debating Team. Grove City would excel in debate, especially in the twenty-first century.[87]

During these years, *The Collegian* featured many essays and poems. This ditty probably captures the sentiment of many students:

Little roots of Greek,
Make the verdant Freshman
Feel extremely meek.
Then a little German,
With a little French,
Make the foolish Sophomore
Think he has some sense.
Then a year of Logic,
And Philosophy,
Makes the best of Juniors

Wise as he can be.
Then comes Analytics,
Turns a fellow's head,
Makes the wisest Senior
Wish that he was dead.[88]

In the early twentieth century, the college's graduation festivities lasted a week. Numerous clubs held banquets, music students gave a recital, art students exhibited their work, a literary club staged a play, and numerous graduating classes had reunions. The college held an oratorical contest for juniors. Hundreds of people watched as a brass band led a procession of trustees, faculty, graduates, and distinguished guests down Main Street, across the bridge over Wolf Creek, and into College Park for the commencement. This ceremony lasted several hours because almost all graduates gave short orations.

In 1912, the college's major benefactor Joseph Newton Pew died. Ketler extolled Pew's wonderful heart, immense reverence for the Bible, and "strong, unswerving, Christian character." Pew had agreed to serve as a Grove City trustee because of its Christian identity and strong "loyalty to the Word of God." Grove City had lost "a wise counselor, a great leader, and a true friend." Further explaining the college's commitments, Ketler argued that Grove City College stood for "a broad, catholic evangelical acceptance of the Bible as the Word of God" and the "fundamental doctrines of grace and redemption," enabling its constituents who belonged to different denominations to be "one body of believers in Christ."[89]

Grove City maintained a close and cordial relationship with the PCUSA during the Progressive years. In 1907, Ketler explained that the college was located "in a Presbyterian community" and was "largely patronized by Presbyterians."[90] Ketler often preached at area PCUSA churches and for twenty-three years served on the board of directors of Western Theological Seminary. Although Grove City was "not organically a Presbyterian institution," he argued, the college "is to all intents and purposes" devoted "to the interests of the Presbyterian Church." It educated many Presbyterian youths and supplied numerous candidates for the denomination's ministry and missionary work at home and abroad.[91] The PCUSA's board of education listed Grove City as one of the denomination's fifty-four colleges, gave scholarships to the school's preministerial students, and regularly sent members to evaluate Grove City's programs.[92]

In 1913, Grove City created an alumni association to enhance communication among graduates and raise funds to aid the college. Alumni could pay annual dues of fifty cents or purchase a lifetime membership for ten dollars ($323 today). In spring 1913, Ketler convinced the trustees to buy a farm across Wolf Creek adjacent to the lower campus, a decision that greatly furthered the development of the college.

His physician told Ketler the previous summer that he needed to have his appendix removed, but preoccupied with his many responsibilities, the president kept putting it off. On June 29, 1913, Ketler suffered an appendix attack. By this time, it was too late to operate. As he lay dying, the sixty-one-year-old president told professor Alva Calderwood that founding and directing the college had been "a labor of love." He asked Calderwood to exhort the trustees and faculty to "always let it stand for the best things." After speaking with Ketler just before he died on July 2, college pastor Robert Calder reported that the president affirmed his deep belief in "the sovereign goodness of God."[93]

At his funeral, W. L. McEwan, pastor of Third Presbyterian Church in Pittsburgh and vice president of board, declared that Ketler strove to equip students to do God's work in the world at a college "established on the basis of evangelical religion." His fellow Western Theological Seminary directors stated that Ketler "worked and planned and lived for the College" to make it a powerful agent for "building the Master's Kingdom."[94] The 1914 *Ouija* praised Ketler's perceptive mind, exceptional administrative ability, magnetic personality, and deep devotion to the college. The editors claimed that he knew every student who had attended Grove City by name, that he had aided thousands of people, and that he "gave God the glory" for all his accomplishments.[95]

Ketler, William Ramsay asserted, had strong religious convictions and was fearless and respected by all who knew him.[96] Weir Ketler asserted that his father's "highest and holiest ambition" was to "serve God and bless the World by establishing a school" that someday might excel all others. His father was a "master teacher" who made metaphysics "understandable to an average student."[97] Calderwood called Ketler "a great master builder" who helped mold the "character of thousands of young people for greater service to God and to humanity."[98]

Prompted by the murder of his niece, her family, and some of her friends serving as missionaries in 1900, Ketler wrote *The Tragedy of Paotingfu* (1902), an account of the Boxer Rebellion in China. In 1910, he published *The Pilgrims*, which defended John Calvin's theory of predestination and detailed how the Pilgrims promoted liberty in America.

Ketler was a Reformed evangelical, a philosophical idealist, and an ecumenicist. He affirmed that scripture was divinely inspired and the principal authority for Christian belief and practice. Ketler believed in Christ's substitutionary atonement and his bodily resurrection. He asserted that the Bible was written by men "as they were moved by the Holy Ghost." Grove City stood for "the integrity of the Bible and for the Gospel of the Son of God."[99] Because people were sinners, Ketler contended, they must be justified by their faith in Christ's righteousness, which only the Holy Spirit could accomplish.[100]

Strongly influenced by Borden Bowne's personalism, Ketler espoused idealism. He asserted in the 1912 college catalog that for twenty-five years, Grove City had "identified itself with the general idealistic movement in Philosophy" and had contributed significantly to promoting "this better way of conceiving fundamental truth."[101] His posthumously published *Studies in Metaphysics: A Text Book for College Students* (1913) defended idealistic metaphysics.

Throughout his life, Ketler enjoyed dialoguing and fellowshipping with people who espoused diverse theological positions. He participated in the 1908 Social Gospel lecture series at Union Theological Seminary in New York City, which included pastors and professors espousing a wide variety of theological perspectives. Most significantly, Ketler invited theological conservatives, moderates, and liberals to teach at the college's summer Bible conferences. The annual summer Bible conferences for college students at Northfield, Massachusetts, and the ones every summer at the Chautauqua Institute in southwestern New York for mainline Protestants were better known, but the ones Grove City hosted attracted several thousand attendees each year and helped shape many lives. These gatherings enabled area ministers to listen to prominent scholars discuss key biblical and theological topics, helped educate pastors who were pursuing the PhD degree in philosophy Grove City, and raised the college's profile. Ketler continually prodded faculty and students to engage with thinkers and ideas across a broad theological and philosophical spectrum. Throughout his life, Ketler strove to promote "a deeper and broader understanding of truth."[102] Ketler, William Ramsay argued, longed to possess "treasures of wisdom and knowledge" and impart them to his students.[103]

By Ketler's death, more than ten thousand men and women had studied at Grove City College; the average attendance for a trimester was about 350 with about six hundred different students attending annually; about 250 graduates had entered the ministry, and more than sixty had become missionaries. The value of GCC property and buildings was about $425,000 ($13.7 million today), and the endowment was about $100,000 ($3.23 million today).[104] Greater trials, troubles, and triumphs lay ahead.

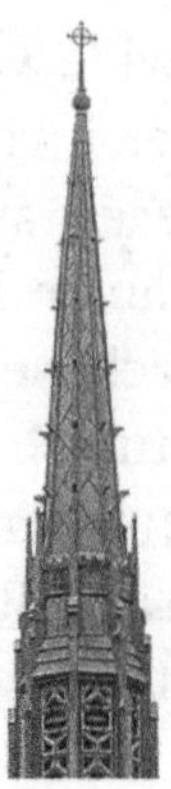

Alexander Ormond, Weir Ketler, and World War I, 1913–1920

In his funeral sermon, longtime college trustee William McConkey compared Isaac Ketler's death to that of Moses but insisted that God would raise up another Joshua to continue the founder's work.[1] Grove City's Joshua was Alexander Thomas Ormond. The death of the beloved founder of an institution or organization is often devastating to that enterprise. But in this case, a smooth transition occurred. Ormond was a highly respected Princeton philosophy professor, a devout Christian, a close friend of Ketler, and a popular lecturer at the college's summer school who had helped arrange Grove City's summer Bible school and school of philosophy from 1908 to 1912.[2] Ormond shared Ketler's convictions and goals. At Princeton, he earned an AB in 1877, an MA in 1878, and a PhD in 1880, and he had taught at the Ivy League institution for thirty years. Ormond wrote numerous books including *Concepts of Philosophy* (1906). He was good natured, congenial, and an innovative administrator. Ormond suffered from diabetes before any medicine existed to control the disease.

Responding to a "Divine call," Ormond accepted the presidency of Grove City College on July 28, 1913. The philosopher wanted to increase Grove City's student body to one thousand in ten years. He pointed out that educating each student cost $125 annually, but tuition was only eighty dollars. Ormond therefore asked the trustees to raise Grove City's tuition to increase revenue, but they refused, fearing it would reduce enrollment and prevent low-income students from attending. If tuition were not increased, Ormond argued, an endowment of $400,000 was needed to pay the college's expenses. He also implored the trustees to raise $1 million to construct a new recitation building and a chapel, enlarge the library, hire more instructors, and boost faculty salaries. In 1913, the trustees pledged to procure $500,000 to fund these projects and planned to increase the endowment to $500,000 ($15.9 million today).[3] Concerned about the college's rising debt, however, a year later, the trustees postponed and effectively ended Ormond's million-dollar endowment campaign.

Delegates from forty colleges attended Ormond's inauguration in November 1913. A forty-member college choir performed. President Woodrow Wilson, Ormond's colleague at Princeton, expressed his regret that he could not attend and declared, "There is no finer man in the country than Alexander T. Ormond," who had a "pure conscience, extraordinary intellectual power," and "a lovable and sound character." "Associating with him," Wilson promised, "will be inspiring." In his inaugural address, Ormond asserted that Grove City College had been "founded and developed largely by the faith, energy and vision" of Isaac Ketler, "who under the providence of God," had been adroitly assisted by Samuel Harbison and Joseph Newton Pew. The "fundamentally Christian" institution had educated many who could not afford more expensive colleges. "Founded on the ideal of sound and liberal culture, vital religion and practical efficiency, [and] animated by the spirit of service to God and humanity," the college, Ormond maintained, had "done a noble work." But its friends must rally around Grove City to help it realize its "higher mission."[4] After the ceremony, while guests dined in the gymnasium, students, led by the band, heartily sang college songs and gave college yells. The football team's 13–6 victory over archrival Geneva was a fitting climax to the festivities.

Ormond's two and half years as president were momentous. He enlarged the faculty (from twenty-one to twenty-nine) and strove to improve its quality.[5] He created a committee system, raised salaries, strengthened the college's philosophical offerings, increased the library's holdings, and worked to boost the endowment. Faculty committees oversaw advising and matriculation, courses of study, discipline, athletics, intercollegiate debates, the library, publicity, and publications. The college reorganized its graduate programs. Grove City offered two master's degrees—one for students in residence and one for those who took two summer sessions and did the rest of their work independently. Students could earn MA degrees in Latin, Greek, English literature, composition, oratory, Bible, modern languages, history, economics, politics, philosophy, education, mathematics, and science. Grove City continued to offer a PhD program in philosophy; degree candidates had to attend three summer sessions and complete substantial independent study.[6] Only undergraduate students with all A's and B's were allowed to take more than fifteen credit hours a semester.[7]

In 1913, Grove City established a department of physical education and medical inspection. Two years later, the Grove City Commercial School was organized in close connection with the college; its students, like their earlier counterparts, could earn a business degree in a Christian environment safe from the temptations and evils of large cities for a very low tuition (twenty-eight dollars per term, about $900 today) and take college courses in the humanities and social and natural sciences to supplement their business ones.[8] Indiana Normal School was the only other Pennsylvania institution offering a degree in commerce. Meanwhile, Grove City emphasized ancient languages. The 1915–1916 catalog listed forty-four courses in Greek, seventeen in Latin, and seven in Sanskrit.[9]

In 1913, Hermann Poehlmann compiled *Songs of Grove City College* containing about 175 musical pieces produced by composers from around the world. It included patriotic, club, and fight songs, popular hymns, and the college's alma mater, whose music he created to enhance school spirit and pride. George Seel, '12, who had a long career as a Presbyterian missionary in Colombia, wrote the lyrics for the alma mater. Students and faculty sang these selections for half an hour at Friday morning chapels. By the 1910s, mandatory chapel provoked problems. Some students carped that numerous professors did not regularly attend services and that many of their classmates did not pay attention. One complained in 1915, for example, that scores of students spent Sunday chapel doing things which were "beneath the dignity of college students," such as reading newspapers and talking.[10]

In March 1914, a typhoid fever epidemic broke out at the college; its cause was traced to the town's water supply. Chemistry professor Otto Sieplein and Pennsylvania Board of Health engineers discovered that a defective well casing near Wolf Creek had allowed surface water to pollute the well. About two hundred students became sick and four died, prompting the college to close for two weeks and the third-term enrollment to drop from four hundred to three hundred.[11] The calamity motivated the town to build a modern hospital.

World War I, which began in late July, raged in Europe during fall 1914. Multiple factors, not one country or cause, *The Collegian* declared, had produced the Great War.[12] The September 1914 alumni magazine lauded the college's new gymnasium, enlarged and improved athletic fields, better equipped library and labs, and the opening of Memorial Hall. Nevertheless, its editors agreed with Ormond that Grove City needed to increase its endowment, provide more scholarships, and erect a science building and a new chapel, which required "the loyal and active support of all alumni and friends." As millions were killed and maimed, campus life went on. In the annual tug-of-war across Wolf Creek, the freshmen defeated the sophomores. The faculty recommended that all women students spend at least two hours per week swimming, playing basketball, field hockey, or tennis, or doing gymnastics or some other physical activity. The governor-elect of Pennsylvania, Martin Brumbaugh, who spoke in chapel on moral issues, lauded Grove

City as "an A1 institution," which had produced more teachers than any other similar size college in the state.[13]

The November 1914 alumni magazine argued that Grove City College stood for "pure athletics, for nonprofessionalism and clean practices."[14] The faculty had to approve almost every aspect of campus life from the dates and casts for plays to the schedule for home basketball games to student requests to change their courses. Students gained greater participation in decision-making in 1914 when an athletic association, composed of three students, two alumni, and two faculty, was formed to manage all athletic activities.[15] Moreover, students, instead of faculty, were permitted to elect the managers of athletics teams.

In 1914, students established an English club and the college opened a bookstore to sell textbooks at reduced prices. *The Collegian* switched from being a monthly magazine that comprised primarily literary works to a weekly newspaper that covered campus news and sports and featured "unbiased" opinion pieces.[16] An October 1914 op-ed sounded themes that resonated throughout the college's subsequent history. Students did "not need to learn a lot of rules and principles with parrot-like precision," the editors asserted. Instead, they must learn to think and act independently to accomplish their God-given callings in the world. If students did not do so, they would be "the dupe of every knave" they encountered. On Charter Day, November 21, 1914, Memorial Hall, built on the upper campus and housing 110 men, was dedicated with speeches, singing, and a well-attended alumni luncheon.

Religious activities remained very important during Ormond's tenure. Grove City was one of the few Pennsylvania colleges that had a full-time pastor. Ninety women participated in seven Bible studies the YWCA sponsored the fall 1914 term, while about one hundred men participated weekly in six discussion-oriented YMCA Bible study groups focusing on personal problems.[17] Every year, the college held a week of prayer in early February. Classes were shortened, and guest pastors spoke at five morning chapels and four special evening chapel services. Meanwhile, many students regularly attended local Sunday morning church services and Sunday school classes. A 1915 study by Princeton Theological Seminary found that 346 of Grove City's 356 students professed to be Christians and that twenty-five men were preparing to become ministers.[18] Six of the ten prizes awarded at Western Theological Seminary's commencement in May 1915 went to Grove City alumni.[19]

In October 1914, an official debating league was formed, and Grove City hosted two debates in 1915. At the first one, Grove City handed Juniata College, a debating powerhouse, only its second loss in eleven years. A winning debate team, *The Collegian* editors insisted, was as great a credit to a college as a victorious sports squad.[20]

In March 1915, two student groups staged plays. Seniors performed *Mose,* a comedy portraying the results of "careless living" by fraternity men.[21] The Philokalian Club performed *The Third Degree,* a drama examining police brutality and corruption.[22] The senior play *Arabian Nights,* directed by Joe Ketler and performed during commencement week, was "one of the most amusing and interesting" shows in years.[23]

In March 1915, a male student had to be pulled from Wolf Creek with a rope after he broke through the ice while skating and almost drowned.[24] In May, seven students and alumni were injured when two cars collided at the corner of Main Street and Center Street. Two female students were thrown out of one car high into the air but fortunately landed on the grass instead of the sidewalk or pavement.[25] In February 1916, two groups of students were injured when the vehicles in which they were riding to a basketball game at Slippery Rock had accidents. A truck ran into a ditch, and a four-horse wagon careened over an embankment. Two female students were hospitalized.[26]

In spring 1915, new tennis courts were being built, and forming a girls' or coed team, *The Collegian* argued, would be a "progressive step."[27] On April 26, members of the four literary clubs serenaded president Ormond to celebrate his sixty-eighth birthday.[28] Students organized the first campus sing-a-long in late April to become "better acquainted with our college songs."[29] A large crowd of students gathered in front of Colonial belted out many college favorites including "Here's to Our Grove City and the Team." Soloists, quartets, and the Speedwell Club entertained the throng.[30] The 1915 yearbook, the *Ouija*, which cost two dollars (sixty-three dollars today) was, according to *The Collegian*, "second to none."[31]

In February 1914, a senior called for establishing a student government to empower students to regulate many of their own affairs and to transform the college from a monarchy to a democracy. Moreover, it would enable the faculty to focus on teaching instead of supervising student conduct. The author also advocated establishing an honor system, the first salvo in a battle that would last until the 1960s.[32] The desire has been growing, another student claimed, to eliminate unfair examination practices that allowed the incompetent to do as well as the industrious.[33] Everyone knew that cribbing occurred at Grove City, and almost everyone agreed that this "evil" should be eradicated. After several years of discussion, a plan was devised to create a student senate chosen by the student body to oversee student affairs and investigate and impose penalties for all misdemeanors on campus. Students voted on whether to adopt a student senate and an honor system to organize and supervise campus activities and govern examinations.[34] Students voted 116 to 94 to establish both, but a three-quarters positive vote was required to pass these measures, so they were defeated.[35] In 1916, *The Collegian* again called for instituting an honor system. At other colleges where this had been done, student conduct had improved and "undesirable" students had been expelled.[36] The next year, its editors noted that president Ormond had been bitterly disappointed by the defeat of the honor system. Their love for Ormond, "earnest desire for betterment," and respect for faculty should prompt students to reconsider instituting an honor code.[37]

In fall 1915, Ormond warned students that college policies against hazing would be strictly enforced.[38] That term, Alva Calderwood became the college's dean, a college band was created to perform at football games, and Robert Thorn was elected senior class president. *The Collegian* called Thorn, who earned letters in basketball, football, baseball, and tennis, "the most consistent all-round athlete" in college history.[39] Thorn would later coach basketball, soccer, and tennis, serve as the college's athletic director, and have the football field named for him. Students formed another prohibition club. In November, Grove City hosted the annual convention of the Student Volunteer Association of Western Pennsylvania. Later that month, in what *The Collegian* termed one of best games in college history, the football team defeated "invincible Allegheny" 9–6 to climax a sensational season.[40] The Speedwell Club and the athletic association combined to produce *The Fortune Hunter*, a 1897 play written by W. S. Gilbert (of Gilbert and Sullivan fame) about an heiress who lost her fortune. The choir performed Georg Friedric Handel's *Messiah* for the advent concert, which college choirs would sing many more times over the years.

On December 18, 1915, Ormond died of a heart attack. At a memorial service on January 16, 1916, Weir Ketler asserted that the philosopher had done an incredible amount in his short tenure to inspire the faculty to improve their work. The president had experienced many trials, disappointments, and "unusual burdens," but he had never flinched. All who knew Ormond, Ketler declared, "respected, loved and admired" him.[41] In his funeral sermon, college pastor Robert Calder contended that the deeply religious visionary had enhanced the prestige of Grove City.[42] A faculty resolution praised Ormond's many publications on varied educational, philosophical, and literary topics, brilliant mind, "great heart," Christlike character, and grand vision of what Grove City College might become.[43] The trustees asserted that by his impressive scholarship, just actions, wise "methods of administration," and "unselfish devotion" to the college, Ormond had made "an indelible mark on the institution." The "devoted Christian" had strengthened "evangelical truth."[44]

No heir apparent was waiting in the wings when Ormond died unexpectedly, but there was a natural successor—the son of the founder, Weir Ketler. He had graduated from Grove City in 1908, earned a second AB at Yale, taught mathematics and other subjects for three years at his alma mater, coached the basketball team, and briefly served as Ormond's assistant. Ketler was intelligent, hard-working, and well-liked by his peers, but he was only twenty-seven years old and had little administrative experience. Nevertheless, on December 20, 1915, the trustees named Ketler acting president. He "tried to avoid" accepting the position because he thought he was too young, but on June 13, 1916, the trustees elected him the nation's youngest college president.[45] *The Collegian*'s editors were delighted. "No choice so universally and enthusiastically satisfactory could possibly have been made," they effused. "A thorough scholar, an effective and inspiring teacher, an administrator of proved ability, he has an intimate knowledge of the traditions, purposes, problems, and personnel of the college." Ketler had "the loyalty and affection of students and faculty," the confidence of the alumni, and the "cordial support of the community."[46] At this point, Grove City College consisted of about fifty acres, nine buildings, and a physical plant valued at more than $700,000 ($20.5 million today). Of the college's twenty-eight faculty, six had no baccalaureate degree, six had only a baccalaureate degree, seven had a master's degree, and nine had a doctorate, four of which had been granted by Grove City College.[47] In 1915–1916, a total of 1,019 students attended Grove City's various programs.

Ketler wanted to erect a new science building, which he hoped the state would help fund, and a chapel "to help deepen the spiritual atmosphere on campus." Neither would be constructed until 1931. Like Ormond, Ketler wanted to eliminate the college's debt and increase its meager endowment. The Pew estate agreed to give $15,000, the trustees pledged $60,000, and Andrew Carnegie promised to provide $20,000 to raise the endowment to $220,000.[48]

The likelihood of the United States being drawn into World War I prompted the trustees in June 1916 to reestablish a military department; all male students unless physically disabled were required to participate. Members of the trustee committee on faculty and instruction were expected to regularly visit the college.[49] The 1916 summer term had the highest attendance in history; 726 students and seventy professors participated in a six-week school of pedagogy designed for elementary school teachers, a nine-week program devised to help secondary school teachers complete their AB, or the twelve-week term for undergraduates. In addition, thousands of people participated in the two-week Bible school.

The college announced in October 1916 it would no longer accept any more candidates for the doctor of philosophy degree, ending a pet project of both Isaac Ketler and Alexander Ormond. In 1916–1917, the college's two religion professors offered seven Bible courses: two in Old Testament history, Hebrew Prophets, Hebrew Wisdom Literature, the Life of Christ, the Apostolic Church, and the History of the English Bible. The next year, the trustees raised $55,000 to endow the Samuel P. Harbison Chair of Bible.

The trustees stated in 1917 that Grove City College had received "Presbyterian approval." This entitled the synod to send a team to evaluate the college's "quality of religious work." The synod was also charged to certify annually that all Grove City faculty members regularly attended "evangelical churches" and were "in full sympathy and accord with the fundamental teaching of evangelical churches."[50] A leading professor in the 1910s was Samuel Oliphant. Oliphant, the head of the Greek department, was named a Fellow of the Royal Society of Arts, one of the highest honors in the scholarly world, and a Fellow of the Sanskrit Society of India.

Administrators, faculty, and students promoted faith formation through a spiritual emphasis week, campus organizations, chapel services, and courses. For many years, the college held a weeklong series of events to foster spiritual growth. Classes were shortened to provide more time for the activities of the spiritual emphasis week, including chapel talks by guest pastors and professors. After operating on campus for twenty-five years, the YMCA became funded by the college in 1916 and no longer needed to charge a membership fee.[51] In fall 1916, the YWCA announced it would engage in "aggressive, effective" work with "renewed zeal" and sponsor group Bible studies.[52] A "Mission Study Class" for women met on Saturdays during the late 1910s. Its leaders asserted that the YMCA promoted men's "real spiritual development" by hosting weekly gatherings that included speakers, Bible studies, prayer meetings, and fellowship. Under YMCA auspices, students helped with Sunday evening church services and Sunday school classes at local churches, religious activities at George Junior Republic, and devotional exercises in local schools.[53] For many years, Grove City had a campus pastor who taught Bible courses, conducted Sunday chapel services, and oversaw campus religious organizations. In 1916, *The Collegian* boasted that no other college's "Christian atmosphere" excelled the one "which pervades Grove City College."[54]

Many prominent individuals spoke in chapel or addressed various campus groups. For example, in February 1916, George Nasmyth, a leader of the World Peace Foundation, preached in chapel. Grace Richardson, secretary of the National YWCA, exhorted students to support the war effort by limiting their consumption and raising money.[55] That month, smoking was prohibited on campus by popular vote after Herbert Harmon made a stirring chapel speech and several student meetings endorsed the ban.[56]

Upperclassmen devised a set of initiation rites and rules for freshmen, purportedly designed to help them adjust to college life. Freshmen were required to wear dinks—felt hats with small brims. The rules were more rigorously enforced some years than others. A 1916 *Collegian* article argued that toning down "hazing" had made it a "sane and successful affair."[57] Each year in September, upper-class Colonial Hall women awoke freshmen at 3 a.m. and required them to pledge "reasonable obedience and submission." As part of their initiation into campus life, female freshmen came to chapel with their hair in curlers or adorned with green ribbons.[58] The annual "sodbuster" gave freshmen an opportunity to meet upperclassmen by completing an obstacle course, engaging in rotating three-minute conversations, playing various games, and dancing. Freshmen were expected to quickly learn a half dozen college yells such as: "O-h-h-h-h for the Undertaker; 'Nother job for the Casketmaker. Up in the Woodland Cemetery, they've been very busy on a brand new grave for poor old _______."[59]

Parties and intramural sports abounded for men and women. For example, in 1916, the faculty entertained students at a Halloween party at which prizes were awarded for the best costumes, and female freshmen hosted a left-handed party for upperclasswomen and female professors.[60] Class spirit was very strong; all four classes had their own colors, mottos, cheers, yells, and songs. That fall, a large crowd watched a gym classes exhibition, which featured drills, marching, folk dancing, apparatus performances, tumbling, and pyramid building.[61]

In March 1904, twelve students, including the editor in chief of *The Collegian*, the captain of the football team, and the son of professor had been expelled for creating an underground fraternity called the Possum Club, infuriating many students and alumni.[62] During the 1910s, sanctioned fraternities and sororities were finally organized. Pan Sophic was formed in 1911, Adelphikos in 1913, and Delta Iota Kappa in 1917; the Sigma Sigma Sigma sorority began in 1917. The administration tolerated, but did not approve of, these Greek organizations. They would play a major role in campus life, especially from the 1930s to the 1970s.

Drumming up support for athletic teams was a perennial challenge despite many teams' superb play. *The Collegian* complained in 1916 that the college had not had "regular, well-attended, enthusiastic mass meetings" for several years.[63] Another editorial that year, however, exulted that Grove City's school spirit was evident in athletic contests, religious endeavors, and other extracurricular activities.[64] While praising the gymnasium's pool, batting cages, and locker room, *The Collegian* urged the college to construct a football complex "second to none" by building an imposing fence around the stadium and concrete stands and improving the track around the field.[65]

In a 1916 chapel speech, Ketler exhorted students to reduce their extracurricular activities and spend more time on their academic work, their principal reason for attending college.[66] So many plays were being staged each year that attendance was poor. Ketler proposed that the seven organizations producing plays pool their resources to produce one play each term, which their leaders concluded was a good solution to the problem.[67]

Ketler beseeched students in a 1916 chapel address to embody the college's ideals of clean living, right thinking, fair play, and hard work.[68] Speaking at a Pittsburgh alumni banquet that year,

Ketler declared that Grove City College engaged in "thorough and accurate scholarship" and strove to produce graduates who had "well-trained minds" and "well-rounded personalities," espoused "high ideals," and exemplified "solid, vigorous, aggressive Christianity." Ketler argued that the faculty compared favorably with those of other institutions, the trustees were "second to none," the students were earnest and enthusiastic, and the alumni were loyal and faithful; together, these four groups enabled Grove City College to accomplish more good than any other school.[69]

As the Great War ripped European civilization apart, the college's four literary societies hosted numerous debates on campus, and men's and women's teams competed in intercollegiate contests. *The Collegian* exulted in March 1916 when the men's team, led by senior Harold McCamey, defeated Pitt's very experienced squad. This impressive victory, *The Collegian* argued, validated the quality of Grove City's education.[70] The *Ouija* added that Grove City's success in debate, even more than its victories in athletic contests, demonstrated the college's distinctiveness.[71]

To earn enough money to pay their expenses, forty-one Grove City students worked for the college in 1916–1917, while others held jobs at stores and manufacturing plants. In addition, numerous students were employed during school breaks. The trustees discovered that sixteen of Grove City's competitors were offering scholarships, often using the interest generated by their endowments, and that many colleges also gave loans to high-achieving students. The trustees noted that the cost of college had doubled in the previous fifteen years, making it more difficult for youths to attend, but rather than giving scholarships or offering loans, they decided to keep Grove City's cost as low as possible.[72]

As American participation in the war grew more likely, Ketler announced in January 1917 that the college would soon establish a unit of the Officer's Reserve Training Corps.[73] Meanwhile, *The Collegian* called for requiring physical education classes and urged men to join college sports teams to help prepare for military service.[74] Faculty wrote numerous articles about various aspects of the war in Europe.

Shortly after the United States entered World War I on April 6, the faculty recommended that any students who were drafted or left college to do vital farm work receive credit for their current courses and that all seniors be granted diplomas. The beginning of the fall term was moved back ten days to aid students who were harvesting crops or doing other crucial jobs.[75] The college organized a student military company, which drilled four times a week. As a precaution, the federal government ordered Harmon to dismantle the college's wireless station (which transmitted telegraph signals without wires).[76] Grove City coeds worked through a local Red Cross chapter to knit clothing for the war effort.[77] At a benefit concert for the American Red Cross in March 1916, a large crowd cheered the performances of the orchestra directed by Hermann Poehlmann and solos by professors Esther Reynolds on the violin and Gustav Mehner on the piano.[78] In March 1917, faculty pledged to President Wilson "our thorough-going support" for whatever measures he deemed advisable.[79] Wilson thanked them for their support for the war effort.[80]

The trustees pondered several questions the war raised: Should the college retrench? Should new courses be devised? Would enrollment be significantly decreased? Influenced by the federal government's encouragement of colleges to continue their normal activities, the trustees decided not to reduce Grove City's program. They acknowledged, however, that the war would likely diminish enrollment, make it difficult to keep qualified faculty, and increase the cost of food, coal, repairs, and labor.[81]

In October 1917, the college's disciplinary committee suspended thirteen men for hazing. At a mass meeting, students selected representatives to confer with this committee. When its members refused to change their decision, almost the entire student body refused to attend their classes for two days. The suspended men returned to campus after a week, but the incident dampened school spirit.[82] Minor protests of the requirement to attend chapel six days a week continued. Students occasionally wore hats to services, festooned with dish pans, brooms, mops, wastebaskets, and tin cans, and rigged up a procedure so that when an alarm clock went off, a sheet and skeleton descended from the ceiling of the chapel.[83] Students were reprimanded for reading Sunday newspaper, not rising during hymns, and doing homework during chapel services. To help justify their actions, students called attention to faculty members who did not regularly attend chapel.[84]

Ketler reported in January 1918 that the college was "keenly feeling" the effects of the war. Prices for many basic supplies had increased, while enrollment had decreased. Summer school attendance declined from 725 in 1916 to 525 in 1917. About two hundred male students were serving the nation in some capacity, many as soldiers in France.[85] College officials praised students' "splendid patriotic spirit" and sacrifices to aid the war effort.[86] Remarkably, the summer Bible school continued to flourish as renowned professors and pastors taught thousands of ministers and laypeople. Ketler claimed in June 1917 that seldom had "such an array of prominent men been assembled at a similar conference in America."[87]

Music has been very important at Grove City College since its beginning. The academy's first catalog promised to supply music teachers for public schools. Eugene Heffley helped organize the music program while teaching from 1890 to 1893. He later became one of New York City's best-known musicians and served as the president of the McDowell Society, one of nation's leading musical organizations.[88] In 1916, Ilse Poehlman, '15, was selected as a soloist for one of New York City's principal Presbyterian churches and several of its major Jewish synagogues. Her success, *The Collegian* claimed, testified that no other institution exceeded the high quality of Grove City's music conservatory.[89] As noted, Hermann Poehlman played the principal role in developing the music program.

Conditions became worse by June 1918. Ketler again informed the trustees that costs were up while enrollment was down (full-time male enrollment decreased from 217 in 1915–1916 to fifty by the end of the June 1918 term). The college still had a large deficit ($134,000, $2.8 million today).[90] Grove City had three options: close until the war ended; retrench (but many departments already consisted of a single professor); or try to keep its debt to a minimum. The college chose the third alternative. Despite the war, Ketler continued to call for increasing the endowment and providing more undergraduate scholarships and aid to help alumni "of exceptional merit" attend graduate school. Although most professors were making financial sacrifices to stay at Grove City and many students had very limited resources, they generously supported the Red Cross, the American Committee for Armenian and Syrian Relief, and other aid organizations.[91]

By the summer of 1918, matters looked even bleaker for colleges. The secretary of war required all men between eighteen and forty-five to register for military service and announced that all male college students would be considered privates in the army and part of the Student Army Training Corps and housed, clothed, and subsisted at government expense.[92] In 1918–1919, 250 men were assigned to Grove City's Student Army Training Corps. Memorial was converted into a barracks for these men who drilled on the college's athletic fields. The faculty and military staff enjoyed a cordial relationship.[93]

About 250 Grove City alumni and students served in World War I, eleven of whom died. After the war ended on November 11, 1918, Grove City quickly resumed normal activities, despite dealing with the global influenza epidemic that between May 1918 and February 1919 killed more than three times as many people as the war had (fifty million versus sixteen million). Numerous staff and students became ill, but no one died, and the college never closed.

The Student Army Training Corps was dissolved in December 1918, but Grove City established an army ROTC detachment in spring 1919, which a government inspector called "a model unit." After visiting twenty detachments, he stated that Grove City's corps was "better organized" and "showed better spirit" and that the college's physical plant was better equipped to handle a unit than any other school he visited.[94] The unit was discontinued in spring 1920, however, because many sophomores and freshmen had served in World War I.

In the 1910s, women had to sign out any time they left their dormitories, and they had strict time limits for how long they could be gone depending upon their destination and activity. Seniors were allowed to go on dates three evenings each week, while underclassmen were permitted to date only on Friday and Saturday nights. In fall 1918, senior Isabelle Blyholder became the first female editor in chief of *The Collegian*. She played on her class basketball team, participated in the YWCA, and belonged to the Philokalian Club, whose members frequently debated the topic of women's suffrage. The 19th Amendment giving women the right to vote was passed by Congress in June 1919 and ratified by the states in August 1920. Blyholder's April 1919 editorial argued that the role women had played in the Great War had brought them to the forefront except in "a few isolated spots," including Grove City College. She insisted that women could do everything men did more efficiently. Blyholder denounced the numerous college rules that applied to only to women, such as curfews and "lights out" hours in their dormitory, which required them to use candlelight to finish their homework and prepare for tests. Many of these rules did not end until the 1960s, and curfews for freshmen women remained until 2005. While men were fighting in Europe, she concluded, women took over many tasks at home. At Grove City College, they served on numerous committees, provided entertainment, and excelled academically. They had ensured that all the college's "vital traditions" had continued. Therefore, she maintained, the college must give women the recognition they craved and deserved.[95] The *Ouija* argued that Blyholder had filled her position "with marked success."[96]

Grove City added a chemical engineering program in 1918 whose majors were required to spend three summers working in industrial plants. In May 1919, a special trustee committee recommended that the college establish scholarships, provide student loans, accept annuities, and create more engineering programs.

That same year, Grove City began offering a four-year bachelor's of music degree program. In 1920, the college established a department of commerce; business majors would be among the most popular for the next century.

In 1919, Ketler claimed that 16 percent of high school principals in western Pennsylvania were graduates of Grove City and that more Grove City graduates had received state permanent educational certificates than those of all other colleges in Pennsylvania combined, despite the state subsidizing its teacher colleges.[97] On the other hand, the president told board members in 1920 that a recent report of the Association of American Colleges judged Grove City to be deficient in several ways. It asserted that a college of five hundred students should have fifty faculty (Grove City had four hundred students and twenty-three faculty); a budget of $333 ($5,300 today) per student (Grove City's was $222 per student), an endowment of $2,215,000 ($35.4 million today) (Grove City's was $261,000), a physical plant and equipment valued at $985,000 (GCC's was $458,000), and total assets per student of $6,400 (GCC's was $1,797).[98]

A trustee planning committee recommended that the college cap enrollment at five hundred, buy land to expand the upper campus, and erect a science building, chapel, and dormitories. The only building project completed in the 1920s, however, was increasing Colonial's capacity to 135 women. The committee acknowledged that the college had been running a sizable debt each year (exacerbated by World War I), its teaching staff was undermanned and underpaid (the top salary of a Grove City professor was $3,000, $48,000 today), and its endowment was substantially less than peer colleges. Therefore, members called for increasing the endowment by $1 million.[99] These and other challenges confronted the college as the 1920s began.

In April 1920, president Ketler gave a speech to the Rotary Club of New Castle, Pennsylvania, over the college radio station WSAJ, which occurred six months before KDKA's famous broadcast of the Warren Harding versus James Cox election results. The *New Castle*

News called the transmission "a remarkable demonstration of wireless telephony," which enabled club members to hear music played and a speech given twenty-two miles away.[100] Grove City College would have many more impressive accomplishments during the next two decades.

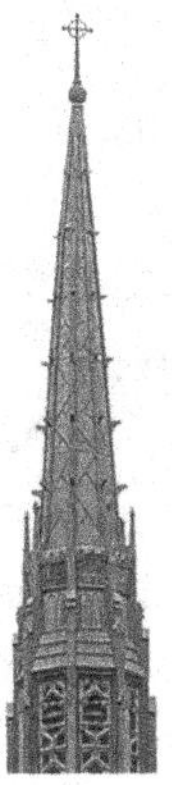

Devising and Implementing the Master Plan, 1921–1940

The 1920s: "Expect Great Things"

Labeled "The Roaring Twenties" and the "Jazz Age," the 1920s was a decade of artistic, cultural, and technological innovation. Prohibition was instituted. Speakeasies flouted the law. Flappers challenged Victorian standards of dress and decorum. The Charleston became a dance craze. Businesses sought to operate more efficiently. Consumerism, fueled by numerous new products and advertising, blossomed. Millions of Americans moved to cities. The middle class grew significantly. Women gained the right to vote. Cultural heroes emerged: baseball slugger Babe Ruth, boxer Jack Dempsey, football star Red Grange, aviator Charles Lindbergh, authors F. Scott Fitzgerald and Ernest Hemingway, actors Charlie Chaplin and Clara Bow, and musicians Louis Armstrong and Duke Ellington. Telephones, automobiles, radios, films, and electrical appliances became popular. The seeming futility of World War I led many young adults to become disillusioned and cynical about life.

Social critics lampooned the greed and hypocrisy they observed. The decade's prosperity abruptly ended with the stock market crash in October 1929.

While affected by these cultural and economic developments, Grove City College, driven by its Christian values, provided an alternative to some trends. In October 1923, Weir Ketler declared that the college's slogan for the year was "Expect Great Things," which Grove City used in its promotional literature.[1] During the 1920s, the college was guided by this motto as college leaders concocted and carried out a master plan that expanded the campus beyond Wolf Creek to a hill overlooking the town. Meanwhile, Grove City emphasized spiritual formation, strengthened its academic program, assembled a larger, better-educated faculty, increased enrollment, incorporated new educational methods, enlarged the endowment, and enriched students' social life. During this decade, many sports teams were highly successful, Greek life became more important (by 1924 the college had six fraternities and ten sororities), and WSAJ aired numerous athletic events, musical programs, dramas, and forensic events.

Weir Ketler told the trustees that the fall 1920 term had the "finest spirit of cooperation" and highest standard of conduct he had witnessed at Grove City.[2] In June 1921, the president reported that Grove City had been trying with "considerable success" to gain accreditation by several standardizing organizations, but he warned that its small endowment might pose a problem. Nevertheless, the Association of Colleges and Secondary Schools of the Middle States and Maryland fully accredited Grove City the next year.

The college continued to strongly emphasize ancient languages. Most departments had only one professor who taught numerous courses. For example, the Department of History, Economics, and Government had a single professor and listed fifteen history, eight economics, and five government courses to be taught on a rotating basis. The college had eliminated its preparatory department, but it provided some remedial courses to help freshmen who were deficient in various subject areas. The Grove City School of Art, closely affiliated with the college, sought "to stimulate an interest in the fine arts in its various forms and phases." The department of athletics and physical training had a director, a medical adviser, and an instructor for women.[3]

A 1921 survey asked students why they chose Grove City. Their principal reason was the encouragement of their parents, relatives, friends, pastors, and high school teachers. But Grove City's religious and moral ideals, courses of study, and athletic program were also very important considerations. To recruit students, the registrar visited most of the leading high schools in western Pennsylvania and the faculty met with students at many high schools during commencement week.[4]

A humorous poem in *The Collegian* in 1921 described the college's four classes:

> *"You can always tell a Senior, he*
> *is so sedately dressed;*
> *You can always tell a Junior by*
> *the way he swells his chest;*
> *You can always tell a Freshman*
> *by his timid looks and such;*
> *You can always tell a Sophomore,*
> *but you cannot tell him much."*[5]

In January 1921, Robert Thorn was appointed the director of athletics, a position he held until 1957. Because the college's gymnasium was small, physical education was not required. In contrast to the effusive praise Ketler received when he was appointed president in 1916, many students complained in the early 1920s that he was too strict and formal. The 1922 *Ouija* declared, however, that Ketler was "firm in his purposes, kindly in disposition, keen in judgment," and an advocate of "fair play and hard work," which were "great qualities" for a college president.[6] In 1924, W. E. Purvis, pastor of Grove City's United Presbyterian Church, was hired to replace Robert Calder as the campus pastor. He was responsible for arranging the Sunday chapel program, overseeing religious organizations, and stimulating the college's religious life.

During the 1921–1922 academic year, 452 of Grove City's 477 students were from Pennsylvania; 129 of them lived in Mercer County. Their denominational affiliation included 201 Presbyterians, ninety-three Methodists, seventy-two United Presbyterians, twenty-three Lutherans, and twenty-two Catholics. The chapel, which seated about four hundred, could no longer accommodate all students and faculty; the Sunday vesper services were especially crowded because many professors brought family members. The 1922–1923 catalog proudly stated that numerous seminaries declared that Grove City graduates "are well trained in habits of thought and study." The college, it added, emphasized Christian character and sent many young men and women into the gospel ministry or other Christian work; it claimed that more Grove City graduates had entered the ministry than those of any other college in Pennsylvania.[7]

In 1922, a student handbook was introduced that contained college history, traditions, rules, and songs. The next year, *The Wolf Pack* debuted, which published student research papers and opinion essays. In fall 1923, students protested the college's lack of a student council and dances by briefly refusing to participate in class recitations or discissions or extracurricular activities.[8] The next spring, students chose senior class president James Tallant and junior J. Stanley Harker to devise a student council constitution. After professors and students agreed on its powers and duties, Clifford Bowden was elected the first Student Council president and Harker was appointed as a representative to the faculty.[9] Students and faculty chose the council's fifteen members. That academic year, the total enrollment for the three terms was 607.

In 1923, the sixty-acre campus included four classroom buildings, Carnegie Library, Ketler Gymnasium, Ivy Chapel, and three dorms—Colonial, Cunningham, and Memorial. Ketler lamented that the college's facilities were inferior to those of some high schools. Most buildings were poorly constructed and had outlived their usefulness; many classrooms and labs were overcrowded. On the other hand, he insisted that the college's moral and religious conditions were excellent and that its winning sports teams were promoting a positive mood on campus and generating much public attention.[10]

The 1923 college *Bulletin* reasserted that Grove City promoted clean living, strength of body and mind through sports and outdoor activities, and right thinking, which included broadmindedness. Grove City stood "for a sane conservativeness," "real Christianity," "public spiritedness," "true democracy," and "hard work." It did not tolerate "idlers and loafers."[11] An article in *The Collegian* in 1923 argued that a college education should furnish students with moral standards based on the Golden Rule; "a religion based on the Sermon on the Mount"; the realization that Christianity harmonized with all truth in every academic discipline; the capacity to observe, reason, and judge; respect for other people's religious views; the ability to write and speak correctly; familiarity with the world's best literature; a knowledge of history and important current events; training for a career; and a spirit of optimism and loyalty.[12]

The Collegian urged students to get involved in activities, and many did.[13] In 1923, the college had four literary societies, YMCA and YWCA chapters, and the Schubert, commercial, science and dramatic clubs. The college established its first academic honoraries in the 1920s—Pi Kappa Delta in forensics, Pi Gamma Mu in the social sciences (the first chapter formed in Pennsylvania), and Kemikos in chemistry, and soon added a Spanish club, another men's glee club, and a college choir. In a 1925 contest, senior Doris Dow was chosen as Grove City's most beautiful coed. The "real nice girl" had received the biblical "ten talents"; she could cook, play sports and musical instruments, and paint; the "winsome lass" also had a delightful personality.[14] During the roaring twenties, a favorite campus game was flag rush, which involved freshmen and upperclassmen competing to put their flag atop the college flagpole. Tactics included freshmen greasing the flagpole after planting their flag and upperclassman shooting the freshmen flag full of buckshot and trying to light it on fire.

Seeking to become less dependent on the Pew family, the college undertook a $750,000 campaign in 1923 to increase the endowment. The next year, the Rockefeller Foundation, the philanthropic arm of oil billionaire John D. Rockefeller, pledged $100,000, while the PCUSA Board of Christian Education promised to give the college 8 percent of the money it raised through its Challenge Fund.[15] J. Stanley Harker chaired a 1925 student drive to help increase the endowment. Almost every senior contributed, and an impressive $31,000 ($566,000 today) was raised in cash and pledges.[16] As schools from the elementary level to state universities were becoming secularized, Ketler argued, institutions like Grove City that emphasized "the Christian spirit and the Christian point of view" were vital.[17]

Grove City offered some athletic scholarships during the 1920s, fielded numerous outstanding teams, and produced several stellar athletes. In 1920, the college reestablished an athletic council, consisting of three trustees, three faculty, three alumni, and two town residents, to oversee college athletics, approve the scheduling of games, and control the athletic budget. Its members argued two years later that the college's athletic success had helped increase enrollment. In 1920–1921, the basketball team coached by Robert Thorn finished 16–1 and won the tristate championship. The next year Grove City went 16–4 and was invited to play in the National Intercollegiate Tournament. The next three years, the squad had a combined record of 50–12; the 1922–1923 team beat Pitt 36–34 and West Virginia University 39–8. Basketball was so popular and the seating capacity was so small that a lottery system was used to dispense tickets. Swimming made a splash on campus in the mid-1920s as a student with lifeguard experience taught classes, many men learned how to swim, and a men's swim meet was held in spring 1926.[18]

Grove City's football teams also excelled in the 1920s, winning four Western Pennsylvania Class B championships. Coach Charles Bowser's football teams compiled a record of 17–6–1 from 1924 to 1926. His 1925 team lost only to West Virginia University and beat Geneva 3–0, which had previously defeated Yale and Cornell.

Bowser's 1926 team went 7–0, outscoring John Carroll, Canisus, Marshall, Allegheny, St. Francis, Geneva, and Thiel 114–19. In 1939, Bowser replaced Pitt's legendary head football coach Jock Sutherland.

Charles Berry served as Grove City's football coach from 1927 to 1931. As a receiver for Lafayette College, Berry had been named to Walter Camp's All-America football team. Berry was a Major League Baseball catcher from 1928 to 1936. Remarkably, the Boston Red Sox, with whom he played from 1928 to 1931, allowed Berry to leave shortly before the season ended to coach Grove City's team. The Chicago White Sox, to whom he was traded in 1932, ended this arrangement. Berry hit.267 in 709 MLB games. After retiring, he worked for many years as an American League umpire and then as a supervisor of NFL officials. Berry's Grove City squads had a superb 27–7–8 record. Berry's team, a *Collegian* sportswriter declared, was "an inspired fighting machine."[19] The 1930 Wolverines opened their season by defeating Morris Harvey College 90–0, the highest score in Grove City College history. They outscored their first six opponents 136–0 and were the fifth-ranked Eastern Collegiate team after Dartmouth, Cornell, Army, and Fordham before losing to Geneva 13–12 and Allegheny 6–0 and finishing 7–2. The 1931 football team scored 149 points to its opponent's twenty-eight. From 1922 to 1931, Grove City's 56–21–10 (.727) record was the best of the nine teams in its district.[20]

Grove City's football stars in the 1920s included Ben Jones, '23, Evans Denver "Butch" Gibson, '27, Ed Waleski, '30, and center Montgomery Lantz '30. After helping lead Grove City to a 20–9–3 aggregate record, Jones, a halfback, played several seasons in the National Football League. He won championships with the Canton Bulldogs in 1923, earning All-NFL status, the Cleveland Bulldogs in 1924, and the Frankford Yellow Jackets in 1926. Gibson, a guard, played for the Canton Bulldogs and Rogers Jewelers teams. He then spent five seasons with the New York Giants, including with the 1934 NFL championship team. Gibson was named an All-NFL player in 1931 and 1934. Lantz played one season in the NFL, while Waleski played professional football with the Philadelphia Legion.

In April 1926, the Student Council petitioned the faculty to permit dancing on campus. Fraternities and sororities had been holding unsanctioned dances off campus for a decade. After the faculty voted eighteen to ten to allow dances, the board decided to permit dances to be held on Saturdays or immediately before holidays.[21] To celebrate the school's fiftieth anniversary during the 1926 commencement week, the college arranged several special events. Clarence Macartney, the moderator of the 1924 General Assembly of the PCUSA, Samuel Black McCormick, the chancellor emeritus of the University of Pittsburgh, and other educators and politicians spoke. In addition, the faculty presented a pageant portraying the college's first half century.

Greek-letter social fraternities began in United States in late the 1820s at Union and Hamilton colleges in New York. They spread quickly to other schools and, at many institutions, replaced literary societies.[22] As noted, Grove City administrators and faculty did not view favorably the fraternities and sororities that were established at the college in the 1910s. The faculty finally approved the Pan-Hellenic Council, which governed sororities, in 1927 and the Inter-Fraternity Council, the counterpart for fraternities, in 1929. Administrators refused to allow fraternity members to live together off campus. Ketler argued that dormitories were less expensive, better furnished, more easily supervised, and more democratic.[23] All students were required to live in dorms unless they received special permission. The battle over off-campus fraternity housing would resurface in the 1960s and persist for more than twenty years.

Grove City's student body and faculty increased significantly in 1925–1926 to 927 students and thirty-six professors. Nevertheless, the college continued to run deficits of about $10,000 ($180,000 today) a year. Although the college raised only about half of its goal in its mid-1920s campaign, Ketler was pleased that the endowment more than doubled between 1925 and 1928 to $619,000 ($11.6 million today). Ketler praised Frederick Raymond Babcock, who served as the board president from 1913 to 1928 and chaired the committee to increase the endowment, for his energetic leadership in guiding the college and improving its finances. Babcock had attended many events on campus, gained the respect of other trustees, and for fifteen years been "a moving and vital spirit" in the college's life.[24]

During the 1920s, some of the world's most renowned pastors, seminary presidents, and religion professors spoke at Grove City's summer Bible school including London minister F. B. Meyer; Mark Matthews, pastor of First Presbyterian Church in Seattle; Charles Jefferson, former pastor of Broadway Tabernacle in New York City; John Timothy Stone, president of McCormick Theological Seminary in Chicago; and Princeton Theological Seminary's former president, Francis Patton, and two of its leading professors, Robert Dick Wilson and J. Gresham Machen.

The 1928–1929 catalog stated that Grove City College "is a definitely Christian co-educational institution." The college was "broadly tolerant" and endeavored to cooperate with all denominations. Grove City had an "exceptionally cordial" relation with the PCUSA, which classified it as a cooperating institution. All students were required to attend chapel services held Tuesday through Saturday mornings and Sunday vespers.[25]

In 1929, the college began phasing out all its MA programs because they required too much faculty time and because standardizing agencies looked negatively at schools with limited resources granting master's degrees. Grove City introduced new majors in English, French, Spanish, Greek, Latin, history, social science, philosophy-sociology, and mathematics for the BA degree (the nomenclature changed from AB to BA in 1920) and chemistry, physics, biology, and chemical engineering for the BS degree. Those receiving a BS in commerce could major in accounting, economics, or business administration. Students could also earn a bachelor's degree in either music performance or music education.[26]

The 1926–1927 catalog asserted that the "college does not publish an exhaustive set of rules," but Grove City did not permit drinking, gambling, dishonesty, or hazing.[27] Throughout the 1920s, however, upperclassmen forced freshmen to act subserviently by walking single file to chapel, wearing dinks, entering buildings by side rather than front doors, stepping off sidewalks to allow upperclassmen to pass, and addressing upper-class women as "mademoiselle." Freshman women were prohibited from using lipstick and required to wear green bows in their pigtails.[28] Hazing, which Ketler despised, continued to produce problems. Numerous upperclassmen violated college rules by the "blindfolding, paddling, and cutting the hair" of some freshmen. Some offenders were suspended, but their penalty was rather mild because no evidence existed that they possessed "a vicious spirit."[29]

The efforts of upperclassmen to enforce their rules often led to conflict, tension, and animosity. Freshmen who did not follow the rules were often brought before tribunals and punished by losing privileges.[30] Upset that numerous freshmen were not obeying the rules, upperclassmen published a list in 1926 of rule breakers to prevent scofflaws from joining any campus clubs.[31] The next year, eleven students were prohibited from dating for one month for various offenses.[32] Upperclassmen declared that freshmen who did not obey the rules not only violated college customs, but failed to contribute "to the spirit of the college." Upperclassmen argued that the college would go "backward if these traditions are not maintained."[33] In the later 1920s, the Student Council usually ended the rules after the last home football game. The battle over freshmen rules intensified in the 1930s.

The Collegian argued that through its classes, dances, parties, literary clubs, and sports contests, Grove City helped students become well-rounded, develop keen minds, and prepare for their lives' work.[34] Despite these belittling initiation rites, freshmen participated with upperclassmen in a wide variety of campus activities including a sodbuster dance, Poverty Day revelries, numerous homecoming events, a Thanksgiving dance, Christmas festivities, a winter frolic, a Pan-Hellenic formal dance in April, the May Pageant, and June commencement celebrations. For Poverty Day, which today would be considered inappropriate, almost all students wore their oldest clothes (dressing as "bums" and "hobos," as *The Collegian* put it) and had a parade.[35] The worst men's and women's outfits received prizes.

Dean of women Lois Cory-Thompson required female students to obey numerous rules. Clinging to a man's arm was forbidden because it was "in wretched taste and very silly." When the electric lights came on, all window shades must be lowered in the women's dormitory. Every woman's room was inspected weekly. Any women caught smoking would be "drastically dealt with." Men escorting women to their dormitory had to leave promptly; conversing by the entrance was "silly and undesirable." Underclasswomen could go to town only on Saturdays. Women could walk with men on only the main streets of town, not on any side streets.[36]

Two months after the stock market crash in October 1929, Ketler told the trustees that offices and conference rooms for faculty, a new science building, a new chapel, additional dormitories for men and women, and a second gym were all needed, which would cost a daunting total of $3 million ($55.4 million today). Despite the bleak economic conditions, the trustees approved a campaign to build a dormitory, a science building, and a chapel.[37] An article in *The Collegian* in 1930 bemoaned the nation's abysmal economic and social conditions: Thousands of businesses had gone bankrupt, drunk driving was commonplace, many Americans smoked or used dope, the United States had a high murder rate, and numerous nations appeared to be preparing for war. The best way to combat these problems, the anonymous author argued, was to faithfully obey God and work to establish his kingdom on earth.[38]

The 1930s: Extending the Kingdom of God

The 1930s were very challenging. The decade began with a worldwide depression and ended with a global war, both of which brought immense suffering to millions. During the 1930s, President Franklin Roosevelt implemented his New Deal policies, which substantially increased the power of both the federal government and the presidency and significantly changed the relationship between the government and the business community. Many colleges struggled during the decade as their enrollment and funds decreased. Although Grove City's student body dipped in the early 1930s and the college faced financial difficulties, it managed to considerably improve its facilities, adding a magnificent chapel, a state-of-the art science hall, two dormitories, and an administration building, and it emerged from the decade as a stronger institution than it had been in 1930. Then the college plunged into the maelstrom World War II caused. In dedicating the Harbison Chapel in October 1931, W. L. McEwan, vice president of the board, declared that small "definitely Christian" colleges like Grove City were "one of the best agencies for the extension of the Kingdom of God."

Academic Matters

The 1931–1932 catalog emphasized that Grove City's fourfold purpose was to promote sound scholarship, Christian morality, spiritual growth, and an aesthetic interest. Grove City, it asserted, was "a Christian college" where "the study of the Bible is an integral part of the curriculum." The faculty "are Christian in belief and influence." Students were required to attend daily and Sunday chapel services.[39] The academic credentials of the faculty were improving; that year, only seven of the college's thirty-nine faculty had only a BA or BS degree, while twenty-one had a master's degree, and eleven had doctoral degrees. In January 1932, Ketler declared his desire to create a retirement plan for faculty (this did not happen, however, until 1955). He also wanted to quickly liquidate the substantial debt the building program and depression had produced and to provide more scholarships.[40]

Ketler maintained in June 1935 that eight hundred was the maximum number of students the physical plant and faculty could accommodate. He argued that the college needed an administration building with a large auditorium and a gymnasium with a swimming pool. Ketler confessed that knowing his limitations, he had accepted the presidency twenty years earlier with "some trepidation," but the trustees' generosity, vision, and courage had enabled the college to overcome many obstacles.[41] The student body increased from 628 in 1932–1933 to 850 in 1936–1937 to an all-time high of 918 in 1939–1940. The freshmen class in fall 1939 consisted of almost three hundred, 46 percent of whom were in the top one-fifth of their high school classes.[42]

Like most other colleges, Grove City struggled financially in the 1930s. The college borrowed money to construct buildings, enrollment declined for several years, and many students had to pay their tuition, room, and board fees on an installment plan. Throughout the decade, tuition remained eighty-five dollars ($1,985 today), while board fluctuated from $135 ($3,150) to $190 ($4,435 today). Aided by funds from the Federal Relief Administration, seventy-five Grove City students performed campus jobs each year during the late 1930s to help cover their expenses. Faculty salaries were reduced. Despite this and other cost-cutting measures, Grove City incurred a large debt during the 1930s. In 1937, the Association of American Universities placed Grove City College on its accepted list, but the American Association of University Professors (AAUP) exhorted the college to decrease its debt, strengthen its faculty, and improve the library and planned to reinvestigate in 1940. In his 1938 reports to the trustees, Ketler admitted that Grove City's "program of development" had been more ambitious that the economic circumstances of the 1930s had warranted. Nevertheless, he called for enlarging the library collection and erecting a new gymnasium (the current one had been constructed in 1912, when the college had three hundred students), an engineering building, and possibly an infirmary.[43] That year, William Stewart, who had previously supported the college very generously, bequeathed $300,000 ($6.8 million today) to Grove City. It was the largest gift the college had ever received.

Various academic and institutional changes occurred in the early 1930s. As many businesses created public relations departments, business professor R. G. Walters was assigned in 1932 to promote the college and to establish a placement bureau for students. During the spring, as many as one hundred prospective students and their families visited the college every Saturday and Sunday. The college hosted two thousand teachers and school superintendents for the eighth annual Northwestern District Pennsylvania State Education Association meeting in October 1932. Almost six hundred Grove City graduates were teaching in Pennsylvania, many of them in this district.[44]

The faculty concentrated on providing quality instruction, supervising extracurricular activities, and helping students grow academically, socially, and spiritually. One outstanding classroom instructor during this period was Elinor Caruthers, the chair of the modern language department, who taught German, French, and Spanish from 1908 to 1940 and led more than twenty student trips to Europe. Colleagues compared Caruthers with the title character of the 1939 movie *Goodbye, Mr. Chips*. Many professors were very involved in church and civic activities. Given their priorities and commitments, most professors spent little time doing research or writing scholarly articles or books. Describing their demanding responsibilities, one student explained "why professors go gray": faculty meetings, "frightened frosh," uncompleted assignments, wisecracking fellows, "undecipherable handwriting, cribbers, evasive answers," and "co-eds who think goo goo eyes bring good grades."[45] In addition to advising student organizations and attending student activities, the faculty in the 1930s engaged in various activities to deepen relationships with students and promote school spirit, including playing a softball game against seniors and debating students about whether Grove City should give athletic scholarships.

Walters wrote five books on marketing, education, and word studies in the 1920s and 1930s, and Miriam Franklin penned *Rehearsal: The Principles and Practices of Acting* (1938). Numerous professors, most notably Walters, dean Alva Calderwood, and history professor Levi Beeler, spoke frequently at churches, civic clubs, parachurch organization meetings, and other venues throughout the region. Moreover, in the 1930s, several faculty distinguished themselves beyond the college. Walters served as the governor of Pi Gamma Mu in Pennsylvania, a member of the executive committee of the National Council of Commercial Education, a consultant on the Educational Policies Commission, president of the Rotary Club and the Grove City Commerce Club, and on the Republican State Committee. Creig Hoyt was elected to Phi Lambda Upsilon, the national chemical honorary. The US Weather Bureau commended Herbert Harmon for furnishing weather reports and submitting weather observations twice every day for twenty-eight years. H. M. Burrowes, head of the English department, was elected the president of Debating Societies of Pennsylvania and as the governor of Pi Kappa Delta's Province of the Lakes.

In 1936, Grove City granted its last master's degree until 1996. It had awarded only seven since 1931. In fall 1937, 105 of GCC's 898 students made the honor roll, eight of whom earned all A's. In 1939, Grove City received 445 applications and enrolled 302 freshmen. Students who had low grades were required to meet with the dean, and their parents were notified. In 1939–1940, the college expelled fifty students because of their poor grades.[46]

The economic depression curtailed attendance at the summer Bible school for several years during the 1930s, but its teachers included some of the world's most respected pastors and professors: A. Z. Conrad, pastor of Park Street Church in Boston; Albert Bevan, president of Colgate-Rochester Seminary; Benjamin Lacy Jr., president of Union Theological Seminary in Richmond; and professors Samuel Zwemer and E. G. Homrighausen of Princeton Theological Seminary. The Bible school, Ketler contended, had enhanced the intellectual and spiritual life of many western Pennsylvania religious leaders.[47]

Facilities

Five important buildings opened in the 1930s—Harbison Chapel, the Hall of Science, Ketler and Mary Anderson Pew dormitories, and Crawford Hall—all situated according to the master plan the Olmstead brothers developed. These famed landscape artists also designed park systems in Cleveland, Portland, and Seattle, roadways in the Great Smoky Mountains and Acadia National Parks, and many other impressive projects. In October 1930, the college held a special chapel service to celebrate the groundbreaking for its chapel and science buildings. Starting the building projects with a chapel service was fitting, Calderwood declared, "since the college was dedicated from the start to Christian service."[48] At the laying of the cornerstone for Harbison Chapel in February 1931, college pastor W. E. Purvis asserted that "spiritual training has always been a first consideration at Grove City."[49] *The Collegian* contended that the chapel and science building were both "living representations of the faith and high ideals of the college."[50]

The college dedicated both Harbison Chapel and the Hall of Science on October 8, 1931, the "greatest day in the history of Grove City College." The sandstone and limestone chapel, which seated nine hundred, was a "tribute to the spirit of Christianity" which had directed the school since its founding, while the science building was "a source of amazement." The chapel's magnificent stained-glass windows portray John Wycliffe, Martin Luther, John Calvin, John Knox, Jesus the Great Teacher, the four gospel writers, scenes from the history of the early church and the medieval church, and various incidents in America's religious development. One window depicts Joseph Newton Pew, Samuel Harbison, and Isaac Ketler at an early meeting of the board of trustees; at the top of the window is an inscription: "We dedicate this college to the development of sound scholarship and Christian character in all aspiring youth." The Hall of Science contained three dozen classrooms, a lecture hall seating two hundred, numerous faculty offices, a library, a museum, and labs for mechanical, electrical, biological, chemical, and physical sciences. Representatives of forty-three colleges, including twenty-five presidents, marched in a processional from the lower campus across the newly constructed Rainbow Bridge spanning Wolf Creek to Harbison Chapel for the dedication ceremony.[51] In helping to dedicate the Hall of Science, J. Howard Pew, the newly elected president of the board of trustees, argued that Christianity and science were complementary not adversarial. "Cosmic questioning," he insisted, would strengthen rather than destroy Christian faith.[52]

Named for Isaac Ketler, the college's second men's dormitory, was completed in 1932 and housed 108 men. It included a kitchen and a dining room that could seat all the male students. In May 1936, the cornerstone was laid for the college's second women's dormitory, Mary Anderson Pew (MAP), named for J. Howard Pew's mother. She strongly advocated women's rights and education and argued that men and women should be treated equally in all areas of life. At MAP's dedication, Pew praised his mother's "life-long interest in expanding the educational opportunity and cultural privileges of young women."[53] MAP, which opened in fall 1937, accommodated one hundred women and had a great hall, a music room, a library, and dining and kitchen facilities.

Hundreds of people attended the dedication of Crawford Hall on snowy January 14, 1939. Barclay Acheson, whom Pew called "our foremost student of the American system of free enterprise," spoke. Harry Jennings Crawford, an Emlenton businessman, oil producer, and Grove City trustee since 1922, gave $150,000 toward its construction. The new administration building, which cost $375,000 ($8.6 million today), included an auditorium seating 1,075, a large social room, many offices, and several classrooms. The college now consisted of nine buildings on the lower campus and six on the upper campus.

Christianity

Numerous factors testify to the importance of Christianity at Grove City during the 1930s. Throughout the decade, catalogs stated that the college strove to promote solid scholarship, "wholesome" social views, "healthy bodies," and "right, moral spiritual, and aesthetic outlooks." They added that "the study of the Bible is an integral part of the curriculum" and accentuated the Christian commitment of the faculty.[54] Many students participated in religious activities. For many years, history professor E. V. Shockley taught a Sunday school class at Grace Methodist Church that attracted more than one hundred students each week. During Religious Emphasis Week, the college brought prominent pastors to campus to preach. Since 1912, Grove City had an organization devoted to helping students consider a call to Christian ministry.

By 1930, it was called the Oxford Society or the Oxford Club. At its weekly meetings, students delivered sermonettes and received constructive criticism from the college pastor. In 1930, its members hosted the Oxford Club's national convention; Grove City's chapter was one of the most active in the nation.[55]

Both the YMCA and YWCA sponsored numerous campus events. In 1932, the college's YMCA hosted the largest and most successful YMCA conference ever held in Pennsylvania.[56] Four years later, Grove City hosted twelve other college YMCAs for a training conference. The YWCA strove to help women "experience a full and creative life through a growing knowledge of Jesus."[57] In 1938, the two organizations cohosted a highly successful convention for Ys and other Christian campus groups from western Pennsylvania and West Virginia.[58] In 1936, a third campus religious organization, the Christian Service League (CSL), was formed to promote "sincerity, service, sacrifice, and spirituality."[59] The coed CSL met weekly. Members of these three religious organizations occasionally met together for special events.

Christian faith thrived on campus in other ways. For much of its history, the college has devoted a week to spiritual formation led by guest speakers, many of whom were ministers of large urban Presbyterian churches. During the 1930s, several pastors were Grove City alumni. Over the years, this event has had various names including religious emphasis week, prayer week, spiritual emphasis week, religion in life week, and faith and life week. During this special period, morning classes were usually shortened to provide more time for chapel speakers who also addressed large groups in the evenings and counseled students. The 1938 speaker, Roy Ewing Vale, pastor of Woodward Avenue Presbyterian Church in Detroit, praised the "high caliber" of GCC students.[60]

In addition, missionaries frequently spoke in chapel and at the meetings of Christian organizations. For example, in 1938, Howard Taylor, who worked with China Inland Mission, founded by his famous father, J. Hudson Taylor, preached in chapel. Numerous campus organizations opened their meetings with prayer and scripture reading. Many students attended local churches and participated in their Bible studies, meals, scavenger hunts, and hayrides. In 1937, the newly organized gospel team began helping conduct services in area churches.

Throughout its history, Ketler asserted, Grove City College had striven adhere to "Christian standards" in all its activities.[61] The college, he added, sought to emphasize "the ideals of democracy" and factors that developed "Christian character."[62] In signing a 1938 agreement with the PCUSA Board of Christian Education, trustees pledged that the content of college courses would be "true to the basic beliefs of evangelical Christianity" and that students would be required to take at least two Bible courses.[63]

Numerous articles in *The Collegian* expressed the Christian convictions that many students shared. For example, a 1931 editorial urged Grovers to ponder the resurrection of Jesus, who alone could give people new life.[64] In 1936, a student urged his classmates to entreat the Holy Spirit to help convince them that "Jesus Christ is our Lord and Savior."[65] In a 1938 series of articles titled "The Cross and the Crown," an anonymous author asserted that believing in Christ's atoning death was the only means of salvation, defended biblical inspiration, and challenged churches to "get back to the Bible" and focus more on "the great teachings of the Word."[66] The author also denounced theological liberalism as taught by theologian Emil Bruner and Baptist pastor Harry Fosdick as contradictory to scripture and "an awful curse."[67]

In February 1940, the three campus religious organizations canvassed all faculty and students to provide aid for needy Chinese students. An op-ed in *The Collegian* stressed that Grove City students who had been given so much and had such fantastic facilities should help suffering Chinese students whose campuses had been destroyed by bombs.[68]

In Harbison Chapel, as in Ivy Chapel, women sat on the left and men on the right. Students were assigned alphabetically by classes, with seniors in the front and freshmen in the back and the balcony; the faculty checked roll at daily and Sunday chapels until 1956, when cards began being collected to monitor attendance. Ketler asserted shortly after the new chapel opened that student attitudes toward services were very positive.[69] Despite his claim, as in other decades, students complained about mandatory chapel attendance. In 1934, R. G. Walters noted that both students and faculty frequently seemed inattentive at chapel services and argued that having student musical and dramatic performances, pep meetings, and songfests would make services more engaging and enjoyable.[70] Disturbed by the extensive chattering and restlessness, a student insisted in 1938 that "our conduct in chapel leaves a great deal to be desired."[71] *The Collegian* lamented the next year that many students did not quiet down quickly when Ketler and others spoke. It also criticized the "puny" singing of nine hundred students who should be able to make the "rafters tremble" by "loudly praising God."[72] A 1940 editorial noted that many students groused about having to attend chapel, but engaging in this shared experience and singing the alma mater together every Saturday promoted school unity.[73] Some disgruntled students occasionally published a record of how infrequently some faculty attended chapel to highlight their bad example.[74]

Pranks

Tomfoolery was prevalent in the 1930s, especially on college campuses. A common prank was for students to sneak onto the campus of their upcoming football opponent and paint their college's name or initials.[75] Students who were caught red-handed typically faced embarrassing punishments. Grove City students both engaged in and tried to prevent these acts. In 1935, *The Collegian*'s editor in chief chastised students for painting "GCC" on Allegheny's campus.[76] In 1938, Geneva students slipped onto Grove City's campus before their football game against the Wolverines and painted "G" on sidewalks, the tennis courts, and the water tower without being apprehended. *The Collegian* urged GCC students not to retaliate but instead to "yell them hoarse" for a Grove City victory to deliver "the most serious blow Geneva could possibly suffer."[77] Unfortunately, Geneva prevailed 13–0 on the gridiron. Two weeks later, Allegheny students painted "AC" behind the chapel and the college's full name on the water tower. However, about fifty male Grove City students prevented them from similar actions on the lower campus. They also bombarded the cars of the invaders with tomatoes and cabbage and forced them to clean the whitewash off the upper campus. A larger group of Allegheny students returned the next night but were scared off by a sizable contingent of Grovers.[78] This time, Grove City did gain revenge, beating Allegheny 13–0 at their homecoming, holding them to a paltry fifty-three yards of offense. The next fall, Westminster students twice whitewashed parts of the Grove City campus, but the Wolverines repulsed a third effort.[79]

Athletics

Although Grove City began to phase out athletic scholarships in 1933, the college's sports teams enjoyed substantial success in the 1930s and had numerous noteworthy athletes. The college's decision to stop giving athletic scholarships significantly impacted its athletic program thereafter. The tristate athletic conference to which Grove City belonged called for eliminating all athletic scholarships by September 1, 1933. Ketler recommended that Grove City comply with this plan, and the trustees concurred. The college thus resumed its original practice of amateur athletics.[80]

In 1932, William Amos, a 1928 Washington and Jefferson (W&J) graduate, replaced the popular Charles Berry as the head football coach. After playing football during World War I for the 28th Army division, Amos starred at W&J, where he received All-American honorable mention as a fullback.[81] His second and third years as coach, the football team went a combined 12–2–2. The 1934 team won the college's fifth Western Pennsylvania Class B championship in fifteen years. The 5–1–1 squad outscored its opponents 140–21.[82] After the scholarship players graduated, however, Grove City had little success on the gridiron for many years.

In 1934, Ketler spoke on "Reform in College Athletics" at a conference in St. Louis. He argued that some administrators saw intercollegiate athletic programs primarily as a means of advertising their colleges, making money, and increasing the interest of alumni and community residents in their institutions. Others, including him, viewed varsity athletics as an integral part of the educational program that stimulated student interest in fitness and helped increase participation in intramural sports.[83]

Students extensively discussed how ending athletic scholarships would affect the college's sports teams. The consensus was that academic scholarships could be given to good athletes and that the college's athletic success would therefore continue. In the short run, they were wrong.[84] A 1935 editorial in *The Collegian* praised the school's athletes for playing for "fun and the glory of Grove City College, not [for] room, board, and tuition, as many college teams are doing."[85] Trying to explain the football team's miserable 1935 season (its 2–4–1 record and being outscored 145–33), another student avowed, "We have de-emphasized football." He urged classmates to appreciate and applaud Grove City's players who were students first and athletes second.[86] On the other hand, most students interviewed for an article in *The Collegian* in 1936 supported subsidizing athletes, especially football players, arguing that not doing so was hurting the college.[87]

Ketler frequently asserted that intramurals were as important as intercollegiate athletics. Because playing sports had both educational and health benefits, he wanted to construct more fields for men and women to play soccer, lacrosse, touch football, softball, and baseball and to provide opportunities for canoeing and rowing. Ketler also hoped to convert part of the basement of Carnegie Library into squash and handball courts and rooms for wrestling and boxing and to create six golf holes on campus.[88] Ketler noted in 1933 that 275 of Grove City's 350 male students were playing intramural sports, which, he argued, helped boost school spirit, improve sociability, and enhance personal development.[89] The next academic year, the men's intramural teams—cross-country, soccer, swimming, basketball, handball, volleyball, water polo, baseball, tennis, and horseshoes—had a combined 563 participants.[90]

Three thousand alumni and friends came to the 1937 homecoming celebration, and three hundred student couples attended the homecoming dance. Unfortunately, the football team lost to Allegheny 3–0 in a sea of mud. After the game, a newspaper reporter pointed out that the Wolverines did not have eleven able-bodied players to use, which was "an all-time low in Grove City football history." Only two solutions existed: Abandon varsity football or reinstate scholarships.[91] Grove City finished the year 1–7 and did not have another winning season until 1947.

Disagreement over athletic scholarships continued. In a 1938 debate in *The Collegian,* junior Judson Heck argued that if athletes were not subsidized, they would need to take jobs to pay their expenses and have less time for training and practicing. Winning teams, he added, helped advertise a college. Senior Marguerite Waterman countered that the classroom performance of Grove City's subsidized athletes had been poor, which had hurt the college's academic reputation. After athletic scholarships were eliminated, the college's scholastic standing had risen, enrollment had grown, and graduates' ability to obtain good jobs had improved. Moreover, a higher percentage of men and women were playing intramural sports.[92]

A varsity golf team began playing in spring 1934. The college's new football stadium debuted in fall 1935. Swimming was introduced as a varsity sport in 1937–1938. The team did not have a winning season until 1951–1952, although no meets were held during World War II. For the next sixty-two years, however, Grove City amazingly did not have a single losing season, and some seasons was among the nation's best small-college programs. In 1938, the GCC Varsity Club was established to promote the college's athletic program and soccer became a varsity sport. In November during the 1930s and 1940s, the Student Council invited all fathers to attend a football game and have dinner afterward. The 1939 homecoming football game was the first to be broadcast on WSAJ and to employ a public address system.

Robert Thorn coached the tennis team from 1930 to 1942. Its best season was 1937, when Grove City won four matches in one week in May and finished 11–3. Thorn coached the team again from 1947 to 1952 and had an overall record of 128–85–2 (.601). Thorn also coached the basketball team from 1920 until 1937, compiling an impressive 227–103 (.688) record.

Several athletes stand out in the 1930s. Guard Lawrence Critchfield, '33 played one season in the NFL. Fullback Tom Shupe, '33, guard George Foti, '34, and versatile Verne Smith, '36, led the football team. Foti and Shupe were named to several regional All-Star squads. In 1934, Smith was selected for the tristate All-Star team and was called the "greatest back to ever play" for Grove City. Smith started every game for four years, starring on both offense and defense; he was also Grove City's punter and could kick the ball sixty yards with either foot. Thorn said he had seen no better player in his twenty years at GCC, while Amos insisted that Smith outshone him as a player.[93] Howard Wilson, '36, excelled on the football, basketball, and track and field teams for four years. Track and field had many exceptional performers. Multitalented Freddie Pusch, '31 often won the one hundred and 220-yard dashes, the low hurdles, the shot put, discus, and hammer. Dick Hoffman, '37 regularly finished first in the one hundred and 220-yard dashes and in 1934 set a school record of 21.8 in the latter, a remarkable time for that era. John Hogg, '37, set a new school broad jump record of twenty-one feet, three inches, in 1935.

Other superb athletes included William Laycock, who led the 1930–1931 basketball team, which finished 14–5, in scoring; the freshman guard was selected for the second team all-district by the Associated Press and named one of the seven best players in the region by the *Pittsburgh Sun Telegraph*. His sophomore year, he again led the team in scoring. Ray Reeves, '31 was a member of the basketball, football, tennis, and track and field teams. The 1932 *Ouija* argued that with his "smashing, killing drives and clever head work," sophomore Mike Koma, the tennis team's number one player, "looked like Olympic material."[94] His senior year, the tennis team went 7–0, and Koma captured the singles and doubles titles at a tristate tournament.

Grove City also had some terrific athletic performers, especially in track and field, during the second half of the 1930s. Mark Graham, '38, named after his father who led the Grove City football team from 1893 to 1897, was a pole vaulter, broad jumper, javelin thrower, and shot putter. Graham, sprinter and broad jumper Paul Hogue, '37, sprinter Glenn Hogue, '40, and shot putter, discus, and javelin thrower Nick Maddalena, '39, scored 50 percent of Grove City's points in track and field in 1937, which went 4–1. Glenn Hogue, a halfback, and Maddalena, a tackle, were also outstanding football players.

Andy Petach, '39, the football team's center, was selected as a third-team All-American by the Williamson System. Bob Bingham, '39, was a halfback and quarterback in football, scored 511 points in his basketball career, and played number three on the tennis team. George Petach, '39, scored 608 points in basketball (the highest point total to that date). Ray Brunton, '39, earned four letters each in football, basketball, and track and field.

Women's Activities

Although Grove City had no varsity women's teams until 1976, in the 1920s and 1930s, the college began to more strongly emphasize exercise, fitness, and athletic competition for female students. In the late 1920s, women were required to complete two hours of physical education each week, and two-thirds of them spent more than two hours.[95] To fulfill their physical education requirement, all female students had to participate in an end-of-the-year sports tournament; tennis and badminton were usually the most popular sports. In the 1930s, women also played intramural field hockey, soccer, basketball, and baseball and held swim meets; *The Collegian* extolled the school's many superb female athletes.[96] The college periodically chose honorary women's teams in various intramural sports. Virginia Crawford, '33, who participated in twelve women's competitions during the academic year, was awarded the Sports Day gold medal at May Day in 1932. That same year, freshman Mary Luzanski was named to the honorary field hockey, tennis, and baseball teams. Two years later, she was selected as the college's "sports queen." The Women's Athletic Association (WAA), formed in 1933, organized intramural contests in field hockey, volleyball, basketball, soccer, tennis, and baseball, as well as tournaments in Ping-Pong, swimming, and archery, and opportunities for hiking, riding, and dancing.

To promote good bearing and robust health, the college created a posture week in 1931, an event that lasted for two decades. The week included a competition in which almost all coeds participated. The judges selected freshman Eleanor McClure as the winner at a well-attended program which included a lecture about posture, a demonstration of corrective exercises, and a guest orchestra performance.[97]

Grove City invited representatives of all Pennsylvania colleges to campus in May 1935 to discuss forming a branch of the Athletic Federation of College Women, which physical education professor Esther Post established the next year. The WAA took over sponsorship of the annual posture contest as well as the May Pageant and hosted an annual play day at which women from numerous colleges engaged in various athletic contests. At a fall 1936 sports day, for example, Grove City coeds competed against peers from seven colleges in tennis, swimming, archery, and bicycling. Grove City women also participated in play days at other colleges, such as an eight-team event at the University of Pittsburgh in March 1936, where they tied for second. In 1939, the WAA sponsored a demonstration at which women physical education students danced and marched and competed in archery and a three-legged race.

WSAJ

As the 1930s began, WSAJ was broadcasting a weekly half-hour program, which included talks by professors, music department performances, orations by speech department members, poetry readings, Christmas carol singing, and short dramas. In 1931, the Radio Club was formed to help Harmon operate the station. The next year, the station moved to the science building on the upper campus, and the best available equipment was installed. The college received numerous postcards from people as far away as five hundred miles in several different directions from Grove City, and even several letters from New Zealand residents who heard WSAJ broadcasts. The station's new license from the federal government permitted WSAJ to broadcast one afternoon and two evenings a week. Its transmissions expanded to include Sunday vesper services, student forums, campus news, athletic contests, music, and other forms of entertainment. Ketler argued that participating in radio broadcasting was a very helpful for students who were studying music, public speaking, drama, and education.[98] In January 1935, WSAJ hosted its first "amateur hour" with dramatic readings, instrumental and vocal solos, and comedy sketches.

In April 1938, WSAJ celebrated its eighteenth anniversary with a tribute to Harmon, its founder and adviser. Harmon discussed the station's history, the college choir and the men's glee club sang, and a twelve-piece orchestra performed. Famous broadcaster Lowell Thomas highlighted the station on his national radio show that month.[99] WSAJ, however, struggled in the late 1930s because of competition with commercial radio stations. After a faculty committee took control of programming, many students felt that their involvement was a waste of time. This situation was unfortunate, *The Collegian* asserted, because WSAJ was an important vehicle for training students in speech and radio work and advertising the college.[100]

Theater

Grove City produced many excellent plays in the 1930s. Joe Ketler was the key figure in Grove City's theater program from the 1910s to the 1930s. Before coming to Grove City, Ketler spent thirty years performing in scores of professional Shakespeare productions and vaudeville shows. In addition to directing dozens of shows at Grove City, he played a leading role in the college's 1932 play *The Middleman* and the 1939 show *Spring Dance*. A play senior Dorothy Turnbach wrote titled *Men Are So Simple* won second place in a 1931 student state contest and was later performed in the chapel. Grove City placed fourth in a Pennsylvania theatrical competition that year with its performance of *Trifles*, with Roy Connor, '31, playing the principal role. Rowland Axtell, '31, had featured roles in *The Witching Hour, Smilin' Through, The Copperhead,* and other productions. *Mignonette,* directed by Ketler in 1935, starred seniors Jane Allen and Don Stitt, two of the college's leading actors during the decade. In 1934–1935, 116 students (one-sixth of the student body) acted in the four college plays, while many other students constructed sets, served on tech crews, and did makeup. In March 1939, *Excursion,* a comedy directed by Miriam Franklin, became first play to be staged in Crawford Auditorium.

Speech and Debate

As noted, from its founding, Grove City strongly emphasized public speaking and debate, and its students excelled in these enterprises in the 1930s. Beginning in the 1920s, the college awarded annual prizes in extemporaneous speaking, with topics often focusing on current events. In 1925, *The Collegian* implored students to support the men's and women's debate teams "100 per cent" to help propel Grove City to "the front in college forensics."[101] That year, sophomore Raymond Walters won the Western Pennsylvania Intercollegiate Oratorical Contest. In 1931, a large crowd watched the men's three-person debating team, led by Roy Connor, defeat Westminster on the topic of free trade. At the regional Pi Kappa Delta convention with colleges from five states participating, senior Anna A'Hearn placed third in extemporaneous speaking and Grove City's men's debate team reached the semifinal in the competition won by Michigan State. The *Ouija* claimed that 1932–1933 was the most successful year in college debate history. During the year, the men's team outscored twelve colleges, including Akron and Kent State, in various contests. Juniors John Fife and Furman Walters finished 7–1 at the Pi Kappa Delta regional convention, making Grove City cochampions with Bowling Green.[102] At the 1938 national Kappa Delta convention, the men finished second in the twelve-state Province of the Lakes. At a 1939 regional Pi Kappa Delta convention, senior Beva Huskin was second in women's extemporaneous speaking and freshman Louise Christie was third in women's debating. In February 1939, the college's women's squad finished second in an eight-team debate at Heidelberg College. In February 1940, the Grove City men's team hosted and won a debate tournament with seven other colleges, including Penn State, Toledo, and Carnegie Tech.

Student Achievements

Grove City students had other significant achievements during the 1930s. The Plymouth (Massachusetts) Drama Festival selected Alex Reed, '39, as one of forty students from one thousand applicants to receive a scholarship. In 1938, twenty-seven Grovers were among only three hundred students who received certificates of merit from the National Office Management Association. In 1939, *The Atlantic Monthly* chose junior Emilie Greenwood's essay "America Speaks" as one of its top entries. Two of junior Sarah Flanagan's poems were included in *American Voices of 1939*, an anthology of American and Canadian poems, while poems by Lois Thompson, '40, and Janet Lebo, '42, were included in *The World's Fair Anthology* (1939).

The accomplishments of several other students were equally impressive. Three decades before Omicron Delta Kappa introduced the Senior Man of the Year award, the faculty annually awarded the Silliman Prize to a senior who did outstanding academic work and gave promise of beneficial Christian service. The 1931 recipient was Roy Connor, who belonged to the Oxford Club, served as an officer in the YMCA, starred in several plays, and lost only one high jump competition in his career. Myra Belle Botsford was the 1932 valedictorian, a graduation speaker, and the editor in chief of *The Collegian*. The 1934 valedictorian, Betty Mark, was the president of Pi Gamma Mu, the faculty representative on Student Council, the vice president of Philokalian Club, and a member of the Pan-Hellenic Council, the House Council, and the *Wolf Pack* staff. Three outstanding 1935 graduates were Peter Pugliese, Virginia Perrine, and George Greenwood. Pugliese had major roles in five plays and was the president of the theater honorary, a top college debater, a WSAJ program leader, an assistant for two professors, and an editor for *The Collegian*. Perrine was an assistant for two professors, the president of Pi Gamma Mu and the Gamma Chis, the secretary of the Pan-Hellenic Council, and a poet and who read her compositions to many campus groups. Greenwood served as *The Collegian*'s editor in chief, played in the college orchestra, sang in four vocal groups, participated in the Shakespeare Club and Kemikos, served on the YMCA cabinet, ran on the track and cross-country teams, and acted in four plays.[103] George Bowles '36, a stellar varsity debater, a Student Council member, and the winner of the 1935 Pennsylvania oratory contest, received the Silliman Prize his senior year. Robert Frazier, the 1937 Silliman Prize winner, was president of the YMCA, vice president of the Western Pennsylvania YMCA, a professor's assistant in English and education, a *Collegian* writer, and a member of Student Council, the Webster Club, and Pi Gamma Mu.

Two other men who stood out were John Calderwood, '38, and James Walther, '39. Calderwood was editor in chief of *The Collegian*, a head WSAJ DJ, a skillful debater, and a member of the YMCA, Webster, Pi Gamma Mu, the football and track teams, and the French, German, and men's glee clubs. He graduated from Harvard Law School in 1941, worked briefly for a US appeals court judge in New York City, and then served as a lieutenant second grade in the navy during World War II. Walther, the 1939 valedictorian, was active in the Christian Service League, the YMCA, TAP, and the Shakespeare, German, Latin and Varsity G clubs, and played in the college band. After earning degrees at Western Theological Seminary and several universities and serving as a navy chaplain during the war, he returned to his alma mater to teach classical languages.

Campus Life

In the 1930s, playing bridge and going to movies were popular Grover activities. Bell Telephone advertisements in *The Collegian* encouraged students to call home weekly, which cost thirty-five cents ($6.70 today) for three minutes. In the 1930s, men usually dressed in suits and women wore skirts and sweaters to class; only a few commuters had cars. Despite the ban on smoking on campus, *The Collegian* contained ads for Chesterfield cigarettes and Granger pipe tobacco. The college's four literary societies continued to hold debates among their own members and with each other. For example, in 1936, Speedwell members debated whether Grove City should have a five-day class week. That would not happen until 1999. Bull sessions discussing fellow students, professors, campus and administrative policies, and politics were common in the dorms.[104]

Grove City began celebrating a May Day pageant in 1915 that featured dances performed by hundreds of coeds around a maypole and the crowning of a queen. The pageant was initially held along Wolf Creek, then moved to the lower campus quad, and, in 1922, to the football field. In 1933, five thousand spectators viewed a pageant that portrayed George Washington crossing Wolf Creek, the arrival of the first settlers to the area, and the granting of the borough charter. In November 1934, the college held its first Leap Week, which continued for many years. During this week, women had to initiate and pay for all dates and hold doors open for men. About seven hundred parents attended the first Parents' Day, held in 1936 on May Day. In 1938, men voted along with women for the May queen for the first time. In spring 1939, Poverty Day was revived. The festivities featured a parade, a pageant mocking Adolf Hitler, and a dance at which Bob Bingham's highly respected student orchestra played.[105] That year, *The Collegian* gave awards to the "most typical Grove City student," "best dressed," "best looking," "wittiest," "class personalities" (all four classes), and "best matched couples."

During the decade, *The Collegian* complained about student apathy, the lack of school spirit, student priorities, the ineffectiveness of the Student Council, improper decorum in leaving chapel, and misbehavior at dances. One writer protested that not even 50 percent of students voted in Student Council elections. Moreover, in these elections, personal popularity, not issues, determined who won.[106] Another writer asserted that some students focused on having fun and cared little about academics beyond getting their diplomas, whereas others sought to obtain only "book-knowledge" and had little interest in social activities; neither group would be adequately prepared for life.[107] A common complaint throughout the 1930s was that students did not enthusiastically support the college's sports teams.[108] Making an argument that was repeated frequently in subsequent college history, *The Collegian* editor in chief asserted in 1934 that the Student Council was "not serving any adequate function."[109] In 1938, *The Collegian* admonished students for rushing out of chapel like hogs going to a slaughterhouse. The editors urged students to observe the long-standing custom that seniors went first, followed by juniors, sophomores, and freshmen.[110] The following year, a *Collegian* article complained that at a dance in the Crawford Social Room, some students smoked, others wondered around the building, and still others engaged in "extreme shagging."[111] To try to prevent the "four hours of shagging" that demeaned the last dance, students were forbidden to come as couples to the next dance.[112]

During the 1930s, numerous well-known swing bands including the Tommy Tucker Orchestra and Ray Pearl's orchestra, which performed three times, played at homecoming, Valentine's Day, May Day, and other major dances. Students entered these dances through receiving lines that typically included President Ketler and his wife and the Student Council president. Over the years, numerous popular student-led vocal and musical groups also performed at dances and other events. Three outstanding groups in the 1930s were the vocal trio Two Maids and a Man and orchestras led by Jack Kennedy, '37, and Robert Bingham. In addition, many teas were held, which often featured student vocal and piano solos, other musical performances, and dramatic readings.

Robert Jewell, '37, *The Collegian* editor in chief, called 1936–1937 a splendid year. MAP opened, and the college had its highest enrollment in history. Grove City was Pennsylvania's "up-and-coming college" and the state's largest liberal arts college (Grove City had 842 full-time students while Allegheny had 645 and Westminster

530). His one criticism was that many students were taking the slogan "don't let your studies interfere with your education" too far.[113] For many years, Ketler made an annual appeal in chapel to students to keep off the grass. In 1938, the Student Council undertook a campaign convince students to walk on walks. *The Collegian* frequently exhorted students to use the sidewalks and keep the main quad beautiful.[114]

In 1937, the college employed one of every six upperclassmen (about one hundred) as student assistants. Some of them made $300 a year, almost double the college's $170 annual tuition. *The Collegian* complained that these student assistants sometimes did not assign grades impartially.[115] Herman Rodgers, '38, disputed *The Collegian*'s claim that in their grading, these assistants were "influenced by personal likes and jealousies [and] fraternity affiliations." This rarely happened, he declared, and disgruntled students could appeal to professors.[116] The editors argued further that one hundred was "an absurd number" of student assistants. They wasted considerable time, and paying assistants cost ten dollars per student per semester. In some courses, assistants had complete control over grades, and there were definitely "cases of dishonesty and favoritism." *The Collegian* maintained that student assistants should grade only objective questions and that faculty with large teaching loads should be paid extra to mark their own exams and lab reports.[117]

In the late 1930s, the question of whether Grove City should have an honor system, which had arisen in the mid-1910s and would cause controversy for the next three decades, was rekindled. If adopted, senior Ken Weber argued in 1938, this system would eliminate the need for student assistants to proctor exams, help create more cordial relationships between professors and students, and produce a fairer assignment of grades. Tom Watson countered that the system sounded great, but in practice it would not work well. If they were in danger of failing, "weak-willed" students would resort to cheating if their only penalty would be a guilty conscience.[118] A *Collegian* article the next year called for establishing an honor system to eliminate cheating, increase personal integrity, ensure that people's grades reflected their performance, and prod some students to study more.[119]

In the late 1930s, *The Collegian* boasted about Grove City's resources and accomplishments. No college in the region had such "fine, well-equipped buildings," and its commerce department was widely recognized as one of the best in the nation.[120] Grove City had more graduates teaching in Pennsylvania schools than any other college or university in the state. No other school had finer dorms, such an inspiring chapel, or more beautiful grounds.[121] *The Collegian* editors happily noted in 1939 that four new clubs and two new varsity sports had begun the previous two years; more men and women were participating in intramural sports; a spirit of cooperation prevailed among the college clubs; the Radio Club, the three Christian organizations, and the four literary societies had all "grown in size and vitality." Moreover, the college's academics were constantly improving.[122]

In May 1939, the largest crowd in college history, *The Collegian* claimed, packed Crawford Auditorium to see the Webster Club's variety show, which featured comedy sketches, humorous readings, and musical selections.[123] In November, the *Ouija* sponsored another revue comprised of musical, dancing, and comedy acts. This "epic" revue set "a record for entertainment" excellence at Grove City. The editors especially lauded Jack Kennedy's twelve-person orchestra, the Kollegiannaires, whose performance met professional standards.[124] *The Collegian* beseeched the trustees to implement a student activity fee to support student publications and plays.[125]

Throughout the decade, *The Collegian* included editorials and articles on numerous topics including criticism of New Deal programs and denunciation of Germany's ruthless persecution of the Jews during Kristallnacht. In the late 1930s, *The Collegian* strongly promoted isolationism. A November 1937 editorial, for example, repudiated the contention that the United States must save "our little yellow brothers" and protect American commerce. The United States must not be duped by England and militarists at home into fighting another war.[126] As many called for stopping Hitler's advance in 1939, numerous editorials implored the United States to stay out of the European war.[127] A January 10, 1940, article contended that contemporary youth must not commit the same mistake their elders did in 1917. America must make its defense invulnerable but not fight aboard.[128]

The Collegian's editors had to deal with censorship and sexism. Expressing the tension that numerous editors experienced, John Calderwood wrote in 1938 that he felt caught between trying to please students and the faculty. His battle against "rigid" faculty supervision of the paper had upset some members of the publications committee.[129] Before 1940, only three women had served as editors in chief of *The Collegian*—the aforementioned Isabelle Blyholder in 1918–1919, Helen Calderwood (the future wife of the college's fourth president, J. Stanley Harker) in 1922–1923, and Gladys Monroe in 1933–1934. In 1940, senior twins Donna and Phyllis Conner were selected. They complained that they faced "severe criticism" from some who thought women "are not [as] capable [as men] or lack initiative."[130]

In 1940, students satirically listed Grove City College's benefits: Students had too many dates, received too many A's and B's, and enjoyed delightful weather and delicious cafeteria food. Students wanted to have two hours of daily chapel, abolish fraternities, and prohibit women from leaving their dormitories after sunset. Some flippantly called the college's coeds "the downfall of men."[131]

Robert Kimberly's poem probably expresses the views of many of Grove City College's recently graduated students in the 1930s:

Back to thee our alma mater,
Now we come, thy sons and daughters.
You tried to fit us for the flight
To give us knowledge to find the Light,

To battle for our daily bread.

And yet to keep our souls well fed.
We've tried our best to keep the faith
And live our lives with modest grace.

So here we pledge ourselves to thee
And swear by all eternity
No matter where, or how or when
We vow to live our lives like men.[132]

The freshman rules continued to generate conflict in the 1930s. Freshmen were not allowed to communicate with the opposite sex; they must always wear dinks, black shoes, and signs that included their names, hometowns, and majors; and women could not wear makeup or jewelry. Upperclassmen heckled and endeavored to humiliate freshmen who broke these rules. One initiation rite required male freshmen to kneel in front of Colonial Hall and pray for rain while female residents dumped buckets of water on them. As part of these rites, freshmen women paraded in their pajamas and sang and danced for their upper-class harassers. All freshmen were expected to participate in a snake dance during halftime of the homecoming football game. (This tradition began around 1912 and lasted until the early 1970s). If Grove City won, the freshmen were allowed to remove their dinks and signs and were officially considered part of the student body; if the team lost, their initiation process usually continued for another week. *The Collegian* extolled one freshmen snake dance as "stupendous, super-colossal, positively gargantuan."[133] Most freshman had accepted hazing in good spirit, *The Collegian* reported, so they "may not be so bad after all."[134] Probably speaking for many, freshman Mike Koma wrote:

To college I came in '29
That I might learn a thing or two.
Now I declare the surprise was mine
When I found how little I knew.
I studied hard and harder
As all good students should.
Now shoes I've shined and clothes I've pressed.
But soon this year will be no more.
And you just make this a note,

That when I'm an elevated sophomore
Someone else [will be] the goat.[135]

In 1932, the chair of the freshman tribunal announced that rules would be enforced more strictly because the newcomers were "too cocky." This would help keep the lowly frosh in the humble position where they belonged.[136] Two years later, the Student Council urged freshmen to follow all the prescribed rules.[137] *The Collegian* editor in chief criticized the Student Council for allowing freshmen to attend the homecoming dance despite their failure to obey most of the rules.[138] The Student Council decided in 1936 to strictly enforce the freshmen rules for three weeks instead of until homecoming (usually about six weeks). Despite this reduced period, a freshman lamented, "we are still dirt under the upperclassmen's feet."[139] The Student Council resolved in 1937 to end dating restrictions for freshmen but to require that freshmen apparel continued until homecoming. *The Collegian* insisted that the chief purpose of freshmen rules was not to keep newcomers from enjoying themselves but to help them adjust to college life and dispel their arrogant attitudes.[140] The Student Council forced freshmen who had broken the rules in 1938 to face a "dreaded ordeal." The administration prohibited upperclassmen, however, from using "ridiculous," insulting signs, which had been very conspicuous in previous years, to mock those who violated freshmen rules.[141] *The Collegian* argued in 1939 that without the rules, freshmen would seek to run the college. The regulations benefited freshmen by teaching them about the traditions and customs of the college. Dinks helped identify them; signs introduced them to upperclassmen; freshmen handbooks supplied information and guidance. *The Collegian* counseled freshmen to demonstrate their ability rather than tell upperclassmen what big shots they were in high school.[142] That fall, seventeen freshmen were brought blindfolded before a Student Council tribunal for violations of the handbook—most grievously, disrespecting upperclassmen and disobeying the dating rules.[143]

During the 1930s, fraternities and sororities played a significant role in campus social life and their rushing procedures and "Hell Week" provoked controversy. Greek parties were very popular. In 1935, fraternity and sorority rush (the process of recruiting new members) increased from one to two months. During "Hell Week," sorority pledges sewed on buttons, pressed clothes, and hemmed skirts for actives. Some pledges had to wear one high heel and one low heel, put their coats on backward, and eschew makeup; others were required to wear diapers or woolen bathing suits under their clothes.[144] *The Collegian* called sorority rush in fall 1939 the "most spiteful, jealous, and disgusting" in many years. Women who did not receive bids were often heartbroken; either sororities needed to expand their membership or more sororities should be created. Despite these criticisms, many students liked the rich social life, strong bonds, and athletic competitions Greek organizations provided.[145]

In 1941, senior Bernard Judy assessed the changes that had occurred at Grove City since 1901. He lauded its attractive campus, fine facilities, spiritual emphasis week, and increased number of professors and extracurricular activities. Because of the "loosening of morals and social etiquette," women could wear lipstick, mascara, and rouge, go without stockings, dye their hair, and smoke—provided they did not get caught.[146]

Clubs and Organizations

Along with the varsity sports teams, the speech and debate and theater programs, six fraternities and eleven sororities, the Student Council, campus publications (*The Collegian*, *Ouija*, and *Wolf Pack*), dances, and special events such as homecoming and May Day, the college's many student clubs and organizations were central to its life. By 1938, Grove City had three religious organizations—the YMCA, YWCA, and CSL—four musical organizations—the college choir, college marching band, glee club, and Schubert Club—four honoraries—Pi Gamma Mu, Theta Alpha Pi, Kemikos, and Phi Kappa Delta—five departmental clubs—Commerce, Science,

German, French, and Latin; four literary societies—Shakespeare, Webster, Philokalian, and Speedwell—two athletic organizations—WAA and the Varsity G—and three clubs—outing, radio, and chess and checkers. The most important campus organizations were the three religious groups, the four literary societies, and the Commerce and Science Clubs.

Throughout the 1920s and 1930s, the Shakespeare and Webster Clubs competed in debates, declamations, impromptu speeches, and orations. Literary club meetings often included book reviews, vocal solos and musical groups, skits, spelling bees, and discussions of current events. The Shakespeare Club's annual program featuring vaudeville skits and bedtime stories regularly packed Carnegie Auditorium.

Commerce was the college's largest major in the mid-1930s with about 330 students typically pursuing either a BS in commerce or a secretarial degree. Grove City's Commerce Club, founded in 1919, was the oldest one in the nation. With 235 members in 1935, it was by far the college's largest club and one of the most active commercial clubs in the eastern United States. In the late 1930s, it sponsored several notable exhibitions. Its 1937, three thousand visited its advertising exhibition featuring entries from fifty companies, which was the first of its kind at any college in Pennsylvania. Two years later, four thousand people attended the club's "Story of Oil" exhibition. Rosey Roswell, a noted humorist and Pittsburgh Pirate radio announcer, spoke at the club's exhibition banquet.

The 150-member Science Club, partnering with the science department, staged equally impressive expositions. From 1937 to 1940, between two thousand and five thousand people attended its annual shows. The 1940 show consisted of $700,000 ($15.9 million today) of equipment, displays, and demonstrations. Exhibits on electric welding equipment, the heart, the circulatory system, and other topics filled thirty-five Hall of Science classrooms. Events included a motion picture on mining coal, a lecture on atomic structure, and a demonstration on polarized light. For many years, the art department held an open house to display student work; visitors could also watch students drawing and painting.

The Outing Club, founded in 1938, quickly became popular. Members constructed a cabin about twenty-five miles from campus that slept thirty, engaged in varied outdoor activities including hunting, hiking, archery, roller skating, canoeing, horseback riding, and swimming, and took trips throughout the country and to Canada.

In the 1930s, the chapel choir typically did six out-of-town performances each academic year, while the college band sometimes performed at halftime at home football games and marched in homecoming parades. The band was frequently small in numbers, shoddily outfitted, and poor in quality. *The Collegian* lamented that at the 1939 homecoming parade, the Sharon High School band had "showed us up in uniforms, numbers, music and marching." Having a larger, better band, the newspaper argued, could enhance school pride and provide better entertainment.[147]

The four honoraries, all branches of national organizations, actively supported students in their respective academic areas—the social sciences, chemistry, speech and debate, and theater. For example, Grove City's Pi Gamma Mu chapter sponsored speakers, debates, and student paper presentations at its weekly meetings as well as the Crombie Allen prize. Allen, '95, a newspaper publisher, gave $1,000 in 1928 to establish the award. The authors of the best papers on how to promote "international peace and goodwill among nations" read them before a student assembly. This award was given for the next eight decades.

Political and Economic Conservatism

Grove City's political conservatism and the support for free enterprise of its faculty and students is well known. In numerous presidential polls, beginning in 1932, students consistently favored Republican candidates. In a straw poll in October 1932, 61 percent of students preferred President Herbert Hoover, 23 percent socialist Norman Thomas, and 15 percent Democrat Franklin Roosevelt.[148] In a 1936 survey, 84 percent of students identified as Republicans.[149] In a poll that October, 76 percent of students supported

Republican Alf Landon for president whereas 24 percent favored incumbent President Franklin Roosevelt.[150] In November, students formed a Republican League, the first of several Republican clubs at Grove City. In 1940, students favored Wendell Willkie over Roosevelt by 80 to 18 percent, while the faculty backed the Republican candidate thirteen to one over the sitting president.[151]

J. Howard Pew, Weir Ketler, the economic faculty, and numerous students strongly defended capitalism. History, they insisted, demonstrated that market economies performed much better than planned ones. In several addresses in the late 1930s, Pew argued that the free enterprise system helped provide the intellectual, religious, political, and economic freedom for society to flourish and the opportunity for people to dream, experiment, invest, and "match wits in friendly competition."[152]

This perspective, coupled with his life experience, led Pew to run the college as much as a business as possible, an approach Ketler supported. "Although he often referred to Grove City as 'his' college, over the years," Pew, Lee Edwards maintained, "did not dictate to its presidents" or other administrators. Other trustees usually accepted his recommendations because he had studied problems diligently, carefully considered various options, and offered convincing solutions.[153] However, board members were undoubtedly influenced by Pew's phenomenal business success and generous aid to the college. He did exert substantial pressure on the other trustees to accept policies he preferred, and, in some cases, he prevented the college from adopting constructive policies, including securing a larger endowment and using endowment income for operating expenses and student aid. Pew also long opposed the college offering any need- or merit-based scholarships. His initial antagonism delayed the college's adoption of a retirement program for faculty and staff.

Guest Speakers and Performers

Numerous interesting guest lecturers and performers came to campus in the 1930s. Chapel speakers included Frank Wilson, Negro secretary for the YMCA; Princeton Seminary professor Charles Erdman; 1936 Prohibition Party presidential candidate Leigh Colvin; George Thewer, the secretary of the Student Volunteer Movement for Foreign Missions; and *Reader's Digest* editor Barclay Atcheson.[154] Especially well received was James Graham, an intercollegiate tennis champion, marine, college professor, professional football player, and missionary and teacher in China for sixteen years. The world-renowned Eddie Lango and the Spiritual Jubilee Singers, an African American group, sang in chapel in fall 1937. Katherine Bacon, a distinguished English pianist, performed in Crawford Auditorium in 1939. The spring 1940 semester brought two fascinating visitors to campus: multitalented Turkish American Johnny Karakash and tennis star Don Budge. Karakash, a lecturer, scholar, world traveler, and gifted athlete, spoke in chapel and ran circles around six of the college's best volleyball players. Using tricky serves and smashing returns, Karakash dazzled spectators, singlehandedly beating the six-man team 21–4 during half time of a varsity basketball game.[155] Fifteen hundred spectators watched Budge, who led the United States to a Davis Cup victory in 1938, demonstrate tennis techniques and play an exhibition match.

Among the prestigious men who delivered Grove City's commencement address in the 1930s were Daniel Poling, the president of Christian Endeavor and editor in chief of the *Christian Herald,* who spoke twice; Harold Dodds, '09, the president of Princeton University; and Samuel Parkes Cadman who served as the president of Federal Council of Churches from 1924 to 1928.

Placement

In the 1930s, Grove City College graduates had an excellent placement record. In 1931, a local newspaper claimed that 70 percent of Grove City graduates had obtained "good teaching or business positions" despite the nation's economic recession.[156] In 1932, Grove City ranked highly among the state's thirty-seven colleges in placing alumni in "lucrative positions."[157] The next month, *The Collegian* asserted that in the last eighteen years, one hundred Grove

City graduates had gone into the medical profession.[158] In the 1930s, Grove City was one of only six Pennsylvania colleges whose graduates were permitted to take the CPA exam in New York State without first doing a two-year apprenticeship. Numerous graduates received scholarships at prestigious graduate and professional schools. In 1938, John Calderwood and Craig Hoyt began at Harvard Law School and Penn Medical School, respectively.

The Alumni

In the 1930s, Grove City strove to increase alumni loyalty and financial support. To supplement the active Pittsburgh chapter, alumni groups were established in the Beaver Valley, Butler, Erie, Philadelphia, New York, and Los Angeles. In 1937, the alumni created a loan fund to help financially struggling students. That year, an alumni directory was published, which listed 3,437 graduates, about three thousand of whom were living. Four outstanding alumni during the 1930s were Harry F. Rowe, '94, C. Blaine Smathers, '02, Harold Dodds, and George Southworth, '14. After graduating from Drew Theological Seminary, Rowe worked as a missionary educator in China for thirty-two years. Smathers was Grove City College's only brigadier general before World War II. During his forty-two years of active military service, he fought in the Spanish-American War and commanded Grove City's Company M during World War I. Dodds strengthened Princeton's academic programs and expanded its facilities by adding a gymnasium, several dormitories, and a library and acquiring the Forrestal campus. Southworth gained national prominence for his work as a radio engineer, especially for helping developing waveguides in the early 1930s. After earning a PhD at Yale in 1923, Southworth worked with Bell Telephone Laboratories in New Jersey. He won three national engineering medals and prizes for his cross-country transmission of audio and visual signals.

As the 1930s ended, Grove City was thriving in many ways. It had first-rate facilities, many good professors, and significant enrollment, and the accomplishments of its faculty, students, and alumni were substantial. One problem, Ketler argued, was that the college desperately needed more administrators and support staff. Whereas the student body and faculty almost doubled between 1920 and 1940, the administrative staff had remained about the same.[159] This problem paled compared with the immense challenges World War II brought.

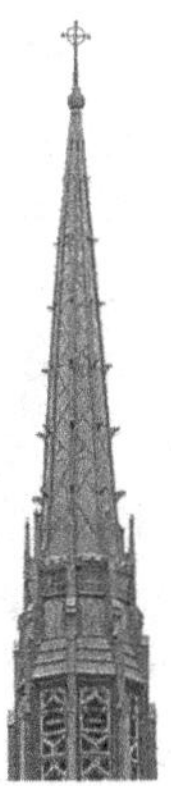

The Challenge of World War II, a Building Program, and the End of the Weir Ketler Presidency,

1941–1956

By 1941, Weir Ketler had served longer as a college president than any of his peers in Pennsylvania, and Grove City's enrollment had grown from about three hundred to 934. World War II caused enrollment to nosedive, but the college reached a record student body of 1,447 in 1948. The college expanded from ten buildings on about fifty acres primarily on its lower campus in 1916 to sixteen edifices on almost one hundred acres on an upper and lower campus in 1940. During the next sixteen years, the college completed seven building projects—three new dormitories, a recreation center, a library, and two Harbison Chapel transepts.

From 1940 to 1956, administrators and trustees worked to upgrade the academic program, but several factors—World War II, an aging faculty, the high student-faculty ratio (exacerbated by the surge in enrollment after the war), low faculty salaries, minimal faculty benefits, the relatively small percentage of faculty holding doctorates, the small supply of professors nationwide, de facto tenure (which prevented underperforming and even most incompetent professors from being dismissed), and a greater focus on other issues—hampered their efforts. Consequently, when Ketler retired in 1956, the faculty and curriculum needed to be significantly improved.

During these years, the college consistently declared its primary goal to be promoting students' intellectual, physical, social, and spiritual development to enable them to contribute to building a better world. Ketler's oft-repeated threefold purpose for the college was to produce "sound bodies, cultivated and disciplined minds and stabilized characters" so that graduates could lead "challenging, happy, and constructive" lives and help strengthen American democracy.[1] On his many visits to the college, board president J. Howard Pew repeatedly declared that "knowledge without good morals and high character is without value."[2]

After World War II, the federal government began to pour more money into funding higher education, especially student loan programs and faculty research. The competition for students intensified, as by 1947, the federal government was supplying half the budget of American colleges and universities. Moreover, the government seemed poised to give even more money to public colleges and universities. A presidential commission appointed by Harry Truman issued a report in 1948 titled "Higher Education for American Democracy" that urged the federal government to invest substantially more money in higher education to enable all Americans who had the requisite ability to complete a college education.[3] His "violent opposition" to federal aid to colleges, J. Howard Pew asserted that year, would lead many to call him a "reactionary," but he feared that increasing government control would, "like a blighting cancer," infect "the entire educational system."[4] Numerous educators wondered what role private church-sponsored colleges would play in the changing educational landscape.[5] Many worried that government aid would lead to "federal dictation or direction, with a consequent loss of autonomy."[6] In 1952, a national academic commission, which included the presidents of Johns

Hopkins, Stanford, and Brown, warned that if federal support increased substantially, "the freedom of higher education would be lost."[7] Nevertheless, only a few schools joined Grove City in refusing federal money because of the danger government largesse posed. Ketler continued to beseech the trustees to raise a larger endowment. Whereas Grove City's revenue came largely from tuition, some state institutions received more than 80 percent of their operating funds from outside sources, Ketler told board members in 1947. In wealthier universities, approximately 50 percent of the operating budget came from endowment income or gifts.[8] Because of its limited revenue, Grove City's administrative team was very small, and professors had heavy teaching loads.

During these years, Grove City primarily relied on its sterling reputation, especially in Pennsylvania, Ohio, and New York, to attract students. The college spent little on advertising and recruiting. In 1944, Grove City mailed about forty-five thousand flyers to high school students and sent issues of the *Alumni Bulletin* to graduates and a special letter to graduates and students serving in the armed forces, urging them to encourage people to apply. Ketler reported in 1953 that the college had been able to fill its classrooms and beds "without resorting to highly competitive methods or to an extensive promotional program."[9]

World War II

Few colleges the size of Grove City made as substantial a contribution to the Allied victory in World War II as it did. Meanwhile, the war dramatically affected the college. Thousands of navy and army personnel received training at the college, and numerous faculty provided instruction in these military programs. Many male and some female students left school to serve in the military. Enrollment declined substantially, and women greatly outnumbered men. The varsity sports program was curtailed. Many clubs ceased to meet. *The Collegian* stopped publication for several months. The college instituted a program to enable students to finish in three years. College finances were extremely tight.

From the outbreak of the war until the bombing of Pearl Harbor, several writers for *The Collegian* expressed the isolationist sentiments many students shared in the late 1930s while acknowledging that increasing numbers of their classmates favored American participation.[10] In fall 1940, the Civilian Pilot Training Program began at Grove City College, using a private landing strip on the edge of town, with Professor Russell Smith providing the ground instruction. In December 1940, the US Office of Education selected Grove City as one of six colleges in its region to operate an engineering defense training program, which lasted six months. Some students contended that all Americans needed to make sacrifices "if democracy is to survive over goose-stepping tyranny."[11] Meanwhile, coeds knitted sweaters, socks, mittens, and scarves for the besieged British people, and students raised $1,500 to aid the World Student Service Fund and British ambulances. Faculty and student defense committees devised blackout procedures and ways to evacuate buildings in the case of air raids, and *The Collegian* called for prayers for peace.[12]

President Ketler argued in chapel on December 9, 1941, that Japan's horrific attack on Pearl Harbor threatened Americans' freedom and security. Most Japanese, like most Americans, he asserted, wanted peace, but Japan's leaders were "skilled, cunning, desperate" and without "moral scruples." Ketler exhorted students to be patriotic, courageous, and magnanimous to help achieve the United States' objectives. A few days later, the trustees passed a resolution calling on the college to "actively and wholeheartedly" support the government's war effort.[13]

Betty Blackmore, '44 remembered that "many girls were crying because they had brothers who would be called" into military service. Male students were "patriotic and anxious to go." After hearing Franklin Roosevelt's address, Donald Kanally, '45, later reported, everyone on campus seemed "stunned." Gerald Householder, '44, explained that "rumors were rampant, excitement prevailed." Without television, Polly Knight, '44, stated, students were not fully aware of "the enormity of the world situation," but "it was a sad, sad time on campus."[14] Mary Love, '44, expressed the fear, frustration, and futility many students felt. She suggested giving Japan some of these "old islands" so that American men would not be killed. She wanted to do something constructive instead of "just plugging away" with psychology, biology, and other courses. Why prepare for the future, Love asked, "when we don't know what it will be?"[15] Faculty weighed in. History professor Levi Beeler contended that the unfairness of the Versailles Treaty had produced World War II. "Japan has gained [an advantage] by attacking on so many fronts without warning, French professor John Nesbitt asserted, but "we shall utterly and forever crush" the "Axis menace."[16] In February 1942, 130 male students registered for draft, as all men aged twenty to forty-four were required to do.

In a September 1942 chapel talk, Ketler urged students to prepare diligently to participate in the war effort. All able-bodied men, he declared, were destined for military service. Colleges must revise their instructional programs to help America win World War II. Ketler warned men that because the draft age might be lowered to eighteen (as it was in November), they must be ready to leave college.[17] Seven faculty members, including Nesbitt and football coach Jim Loveless, fought in the military, while others served on Mercer County's Selective Service Board or as observers for the Army Air Corps, directed Red Cross campaigns, or taught and oversaw the military courses offered at the college.[18] Echoing Ketler, *The Collegian* beseeched students to support the war effort financially, and a December 1942 Pan-Hellenic Council drive raised more than $4,400 ($86,000 today).[19] On February 10, 1943, forty-seven Grove City male students who were members of the Army Enlisted Reserve Corps left for Camp Meade as the high school band played while they walked together down the steps of Crawford.[20] During the 1943 spring semester, the college sponsored a four-part peace forum discussing the political, economic, and spiritual aspects of "a just and durable peace," as put forth by John Foster Dulles. In April, the sororities sponsored a drive that raised $8,500 for the war effort. That year, the college provided eighteen forty-by-one-hundred-foot plots for staff to grow "victory gardens."

Because of the college's advances in radio technology, the federal government chose it as one of only six sites in the nation to host a secret radar training program. On March 1, 1942, Grove City began operating the Naval Training School in basic radio for three hundred servicemen at a time. One hundred of them rotated out every three months and were replaced by one hundred more. Fourteen Grove City faculty taught full-time in this program. Memorial Hall was converted into a barracks with double bunk beds to house program participants, and servicemen also stayed in one-half of Lincoln Hall.[21] Operating this program required the college to buy a substantial amount of scientific equipment and construct or revamp its laboratories. During the more than three years the school operated, 3,759 sailors and marines completed their training. Because of its excellent facilities in basic sciences, Grove City was also selected to host an Army Air Corps preflight school, which began on March 1, 1943, as a successor to its Civilian Pilot Training Program; the college provided the ground school instruction and housed and fed these airmen.[22] When this program ended in spring 1944, almost one thousand pilots, navigators, and bombardiers had been trained.[23] The air corps rated Grove City's program as one of the best in the nation.[24]

During the war, college women held numerous dances for servicemen. These men, *The Collegian* reported, greatly enjoyed spending times with Grove City's "beautiful co-eds."[25] The newspaper acknowledged in March 1942 that things looked bleak for the Allies but urged students not to adopt a defeatist attitude.[26] The editors counseled students to hate the principles but not the people of Germany, Japan, and Italy; they called for loving both America's neighbors and its enemies to help establish world peace.[27]

By 1943, alumni and former students were serving in England, China, India, Australia, New Guinea, Northern Africa, and several other places with the marines, army, navy, merchant marines, and women's auxiliary services. They participated in battles on the land and sea and in the sky. During the war, the college sent a "Wolverine Newsletter" to over three hundred servicemen to inform them about campus events and the activities of fellow military alumni and classmates.

Grove City College contributed to the war in another major way. Companies J. Howard Pew owned fueled more than half of the nation's military planes and built 40 percent of its tankers; by one estimate, Pew's companies constructed 250 major vessels and repaired one thousand two hundred ships during the conflict.[28] Many of the supporting vessels accompanying the D-Day attacking force on June 6, 1944, were built by Pew's Sun Shipbuilding and Dry Dock Company. A jubilant Pew called this pivotal invasion "phenomenal."[29]

The Collegian's "From the Front" series furnished news about Grove City alumni and students fighting in the war, and Weir Ketler's son, David, '43, wrote a column to provide updates on the war. In addition, the newspaper included interviews with and letters from alumni who were fighting in the war. My father, Roger Smith, '42, an ensign in the navy, was interviewed while on leave in December 1942 after fighting in a naval battle in the Mediterranean Sea near Casablanca the previous month.[30] Weir Ketler's older son, George, '39, a marine first lieutenant, fought at Guadalcanal in 1943. Delighted that a large statue of the Virgin Mary was undamaged during a heavy bombardment of a Catholic mission, he declared, "No matter how hard a despot tries to destroy religion," it survived "and it blossoms forth stronger than ever."[31] Most issues of *The Collegian* during the conflict included articles about students or alumni who were killed or missing in action. An estimated five hundred alumni served in the war.[32]

Ketler told the trustees in December 1944 that college personnel needed faith, vision, and courage to carry out their normal tasks in difficult times.[33] As the Allied victory seemed imminent, *The Collegian* urged students in January 1945 to remember the millions of soldiers who had died, stop griping that movie theaters, bowling alleys, and skating rinks had been closed because of lack of fuel, and keep buying war bonds, giving blood, and writing letters to soldiers.[34] It would soon seem strange, the editors asserted, to no longer see hundreds of servicemen marching and drilling and to not be able to spend time with them. Many officers and servicemen expressed regret about leaving the college because their experience had been so positive.[35]

In late April 1945, the *GCC Victory Ship* was launched. The navy named ships for all colleges with more than five hundred students, which were constructed in order of the schools' founding. On April 29, the college held a special chapel service to commemorate and celebrate the lives of twenty-nine Grove City alumni and students who had died during World War II, seven who were missing in action, and five who were POWs. At a May 8 chapel service, students listened to President Harry Truman's proclamation of V-E Day and to Ketler's exhortation to strongly support the war effort until Japan was defeated.[36]

In May 1945, Ketler lauded the "faithful and heroic service" Grove City graduates and students had rendered. The president praised Russell Smith's direction of the naval training program, which was rated one of the nation's best in the field of radar. He extolled Grove City students for their enterprise and enthusiasm during the war, especially their work with theater, radio broadcasting, and the campus newspaper, and was pleased by students' involvement in religious activities.[37] On October 21, 1947, the navy awarded Grove City College a plaque stating "Well Done" at a special assembly to commemorate the college's Naval Training School.[38]

In December 1945, Ketler argued that the college had effectively served the nation and "come through the war "reasonably well," but it now needed to undertake many other tasks to "make an even more constructive contribution" to the world.[39] The college's solid financial circumstances when the war started and limited indebtedness during the first two years of the war, Ketler argued, prevented it from experiencing "serious or crippling" effects. Nevertheless, having an emergency fund or a larger endowment "would be a source of strength."[40]

Enrollment fluctuated substantially during the 1940–1956 period because of World War II and the influx of veterans using the GI Bill to attend college after the conflict ended. Grove City's enrollment was 928 in fall 1940–1941 and decreased to 465 students in fall 1944, 405 of whom were women. In June 1946, Ketler reported that the college had restored normal enrollment more rapidly than he anticipated primarily because of the enrollment of many former servicemen, some of whom were returning students. That fall, fueled by 653 male and female veterans, the student body soared to 1,228, of whom 467 were freshmen, the college's largest freshman class by far and its largest enrollment. A significant number of students were married, and the town had few accommodations for married students. Ketler argued that the grades of veterans were as good as men coming directly from high school, and he praised their "fidelity, earnestness and enthusiasm." Classrooms and labs were crowded, and more professors were needed, but there was a nationwide shortage. Funds provided by the Federal Housing Authority, Ketler explained, were helping the college build eight units to house married veterans and their families.[41] Several faculty returned following their military service, and Grove City added sixteen new professors in 1947–1948, including William Swezey in biology and Eugene Liggitt in religion, but the increased student body still overwhelmed faculty in numerous disciplines. That year, 51 percent of Grove City students were World War II veterans, 6 percent lower than the national average.[42] Consequently, the college's ratio of men to women went from its normal five-to-four to two-to-one, where it remained until the mid-1970s.

In fall 1947, the college had 1,364 students including 175 seniors, 253 juniors, 508 sophomores, and 419 freshmen. For the first time, the sophomore class was larger than the freshman class. Enrollment peaked the next fall at 1,447; 1,019 students were men, about 60 percent of whom were receiving GI benefits. In fall 1949, enrollment was 1,014, and for the only time in college history, seniors were the largest class. In the 1940s, the enrollment of women fluctuated only from 319 in 1943 to 453 in 1949, while the number of men varied from sixty-five in 1944 to 1,019 in 1948. In June 1955, Ketler told the trustees that 1,250 was the maximum number of students GCC could adequately accommodate; Pew preferred, if possible, to enroll 1,350 to help balance the budget.[43]

Academic Life

The SAT was created in 1926, but few students took it until the late 1950s, and the ACT was not devised until 1959. Grove City College has no records of SAT scores for applicants or accepted or enrolled students before 1956 and very limited records of the percentage of applicants who were admitted or of enrolled students who ranked in the top one-fifth or one-tenth of their high school classes prior to this date.[44] Therefore, it is difficult to determine the academic quality of the student body during this period. Their admission to some of the nation's top medicine, law, and graduate schools and their employment records indicate that Grove City's best students were outstanding during the 1940 to 1956 period.

Many students found their coursework at Grove City to be very challenging, as demonstrated both by their frequent complaints and the large number who received low marks. College grades have risen substantially from the 1940s to the present. *The Collegian* advised freshmen to develop good time management skills and ask professors for assistance.[45] Faculty typically met with freshmen in early October to discuss study skills. After the first six weeks of each semester, all students who had one failing grade or two "unsatisfactory marks" (D's or F's) were invited by Alva Calderwood to discuss their difficulties at what students called the "Dean's Tea Party." Calderwood reported in November 1940 that 190 students had received unsatisfactory cards, while 170 had been sent flunk cards; the main reason for poor grades was that they were not studying enough, especially in English and math courses.[46] In fall 1948, 250 of the college's 1447 students received a dean's invitation.

As noted, after the war, the faculty faced the challenge of educating large numbers of veterans. Ketler explained in December 1946 that many veterans were having trouble meeting professors' standards in some science and math courses because they had not studied this material for several years, but their overall work had been very good.[47] Another problem was that many required courses were bursting at the seams.

"Tension Mounts as Exam Week Nears," *The Collegian* declared in 1949. "Black coffee and black circles under the eyes from lack of sleep are the order of the day."[48] The college did not yet have review sessions, a study day, or therapy dogs to help students reduce their anxiety and prepare for finals. Some students protested that finals counted for too much—25 to 50 percent—of their final grades. Many complained that few professors recognized how much material had been covered in a semester. The faculty insisted that reviewing for finals was more important than the grade students received, but few students agreed.

In fall 1948, 217 students (15 percent) made the honor roll (all A's and B's). The next fall, ninety-nine women and ninety-eight men achieved this distinction. In the late 1940s, the college began honoring the 10 percent of students with the highest grades in a chapel program.[49] In addition, students who maintained superior marks for three years were admitted to an honor society.[50] In 1954, Grove City adopted the quality point average. Professors, a writer from *The Collegian* joked in 1955, seemed intent on flunking out any students with IQs below 150. Upperclassmen did freshmen a disservice by not warning them before they enrolled how hard academics were (and how bad the weather was) at Grove City.[51]

The college added a religious education major in 1946, a Latin-Spanish major in 1947, and a sociology major in 1954. In 1949, Grove City replaced the Bible-philosophy major with a philosophy-psychology major, divided the biology major into zoology and botany majors, and established one-year programs for prelaboratory technicians and pre-nursing students. That year, the general engineering major was replaced by separate ones in mechanical and electrical engineering. These curriculum revisions made the science and engineering curriculum the strongest it had ever been.[52] Unfortunately, similar improvements did not occur in other disciplines during these years. Students called for devising a faculty evaluation system to weed out poorly performing professors and help improve the academic program, but this was not implemented until 1971.[53]

Facilities

The opening of five new buildings between 1940 and 1956 significantly improved the college's living conditions and athletics facilities. Lincoln Hall, a third men's dormitory, began housing students in January 1941. Three building projects were completed in 1947: An addition to MAP accommodated two hundred women, a transept added to Harbison Chapel seated 180, and apartments were constructed for married students. That year, the trustees evaluated a plan to erect for an estimated \$2.7 million (\$38.7 million today) an athletic and recreation center, a new library, another men's dorm, a women's dorm, and an engineering building.[54] In 1949, they decided to proceed with several of these projects and broke ground for Hopeman Hall and another annex to MAP. With its basketball arena, swimming pool, and bowling alleys, an exuberant writer for *The Collegian* declared, the new recreation building would include almost everything "except carbon copies of all final exams."[55] In 1949, the trustees expressed thanks for the "magnificent generosity" of the Pew family in constructing the college's dormitories. Its "record of philanthropy and public service" had "few equals in the history of American education."[56] More than two-thirds of students contributed in 1949 to the building fund. For the first time, the board hired a public relations firm to help raise money for a building campaign. An agent for this firm, the John Price Jones Corporation of New York, argued that corporations and individuals "outside of the immediate college family" needed to be enlisted in the financial drive.[57] Hopeman Hall and West Hall, an annex to MAP, were both dedicated on June 5, 1950. The Pew Memorial Foundation gave \$300,000, and J. Howard Pew personally donated \$100,000 to help erect the recreation building, which included Alumni Hall. Although many other gifts were received, the college had to borrow \$250,000 to complete the edifice that cost \$1,400,000 (\$18.6 million today). The facility included a basketball arena seating one thousand eight hundred, an Olympic-size swimming pool, bowling alleys, a large intramural room, handball courts, a snack bar called the "Gedunk," offices, and accommodations for students. The building was dedicated before a basketball game on December 5, 1953, which was attended by dozens of Grove City letter winners and numerous area coaches. The ceremony included a banquet to honor Robert Thorn at which Ketler praised Thorn's moral integrity, inspiring teaching, and coaching.[58] The recreation building quickly became the center of student life. The Buhl Foundation gave $150,000 to help build the new library. Named for Henry Buhl, who served as a trustee from 1898 to 1927, it opened in February 1954. The 1957 Middle States evaluation team called Buhl Library "a gem" and the recreation building "magnificent."[59] A second transept was added to Harbison Chapel in spring 1956, enabling the entire student body to worship together.

Christianity

During the last fifteen years of Ketler's presidency, Christian faith and values remained at the center of the college's identity and enterprises. As many church-related colleges downplayed their religious connections and commitments, Grove City repeatedly affirmed its Christian mission and relationship with PCUSA.[60] The 1950 *College Bulletin* expressed Grove City's aims during these years: "The college is animated by the spirit of service to God and humanity" and strove to foster "sound and liberal culture, vital religion, and practical efficiency," virtuous conduct, "right thinking, fair play, and hard work." Christian training was "a large part of a true education."[61] Bible courses were a key part of the curriculum. The annual Prayer Week (soon called Spiritual Emphasis Week) continued. The three major campus religious organizations—the YMCA, YWCA, and Christian Service League—held well-attended weekly meetings, sponsored special events, and ministered to people at local churches, George Junior Republic, and a home for the elderly. *The Collegian* articles defended basic Christian doctrines and challenged students to profess and practice their faith. Most clubs still began their meetings with devotions, and numerous Bible study groups met regularly in the dorms. Dozens of missionaries spoke in chapel and to campus groups.

During Spiritual Emphasis Week, all morning classes were shortened by ten minutes to extend chapel services from thirty to sixty minutes. The week's keynote speakers included Louis Evans, president of the Board of National Missions; Peter Marshall, soon to become the US Senate chaplain; and Robert Lamont, pastor of First Presbyterian Church in Pittsburgh. During this week, guest ministers gave morning chapel talks and held informal discussions in the dorms and private counseling sessions with students. Students often performed a short religious play or a tableau. Methodist pastor Russell Humbert, the 1949 speaker, praised Grove City's "congenial Christian atmosphere."[62] That year, *Good Housekeeping Magazine* named Grove City one of its outstanding liberal arts colleges, citing its Spiritual Emphasis Week as a chief reason for this designation.[63] The 1950 week included dramatic scenes based on James Weldon Johnson's *God's Trombones*. Selections of the book were read while organ music sounded in background; a Black soloist sang several Negro spirituals, and the pastor of the Mt. Lebanon Presbyterian Church in Pittsburgh preached sermonettes between the scenes.[64]

The YWCA sponsored a series of talks on Catholicism, Protestantism, and Judaism in 1941. That year, the college hosted a conference on "The Changing Orient," featuring religious leaders from China and Japan. In 1947, the YMCA invited a Presbyterian pastor, a Catholic priest, and a Jewish rabbi to give talks. Hundreds of students attended several series the YWCA and YMCA arranged on the physical, mental, and spiritual aspects of marriage. For example, 350 students heard J. Calvin Rose, a YMCA Marriage Institute leader, exhort them in their dating to focus more on intelligence and spirituality and less on physical attractiveness, dancing ability, and petting prowess.[65] Each year, the CSL and the two Y's led a chapel service, and they held frequent retreats at nearby church camps attended by as many as 125 students. YMCA and CSL members taught Sunday school at George Junior Republic, assisted with GJR's plays and newspaper, and hosted parties for them. They also preached, read scriptures, led prayers, and did vocal and instrumental solos at Sunday church services at GJR.[66]

Many Catholic students actively supported the Newman Club established in 1947. Hundreds of students regularly attended local Presbyterian, United Presbyterian, Methodist, Episcopalian, Lutheran, and Catholic church services, Sunday school classes, and college fellowship groups. Ketler estimated in 1949 that half of Grove City's one thousand students were Presbyterian and that 95 percent of students were church members."[67] The next year, Ketler claimed that the many campus religious organizations and college groups meeting at local churches contributed significantly to the college's "wholesome, vital religious spirit."[68]

Despite the college's Christian mission and these many opportunities for worship, fellowship, and service, spiritual lethargy occasionally surfaced. In 1945, Ketler called for reviving "a truly Christian spirit and outlook" on campus. "Christian attitudes and conduct," he maintained, "can do much to heal and lead forward a broken world."[69] On the other hand, many graduates probably did what physician John McMillan, '45, advised: Consider "your enrollment at GCC as one of the greatest blessings you will ever receive and join me in a brief prayer that I often make: 'Thank you God, for allowing me to attend Grove City College.'"[70]

Their faith in Christ helped students deal with the sudden loss of friends, the horrors of World War II, and the anxieties of the Cold War. Responding to the death of a classmate in a car accident, a writer for *The Collegian* declared, "Our faith in our Saviour makes us believe that Bob Parks is well and happy in a world of life eternal."[71] A 1951 Easter op-ed exhorted students to recognize that Jesus "gave everything he had for us." Without him, only "doom and ultimate failure" awaited people.[72] Two months later, another editorial asserted that neither an ingenious scheme nor a more powerful bomb could restore human meaning and hope; the only remedy for people's ills was to recognize that God created and controlled the universe and that trying "to rule our affairs apart" from God's guidance brought ruin.[73] A third student declared similarly in 1955, "Neither the building of a powerful armed force nor the world organization holds our real hope. Our hope lies in Jesus Christ." We must "put our faith in Him, our Lord and Savior."[74]

One example of *The Collegian* articles affirming fundamental Christian doctrines and beseeching students to accept Christ as their savior or to follow Jesus faithfully is Dave Prince's 1954 series. He discussed biblical authority, Christ's bodily resurrection, Christ's nature, heaven, and other topics, usually including an evangelistic message. One article criticized those who received "the free gift of salvation through faith in Christ" and then lived as they pleased.[75]

Until World War II, many church-affiliated colleges required chapel attendance and numerous state universities held chapel services.[76] After the war, however, many church-related colleges made attending chapel voluntary, and most state schools stopped arranging services. At Grove City, chapel attendance continued to be required Tuesday through Saturday mornings and Sunday afternoons, prompting some disgruntled students to engage in disruptive behavior. In October 1942, *The Collegian* chastised men for persistently talking in chapel and whistling at the Manhattan Singers' special assembly and at coeds during a merit award presentation.[77] In 1946, the editors complained that numerous students were doing their homework and chattering during the hymns, sermons, anthems, and prayers.[78] The editors doubted "the advisability of required chapel" but urged students to be respectful.[79] In 1954, the editors asserted that not all those enrolled at Christian colleges were "devout, pious youth." However, Grove City students were "expected to be mature adults" who acted "properly in polite society." They lamented that "irreverence in chapel services is entirely too common." "Particularly disgusting," the editors averred, was "the perennial ringing of an alarm clock" during Sunday services. They regretted that many "students at a Christian college show so little respect for the things of God." Some students argued that this impertinence would cease if chapel were not compulsory, but as long as chapel was required, the editors maintained, Grovers must be "courteous adults." The long-standing practice of men and women sitting on different sides, *The Collegian* contended that year, was a century out of date.[80] Senior Barbara Kober maintained that ending segregated seating would reduce sleeping, reading, writing letters, knitting, laughing, and other disrespectful, detestable conduct.[81] Greater faculty attendance at the Sunday chapel service, *The Collegian* avowed, would make it more important to students.[82]

The Faculty

Grove City's efforts to provide a high-quality education in the post–World War II years were hindered by professors' numerous course preparations and the high student-faculty ratio. The faculty's teaching load, coupled with their responsibilities in advising campus organizations and chaperoning student events, gave them little time to improve their courses, supervise independent studies, assist struggling students, or engage in their own research and writing projects. Consequently, faculty published few books or scholarly articles during these years. Ketler declared in 1947 that professors had "responded cheerfully and enthusiastically to the challenges" substantially increased enrollment caused. By assuming some routine faculty responsibilities, student assistants had increased the "efficiency" of professors' teaching and deepened their own understanding of course subjects.[83] That year, Ketler proposed providing periodic sabbaticals or at least permitting some faculty to have a summer term off from teaching. (Sabbaticals were not introduced until 2004.)[84] Ketler beseeched the trustees for many years to institute a faculty retirement program, which was finally established in 1955 for all professors or staff who had served at least ten years and were sixty-five or older.[85]

The primary contribution Grove City professors made beyond the classroom between 1941 and 1956 was the military service some of them rendered as soldiers, sailors, or chaplains. Their demanding teaching and extracurricular duties limited faculty activities beyond the campus. John Nesbitt hosted a weekly Pittsburgh radio show called *News by Nesbitt* in 1941 that analyzed international developments. During the war, R. G. Walters edited several business textbooks used in army and navy educational programs. Head football coach Jim Loveless was elected president of the Tristate Track and Field Coaches in 1949. French professor Jonathan Ladd served as the president of the Bowling Green University Alumni Association, and its ODK chapter named him the 1953 alumnus of the year.

The faculty had hundreds of daily interactions in and outside the classroom with students. They counseled scores of students about personal issues. Professors also organized or participated in varied events to entertain students and build rapport. At a May 1941 faculty-student day, for example, thirty-three of the college's forty-three professors engaged in a dishpan relay, a "silly track meet," and other activities to "let their hair down." They also competed against students in tennis matches, softball games, and a golf driving contest and put on a variety show.[86] Throughout the 1940s, women students hosted the faculty for a chicken dinner in MAP dining hall. In 1945, the faculty resumed their efforts to amuse students and get to know them more personally. A faculty variety program showcased monologues, musical numbers, and a sing-along. Classes were canceled in mid-May so that faculty and students could enjoy a play day. Its activities included a Truth of Consequences program with dean of men Addison Leitch, registrar H. O. White, and academic dean Alva Calderwood revealing some of their hidden talents as well as a three-legged race, wood chopping, a tug-of-war, a softball game, and dinner.[87] A May 1949 student-faculty day featured a softball game, a chariot race, a costume competition, log cutting, and an obstacle course. In the 1950s, the Woman's Athletic Association sponsored an annual meet and greet with the faculty. In a 1952 student contest, religion professor Eugene Liggitt and history professor Wilfred Black tied for professor of the year.[88]

Campus Life

Hundreds of dances, talent shows, debates, plays, musical performances, athletic contests, club programs, and guest speakers and entertainers made campus life rich and robust during much of this era. During World War II, however, many activities were curtailed. Varsity sports and intercollegiate debate were suspended, most clubs did not meet, and few parties were held. In 1944, when only sixty-five male students were enrolled, the only active men's organization was the YMCA, and the only sports were intramural football and basketball.

Dances were popular, and during the war, military personnel living in the dormitories attended USO dances at the town armory and on campus. In May 1946, the Inter-Fraternity, Pan-Hellenic, and May Day dances were all revived. Prominent bands played for major dances. Elliot Lawrence and His Orchestra, voted the most promising new big band in *Billboard*'s college polls in 1947 and 1948, provided music for the 1948 Inter-Fraternity Ball. Many dances had innovative decoration themes such as "The Courtship of Miles Standish" (for which all faculty were asked to dress as Pilgrims), Madri Gras, April in Paris, and Alice in Wonderland.

A 1941 talent show featuring skits, comedy routines, dances, and popular music raised money for needy and imprisoned students in war-torn Europe and Asia. Acts by students and professors at the 1947 winter carnival included a magic show, a humorous dance, sketches, and vocal music. Freshmen stunt nights were held annually. The 1947 one consisted of twenty-four acts featuring a skit by women who were trying to get into heaven, forty-five guys singing "Tell Me Why," and a vocal quartet including future director of admissions John Moser.

During Leap Week, which was popular from the mid-1930s to the mid-1950s, women had to ask for, plan, and pay for all dates, hold doors and coats for men, carry men's books, and whistle at truck drivers. Promotions for the event in 1947 declared that the woman who secured the most dates would be crowned Wolf queen.[89] The next year, Leap Week featured a twin sweaters dance;

if couples did not have matching sweaters, women were encouraged to knit them. Throughout most of the 1940s, the college also had an annual Dutch Treat Week.

Other forms of entertainment during these years included a WAA fashion show and a Halloween party at which women won prizes for their costumes and students traversed a "House of Terrors" filled with strange-looking creatures. At occasional "panty raids," male students tried to climb in the windows and pry open the doors of MAP while beseeching coeds to toss them their underwear, adding spice to campus life while irritating administrators.[90]

After the war, dozens of campus groups sponsored fundraising drives to support scores of worthy causes. For example, in 1947, the YMCA raised money to provide care packages for war-ravaged Europeans by posting baby pictures of faculty and students. Students paid a nickel to vote for the cutest one; dean William Swezey won.

Sexism abounded in the 1940s and 1950s. During the late 1930s, profiles of female students routinely listed their height and weight. Some women tried to shed pounds. In fall 1940, sixteen women pursuing this goal ate at two "diet tables" in MAP dining hall. They agreed not to eat snacks or drink Cokes between meals. Many more women wanted to participate than the spaces allotted.[91] In 1942, the *Ouija* began featuring six "charm queens" chosen by a student vote based on their allure, personality, versality, and popularity. *The Collegian* described women as attractive and "blushing beauties," praised their pulchritude, lauded majorettes for wearing "morale-boosting" skirts, pictured numerous "curvaceous co-eds," and referred to women as the "weaker sex." An alliterative Valentine's Day's headline in *The Collegian* proclaimed, "Cupid's Casual Capers Captivate Campus Cuties With Romance, Music."[92] A 1941 article in the campus newspaper titled "Men Disprove Female Worth at Outing Club" unabashedly declared: "To prove that women are more or less worthless in every sense of the word," male club members made a good dinner at the cabin by themselves; the "consensus was that women are all right in their place, but when they are not there, man makes a darned good substitute."[93] WSAJ did not have any female announcers until 1945.

From 1950 to 1955, *The Collegian* regularly featured photos of coeds in bath suits. Meanwhile some students urged the college to offer a marriage and family course. Bernard Judy protested that Grove City's "ultra-conservativism" prevented the college from teaching courses that discussed sex. Students were mature enough to handle this content, he maintained, and the large attendance at the recent lectures on marriage and family issues demonstrated their interest in the topic.[94]

During these years, campus rules became somewhat less restrictive. In spring 1942, junior and senior women's hours were extended until 10 p.m. every night, while sophomores were given two 10 p.m. curfews per week and freshmen received one. Women could receive occasional permission to stay out until midnight or 1 a.m. Deans periodically conducted a bed check, and women were required to have written permission to leave the college overnight. Same-sex dining continued. Ten years later, men were finally permitted to stay in the lobby of women's dorms until 10 p.m., but "making out" was not allowed. To help freshmen women adjust to campus life, senior women held meetings to discuss college history, traditions, study habits, extracurricular activities, sororities, campus rules and regulations, and vocational topics.

School spirit was like a yo-yo. Laments bemoaning its absence were typically followed by reports asserting its rejuvenation.[95] *The Collegian* insisted in 1942 that Grove City needed new cheerleaders every year because the previous ones became discouraged by lackluster rooting.[96] Soon thereafter, however, a booster club was created, students exuded enthusiasm at home football games and pep rallies, females were finally permitted to be cheerleaders, and buses transported students to away football games.[97]

Summarizing the 1942–1943 year, *The Collegian* declared that despite all the hardships the war had brought, students would long remember dances, special chapels, the rivalry among the navy, army, and marine servicemen stationed on campus, bond drives, students departing for military service, friendships, plays, measles and mumps outbreaks, Alva Calderwood's prayers in chapel, the suspension of varsity sports, the small enrollment, and Cokes.[98]

In 1945, some students revived the idea of establishing an honor system. After investigating honor codes at two hundred colleges, a committee presented plans to the Student Council to create an honor system to increase trust and integrity on campus. For the honor system to be successful, *The Collegian* argued, all students must support it.[99] The newspaper complained the next year that some students bragged about how they passed tests and quizzes with the help of friends or by cribbing; these cheaters would pay a price later when they could not properly do their jobs.[100] The Student Council endorsed this proposed honor system, but it was not adopted. A decade later, *The Collegian* editors again contended that implementing an honor system would increase student maturity and boost the college's reputation.[101]

After World War II, many students expressed concern about the world beyond campus. One beseeched his classmates to conserve food because one-third of the world's people did not have enough to eat.[102] Others called for world peace. In a letter to the *Pittsburgh Post-Gazette,* Grace Colwell, '49, argued that unless peace prevailed, the Allies would not have truly won the war. An editorial in *The Collegian* expressed hope that the United Nations could achieve Woodrow Wilson's goal of world peace.[103] Editor in chief Bill Weil, '50, labeled the US government "an oversized Machine," which was "stumbling blindly with bunglers at the controls." Sadly, it promoted dependency by instilling in people the conviction that the government owed them a living.[104] Yugoslavian George Werbizky, '54, who had endured the horrors of World War II, exhorted classmates to combat communism and work to prevent World War III.[105] In 1950, Grove City students joined those at many other colleges in the Crusade for Freedom to combat communist aggression. Before a home football game, Dwight Eisenhower's speech opening the crusade was rebroadcast, and at halftime, the presidents of five campus organizations signed the Freedom Scroll to enlist in this campaign.[106]

The battle over freshmen rules persisted in the late 1940s and early 1950s. Freshmen were still required to wear dinks and signs, display no high school insignia, not smoke, tip their hats to and open doors for upperclassmen, be in their dorms by 10 p.m. every weekday, know the alma mater and the history of all campus buildings, generally do everything upperclassman asked them to do before 8:30 p.m., and sit in a special section at all home football games. Scofflaws were brought before a tribunal.[107] Everyone agreed that freshmen traditions aimed to unite first-year students and help them to get to know upperclassmen, but many freshmen protested that the rules were too harsh. In October 1949, freshmen implored sophomores to help them adjust to college life rather than heckle them. Sophomores countered that freshmen had never been treated so well.[108]

The Collegian often published an April Fools' edition. The 1945 issue reported that the deans were urging women to wear shorts to class, a subway would be built to connect the upper and lower campuses, and students should walk and play on the grass and keep off the sidewalks.[109] The 1947 edition announced that for the first time in college history a Democrat, President Harry Truman, would speak at commencement. Four years later, this issue announced that Joseph Stalin would deliver the commencement address, a large dam would be built on Wolf Creek, and students would not be granted any class cuts.

A common postwar complaint was that the dearth of social activities led many students to leave on the weekends.[110] Some countered that the Student Council was providing numerous interesting programs to encourage students to stay.[111] Students also grumbled about the inclement weather. For the sixth time in the last seven years, *The Collegian* bemoaned in 1947, it had rained on homecoming. Sports reports often mentioned that many contests had been postponed or canceled because of rain or snow.

During much of the postwar period, the college's touring choir maintained an active concert schedule. On a trip to sing Handel's *Messiah* in nearby Franklin in March 1947, the "bloody but unbowed" choir encountered some major problems. On the way to the concert, one of its buses caught on fire, and one of the cars transporting students crashed into a telephone pole. On the return trip, snow prevented one bus from ascending a large hill outside Franklin, requiring another bus to pick up the stranded choir members.

Before 1947, the YMCA and YWCA organized campus tours, brunches, mixers, and parties to help acclimate freshmen to campus life. That year, the college hired upperclasswomen to serve as counselors to help freshmen women adapt to college life academically and socially. This resident assistant program (for women and men) quickly became a key ingredient of campus life.[112] In fall 1953, the college introduced a social and educational orientation program for freshmen held for two days before upperclassmen arrived. Over the years, this program became longer, more important, and more focused on vocation and Christian discipleship.

After the Korean War began in 1950, some Grove City students were drafted. The college's Air Force ROTC unit was activated in July 1951, and all male freshmen were required to participate in its program beginning in 1951–1952. As at most other campuses, the Korean War engendered neither strong opposition nor enthusiasm nor caused any protests at Grove City College.[113] After inspecting the college's ROTC program in May 1953, Colonel Adolf Wright ranked it among the best in the country in terms of its facilities and effectiveness. Four graduates of the first class commissioned at Grove City who were serving at an Air Force base in Texas thanked their instructors for preparing them so well to fulfill the responsibilities assigned to second lieutenants.[114]

A 1951 article in *The Collegian* exhorted students to cheer at football games, stay off the grass, and act respectfully in chapel.[115] The next month, the editors argued that school spirit, which had declining since the end of World War II, needed a "transfusion" to preserve its life. Some blamed this on the college's many veterans who did not care about extracurricular activities, but most of them had graduated, and the problem had become worse. In addition, the editors renewed their call for an activity fee to help fund *The Collegian,* which depended on subscriptions. This fee would also encourage more students to attend dances and plays to get their money's worth.[116]

In 1951, *TIME* magazine described American college students as "fatalistic, security-minded, conservative, grave, morally confused, tolerant of almost anything," and concerned about a good job above all else. Many women allegedly believed that staying at home alone with children "would be a fate worse than death."[117] The next year, Harvard English professor Howard Mumford Jones argued that college women were interested in jobs, husbands, and lucrative salaries rather than intellectual adventure and inquiry. Moreover, few students supported social causes or joined movements; they were obsessed with personal security; self-absorption ruled, and civic spirit had waned.[118] Although many Grove City coeds planned to work after graduating, most of them wanted to marry, raise children, and provide a loving home for their families. For many years, columns in *The Collegian* regularly listed the numerous women who had become keyed, pinned, engaged, or married.

In the early 1950s, the college still required faculty to chaperone many student events, placing a burden on professors and requiring some events to be canceled. After students complained about the faculty's unwillingness to chaperone all their activities, Jonathan Ladd beseeched students to give professors sufficient advance notice, ask all faculty, not simply a select few, and treat chaperones cordially at their functions.[119]

As noted, other common student gripes included compulsory chapel, the length of freshmen traditions, early curfews, and the lack of an activity fee and a resident nurse; students also often called for improving faculty-student relations.[120] In 1954, students petitioned the administration for an activity fee to cover receiving the *Ouija* and all *The Collegians* and attending four plays.[121] Some called for coed dining; men eating alone, a male student avowed, was not good for "conversation, manners, or digestion."[122] Throughout the 1950s, women wore skirts to all classes and were required to wear skirts to all meals except Saturday and Sunday breakfast.

Senior David Prince insisted in November 1954 that the college was concerned about both spiritual growth and intellectual development and that students could freely express their views in *The Collegian*.[123] From 1940 to 1956, most of *The Collegian*'s editors in chief insisted that neither the faculty committee that oversaw the newspaper nor administrators interfered with their work. They reported that the newspaper had never been subjected to prepublication censorship, and they had not been called on the carpet for criticizing the college.[124] One editor in chief complained that he felt caught between defending the administration and expressing student grievances, leading him to try to straddle the fence.[125]

In 1949, the college elected its first homecoming queen and court who were feted at the football game. A water show began in spring 1956 featuring seventeen women performing synchronized swimming routines. It quickly became one of the college's most anticipated and appreciated annual events. May Day included the coronation of a queen, a dance pageant, plays, and sporting events. In 1948, senior Betty Reed Finnessy became the first married May queen. Queens were supposedly chosen based on their beauty, charm, character, leadership, and scholarship, but their personal popularity played a major role in winning the student vote.

In May 1955, *The Collegian*'s editor in chief argued that students progressed from frightened newcomers who dealt with freshmen traditions, pledging, and their first college dates, to sophomores who dominated freshmen, to high-achieving juniors, to privileged seniors who were going into the world as the college's "finished products." Those about to graduate had learned to turn to God for guidance and had become "intelligent, cooperative, friendly, and mannerly" people of whom Grove City College was proud.[126]

The sounds of music filled the air in the early 1940s. The chapel choir, which had performed at the 1938 PCUSA General Assembly in Cleveland, enriched the Sunday vesper services and sang at several nearby churches each year.[127] The college symphony orchestra performed several times each year, and the music department held monthly recitals. In spring 1941, Grove City hosted six colleges at a festival of applied music. Robert Bingham enlarged and improved the band after he joined the faculty in 1939. Most musical activities were suspended during the war. One exception was the almost all-female chapel choir with which a few Air Force men sang.

The college's men speech and debate team was highly successful from 1940 to 1942. In December 1940, the squad tied for third at a seventeen-team debate tournament at Westminster College. In April 1941, Grove City tied for fifth at a large tournament at Michigan State University, and senior Fred Van Vorhees captured second in radio speaking. In December 1941, the squad finished fourth at an eighteen-team debate tournament at Westminster College. The national Pi Theta Kappa organization awarded junior Vin LaBarbera a Special Distinction in Debate in March 1942. That month, Grove City, led by LaBarbera and senior Thomas Shearer, won the eight-team Northeastern Ohio Speech Tournament.

The speech and debate team resumed its impressive performance after the war. In 1946, Bill Dean finished second in impromptu speaking at a tournament at Georgetown, Kentucky, and the debate team tied Penn State for second at a tournament at Seton Hill. In March 1949, Grove City made it to the semifinals of a twenty-four-college tournament at Allegheny College. In spring 1950, sophomores Don Powers and Vincent Wilson propelled Grove City to second place at the Pi Theta Kappa Province of the Lakes tournament. In January 1951, the Wolverines, again spearheaded by Powers and Wilson, defeated many teams at a twenty-one-school tournament at the University of Pittsburgh.[128] In 1951, Powers and Wilson took high honors at a national debate tournament at Oklahoma A&M University; in 1952, the duo had the highest score at the state debate tournament at Lehigh. Wilson also won second place in the twenty-seven-team Pennsylvania state oratory contest.

The theater program had no lull in activities during the war years. Miriam Franklin directed *The Philadelphia Story* in 1942 and *Letters to Lucerne* in 1943. Joe Ketler directed *Twin Beds* in 1943, whose cast had to be changed several times because of military call-ups, measles, and an auto accident. Four one-act plays were staged in Crawford Auditorium in March 1945, and *Arsenic and Old Lace* was performed the next month. After the war, several notable plays were produced—*Junior Miss* directed by mathematics professor Philip Carpenter; Noel Coward's *Blithe Spirit* directed by Franklin; the college's second staging of *Our Town*, directed this time by English professor Maude Jamison; and Tennessee Williams's smash hit *Glass Menagerie*. The leading actors during these years were Betty Camera, '42, who played the principal role in *Stage Door, You Can't Take It with You,* and *Spring Dance*; Jane Urey, '44, who starred in *Letters to Lucerne*; and Bob Gregory, '47, a military veteran who had the major role in *Blithe Spirit*. Alice Bartlett, '48, who starred in *Our Town* and *Junior Miss* and was the student director of *Ten Little Indians,* and Frank Ketler, '48, who played the chief role in *Dear Ruth* and *The Man Who Came to Dinner,* won the TAP award for best actors in 1948. In the new decade, plays included *An Inspector Calls, Macbeth, Harvey,* and *Hedda Gabler.* Future French professor Robert Sisler, '52, played the title role in *Macbeth*. Future dean of the chapel Richard Morledge, '54, played the lead in *Harvey*. Jay Frey, '54, and Edwina (Eddie) Adams, '54, who starred in *Hasty Heart,* received the TAP best actor awards in 1953. The next year, TAP honored sophomore Dot Turk, who had played roles in five shows, as best actress, and junior Don Maclay, who had major roles in several plays, as best actor.

Clubs and organizations continued to play a central role in campus life. In April 1941, the Commerce Club sponsored an exhibition titled The Industry of America, to which numerous corporations contributed displays. The club was inactive during the war years, but by 1946, it had 150 members. The four literary clubs resumed many of their activities after the war. Ketler called 1949 "an unusually significant year" for student extracurricular activities. He especially praised the work of the literary societies, theater program, departmental clubs, touring choir, and debating team.[129] By 1954, however, all four literary societies were defunct. Ketler praised numerous groups the next year for their community service. The theater society performed several times each year at the Deshon Hospital in Butler; the touring choir sang in local churches; religious organizations taught Sunday school at George Junior Republic; the CSL and gospel team led services at local churches; several groups visited the elderly at the Odd Fellows Home; and scores of students raised money every year for the World Student Service Fund.[130] In 1947, the faculty, prodded by Ketler, who had earlier belonged to the organization at the University of Pittsburgh, established an Omicron Delta Kappa circle on campus. Since then, this organization, which honors student achievements in academics and leadership, has played a major role on campus. In 1950, a chapter of Cwens (later Crown and Sceptre), a sophomore women's honorary, began. In May 1951, the Science Club held its first open house since 1940 to conduct experiments and display products of classroom work.

Grove City students captured additional honors during this sixteen-year period. Vin LaBarbera's editorial titled "Youth Need Union Now" won fifth place in a national 1941 Pi Delta Epsilon contest. In 1942, *The Collegian* earned three second-class honor ratings from the Associated Collegiate Press. In 1949, two of senior Pat Belknap's short stories were published in the *Atlantic Monthly*'s national contest for college students. That same year, *Mademoiselle* named freshman Mary Everly to its college board to report on campus news, fads, and fashion. In 1952, junior Sally Coutts was elected president of the state's Women's Athletic Association. The next year, freshman Don Maclay won first place in a national contest sponsored by the Thomas Paine Foundation. Sophomore Dick Ridenour won a national essay contest on "America's Place in the Arab World" in 1954. Finally, in 1956, sophomore Barbara Myers was elected chair of the state convention of the Athletic Federation of College Women.

Several other students excelled during this period. Premed major George McCloskey, '41, was president of the Student Council, Varsity G, and the Webster Club, and the sports editor of *The Collegian*. Vin LaBarbera was the editor in chief of *The Collegian*, president of the freshman, sophomore, junior, and senior classes, Pi Kappa Delta, and the EPs, an outstanding debater, and a member of the Shakespeare Club and Pi Gamma Mu. Claire Winters, '53, was a basketball star, the ODK Sportsman of the Year, and the president of the senior class and the Leadership Club. Nancy Lee (Paxton), '54, a later vice president of Student Life and Learning, was president of the Women's Governing Board and a member of the Judicial Board, Alpha Theta Mu, CSL, and the YWCA. Bob Buckham, '55, was president of both the Student Council and ODK.

Many interesting guests spoke on campus between 1940 and 1956. In 1941, Jim Thorpe, "universally regarded" as America's greatest all-around athlete, spoke in chapel. The 1912 Olympic decathlon champion discussed the importance of training and fitness to a successful career.[131] Anauta, a nomadic Eskimo; Canadian prohibitionist Ben Spence; and noted sculptor Leonard Craske also spoke in 1941 or 1942. At a January 1945 chapel program, Major Compton Packenham of *Newsweek* tried to temper the hate-Japan message promoted during World War II. In November, James Whittaker, Eddie Rickenbacker's copilot, described the twenty-one perilous days in October 1943 they and six other men spent on a raft in the Pacific Ocean after their plane was shot down. Between 1946 and 1955, students heard adventurer Sydney Montague; M. Thomas Tchon, a Chinese scholar, soldier, and statesman, and former secretary for General Chiang Kai-Shek; Bob Mathias, an American decathlete, two-time Olympic gold medalist, and US congressman; Jesse Hays Baird, the moderator of the PCUSA General Assembly; and Michális Dórizas, an Olympic medalist, collegiate wrestling champion, and geography professor at the University of Pennsylvania.

An interesting array of guest performers also visited Grove City during these years. The Kryl orchestra, led by Bohumir Kryl, played in both 1941 and 1942. Helen Holloway Steigman, an American opera composer, performed in 1941. The Guardsman's Quartet received the largest special chapel applause in four years in November 1941. In 1945, acclaimed opera singer Hilda Ohlin performed, and one thousand one hundred people packed Crawford Auditorium to hear David Rubinoff play his $100,000 Stradivarius violin. In 1949, the celebrated General Platoff Don Cossack Chorus and American lyric soprano Helen Jepson presented concerts in Crawford Auditorium. Two years later, actor Hal Holbrook portrayed Mark Twain, Moliere, and other celebrities. In 1954, British tennis star Mary Hardwick played an exhibition match on campus. In spring

1956, American jazz pianist and composer Erroll Louis Garner performed in the Arena.

Greek Life

The Greeks were a major part of campus life from 1940 to 1956, although they became even more important after 1960. During the latter Ketler years, Greeks were frequently criticized for their rushing and pledging activities, especially "Hell Week," and their preoccupation with parties. In 1942, the college had six fraternities and eleven sororities. Fraternities were suspended from May 1943 until February 1946. They received fifty-two pledges two months later and 102 the following February. In March 1948, seventy-seven women joined sororities, the highest number in history.

Bernard Judy contended in 1941 that fraternities and sororities caused "much ill-feeling on campus."[132] *The Collegian*'s editors claimed the next year that administrators viewed fraternities negatively and that they contributed little to campus life. They complained that fraternities were engrossed with social activities and often had a detrimental effect on independent students and on their own members' classroom work.[133]

As in the 1920s and 1930s, female pledges did errands for upperclasswomen, cleaned their rooms, and pressed their clothes. Pledges wore necklaces made of clothespins, dog biscuits, bottle caps, and baby blocks. Male pledges were required to serenade women before dawn, wear bow ties and burlap "sweaters," and sport crews cuts. Male and female pledges attempted to outdo one another by hollering, wearing outlandish apparel, and capturing "the hallowed rock" on the lower campus. As "Hell Week" began in March 1948, *The Collegian* announced that "flattery turns to jeers." No longer telling pledges, "You look mighty sharp today," actives were screaming, shouting, and hissing at weary initiates.[134] After "Hell Week" ended, many new actives claimed that they had no "hard feelings"; they viewed their experience as a rite of passage.[135] Others maintained that pledges quickly forgot the sting of paddling, the hideous taste of food, and the sleepless nights. They did not hold grudges against actives, and many of them wanted next year's pledges to undergo the same activities.[136] When "Hell Week" was reduced from three to two days in 1950, actives insisted that "anything that happens on Friday or Saturday can be forgotten by Sunday and we'll all be friends again."[137] A March 1950 headline in *The Collegian* probably expressed the feelings of many new initiates: "119 Pledges Survive as 'Cessation of Hostilities' Is Declared Saturday. Lack of Sleep Named as Hell Week's Worst Hazard."[138]

In 1948, the conflict between Greeks and the administration erupted. Dean of men Robert Thorn accused fraternities of "irresponsible pranks, physical torture, [and] disreputability" and asked them to surrender their constitutions. Leaders, many of whom were veterans, pledged to eliminate problematic behaviors and refused to turn in their constitutions.[139] The same year, dean of women Mary Taylor demanded that the college's sororities change some of their rush policies, which sororities had previously voted against doing, to enhance the welfare of female students.[140] Both the fraternities and sororities acceded to the ultimatums of the administration, enabling them to continue their good standing.

In 1951, Taylor chastised actives for requiring pledges to work for them during the entire pledging period; this was permitted only during "Hell Week," which was restored to three days that year.[141] The next year, sororities changed "Hell Week" to "Help Week"; instead of pledges cleaning the football stadium steps with toothbrushes, scrubbing Rainbow Bridge, or doing other useless tasks, they would help at the two local hospitals, several area churches, and the Odd Fellows Home, and do other worthwhile projects.[142] In subsequent years, pledging would entail plenty of both pointless and helpful activities. In the mid-1950s, the numbers of Greeks increased significantly, and interfraternity sports became even more important after flag football was added in 1953.[143]

Athletics

Overall, the college's sports teams did not fare as well from 1940 to 1956 as they did in the preceding or subsequent years. The ending of athletic scholarships by 1936, coupled with physical education professors' time-consuming classroom responsibilities that limited their recruiting, strategizing, and mentoring of players, contributed to this outcome. From the 1890s through the early 2000s, Grove City coaches were overloaded. Many of them oversaw three different sports. Remarkably, Jim Loveless simultaneously coached swimming and basketball for most years from 1937 to 1954.

The college did have some very good teams, especially in soccer during the first half of the 1950s, and numerous outstanding athletes. The basketball team had a 25–9 record in the 1940–1941 and 1941–1942 seasons combined. The golf team played thirteen consecutive matches without a defeat in 1941 and 1942. In spring 1942, the track and field team had only one loss, while the tennis team finished 9–2, shutting out six teams including Youngstown State and defeating Pitt 5–4. The premier athletes during these years were senior Bob Hulton, '42, who his senior year led the basketball team in scoring and had a 9–2 record playing first singles in tennis; Walt Moore, '42, who scored 528 career points in basketball in 1942; Jack Blakely, who set records in the half mile and the mile; and senior Ted Penar (a future Grove City academic dean), who received honorable mention on the AP All-State team as a football halfback and won many races as a sprinter. From fall 1942 until fall 1945, only the basketball and soccer teams played a few contests, and football and golf did not resume play until 1946–1947. During the war, many students played intramural sports, and women took physical conditioning classes that included calisthenics and an obstacle course.

Some sports teams excelled between 1947 and 1956. The 1947 football team reeled off six straight victories and held its opponents to an average of seventy-three yards from scrimmage per game (one of lowest averages in the nation). Grove City was ranked fourth in the state after Penn State, Penn, and Geneva. Before basketball games were played in the new Arena in the recreation building in December 1953, the eight hundred seats in Carnegie Gym were usually all filled. Freshman forward Mike Bish was named to the 1947 AP All-Pennsylvania Collegiate Basketball

Team. In 1948–1949, Bish set a record for the most career points with 614 and the 11–6 team had the highest average in college history—sixty points per game. Danny Hill, '52, Mike Robertson, '52, and Claire Winters, '53, successively set the record for most career points between 1950 and 1953.

Grove City's track and field and golf teams were outstanding from 1948 to 1950. In 1948, the Wolverines finished 5–0 and won the Class B intercollegiate tristate championship. Charlie Sutcliffe, '49, regularly won the high hurdles and broad jump, while Bill Kroske, '49, frequently captured the mile and two-mile runs. The next spring, led by Homer Bechtell, '51, the team finished 4–1 and placed second at the tristate championship. In 1950, the squad again captured the championship, as Bob Baughman, '52, in the 440, Dick Hettish, '53, in the 880, and the mile relay team set tristate meet records. Ned Hamilton, '52, who ran a leg on this relay team and won the broad jump and pole vault, was Grove City's top point scorer. The golfers went 7–1 in 1948 and 6-2-1 in 1949, winning the tristate championship.

The 1948 football team defeated perennial powerhouse Geneva 16–7, Allegheny 13–0 at homecoming, Hiram 40–0, and Thiel 33–0 before losing a heartbreaking game 20–12 to Slippery Rock at home. After Slippery Rock students tried to tear down the goalposts, Grove City decided to discontinue playing sports against their next-door rivals. The 1949 football team, which many at the time called the best one in Grove City history, finished 7–1. The Wolverine offensive line averaged 215 pounds, just twelve pounds less than the nation's heaviest one. Quarterback Hal Foster, '51, was an AP first-team All-State selection, while wide receiver Ned Hamilton was named a Little College All-American. That fall, Willie the Wolverine, the college's mascot, made his first appearance. As the fall 1951 season began, the football team's record was 240–175–41, and its tally against Westminster College was 32–21–6, but the team did not have another winning season until 1957.[144]

The shining star among Grove City's sports team in the postwar years was the soccer squad. In 1948, the team finished 5–0–3, its first undefeated season in history. One of its leading players, George Ramsey, '49, flew more than eighty missions during World War II as an Army Air Corps pilot before being shot down and imprisoned by the Germans. Between 1952 and 1956, the team compiled a superb 31–4–2 record. The 1954 team, spearheaded by sophomore Frank Sbrocco, beat Wheaton, ranked second in the nation, 2–1, as well as Pitt (4–2) and Indiana State Teachers College (8–1) in going 7–1. Sbrocco received honorable mention on the New Jersey, Delaware, and Pennsylvania All-Star team, played number one in tennis, and started in basketball. In 1956, Bob Thorn's final year as the coach, Ross Emerson, '57, who still ranks second all-time in goals scored, led the soccer team to 7–0 record. Emerson spent two years in the middle of his college career as a paratrooper in the Korean War and is the only man in college history to play on two undefeated soccer squads.

While extolling the "sterling performance of Grove City's athletic teams, a sportswriter for *The Collegian* argued in 1949 that for the college and its athletes, scholarship, sportsmanship, and character formation were more important than winning.[145] Ketler heartily agreed. He insisted (incorrectly) in 1951 that Grove City had never tried to use athletics to promote the college. Instead, the college encouraged all students to participate in athletic activities to improve their health and vigor and develop attitudes that were very beneficial in all aspects of life.[146] After Westminster shellacked Grove City in football 48–6 in 1954, *The Collegian* argued that all colleges should have the "will to win," but "winning is not paramount." Colleges had been established first and foremost to educate students, not to triumph in athletic contests. Grove City's soccer team proved that good coaching could produce good teams without giving athletic scholarships.[147]

In March 1952, sophomore Paul Cuffari set the tristate shot put record, and the next May, he extended Grove City's record to 49 feet 8⅜ inches. Led by John Hopkins, '55, and Hub Garver, the golf team went 6–1 in 1954 and 6–1–1 in 1956. After many years of losing records, the swimming and diving team, aided by the new state-of-the-art pool in the recreation building, which included diving facilities, finished 9–1 and captured its first Penn-Ohio championship in 1955, beating seven other schools. Scott Johnston, '55, set the Penn-Ohio record in the fifty freestyle, while Lee Steller, '57, established records in the 100 freestyle and the 150-yard individual medley, and Chips Koehler, '56, won the fancy diving event. In 1955, Grove City created a rifle team, which was quite successful in subsequent years. The 1955–1956 basketball team, led by Jim McElrath, '57, Gary Peters, and Dutch Leonard, '59, (the first one-thousand-point scorer in college history), went 13–5 and averaged 77.1 ppg, the highest in school history.

In 1948, ODK introduced its Sportsman of the Year award. Sophomore football center Hal Kelly won the inaugural award in an all-college election. Senior halfback Jack Shankle captured the award in 1949, while Fred Leetch, '51, a basketball and soccer player, received it in 1950. Senior Dick Brock, the 1954 Sportsman of Year, scored 457 points in his basketball career and played number one in tennis, winning six letters.

From 1940 to 1956, many women played intramural sports, and some participated in play days at nearby colleges, engaging in tennis, badminton, rifle shooting, bowling, and other sports. At gymnastic exhibitions, Grove City coeds displayed their prowess in square dancing, modern dancing, archery, relay races, basketball, and volleyball. Several years, a women's club field hockey team played intercollegiate contests. Women became eligible to join the WAA when they accumulated twenty-five points by participating in individual sports, dual sports, and group sports and by being chosen for honorary varsity teams. In 1940, the WAA hosted thirteen colleges for a conference to discuss mutual problems and exchange ideas, and in 1948, the organization welcomed almost one hundred Athletic Federation of College Women delegates representing twenty-five colleges to work on enhancing athletic opportunities for women. In 1954, Grove City women, led by Donna Bingham, '56 and Jane Powers, '55, won a national intercollegiate telegraphic duckpin bowling tournament.

Placement

Grove City's excellent placement record continued in the final Ketler years. For example, in 1941, seven Grove City graduates were admitted to seminaries (four at Princeton), four went to medical or dental schools, two went to law school, and seven attended graduate school in various fields.[148] The next year, *The Collegian* claimed that all fifty-seven graduates who had sought teaching positions received them.[149] In the first half of the 1950s, about fifty companies, including US Steel, ALCOA, General Electric, and Gulf Oil, came to campus each year to recruit. In 1954, academic dean Creig Hoyt reported that many Grove City alumni were presidents, vice presidents, and other top executives at corporations.[150]

The Trustees

The college lost several very long-serving trustees between 1940 and 1956: banker William McKay of Grove City, a board member from 1907 to 1945; another banker, Edwin Harshaw, also of Grove City, the board's treasurer from 1906 to 1945; oil producer Mark W. Graham, a trustee from 1902 until he died in an automobile accident in 1949; Pittsburgh City Council member Robert Garland, a trustee from 1912 until 1949; industrialist Edwin Fithian, a third trustee from Grove City, served from 1902 to 1953; prominent Protestant church leader William Albert Harbison, who also died from a car accident, served from 1902 until 1950; and Harry Jennings Crawford, president of Quaker State Oil Refining Co. and of two banks, a board member from 1922 until 1953.

Prodded by J. Howard Pew, who argued that women should be added to the board because 40 percent of Grove City's students were coeds, women owned 60 percent of the nation's wealth, and women would raise the quality of the board, the trustees appointed four female members in 1949: Pew's sister, Mary Ethel Pew; Sara Mathide Soffel, a judge in the Common Pleas Court of Allegheny County; philanthropist Jane Torrance Baker of Sewickley; and Harry Crawford's daughter Katherine J. Breen.

An Era Ends

Weir Ketler considered retiring for five years, but Pew persuaded him to remain. In January 1956, Ketler finally announced his retirement. Ketler had completed forty years as Grove City's president and finished all his major building projects. Pew called Ketler, the nation's longest-serving college president, "a scholar of distinction, an educator of unusual ability," and an executive with "a genius for efficient business management."[151] Pew praised Ketler's devotion to training young people in the interconnected "fundamental truths of Christianity and freedom."[152] Under Ketler's leadership, Pew added, the college had emphasized moral and spiritual values, developed "high intellectual standards," and procured "an excellent faculty." He had also maintained the college's Christian heritage.[153] The trustees asserted that when Weir Ketler became president, Grove City was one of the least-conspicuous colleges in Pennsylvania in terms of its physical plant, equipment, reputation, and financial resources. Few Christian colleges, Pew maintained, had exceeded Grove City in growth and development during Ketler's forty-year tenure.[154] *The Collegian* lauded Ketler as an exceptional leader who had helped Grove City become "an institution of unusual stability and quality." William Tolley, the chancellor of Syracuse University, extolled Ketler's modesty, generosity, unselfishness, and thoughtfulness.[155] Charles MacKenzie later praised Ketler's "genius and moral character."[156]

Ketler declared that he had been privileged to serve the college during "a challenging and interesting period." The most important factor in Grove City's success, he avowed, had been the trustees' "unity and continuity of purpose." Their loyalty and commitment to the college, guidance, and friendship had made his experience "happy, memorable, and rewarding."[157] While serving as president, Ketler participated in numerous educational, religious, and civic affairs. He served as the president of the Higher Education Society, the College Presidents Association of Pennsylvania, and the Pennsylvania State Education Association. He was a member of the PCUSA Board of Christian Education, the State Council of Education, and the Board of Directors of Princeton Theological Seminary, and he was a trustee of the Grove City Hospital.

The Ketler era ended, and leadership passed to other men and women. *The Collegian* insisted that the college had made "sure, steady, constant progress" during his presidency.[158] Indeed, it had, but many challenges awaited Ketler's successor. Despite Pew's glowing assessment, the academic program needed to be significantly upgraded as the college confronted the increasing secularization of higher education and the social upheaval of the 1960s.

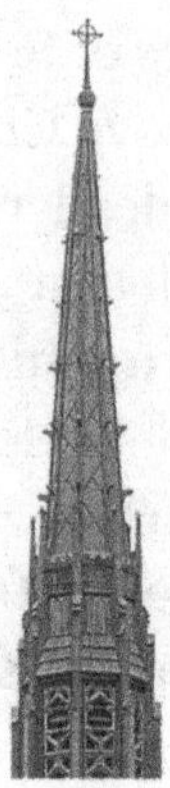

The Harker Years:

Strengthening the Academic Program and a Drift Toward Secularization,

1956–1971

In 1956, the trustees selected John Stanley Harker, '25, (who went by J. Stanley) to succeed Weir Ketler. As a student, Harker was the editor in chief of the *Ouija* and *The Collegian*, president of the Beta Sigma fraternity, and an outstanding debater; he helped organize the Student Council and coauthored its constitution. In 1928, he married Helen Francis Calderwood, '23, the daughter of dean Alva Calderwood. Helen was a straight-A student, the editor in chief of *The Collegian*, an associate editor of the *Ouija*, a class and YWCA officer, a debater, and the center on the senior girls' basketball team. The yearbook praised Helen's "intelligence, wit, humor, poise," charm, and "pleasing and lovable personality."[1]

Harker earned a bachelor of divinity degree at McCormick Theological Seminary and an MA and PhD at the University of Pittsburgh and pastored Presbyterian churches in New York, Pennsylvania, and Ohio. From 1951 to 1956, he served as the president of Alma College, a small Presbyterian liberal arts institution in Michigan. Harker was elected the moderator of his presbytery and helped found the Presbyterian new life movement to promote evangelism and spiritual renewal. He was a Republican, a Rotarian, and a Mason. All three of Harker's daughters, like the four children of Weir Ketler, graduated from Grove City College.

Harker was a logical choice to succeed Ketler. He had headed the alumni association for several years, and many trustees knew him well. He was a PCUSA minister, a theological and political conservative, held a PhD, had shepherded large churches, and had served for five years as the president of another Presbyterian-affiliated college. He was "energetic, experienced, and exceedingly direct."[2]

During Harker's presidency, the quality of the college's academic improved significantly as indicated by the credentials and scholarly achievements of the faculty, the upgrading of the curriculum, two positive Middle States reaccreditations, the high school rank and SAT scores of enrolled students, and the admittance of numerous alumni to prestigious professional and graduate schools. On the other hand, during these years, the college watered down its historic evangelical Christian mission despite the orthodox Christian convictions of Harker, J. Howard Pew, and several other leading board members and the college's continued affirmation of its Christian mission in catalogs and other publications. It is difficult to explain why and how this occurred. But given the battle to restore the college's evangelical Christian orientation during the presidency of Harker's successor, Charles MacKenzie, mission drift clearly happened. Several developments during Harker's tenure are suggestive: The worldviews of guest lecturers and chapel speakers, the discontinuation of Spiritual Emphasis Week, the dearth of articles in *The Collegian* affirming or defending Christianity, the types of plays performed, the worldview of professors hired between 1956 and 1971, and the perspectives presented in classrooms. This last point is extremely difficult to document, and here I rely on *The Collegian* articles as well as my own experience and that of classmates interviewed for this book. Also contributing to diminished Christian emphasis at Grove City during the 1960s was its less religiously committed student body. During the turbulent decade, the college was affected by the nation's increasing social protests, cultural upheaval, personal alienation and bewilderment, drug usage, and controversy over the Vietnam War.

As his presidency began, Harker stated that his major goals were maintaining the college's "Christian ideals and high scholarship."[3] Most students liked Harker. *The Collegian* declared that the Harkers had quickly brought many "wonderful changes" to the daily routine and spirit of students. Admirers called the Harkers "a fine example" of a Christian family. The president was never too busy to listen to, advise, or help a student.[4] Harker's highest priority was to improve the academic program. This required paying higher faculty salaries, increasing library resources, enlarging the staff, and erecting a new classroom building on upper campus. Harker also strove to boost alumni giving, produce a better alumni magazine, enhance public relations, and decrease the attrition rate.[5] In 1959, Harker declared that he wanted Grove City to "become one of the top small colleges in the nation."[6] By describing itself as a Christian college, the 1959 self-study stated, Grove City affirmed that "religion and education are inseparable, and that Christianity is the true religion." The college argued that American life was "based largely upon the Judeo-Christian philosophy, principles, and practices" and endeavored to promote these fundamental aspects of the American heritage.[7]

Enrollment

Enrollment increased from 1,487 students in fall 1959 to 2,050 in fall 1971. The acceptance and attrition rates steadily decreased during Harker's tenure, while the high school rank and SAT scores of enrolled students rose significantly. Two hundred twenty-five of the four hundred men and 216 of the 323 women who applied for the class of 1961 were accepted. Four years later, one thousand six hundred students applied for a freshman class that numbered 462. Seventy-eight percent of the class of 1965 were in the top two-fifths of their high school classes; they averaged 931 on the SAT. Grove City, Harker argued, was accepting "well-rounded applicants," not "egg-heads." [8] In 1962, Grove City enrolled one of almost every six applicants. In fall 1963, 26 percent of freshmen were in the top tenth of their high school class. The average SAT scores of the 1965 freshmen rose to 1144. That year, 43 percent of women and 11 percent of men were in the top 10 percent of their high school classes. The college enrolled 608 of the 2,560 applicants for the 1966 freshman class. The percentage of students who graduated in four years rose from 44.5 percent of the class of 1955 to 90 percent of 1964.[9] In the late 1960s, Grove City usually accepted about one-third of applicants and enrolled about one in four applicants.[10] In 1970, 72 percent of freshmen women and 20 percent of freshmen men finished in the top tenth of their high school classes. In 1961, 54 percent of Grove City students were Presbyterians, followed by Methodists, Lutherans, and Roman Catholics in descending order.[11] Throughout the decade, a majority of students were Presbyterians. Most Grove City students came from middle-class, rural or suburban Christian families.

Enrolling significant numbers of minority students, especially African Americans, has been a perpetual challenge for Grove City. Music major Dolores Ginyard from Norristown, Pennsylvania, a Philadelphia suburb, became the first Black student to graduate from the college in 1958. Marcia Hammond served as the college's first African American editor in chief of the *Ouija* in 1960, and Bradley Scott was the first Black Student Government Association president in 1968. Only about a dozen of the twenty-three to twenty-five hundred applications each year in the late 1960s were from African Americans, who were required to meet the same standards as other applicants.[12] To enroll these students, Grove City competed against Ivy League schools and the nation's best public universities, which typically lowered their SAT requirements for African Americans. And, unlike them, Grove City gave no special scholarships to minority students. Additional obstacles were the college's small number of Black students (six in 1969), the lack of Black faculty, and the difficulty of attracting urban Blacks to a small town. In short, few inner-city or minority students applied because of Grove City's religious affiliation, substantial cost to lower-income students, geographical location, and refusal to lower academic standards for these students.[13]

Facilities

Numerous improvements to the physical plant occurred during Harker's tenure. A president's home was completed in 1957. Memorial Hall was renovated in 1958. An academic building named for former dean Alva Calderwood that had twenty-two classrooms, which could seat 1,346 students, began use in 1958. Sixteen more classrooms were added to Calderwood Hall in 1962. North Hall, a woman's dormitory, opened in 1961. Willard Rockwell Jr. donated $150,000 to remodel the Hall of Science, which was rechristened Rockwell Hall of Science in 1965. Classes began in fall 1966 in Hoyt Hall, an engineering building honoring former dean Creig Hoyt. Hicks Hall, named for deceased board member Lewis Hicks, a $1.6 million structure housing 164 men and seating five hundred diners, opened in 1967. Colonial Hall was converted from a women's residence to a freshmen men's dormitory in 1966. Zerbe Health Center, named for alumnus benefactor Arthur Zerbe, opened in 1970. Carnegie Library was refashioned to serve as a music building. The former music hall on the lower campus was converted into classrooms and offices for the ROTC detachment. In April 1970, the trustees announced a $2.5 million ($20.6 million today) campaign to add more classrooms and offices to Calderwood, enlarge women's dining facilities, and erect a new women's dorm. The Association of Women Students petitioned the trustees to name the dormitory for Helen Harker who had created "a warm and friendly spirit on campus."[14] Helen Harker Hall, which housed 137 women, opened in 1971.

Academic Life: Raising the Bar

The quality of Grove City's academic program increased substantially during the Harker years, as indicated by the Middle States Association of College and Secondary Schools' reaccreditation of the college in 1960 and 1970; the Commonwealth of Pennsylvania's Committee of Public Instruction's glowing assessment of the college's teacher education program in 1963; the high SAT scores and high school rank of accepted students; and the growing number of alumni admitted to top professional and graduate school programs. During these years, significant changes occurred in some curricular areas and in the reporting and assigning of grades and honors.

Harker's plea to improve the academic program became more urgent when a Middle States team refused to accredit the college in 1957. The organization had not evaluated Grove City College since 1922. Its 1957 team discovered "serious problems" with the college's organization and policies. Its members were especially disappointed with the college's self-study, which was "shallow, evasive or non-responsive to many [of their] questions." The evaluators argued that faculty and staff salaries and fringe benefits were inadequate, the college's chain of command was unclear and inefficient, student health services were poor, and science laboratories had insufficient equipment. They also criticized the college's large class size and faculty teaching load, limited library collection, and high student drop-out rate. The Middle States team called for giving the faculty a greater role in the governance of the college. They were impressed by Grove City's physical plant, bright and loyal students, and devoted faculty, but they required the college to fix these problems and upgrade its academic program to receive reaccreditation.[15] William Sweezy was named the academic dean in 1957 and organized the faculty into more discrete departments, eliminated some weak majors, introduced an elementary education major, and discontinued the long-standing two-year secretarial course.

Two important additions to the faculty in fall 1956 were economics professor Hans Sennholz, who became the college's best-known professor, and Fred Kring, who significantly shaped student life policies in the 1960s as dean of men and dean of students. Led by Sennholz, the college's economics department became one of the nation's leading proponents of Austrian economics and one of its most staunch defenders of the free enterprise system.[16] The charismatic Kring was interested in hypnosis, telepathy, and occult literature.

In fall 1957, for the first time, all students received midterm grades instead of only those with D's and F's. In January 1958, the faculty established QPAs for graduating with honors in students' major fields—3.4–3.69, honors; 3.7–3.89, high honors; 3.9 and above, highest honors. In 1958, sixteen new faculty began, and course offerings were expanded. Faculty salaries were slightly below the average for Pennsylvania professors, and professors approved participating in Social Security.[17]

For the 1960 Middle States evaluation, Harker and his team prepared a much more analytical self-study documenting that many deficiencies accentuated in the 1957 Middle States report had either been remedied or were being addressed. This self-study asserted that the college engaged in "a courageous and persistent search for the truth" and wanted students to arrive at their own conclusions based on "broad knowledge, wide experience, and careful thought." It declared the college's intention to enroll students from a wider geographical area and to increase "the intellectual, cultural, and moral caliber" of the student body. Only individuals who were "receptive to the ideals and philosophy of the small Chrisian college" could succeed at Grove City.[18]

The 1960 Middle States team applauded the college's "impressive progress in the past three years" in almost "every field of activity." They commended the college's reasonable goals, division into departments, improved committee structure, increased salaries, and upgraded library and instructional facilities. They called, however, for reducing class sizes, offering more upper-level courses, and improving faculty benefits by providing tenure, sabbaticals, sick leave, and tuition remission for faculty children.[19] When examiners returned in 1960, Harker declared, they "enthusiastically congratulated" Grove City College for enriching its academic program.[20] They reaccredited the college.

Harker argued in 1960 that the college had strengthened its academic program by adding eighteen faculty, three-fourths of whom held PhDs "from the best universities in our land." One-quarter of graduates were going to graduate school, many of them at prestigious universities.[21] To help recruit and retain excellent faculty, the trustees in June 1960 granted a 50 percent reduction in tuition for faculty children and increased professors' salaries by 10 percent.[22] In 1961, Harker claimed that he had received hundreds of letters "rejoicing that Grove City is tightening its academic standards"[23]

The firing of Larry Gara rocked the campus in the early 1960s and brought Grove City adverse publicity. The controversy caused by Gara's dismissal engulfed the history professor, the college, the AAUP, the PCUSA's Pennsylvania Synod, and the parts of the higher education community in "a spirited debate about the limits and conditions of academic freedom, tenure, local educational autonomy, and due process."[24]

Gara began teaching at Grove City in 1957. He held a PhD from the University of Wisconsin, was an accomplished scholar, and had been a conscientious objector during World War II. Gara was not offered a contract for the 1962–1963 academic year on the grounds that he was deficient as a teacher and a department chair. Harker claimed that Sweezy had spoken with Gara for the last three years about his shortcomings in both capacities. Harker accused Gara of overly demanding grading, poor pedagogy, and administrative ineffectiveness.[25] Harker asserted that Gara had been given the opportunity to resign, and the college promised to help him find another job, but the professor refused to do so. Gara objected that he had been given no formal opportunity to answer the charges against him, including that he was "a dreary," incompetent teacher; he noted that six of his colleagues had resigned to protest his dismissal.[26] Led by his fellow historian Raymond Lorantas, '53, these professors also informed the media, wrote letters to the trustees, and appealed to their colleagues to support Gara. A sizable group of students also strongly opposed Gara's dismissal.[27] Gara stressed that he had received raises and supportive notes from the dean every year. A major reason for his firing, he maintained, was that Harker disliked his interest in research and writing. Gara also claimed that Harker never provided any evidence to justify his dismissal.[28]

Most faculty supported the administration. Many of them had earned degrees at regional universities, did not possess terminal degrees, and had little interest in the hot-button issues of the 1960s—tenure, academic freedom, and unionization. These issues seemed irrelevant to them, provided administrators did not interfere with their classroom teaching.[29]

Gara protested his dismissal to the AAUP, which promised to conduct its investigation with minimal publicity. When the AAUP instead issued several press releases about the case, the trustees instructed Harker and other administrators not to cooperate with its inquiry. After concluding its investigation, the AAUP censured Grove City, faulting the college for failing to provide a fair procedure for Gara to defend himself and to protect the academic freedom of its faculty.[30] Although the trustees were upset by articles in newspapers including *The Pittsburgh Press* criticizing the college for firing Gara, they unanimously commended Harker for how he handled the Gara situation.[31]

Supporting Gara's contention, Harker later insisted that the college dismissed Gara because he had utterly neglected his teaching responsibilities, which he viewed "a mere meal ticket." Since Gara's dismissal, Harker griped, "the AAUP has viciously attacked us." He claimed that 89 percent of the faculty endorsed firing Gara.[32] Actually, forty-nine of the eighty faculty signed a letter expressing confidence in the administration.[33]

In private letters, Harker lambasted the AAUP. While "blasting" Grove City, he told an applicant for a faculty position, the AAUP was also "attacking many of the finest schools in America for dismissing card carrying communists" and "sexual deviates." Harker claimed that Princeton Seminary, the University of Michigan, and many other outstanding institutions were on its list.[34] Harker told an alumnus that only one-eighth of American faculty were members of the AAUP, that the organization had sought to smear Grove City, and that the AAUP secretary had requested a bribe to hush up the case. To be censured by the AAUP, Harker concluded, was to be on "the honor roll of American institutions of higher education."[35]

Stephen Taaffe argued that to try to avoid a public relations disaster and protect Grove City's reputation, Harker had three basic options: He could have revealed that J. Howard Pew forced him to fire Gara because the board president despised Gara's political ideology, declined to comment and hoped the matter blew over, or "lie[d] indiscriminately to faculty, students, alumni, Presbyterian church officials, and even members of the board of trustees." Choosing the third option, Harker "developed a false narrative to explain and justify the decision to remove Gara based on hearsay, half-truths, distortions, exaggeration, and innuendo."[36]

After evaluating the college's teacher training program in 1963, the Commonwealth of Pennsylvania's Committee of Public Instruction deemed it "excellent." In 1971, the organization approved all eight of Grove City's education programs. The chair of its evaluation team declared that Grove City's preparation of teachers surpassed that of all other schools in the state except for the two teachers' colleges.

Despite these improvements, academic problems persisted. Overcrowding in classrooms was so great in the early 1960s, especially in the Hall of Science, that the trustees considered discontinuing the engineering program before deciding to erect a new engineering building. In a 1963 letter, Harker argued that the number of students in classes was being reduced (the average was 26.5 the previous year). The faculty had doubled since 1953, while the student body was only one-third larger.[37] The trustees appropriated $70,000 in 1964 to give raises to faculty, including providing merit pay to upgrade the quality of instruction.[38] The trustees acknowledged that academic facilities, including faculty offices, were "strained to the utmost." The trustees wanted to increase the percentage of professors holding a PhD from one-third to one-half. By 1965, the summer school enrollment was only about two hundred students; if low-enrollment courses were dropped, professors would need to teach only once every six years.[39] In fall 1965, the college purchased its first digital computer. The IBM computer, which was as large as a normal-size desk and could store 4,096 words of memory, would be used primarily for problem-solving.

In addition to complaining that large classes and the teaching style of most professors limited discussion, some students protested that professors' attitudes inhibited a frank exchange of ideas. One argued that while Grove City professors had academic freedom, students did not. Students were taught not to ask questions, and to pass their courses, they must echo faculty views. The author exhorted his classmates to break the bondage of "I lecture and you keep still because you are wrong."[40] Students who challenged the perspectives of some narrow-minded professors on exams, Ann Lewis asserted, even when asked "in your opinion," risked getting a lower grade.[41]

Students criticized academics on other grounds. One maintained that many professors' material and teaching methods were outdated and called for student course evaluations, a plea repeated throughout the 1960s.[42] Numerous students protested that some professors were incompetent. Some asked for higher tuition fees to enable the college to hire more and better qualified professors.[43] Senior Dick Jewell called in 1967 for creating a more challenging academic environment, increasing student engagement in the classroom, reducing teaching loads and class size, expanding honors work, and raising tuition one hundred dollars a semester to help hire twenty more professors.[44]

In November 1965, Harker asked retired Princeton president Harold Dodds, '09, whose father Samuel had taught at the college from 1889 to 1911, to help him upgrade the academic program. "Where we do sin terribly," Harker lamented, was in what was demanded of the staff; at Alma College, he had four secretaries; at Grove City he had one. At Alma, he also had two assistants, a vice president, and a director of publicity; he had none of these at Grove City. He did all the fundraising. In the past year, he had raised more than $1 million ($10.2 million today) while also teaching a course (ancient history) that regularly had fifty to eighty-five students. This excessive workload prevailed "throughout the entire staff." Many professors he wanted to hire refused to come because of the "absurd class loads" of fourteen instructional hours each week.

Harker urged Dodds to ask trustee Albert Hopeman to help rectify these problems.[45]

That fall, Dodds returned to Grove City for the first time in several years and observed conditions firsthand. Granting Harker's request, Dodds bluntly told Hopeman that the college was not achieving its full potential. Grove City's shockingly low tuition of $600 ($6,000 today) a semester, he maintained, kept it from effectively competing with high-quality colleges. Many other colleges had substantial endowments that generated income to supplement their higher fees. He argued that Grove City could charge $600 more a year and still maintain its financial advantage, which would enable the college to attract better faculty and keep them "loyal and enthusiastic." The college's "abnormally high" teaching load was "a serious handicap to [academic] excellence." To remain "abreast of his subject," Dodds contended, a professor needed "more time for study and reflection than the present teaching schedules at Grove City allow." He also suggested using some of the money increased tuition would produce to give scholarships and loans to needy students. Sadly, their "inadequate preparation" was preventing some Grove City graduates from gaining admission to top-flight postgraduate and professional schools, which was the most significant measure of a college's standing in the public mind.[46]

In 1968, only thirty-four of 107 faculty members (32 percent) had PhDs, well below the trustees' 50 percent target. The next year, the faculty teaching load was reduced from fourteen to twelve hours. In the late 1960s, the SGA's Academic Affairs Committee strove to change the school calendar, provide honors courses for underclassmen, and institute faculty course evaluations.[47] A 1968 survey found that 74 percent of students wanted to take finals before Christmas.[48] In January 1970, a study day was introduced before finals began.

In spring 1969, the faculty endorsed the SGA proposal to have course evaluations but made participation optional. An SGA committee explored the possibility of initiating a five-day class week. Some objected that it would make Grove City a suitcase campus and lead to more cutting of Friday classes and that rescheduling

Saturday classes would be difficult.[49] Others countered that Saturday classes were unpopular and a burden to their instructors.[50] In spring 1970, the committee discontinued its work because its members could not envision how to make a five-day week work effectively.[51]

In November 1970, another Middle States team evaluated the college. Its members commended the college for its well-maintained physical plant, affordable, high-quality education, focus on classroom instruction rather than research, friendly community, increased alumni interest and support, and "well prepared student body which understands and accepts, as does the faculty, the college's aims, programs and objectives."[52] The college's contribution to American higher education was "excellent." Like the 1960 team, however, evaluators called for faculty tenure, a more clearly delineated administrative structure, and a better retirement program.[53] A large majority of students surveyed in 1970 believed that faculty were genuinely interested in teaching, but most agreed that students were not required to do "their best work."[54]

Most students sampled for the 1970 self-study identified their major goals as broadening their intellectual interests, developing career skills, and learning to work effectively with others. Eighty-two percent said that the college had helped them achieve these goals. Seventy-nine percent of respondents said they would recommend Grove City to high school students, and college officials expected their opinion of the college to improve after they graduated.[55] Linda Croushore, a 1968 graduate and professional educator, probably speaking for many, declared that Grove City encouraged her to "think hard and develop higher-level thinking skills."[56]

In fall 1970, the AAC developed a course prospectus to help students decide which courses to take, which the faculty approved in spring 1971. Evan Adair reported, however, that many professors questioned its validity and viewed the prospectus as "a course evaluation." No other words, Adair opined, caused such fear among the faculty. The proposed course information guide was the most contentious issue at a May 1971 bull session. Fred Kring, English department chair Jim Paton, and several other administrators and faculty opposed the course prospectus because of "its methods, basic concepts, ethical connotation, psychological influence, or techniques."[57] That spring, 90 percent students favored having finals before Christmas.

As in earlier eras, the faculty strove to develop cordial relationships with students through activities outside the classroom, including playing student All-Star basketball squads, fielding teams in the independent men's basketball and softball leagues, and participating in bull sessions to discuss student grievances, dispel myths, and improve communication. In 1967, Kring stressed that students could visit the homes and offices of the president, the dean, and faculty without an appointment; he knew of no other institution where this was the case. Kring and his wife modeled hospitality, and students flocked to their farm on the outskirts of Grove City to picnic, chat, and swim in their pond. Every year, Helen Harker hosted many student groups in her home."[58]

The faculty chalked up notable achievements during the Harker years. Hans Sennholz was elected a lifetime board member of the Intercollegiate Society of Individualists in 1960. The Department of Vocational and Practical Arts Education of the Pennsylvania State Educators Association chose Ted Penar as its vice president in 1961, and he was selected as the 1965 Pennsylvania business professor of the year. R. Clark Dawes was awarded Knighthood in the Royal Order of Scotland in 1965 and named an Outstanding Educator of America for 1971. In 1966, William Teufel was elected president of the Pi Kappa Delta province consisting of New England and the Mid-Atlantic states. In 1969, ODK headquarters gave Philip Carpenter a certificate of honor for his long service to the Grove City circle, and Jonathan Ladd received Bowling Green's Alumni Service Award. Hilda Kring was listed in the Outstanding Educators of America in 1970 because of her civic and professional achievements.

Harker declared in 1966 that "We employ only evangelical Christians for teaching positions,"[59] but he hired numerous faculty who were not evangelicals. Harker appointed numerous professors who were either theologically liberal Christians or held secular humanist presuppositions. Illustrating the worldview of numerous faculty, Fred Kring, when asked in 1967, "What does Grove City being a Christian college mean?" replied that this designation expressed belief that Western Christian culture was "the best way of life," and Grove City students had higher values than the larger society.[60] He said nothing about Christian doctrines, faith, or mission. SGA president Bradley Scott maintained that Christianity was at a low ebb at Grove City during the late 1960s. Few students had "a wholesome, fulsome commitment" to the college's religious traditions, and many disliked taking required religion courses.[61]

Both secular humanism and what sociologist Christian Smith terms moralistic therapeutic deism flourished in classrooms, and few professors espoused distinctively biblical perspectives.[62] The worldviews of many professors clashed with orthodox Christianity. Faculty had free rein in the classrooms and were not closely monitored by the dean or their departmental chairs. In addition, emphasis on the integration of faith and learning began only in the 1970s; before this, most Christian faculty had little understanding of how to present an explicitly biblical perspective of their disciplines.

Political and Economic Conservatism

From 1956 to 1971, Grove City College remained a bastion of political and economic conservatism. In an October 1956 poll, students gave Republican President Dwight Eisenhower 430 votes to eighty-eight for his Democratic challenger Adlai Stevenson. Harker declared in 1960 that Grove City "is a very staunch Republican institution. Virtually all members of our staff are members of the Republican Party." He also noted that the Republican campus organization was very active.[63] In a straw poll that fall, Republican Richard Nixon received four times as many votes as Democrat John F. Kennedy.[64] On the other hand, in a November 1964 mock election, ultraconservative Republican Barry Goldwater received 324 votes to 216 for Democratic President Lyndon Johnson, indicating that such candidates were not as popular with Grove City students as moderate Republicans were.

At the opening convocation in fall 1964, Harker deplored how the "creeping paralysis of socialism" was damaging "the American spirit."[65] Harker insisted that Sennholz's economic position accurately represented Grove City, which was an independent, conservative Christian college; it was not "a tale to the kite" of either the liberal National Council of Churches or of Carl McIntire's fundamentalist American Council of Christian Churches.[66] Harker hired faculty who either endorsed the free enterprise convictions of J. Howard Pew and most other trustees or at least did not publicly criticize them.[67] Sennholz extolled the benefits of free enterprise in dozens of scholarly and popular articles, while history professor Clarence Carson staunchly defended political conservatism in several books. Carson contended in *The War Against the Poor* (1969) that government programs designed to aid the destitute had instead harmed them. Numerous articles in *The Collegian* in the mid-1960s criticized Lyndon Johnson's Great Society program. In a national collegiate presidential primary in May 1968, Grove City students gave Nixon 46 percent of their votes, Democrat Eugene McCarthy 11 percent, and Republican Nelson Rockefeller and Democrat Robert Kennedy each 10 percent.[68]

The faculty published little in the 1956–1971 period because they were more interested in teaching than research, and the heavy teaching load left little time for scholarly activities. Faculty books included Larry Gara's *The Liberty Tree: The Legend of the Underground Railroad* (1961), Carson's *The Fateful Turn: From Individual Liberty to Collectivism 1880–1960* (1962), *The American Tradition* (1963), and *Throttling the Railroads* (1971), and Carroll Edgar's *Fundamentals of Manufacturing Processes and Materials* (1965). Sennholz published dozens of articles during this period. A few professors wrote journal articles or contributed chapters to books.

Guest Speakers

To enrich the academic atmosphere and stimulate thinking, the college hosted a wide array of guest speakers during the Harker years. In the late 1950s, they included Minnesota Republican congressman Walter Judd, Countess Alexandra Tolstoy, MLB Hall of Famer and sportscaster Frankie Frisch, foreign correspondent William Shirer, post-war British Prime Minister Clement Atlee, and Filipino ambassador to the United Nations Carlos Peña Rómulo.

During the first half of the 1960s, the college community had the opportunity to hear Hal Holbrook's impersonation of Mark Twain and lectures by aerospace engineer Wernher von Braun, labor columnist Victor Riesel, Pulitzer Prize–winning novelist Allen Drury, renowned historian Kenneth Scott Latourette, former president of the United Nations General Assembly Frederick Boland, Foundation for Economic Education president Leonard Read, and cartoonist Al Capp.

The final Harker years featured WWII commando leader General Edwin Walker; polyglot Erik von Kuehnelt-Leddihn; Olympic champion Bob Richards; satirist Art Buchwald; novelist and biographer Alex Haley, who discussed his research for the book that became *Roots* (1976); *The New York Times* correspondent Harrison Salisbury; Congressman Gerald Ford (later president); Senators Edmund Muskie (D-ME), Abraham Rubicoff (D-CT), and John Tower (R-TX); comedian and civil rights activist Dick Gregory; talk show host David Susskind; sportswriter Heywood Hale Broun, John Birch Society founder Robert Welch; John F. Kennedy's press secretary Pierre Salinger; economist Ludwig von Mises; Boston Celtic great Bill Russell, and Ghanaian official Daniel Nyaho.

Walker (because of his scathing criticism of Dwight Eisenhower), Gregory (because of his denunciation of American economic and political systems), and Welch (because of his claim that Eisenhower, Kennedy, and Johnson all promoted a communist conspiracy) provoked some controversy. Two speakers, however, were especially provocative during Harker's tenure: radical feminist Ti-Grace Atkinson and abortion rights advocate Bill Baird, who both spoke in spring 1971.[69] Atkinson, who helped lead the fight to legalize abortion, censured marriage as "legalized rape" and demanded that women receive more rights. Marilyn Wolfe argued that Atkinson had presented "many thought-stimulating propositions," whereas a *The Collegian* writer denounced Atkinson's disappointing "110-minute ramble through her maze of bitterness and past experiences."[70]

Baird founded and directed the New York Aid Society, which promoted birth control and legalization of abortion. *The Collegian* praised his advocacy of abortion and birth control and pointed out that some women could not afford birth control products and that ten thousand women had abortions in 1970.[71] Alleviating suffering, Baird contended, was much more Christian than forcing women to have unwanted children.[72] One student challenged the common reasons for allowing abortion and insisted that women who did want to raise their children could put them up for adoption.[73] Baird's visit prompted students, with support from chaplain Dudley Rose, to create a birth control and abortion assistance service.

The college's numerous politically liberal lecturers prompted *The Collegian* editor in chief Alan Mesches to complain in 1969 about the lack of balance among college speakers. Ironically, Grove City had trouble bringing a major conservative figure to campus; William Buckley Jr. declined to speak three times.[74] No one protested in the newspaper the dearth of speakers offering distinctly biblical analyses of their topics.

Financial Matters

Grove City College steadfastly refused to accept the largesse of the federal government. Board members voted not to participate in a federal student loan program created in 1958. Aided by a $750,000 ($8.3 million today) bequest from trustee Bertram Hopeman, the college established a private loan program with better terms than those offered by the National Defense Act. "With adequate loan funds of our own" Harker explained, "we saw no reason for becoming involved in the Federal red tape."[75] In 1962, he told a magazine editor that Grove City has "never considered accepting a penny of Federal money." Handouts from "the welfare state," he averred, always came with strings attached.[76] Grove City, Harker insisted, "would rather do without some things" than "sell our birthright for any mess of potage."[77] Contrary to popular perception, the college frequently borrowed money to help construct buildings. In 1962, Grove City liquidated $770,000 of debt and became debt free for the first time in thirty years. Fund drives covered the cost of new buildings erected during Harker's presidency, but the endowment remained paltry—$4.84 million ($49 million today) in 1964. Harker explained in a 1968 letter that declining denominational support was hurting many church-related colleges, but for Grove City, this funding had never been more than a "bag of peanuts."[78]

Throughout the Harker years, Grove City prized its low tuition. Officials claimed in 1964 that its tuition was the lowest of all private colleges in the East. For the 1965–1966 academic year, tuition was $600 per year, while room, board, and fees were $850. Harker prodded the trustees to raise tuition, but Pew and Hopeman considered the college's low tuition to be "a mark of distinction" and were unwilling to increase it if the college budget was balanced.[79] Grove City students did accept state scholarships; one-third of them received Pennsylvania scholarships in 1970.

Recruitment and Placement

In spring 1957, the college produced a thirty-minute film, *A Year at G.C.C.*, which staff, alumni, and trustees used for recruiting. In October 1957, the college hired its first full-time public relations director. Admission staff visited almost all the large high schools in Pennsylvania, Ohio, and New York and prodded alumni to help recruit students. Despite Harker's boast in 1959 that no other American college could match what GCC offered "American youth for $500 tuition,"[80] the college did little to promote itself beyond its own region. Grove City received little national attention or recognition. One exception was when *McCall's Magazine* listed Grove City as among the country's thirty-seven "better bargain" small colleges in the early 1960s. In April 1967, Grove City participated in a three-day promotion at Northway Mall in the North Hills of Pittsburgh. The college band, orchestra, touring choir, ROTC drill team, and Marquettes performed. A magic show, a comedy routine, piano solos, folk singers, and numerous vocalists including Bradley Scott entertained shoppers. Highlights of the undefeated 1966 football team were shown. Almost two hundred students participated in what the mall's promotion manager deemed "a tremendous success."[81]

The placement record of Grove City graduates during the Harker years was very good. In 1964, for example, 25 percent of graduates went immediately to graduate or professional programs, and the air force commissioned thirty-three men. This pattern continued throughout the 1960s.[82] Many graduates earned good salaries.[83]

Religious Matters

During Harker's presidency, the YMCA and the YWCA ceased meeting and the Christian Service League declined in numbers and influence.[84] Moreover, biblical principles and moral values were less evident in the classroom and campus activities than during other periods of the college's history.

When Harker assumed office, the campus's three major religious organizations were thriving. In 1956, Saturday morning chapel was eliminated, and students were allowed to sit wherever they wished for the five other services. While some students were apathetic or misbehaved in chapel, a freshman maintained in 1958, the majority were attentive and sang enthusiastically.[85]

A December 1957 editorial in *The Collegian* asserted that Grovers were being trained in Christian principles, and many were practicing their faith.[86] Forty CSL members taught Sunday school at George Junior Republic.[87] Beginning in 1957, about thirty-five students traveled weekly to Polk State School to teach classes in religion, creative writing, folk dancing, and art to residents with intellectual disabilities. In spring 1960, CSL sponsored programs on evolution and missions and a Q&A with religion professors. That year, Harker wrote a friend, Grove City College was "indoctrinating youth in a faith we sincerely and firmly hold."[88]

Nevertheless, disinterest in spiritual matters increased. Senior James Allen Nash argued that most students had avoided the 1960 Religion in Life Week activities as much as possible; did this signal "the twilight of Christianity" at Grove City College?[89] After the 1961 Religion in Life speaker, Roe Johnson, the first president of the Fellowship of Christian Athletes, discussed how students could apply their faith to everyday life, junior Carl Hull complained that many Grove City students were apathetic toward Christianity.[90] That fall, Harker admitted to a Presbyterian pastor who had recently spoken in chapel that "we have a drinking problem" at Grove City but "we are working to make it a school worthy of the high name 'Christian college.'"[91] A 1963 survey of religion at twelve colleges, secular and Christian, conducted by *The National Review*, concluded that Protestant liberal arts colleges had "a generally destructive influence on students' religious convictions."[92] A Grove City student lamented that few of his classmates carefully examined what they believed.[93]

Disruptive pranks, including setting off alarm clocks during speakers' sermons, continued in chapel. A 1962 letter to the editor protested that many viewed chapel as "Harbison Social Hour." At a recent service, the letter said, one student reviewed French vocabulary cards while another wrote a "Dear John" letter, and a couple chattered away.[94] A writer for *The Collegian* argued (incorrectly) that the PCUSA Board of Education provided much of the cost of students' education. Consequently, students should happily attend chapel at a Presbyterian-affiliated college.[95] ROTC squadron commander junior Dick Conners contended that chapel was a waste of time because few preachers spoke directly to students.[96] Senior Robert Dent countered that by choosing to attend Grove City College, students agreed to go to chapel services.[97] Deeply religious students, David George averred, disliked being surrounded by "the openly scornful," but chapel should remain mandatory because religious experience was a crucial part of a complete education.[98] In 1965, sophomore Richard Conolly argued that Grove City had enough "true Christians" to make a voluntary chapel program successful if its programs were stimulating.[99] In 1967, a student criticized the college for holding beauty contests and tapping ceremonies, presenting athletic awards, honoring sports teams, and making announcements in chapel. Many students, he contended, wanted chapel to have an exclusively religious focus.[100]

In a February 1966 talk to Pittsburgh Presbytery, J. Howard Pew criticized the proposed Confession of 1967's low view of biblical authority and faulty description of such key theological terms as justification, redemption, atonement, and the deity of Christ. Like Pew, Harker strongly supported conservative Presbyterianism; he implored ministers to join a laymen's organization Pew founded to oppose the Confession of 1967, which would "water Presbyterianism down to Unitarianism."[101]

A major problem Harker faced was hiring deeply committed Christian faculty. In a February 1967 letter to Carl Henry, the editor of *Christianity Today*, a leading evangelical magazine, Harker exhorted Henry to help establish a Christian university to provide professors for church-affiliated colleges. The toughest job Christian college presidents had, Harker asserted, was finding well-prepared Christian professors. "Some of us," Harker declared, "stand willing to beat the bushes to find the dollars" to help create such a university."[102]

Although its Religious Emphasis Week was discontinued, the college brought former NBA player Bob Davies to headline a special Lenten program in March 1967 and Elton Trueblood, a Quaker author of twenty-five books, to speak on "The Rationality of Basic Christianity" in February 1969. As part of the ten-day 1967 Lenten program, fraternity and sorority members led religious discussions, communion was celebrated, the chapel choir sang Easter music, the touring choir performed, and CSL staged a religious drama. In a 1967 essay, Harker argued that the goal of Christian colleges was to help students grow up into the full stature of Christ.[103]

In 1969, protests about mandatory chapel intensified. In February, a group of seniors proposed giving students greater involvement in designing chapel programs and making services voluntary on Tuesday, Wednesday, and Thursday.[104] Many students did assignments, wrote letters, and listened to the radio at services.[105] SGA president Bradley Scott argued that Grove City was founded on a "strong Christian basis," which would continue even if chapel were made voluntary.[106] In March, the Conservative Club passed a resolution condemning mandatory chapel because it promoted disrespect for and was detrimental to religion. The Ad Hoc Committee for Voluntary Chapel was created to work with SGA to end mandatory chapel. The newly created Religious Activities Committee, composed of twelve students and twelve faculty, sought to make chapel more meaningful.[107] In March 1969, Scott maintained that students wanted chapel to be voluntary or required less frequently. Their donation of large sums of money to the college, he argued, did not entitle the trustees to unilaterally set the chapel policy; students who paid tuition should also have a voice in this matter.[108]

An April 1969 survey found that 65 percent of students strongly opposed mandatory chapel, and 25 percent were mildly opposed. Forty percent of students believed that chapel speakers were mediocre; 43 percent judged them poor; and 10 percent thought they were ridiculous. Sixty percent of students claimed that chapel messages had no effect on their faith, while 24 percent declared that speakers had weakened their faith, Moreover, 96 percent thought that mandatory chapel was not "consonant with Christian principles."[109]

In May 1969, Scott presented the SGA's request to Harker to significantly reduce the number of daily and Sunday chapels students must attend. Decreasing the chapel requirement, Scott argued, would increase Sunday church attendance and participation in campus religious organizations.[110]

Board members lamented that required chapel had become a "very serious problem."[111] To improve the chapel program, they hired Jack Heinsohn, a Presbyterian minister in Philadelphia who had worked as a circus trapeze artist from age ten to twenty-one, as the college chaplain in fall 1969.[112] Heinsohn, however, stayed for only one year even though *The Collegian* editor, an SGA resolution, and several student petitions implored the popular pastor not to leave. Many thought that he had made the chapel program more interesting and meaningful.[113] Dudley Rose, another Presbyterian minister who had been a football star and a campus leader at Muskingum College, replaced Heinsohn.

Grove City's 1970 self-study declared that it strove to educate students in a Christian context and to help them apply "Christian principles to daily life."[114] Harker sent incoming 1970 freshmen a letter stating, "We are a Christian college" which entailed "required courses in Bible," regular chapel attendance, and "a Christian climate" where they could "find deep meaning and real values."[115] Rose insisted that students were amazingly receptive to chapel services considering that they were required.[116] Nevertheless, students continued to protest that required chapel violated their First Amendment right to worship as they pleased, that the atmosphere in chapel was not conducive to worshipping or listening to speakers, and that the trustees wrongly assumed that attending chapel would mold them into good Christians.[117]

Meanwhile, as CSL died, a new religious organization, eventually called Campus Christian Union, arose on campus. Initially led by Dave Diehl and Dave Nissly, CCU brought dynamic speakers to campus including Pittsburgh-area Young Life leader Reid Carpenter; Millard Fuller, who later founded Habitat for Humanity; and John Guest, who soon established the Coalition for Christian Outreach. These speakers presented "the claims of Christ in an exciting, straight-forward manner."[118] More than 350 students attended CCU meetings, which also included vibrant singing, humorous skits, and engaging student testimonies. CCU also sponsored retreats that featured charismatic pastors, youth leaders, and professors and attracted as many as three hundred students. Paralleling the Jesus movement in California and a major college revival at Asbury College in 1970, dozens of Grove City students committed their lives to Christ in 1970 and 1971.

Soccer player Bob Scott, '72, shared that he surrendered his life to Christ at one of these retreats. Scott argued that Diehl's "influence on the lives of hundreds of students was amazing. The Lord worked through him and others to create the revival at GCC." Scott attributes the student revival at Grove City to extensive prayer, enthusiastic student leaders, a few zealous faculty, and the power of God.[119] Diehl, who worked with the Coalition for Christian Outreach at Indiana University of Pennsylvania and then as a PCUSA pastor in the Seattle area, had an amazing "instinct for how to grow the kingdom on campus."[120] Another leader, Ralph Pointer, who spent his career as a Reformed minister, shared Christ with his students as a freshman RA, led several dormitory Bible studies, and served as a big brother at George Junior Republic.[121]

CCU revived the practice of sending gospel teams to sing musical numbers, perform skits, and deliver children's talks and sermons primarily in area churches. CCU members, led by Terry Thomas, began Young Life clubs in local high schools. In 1970, Tom McWhertor and I created the New Life program at George Junior Republic to supplement the long-standing Sunday school classes Grove City students taught. It included a weekly evening meeting featuring songs, skits, and speakers; Bible studies for the most interested GJR boys; and a big brother program that paired about seventy-five Grove City male students with GJR youth who attended church, movies at the Guthrie, and events on campus together.[122]

Despite Harker's orthodox theology and desire to maintain the college's historic mission; the strong faith of J. Howard Pew and numerous other trustees, including Robert Lamont, pastor of Pittsburgh's First Presbyterian Church; statements affirming the college's Christian mission; and a religious revival in which a quarter of students participated, the college capitulated in some ways to the prevailing secular zeitgeist, as evident in faculty worldviews, classroom instruction, and students' convictions and behavior. Unfortunately, the trustees relied too heavily on Harker's glowing reports rather than carefully investigating academic and campus life themselves.

"A Beehive of Activities"

As his presidency began, Harker professed hope that the college would be "a beehive of activities."[123] Students granted his wish, as extracurricular activities abounded. In addition to the college's highly successful athletic program, Grovers excelled in speech and debate, theater, and music. Many clubs and organizations flourished. As Harker's tenure progressed, increasing numbers of students questioned or disobeyed college policies prohibiting drinking on campus or at college functions off campus. Many students beseeched the college to abolish women's curfews, prolong intervisitation hours, and permit them to communicate directly with the trustees. Like students at campuses across the nation, some Grovers experimented with illegal drugs, and many protested the United States' involvement in Vietnam. One extensively debated issue was whether Grove City should adopt an honor system.

Debate over creating a college honor system, first broached in the 1910s, reached a pinnacle in the early 1960s. In February 1957, Student Council president Bob Johnson, '57, deplored the prevailing perspective that stealing exams in "uninteresting" and unpopular courses was morally acceptable but not in "valuable or stimulating" ones. He warned students that their honor and the reputation of the college were at stake. Johnson led the Student Council to devise "Our Principles of Honor" to inspire students to act more honesty in writing papers and taking examinations. Sadly, John Werren, '58, claimed, some upperclassmen were teaching freshmen that cheating was acceptable if they did not get caught because everyone was doing it. Grove City was "graduating its share of fine Christian young men and women but also its full share of cheats, dishonest people, and society parasites."[124] Some professors also called for establishing an honor code.[125]

In March 1960, students debated the issue in *The Collegian*. The key questions included if students were truly honest, why did they need to sign a pledge?; would students self-report violations?; would honest students confront cheaters?; and would troublemakers make false accusations? Many insisted that the system could work only if almost all students supported it and professors had confidence in it.[126] That month, the college's Speech Week included a debate over whether to adopt an honor code. Supporters argued that the system was working well at other colleges and that it would build student character. Opponents countered that human nature would prevent the code from being successful, and reporting violators would be like informing on dissidents in communist countries.[127]

English professor Margaret Ford, who chaired the joint faculty/ student President's Honor System Committee, argued in 1963 that if it were adopted, the cheater would become "a moral leper."[128] That year, 67 percent of respondents claimed that they had never violated the honor system outlined in a questionnaire, while 33 percent admitted they had. Ninety percent promised that they would abide by an honor code, but only 34 percent said they would report cheaters.[129] In November 1963, sororities adopted an honor code for rushing that some saw as a model for a campus-wide honor code.[130] ODK made the honor system its key project in 1963–1964.

In February 1964, *The Collegian* argued that approving an honor system would help validate the maturity of students, produce greater respect for knowledge, and enhance school pride. Ford urged students to vote yes if they wanted other colleges to view Grove City more positively, were mature enough to follow the code, and thought that professors and students could trust and respect each other.[131] Clarence Carson countered that an honor system "would undermine some of the main safeguards to liberty, promote social discord, and develop servile minions of an all-powerful state."[132] In March 1964, faculty voted 49–45 for and students voted 1,200–373 against establishing an honor code. Ford lamented that many students had voted no based on "simple ignorance," misinformation, "silly rumors," or "outright lies."[133] The college has not had another campaign to institute an honor system.

During the Harker years, students elected both fashion queens and the ugliest man. The latter contest raised money for the World University Service Fund, which aided colleges and students in underprivileged areas. Big-name bands such as the Tommy Dorsey Orchestra and Bobby Vinton and His Orchestra played for major campus dances including the ROTC Ball, which began in the mid-1950s.

In the late 1950s and early 1960s, students continued to deplore various problems. One complained that many Grovers walked on the grass, that the school was becoming a "suitcase college," that the administration was grudgingly accepting student drinking, and that fraternities employed "sadistic and medieval tactics" during "Hell Week."[134] Another groused about indoctrination in the classroom and campus policies on drinking; he urged administrators to allow responsible drinking and act like a "modern Presbyterian college" rather than the "medieval church or a Puritan witch hunt."[135] *The Collegian*'s writers argued that students at other colleges also bemoaned that there was little to do on weekends, and estimated that only about 3 percent of Grovers violated campus rules on drinking alcohol.[136] Editor in chief for *The Collegian* Joanna Hartley Jones, '64, acknowledged that students tacitly agreed not to consume alcohol on campus by attending Grove City, but she urged the college to punish drunkenness, not moderate drinking.[137] Harker insisted that the college was "making a sincere effort to maintain Christian standards." Only a few students drank liquor on campus, he claimed, but the college dealt "firmly" with all cases that came to its attention.[138] Harker did not mention that the college made little effort to police drinking on campus and prosecuted only the most egregious violations.[139]

During the Harker years, two traditions began that became an important part of the May Day weekend celebration—a recognition ceremony on Saturday morning in Harbison Chapel and Greek Sing on Saturday night in the Arena. At the recognition ceremony, honoraries announced their new members, and students received awards for academic achievement. In 1959, Parents' Day was moved from the fall to May Day weekend. The Arena was always crammed full for Greek Sing, which featured nostalgic, patriotic, religious, and romantic songs. Greek Sing (later All-College Sing), a dance pageant, and the crowning of a queen have continued to be staples of the weekend.

In May 1960, ODK selected its first Senior Man of the Year. A faculty/student committee submitted a list of seniors with CQPAs above 2.6 for the student body to vote on; the five men who received the highest total were then voted on by ODK members. The top three in this election were submitted to Harker, the dean of men, the presidents of the Student Council, the senior class, and the Athletic Council, two faculty ODK members, and one junior ODK member to make the final selection.

In 1962, the campus literary magazine, *The Quad*, was renamed *Perspectives* and revamped to publish student poetry, satire, short stories, and nonfiction. Meanwhile, articles in *The Collegian* discussed whether the United States should implement compulsory health insurance, the best way to combat communism, and the Cuban missile crisis.[140]

During the Harker years, the traditional senior week included a picnic and swimming party at the country club, a farewell dance, and a co-recreation day. In mid-March 1963, Grove City held its first All-College Weekend. Woody Herman and His Herd played for the dance that climaxed the weekend. After President John F. Kennedy was assassinated, grieving Grove City students watched his funeral on television and attended a memorial service in the chapel; the ROTC unit conducted a military memorial drill around the flagpole at the end of the main quad.[141] In 1964, the Independent Men's Organization was founded to provide scholastic, social, and athletic activities for the college's approximately seven hundred independent students.[142]

The Collegian argued in October 1964 that many students were now more interested in academics than extracurriculars. Belonging to a fraternity or sorority was "no longer essential"; fraternity life "has lost much of its glamor." What remained the same at Grove City was political conservatism, certain traditions, and low tuition.[143] Dick Jewell, on the other hand, argued that students were focusing on grades rather than learning.[144] Probably speaking for many classmates, John Reitinger, '64, who was serving in the air force, wrote to Harker in 1966 to commend the wonderful relationship between and shared faith of faculty and students. He appreciated attending a school free of LSD "where unity and the spirit of brotherhood prevailed." Reitinger now recognized the true academic and social value of his four years in college and deeply loved his alma mater.[145]

In the 1960s, the Orientation Board was reconstituted and enlarged to better introduce freshmen to the college's academic and social life. "Extended Orientation" replaced the "Freshman Traditions Program." Constructive activities such as book discussions, tug-of-war, and pep rallies were incorporated to build school spirit; freshmen organized a stunt night and built a float for homecoming. In addition, a fair was held to help students decide which clubs and organizations to join. Many students rejoiced that the "tortures" upperclassmen had stayed up all night to devise had ended.[146] In fall 1963, David Blackmore, '64, lauded OB's more constructive approach to helping freshmen adjust to academic and social life. "Hours of senseless activities [had been] replaced by purposeful ones."[147] In 1967, dean of students Ben McClelland beseeched OB leaders to appeal to "high ideals and intellectual purposes" to compete with "the allure of Greek goddesses and the prestige of the BMOC."[148] Bill Rundorff, '70, labeled the 1969 OB program a "Five-Day Party." By focusing almost exclusively on social life, OB gave freshmen the wrong impression of what college should be.[149] The 1970 OB program included faculty workshops, faculty counselors, and an imaginative chapel service.[150] Freshmen were increasingly better educated and more sophisticated and the transition from high school to college was less difficult than in previous years, a writer for *The Collegian* argued, so treating freshmen in a "Mickey Mouse" fashion was a waste of time.[151] Describing this transition, freshman Evan Adair wrote that two major challenges newcomers faced were that their workload was much heavier, and no one made sure they did it.[152]

In 1968, the Student Council was renamed the Student Government Association. Since its inception in 1925, the organization had worked to oversee student activities, improve student-faculty relationships, and represent students to the administration and board. It sponsored freshman orientation, musical concerts, homecoming, All-College Weekend, and May Day and published *The Crimson*, a student handbook, containing pictures of all freshmen.[153]

Dating and engagements were very important aspects of campus life, especially during the first half of the Harker years. In the early 1960s, *The Collegian* featured a "Romance Corner," regularly announced student pinnings, keyings, and engagements, and provided profiles of many engaged couples. A 1966 survey reported that 40 percent of Grovers dated every weekend, while 32 percent dated very little or not at all.[154] An anonymous student argued that if freshmen women sounded too intelligent on dates, they were considered eggheads, but if they did not display substantial brainpower, they were deemed airheads.[155]

In a concerted effort to enlist nonteaching staff in their union in spring 1968, members of the Carpenters' Union picketed the college. Less than half the staff joined the strike. Refusing to participate, hundreds of students, assisted by numerous professors, mowed grass, hauled garbage, cooked and served food, drove trucks through picket lines, and prepared the campus for Parents' Day. The college's PR director termed the actions of Grove City students and faculty "an oasis in a desert of seething trouble." Letters of "surprise and pleasure," he declared, were pouring in from all over. Harker effused, "This is the finest student body to ever grace an American campus."[156] A Pittsburgh journalist asserted that their actions demonstrated that some students still took pride in their institutions and were willing to do good deeds without calling a press conference.[157] The Pennsylvania Senate passed a resolution on June 17, 1968, commending Grove City students and president Harker.

In 1969, Peggy Matzie pointed out that many schools were abolishing or at least liberalizing curfews for women. Why could Grove City not permit women to assume responsibility for themselves, she asked.[158] In a poll that year, 67 percent of women wanted all coeds to have a 1 a.m. curfew.[159] Judicial Board president Karen Larson, '71, complained in 1970 that many women were staying out all night; if this did not stop, the administration's response would be "severe."[160]

The 1970 Middle States report asserted that Grove City students seemed to be more interested in "internal issues" than national and international ones and expressed little passion about major political events and developments.[161] Many Grovers, however, were concerned about the Vietnam War. As violence erupted on college campuses around the nation protesting American involvement in Vietnam, Grove City faculty and students engaged in peaceful, if sometimes heated, discussions about the war. Both the faculty and students held conflicting views about the United States' mission in Vietnam. Almost four hundred students attended a November 1965 "teach-in" at which professors analyzed communist tactics and the United States' aims and options in Vietnam.[162] Senior John Sparks and juniors William Nutt and Robert Nutt argued in April 1966 that Americans were fighting "the most immoral and cruel war in our history" primarily to preserve our "honor."[163] In September 1967, students expressed many different perspectives on the Vietnam War: The US should either get out or let troops fight all-out; the communists would again quickly infiltrate South Vietnam even if the United States won; the war was benefiting the US economy; Americans had no valid reasons for being there; stopping the spread of communism justified the death of US soldiers; the war was a mistake; the US must end the war as quickly as possible; and Americans should help its own poor rather than fight abroad.[164] At a November 1967 panel discussion, six professors expressed positions that varied from immediate withdrawal to cautious escalation.[165] In March 1968, the Selective Service System ended all graduate school military deferments except for medicine and the ministry, making it more likely that college graduates would be drafted. After George Hamilton, '65, was killed in October 1968 when his reconnaissance plane crashed in Vietnam, a local newspaper proclaimed that Grove City students "have won high praise in the press all over the nation" for paying "tribute to those who have died in the service of their country" instead of burning their draft cards.[166]

On Moratorium Day, October 15, 1969, three professors spoke at a special chapel service and CSL members led prayers for peace. A late afternoon program featured five speakers including a student who was a Vietnam veteran.[167] In December, the Selective Service conducted two lotteries to determine the order of conscription for American men, further ratcheting up tension for those who received low numbers. In the aftermath of the National Guard's killing of four students at a protest rally at nearby Kent State University in May 1970, two Grovers implored their classmates to use constitutional processes, persuasion, and peaceful means to effect change.[168] In November 1970, 16 percent of Grove City students agreed with pulling out of Vietnam immediately compared with 36 percent of college students in a national *Playboy* poll.[169]

Although the Vietnam War was much discussed, Grove City students were more concerned about campus policies and life, especially required chapel, women's hours, the prohibition of drinking on campus, and mandatory ROTC for freshmen and sophomores. Many also wanted to change the college calendar, upgrade academic life, and institute faculty evaluations. In November 1968, Kring formed a "Committee of 13" students to discuss ending mandatory chapel and the AAUP censure, reducing women's dormitory regulations, improving classroom instruction, and revising the curriculum.[170]

Students usually strove to change policies with which they disagreed through official channels—the Student Government Association, other student organizations, and committees created to address specific issues. In October 1968, *The Collegian* editor in chief Larry Griswold, '69, criticized an *Esquire* magazine article on college protests that included Grove City College as among the places "Where the Action Ain't." Grovers were being mocked, he declared, for not becoming "bearded, pot-smoking, draft-dodging, leftists."[171] Trustees were pleased in June 1969 that there had been no violence or threat of violence at Grove City.[172]

The *Esquire* article also described Grove City College as wholesomely American as apple pie, "worthy in every respect of the hearty endorsement of the John Birch Society." When *Esquire* asked various organizations which colleges they would recommend "where American traditions are strongly supported," *The National Review* and the John Birch Society chose Grove City. Tate DeWeese, '69, deplored identifying the college with this "despicable" organization, which was "a dangerous mix of theology, superpatriotism, capitalist mythology, political anarchism," and "simplistic thinking"; like communists, the society used fear, innuendo, subversion, and suspicion to advance its cause.[173]

Joanna Hartley Jones argued that in their conflicts with administrators, students often did not understand the big picture. She urged administrators, however, to be more open to student ideas.[174] Dick Jewell maintained that contrary to student opinion, administrators frequently considered their ideas and interests.[175] *The Collegian* editors rebutted the common complaint that administrators censured the newspaper, arguing that they had the freedom to print whatever they wanted.[176] Fred Kring argued that current students pursued academics "more seriously" than ones fifteen years earlier. They were more interested in attending graduate and professional schools; they were more mature and more committed to reducing bigotry, poverty, and war.[177]

In the final Harker years, students protested their lack of opportunity to talk with board members, women's hours, and the intervisitation policy. SGA members were disappointed that they had no direct communication with the trustees, and many women felt overprotected.[178] *The Collegian* argued that Harker could not adequately represent the faculty and the students; both groups needed to have their own representation on the board.[179] The trustees refused in 1969 to change the hours for senior women or to increase the hours of intervisitation, which the women's Judicial Board had requested. The limited hours of intervisitation, students contended, was retarding their social and spiritual development.[180] Administrators did introduce some evening open house hours to supplement weekend hours on a trial basis in spring 1971. One policy the administration was willing to change was to provide coed dining, but many students resisted.[181]

Like their counterparts on other campuses, numerous Grove City students challenged traditional moral standards in the late 1960s. By the late 1960s, the use of legal drugs had become widespread on campuses across the nation. Don Steighner, '69, alleged that significant numbers of Grovers had smoked marijuana a least once, while two sophomores asserted that less than 1 percent of Grovers had taken drugs stronger than NoDoz. Kring estimated that 10 to 20 percent of students had tried marijuana. Dean of men Bruce Smith explained that administrators tried to counsel rather than expel students who were caught using drugs.[182] Steighner argued against using marijuana because it was illegal and was a gateway drug.[183] Other students maintained that smoking marijuana was beneficial and should be left to individual discretion.[184] The college sponsored several seminars on the drug problem.[185]

As the Harker years ended, *The Collegian* asserted that OB had improved its program, intervisitation hours had increased, academics had been upgraded, and campus social life had been enriched.[186] In a 1970 survey, a quarter of students said they would heartily recommend the college to high school seniors, while 50 percent stated they would recommend it with reservations.[187]

Speech and Debate

In the Harker years, the college's speech and debate team made a strong showing led by Bonnie Barr, '59, Pat Rickert, '60, Judy Myers, '61, brothers Robert and Bill Nutt, Lee Kessler, '68, Bruce Gridley, '69, Donald Steighner, Kevin Kelly, '73, and Darrell Kadunce, '71. Barr finished second in extemporaneous speaking at a nineteen-college tournament Grove City hosted in 1958, while Rickert won first place in women's oratory. Myers took first place at the Women's Division of State Oratory in 1960 and received an "excellent" in Women's Oratory at the National Pi Kappa Delta convention in 1961. Robert Nutt ranked fourth at the Oratorial Association's national collegiate competition in 1965, while Bill Nutt won first place in impromptu speaking at a twenty-school debate tournament at Penn State in 1966. Kessler and Gridley won high honors at a large tournament at Susquehanna University in November 1966. Kessler captured the Pennsylvania state championship in women's oratory in April 1967. That same month, Kessler and Gridley both received an excellent rating in oratory at the national Pi Kappa Delta convention. Steighner was one of five competitors to receive the highest award in debate at this convention. At November 1967 tournaments, Gridley received an exemplary debater award, while Kessler finished second in women's oral interpretation. In 1968, Gridley won first prize and Kessler placed third in an oratory contest at the Pi Delta Kappa Province Convention. At a 1971 fifty-school tournament at Columbia University, Kelly and Kadunce placed fourth and sixth, respectively, in impromptu speaking. In 1965, the debate team placed second at two tournaments and was ranked in the top 15 percent of teams nationwide. The 1966 team tied for third at a large tournament at Columbia University. At the 1967 national Pi Kappa Delta convention, the Wolverines won awards in five categories and again ranked in the nation's top 15 percent. In 1969, debaters defeated squads from Temple, West Point, Columbia, Cornell, and many other top schools.

Theater

The theater department staged many splendid shows during the Harker years. Led by directors Jim Paton, Jonathan Ladd, Robert Sisler, and William Teufel, the college produced three to six shows per year. In fall 1957, Grove City performed its first musical, *Brigadoon*. From 1956 to 1971, the theater department presented Shakespearean plays (including *The Taming of the Shrew* and *Twelfth Night*), contemporary comedies and dramas (most notably *Auntie Mame, Glass Menagerie*, and *She Stoops to Conquer*), other musicals (*HMS Pinafore* and *Oklahoma*), satires (*Squaring the Circle* and *Inherit the Wind*), an operetta (*The Mikado*), mysteries, theater of the absurd productions, and experimental theater performances.

Among the college's many superb actors, two stand out who went on to impressive careers in television and film—Lee Kessler and Lauren Levian, '67. Kessler starred in *Inherit the Wind* in 1966 and *Goodnight Mrs. Puffin* the next year. *Collegian* reviewers extolled her "striking performance," flawless British accent, and "captivating character" in playing the title character in the latter play.[188] In addition, Kessler served as the student director for *The*

Fantasticks, directed *The Good Woman of Setzuan* as an honors project, and shone in *Six Characters in Search of an Author*. Levian excelled in pantomime, improvisation, and puppeteering, winning prizes at several all-college talent shows. *The Collegian* called her "a walking talent show."[189] She played the lead in four shows including *Mary, Mary*. A reviewer declared in *The Collegian* that Levian "lit up" the play by her "great pose and naturalness."[190]

Other leading actors between 1960 and 1971 were Carl Finck, '61 who starred in *HMS Pinafore,* Barb Holes, '61, who excelled in *A Corn in the Green*, Bob Kuncio, '62, who played the title character in *Cyrano de Bergerac*, Dick Westefeld, '64, who headed the cast in *The Mikado*, and future dean of men Ben McClelland, '65, who starred in *Uncle Vanya* and *Bonds of Interest*. Bob Bronson, '67, had featured roles in several shows. Bradley Scott played major roles in *A Good Woman*, Samuel Beckett's *Krapp's Last Tape, Carnival!*, and several religious plays performed in chapel. Dan Stumme, '71, starred in *The Caretakers, Aristophanes' The Birds, Anastasia,* and as Sir Thomas More in *A Man for All Seasons*. Kathy Beddow, '73, had the lead in *Auntie Mame* and *Oklahoma*.

Music

The quality of the college's musical program improved during the 1956–1971 period. Under Edgar Cole's and Francis Pittock's direction, the marching and symphonic bands, respectively, became better, and the latter band held several concerts a year. The eighty-plus-member chapel choir, directed by Oscar Cooper, performed at the PCUSA General Assembly in Pittsburgh in 1958 and at the 1961 General Assembly at Buffalo. Cooper reinstituted the touring choir in 1960 and arranged annual spring singing trips to Pennsylvania and nearby states. The Men's Glee Club was also revived in 1960. In April 1964, the touring choir performed in the Old Senate Office Building in Washington, DC, at the request of Pennsylvania Senator Hugh Scott, who lauded its "outstanding and beautiful musical program."[191] The sixteen-member college stage band gave two concerts at the World's Fair in New York City in May 1965.

Men's Athletics

Grove City athletics team enjoyed substantial success during the Harker years, especially from 1966 to 1969. Harker's first year, the football team lost to Westminster 60–0, finished 0–8 and surrendered 338 points, the second highest total by any D3 team in the nation, which was deeply disappointing to the sports-loving president. In 1956, Robert Thorn's last year as coach, the soccer team finished 7–0, and Frank Sbrocco was selected as a first-team All-American. That year, Jack Behringer became the head football coach, and the next year, he replaced Thorn as the athletic director. When the college played its five hundredth football game in 1957, its overall record was a respectable 240–214–45. Behringer's second team finished 5–3, and he was named the small college coach of the year in the tristate area. That December, Grove City joined Carnegie Tech, Duquesne, St. Francis, St. Vincent, Geneva, Westminster, and Waynesburg in forming the Western Pennsylvania Intercollegiate Athletic Association (WPIAA), also called the West Penn Conference.

In February 1958, junior Gary Peters, one of the basketball team's top scorers, left school to play professional baseball. In fourteen seasons with the Chicago White Sox, he had a 124–103 record and an excellent 3.25 ERA. Three members of the 1958 soccer team—senior Travis Young, junior Christos Takoudes, and sophomore Pete Buttner—were named to the all-eastern (Pennsylvania, Maryland, New Jersey, and Delaware) soccer team. Buttner was selected for the 1959 All-American second team, becoming the first Grove City player to be chosen for one of the nation's top two squads. From 1955–1958, the Wolverines went 23–7–1.

In 1958–1959, baseball was reestablished as a varsity sport and wrestling was introduced. That fall, Ruth Bogert '63 became the first woman to compete on a Grove City varsity squad. She earned four letters and was a leading scorer for the rifle team. In 1959–1960, the team went 12–1 and captured the Pennsylvania Collegiate Rifle League trophy.

Ron Plano, '60, who also started as a halfback and defensive back and punted and place kicked for the football team, was the baseball star in the late 1950s. In 1959, he led pitchers in wins, strikeouts, and ERA, and in 1960 he led the squad in ERA and batting average, home runs, and runs batted in (RBIs). The swimming and diving team captured the conference crown in 1959, as Ubbo VanderValk, '60, became the first of many Grove City All-Americans in swimming. In 1960, the swimmers and divers repeated as WPIAA champions.

In 1960, senior football fullback Jake LaMotta won the ODK Sportsman of the Year. LaMotta scored 136 points in his career, surpassing the record of Verne Smith, '34. LaMotta's 829 rushing yards in 1959 was also a college record. The Associated Press named him first-team All-State, making him the first Wolverine player ever selected. LaMotta also achieved Little All-American status in baseball in 1959.

In March 1961, sophomore Myron Michaels finished seventeenth in the National Intercollegiate Bowling Tournament. The next month, Dave York, a member of the soccer, swimming and diving, and track and field teams, posted the highest ever score on the physical fitness exam administered to all freshmen. In 1961, the swimming and diving, track and field, and golf teams all brought home WPIAA crowns. That spring, Jim Longnecker, who coached swimming and diving, track and field, and cross-country, was chosen as the Area College Coach of the Year by the *Erie Times-News* from among all the coaches in New York, Pennsylvania, and Ohio. Sprinter Jerry Smoyer, '62, was voted the outstanding athlete at the 1961 WPIAA championship meet and earned four letters in both track and football. The golf team won eighteen consecutive matches in 1960 and 1961. The latter year, the golfers crushed their eight opponents by a combined score of 50.5 to 4.5.

During Harker's presidency, *The Collegian*'s sportswriters repeatedly praised small college amateur athletics for focusing on athletes' character development, while criticizing the "professionalism" at large colleges and the pressure their alumni exerted on them to win.[192] When Harker attended Grove City in the 1920s, it subsidized athletes and frequently beat "the best teams in the land." However, Harker wrote, "we saw the folly of such nonsense" and restored "our strictly amateur program."[193] After the 1961 football team upset archrival Westminster 21–13, the first victory over the Titans in many years, Monday classes were canceled, and students danced in the streets.

In January 1962, the wrestlers beat St. Vincent for their first-ever win. The 1961–1962 swimming team, led by Mike Monahan, '64, and Tom Tulenko, '66, went 12–0 and won the Penn-Ohio championship for the first time. A February 17, 1962, contest against Allegheny was the basketball team's one thousandth game. At halftime, the Betas and members of an Allegheny fraternity, sporting mustaches, long sideburns, and 1890s basketball attire, played a demonstration game using James Naismith's 1891 rules. The 1961–1962 basketball team's 18–5 record was the best in forty years. Senior Tom Robinson racked up 1,181 career points, becoming the highest scorer in Grove City history; he broke thirteen other college records including the most points (415) and rebounds (288) in a season.

In fall 1962, Cliff Wettig began coaching soccer, basketball, and tennis. Wettig's soccer teams went 9–0 and 8–0-1 in his third and fourth seasons. Wettig's career record as the soccer coach was a very impressive 65–20–4 (.765), especially considering the first soccer match he ever saw, he coached. During his nine-year tenure, the team beat Pitt several times and produced several All-Americans.

The 1962–1963 swimming and diving team finished 11–1, won the Penn-Ohios, and set twenty-five varsity and seventeen pool records. Bill McGarry, '66, established twelve of these records and participated on several relay teams that broke records. Longnecker's 1963 track and field team finished 9–0 and won the conference championship for the third consecutive season. The tennis team was also undefeated. Grove City won six of the eleven WPIAA championships in 1962–1963. Senior Don Shockey, the cocaptain of the football and track teams, received the 1963 Sportsman of the Year award.

In January 1964, the swimming and diving team beat Kent State 57–38 before a capacity crowd, avenging its only loss during the last three years. The mermen, as *The Collegian* often called the members of the swimming and diving team, defended their Penn-Ohio Relay crown by tallying 127 points, one less than a perfect score. In mid-March, Grove City hosted the First Annual NCAA College Division Swimming Championship for small colleges and finished ninth in the country. McGarry, junior swimmer Charles Stadler, and junior diver Jim Livermore earned All-American status.

In April 1964, Cliff Wettig argued that Grove City's biggest problem in recruiting was not being able to give athletic scholarships. To recruit successfully, the college needed to have winning teams, play strong competitors, and receive recognition for its athletic achievements. Grove City's educational program, athletic facilities, and friendly students also helped.[194]

In spring 1964, the tennis team finished 10–0 and won the WPIAA singles and doubles titles. The underdog track and field captured the conference title by four points over Westminster. Senior Todd Alexander, the 1964 Sportsman of the Year, set a varsity record in the discus and won four letters in football, starring as a halfback and a quarterback, and in baseball, excelling as a pitcher and an outfielder.

The 1964 soccer team finished 9–0, including victories over Pitt, St. Bonaventure, and Western Reserve 12–0, the highest total in team history. The team outscored its opponents 49–7. Fullback senior John Mulholland was named to 1964 soccer NCAA All-American team. The cross-country team again captured the conference championship.

In January 1965, the mermen walloped WVU 66–28, winning every event except one, with Dick Jewell placing first in diving. The team won the Penn-Ohio championship. Unfortunately, the Wolverines were not permitted to participate in the small college championship in Chicago because of the college's policy that students could not miss three or more consecutive days of classes. The track and field squad won its fifth straight WPIAA title. The 9–0 tennis team won another conference title, with John Knarr, '66, triumphing at first singles and first doubles. *The Collegian* called 1964–65 the college's finest sports year ever, noting that he eleven varsity teams had a combined record of 81–47 (.633).[195] The soccer and tennis were undefeated. Even better years lay ahead.

The 1965 soccer squad pounded Mt. Union 8–1, perennial power Frostburg State 7–0, and St. Francis 15–0, in recording its second consecutive undefeated season and an eighteen-game win streak. Seniors Bob Bishop and Paul Fletcher received honorable mention on the Pennsylvania-New Jersey-Delaware All-Star team. The 1964 and 1965 soccer teams outscored their eighteen opponents 110 to 14.

As the 1965–1966 basketball season began, *The Collegian* told readers to watch out for 6'7" forward newcomer Jeff Claypool.[196] In December 1965, the hoopsters upset Westminster 97–84 at home, ending the Titans' streak of twenty-four straight victories over the Wolverines. The victory "launched the capacity crowd into a frenzy." Fans hoisted Coach Wettig and team members onto their shoulders and paraded around the Arena.[197] His freshman year, Claypool averaged 19.7 ppg and 13.9 rounds per game, broke the varsity rebound record, and shattered the record for best shooting percentage, making 58.2 percent of his shots. In March 1966, freshman Ted Thilly became the college's first conference wrestling champion, and mermen easily captured their fifth straight Penn-Ohio title.

In April 1966, the college's outstanding junior goalie, Dick Manley, competed for a spot on the United States Pan American and Olympic teams. The tennis team's twenty-three-match winning streak ended that month, but the team again captured the conference championship, with John Knarr earning titles in first singles and doubles. The track and field team scored double the total points of the second-place squad to win the conference title. Overall, Grove City was 34–11 (.760) in spring sports, the best record since 22–5 (.820) in spring 1948. Senior halfback Thom Shear won the 1966 Sportsman of Year award. He was also an outstanding javelin thrower and member of track team's record-setting mile relay foursome. *The Pittsburgh Press* named him to its all-district small college football team. In a 1966 letter, Harker argued that "the terrible subsidy program that prevails in this country in both football and basketball is a curse to education, not only financially but ethically."[198]

The 1966 football team, loaded with veterans, vanquished Lycoming 27–8 and Brockport 20–0 before five thousand rain-soaked fans at homecoming. After beating W&J 28–10, the Wolverines throttled Carnegie Tech 52–35 as junior quarterback Mike Zeigler ran for four touchdowns. The team crushed Geneva 41–6, squeaked by Delaware Valley 8–6 in a mud bowl, and dominated Hiram 38–6 and Thiel 34–0 to finish 8–0–1, its first undefeated season since 1926. Zeigler, who was compared with the Minnesota Vikings' scrambling quarterback Fran Tarkenton, completed 63 percent of his passes for 883 yards and fifteen touchdowns and ran for 394 yards on ninety-four carries. Zeigler was also the team's punter and placekicker. The Wolverines broke the school's scoring record with 269 points (thirty per game); while holding opponents to an average of 10 ppg.

The 1966 harriers, led by Art Ruff, '68, who set a new college record for the 4.1-mile course, finished 7–3. The 7–1–1 soccer squad won the WPIAA title. In December 1966, Jack Behringer announced that Grove City was leaving the conference after the spring season primarily because other members were giving large scholarships to top athletes.

Before a capacity crowd in March 1967, the basketball team lost to Clarion 79–71 as the sophomore forward, Jeff Claypool, scored thirty-five points and ended the season with 602 points. His 25.1 ppg was the highest average in western Pennsylvania, eastern Ohio, or West Virginia. Claypool set ten school records including most points in a game (forty-four) and the most rebounds in a season (319).

After going 49–5 the previous five years, the swimming and diving team faced the toughest schedule in its history in 1966–1967.[199] Outscoring Youngstown State, Carnegie Tech, Slippery Rock, Lock Haven, Cleveland State, and Westminster by a large margin, Grove City took its sixth straight Penn-Ohio championship. The wrestlers finished 7–3 as sophomore Jack Evans was undefeated, and freshmen Jim Poole and Charlie Purdue were both 8–1.

The 1967 track and field team went 10–0 for the season, while the golfers were 6–1. Both squads won the WPIAA championship. Dick Manley was named the All-Eastern Conference goalie both his sophomore and junior years and selected as the first alternate goalie for the US Olympic team. Senior Pete Anselmo, the soccer team's high scorer, was named to the second team All-Pennsylvania-New Jersey-Delaware. Meanwhile, the faculty voted not to permit students to miss more than three consecutive days representing the college in any capacity, a policy with which Harker agreed. "No man is more interested in athletes than I am," he explained, "but they are not so important that teams can go off on junkets whenever they wish."[200] For the 1966–1967 academic year, Grove City's teams had a stellar combined record of 84–30–2 (.740).

Zeigler, who started at quarterback all four years, finished his career in 1967 with 3,997 total yards from scrimmage. He set records for the most touchdown passes (thirty-two) and the highest punting yard average (39.1). Twice he was named the conference MVP, and he was selected as a Little All-American.[201] The 1967 cross-country team finished 10–1.

Before the 1967–1968 basketball season, a *The Collegian* sportswriter predicted that this would be "an exciting, entertaining" team.[202] In December 1967, Grove City beat Alliance 91–77 as Claypool had twenty-five points and twenty rebounds. The same day, the wrestlers beat Western Reserve 32–0, and the swimmers and divers crushed Indiana 71–32. In January, the hoopsters upset Baldwin-Wallace 81–78 as Claypool scored thirty-three, surpassing Tom Robinson's 1,181 total points to become Grove City's all-time leader scorer. That month, both Bob Richards, a former Olympic gold-winning medalist, and future Pittsburgh Steeler radio announcer Myron Cope, pronounced the college's athletic facilities excellent.[203] The basketball team finished 15–4, and the NCAA named Claypool the best player in District 2, which included parts of Pennsylvania, West Virginia, Ohio, and New York. Despite being constantly double- and triple-teamed, he averaged 29.6 ppg his junior year.[204]

The 1967–1968 swimmers and divers dominated Pitt 66–38 and beat WVU 57–47 to end the season 9–2 and win their seventh consecutive Penn-Ohio championship. Freshman Skip Arbuckle established the Penn-Ohio record in the 200 freestyle, while junior Mickey McCollum set meet records in 200 IM and 500 freestyle. The wrestlers finished 9–3 led by Charlie Purdue. The three winter sports teams had a combined 33–9 record. Harker estimated that during 1967–1968, 350 men had played on ten varsity sports teams, and five hundred men had participated in the intramural program.[205]

Returning with several record holders from a squad that had gone 50–3 during the three previous seasons, the 1968 track and field team crushed all its opponents to finish 10–0. A sportswriter explained that Jim Longnecker had achieved great success as coach by continually stressing four factors: mechanics, conditioning, endurance, and the pursuit of excellence. He also painstakingly scouted opposing teams.[206] In 1967–1968, Grove City went 91–22–2 (.806) in its ten sports.

The football, cross-country, and soccer teams were outstanding in fall 1968. Junior Greg Magness scored fourteen touchdowns, ranking fifth in D3, as the Wolverines finished 7–2. The harriers went 8–2, while the booters were 7–3. John Pontier, '68, earned eight total letters at Grove City while leading the track and field and soccer programs to phenomenal success. The four-year soccer starter helped the Wolverines compile a 30–5–2 overall record. The 8–0–1 1965 team scored fifty-four goals and played in the NCAA tournament. Pontier set the school record in the high jump and helped Grove City win three WPIAA crowns, as the Wolverines went 28–0 in dual meets during his final three seasons.

In mid-December, the basketball team upset Ashland 41–40, ranked second in the nation. In January, Claypool tallied forty-six to break the school record in a 109–88 defeat of St. Vincent, the highest total in college history. In a 78–62 victory over Slippery Rock in February 1968, Claypool became only the fourth college player in the region to score more than two thousand points. The basketball team finished 19–5, as Claypool ended his career with 2,234 points. His senior year, he averaged 29.8 ppg (sixth in nation) and made 64.6 percent his field goal attempts (third in nation). For second season in a row, Claypool was named both the small college player of the year in western Pennsylvania by the Pittsburgh sportswriters and an honorable mention small college All-American. At that point, he held twenty-four of the college's twenty-eight basketball records. For his career, Claypool averaged 26 ppg and made 59 percent of his field goal attempts. Grove City ranked second in nation among small colleges in shooting percentage in 1968–1969 at 52.3. The star inspired and routinely gave credit to his teammates.[207]

The 1968–1969 mermen defeated Pitt and WVU en route to an 8–2 season. Swimmers and divers who qualified were finally permitted to compete at the NCAA D3 nationals. Skip Arbuckle placed fourth in the 200 freestyle, becoming the college's first All-American in five years. The wrestlers were led by seniors Tom MacRae and Ted Thilly, who had career records of 30–9–3 and 30–11–1, respectively.

During the 1969 season, freshman Paul Cameron set records in the one and two-mile runs. The cross-country team's thirty-two-meet winning streak finally ended in mid-May. The golf team, led by junior Barry Bowen, who averaged 74.4 per round, finished 10–3, while the tennis team, led by sophomore Bruce Whaley, went 8–2. Senior centerfielder Rennie Petre hit .440, the highest average in District 2 of NCAA's College Division. From 1966–1967 to 1968–1969, Grove City ten sports teams had a remarkable 297–99 (.750) record.

Spearheaded by Paul Cameron and freshman Keith Fox, the 1969 cross-country squad finished 9–1. Cameron broke the 4.1-mile course record by a whopping forty seconds. The soccer team finished 9–2. After eight seasons, Wettig's teams had a stellar 42–12–3 record, despite playing one of the nation's most demanding schedules.[208] Fullback Matty Lux, '70, was named a second-team All-American.

John Cochran's smothering defense and scoring prowess powered the basketball team in his junior and senior years. As a senior, Cochran averaged twenty-one points and 12.8 rebounds per game, and the team had its highest ever ppg average—82.3. He ended his career with 1,352 points and ranked second behind Claypool in scoring and seven other categories. Heavyweight wrestler Charlie Purdue finished his career with an outstanding 35–4–2 record.

Both the college's high academic standards and lack of scholarships, a *The Collegian* sportswriter contended in 1970, were hampering its recruiting efforts. Prospective athletes needed to be in top two-fifths of their high school classes and have at least 1000 on their SATs, which eliminated 75 to 80 percent of male students. Only five of the thirty-five colleges against which Grove City was competing in its ten varsity sports were as highly ranked academically. Moreover, many colleges offered exceptional athletes with good grades scholarships. Numerous Grove City athletes, Behringer explained, had been rejected by larger schools because of their size and speed, but they had produced winning teams because of their "pride, desire, and dedication."[209]

At the 1970 nationals, junior Dan Reid placed fifth in the 100 backstroke, while Skip Arbuckle finished sixth in the fifty freestyle and twelfth in 100 freestyle, as they earned All-American status and the team finished twenty-fifth in the nation among colleges of all sizes.

In spring 1970, choosing the Sportsman of the Year award by a student vote was replaced by having the athletic director, the sports editor of *The Collegian,* the sports director of WSAJ, the SGA president, and the Grove City publicity director create a slate of ten candidates to be voted on by students and faculty. Later, the coaches would become involved in the selection process.

In spring 1970, Paul Cameron broke his own records in the mile and two-mile. Pitcher Larry Sawyer, '70, finished his baseball career at Grove City with a sparkling 2.04 ERA; when not pitching, he played outfield and had a career batting average of .351. He was selected for the 1969 first-team western Pennsylvania All-Star team.

The fall 1970 cross-country team went 11–0 and defeated Slippery Rock, the defending Pennsylvania state university champion. Cameron finished first in every meet and set a new course and varsity record. The Wolverines won the Penn-Ohio championship, beating the favored Ashland and Akron squads, with Cameron placing first. Grove City finished thirty-second at nationals for colleges of all sizes.

The basketball team's 71–67 defeat of Carnegie Mellon University (CMU) in February 1971 gave Jack Behringer his one thousandth win as the athletic director and an overall record of 1,000–603–25 (.624). Reid and Arbuckle again earned All-American status by both finishing in the top twelve in two events, placing the team twenty-seventh in the nation. In March, Wayne Bissell, '71, explained that Longnecker's swimmers believed they could accomplish whatever he said they could. During Longnecker's tenure, Grove City's record against Pitt, West Virginia University, and Youngstown State University was a combined 16–5, and twelve swimmers had become All-Americans.[210]

Women's Athletics

Although women's varsity sports still lay in the future, the Women's Athletic Association provided numerous athletic opportunities from 1956 to 1971. Women hosted conferences, participated in play days, organized a field hockey team, and played several intramural sports. A 1956 WAA conference at Grove City included discussions, a campus tour, a style show, an archery contest, a trip to the Outing Cabin, and a synchronized swimming symposium. The WAA hosted a play day in 1961 with competitions in bowling, Ping-Pong, volleyball, and badminton. That year, women also participated in play days at Slippery Rock and Thiel. The WAA organized leagues in archery, tennis, field hockey, volleyball, basketball, and tennis. In 1970, three hundred women played on twenty-four intramural volleyball teams.

WSAJ

In the late 1950s, WSAJ aired two ninety-minute segments of campus news and music weekly. The Student Council used fifteen minutes a week to update students about its activities, and other campus organizations were invited to do fifteen-minute programs. In October, the station added an FM component to gain additional airtime and give more students radio experience. In April 1970, WSAJ celebrated its fiftieth anniversary by having Weir Ketler reprise his 1920 address to the New Castle Rotary Club.[211] Dean Burch, the chair of the Federal Communications Commission, congratulated WSAJ on its pioneering efforts and its longevity.[212]

Clubs

Three honoraries—Beta, Beta, Beta (a biological honorary), Kappa Mu Epsilon (a math honorary), and Alpha Mu Gamma (a foreign language honorary)—and numerous clubs were established during Harker's presidency: the Young Republican Club; the Conservative Club; Campus Democrats; the Chess Club; the American Management Association; and clubs in physics, English, math, foreign language, metallurgy, sociology, business, and philosophy. In 1960, the Republican Club brought both Hugh Scott and West Virginia Governor Cecil Underwood to speak. The Conservative Club published *The Entrepreneur*. The Alpha Phi Omega service fraternity was chartered in 1965 to provide leadership and service opportunities.

Greek Life

Throughout Grove City's history, its fraternities and sororities differed from those of most other colleges in that they were local rather than national and most Greek members lived in dormitories instead of in off-campus houses. This enabled Grove City's Greeks to control their affairs instead of having to follow policies dictated by national organizations.[213]

The Harker years were the heyday of the Greek system in terms of the percentage of students who belonged to fraternities and sororities and Greeks' influence and prestige. Collectively, fraternities and sororities typically took two hundred to three hundred members per year. Until the mid-1970s, only Greeks built floats for the homecoming parade, and until 1973, they alone competed in the singing contest on May Day weekend. Greeks filled most SGA offices, served as many club presidents, won many ODK Senior Man of the Year awards, and supplied numerous varsity athletes. Greek parties were an important part of campus social life. *The Collegian* extensively described Greek athletic contests, social activities, dating relationships, and campus and community projects. Greeks' rushing, pledging, and drinking at parties caused substantial controversy. Pledges did errands for actives including ironing their clothes, making their beds, and carrying their books; women pledges carried pails of candy, bubble gum, and cigarettes, and curtseyed to upperclassmen.

In 1959, senior Lynne Sayer asked, "Is Hell Week Beneficial?" She noted that administrators and faculty at most PCUSA colleges opposed having a Hell Week and inquired, "How does it create school spirit or better Christian social relations?"[214] *The Collegian* edition in chief Ronald Curran argued in 1960 that the "longer pledging was supposed to produce more tight-knit groups and improve pledges' grades," but it was "a complete flop." Pledging was based on revenge, and many actives displayed "the nasty side of their nature" in treating "defenseless pledges." He implored Greeks to redesign pledging to do constructive work projects.[215] Harker insisted that fraternities and sororities added "little value to campus life," but he recognized that many students highly valued them.[216]

Critiques of Hell Week continued. *The Collegian*'s 1964 editor in chief observed that fraternities claimed that the week strove to prove pledges' mettle, unify the pledge class, and uphold tradition. He questioned whether humiliating pledges and causing them to temporarily dislike actives strengthened their grit. "If Hell Week has become merely an outlet for immature, sadist actives," he concluded, then "feelings of pride and purpose can never be achieved."[217] "If these guys are going to be your brothers someday," sophomore Gary Brook asked, "why do you make them look like fools?"[218]

Another student criticized fraternities for limiting the studying of pledges for a month, destroying college property, acting rudely toward independents, and flooding the dormitory halls so that their members could surf.[219] Alumnus James Hanushek, '66, argued that fraternities had been established to promote brotherhood and serve the college, the community, and other students. Sadly, however, fraternities were instead breeding disrespect for other people, property, and college-sponsored functions.[220] Senior Nancy Jaques contended in May 1969 that Greeks strove to mentally and physically humiliate pledges and sometimes produced psychological wounds. She denounced forcing pledges to wear burlap underwear, swallow goldfish, eat disgusting "food," get little sleep, grovel on the floor, and be shocked by an electric current. Pledging was causing Greek organizations to lose favor with administrators, faculty, and students and needed to be revamped.[221]

Future Phi Tau Alpha president Clint McCoy, '70, exhorted fraternities to stop preventing pledges from studying and to cease paddling and other abusive acts.[222] Another Phi Tau complained that a "maniac fringe," guided by pent up frustration, was employing harsh pledging policies.[223] In spring 1971, many faculty complained that during Hell Week, numerous students fell asleep or were listless in class. At a raucous faculty meeting, some professors demanded having more control over pledging. *The Collegian* faulted the Inter-Fraternity Council for failing to properly monitor and enforce pledging rules.[224]

More positively, Greeks contributed significantly to campus life by providing rich camaraderie and splendid athletic and service opportunities.[225] Their services projects during the 1960s included entertaining residents of Polk State School and the Odd Fellows Home, hosting dances at George Junior Republic, working at the community library and the Mercer County Children's Home, conducting a food drive for local families, and sponsoring a Brownie troop. During much of the Harker years, fraternities and sororities also organized a Greek weekend that featured a raft race on Wolf

Creek, a sorority kissing stand, a dunking booth, a car demolition, a picnic, and an all-campus dance. Fraternities and sororities worked diligently to build homecoming floats and prepare songs for Greek Sing on May Day weekend, which were judged on intonation, vocal balance, direction, and interpretation. A 1970 editorial argued that as individuality and independence became more important, Grove City's fraternities must enlarge their functions to survive.[226]

AFROTC

During the Harker years, all male freshmen and sophomores were required to take ROTC classes for credit and drill during a weekly common hour. Juniors and seniors could choose to continue in the advanced program. On a rotating basis, five air force officers served as instructors. Graduates of the program were commissioned as second lieutenants in the air force. From 1966 to 1970, about 10 percent of male graduates were commissioned each year. ROTC also had a rifle team and a drill team, which, *The Collegian* declared, added "pomp and splendor to campus." The detachment sponsored an annual ball and an angel flight of women who supported the cadets. Beginning in 1963, the thirty-three-man ROTC Blue Crusaders singing group provided campus entertainment.

As other colleges made ROTC voluntary and dissent toward the Vietnam War mounted, many male Grovers called for ending mandatory ROTC. The air force endorsed this change, but Harker resisted, fearing that it would reduce the number of students who joined the advanced program.[227] The SGA, led by Dave Thayer, '71, formed a committee to work to end the requirement.[228] The trustees decided to make ROTC optional for all men beginning in the fall 1970. Grove City was the last college in the Northeast to have a mandatory ROTC program.

Student Achievements

Dozens of students stand out during the Harker years. Bruce Smith, '58, was the vice president of the Student Council, an editor for *The Collegian*, a cheerleader, an RA, and an OB member who played on the tennis team and in the band and sang in the chapel choir. John Werren, '58, was a leading actor, the OB chair, the student director of *Brigadoon*, the coeditor in chief of *The Collegian*, and the vice president of the Student Council. Rick Howard, '59, played a principal role in several theatrical productions, had his own radio show on WPIC in Sharon, and was a leader in CSL and Pi Kappa Delta. Barbara Montgomery, '60, was a member of the Alpha Theta Mu honorary, CSL, the chapel choir, OB, Cwens, and vice president of the Women's Governing Board. Gerald Russo, '60, the first ODK Senior Man of the Year, was the president of the senior class and of the college's Music Education National Conference chapter, and he was a member of the Newman Club, ODK, various musical groups, and the Student Council. Bob Loch, '62, chaired two state Republican student committees and was the Student Council president and the head of OB. Dick Swope, '63, was the deputy commander of ROTC, the president of Betas, a head RA, a varsity wrestler, and the chair of homecoming. Sue Wherry, '64, served on the Student Court and the Judicial Board and was the ROTC and homecoming queen, a cheerleader, and a member of Alpha Mu Gamma. John Sparks, the 1966 Senior Man of the Year, was the OB chair, the president of the Conservative Club, an RA, and the editor in chief of *The Collegian*. The 1970 Senior Man of the Year, Jim Evans, was the president of SGA president and Kemikos, a member of touring choir, a head RA, the chair of Greek Sing, and an ex officio member of Middle States Evaluation Committee.

Student achievements beyond the campus were plentiful during the Harker years. In 1958, senior Donald Galbraith won second place in botany in a national essay contest. The next year, *Mademoiselle* magazine chose Martha McDougle, '60, as one of its twenty campus board members, and Neal Shipley received a Danforth Scholarship to study at Harvard. In 1960, Bob Loch was elected to serve on the Republican Party's national steering committee. The class of 1960 was especially impressive. Ray Guarnieri earned a Woodrow Wilson Scholarship to study at New York University and an Earhart Scholarship to attend the University of Geneva. Other students received assistantships: Ron Curran at Northeastern University, David Dayton and Jim Watson at Duke, Marcia Hammond at Cornell, Ruth Wheeler at Ohio University, Ronald Montgomery at the University of Arizona, Joan Spak at the University of Iowa, and Grant Pribanic at Iowa State University.

In 1964, the college's Cwens affiliate was named the most outstanding chapter in the nation. The 105 Grove City seniors who took the GRE in 1964–1965 collectively scored in the sixtieth percentile. In 1966, Grove City's Pi Gamma Mu chapter was one of twenty-five of the nation's one thousand to be placed on the society's Roll of Merit. That year, Tom Andrews and John Sparks were semifinals for the Woodrow Wilson National Foundation Scholarship. Judy Altman, '68, was elected president of Student Pennsylvania Educational Association in 1967. *The Collegian* earned a first-class rating (outstanding) from the Associated Press in 1968 (its first ever), 1970, and 1971.

Guest Performers

Some of the nation's most exciting vocalists, instrumentalists, bands, musical ensembles, touring theater groups, and comedians, performed at Grove City during Harker's presidency. Between 1956 and 1965, these luminaires included Louis Armstrong who, along with a six-member band, put on a fabulous show in a packed Arena in October 1958; opera stars Jean Madeira, Roberta Peters, and Mary Costa; opera tenor Loren Driscoll; jazz artist Stan Kenton; trumpeter Dizzy Gillespie; The Kingston Trio; the US Marine band; jazz composer and band leader Duke Ellington; actor Basil Rathbone; jazz pianist Dave Brubeck; folk singer Odetta; Flamenco guitarist Carlos Montoya; comediennes Anna Russell and Cornelia Otis Skinner; The Coasters; The Highwaymen; and Traveling Broadway. From 1966 to 1971, several famous music groups and singers performed: The Lettermen, The McCoys (best known for "Hang on Sloopy"), Simon and Garfunkel, The Temptations, Dionne Warwick, The Vogues, Peaches and Herb, The Happenings (best known for "See You in September"), and The Guess Who. Other entertainers during these years included pianists Arthur Ferrante and Louis Teicher (known as Ferrante & Teicher), jazz musician Peter Nero, the Roger Wagner Chorale, Sam the Sham and the Pharaohs, Smokey Robinson and the Miracles (Robinson called the Grove City audience "fantastic, beautiful, and tremendous"),[229] the Jimmy Dorsey orchestra, Les Ballets Africains (thirty-five dancers, singers, acrobats, and instrumentalists from Guinea), the Vienna Boys Choir, and the Canadian ballet company.

Alumni and Trustees

The alumni association became more active during the Harker years, and many alumni strove to recruit high-performing students. The first Alumni Achievement Awards were given at the 1964 homecoming to J. Howard Pew, '00, in the field of industry, Weir Ketler, '08, in education, George Southworth, '14, in science, F. Paul McConkey, '09, in the professions, and Robert Thorn, '16, in sports. In 1967, Fred and Hilda Kring created an annual tour for alumni and friends. In 1970, ninety alumni from the classes of 1915 to 1970 and guests toured Europe with them. In 1969–1970, 2,778 alumni (almost double the number who had contributed in 1965) donated $113,000 ($931,000 today) to the college. Several other alumni stand out during the Harker years. Walter Moser, '15, the father of admissions director John Moser, was a Presbyterian minister, educator, and author who received an Alumni Achievement Award in 1969. Henry Wycis, '34, a professor of neurosurgery at Temple University School of Medicine and one of the top brain surgeons in the East, received an honorary degree in 1965.

The college lost three influential trustees in 1958. MIT graduate Bertram Hopeman served from 1941 to 1958. He founded Hopeman Brothers, a company that furnished ship interiors, and donated generously to the college. Hopeman Hall is named for him. Judge Marshall Thompson, the University of Pittsburgh Law School's dean and a judge on the Court of Common Pleas for twenty years, was a trustee from 1925 to until 1958. Stuart Nye Hutchinson, a trustee from 1928 to 1958, pastored East Liberty Presbyterian Church in Pittsburgh for twenty-six years, was a moderator of the PCUSA General Assembly, and penned eleven books. Attorney William Robinson, who served as an elder at Eastminster Presbyterian Church for forty-three years, was a trustee from 1928 to 1961.

Conclusion

J. Stanley Harker, *The Collegian* argued, brought "vast improvements" to the college. When he arrived, the faculty members were old and poorly paid, women's hours were "hideous," no fee funded student activities, admission standards were low, "stagnation" reigned, and the college received a dismal Middle States evaluation soon after he began. Harker helped establish a faculty pension plan, raised salaries, hired more professors with PhDs, and doubled the size of the faculty. During his tenure, the student body increased from 1,250 to 2,050, the chapel requirement was cut in half, women's hours were liberalized, and admission standards became more rigorous. Harker had "tenaciously" pursued funding for building projects.[230] During Harker's presidency, eight buildings valued at a total of over $7.5 million ($59.22 million today) were constructed, academic standards were elevated, the curriculum was enriched, library books more than doubled, the academic ability of students increased, alumni relations improved, and alumni giving rose.[231] When Harker retired, alumni praised the "dedication and devotion" of both the president and his wife as well as Harker's "dynamic leadership" and his wife's "gracious manner."[232]

J. Howard Pew praised Harker's work as president and credited him with assembling the finest group of students in college history.[233] Pew called Harker one of Grove City's "immortals" along with Isaac and Weir Ketler. [234] Albert Hopeman thanked Harker for keeping the college "morally and economically strong."[235] Historian Stephen Taaffe, by contrast, accused Harker of being "brittle and blustering" and "willing to bend the truth" when "it served his purposes." He was understandably unwilling to confront or cross Pew, "the formidable board chairman."[236]

Pew told a large Parents' Day audience on May 1, 1971, that Grove City College's "prime responsibility" was to teach Christian ethical principles "without which neither our College nor our Country can long endure." Grove City, he insisted, must balance its budget every year. Its trustees, administrators, and faculty must prevent "the taxers, the planners, the equalizers and the socialists" from "further encroaching on the freedoms" of the American people. Pew exhorted his listeners to serve God and others and faithfully follow biblical teaching rather than strive for success, power, or wealth.[237] His address encapsulated the goal that he, Harker, many other trustees, and numerous faculty had: promoting Christian morality, free enterprise, and God's kingdom on earth. Impressive improvements occurred during the Harker years, but the college's historic Christian mission was sidetracked during his watch.

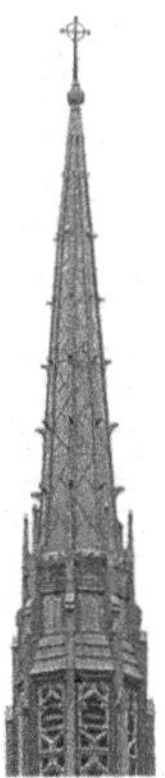

The Presidency of Charles S. MacKenzie:

Reversing Course and Restoring the Mission,

1971–1991

Introduction

In the 1970s, African Americans, Hispanics, Native Americans, women, gays and lesbians, and other marginalized groups intensified their fight for equality. Upset by antiwar protests, urban riots, and the counterculture's drug usage and sexual promiscuity, the "new Right" mobilized to promote political conservatism, the free market, and traditional family roles. Many television shows, including *M*A*S*H,* and *All in the Family,* addressed the nation's leading political and social issues. Some called the 1970s the "Me" generation because many Americans focused more on their own "self-actualization" and "self-fulfillment" than on trying to improve society. Health and exercise fads, spirituality, and self-help books were all popular. The New Right continued its resurgence in the 1980s as a diverse coalition of evangelicals, free-market enthusiasts, disenchanted White liberals, and citizens who wanted a stronger American military and foreign influence. Its members helped elect Ronald Reagan in 1980. The Republican sought to decrease government regulations and spending, build up the military, crush communism, and provide tax cuts for both corporations and individuals as part of "supply-side economics." In the 1980s, CNN, MTV and other cable networks emerged, and computer games became popular. The Reagan administration fought a "war on drugs," Americans coped with the AIDS crisis, and the Cold War ended. Some pundits argue that the phrase "greed is good" defined the decade, as materialism, consumerism, and self-indulgence, as depicted in the popular television show *Dallas* (1978), were rampant. Amid these developments, Grove City College reaffirmed its Christian mission and greatly strengthened its academic program during the presidency of Charles MacKenzie.

Reclaiming the College's Historic Mission and the Integration of Faith

By 1971, Grove City was not fulfilling its original mission to provide an education and campus environment thoroughly grounded on biblical presuppositions and values. Although the college still professed to be a Christian institution, a distinctively biblical worldview was not undergirding its educational philosophy, curricular offerings, classroom instruction, and extracurricular activities. Grove City had journeyed far down the road to secularization traveled by hundreds of other colleges founded by Christian denominations, groups, and leaders.[1]

Numerous trustees, however, spearheaded by J. Howard Pew, wanted to rejuvenate the college's Christian mission. In the mid-1950s, Pew met Charles S. MacKenzie, a PCUSA minister who had earned a PhD at Princeton University in philosophy, on a Mediterranean cruise. The pastor and the business tycoon developed a friendship based on their shared Christian convictions and concern about the PCUSA's liberal theological drift.

In April 1971, the board endorsed MacKenzie, Pew's choice to succeed J. Stanley Harker as president. The trustees admired his education, vigor, and success in transforming three declining congregations into thriving ones. They charged him to restore the college's original mission, which MacKenzie seemed well suited to accomplish.[2] Hungry for a new challenge, the forty-six-year-old pastor of the First Presbyterian Church of San Mateo, California, and a lecturer in philosophy at Stanford University, accepted the presidency.[3] Pew reportedly told MacKenzie, "Everything I am and everything I have is dedicated to bringing America to Jesus Christ." The college, he complained, had "drifted very, very badly" in both its academic quality and Christian commitment. "You," he informed MacKenzie, "are my last hope for a renewal of Christian teaching and morality at Grove City. If you don't succeed, I probably will sever ties with my school."[4]

Under MacKenzie's s leadership during the next two decades, the college hired many faculty members who strove to base their instruction on biblical principles, and in 1973 and 1974, introduced the all-college interdisciplinary Keystone Curriculum—composed of courses in religion and philosophy, the social sciences, the natural sciences, and literature and the arts—to help students develop a Christian perspective of life and learning. The faculty who taught these Keystone courses were aided greatly by the quest at numerous Christian colleges beginning in the 1970s to integrate faith and learning.[5]

To understand Grove City's story, it is necessary to provide a brief overview of secularization in American society and the meaning and practice of the integration of faith and learning. After 1920, secularization deeply impacted all American institutions, including colleges and universities, as hundreds of them abandoned their historic Christian identity and adopted educational philosophies, curricula, and classroom instruction similar to those of state universities. Beginning in the 1970s, the integration of faith and learning became one of the most distinct components of Christian higher education, and by the 1980s, this educational approach became pervasive at evangelical colleges including Grove City.

The Secularization of American Higher Education

Historian George Marsden describes the secularization of American colleges and universities as "the transformation from an era when organized Christianity and explicitly Christian ideals had a major role in the leading institutions of higher education to an era when they have almost none."[6] This development was driven by insights and arguments many academicians drew from the natural and social sciences that caused Christianity to become implausible to them.

Although Christian groups and individuals established almost all private college founded before 1860, and many state-sponsored universities initially promoted biblical principles in their classrooms and Christian morality through their campus rules, by the 1920s, a strong secular spirit pervaded many institutions of higher education, and traditional religious perspectives had been pushed to "the periphery of student life and consciousness."[7] Beginning in the 1920s, Marsden argues, liberal Protestants and secularists saw orthodox Protestant views "as intellectually reactionary, and within about only fifty years they effected a remarkable revolution that eliminated most traditional [Christian] views from respectable academia."[8]

Numerous factors pressured many religiously affiliated colleges to abandon their founding mission: the need to secure greater funding (supplied primarily by government and businesses); American's growing ideological pluralism and ethnic diversity; the increased demand to offer STEM majors; agnostic and naturalistic perspectives in most academic disciplines; the desire to escape ecclesiastical control; the decreased involvement of sponsoring denominations in college governance; the smaller number of clergy serving as their professors and presidents; presidents and faculty who did not want to maintain their colleges' Christian mission; and the desire to be accepted by secular institutions "as true academic colleges and universities."[9]

In 1950, Howard Lowry, president of Wooster College, warned that Presbyterian colleges were experiencing "varying states of fiscal trouble" as the flood of dollars from GI benefits was ending. Many of these colleges, he complained, said little in their catalogs about the distinctive character of Christian higher education.[10] Eleven years later, a scholar of higher education argued that church-related colleges ranked "only fair or poor on items" that most of them used "as their raison d'être": outstanding teaching, the insightful study of religion, flourishing campus religious life, and the benefits of small size.[11] Moreover, in the 1950s and 1960s, many church-related colleges abandoned "the specifics of their Christian heritage" and toned "down their religious emphases."[12]

By the 1970s, conditions at church-related colleges had changed substantially. Minister presidents were rare, chapel attendance was voluntary, and humanistic and relativistic rather than Christian perspectives prevailed in most classrooms. These colleges emphasized their academic excellence, small classes, personal concern for students, and welcoming environments rather than their religious convictions and values.[13] The academy's favoring of "purely naturalistic and materialistic worldviews" and view of religiously-informed higher education as antiquated and substandard deeply affected numerous administrators, faculty, and trustees at church-related colleges. Many of these colleges strengthened their campus ministries, employed dynamic chaplains, built impressive chapels, and offered more courses to promote religious life, but their classroom instruction differed little from that of secular schools.[14] Most church-related colleges accepted the academy's prescription of "what, how, and who a college should teach," leading them to focus much more on scholarly research than on the character development of undergraduates.[15] Many professors considered their personal religious beliefs and practices irrelevant to their teaching and scholarship.[16] In the academy at large, many strongly opposed religiously informed perspectives "getting a hearing in the university classroom."[17]

The Integration of Faith and Learning

These developments prompted many evangelical colleges in the 1970s to work to integrate faith and learning. The Christian College Consortium, founded in 1971, and renamed the Christian College Coalition in 1976, made this a key objective. In **the 1980s and 1990s, evangelical professors increasingly argued that Christian perspectives made a major difference in teaching and scholarship.**[18] The integration of faith and learning became a hallmark of evangelical colleges as they sought to do more than provide a safe haven where Christian students could study the Bible, attend chapel, avoid the world's contamination, and prepare for vocations.[19]

The integration of faith and learning entails intentional, systematic efforts to base both the curriculum and campus life on Christian presuppositions and practices. It involves bringing all college life "under the Lordship of Christ, of taking every thought captive" to Jesus.[20] Faith and learning integration involves an institution's total program and ethos and the design and delivery of its courses and takes place in the mind of students.[21] It involves assessing the foundational assumptions of academic fields, interpreting their claims and conclusions in light of biblical teaching, and applying the knowledge gained to glorify God and strengthen the faith of Christians.[22] The goal of faith/learning integration is to help students internalize beliefs, values, and knowledge that is biblically based, Christ centered, kingdom inspired, and service focused.

While most evangelical colleges adopted this approach in the 1980s and 1990s, the faculty at many church-related ones did not. During the final quarter of the twentieth century, when Presbyterian colleges had substantial funds and faculty with requisite scholarly training, most of them became controlled by academics who viewed the integration of faith and scholarship as "an unattractive ideal."[23]

The Road Not Taken and the Mission Rejuvenated

The 1970s were turbulent, troubled, traumatic years for higher education. Colleges and universities faced many challenges, including maintaining their enrollments, containing their costs, revising their curricula, and responding to students' requests to stop in loco parentis, make courses more relevant, and better prepare them for careers. Christian colleges confronted the additional challenges of trying to upgrade their academic program and reputation while resisting the forces of secularization that had led hundreds of their sister institutions to abandon their historic commitments and values. By 1971, Grove City seemed poised to emulate many other church-related colleges that had abandoned their founders' mission and become essentially secular institutions.

In 1971, however, Grove City became one of a handful of American colleges to turn back from the road toward secularization and restore and strengthen its original mission. The impetus for this reversal came from a small group of faculty, a larger group of students, and the board of trustees led by J. Howard Pew. In the late 1960s and early 1970s, a revival occurred at Grove City, as it did at many other church-related colleges. Students created a Committee of Concerned Christians that through a chapel presentation, a letter to *The Collegian*, and other means, prodded college officials to reinstitute Grove City's original mission. They criticized the college for failing to make God "central to every discipline of study" and exhorted administrators and faculty to help students develop "an intimate, personal relationship" with Jesus. Would the college return to its founding objectives, they asked, or would "it take the secular route and become just another indistinctive little school?"[24]

Individual students also challenged the college to restore its original mission. For example, in a November 1971 letter to *The Collegian*, I argued that Grove City could "become a typical secular college" or the "Christ-centered institution" its founders intended. The catalog, I noted, stated that the college sought to provide a "Christian interpretation of all fields of learning," which required hiring faculty who were both experts in their disciplines and "thoroughly loyal to the Christian purpose of the College." The catalog further declared that the college sought to help students apply "Christian principles to everyday life." Would Grove City, I asked, diligently seek to understand Christ's teachings and apply them "to our everyday experiences"?[25]

Pew died in November 1971, three months after Charles MacKenzie assumed the presidency, but he would have been delighted by the institution's return to its founding mission during MacKenzie's twenty-year tenure. Albert Hopeman, an MIT graduate, a builder of ship interiors, and a board member since 1953, succeeded Pew as the board president and helped the college restore its original mission. Hopeman and MacKenzie worked to strengthen the "Biblical world view and a Judeo-Christian ethic, as espoused by the Ketlers, the Pews and by generations of Trustees and Faculty."[26]

The challenges confronting MacKenzie, Hopeman, and others who sought to achieve this goal were immense. To succeed, the college would have to buck educational trends that had driven hundreds of other institutions to give up their distinctive Christian identity and mission. MacKenzie and the trustees also faced entrenched opposition from numerous faculty who either espoused humanistic or naturalistic worldviews or assumed that education could be value neutral and from many students who disliked the college's strict conduct regulations.[27]

MacKenzie emphasized his mandate to provide Christian perspectives of all academic disciplines in his board reports, chapel addresses, faculty meetings presentations, articles and interviews in *The Collegian*, and countless discussions with professors and students. In a September 1971 chapel address, MacKenzie declared that he wanted to enhance academic excellence and increase excitement about learning. He wanted to bring "a rebirth of basic spiritual, moral, ethical values" at Grove City and in American society.[28]

In his November 1971 board report, MacKenzie asserted that humanistic and Christian philosophies were "struggling for supremacy" at Grove City. Secular ideas had made "deep inroads into college life." If this trend were not arrested, it would soon alter the "college's philosophy and historic mission. "A committed and determined" board, MacKenzie argued, could play the decisive role in determining which position prevailed.[29] One year later, he told the trustees that "slowly the tide is turning" as an increasing number of students and faculty were supporting the college's Christian heritage. Adding "some articulate, young scholars" with strong Christian commitments to the faculty in fall 1972 was helping the college reclaim its original mission. "Though we still have a long way to go," MacKenzie asserted, "significant progress is being made in realigning the institution with the convictions which gave it birth."[30] In May 1973, MacKenzie asserted that recently hired erudite faculty "with deep Christian convictions" were "having a profound impact on the college." They and some longer-serving Christian faculty were rejuvenating "the Christian perspective on campus" and counterbalancing professors who espoused a "liberal, humanist" worldview.[31]

MacKenzie's assessment was overly optimistic. He later explained that his first decade as president was "traumatic," "bitter," and "painful." MacKenzie greatly underestimated how long it would take to turn the college around. He complained that "self-interest, the protection of departmental turf, different philosophic presuppositions," and the opposition of many faculty members thwarted his objectives.[32] The quest to "revive the moral and spiritual values which had been the soul of the college," MacKenzie stated, "took an incredible amount of time and energy" during his presidency. He worked tirelessly to convince "various constituencies, some of whom had opted for contemporary, secular values and therefore had little sympathy with the Christian values upon which the school was founded," of the benefits of this approach.[33] Many faculty who resisted restoring the college's Christian commitment retired or resigned, but other stayed and fought the changes. Some professors wrote anonymous protest letters to the trustees, criticized the college's renewed Christian emphasis in their classes, and schemed about how to thwart this objective.[34]

To strengthen the academic program and address students' complaints about the college's copious required courses and mandatory chapel attendance, MacKenzie took several steps. He strove to improve classroom instruction, hired faculty with PhDs who supported the college's Christian mission, upgraded the chapel program, and created a faculty committee to redesign the all-college course requirements. The college hired a full-time chaplain, sought to make students' chapel experience more stimulating, and offered varied ways to fulfill the attendance requirement. Many students complained that they were forced to take numerous "Mickey Mouse" courses that duplicated their high school subject matter. The college introduced in 1973 and 1974 a new eighteen-hour core consisting of six team-taught, interdisciplinary courses—the Keystone Core—which entailed yearlong courses in the humanities, religion, and philosophy and semester courses in the social sciences and the natural sciences.[35]

MacKenzie argued that the Keystone Curriculum was designed to show that all areas of knowledge were interrelated and to help all student develop their own worldview.[36] The core, the campus newspaper reported, was designed to be "both intensely stimulating and educationally superior."[37] MacKenzie argued that it strengthened the college's academic program by teaching students about "the methodologies and principles" of all the major academic disciplines. Its interdisciplinary approach helped students understand the "unity of knowledge" and taught them how "Christian truth and values relate to all dimensions of life."

The heart of the Keystone Curriculum was the Religio-Philosophic Dimension of Life course, which enabled students "to explore, from a Biblical perspective, many of the important issues of human existence—the meaning of man, God, knowledge, the nature of the world, and social relationships, including ethics." Students were responding much more favorably to this course, MacKenzie claimed, than they had to the formerly required Bible survey courses, which many regarded as a "rerun of Sunday School."[38] The college featured the core in its promotional materials, which helped "attract a higher caliber of student" by offering a unique curriculum.[39] *The Collegian* editor in chief called the Keystone Curriculum the "most progressive" development in the college's history.[40]

Despite the adoption of this curriculum, sophomore Ken Heffner argued in September 1973 that the college had not yet reclaimed its Christian heritage. Most faculty and students," he asserted, did "not understand or accept" biblical presuppositions and instead espoused non-Christian philosophies. Heffner urged the college to hire professors who believed that Christ is the "Lord of History" and "is actively involved" in its ongoing development. The next year, senior George Yates complained that humanistic perspectives permeated many assigned readings; he wanted all subject matter to be presented from a distinctly Christian perspective.[41]

The college strove both to help current faculty understand better how to integrate faith and learning and to hire new professors who were committed to this enterprise. The retirement, departure, and dismissal of many faculty in the 1970s enabled the college to employ new professors who strongly supported its Christian mission and sought to teach their courses from a distinctively biblical perspective. Especially important was the hiring of Andrew Hoffecker in religion and L. John VanTil in history in 1972 and of John Sparks in business in 1976. These men and a cadre of like-minded colleagues hired in the 1970s and 1980s played the decisive role in helping Grove City reclaim its evangelical heritage.

Discussions about the integration of faith and learning, MacKenzie reported, caused substantial "furor among some faculty" who "resented it very much." The hostility of one-third of the faculty toward teaching from a distinctively Christian perspective was so great during MacKenzie's first five years that they had to be let go, although some were dismissed on the grounds of incompetence.[42] In May 1974, MacKenzie claimed that "an articulate but declining minority" continued to challenge the college's "goals and standards." This "handful of well-entrenched" faculty were "making a 'last ditch' effort to prevent the College from reaffirming its great traditions." They called for secularizing the campus, abandoning Grove City's Christian heritage, and liberalizing the college "standards and policies."[43]

To help faculty understand how to base their teaching and research on biblical presuppositions, administrators organized numerous workshops led by outside experts or college faculty. They focused on designing courses and providing classroom instruction that helped students understand biblical perspectives in all academic disciplines and develop a coherent Christian worldview to direct their lives. MacKenzie contended in 1978 that the battle was still being waged. Many students chose Grove City because of its Christian perspective and emphasis, but other students, who had been immersed in "humanistic, positivistic values" before enrolling, rejected or resisted the college's approach.[44]

MacKenzie and some professors produced a "Statement of Identity," which the trustees approved in 1979. It emphasized that the charter stated that Grove City "shall be thoroughly Christian and evangelical in character" and be "guided in its theological understanding by the Apostles' and Nicene Creeds." "Believing that God is the Source of all truth," the statement proclaimed, the college sought to promote "the unity of knowledge." The college strove to explain "the significance of the Word of God for all disciplines" and to create a learning and living environment that helped students grow in knowledge, their relationship with God, and Christian character.[45]

MacKenzie argued in 1982 that prior to his arrival, Grove City had been "nearly as secular as any State school."[46] Testifying to the ongoing battle over restoring the college's original mission, a senior asserted that most "professing Christian students" objected "when a 'non-religious' subject is taught in a consistently biblical manner."[47] MacKenzie bemoaned in 1986 that administrators had expended "an enormous amount of time and energy" responding to "students and faculty whose values were at odd with those of the College."[48]

In 1988, the college issued a revised "Purpose and Identity of Grove City College," which asserted that the college rejected "educational philosophies that deny the possibility of truth or meaning, assert the relativity of values, or emphasize contemporary perspectives" that clash with traditional wisdom.[49] Meanwhile, the struggle to restore the college's foundational mission continued. In 1989, MacKenzie told a trustee that some of the faculty he had inherited accepted "the deconstructionist methodology which denies any ultimate meaning or norms of truth."[50] The next year, however, he claimed the college finally had "a 'critical mass' of students and faculty" who shared its "value orientation." Many student leaders, he declared, "are deeply committed to Grove City's Christian values" and strongly supported the college.[51]

Confirming the college's success in reclaiming its historic commitments, raising its academic reputation, and integrating faith and learning, the 1990 Middle States team applauded the faculty's "tremendously strong work ethic" and "commitment to teaching in a Christian tradition" while maintaining "high academic standards." Grove City College, evaluators stated, was based on the cornerstones of "academic excellence and an open-minded espousal of Christian values," which had given the college a special strength, commitment, and mission. The college, they added, had returned "to its roots with genuine conviction and real dedication."[52]

As MacKenzie's twenty-year tenure as Grove City's president was ending, Presbyterian-related colleges were encountering tough times. An "aggressive pluralist secularism" that had emerged in the 1960s was by the 1990s dominating many colleges, where numerous professors viewed "all beliefs as mere social constructions," attacked the "Western-oriented canon," and repudiated "many conventional ethical assumptions.[53] In 1990, presidents of sixty-nine Presbyterian-affiliated schools warned that "recognizably Protestant colleges," including PCUSA-affiliated ones, might soon disappear. These colleges faced "incredibly difficult pressures in the years ahead" including "increasing competition from state universities for students and gifts"; a diminishing "pool of high school graduates; and changing student populations."[54] Grove City chose to go a different direction.

Finances

Throughout its history, Grove City has striven to be affordable to students from families with modest means. Throughout its history, the college's small endowment made achieving that goal very challenging. It became even more difficult after 1970 as the costs of American colleges rose much more rapidly than the nation's inflation rate and Grove City's competitors received more federal funding. Shrewd financial management and increasing support from alumni, trustees, and friends enabled Grove City to achieve its financial objectives. The college maintained one of the nation's lowest tuition rates for private colleges without deferring maintenance or borrowing large sums to construct buildings. A 1979 survey found that Grove City's tuition was the lowest of any private college in Pennsylvania, New York, West Virginia, or Ohio.[55] In fall 1981, the national average for tuition, room, and board at four-year private colleges was $5,752, while Grove City's was $3,960. Grove City's financial challenges intensified in 1984, when its students could no longer receive federal grants.

Ted Penar claimed Grove City had "never been in the red" because of "good management and generous friends."[56] As noted in previous chapters, for many years, Grove City carried a debt primarily from borrowing money to erect buildings. During MacKenzie's presidency, some faculty and alumni accused Grove City of trying to squeeze water from stones and urged trustees to raise tuition to provide more scholarship aid, better compensate the faculty and staff, and provide more amenities—such as full tuition remission for the children of faculty and staff, and sabbaticals and more travel funds for professors.

The Student Body

During MacKenzie's tenure, the college typically received about three applications for every slot available in the freshman class, and about three-quarters of the students were Pennsylvania residents. About 75 percent of students were usually in the top one-fifth of their high school classes, and the SAT scores of enrolled students were about 1045 to 1075, approximately 150 points above the national average. In fall 1971, 2,223 students applied, almost half of the six hundred freshmen were in the top tenth of their high school class, and the average SAT score was 1057. A significant change in the composition of the student body occurred in the mid-1970s, as the college shifted the male-female ratio from two-to-one to one-to-one. In fall 1977, 60 percent of women and 40 percent of men were in the top tenth of their high school class; 20 percent of them were legacies (sons or daughters of Grove City graduates). In 1988, the college received 1,828 applications, the most since 1971; 75 percent of enrolled students were from the top 20 percent of their high school classes, the average SAT score was 1061, 101 were legacies, and 69 percent were from Pennsylvania. In the 1980s, the most popular majors were accounting, business, engineering, and computer systems.

MacKenzie explained in 1973 that attracting Black students who were academically qualified and could afford to attend Grove City was very difficult; African Americans who could meet Grove City's academic qualifications received full scholarships at state schools.[57] In 1978, Grove City began offering special scholarships to help attract African Americans, but this made little difference in enrolling Black students.

Trying to dispel rumors to the contrary, MacKenzie stressed in 1980 that the college welcomed students of all religious backgrounds and affiliations as well as those with no religious commitments; college leaders believed that ideological diversity benefited the institution. He urged students to respect all philosophical perspectives and to seek to learn from others with whom they disagreed.[58] That fall, the freshman class was 32 percent Presbyterian, 27 percent Catholic, 17 percent Methodist, 9 percent Lutheran, and 6 percent Baptist.

Recruitment

Although the college increased its budget for advertising in newspapers and magazines during the MacKenzie years, for recruitment, it relied primarily on admission counselors, many of whom were recent Grove City graduates, visiting high schools primarily within a five-hundred-mile radius of the college. The admissions department prodded alumni to promote the college. Grove City held two visitation days for high school seniors and one for juniors each year, and for several years, the college had a high school church visitation day to appeal to prospective Christian students. Grove City benefited from positive publicity it received in various guides that rated colleges. Beginning in 1981, Grove City was repeatedly included in *Peterson's Competitive Colleges* and *The Competitive Colleges.* Grove City was also selected for *Barron's Guide to the Most Prestigious Colleges* and chosen as one of the fifty best liberal arts colleges by *The National Review*. Grove City was ranked thirteenth in the category of small comprehensive colleges in the 1988 *US News & World Report*, fifth in the 1990 *Money College Guide* among all private colleges in quality in relation to cost, and third among eighty-seven schools named to the 1991 Templeton Foundation Honor Roll for Free Enterprise Teaching.

Facilities

Several significant construction projects occurred during MacKenzie's presidency. The Pew Fine Arts Center opened in January 1976; 248-bed MEP Hall, named for benefactor Mary Ethel Pew, began occupancy in fall 1982; the Weir Ketler Technological Learning Center was completed in 1984; and the recreation building was significantly enlarged and retitled the Physical Learning Center in 1988. In addition, in 1975, the football stadium was named Robert E. Thorn Field in honor of the former athletic director, and the theater in Pew was called Ketler Auditorium in honor of Weir Ketler. "As a coach, athletic director, and dean," Thorn had influenced thousands of Grove City students, MacKenzie declared, and had "become a legend in his own time." MacKenzie argued that Weir Ketler, by serving as its president for forty years and a trustee for eleven, had "done perhaps more than any other single human being to make Grove City College what it is today."[59]

The decision to construct the fine arts center provoked controversy. Numerous faculty and students thought it was too extravagant for a tight-fisted college that focused on business and the sciences. Others, including English department chair James Paton, insisted that the building was essential to Grove City's mission. He estimated that one thousand students a year would use Pew for drama, and many more would take music and art classes, practice and perform music, and participate in art shows there.[60]

While preparing to expand the recreation building in August 1985, engineers discovered an old coal mine fifty feet below it, forcing the college to close the building and relocate its services and lodgers. An engineering company filled in the mine shaft and reinforced the building. The work was quickly completed, and on October 30, students and services returned to the building. A $6 million expansion of the recreation building began in January 1987 and was completed by September 1988. The forty-thousand-square-foot addition included two basketball courts, four racquetball courts, a second Olympic-size swimming pool, a weight room, and a one-eighth mile track. The Gedunk doubled in size, and the bookstore became 50 percent larger. The college facilities were extensively used during the summers as seven thousand or more people attended twenty or more conferences and sports camps each year.

Academic Matters

During MacKenzie's tenure, the curriculum was enriched, academic rigor increased, more proficient faculty were hired, and higher-achieving students enrolled. As MacKenzie began his presidency, he stated that upgrading academics was his highest priority. Academic Affairs Committee vice president Buddy Hendershot noted that the 1970 Middle States report called Grove City's academic atmosphere unexciting; many professors and students, he claimed, settled for mediocrity.[61] In a 1972 poll, only 20 percent of students said that the academic environment at Grove City was "intellectually stimulating."[62]

Students complained about numerous aspects of the college's academic life. In December 1971, *The Collegian* insisted that the faculty liked Saturday classes "even less than students do."[63] Editor in chief Evan Adair, '72, contended that most Grove City students focused more on grades than learning. Course assignments and examinations, he avowed, involved too much regurgitation and not enough creative thinking.[64] Fred Kring admitted that testing methods were poor in many courses and led to too much cramming.[65] Seniors SGA president David Ottaviano and ODK president Bill Bunt contended that some instructors were lackluster and that many professors placed too much emphasis on memorization.[66] Some professors, *The Collegian* protested, used strict attendance policies to force students to attend their "boring lectures."[67] Because students paid for their education, others asserted, they be able to attend classes only when they wanted.[68] A Continuing Evaluation Committee pinpointed other academic shortcomings: department chairs' lack of leadership, excessive survey courses, the absence of faculty sabbaticals, and inadequate science facilities, student research opportunities, and funds for professors to attend conferences.[69] Some faculty also exhorted the trustees to provide tenure, tuition remission for their children, and a better retirement program.[70]

To respond to widespread student concerns, MacKenzie, Kring, and other administrators held several "bull" sessions. At one in December 1971, students protested that faculty course evaluations were voluntary and viewed only by individual professors. Consequently, poorly performing professors did not permit their students to evaluate them, and administrators could not use evaluations as a basis for firing incompetent faculty. Grove City's unofficial tenure, students complained, allowed faculty who had long been ineffective to continue to teach. Administrators and professors countered that the grapevine identified inept faculty as effectively as published evaluations would. Students also called for significantly reducing the number of required courses, which would soon occur.[71]

All departments except engineering and physics finally agreed to allow course evaluations. Survey questions dealt with such issues as the faculty's fairness in grading, the amount of work courses required, the clarity of course objectives, how organized class lectures were, and how much courses stimulated thinking.[72] After a four-year battle, students finally received permission to publish the results of course evaluations, but only ones done by upperclassmen in their major departments. Many hoped that these evaluations would counter the Grover grapevine, which perpetuated "rumors and distortions," by providing "informative, honest, scrupulously fair" course overviews.[73] The faculty rejected the committee's proposals for a January term and pass/fail physical education courses.

As noted, Grove City adopted a core curriculum in 1973 that significantly changed graduation requirements and reenergized academic life. This "long awaited, progressive innovation," freshman Robb Jones argued, would help end Grove City's "academic lethargy."[74] Numerous faculty members praised the four new core courses—the Religio-Philosophic Dimension (usually shortened to Rel-Phil), the Creative Dimension (focusing on literature, the fine arts, and writing), the Social Dimension (examining the social sciences), and the Scientific Dimension (exploring the natural sciences). Faculty insisted that these courses would help both students and professors grow intellectually.[75] The new core was designed to give students a well-rounded education in both the arts and sciences and aid them in developing a mature philosophy of life. They would also be able to take more electives.[76] Rel-Phil helped students understand the Bible, and the Creative Dimension introduced them to great ideas and historical trends in art and literature and taught them how to write and speak more cogently.

MacKenzie stated in December 1973 that his chief priority in hiring new faculty was candidates' academic credentials and teaching ability.[77] Grove City, he asserted, would continue to stress teaching effectiveness rather than "publish or perish." The college stressed that all knowledge originated from "the God of the Bible," but no students would ever "be pressured to accept this premise."[78] Edward Groesbeck, who replaced William Sweezy in 1974 as the vice president for academic affairs, similarly declared that although

Grove City refused to hire non-Christian faculty, it sought to present a wide variety of non-Christian perspectives in its classrooms and was "not trying to force feed Christianity to anyone."[79]

After resigning in 1974, political science professor Ken Warren protested that faculty could not openly criticize administrative policies. "Neither the president nor anyone else has told me what I can or cannot say in the classroom," Warren avowed, which seemed to be true for all faculty. But by hiring applicants not based on their credentials but on their points of view, the administration controlled what was taught in the classroom. Warren urged the college to seek a better ideological balance among its faculty. He argued that the benefit of tenure—ensuring academic freedom—outweighed its cons—laziness and ineffective teaching. Warren also urged Grove City to get off the AAUP censure list and bring guest speakers who espoused varied viewpoints.[80] Many students proclaimed Warren a hero and plastered his letter outside the Gedunk. MacKenzie's only rebuttal was to point out that Warren had graduated from a state school, which had "different presuppositions and policies" than did Grove City.[81]

The Social and Scientific Dimension core courses were introduced for freshmen in fall 1974. Creative Key employed upperclassmen and upperclasswomen as teaching assistants to lead discussions of course lectures and assigned materials. The course also used films, books, and journaling to help students achieve better self-understanding.[82] In a spring 1976 survey, students rated Rel-Phil the best key course with the Creative Dimension second. Seventy percent of students said that Rel-Phil had improved their understanding of philosophy.[83]

Throughout the MacKenzie years, faculty and students repeatedly expressed concerns about the quality, amount, and use of Buhl Library's resources. In 1976, a student claimed that students needed to go to other libraries to complete their assignments for some courses. Head librarian Diane Grundy countered that Buhl was superior io the libraries at Westminster, Allegheny, and Thiel.[84] From 1972 to 1977, book circulation in Buhl decreased from forty-eight thousand to eighteen thousand, primarily because professors were requiring more reaction and fewer research papers.[85]

Students requested that physical education classes be made pass/fail. Assigning grades discouraged less physically adept students from taking valuable courses.[86] Students also complained that earning A's in physical education courses was very difficult, while varsity athletes received automatic A's. *The Collegian* protested that no comparable credit was given to students who worked for the newspaper or other time-demanding extracurricular activities. Ted Penar maintained that students would not work as hard in pass/fail courses, while Jack Behringer argued pass/fail grades penalized proficient students who could earn A's. Some students suggested a compromise: Allow physical education courses to be taken either for a grade or pass/fail, but no changes were made.[87]

Students continued to lobby to eliminate Saturday classes, which Penar also opposed. He maintained that hundreds of classes and labs would need to be rescheduled, many of them in the evenings and afternoons, which would interfere with extracurricular activities. A five-day week would also negatively affect the quality of instruction and learning by necessitating longer classes and would make Grove City a suitcase college.[88]

Some students maintained that Grove City was striving for competence rather than excellence. One contended that their heavy class loads decreased professors' time to do research and prepare new lectures, which stifled their intellectual growth and decreased their teaching effectiveness. Moreover, the college's many overcrowded classrooms diminished students' ability to learn. If the college could raise $6 million to build Pew, it should be able to procure enough funds to hire more faculty.[89]

By 1980, students believed that Grove City's academic environment was improving. In one survey, 14 percent of students rated Grove City average academically, 28 percent good, 54 percent very good, and 5 percent superior.[90] The 1980 Middle States team emphasized that a "dedicated, hard-working, and extremely productive faculty was making every effort to provide a high quality learning experience for students." On the other hand, less than 20 percent of faculty had engaged in research during the previous two years, primarily because of their heavy teaching loads. The college's emphasis on balancing the budget, team members argued, was thwarting efforts to furnish enough professors and equipment.[91]

The faculty were primarily concerned about the discrepancy between published promotion procedures and actual practices, the minimal support for faculty development, "confusion about how to implement" the integration of faith and learning, and their desire to determine the college's larger curricular issues. The evaluators noted that some professors taught overloads or had heavy advising loads or administrative responsibilities. The faculty wanted smaller classes, more staff support, and better equipment. They had the same job security as tenured faculty at other institutions. Professors believed that they were compensated adequately and equitably. The faculty were dedicated to the college's objectives, and their morale was high.[92]

The 1980 Middle States report noted that administrators, faculty, and students all agreed that the college had three foundational purposes: fostering its Christian mission, promoting academic excellence, and ensuring fiscal integrity. Team members argued, however, that for many faculty and students, defending the American free enterprise system was "more important in shaping institutional policies than the three foundational purposes." The committee exhorted the college to be up front about this matter. The college's most respected majors were those promising high salaries, which, team members asserted, conflicted with the college's emphasis on Christian service.[93]

The Middle States report noted that most Grove City students were "pleasant," talented, "highly motivated," articulate, and "sincerely interested" in their education, and had very positive relationships with faculty. They were concerned about the amount and availability of library resources, laboratory facilities, and the faculty advising process.[94] The team noted that students scored above average in thirteen of the eighteen Undergraduate Assessment Program tests, with a combined 66 median percentile.[95]

In 1982, MacKenzie announced that the college's primary goal for the 1980s was to strengthen the academic program so that Grove City would be increasingly recognized as a premier American educational institution.[96] His "Academic Excellence for the 1980s" program strove to put Grove City on the cutting edge of current technology. To help achieve this, the college established a computer systems major. Beginning in fall 1984, all students received access to computer equipment designed by the Digital Equipment Corporation when the college purchased one hundred Pro-350 terminals and a power disk cluster system. In addition, Grove City spent $4 million to build the Weir Ketler Technological Learning Center, which had 270 computer terminals. Despite the college's improving academic program, *The Collegian* editor in chief Kathy Gardner, '86, complained in October 1985 that students were "the regurgitation generation." For most of them, obtaining a diploma was more important than seeking truth.[97]

Several other new majors were added between 1971 and 1991: religion in 1973, management engineering and social work in 1975, international business in 1981, and Christian ministries in 1982. In fall 1983, the college established a program to improve students' writing skills and initiated the Adult Audit Program, which enabled adults to sit in on any of twenty-five courses in various disciplines. In 1984–1985, the college granted its first full-tuition trustee scholarships.

In fall 1987, Grove City opened the Early Childhood Laboratory School to give elementary education majors practical experience while educating local children. That fall, the college adopted a plus/minus system for grading. The next spring, the minimum QPA required for the dean's list and honors at graduation was raised from 3.1 to 3.4, bringing it closer to the national average. The number of full-tuition trustee scholarships was increased to six beginning in 1989–1990. In the late 1980s, the number of students doing internships rose significantly.

In 1987, Hopeman insisted that although some departments were "superb," others were mediocre, and a few were poor.[98] To improve its academic program, the college hired Jerry Combee as its vice president for academic affairs in 1988. Combee had earned his PhD at Cornell with the renowned Allan Bloom, written or edited seven books on government, and served as the dean of the School of Business and Government at Liberty University. MacKenzie praised Combee as "a fiercely bright, well-organized scholar administrator," while Bloom lauded his understanding of both Christian thought and classical political philosophy.[99] During the next three years, Combee led the college through three major evaluative processes—the 1990 Middle States Association reaccreditation; ABET approval of the engineering department (making GCC one of the few small Christian colleges to receive this prestigious distinction), and the Pennsylvania Department of Education (which recertified the college's teacher training program).

With strong support from the faculty, Combee led a revision of the general education curriculum that increased the core requirements from eighteen to between thirty-eight and fifty hours, depending on students' majors, and included a quantitative, lab science, and foreign language component. The new curriculum, which began in September 1990 for the class of 1994, replaced the Keystone Core and included eighteen hours in the humanities (in a three-year "civilization series"), six in the social sciences, eight in the natural sciences, and six in quantitative and logical reasoning. A writing competency component was also introduced. The goal of the new curriculum was to graduate students who were culturally literate across all fields. It would focus on ultimate truth, not current ideology, and propagate basic Western principles such as human equality and individual freedom.[100]

Hopeman asserted in 1988 that Grove City could have "a profound effect" on the national struggle between "secular humanism and Christian morality" if it came to be widely "perceived as an institution that guided by Christian principles" was "providing a preeminent education."[101] The 1990 Middle States Association report indicated that Grove City was making progress toward achieving this goal. Evaluators declared that the new curriculum had produced "vitality and exciting energy." The team was confident that the college would continue to attract high quality students because of its low cost, "commitment to academic excellence," and "traditional and solid Christian values."[102] MacKenzie claimed that the chair of the team told him that he expected Grove City to enter "the very top echelon of private, undergraduate colleges."[103]

The Faculty

Several important personnel changes occurred during these years. In 1972, William Swezey became the vice president for academic affairs, and Ted Penar became the college's first vice president for business affairs. Nancy Paxton became the dean of women in 1976, and Ross Foster was named the vice president for student affairs in 1977. In 1977, Penar became the vice president of academic affairs, a role he filled until 1989. During his thirty-seven-year tenure, Penar helped establish the college's elementary education program, chaired the education department, and served as an adviser to MacKenzie. Fred and Hilda Kring retired in 1985 with a total of forty-seven years of combined service.

During the MacKenzie years, the faculty continued to provide high-quality classroom instruction and develop cordial relationships with and mentor students. As noted, the high teaching load in terms of both students and course preparations limited the research and publications of most professors. Future Oxford philosophy professor Brian Leftow, '77, maintained that eight courses a year was "an incredibly hard teaching load," which Grove City professors shouldered "manfully and without seeming tired."[104] The amount of research the faculty did and the number of books and articles they wrote, however, increased compared with the Harker years because of professors' academic training and interests. The most significant books were the two-volume *Building a Christian Worldview*, edited by Andrew Hoffecker, published in 1986 and 1988. Designed for use in the Rel-Phil key, the first volume explored God, humanity, and epistemology, while the second examined cosmology, society, and ethics. L. John Van Til wrote *Liberty of Conscience* (1972). Jim Dixon coauthored the sixth edition of *The Principles and Practices of Acting for the Stage* (1978). Hoffecker published *Piety and the Princeton Theologians* (1981). I penned *The Seeds of Secularization* (1985) and edited *God and Politics* (1989). MacKenzie authored *Churches on the Wrong Road* (1986) and *The Trinity and Culture* (1987). Political science professor Marvin Folkertsma authored *Ideology and Leadership* (1987). Combee co-edited *Economic Justice in Perspective* (1991). The most productive professors were biology professor Fred Brenner, chemistry professor John Shaw, and economics professor Hans Sennholz. Brenner coedited *Endangered and Threatened Species Programs* (1986), and he and Shaw both penned numerous articles based on research they did with students. Sennholz published dozens of articles and eleven books during MacKenzie's tenure including *Age of Inflation* (1977) and *The Politics of Unemployment* (1987).

The faculty received numerous accolades during the MacKenzie years. In 1971, admissions director John Moser was elected vice president of the National Association of College Admission Counselors. In 1972, Brenner was selected to serve on the executive board of the Pennsylvania Academy of Science and to edit its newsletter. The next year, he was chosen for "Who's Who in Ecology," and in 1975, Brenner was elected to his third term on the executive committee of the national biology honorary. In 1981, Brenner was elected president of Pennsylvania chapter of the Wildlife Society. French professor Robert Sisler was listed in the Outstanding Educators of America in 1974, while psychology professor Earl Houts was selected for the *Dictionary of International Biography* in 1976. In 1977, Sennholz was named the shadow secretary of the treasury by the two-hundred-thousand-member Conservative Caucus. In 1978, Shaw received a research grant from the Petroleum Research Fund. In 1985, MacKenzie was elected president of the American Association of Presidents of Independent Colleges and Universities. He was also appointed to Rockford Institute's Main Street Committee, a group of eighty scholars, opinion leaders, and public policy analysts. Head football coach Chris Smith worked with the American Football Developmental Program during the summers of 1985 and 1988 in Ireland, Scotland, England, and Italy. In 1989, mechanical engineering professor Mark Reuber received the Society of Automotive Engineers' educational award for his outstanding teaching and research in machine design and robotics. Industrial management professor Bruce Ketler worked to refuel fighter jets with the air national guard during the Gulf War in 1990 and 1991.

Professors strove to build rapport with students through Faculty Follies. Bruce Thielemann, dean of the chapel, created this variety show in 1976 to raise funds to feed hungry people in various locales. In 1987, the follies shifted to providing a scholarship for an ODK or Mortar Board member, the two honoraries that assumed sponsorship of the program. During MacKenzie's presidency, between twenty and forty professors typically performed vocal or instrumental music, magic or juggling acts, lip syncs, or silly skits which they or students devised. Crowd favorites during these years were John Sparks as a mind-reading wizard, computer professors Everett DeVelde and Jack Kendall as the Smothers Brothers, Combee and others performing the rock 'n' roll classic "Johnny B. Goode," and religion department faculty impersonating various bands and individuals, including the Village People and MC Hammer. Professors also played revenue-raising games against the SGA officers, the women's basketball team to fund its trip to play in Hawaii, and the Pittsburgh Steelers.

Celebrating the Centennial

The college hosted a variety of events during the 1976 spring semester to celebrate its centennial. MacKenzie initiated the festivities with a convocation address titled "Founders of the Future."[105] The college hosted a Freedom in America speakers series that included Robert Dunlap, the president of Sun Oil. In April, the Fine Arts Festival gave prizes for student entries in poetry, photography, painting, pottery, film, and crafts. Founders Day, April 11, featured a multimedia show, a ballet, an ROTC drill, a Scottish "kiltie" band, guest speakers, and a pageant written by Hilda Kring depicting events from the college's first one hundred years.

Guest Speakers

During the MacKenzie years, many luminaries appeared at Grove City College. Three major speaker series during these years were the Pew Memorial Lectures, the Thomas Staley Distinguished Christian Scholar Lectures, and a twelve-person special series in 1987–1988. The Pew Lectures, which began in 1973, continue today. The Staley Lectures were given from 1976 until 1999. Speakers included former Black Panther leader Earl Anthony, actor Vincent Price, soon-to-be Surgeon General C. Everett Koop, Harvard psychiatrist Robert Coles, U.S. Commissioner of Education Ernest Boyer, Soviet dissidents Alexander Ginzburg and Vladimir Sakharov, undercover cop David Toma, social theorist Jeremy Rifkin, political commentators James Kilpatrick and William F. Buckley Jr., and activist Phyllis Schlafly.

Several authors lectured: Erich Segal, who penned *Love Story*; Raymond Hull, the coauthor of *The Peter Principle*; Thomas A. Harris, who wrote *I'm OK, You're OK*, award-winning poet and novelist Madeleine L'Engle, and public policy pundit David Eisenhower. Two astronauts spoke—Jim Lovell and James Irwin—as did Robert Jastrow, founder of NASA's Goddard Institute for Space Studies. Other scientists included Stanford electrical engineering professor Richard Bube, Nobel Prize–winning physicist William Fowler, eminent Harvard astrophysicist Owen Gingerich, and University of Minnesota geneticist Elving Anderson. Sociologist Robert Nisbet of Columbia University, Austrian economist Erik von Kuehnelt-Leddihn, Harvard Medical School professor Armand Nicholi II, Johns Hopkins University historian Timothy Smith, Middle Eastern expert Ken Bailey, Catholic philosopher Michael Novak, librarian of Congress Daniel Boorstin, and Vanderbilt education professor Chester Finn also spoke.

Religious leaders included Louis Evans Jr., pastor of National Presbyterian Church in Washington, DC; Calvinist philosopher Rousas Rushdoony; and Clinton Marsh, former PCUSA General Assembly moderator. In 1985, Christian educator Melicent Huneycutt became the first female baccalaureate speaker. Politicians included Senators Jesse Helms (R-NC) and Pete Wilson (R-CA); US Congressman Ron Paul, a Libertarian candidate for president; and former Secretary of the Interior Stewart Udall.

Legendary UCLA basketball coach John Wooden, whose teams won ten NCAA championships, spoke. Several journalists lectured: sportswriter and participant observer George Plimpton; Edward Fiske of *The New York Times*; Norman Podhoretz, editor in chief of *Commentary* magazine; and David Gergen, editor of *US News & World Report*. Leading African American voices were economists Thomas Sowell of Stanford, Walter Williams of George Mason (a later Grove City trustee), Clarence Pendleton, who chaired the US Commission on Civil Rights, and journalist William Raspberry.

The most controversial speakers were astrologer Jeane Dixon and Merle Miller, who wrote *On Being Different* (1971), which discussed his life before and after publicly acknowledging that he was a homosexual. Especially notable was judge Robert Bork's speech in February 1988, the first talk he gave after the Senate refused to confirm him as a Supreme Court justice, which drew more than two thousand five hundred people, the largest college audience since the Simon and Garfunkel concert in 1966.

David v. Goliath: The Grove City Case

From 1976 to 1985, a matter that took much of MacKenzie's time was a battle with the US Department of Health, Education, and Welfare (HEW) and later the US Department of Education over how Title IX applied to Grove City College.[106] This confrontation, which culminated in a 1984 Supreme Court case, was expensive (costing the college about $500,000) and brought Grove City considerable positive national publicity. Passed by Congress in 1972, Title IX of the Education Amendments Act declared that "No person in the United States shall, on the basis of sex, be excluded from participation in, be denied the benefits of, or be subjected to discrimination under any education program or activity receiving Federal financial assistance."

In July 1976, Grove City was told it must sign an "assurance of compliance" with Title IX. College officials refused to sign this form, arguing that Grove City had been coeducational from its founding and did not discriminate against women. MacKenzie contended that by signing the form, the college would be agreeing to abide by all future amendments to and government interpretations of Title IX. Doing this, MacKenzie averred, would turn "over control of the college's future to the federal government."[107] This would force the college to abandon its Christian perspective, reduce the quality of its academic program, and greatly increase the college's cost.[108]

HEW argued that if any students received federal assistance through Pell Grants or guaranteed student loans, it made their college a "recipient institution" as much as universities receiving millions in federal grants. In the late 1970s, about one-quarter of Grove City's two thousand two hundred students were getting either federal grants or government-secured loans through their own initiative. HEW threatened to cut off these grants and loans to Grove City students and those attending thirteen other schools including Hillsdale College that refused to sign the compliance form. Grove City officials argued that these loans and grants were arranged between students and the government and therefore did not constitute federal aid to the college. This would be similar, MacKenzie reasoned, to supermarkets or churches being subject to federal regulations because customers or contributors used Social Security funds or food stamps to purchase products or make donations.[109]

In September 1978, administrative judge Albert Feldman of the Federal District Court of Western Pennsylvania ruled that Grove City students should not be allowed to receive federal grants (BEOG) or guaranteed student loans (GSL) from private lenders because the college refused to sign Title IX compliance forms. The college insisted that his decision raised an alarm about "the awe-inspiring growth of bureaucracy interfering in private affairs." The Inter-Fraternity and Pan-Hellenic councils sponsored a raffle to raise money for the college's legal defense drive, and numerous television news shows interviewed MacKenzie. This administrative ruling prompted the college and four of its students to file a complaint against HEW in November, arguing that it had exceeded its constitutional authority by trying to regulate a private college that accepted no federal funds. "Once the nose of the camel gets into the tent," MacKenzie warned, "the whole camel moves in."[110] Albert Hopeman Jr. similarly cautioned, "Once control is established, complete domination will follow."[111] Many private colleges, Hopeman complained, had become "so dependent on government funds that their administrations are afraid to stand up and fight."[112] Because Grove City was "free from government entanglement," it could wage war against the forces of secularism and assaults on traditional morality.[113]

The college's stance received considerable support. The Republican College Council of Pennsylvania endorsed it. Alumni provided "generous and enthusiastic" backing.[114] Senator Gordon Humphrey, R-New Hampshire, maintained that no valid arguments existed for subjecting institutions that received no federal funds to HEW regulations.[115]

After hearing arguments brought by HEW and Grove City in November 1979, federal judge Paul Simmons, the grandson of a slave, asserted that this "difficult" case might be a "crossroads" for private independent higher education.[116] In his March 1980 ruling, the Pittsburgh-based judge declared the HEW compliance form to be "invalid, void and of no effect whatsoever." Simmons stated that BEOGs could be terminated only if hearings were held for Grove City students to present their cases and actual discrimination was shown to exist at the college in admission or education programs, which HEW had not attempted to prove. Moreover, HEW did not have the authority to stop Grove City from accepting GSL.[117] The college celebrated Simmons's ruling by thanking God for a favorable outcome and holding a party where the stage band played and students ate ice cream sundaes.[118] The college issued a press release declaring: "Without government interference, the college will continue to maintain its Christian values, its quality programs and its very low cost to students." Echoing MacKenzie's arguments, *The Collegian* editor in chief Dave Peiffer, '81, avowed that federal funding of education inevitably brought government control, secularization, lower educational standards, and harmful affirmative action programs.[119]

MacKenzie acknowledged that this was only round one; HEW would either appeal the decision or rewrite its regulations. "Surely HEW has enough tame horses to ride," declared political commentator George Will, "that it can leave alone the spirited, endangered species represented by Grove City College." Newspapers around the nation extolled the decision; the Lewistown *Sentinel* proclaimed, "Hooray for Grove City," while *The Indianapolis Star* announced, "Goliath Loses One."[120] An August 1980 *Reader's Digest* article argued that HEW should stop harassing Grove City and other colleges, eliminate meaningless paperwork, and cut costs by reducing its interference in their affairs.[121]

The Department of Education, which had replaced HEW, appealed Simmon's decision to the US Court of Appeals for the Third Circuit in Philadelphia. Its officials chose not to contest his ruling that Title IX did not cover federally guaranteed student loans. But they contended that students' use of federal grants to pay for their education was sufficient to bring their colleges under Title IX coverage.[122] Accepting this argument, the US Third Circuit Court ruled in August 1982 that because some Grove City students received Pell Grants, the entire college was subject to government jurisdiction. The court authorized halting grants to Grove City students. The judges asserted that no evidence existed that Grove City had practiced discrimination; its refusal to sign was "obviously a matter of conscience and belief."[123] MacKenzie insisted that the case had significant ramifications for the nation's eight hundred church-related colleges because of the government's "secularizing influences." The president pledged to take the case all the way to the Supreme Court. "I hope everyone who prizes freedom will join us," he declared.[124] John Dellenback, the president of the Christian College Consortium, which represented more than seventy private colleges, contended that the Third Circuit's ruling distorted Title IX's intent.[125]

Meanwhile, the college began working to establish a fund to replace federal grants with private ones to help students pay for their education. MacKenzie insisted that Grove City's skirmish with the federal government was primarily about educational freedom, not sexual discrimination. Grove City was fighting to "preserve its independence and Christian identity."[126]

The Supreme Court agreed to take the case, and hearings began in late November 1983. Grove City's attorneys, David Lascell and Robb Jones, '76, members of Nixon, Hargrave, Devans & Doyle in Rochester, New York, exhorted the justices to maintain two constitutional principles—preserving "a pluralistic system of higher education" and preventing "invidious discrimination" without imposing the "heavy hand of government regulation."[127]

The next month, three-fourths of the student body signed a petition titled "Preserve Our Independence," which outlined Grove City's position, and forty-eight students traveled to Washington to hear the college's attorneys present its case. Lascell argued that the central issue was whether to avoid "government entanglement," retain its independence, and operate efficiently, Grove City "must either expel students who receive federal scholarships or must agree that it is subject to government regulation." He emphasized that Grove City College had never sought federal aid and grants.[128] Charlene Finnegan, '84, the president of Mortar Board, insisted that the college's stance was an "object lesson of what is taught in the classroom." A classmate stated that students "are solidly behind the school." In interviews with hometown newspapers, dozens of students emphasized that Grove City did not discriminate against women and explained the college's case.[129]

In late February 1984, the Supreme Court ruled that BEOGs given to Grove City students constituted direct aid to the college and therefore triggered the provisions of Title IX. By a 6–3 vote, however, the justices rejected the government's position that this placed the entire college under government jurisdiction; only the school's financial aid office was subject. Justice Lewis Powell Jr. called the ruling "an unedifying example of overzealousness on the part of the Federal Government" and stressed that the case had "nothing whatever to do with discrimination past or present."[130]

This court's program-specificity ruling prompted Congress to seek to expand it so that if an institution received any federal funding, every facet of it would be subject to federal jurisdiction. At a US House Judiciary Committee hearing on the Civil Rights Restoration Act of 1985 in March, MacKenzie beseeched representatives to accept an amendment to the Hatch Bill (a much narrower bill with the same intention) to allow students attending schools that had been found not to discriminate to receive federal grants and to allow church-controlled and religious-oriented schools to be exempt from Title IX. Testifying before a Senate Judiciary Subcommittee about the Civil Rights Restoration Act in September, MacKenzie argued that passing the bill would destroy "mediating institutions, vastly expand government control of American life, and greatly diminish freedom."[131] While many colleges admired and appreciated Grove City's strong stand, their acceptance of federal money kept them from imitating it.

After several attempts, Congress finally passed the Civil Rights Restoration Act in March 1988, which declared that Title IX applied to all areas of institutions that received federal aid, not just their financial aid offices. The bill was passed over the veto of President Ronald Reagan, who argued it "would force court-ordered social engineers into every corner of American society." The next day, MacKenzie told students that Grove City had lost its "effort to limit government power," but its leaders did not anticipate any negative short-term impact from this act. He promised, however, that it would "remain vigilant" in its fight to avoid both federal funding and jurisdiction.[132]

Overall, the publicity Grove City received in its David v. Goliath battle against the federal government was positive and fortified its reputation as a premier Christian liberal art college. President Paul McNulty, '80, later asserted that "Losing the Supreme Court case was one of the best things that has happened to Grove City" because it "strengthened the college's financial sustainability and affordability." It also allowed the college to remain independent and provide a Christian perspective of all aspects of life.[133]

Christianity

The 1970s, Brian Leftow explained, "were exciting times, for Christians. Jesus freaks, the Jesus Movement, 'born again' Christianity, the growth of Pentecostalism, [and] febrile discussions of the end times all had echoes on campus."[134] During the MacKenzie years, the percentage of students involved in religious activities increased as larger numbers of more strongly committed Christians enrolled and many Grovers grew in their faith. Numerous Christian organizations thrived, most notably Salt Company, which sponsored speakers, Bible studies, retreats, concerts, barn bashes, ice skating trips, coffeehouses, Christmas caroling, and other activities. Students continued to minister at local churches, George Junior Republic, Polk State School, Young Life clubs, and the Odd Fellows Home. Although chapel was still mandatory, many students found it to be interesting and even inspiring thanks to the superb leadership of Presbyterian deans of the chapel Bruce Thielemann, who served from 1974 to 1984, and his successor Richard Morledge. Faith and Life Week was reinstituted in spring 1973, and some of the nation's most scintillating religious leaders served as speakers. The faculty-student Religious Activities Committee stove to foster students' spiritual formation. Its members selected Red Box missionaries, Faith and Life Week speakers, and Staley lecturers, directed the annual hunger drive, and allocated money to and supervised all campus religious organizations.

Koinonia and Gospel Team members led church services throughout the region. Some new organizations and programs began: Sweet Manna (a Christian dance and drama group created by Bill Liegel, '73), Clowns for Christ, the Fellowship of Christian Athletes, Lamplighters (a ministry to the blind), Revelation Bookstore (a Christian bookselling enterprise), Adopt a Grandparent, Life Advocates, the Fellowship of Christian Educators, New Grace

Singers (talented vocalists who performed in churches), and Student Missions Fellowship.

In November 1971, the board approved devising a chapel program that provided "maximum freedom and flexibility."[135] Students would be required to attend thirty-five of 138 religious and cultural programs, including seven daily chapel programs and four Sunday vesper services. Despite these changes, some students continued to complain. Evan Adair argued that to be meaningful, religion must be voluntary.[136] In February 1972, SGA representatives passed a resolution 29–2 to end mandatory chapel.[137] Eighty-two percent of respondents to a spring 1972 poll wanted to abolish required chapel attendance. The trustees met with six students in spring 1972 to discuss mandatory chapel—three who supported it and three who opposed it. The trustees decided to continue to require students to attend thirty-five events per semester but not any Sunday night vespers. Moreover, Sunday morning church attendance would count toward the total; morning chapels would be educational, while Sunday evening chapels would be worship services. Some students were still not satisfied. Adair accused the board of providing palliatives rather than addressing the fundamental issue—that chapel was compulsory.[138] Other students denounced the college's effort to mold Grovers into "good Christians" by mandatory chapel attendance.[139] A disillusioned Dudley Rose left after the 1972–1973 academic year. In accepting the college pastor position two years earlier, he had not realized how much antagonism mandatory chapel provoked among students.[140]

In March 1972, the world-renowned evangelical apologist and author Francis Schaeffer, an American who in 1955 had founded L'Abri in Switzerland as a refuge for people investigating Christianity, spoke at Grove City. While turning down hundreds of other offers to speak, Schaeffer agreed to lecture at the college because in the 1930s, he had pastored the town's Orthodox Presbyterian Church. People came from miles in all directions and filled the Arena to hear Schaeffer discuss fundamental Christian truths.

Numerous students exhorted their classmates to acknowledge Jesus Christ as the Lord of life,[141] serve as agents of God's kingdom,[142] be guided by scripture in everything they did,[143] view all life in light of God's word,[144] and to emulate Christ.[145] During the MacKenzie years, scores of students committed their lives to Christ, and hundreds developed a deeper, more intellectually grounded faith. Speaking for them, Leftow explained that through Christian friends, faculty and student role models, and courses, he "emerged with beliefs and habits of life settled enough to remain unshaken through a very secular graduate school [Yale] and an academic career largely in very secular places."[146]

Despite the college's strenuous efforts to restore its historic mission, Leftow explained, students in the 1970s could go from a class taught by an orthodox Christian to one taught by a professor espousing a Buddhist worldview that attacked everything they had just learned. Many students objected to the institution's "blatantly Christian perspective," and "seething academic conflicts" existed. He praised administrators for "holding fast to an extremely unpopular position" as they strove "to Christianize the daily life of campus." Many students did not respect Grove City's efforts to base all facets of its life on biblical principles, producing "frequent and vehement" clashes.[147]

In fall 1974, Bruce Thielemann, the senior minister of the two-thousand-five-hundred-member Glendale Presbyterian Church in a Los Angeles suburb and one of the nation's most enthralling and esteemed preachers, became the dean of the chapel. Leftow called his sermons "spell-binding. For sheer power as a speaker—the ability to hold a large audience rapt—I haven't seen his equal."[148]

In 1974–1975, Campus Christian Union alternated between sponsoring weekly worship services and faculty-led Bible studies. In spring 1975, Thielemann initiated a chapel film series that dealt with essential questions about faith and morality. He also created a photograph contest to help portray the relationship between Christianity and the arts. In five months, *The Collegian* opined, Thielemann had changed the dean of chapel position from one of derision to respect and had significantly elevated the intellectual level of Christianity on campus. Thielemann had shifted focus from "blue-stocking morality to a caring, sharing concern for humanity."[149] The WSAJ editorial board insisted that the friendly, down-to-earth Thielemann had provided "leadership, guidance, inspiration, and direction."[150] In December 1975, the first annual all-college Christmas candlelight service was held in Harbison.

Shortly after arriving, Thielemann created Salt Company to appeal to a broader variety of students than Campus Christian Union did. Because of Thielemann's support and influence, Salt Company had greater visibility on campus and drew more students than CCU, and Salt Company soon subsumed CCU. Thielemann chose four to six chapel aides each year to help lead services and plan programs, while several members of the Coalition for Christian Outreach, most of whom also served as head residents, supplemented his work.[151]

Scores of students continued to lead programs at George Junior Republic, which strove to rehabilitate delinquents sent there for truancy, drug use, assault, theft, and incorrigibility.[152] Students taught Sunday school classes, held evening New Life meetings, and sponsored chess and arts and crafts clubs. The big brother program was expanded to include big sisters. Working in pairs, male and female Grovers took GJR youth to dinners or movies, played cards and sports, and talked. Forty Grovers went weekly to Polk State School to build relationships with residents through singing, art, dance, drama, and Bible studies. In 1977, the Religious Activities Committee began choosing students to go on a funded summer mission trip. The first missionary, Jim Leuenberger, spent the summer ministering in Guatemala. This "red box" program eventually expanded to eight students each summer. In fall 1977, Tony Campolo, a sociology professor at Eastern Baptist College and a remarkably engaging and entertaining speaker, served as the college's Staley lecturer. In spring 1978, the college held a Faith and Fine Arts Festival that featured architecture, music, dance, and poetry, and a talk by children's television host Fred Rogers. The Phi Taus and Gamma Sigs began a runathon to raise money for summer missionaries.

Numerous articles in *The Collegian* had Christian themes. For example, a 1980 Easter piece by Paul McNulty argued that Christ's resurrection from the grave had "split nations, built empires, ruined dynasties, brought civilization to new continents," and "changed the course of history."[153] The 1980 Faith and Life Week speaker, William Pannell, an evangelism professor at Fuller Seminary, was "impressed with the Christian attitude on campus" and praised Thielemann's colorful preaching.[154] In fall 1981, senior Michael Jensen became *The Collegian*'s first religion editor, paralleling the paper's long-standing sports editors, and Christian content became much more extensive.

During spring 1982, Salt Company sponsored Robert Short, author of *The Gospel According to Peanuts,* who discussed whether psychology and Christianity were teammates or rivals, and Paul Bromley, who spoke about the Shroud of Turin. In September 1982, Faith and Life Week speaker author Elisabeth Elliot Gren beseeched students and faculty to the totally surrender their entire lives to Christ. Her first husband, Jim Elliot, was killed by the Auca Indian of Ecuador (now called the Huaorani) in 1956. Her second husband, Addison Leitch, taught at Grove City fand served as dean of men from 1940 to 1946.

In spring 1984, Thielemann resigned to become the senior pastor of First Presbyterian Church in Pittsburgh. *The Collegian* noted that his successor, Richard Morledge, '54, was highly regarded for his speaking ability and personal warmth.[155] That fall, Tony Campolo strove to sensitize students to the needs of the poor and the oppressed.[156] Salt Company sponsored the first of its many highly attended coffeehouses featuring student performers. The Newman Club, advised by physical education instructor John Barr and math professor John Ellison was quite active during the MacKenzie years.

In spring 1989, trustee Truman Davis discussed the medical implications of Christ's death at Salt Company, while Max McLean did a dramatic presentation on the gospel of Mark. That fall, Salt Company meetings attracted two hundred to three hundred students for an hour of speakers, praise, and fellowship. The next spring, the college held its first annual Christian Leadership Conference featuring Leo Wisniewski, a former NFL tackle, and Paul McNulty, minority counsel for the US House of Representatives' subcommittee on crime. New Life began holding weekly Bible studies in group homes at George Junior Republic.

From 1971 to 1991, numerous Christian bands and artists performed including Danny Taylor, Phil Keaggy (twice), James Ward (five times), Randy Stonehill (three times), Kenny Marks, Randy Matthews, Petra, Kathy Troccoli, Scott Wesley Brown, Michael Card (twice), DeGarmo and Key, and Steve Camp.

It is difficult to assess how their experience at Grove City affected students' faith development in the aggregate. However, a 1980 survey of the class of 1975 is suggestive. Sixty-five percent of the respondents said that Grove City "had trained them how to seek a Christian view of life"; 34 percent of them said that were deeply religious and 39 percent were fairly religious, while 27 percent had no interest in religion.[157] Various considerations indicate that the number of devout Christian students grew throughout the remainder of the MacKenzie years. This, coupled with the college's increased emphasis on the integration of faith and learning, make it likely that higher percentages of the graduating classes after 1975 would have stated that they had developed a Christian worldview and were deeply religious.

Campus Life

Throughout the MacKenzie years, activities and organizations abounded while several issues continued to provoke controversy, especially required chapel, off-campus housing, alcohol consumption policies, intervisitation hours, and rules for women. MacKenzie strove to better understand student concerns by visiting with them in the dining halls and attending campus social events.[158] SGA president David Ottaviano praised MacKenzie's "sincerity and openness."[159]

In November 1971, a Mortar Board chapter was established, a national organization that recognized leadership and scholarship and was the female counterpart to Omicron Delta Kappa. The next spring, the first Senior Woman of the Year was chosen, paralleling the award for males that began in 1960. Thereafter, the two organizations worked together on many important college activities. ODK became coed in 1974 and Mortar Board in 1975, and that year they began to jointly sponsor the Senior Man and Woman of the Year awards.

The Collegian's faculty advisers and editors both maintained that the college did not control or censor the newspaper's content. On the other hand, Brian Leftow, the 1976–1977 editor in chief, sometimes felt pressured not to say things with which the college disagreed.[160] In 1980, an adviser expressed surprise at how much discretion *The Collegian* editors had, while the editor in chief asserted that college had never used the purse strings to control the newspaper's content.[161] Another editor in chief insisted that *The Collegian*'s role was not to be a cheerleader or public relations agent for the college, while a fourth maintained that the newspaper strove to be "the loyal opposition," "to serve as an outlet for criticism and suggestions," and provide information objectively, fairly, and accurately.[162] Editor in chief Kathy Gardner declared that *The Collegian* was not procontroversy, proscandal, or proadministration, but only protruth.[163]

Despite MacKenzie's leadership of curriculum revision, efforts to build rapport with students and willingness to discuss their grievances, problems of distrust arose, primarily because of students' dislike of college policies. Mark DeWalt, '72, accused the administration of forcing housekeeping staff to serve as its spies.[164] MacKenzie insisted that cleaning personnel were expected to report obvious violations of the campus drinking policy but not to snoop around. College officials would not "spy" on off-campus housing, but they would respond if the police became involved or neighbors complained about noise.[165] The college's policy, *The Collegian* observed, seemed to be that if students did not attract "undesirable" attention and thereby hurt the college's reputation, administrators would leave them alone.[166]

In reviewing his senior year in May 1972, Ottaviano argued that the college needed more interaction between faculty and students, better communication and cooperation among campus organizations, a counseling center, and equal campus employment opportunities for female students.[167] Meanwhile, some students argued that women's rules stifled their growth.[168] The next year, a student contended sarcastically that women's curfew had taught them to "lie, sneak, and prevaricate."[169]

The Collegian staff declared in October 1973 that although they disagreed with some of MacKenzie's policies and actions, they were impressed with the president's "energy and devotion" in pursuing what he believed was best for the college; they appreciated his accessibility and willingness to meet with student groups, and they recognized the conflicting interests with which he was dealing.[170]

If disgruntled Grovers wanted to be treated as adults, a student argued, they must approach the administration and board "as mature, responsible individuals with concrete proposals," which would be more appealing to the board's "hard-headed businessmen."[171] Thomas Sweet, '77, disagreed with *The Collegian*'s contention that trust and honesty between students and administrators was absent at Grove City; he had found MacKenzie and Ross Foster to be very willing to discuss issues.[172] *The Collegian* urged students to use normal channels to try to change college policies. Jay Porter, '75, claimed, however, that this was a dead end. When 350 students assembled outside Memorial Hall in May 1973 to protest college policies, administrators' only response had been to threaten them. Faculty members, he alleged, feared that challenging the trustees and administrators might jeopardize their jobs.[173]

In 1973, three students created *The Entrepreneur* to promote free-market economics, a strong national defense, laissez-faire government, and the death of communism. That May, independent groups began participating in the singing contest on Parent's Weekend and its name was changed from Greek Sing to All-College Sing. In September, *Collegian* staff questioned the college's "unqualified support of the American way of life with its traditional rights and freedoms" asserted in the catalog. "Is our country so righteous, progressive, and responsive to our needs," they asked, "that its every action deserves our 'unqualified' support?" Where, they added, can we find a list of these "traditional rights and freedoms"?[174] A month later, *The Collegian* emphasized the aspects of college that made it special: its Christian heritage, friendly students, and dedicated faculty with whom students could have meaningful personal relationships.[175]

MacKenzie wanted all students to be exposed to "a mature Christian world view," not to have a Christian worldview forced on them. He hoped that students would develop the "capacity to evaluate and weigh the concepts and ideas underlying government, business, and personal living" and to analyze the worldviews currently competing for allegiance.[176]

In 1973, *The Collegian* saluted the Gedunk, which had opened in 1954 and received its name from men who had served in the navy and used this word for dunking donuts in coffee. For two decades, it has been the hub of college social life. Students met there for recreation and relaxation, discussion of "innovative and invigorating ideas," and strengthening interpersonal relationships.[177]

In a January 1974 survey, 47 percent of juniors rated the quality of the faculty on a four-point scale, a four, while 38 percent gave it a three. Asked to choose which three among a variety of factors led them to attend Grove City, 76 percent said low cost, 65 percent said academic quality, and only 16 percent said Christian philosophy.[178] That month, SGA president Bill Sparks, '74, regretfully reported that students had been unable to increase self-rule and individual responsibility in large part because the trustees had set ways of how to run the college. Sparks urged the trustees to come to campus more often and talk with students to gain a better understanding of their concerns.[179] Former *The Collegian* editor in chief senior Chip Mander argued in April 1974 that the four main complaints at Grove City were its favoring of conservative perspectives, "force-fed Christianity," lack of variety in student backgrounds, and limited social and cultural opportunities.[180]

Although they welcomed the chance to have greater interaction with men, women had long opposed coed dining because of their concerns about long lines, going out in inclement weather, and poorer food quality in the men's cafeteria.[181] After both women and men women voted decisively for coed dining in February 1974, complete coed dining was adopted that spring. In response, *The*

Collegian derisively declared, "Grove City finally entered the 19th century last week."[182]

Many students called for lowering the drinking age in Pennsylvania to eighteen. One stressed that Pennsylvania was surrounded by other states with a lower drinking age and Grovers who drove to nearby states to drink risked being arrested or having a car accident. Moreover, eighteen-year-olds could marry and serve on juries and had to pay income tax.[183] Others contended that students who were twenty-one or older should be permitted to drink in moderation on campus.[184]

In 1974, the college announced that it would begin admitting equal numbers of women and men. *The Collegian* hoped that a balanced sex ratio would lead more women to SGA executive positions, the college establishing women's sports teams, and men having less awe of "the feminine mystique."[185] Administrators announced in February 1974 that freshmen whose social and academic records demonstrated their successful adjustment to college life and had parental approval would receive self-regulated hours after the spring recess of their second semester.[186]

In September 1974, the Discipline Committee was established to replace the Student Court and the Venue Committee (which had both heard cases). The committee consisted of the academic dean, five faculty appointed by the president, and the five former members of the Student Court. *The Collegian* objected to the committee's intention to keep its proceedings strictly confidential; the benefits of an open trial far outweighed "the detrimental effects of public embarrassment."[187] That fall, the college statements forbidding violations of "Christian sexual standards" and gambling on college property were eliminated.[188]

After arriving in fall 1974, dean of the chapel Bruce Thielemann strove to raise the social consciousness of students, especially about the world hunger crisis. Each fall, several chapel programs and numerous classes focused on world hunger. Beginning in 1974, for several years, students fasted for twenty-four hours each fall to raise money for various organizations working to alleviate hunger.

The town's mayor, James Perry, insisted in 1974 that community residents regarded Grove City as one of the finest liberal arts colleges in the nation. He was impressed with the sterling character and admirable conduct of most students; during the past three years, the police had had few problems with students. He thanked fraternities and sororities for their service projects.[189]

In 1975, the college finally made block housing, which had long been granted to fraternities, available to sororities and independent women's and men's groups. In spring 1975, Hilda Kring created the Orchesis dance troupe, whose annual shows quickly became among the most popular ones on campus. A large crowd watched the first full-scale Orchesis production in late February 1976.

In a May 1975 survey of all four classes, 38 percent of students rated the faculty average, 45 percent above average, and 6 percent excellent. Women rated the college's athletic facilities above average, while men rated them below average. Women rated their dorms above average, while men rated theirs below average.[190] Eighty-six percent of respondents to a December 1975 survey said they were content with their overall experience at Grove City, a substantially higher percentage than the national average.[191] Moreover, in a 1980 survey, 34 percent of the respondents from the class of 1975 rated their experience at GCC as excellent, 49 percent as good, 14 percent as fair, and only 2 percent as poor.[192]

Nothing created more problems for MacKenzie's administration than the college's policies on and the ending of off-campus housing in 1981. In 1971, Fred Kring explained that students living off campus were expected to act responsibly, follow community standards, and obey local, state, and federal laws. Those under age twenty-one were prohibited from consuming alcohol.[193] Many students defended off-campus living. One objected that this housing was often viewed as a den of immorality that produced bad habits, but it had educational benefits and cost less.[194] *The Collegian* complained in 1977 that the college's strict rules for off-campus housing very negatively affected student morale and student-administration relations.[195]

In fall 1978 *The Echo* replaced *The Gyre* as a creative outlet for students. That December, Julie Furber, '80, became the first woman to be elected SGA president, while a writer for *The Collegian* praised how well social affairs operated under the "astute leadership" of Paul McNulty.[196] A Middle States survey in May 1979 found that students believed the faculty were genuinely interested in them, that students were encouraged to think for themselves, and that 85 percent of Grovers would recommend the college to high school students.[197]

In response to an SGA survey in October 1979, 80 percent of students said they were not "fully aware of the extent of the rules and penalties at GCC before attending"; 62 percent believed that the college rules "were deliberately withheld" to encourage them to attend; 67 percent thought that students had no voice in determining these rules; and 43 percent said they would not have enrolled if they had fully understood the rules. *The Collegian* editor in chief Tom Michaelian, '80, was appalled. If students were unaware of the rules, it was because of their ignorance, not the college's deception. Why anyone would devote $13,000 and four years of their lives without carefully checking an institution's regulations, he maintained, was a mystery. Many alumni, he added, also had gripes about the college, but most of them would call their experience at Grove City "invaluable."[198]

Tension continued, and in mid-October 1979, about five hundred students attended an open forum to discuss campus issues. Two primary student concerns were the enforcement of the "twelve-inch rule" in intervisitation and rumors of an administrative crackdown. Ross Foster emphasized that board played a very active role in college life, and he and MacKenzie stated that the trustees viewed expanding intervis hours as "nonnegotiable."[199] The forum made it clear, MacKenzie lamented, that some students strongly disagreed with college rules even though they had been "carefully and prayerfully" crafted for the long-term well-being of the college community.[200]

The 1980 Middle States team reported that most students supported the college's rules and regulations except for the intervis policy. Students wanted to meet regularly with the trustees about matters that affected them. The evaluators were concerned that many students thought that their views could not be effectively conveyed to administrators and trustees through regular channels. Many students wanted more counseling services.[201]

In 1980–1981, seventy-two students resided in thirty apartments or houses. The trustees' decision to end off-campus housing in fall 1981 unleashed a torrent of frustration and dissent. Eighty-four percent of Grovers disagreed with decision, and 93 percent of upperclassmen thought that the trustees should have had discussed it with students before making the decision.[202] Unilaterally eliminating off-campus housing offended many students' "sense of right and wrong," and they protested that a privilege had been unjustly taken away.[203] MacKenzie asserted that problems with off-campus housing had increased substantially in the last six years. Numerous "loud and crowded beer blasts" held there had violated the school's standards and threatened its reputation. Sixty percent of all recent disciplinary cases were related to off-campus housing, where only 5 percent of students lived.[204] MacKenzie repudiated rumors that the trustees and administration planned to make regulations even more restrictive; they wanted to keep rules to a minimum, while maintaining the college's values and standards.[205]

In 1982, *The Bridge* was chosen from fifty-two submissions to replace the *Ouija* as the name of the college yearbook. The change was made both because of the *Ouija*'s Satanic implications and because this name had no significance for the college.[206] That May, half the student body performed in Parents' Day's twenty-five events, including the first crowning of a spring king.

In 1983, the Florence MacKenzie Campus-Community Award, named in honor of the president's wife Florence, who had died of cancer in 1981, was created to celebrate annually the contributions a town resident and a college professor, staff member, or student made to the life of the community. The first winners were Hilda Kring and borough council president James Montgomery.

In October 1984, MacKenzie reported that since off-campus housing had been terminated, the number of discipline problems had decreased dramatically.[207] That fall, a poll in *The Collegian* found that a high percentage of respondents wanted more intervis hours, principally because there were few places on campus where men and women could study together. Many students were frustrated that they were told to act as mature adults but were not given the chance to demonstrate their maturity.[208]

When Grove City students were asked in 1985 to select the two most important reasons they attended college, to get a good job received 56 percent of their votes, to be trained in a specific field received 40 percent, and formulating goals and values for life received 30 percent (which was very similar to the results of a national survey). The poll also found that students were much more focused on obtaining happiness, affluence, and security than on working to procure justice, equity, and integrity.[209]

In mid-March 1986, about five hundred students, led by seniors Kathy Gardner and Matt Price, gathered outside Crawford Hall, and one thousand students signed a statement calling on the administration to create a student board to help remedy various problems, set more clearly defined rules for conduct, and establish specific time periods for the revocation of Greek charters. They sang Greek songs and the alma mater and presented their petition to administrators. It expressed support for the college's traditions, "high academic standards," and Christian values and argued that the Greek system was valuable. Signers acknowledged that Greeks had made mistakes, but they protested that administrative policies were threatening to destroy the Greek system.[210]

In the late 1980s, hacky sack was a favorite pastime at Grove City. To graduate without ever playing the game was "a fate almost as bad as never have being kissed" on Rainbow Bridge."[211] In 1987, ballroom dancing lessons were offered for the first time, and a fitness craze swept campus. The next September, the college celebrated the two hundredth anniversary of the US Constitution with a program featuring speeches, band performances, and a historical reenactment, underscoring Grove City's commitment to America's democratic values. In the late 1980s, women gained more key campus leadership positions as Laura Ritchey, '87, was elected the

SGA president and Allyson Baird, '88, the ODK president. In 1989, one thousand three hundred people attended the Tri Rhos men's housing group's fifth extravaganza, one of the college's major social events. In fall 1990, the Visiting International Students Association (VISA) was created to help international students adjust to college life. Orchesis, now involving two hundred participants, celebrated its fifteenth anniversary.

Abortion generated more debate and activism among students than any other social issue during the MacKenzie era. Bill Baird returned to campus in September 1971 and called for repealing all laws prohibiting abortion. Evan Adair asserted that many Grove City students agreed with Baird that laws forbidding the dissemination of birth control material should be repealed.[212] Some students praised the Supreme Court's 1973 *Roe v. Wade* decision, while others deplored it. Junior Samuel Kramer argued that abortion killed innocent, helpless human life and therefore was murder.[213] Political science professor Angelo Codevilla, warned that *Roe v. Wade* would lead to many "chopped-up infant bodies."[214] Agreeing with the court's decision, philosophy professor Richard Trammell countered that an embryo deserved more protection the further it progressed.[215] Senior Jan Diehl averred that because God knew people in the womb, he alone should determine their life and death.[216] Other students urged women contemplating abortions to consider adoption instead.[217] Throughout MacKenzie's presidency, a large Life Advocates contingent strongly promoted the pro-life position through writing newspaper articles, participating in local fundraisers and protest events, and joining the yearly National March for Life in Washington, DC.[218]

The Collegian articles discussed a host of other issues during MacKenzie's two decades as president, including the Israeli-Arab conflict, whether Richard Nixon should resign, the energy crisis, the legalization of drugs, AIDS, homosexuality, the nuclear freeze movement, prayer in public schools, apartheid in South Africa, gun control, and capital punishment.

The activities of numerous clubs and honoraries enriched campus life. A business honorary, Delta Mu Delta, was established in 1972. In February 1978, the college's Pi Gamma Mu chapter became one of only nine in the nation to have initiated more than one thousand members. In March 1976, the Management Association held its second annual J. Howard Pew Memorial Management Day featuring future board of trustees' president J. Paul Sticht. Operation Top Management was established in the mid-1970s to enable juniors and seniors to interact with chief corporate executives. Since its creation in 1938, the Outing Club had been often one of the college's most popular organizations. Its activities included canoeing, white-water rafting, caving, rock-climbing, white-water rafting, and parachuting. In the 1980s, Circle K and Student Activities for the Elderly engaged in numerous community service projects. In 1989, the Law Club was formed.

In an October 1980 student poll, 64 percent supported Ronald Reagan, 18 percent independent John Anderson, and 12 percent Democratic incumbent Jimmy Carter. The following March, David Peiffer argued that conservativism abounded on campus. The "free market economic philosophy, Creationist speakers, a John Birch Society speaker, and a growing Christian Action Council" all testified to the visibility of the right. He beseeched politically liberal students to come out of hiding and engage in dialogue and debate.[219] In a 1984 student poll, Reagan received 90 percent of the votes compared with Democratic challenger Walter Mondale's 10 percent. In a tongue-in cheek 1987 article, sophomore Donna Kosik presciently, if prematurely, wrote, "I have the perfect presidential candidate: Donald Trump, the American business tycoon who flaunts his triumphs."[220] The next year, Republican George H. W. Bush received 82 percent of student votes compared with Democrat Michael Dukakis's 9 percent.[221]

Numerous student and organizational achievements were significant. *The Collegian* received a first-class rating for both 1972 semesters. In May 1973, junior Craig Jones was elected an ODK Student Province Deputy, giving him oversight of seventeen circles. The next year, Anne Church, '75, was named the tri-state's most outstanding angel flight member. That year, the George Washington Honor Medals gave Lawrence Reed, '75, the editor of

The Entrepreneur, an award for the journal and another for an article he wrote. In 1976, junior Jodie Mathie received a national award for best fulfilling the angel flight mission, while senior Stanley Larimer received the AFROTC's top engineering award. In 1980, Steve Lowry, '82, won the Pennsylvania Ping-Pong Championship for ages twenty-one and under and finished fourth among contestants of all ages. Lowry was also the MVP for the junior national team that year. Senior Karen Smith received an award for the outstanding research paper at a Beta Beta Beta district conference in 1986. In 1989, Grove City's chapter won an ODK Province Circle of the Year award and a team of four engineering majors earned first place at the Micro Truck Baja National Design contest. In 1990, another team of engineering students won four first place awards for their "Bigfoot" at a competition at Central Florida University. The 97 percent pass rate of the teacher certification test by Grove City education majors in 1990 was the highest of any college in Pennsylvania. In 1991, Grove City took first place in the Fifth Annual Walking Machine Decathlon and received the SAE's Allied-Signal Outstanding Student Performance Award, the first time in the twenty-eight-year history of the award that it went to an undergraduate church-related college.

Greek Life

Greek life flourished during the MacKenzie years, as fraternities and sororities supplied many campus leaders, organized numerous dances and parties, engaged in hotly contested athletic events, and did various service projects. The Greek organizations typically received 250 to 325 members each year until 1986, when the number was reduced because several fraternities were suspended. Many students continued to question the value of Greek organizations and to criticize the conduct of their members. Almost all the fraternities and a few sororities lost their charters at least once between 1971 and 1991, primarily for violations of college alcohol, rushing, or pledging policies, but also for behavior that disgraced the college at All-College Sing, food fights, damaging college property, renting houses to hold parties, and various pranks. Some students contended that independent life was superior to that of the Greeks.

In November 1971, Mark DeWalt argued that independents had superior sports programs than Greeks, sponsored more campus activities, produced more varsity athletes, and participated more frequently in musical groups and campus forums. Herb Goetz, '72, accused Greeks of elitism and incorrectly painting independent life as boring.[222] Freshman David Bailey contended that many Greeks were not living according to Christian values and that some of them were hostile to Christianity.[223]

Defenders of Greek organizations emphasized their many good works. They built homecoming floats, participated in Greek Sing, completed numerous services projects, and led many campus organizations.[224] Fraternity members were a positive force on campus, not "beer-swilling troublemakers," two Greeks argued. They raised funds for many charitable causes, furnished the heads of student governmental and religious organizations, provided most OB members and varsity athletes, and fostered brotherhood and loyalty.[225] Kathy Gardner maintained that Grovers could be both dedicated Greeks and devout Christians, demonstrated by their roles as chapel aides and Salt Company board members.[226]

Pledging continued to generate considerable controversy. Brian Leftow was "constantly astonished" by what students were willing to endure to attain "the exalted status" of active brothers. Fraternities, he joked, spent more to win and woo new pledges than medieval squires did to court their fair ladies.[227] Henry Pearce, '76, challenged Leftow's assertion that pledging was based solely on seeing "how much idiocy" students would endure before becoming "revolted and revolting." He countered that pledging was designed to familiarize initiates with active members and fraternities' goals and pursuits. Pearce insisted that his brothers had never pressured him to do anything contrary to his "Christian standards."[228] Another Greek argued that pledging instilled "unity and a sense of accomplishment and pride."[229]

The campus was rocked in mid-February 1974 when four Adel pledges were struck and killed by a car as they were walking back to campus on the highway south of Grove City with thirteen other initiates after a "drop off." Fraternity pledging was suspended for five days until their memorial service was held in Harbison Chapel.[230]

Many students protested in February 1979 that the college punished the Diks too severely by revoking their charter for a year because of rushing violations. MacKenzie and Foster met with the Inter-Fraternity and Pan-Hellenic councils to address Greek grievances. Fraternity leaders strove to dispel the image of their members as heavy drinking hell-raisers.[231]

In 1983 fraternity pledging rules were revised to shorten the initiation period and place greater emphasis on moral values and personal development. In 1986, the Pennsylvania legislature passed an antihazing law that substantially changed Grove City's fraternity pledging. The initiation process at Grove City was significantly modified to conform to these new laws, and pledging was renamed "gadding"—going active days.

The college began recognizing men's housing groups in 1975, and by 1987, nine groups were functioning. In February 1987, simmering controversy between housing groups and fraternities intensified. Members of the housing groups stressed that like fraternities they built floats, played sports against each other, and had parties. They protested that some fraternity members seemed to assume that certain privileges, including using Greek letters, belong to them alone.[232]

Throughout the MacKenzie years, fraternities and sororities sponsored a Greek weekend that included a water balloon fight, a three-legged race, a root-beer chug, hot dog- and pie-eating contests, a tug-of-war, and a dance. Many years Greeks also held a Help Week, during which they hosted basketball clinics, did handyman work at churches, cleaned and painted community buildings, improved hiking trails at the Krings' farm, remodeled the Borough Recreation Center, and engaged in other service projects.

Music

The quality of Grove City's music program increased significantly during MacKenzie's presidency, thanks in large part to the arrival of Ed Arnold in 1976, who directed the marching band, and Doug Browne in 1981, who oversaw the touring choir. In 1972, under Oscar Cooper's leadership, the forty-three-member touring choir undertook a three-thousand-three-hundred-mile trip, performing eleven concerts, and singing at Disney World, Maxwell Air Force Base in Alabama, and an Easter sunrise service in Miami, where Billy Graham spoke. In spring 1975, the marching band had seventy-five members, ten more than the college's symphonic band. Arnold's first year, the marching band swelled to 127 participants—ninety instrumentalists, a sixteen-woman dance team, a twelve-person flag core, six rifle bearers, and three feature twirlers. In 1980, the band numbered 160 when it performed between games of a Pirates-Astros doubleheader at Three Rivers Stadium. Two years later, the 211-member college band again performed there, this time before and during half time of Grove City's football game against Duquesne. Under Browne's leadership, the touring choir sang at Pennsylvania Music Educators Association conferences in 1984 and 1991 and the Music Educators National Conference at Baltimore in 1987.

WSAJ

WSAJ, operated entirely by students, began its fifty-fifth year in fall 1974 by airing soft rock, classical music, jazz, news, live broadcasts of football and basketball games, and some chapel services and public service programming. The next spring, the station was on the air thirteen hours a day. In 1980, WSAJ strove to upgrade its image on campus as it broadcasted world, national, and campus news, sports, and jazz, classical, and rock and roll music 110 hours per week. In 1985, programming consisted of contemporary Christian music, top-forty songs, live vesper services, nightly news, interviews of faculty and other guests, "entertainment this week," a sports show, and broadcasts of all football and men's and women's basketball games. In 1987, WSAJ increased from ten to two hundred watts, giving it a thirty-mile listening radius. In 1989, Joe Klimchak, '91, became the sports programs director at WSAJ; the college's future sports information director sought to make his new morning show "the hottest thing on campus." The next year, Klimchak became the station's program director, as WSAJ aired classical, jazz, modern progressive jazz, and big band music, college sports, and a morning news program.

AFROTC

In spring 1976, Christine Cicotello, '77, became the first woman to head the ROTC cadets, who numbered one hundred. In 1987, the air force decided to close Grove City's long-standing ROTC detachment because of federal budget cuts, marking the fourth time in college history that a military program had been discontinued. Since 1951, the detachment had been an important part of college life, sponsoring an annual formal ball, parade reviews on Parents' Day, and Veterans Day chapel services. Most significantly, the program produced six hundred officers for the air force. To celebrate ROTC's distinguished history at Grove City, on April 18, 1989, a ceremony was held at the flagpole on the upper quad.

Guest Performers

From 1971 to 1991, numerous popular performers entertained faculty, students, and community residents. Musician headliners included: Alice Cooper; Kris Kristofferson; Rita Coolidge; the McCoys; the Nitty Gritty Dirt Band; John Sebastian; Don McLean (renowned for "American Pie"); Blood, Sweat, and Tears; Kansas; opera singer Jerome Hines; organist Virgil Fox; Pure Prairie League; the Atlanta Rhythm Section; England Dan and John Ford Coley; Disney World keyboard synthesizer wizard Michael Iceberg; the Canadian Opera Company; Fred Waring; the Preservation Hall Jazz Band; the Eastman Philharmonic; and contemporary Christian singer Twilia Paris. Other entertainers included pantomimist Marcel Marceau, William Windom doing a one-man show on James

Thurber, magician Harry Blackstone Jr., and touring companies performing *Company, Godspell,* and *Fiddler on the Roof.*

Women's Athletics

Women continued to play only club sports against teams from other colleges and intramurals among themselves until the college joined an athletic association that enabled them to compete in three varsity sports beginning in fall 1976. In 1973, "pretty freshman Betty Zembower" was the only diver on the men's swimming team.[233] In 1973–1974, 950 women participated in fourteen intramural sports (some women played multiple sports); the most popular sport was volleyball. Led by number one player freshman Joanne Landis, a club tennis team finished 11–1 in 1974, while the club volleyball team went 14–4, foreshadowing the great success both varsity teams would enjoy throughout the 1980s. In 1976, her coach Terry Ellis argued that Betsy Young, '77, who led the volleyball team to a 13–1 record, probably had no peers in the tristate area.[234] In 1975, Ellen Pollock, '77, became first woman to run on the men's cross-country team. That fall, she finished second and fifth at large women's invitationals. The next fall, she placed second at a three-mile race in Schenley Park in Pittsburgh, featuring fifty of the region's top women runners.

The passage of Title IX in 1972, mandating gender equality in college sports, and the organization of women's athletic teams at nearby colleges led Grove City to create several varsity women's teams during MacKenzie's presidency: basketball, volleyball, and tennis in 1976; cross-country in 1979; softball in 1980; track and field in 1987; and swimming and diving in 1988. Grove City participated in the Women's Keystone Conference from 1976 to 1985 and the President's Athletic Conference beginning in 1985 (in 1985, women from Grove City played in both leagues). While all the women's teams fared well, volleyball, tennis, and basketball were especially successful.

Under coaches Terry Ellis, Judy Zarenko, and Susan Roberts, Grove City's team was among the best D3 volleyball ones in the nation from 1976 to 1991. While playing numerous D1, D2, and top D3 schools, all three coaches compiled extraordinary records, and their teams were often ranked in the top ten in the nation. From 1976 to 1982, Ellis had a record of 181–54–1 (.770); her squads captured five WKC championships, finished in the top eight four times in the Eastern Association for Intercollegiate Athletics for Women, and participated in two NCAA D3 postseason tournaments. Zarenko's record was 67–17 (.798), and her teams won two WKC titles and an NCAA first-round playoff game in 1984. Roberts's teams went 104–16 (.867) from 1985 to 1987. From 1985 to 1991, the squad claimed four PAC titles and played in two NCAA tournaments.

The two most successful volleyball teams were the 1982 squad, which finished 37–8 and won two games in the NCAA playoffs before losing in five sets to archrival Juniata, and the 1985 team, which went 41–1. This team was ranked number two in the nation for much of the season. Unfortunately, the team lost in the first round of the NCAA playoffs. Roberts was chosen as the D3 volleyball coach of the year, and setter Barb Beck, '86, and middle hitter Sue Shadle, '87, were named All-Americans. Shadle was selected as a first-team All-American the next fall.

Other noteworthy volleyball players are Carla Wetzel, '82, Natalie Sutyak, '83, and Lisa Lippincott, '93. Wetzel earned eleven varsity letters—four in volleyball, four in basketball, and three in softball. Sutyak was honorable mention for the 1982 All-American D3 volleyball team, becoming Grove City's first female athlete to earn All-America honors. Ellis called her the best middle blocker/middle hitter in the East.[235] Lippincott earned second team All-America laurels in 1992 and helped lead the Lady Wolverines to conference titles in 1989 and 1992.

Under coach Patti Zbell, the tennis team had an astounding 110–9 record (.924) between 1979 and 1990 and won the PAC championship five of the six seasons in which the college belonged to the conference. The leading tennis players were Betty Rae Gray, '82, Tracy Penn, '86, and Anne Kister, '88. Gray had a 34–7 record at first singles and led the team to a 31–1 mark her final three years. Penn went 63–2 at number one singles and doubles between 1981 and 1985. Kister, a math secondary education major with a 3.99 QPA, was 26–3 in singles and 28–1 in doubles her junior and senior years and was named to the first-team GTE Academic All-American At-Large Team; she was the first Grove City player in any sport to be named to the first team since 1973.

Spearheaded by Jodie Imbrie '83, the program's all-time leading scorer with 2,288 points, and Karen Watkins, '82, who is third all-time in rebounds, the basketball team, under Terry Ellis, had a fantastic 89–16 (.847) record between 1978 and 1983. The team went 16–1 in 1979–1980, losing in the first round of EAIAW tournament. Imbrie averaged 22.6 ppg and was second in scoring among D3 schools in the eastern region. She was the third-highest scorer in D3 in 1981–1982, averaging 24.8 ppg. Imbrie was an EIAWA all-region team selection, as the team went 19–6 and lost its first-round NCAA tournament game. She scored forty-one points against Youngstown State in late January 1983 to set a college record for most points in a game. Her senior year, Imbrie averaged 28.5 ppg and was named to the Kodak Women's Basketball Team, consisting of the top ten small college players in the nation. Ellis praised her intensity, work ethic, and love and respect for her teammates. On the court, Imbrie was a "tiger" who played with her head and heart; a coach had an athlete like her only once in her career.[236] The 1982–1983 team finished 22–5 and defeated Susquehanna, ranked second in the nation, 60–58 in round one of the NCAA tournament, before losing 59–55 to Elizabethtown in the next round.

In 1986–1987, the basketball team went 17–3 and won the PAC. The team was led by PAC MVP Monica Yustak, '87, who is third in career ppg (15.5) and Carolyn Cochrane, '89, who had 1,153 points and 1,110 rebounds (first all-time) in her career.

The Wolverine women won their five consecutive WKC all-sports trophies from 1980 to 1984, besting seven other schools including Mercyhurst. In 1983–1984, the women's sports teams collectively went 73–22 (.768).

Martha Fox, '81, led the first two women's varsity cross-country teams. In 1979, the women won all four meets in which they participated; Fox finished twelfth of 240 runners at the California (PA) Invitational that fall. In fall 1987, the women were ninth at the NCAA Mideast Regional Qualifier and senior Cindy Langwig finished forty-fourth at nationals. Three years later, Cathy Williams, '92, was sixty-third at nationals. The women won the PACs in 1989, 1990, and 1991.

The best stretch for the softball team was from 1985 to 1988, when the Lady Wolverines went a combined 60–28. Softball stars included Dianna Cokain, '85, whose career batting average of .375 is fifth all-time and shortstop Tammy Leonard, '88, who helped lead the Wolverines to their first two PAC titles in 1986 and 1987 and hit .400 in 1988. Pitcher Michelle Kirin, '90, is first all-time in complete games and in career wins with 44, second in innings pitched, and fourth in strikeouts and career ERA at 2.58.

The women's track and field team won all its conference meets in its inaugural season. In 1988, the squad placed first at an eight-team meet at Hiram. Patty Brain, '88, is second all-time in the high jump; Leslie Long, '89, ranks third in the long jump; and Connie Houston, '91, is third in the shot put.

Men's Athletics

During the MacKenzie years, three men's teams coached by Jim Longnecker—cross-country, track and field, and swimming and diving—and the tennis team coached by Joe Walter consistently had outstanding results, and the basketball, soccer, golf, and wrestling teams had some superb seasons. Chip Mander argued in 1973 that Grove City was facing increasingly good competition and that the college needed to provide better athletic facilities, give more academic scholarships to athletes, and recruit more effectively.[237] To a large extent, Mander's plea was answered.

During fall 1971, the men's cross-country team, led by All-American Paul Cameron thumped several opponents 15-50 (all seven Grove City runners finished before any of their opponents). In two meets in October, Cameron lowered the college's 4.1 course record by a combined one minute. The harriers finished 10–1 as Cameron won his twenty-second consecutive meet and set course records in his last six meets. The team finished nineteenth among the nation's small colleges, and Cameron earned All-American status by finishing seventeenth. The next season was equally memorable for Cameron and the team. In October 1972, Cameron placed second at the prestigious Malone Invitational, broke Westminster's course record, and won his thirtieth consecutive dual meet. The team finished 10–1 and tied for thirty-second at nationals, which was won by North Dakota State; by finishing twenty-third, Cameron again gained All-American recognition. The 1976 harriers, spearheaded by Cliff Winkler, '78, ranked thirtieth in the nation. At a meet in April 1978, Winkler set a three-mile record of 14.24.5. Led by senior Vern Anderson, the 1989 cross-country team was 8–0, the first undefeated season since 1970. In 1990, the harriers won the Case Western Invitational and the PAC title.

The powerhouse track and field team had the best record of any men's sport during MacKenzie's presidency. Paul Cameron set college records in the two-mile in 1971 (9:31.4) and in the one-mile (4.16) in 1972. That year, senior Jim Thoma established a javelin record and sophomore Chuck Fitz set the 880 mark. From 1957 to 1972, Longnecker's team compiled a 113–28 (.820) record. The squad continued to win at this clip during the MacKenzie years. In 1973, sophomore Wayne Sedlak established a record in triple jump of 48'3" (which still stands today), won first place in the triple jump at the All-Pennsylvania Track Classic, and achieved All-American status; in 1975, he set a college broad jump record (which ranks second today). That year, he won titles at invitationals at Penn State and the University of Pittsburgh and became a D3 All-American by placing fifth in the triple jump.

The principal star of the mid-1980s was thrower Jim McElhaney, '86. In May 1985, he became the second Wolverine to earn All-American status in track as he finished second in the javelin and seventh in the shot. In 1986, McElhaney set college records in the shot (53'6") and the javelin (222') (which both still stand today) and the discus (155'8") (which ranks third today). That year, McElhaney earned All-America honors in the discus, javelin, and shot put by finishing second, fifth, and tenth respectively at nationals, singlehandedly placing Grove City nineteenth. In May 1985, CMU defeated Grove City 73–72, breaking the Wolverines' twenty-six straight victory streak. Other standouts in the late 1980s were middle distance runner Brian Herrick, '87, and sprinter Jeff Cass, '89. Herrick is third in college history in the 800 and 1500 meter race. Cass was a PAC MVP and won five individual conference titles and three additional relay titles to help Grove City capture conference crowns three of his four years. Cass holds the school record in the 200 meters (21.26) and is second in the 100 meters. McElhaney, Herrick, and Cass were all selected for the PAC sixtieth anniversary team in 2015.

Longnecker's swimming and diving teams had a remarkable record of 184–52 (.780) during MacKenzie's presidency. Between 1971–1972 and 1983–1984, the Wolverines finished second five times in the Penn-Ohios, competing against mostly D1 and D2 programs. The squad won four PAC championships after Grove City joined the league in 1984. From 1974 to 1984, the team finished in the top seventeen colleges in D3 eight times. The 1974–1975 team went 12–1, sent twelve members to nationals, and finished thirteenth in the country. Eight swimmers—diver Marty Wurl, '78, who placed second in three-meter diving, backstroker Dave Tomashewski, '78, and six relay participants—were named All-Americans. The next year, the college also had eight All-Americans—three in individual events and five in relays; Tomashewski was a double All-American in the 100 and 200 backstroke; Rick Durstein, '77, finished second in the 100 butterfly, and Wurl was ninth in one-meter diving, as the team finished eleventh in the country.

In 1976–1977, the swimmers were fourteenth at nationals. Six Wolverines gained All-American status, including Durstein in the 100 butterfly, Tomashewski in both the 100 and 200 backstroke; Wurl in the low board, and Pat Walsh '78 in the high board. In 1977–1978, six swimmers and divers achieved All-American distinction including Wurl who was second in both diving events and Tomashewski who was fifth in 200 backstroke, and eighth in the 100 backstroke, giving him nine All-American awards; the team again finished fourteenth. In March 1980, six swimmers and divers captured All-American honors, including Chris VanDeMark, '82, who was second in one-meter diving and ninth in three-meter diving and Randy Galm, '81, who finished ninth in the 200 freestyle. In 1981, the team finished tenth in the nation, propelled by VanDeMark's first place finishes in one-meter and three-meter diving. He was the first Grove City swimmer or diver to win a national champion, and the first diver in D3 history to win both events.

After Longnecker's squad beat Indiana University of Pennsylvania 65–48 in February 1982, *Swimming World* magazine called Grove City one of top ten teams in D3. The team finished 12–0, its second ever undefeated season. Dan Young, '83, placed first in one-meter diving at nationals in 1983; for the third year in a row, a Wolverine diver won this event. The 1983–1984 team finished 11–1. Clark Johnson, '84, won the high-board diving national championship and finished seventh in the low board. Eric Sluss, '86, earned All-American status in the 100 butterfly, 200 butterfly, and with the 400 medley relay team, as Longnecker's troops were twelfth in the nation.

The 1986–1987 squad went 10–0 and won its third consecutive PAC title. The next year's team extended the winning streak to twenty-two before losing to CMU in mid-February 1988. When the college celebrated the fiftieth year of its swimming and diving program in 1990, the teams had a combined 356–180 (.664) record, had captured thirteen conference championships, and had thirty-nine consecutive winning seasons.

The men's tennis team record during MacKenzie's presidency was 129–62 (.675). The 1991 team went 11–1, tying the 1937 and 1965 teams for the most wins in college history. Freshman Srinivasan Balaji from India was 20–1 playing number one singles and doubles as the squad won the PAC title decisively.

The best men's golf teams were in 1974 (12–4–2) and 1990, when the squad placed high in three invitationals and won its first

PAC championship. The best golfers of this period were Bruce Pollock, '74, (who had a 77.7 average in 1973), Rick Hangliter, '88, and Drew Moore, '92, the 1990 PAC medalist.

Under Don Lyle's leadership, the men's soccer team compiled a 149–102–19 (.594) record from 1972 to 1991. The 1976 booters finished 10–3–1, beating Pitt 3–0, recording six shoutouts, and defeating Lynchburg, the number one regional seed, 2–0 in a first-round NCAA tournament game. The 1980 team lost 2–1 to Scranton, the top seeded regional team, in double overtime in the opening round of the NCAA tournament. The 1986 Wolverines were 11–2–1 and ranked seventh in the southern district of D3. Center halfback Phil Ahlschlager, '73, was selected for the West Penn All-Star squad in 1972 and invited to try out for 1975 Pan American games and 1976 Olympics. Doug Hagen, '78, is first in college history in career save percentage and third all-time in fewest goals allowed per game at 0.92, while Tom Shupe, '85, is fifth in career saves and was selected for the All-Pennsylvania-New Jersey-Delaware second team in 1984. In 1986, senior sweeper Bill Juergens became only the fourth Grove City player to be named to the D3 All-American soccer squad.

The men's basketball team, coached by John Barr, earned a berth in the NCAA tournament four times between 1971 and 1991. Led by freshman Bill Fox, the 1975–1976 squad was 16–6. Fox and fellow senior Mike Donahue, both one-thousand-plus-point career scorers, propelled the 1978–1979 team to an 18–7 record. The team lost to Elizabethtown 58–53 in the NCAA tournament but beat Albright 79–73 in the consolation game. In 1979, Donahue, a premed major with a 3.83 QPA, became the first Grove City basketball player to be named to the Academic All-American first team.

Led by senior forwards Bob Crow, the college's second leading scorer with 1,450 points and Mark Smith who tallied 1,171 career points, the 1982–1983 team finished 21–4. The Wolverines lost to Widener University 56–52 in the first round of D3 tournament but beat Moravian 76–54 in the consolation game. *The Pittsburgh Press* selected Crow as its Co-Player of the Year and as a member of the 1982–1983 All-District Small College Team. The newspaper named

Barr named the District Coach of the Year. Led by senior forward Joe Buckley, the college's third leading all-time scorer with 1,415 points, the 1988–1989 Wolverines finished 20–6 and won the PAC. The 1990–1991 hoopsters captured their third consecutive PAC title and had the eleventh-best defense in D3.

The 1971–1972 wrestling team, led by senior Dave Cox (11–0), junior Bob Lewis (9–1), and freshman Eugene Brown (9–2), who all went to nationals, was 7–4–1. Cox finished with a career record of 36–12–2, surpassing Charlie Purdue for most wins as a wrestler. Dave Baughman, '78, earned All-American distinction in 1976 and 1978. He finished his career 36–16–4 to tie Cox for the most wins in wrestling history. Grove City discontinued its wrestling program in 1980.

The baseball team program produced several exceptional players. Baseball captain Dave Kerestly, '72, was chosen along with football player Jeff Lane, '72, for the *Outstanding College Athletes of America* in 1972 based on their athletic achievement, community service, extracurricular activities, character, and leadership. Kerestly is seventh in career ERA (2.57) and fifth in single-season ERA (1.59). John Senkowitz, '87, has the fourth-highest career on-base percentage in college history. Sophomore John Avdellas's .493 batting average in 1988 is the highest ever. Pitcher Dave Meadows, '91, is second in complete games.

Jack Behringer stepped down after sixteen years as the head football coach following the 1972 season. After Joe Kopnisky led the team for a decade, Chris Smith, '72, the college's recordholder for career interceptions, took the helm in 1984. During the MacKenzie era, the program produced many superb players. Halfback Chuck Gaetano, '74, ranks sixth in rushing in college history with 2,403 yards. Wide receiver Jeff Mateer, '87, is third all-time in receptions (145) and fifth in receiving yardage (1,857). Defensive back Tony Colangelo, '91, is second in career interceptions with sixteen. Quarterback Jeff Cass finished his career with the most passing yards in Grove City history, was named to the regional GTE All-Star team, and is currently second all-time in career punt return yardage. Doug Hart, '89, made the most career field goals (forty), set the PAC record for most field goals in a career, and in 1987, became Grove City's first-ever first-team Kodak All-American Team, Division 2 selection.

The 1976 men's and women's fall sports teams had a phenomenal combined record of 43–8–1 (.843). In 1981–1982, Grove City teams were 140–70 (.667), the highest winning percentage since 1968–69.

Several Grove City club teams competed against other colleges during the MacKenzie years. Rifle team member Paul Whitworth, '71, placed fourth in 1972 US Olympic trials, just missing a trip to Munich. Club teams were organized in ice hockey in 1973, water polo in 1974, and volleyball in 1980. In spring 1982, the Grove City club team won the northern division of the Western Pennsylvania Intercollegiate Bowling Conference.

In addition to its many stellar varsity and club teams, the college had a strong intramural program, with separate Greek and independent leagues that involved hundreds of men and women playing a wide variety of sports. *The Collegian* sports editor Paul Simoff, '75, argued that no college of comparable size had a program with so many sports and participants and such intense competition as Grove City.[238]

Alumni

During MacKenzie's presidency, the alumni became more involved in the life of the college, increased their donations to the college, and had many significant achievements. Grove City's centennial year celebration featured exhibitions of alumnae artists Maude Winder and Margaret Williams. With Betty (Casey) Prince, '38, serving as the director of alumni giving, a record high $336,000 was donated in 1983. Two years later, the former May queen and president of Pi Gamma Mu received an Alumni Achievement Award. The wife of Pirate announcer Bob Prince was a community activist and a longtime board member of Presbyterian Association on Aging. Other award winners in the 1980s included television, stage, and recording artist Marcia D'Arcangelo, '67; James Hunter,

'63, the Pennsylvania Commissioner of Higher Education; twins Elizabeth (Graham) Lotz, '50, and Janet (Graham) de Araujo, '50, who served on the mission field for several decades in Bolivia and Brazil, respectively; Judith (Chittum) Flynn, '66, who held numerous executive positions in the business world; Patricia Ecker, '63, an Emmy-winning television reporter in Los Angeles; Michael Mawhinney, '67, an authority on hormone action in neoplastic tissue; and Don Hayes, '59, the president of GTE Data Series, the third-largest company of its kind in the United States.

The Trustees

During MacKenzie's tenure, students often complained that the trustees had too much power and were unaware of what was happening on campus, while the president defended their status and understanding of student concerns. MacKenzie argued that the trustees were very open to meeting with student groups; they were more attentive to the problems students perceived than students realized and were "sensitive and eager" to meet their "real needs."[239] Some students recognized the significant financial contributions the trustees made to the college and their strong interest in its well-being. Student dissent prompted the trustees to visit the campus in late October 1972 and meet privately with faculty and student leaders about a five-day class week, self-regulated hours, coed dining, and other topics.[240]

In December 1973, senior Mark Ketterer protested that MacKenzie and the board were trying to preserve the era in which they grew up and did not respect his generation's independently minded people. MacKenzie responded that many changes during the last two years had reduced in loco parentis.[241] Other students, including SGA president Julie Furber, complained that board members received too little input from students.[242] *The Collegian* editor in chief Chris Klicka, '82, argued that the trustees apparently made their decisions "very arbitrarily" and needed to better understand what students thought about key issues.[243] Several trustees visited campus regularly, especially Robert Lamont, Phillip Smith, R. Heath

Larry, and Fred Fetterolf. One of his most difficult jobs, MacKenzie explained, was "keeping six constituencies in harmony": the trustees, students, faculty, alumni, townsfolk, and major donors; five of them had a long-term perspective; the students' short-term one often produced conflict between them and the trustees.[244]

Shortly after MacKenzie's presidency began, J. Howard Pew died on November 27, 1971. Born in 1882, Pew became one of America's greatest twentieth-century industrialists and philanthropists. After graduating from Grove City College in 1900, he studied thermodynamics and structural design at Boston Tech (renamed MIT). He worked at Sun Oil Company, founded by his father Joseph Newton Pew, as an engineer, assistant superintendent, superintendent, vice president, and finally as president from 1912 to until 1947. During his presidency, Sun Oil immensely expanded it work, operating in thirty-five states and Canada. Pew was a key leader of the American Petroleum Institute and a principal spokesperson for the oil industry. During World War I, he served on the federal government's National Petroleum War Service Committee, and during World War II, he was a member of the government's Petroleum Industry War Council.

Pew was the president of Grove City's board of trustees from 1931 until his death. John Van Til argued that Pew's devotion to and interest in Grove City College "may be unmatched in the annals of higher education."[245] For more than thirty years, Pew was the president of the board of trustees of the General Assembly of the Presbyterian Church, USA. In 1950, Pew chaired the National Lay Committee of the National Council of Churches, which represented thirty-four million Protestants. He urged the council and congregations to focus on evangelism, Christian education, and spiritual nurture rather than on political and social activism. Pew helped establish the Presbyterian Lay Committee, which concentrated on promoting evangelism and biblical teaching and trying to revitalize the PCUSA. Pew and other PLC members adamantly opposed the Presbyterian Confession of 1967, arguing that it diluted Christian faith and denied the authority of scripture.[246] In addition, Pew served as an elder at First Presbyterian Church in Ardmore near Philadelphia, a director of the National Association of Manufacturers, president of the United Presbyterian Foundation, and a trustee of Jefferson Hospital in Philadelphia. On November 30, 1971, the college held a memorial service in Harbison Chapel simultaneously with Pew's funeral service at his church in Ardmore, at which Billy Graham spoke. Graham, who partnered with Pew to found *Christianity Today*, described him as one of America's best-informed laymen "on the Bible and on religious matters." A writer for *The Collegian* asserted that Pew strongly defended the free enterprise system, generously supported conservative political, social, and economic causes, "lived austerely," and "avoided publicity."[247] Pew was well known for his devout Christian faith, remarkable stamina, robust work ethic, and deep love of human liberty. Van Til described Pew as "a rugged individualist," "integrity personified," a "great Christian steward," and a "genius of enterprise."[248] Albert Hopeman told Grove City faculty in June 1972, "I will always remember Mr. Pew admonishing us to 'inculcate in the minds and hearts of the students an abiding faith in God and country, a love of freedom, a respect for truth, an acceptance of personal responsibility, and a desire to contribute to the betterment of the human race.'"[249]

Conclusion

After trustee search committee members evaluated 150 candidates, they chose Jerry Combee as Grove City's sixth president in 1991. MacKenzie was confident that Combee would lead with "great vision and insight." Combee promised the college would continue to promote excellence as it built upon its Christian foundation.[250]

MacKenzie led a major curricular revision, hired more gifted faculty, balanced the male-female ratio, instituted coed dining, and oversaw several building projects, most notably the Pew Fine Arts Center and a major addition to the Physical Learning Center. Since the Keystone Curriculum was devised in 1973–1974, Grove City's core courses have been the centerpiece of its educational enterprise. The core has given students a common intellectual foundation and expressed the college's commitment to teaching and embodying truths about God, the created world, and human flourishing as revealed in scripture and the natural world to equip students to love and serve God. The faculty praised MacKenzie's commitment to academic excellence, breadth of knowledge, and effort to base the curriculum on a biblical foundation. During his twenty-year tenure, the college's quality and reputation improved significantly.[251] By 1991, an evangelical ethos pervaded campus and that persists today. MacKenzie faced many difficulties, but he stayed because he "recognized the College's incredible potential for greatness."[252] Trustee Richard Jewell lauded MacKenzie for leading Grove City to "its unique place in American higher education" as "a school with true vision and values" whose faculty and students "profess and practice those values."[253]

The 1903 men's basketball team.

The 1909 men's track and field team.

Isaac Ketler, founder of the college and president, 1876–1913.

Tug of war across Wolf Creek in 1913.

May Day celebration in front of Founder's Hall in 1915.

Alexander Ormond, college president, 1913–1916.

Faculty and students at the 1920 summer term.

Samuel Harbison, a college trustee for whom Harbison Chapel is named.

Eleanor Ketler, the 1937 May Queen, and her court.

Military training on campus during World War II.

Navy cadets in 1943.

The Adels in 1943.

Mary Anderson Pew dormitory lounge in the 1940s.

Alva J. Calderwood, dean and professor, 1896–1949.

The 1952 May Day court, the first year the Arena was used for the celebration.

AFROTC cadets in 1953.

Colonial dormitory in the 1950s.

Weir Ketler, college president, 1916–1956.

The Epsilon Pis in 1961.

A Christmas service in Harbison Chapel in the early 1960s.

Freshmen in 1966.

J. Stanley Harker, college president, 1956–1971.

J. Howard Pew, president of the board of trustees, 1931–1971.

Commencement during the 1970s.

The All-College Sing in 1986.

The Gamma Chis at table pounding in 1989.

Charles MacKenzie, college president, 1971–1991.

The ABTs at the 1992 homecoming parade.

Jerry Combee, college president, 1991–1995, with the first class of students to receive notebook computers in 1994.

Albert Hopeman, president of the board of trustees, 1972–1998.

The college marching band at the 2001 homecoming parade.

John Moore, college president, 1996–2003.

Richard Jewell, college president, 2003–2014.

A children's theater production during the 2010s.

Inside Breen Student Center in the 2010s.

David Rathburn, president of the board of trustees, 2003–2020.

President's Athletic Conference football champions, 2023.

Paul J. McNulty, college president, 2014–2025.

Edward Breen, president of the board of trustees, 2020–.

Brad Lingo, college president, 2025–.

The administration building on the lower campus.

Carnegie Hall.

Smith Hall of Science and Technology (formerly known as Rockwell Hall).

Ketler dormitory.

Crawford Hall.

Calderwood Hall.

Pew Fine Arts Center.

Staley Hall of Arts & Letters.

Breen Student Center.

An aerial view of the campus.

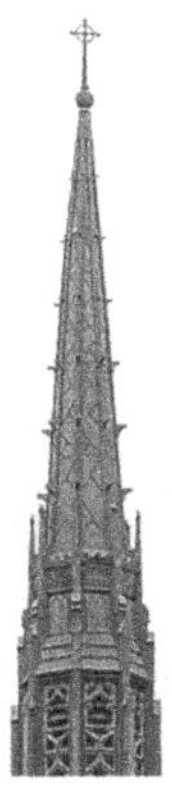

Jerry Combee, Garth Runion, and John Moore: *"We Are Ready to Attain National Leadership in Christian Higher Education,"* 1991–2003

Introduction

During the presidencies of Jerry Combee (1991–1995), Garth Runion (interim, 1995–1996), and John Moore (1997–2003), Grove City strengthened its Christian identity and reaffirmed its mission, and the Christian commitment of students intensified. At Combee's inauguration ceremony in 1992, head librarian Diane Grundy aptly described the role of Grove City's president as the "resident policy maker, visionary, money raiser, building superintendent, and chief cheerleader. A most awesome task."[1]

Under these three presidents, the college improved its academic program and national reputation; the SAT and ACT scores and secondary-school class ranks of enrolled students increased substantially, and many publications accorded the college high ratings. New all-college requirements were implemented, modified, and effusively praised by faculty and students. Grove City's athletic teams won several dozen PAC championships and fifteen all-sports trophies. Several athletes had phenomenal achievements that brought significant attention to the college, most notably record-setting football halfback R. J. Bowers and three-time national swimming champion Peggy Whitbeck. The resurrected speech and debate team placed highly at many tournaments. Faculty and students, especially those in engineering, won numerous awards. As many colleges and universities rejected core curricula, eliminated long-standing course requirements, censured Western culture, and promoted multiculturalism and political correctness, Grove City continued to emphasize the principal ideas and moral values, influenced by Christianity, that shaped and sustained the best features of Western culture and life. In 1998, the college mourned the death of Albert Hopeman Jr., its board of trustees president since 1971. In 2001, Grove City celebrated its 125th anniversary with a yearlong series of events called "Faith, Freedom, and the Future."

Between the Soviet Union's demise in 1991 and China's rise to global economic and political prominence in the early 2000s, the United States was the world's only superpower. Americans enjoyed relative peace and prosperity during these years. The creation of the internet helped fuel major innovations in communications, business, and entertainment. The United States was shaken by violence and tragedy, including the LA riots in 1992, the bombing of the World Trade Center in 1993 and of a federal building in Oklahoma City in 1995, the Columbine High School shooting in 1999, and deadly standoffs between federal agents and armed civilians at Ruby Ridge, Idaho, and Waco, Texas, culminating with the horrific Islamic fundamentalists' attack on September 11, 2001. These years were marked by increased globalization, international trade, multiculturalism, and environmental concern. The end of the Cold War sparked the rise of ethnic-nationalist separatist movements in the Balkans, Tibet, Chechnya, Spain, and other regions and countries, while the 9/11 attacks prompted US invasions of Afghanistan and Iraq. Some commentators argued that a major realignment was transforming American politics and culture. Two identifiable camps debated such "hot-button" issues as abortion, gun control, the separation of church and state, censorship, and privacy. The combatants were defined primarily not by religion, ethnicity, race, social class, or political affiliation, but rather by differing ideologies or worldviews. All these developments affected Grove City College from 1991 to 2003.

Jerry Combee pledged to follow what J. Howard Pew called "those Christian, moral and ethical principles without which our country cannot long endure." Isaac Ketler, he asserted, strove to create "an institution equal in academic quality to America's best, dedicated to Christian principles, at a price within the reach of families of modest means."[2] Combee stressed that Grove City rejected relativism and secularism and promoted "Christian truth, morals, and freedom." The college made "great books, thinkers, and ideas" that had inspired people throughout history the centerpiece of its curriculum.[3] In his April 1992 inaugural address, Combee proclaimed that God had richly blessed Grove City because of its dedication to furthering his "purposes in the world."[4] Combee insisted that Grove City fostered the values of work, family, faith, and freedom. He urged student to repudiate the 1960s quest to find oneself and instead lose themselves "in service to God."[5]

In September 1991, the trustees declared, "We oppose federal regulation of education" because it destroys the independence of private colleges and their freedom to govern their own affairs. They also denounced efforts by any public or private agencies to prevent institutions from pursuing their "self-defined missions, goals, and objectives."[6]

Combee oversaw the implementation of the new all-college requirements, which included an eighteen-hour Civilization Series consisting of courses in the Bible, theology, ethics, Western and international history and culture, the fine arts, and literature. He strove to further upgrade the academic program, including by giving laptop computers to all students, to advertise the college more effectively, and to communicate better with alumni.

In November 1993, the board's executive committee reaffirmed the college's goals and objectives. Grove City's three basic goals were to furnish a high-quality education in a "thoroughly Christian and evangelical" setting; to provide a Christian perspective of all fields of learning; and to maintain charges that families of modest means could afford. The college sought to help students develop academically, spiritually, morally, socially, and physically and to increase their "sense of responsibility to the larger community."[7]

In summer 1995, Combee resigned under pressure. No reasons were publicly stated for his sudden departure, but some trustees thought that Combee was moving too fast and spending too much money. He argued that the college could afford his new programs and initiatives, but apparently, some trustees were alarmed by the nature and alacrity of some changes he implemented or proposed.

After executive vice president Garth Runion "performed beautifully," according to board president Albert Hopeman Jr., for one year as the interim president, John Moore became Grove City's seventh president in 1996. Moore brought impressive credentials and a wide range of experiences to the job. He earned his PhD at the University of Virginia and had a background in both business and education. Moore was the president of Sigma Xi, the scientific research society that had eighty thousand members in more than five hundred chapters at colleges, industrial research centers, and government laboratories. He had been the deputy director of the National Science Foundation, the associate director of the Hoover Institute, and the president of the Thomas Jefferson Center Foundation, and he had taught at the University of Virginia, Emory University, the University of Miami, and George Mason University. He knew little about Grove City before being approached by trustees Richard Larry and Albert Hopeman Jr. about accepting the presidency. The more he learned about Grove City, the more he became intrigued about the institution. Moore's entire career had been spent in large secular research universities, but he thought that his understanding of academia and broad experience could help Grove City fulfill its historic mission. Hopeman was "a great salesman," and Moore agreed to come.[8] "We are very pleased and excited," Hopeman declared, "that a man of John Moore's caliber" agreed to serve as president.[9]

On April 21, 1997, Ed Feulner, the president of the Heritage Foundation, spoke at Moore's inauguration.[10] Moore, who led wisely and courageously, according to The *Bridge* ,[11] helped steady the ship after Combee's abrupt dismissal, and his extensive experience, astute leadership, winsome personality, and congenial nature contributed to improving relationships between administrators and professors and enhancing faculty instruction and research. He praised Grove City's "great spirit," sense of community, superb students, loyal alumni, excellent faculty and staff, and these groups' "shared commitments and values."[12] The 1998 Middle States report commended Moore for swiftly gaining the respect of all the college's constituencies and grasping Grove City's current conditions and priorities.[13] Moore credited dean of the chapel Richard Morledge with helping him better understand the college's historic mission and develop a deeper spiritual life.[14]

The 1998 Middle States report applauded Grove City for "expanding its programs and services to students," sustaining its fiscal stability, and "refurbishing and enlarging its physical plant," while providing "a quality education" undergirded by Christian principles. Grove City had attained its "unique niche in higher education" by keeping its cost affordable for families of "modest economic means," developing curricula and programs that nurtured students, "capitalizing on the technological revolution," and effectively utilizing "faculty innovation and subject-matter expertise." Grove City, the evaluators asserted, occupied "a distinctive position in higher education" based on its teaching and modeling of a Judeo-Christian value system; promotion of traditional Western values including personal freedom, free enterprise, and individual dignity; quest for academic excellence; and efforts to develop the whole person and students' sense of social responsibility." The team maintained that Grove City had remained faithful to the vision and values of its founders.[15]

The Student Body

From 1991 to 2003, the scholastic credentials of Grove City students rose remarkably. Combee's first year, the average SAT rose twenty points to 1124 and applications, which were submitted from eleven more states than the previous year, increased by 15 percent. The 628-member 1995 freshmen class, the largest in college history, contributed to a record enrollment of 2,325. This class's average SAT was 1240 (after scores were recentered), and one of every seven students was a valedictorian or salutatorian; 56 percent of freshmen were in the top 10 percent of their high school classes, and 81 percent were in the top 20 percent. The next fall, 2,299 students applied for 626 spots. Twenty-one percent of enrolled students were Presbyterians, 13 percent Catholics, 10 percent Baptists, 8 percent Methodists, and the rest belonged to other denominations, attended nondenominational churches, or had no church affiliation.

Admissions director Jeff Mincey called the class of 2002, which had an average SAT of 1257 and included seventy-seven valedictorians, "our brightest yet."[16] The 631-member class of 2004, which included a record eighteen National Merit scholarship winners, had an average SAT of 1258; 80 percent of freshmen were in the top one-fifth of their high school classes. Grove City continued to struggle to enroll minorities even after hiring Samuel Heastie from the Bahamas in fall 2001 as part of an initiative to increase minority students. In spring 2002, only twenty-three students, 1 percent of the student body, were minorities. Some faculty argued unsuccessfully that given the difficulty of enrolling qualified African American students, the college should instead focus on recruiting Asian Americans and Hispanics.

Facilities

The 1998 Middle States report lauded Grove City's "efficient facilities." Team members were "greatly impressed" by the college's natural topography and "beautiful and visually satisfying" appearance.[17] Two major building projects were completed between 1991 and 2003. The 169-bed Memorial Hall opened in 1996, replacing the namesake dormitory that began occupancy in 1914. In January 2003, the Hall of Arts and Letters (HAL) replaced Calderwood Hall as the campus's principal classroom building. Spearheaded and designed by Charles Dunn, the dean of the Calderwood School of Arts and Letters, HAL was a state-of-the-art marvel with an attractive atrium, a two-hundred-seat lecture hall, four sixty-seat and many forty-seat tiered classrooms, numerous seminar rooms, several dozen offices, and a childhood learning center. Dunn argued that it would "raise the national profile of GCC architecturally and academically," while provost William Anderson called it "a monument to the love of learning and liberty and the God who gives them to us."[18] Professors praised HAL as a "carefully designed and beautifully crafted" "technological wonder" that combined the very best of "Grove City's heritage with the technological capabilities of the future." Comparing HAL and Calderwood, one professor declared, was like comparing jeans and a sweatshirt with a tuxedo. The faculty believed that HAL would enhance student learning and that its office suites would foster collegiality.[19]

Academic Life

During Jerry Combee's last year as provost, the college implemented a new set of all-college core courses totaling between thirty-eight and fifty hours, depending on students' majors and whether they could meet the two-year language competency requirement through their high school courses. The new core consisted of an eighteen-hour humanities sequence called the Civilization Series, six hours in the social sciences, eight hours in the natural sciences, six hours in quantitative and logical reasoning, and between zero and twelve hours in a foreign language. Initially, all the six interdisciplinary humanities courses were team taught, and content was delivered in lectures to about six hundred students. There were also weekly discussion sections of twenty-five students. These courses focused on "great ideas, books, and thinkers proven across the ages" to be invaluable "in the quest for knowledge."[20] The core affirmed basic Western values, especially human equality and individual freedom, rejected the relativism and secularism rampant in American higher education, and strove to help students embrace "ultimate truth rather than current ideologies."[21]

Combee recognized that many students were finding these interdisciplinary courses very challenging as they moved from literature to philosophy to theology to art in large lecture halls. Therefore, he and the civilization faculty decided to subdivide the same basic material into six courses focusing on the Bible, literature, the arts, theology and philosophy.[22] In fall 1992, these core courses became HUMA 101: Civilization, an overview of "seminal ideas, major movements and decisive turning points" in human history; HUMA 102: Civilization and Biblical Revelation, a study of the Old and New Testaments; HUMA 201: Civilization and the Speculative Mind, an examination of pivotal thinkers and ideas and "decisive moments in theology, philosophy, and science"; HUMA 202: Civilization and Literature, an exploration of great works of literature; HUMA 301: Civilization and the Arts, an analysis of outstanding artists, musical works, and visual art; and HUMA 302: Civilization and the Modern World, a survey of "seminal ideas, major movements," and pivotal events in world history. Four of the courses were reduced in size to sections of forty students and taught by individual professors with expertise in these subject areas. In addition, all students were also required to take one three-credit course from a grouping of international courses. Combee continued to lecture to the entire freshman class in HUMA 101, using a book he wrote, *Forward to Freedom,* as the primary text.[23]

In 1991, the college's engineering program received ABET accreditation, a communications major was added, and a computer-aided engineering lab was constructed. In September 1992, *The Collegian* editor in chief senior David Pisani argued that Grove City demonstrated that private, Christian education was not "outdated, unresponsive to modern problems and financially inaccessible to most families."[24] In surveys in the early 1990s, about one-third of seniors maintained that the faculty and academic program were the strength of the college.[25] In fall 1993, a Washington, DC, internship began in the nation's capital with Paul McNulty, '80, as the instructor.

Three major developments occurred in 1994. In March, the college introduced a program to help students arrange internships, and by 2000, about two hundred students were doing internships annually either in the summer or during the spring or fall semester. (International internships began in fall 1997.) In fall 1994, Grove City became one of the nation's first colleges to give all freshmen laptop computers. Faculty members were offered intensive computer training in word processing, spreadsheet usage, and presentation software to better use computers in their classrooms. Students received extensive training in word processing, program installation, and file management.[26] Combee called the first year of the Information Technology Initiative "a resounding success."[27] In fall 1994, the Counseling Center Service was established under the direction of Warren Throckmorton.

In January 1995, the college offered its first intersession courses. These two-week, three-credit courses, held on campus in January and May or as travel interims around the world primarily in May, became a popular way to earn credits, with as many as four hundred students taking courses during some intersessions. Over the years, professors took students on travel courses to Civil War battlefields, China, Russia, western and eastern Europe, Greece, Italy, England, Israel, and other countries. In fall 1995, the college began a master's of science in accounting degree (which was discontinued in 2001) and introduced an all-college requirement called Fitness and Wellness focusing on nutrition, conditioning, physical endurance, and body composition to help students maintain healthy lifestyles during and after college.

In April 1996, SGA officials called for ending Saturday classes, claiming that only 6 percent of American colleges and universities still held them.[28] In November 1999, the board voted to halt Saturday classes, which had been part of the schedule since the college's inception, beginning the next fall. The trustees asserted that this change this would "enhance the quality of education and student life" and provide more time for class preparation and team projects.[29]

The college's 1998 self-study reported that student and alumni surveys conducted that year indicated that the "faculty effectively integrate Christian values into course content"; the college provided a "distinctly Christian environment for living and learning"; principles of freedom and responsibility guided campus life; and many students lived out their Christian commitment by participating in domestic and international internships and mission trips.[30] The 1998 Middle States report affirmed these same points. Grove City College, evaluators stated, provided "a high quality education within a Christian context." The founders' vision and values continued to undergird its "mission, goals, and objectives." Evaluators declared that Grove City's curriculum, which included forty-eight undergraduate majors, was grounded upon Christian principles and provided both excellent liberal education and professional preparation. The college effectively balanced teaching the theoretical and practical aspects of various disciplines. The college's information technology initiative, the team added, had made "computing convenient, economically efficient, and readily available" to faculty and students.[31]

In April 2002, preregistration, long a tedious process for faculty and students, was done online. Freshmen were encouraged to take a free diagnostic program to help them identify possible career fields. An entrepreneurship major began in fall 2002, and the next spring, the college held its first annual business plan competition; a $4,000 ($7,000 today) prize was awarded to members of the first-place team. Paul Kemeny created a website to help students evaluate the quality and value of books, articles, and websites.

Despite Grove City's continually improving academic program, abetted by more gifted faculty and students, complaints and problems persisted. Some students protested that numerous professors taught that "greed is good" and promoted pragmatic capitalism.[32] Others contended that a class attendance policy protected incompetent faculty.[33] In 1996, sophomore Stephanie Barnes observed that Catholic and politically liberal students were frustrated that their classmates did not seriously consider their perspectives. She noted, however, that professors often presented devil's advocate positions to stimulate thinking and discussion.[34] Even though most professors believed that only a small number of students cheated in some way, the faculty took steps in 2002 to reduce plagiarism. *The Crimson* provided an extensive definition of what it entailed; a software program was introduced to detect plagiarism in HUMA papers; and many faculty included an "honesty in learning" statement in their course syllabi. More positively, *The Collegian* editor in chief Rachel Leonard, '03, declared, professors and fellow students through their teaching and examples, had given her "a thirst to seek God and serve Him."[35]

The Faculty

The 1998 Middle States evaluators were impressed by the faculty's credentials (more than 70 percent of professors held doctoral degrees), enthusiastic support for the college's mission, and modeling of lifelong learning. They noted that the faculty wanted more dialogue with administrators, enhanced collegiality, and greater participation in institutional decision-making, especially in hiring new faculty.[36]

In 1992 Hans Sennholz, a prolific author who had chaired the economics department for thirty-six years, retired. Two key faculty additions in fall 1999 were Charles Dunn and Stan Keehlwetter. Dunn, the former chair of the political science department at Clemson University and of the Fulbright Committee and the highly respected author of ten books, wanted to teach at a Christian institution. The dean worked to enhance the college's national reputation. Keehlwetter replaced Richard Morledge as the dean of the chapel. Morledge asserted that God had called him "to try to unify and harmonize the campus under the Lordship and in the spirit of Jesus Christ." The beloved campus pastor was known for his upbeat attitude and compassion.[37] Many students said they would greatly miss Morledge, whose "blood really does run crimson red."[38] Keehlwetter had served as the senior pastor at Bethany

Presbyterian Church in Mercer since 1982 and earned a DMin from Fuller Theological Seminary in 1995. In addition to directing the chapel program, Keehlwetter taught HUMA 101, served an assistant women's soccer coach, and, like Morledge had done, initially continued to pastor his church.[39]

Biology professor Mark Weber took seven students on a medical mission trip to India in spring 1994. In subsequent years, dozens of students, under his leadership, shared God's love and provided medical assistance in many underserved locales around the world. One of the most memorable faculty classroom presentations was physics professor Richard Leo's annual portrayal of Galileo, for which he dressed as the seventeenth-century astronomer.[40]

As the 1990s ended, three noteworthy faculty members retired—R. Jack Behringer in 1996, Cynthia Walters in 1998, and Ross Foster in 2000. Runion averred, "For 40 years, Behringer has played a vital role in the life of Grove City College."[41] Known as the "Emperor" and "Gentle Jack," Behringer coached football, track, and wrestling, helped expand men's varsity sports and institute women's intercollegiate sports, and expected "nothing less than the best" from his athletes.[42] During her thirty-two-year career, Walters taught physical education classes, directed the women's water show, coached women's field hockey, and oversaw Parents' Weekend. She played the principal role in developing the women's varsity sports program and help found and served as the inaugural president of the Women's Keystone Conference, the first women's athletic conference for private colleges in western Pennsylvania.[43] Foster taught philosophy from 1969 to 1973, worked in student affairs from 1973 to 1990, and then returned to teaching from 1990 to 2000. Without "the courage and faithfulness" of Foster and others "who stood firm for what was right," Charles MacKenzie declared, the Christian values of the Ketlers, Pews, and Hopemans might not have prevailed. "His profound Christian influence on the campus, in the classroom and in the community is testimony to his faith in Jesus Christ."[44]

In fall 1999, ODK created the Professor of the Year Award to honor faculty members for "exemplary character, enthusiastic and high quality teaching, genuine rapport with students, wise advising, significant scholarship, responsible leadership, and faithful service to campus and community." Recipients were to be chosen in part by a vote of seniors, faculty, and ODK and Mortar Board members. A selection committee composed of administrators, faculty, and ODK and Mortar Board members made the final decision. Winners received $2,500 ($4,600 today) and gave a chapel address. I was selected as the award's first recipient in 2000, followed by business professor John Sparks in 2001, chemistry professor Tim Homan in 2002, and English professor Jim Dixon in 2002.

In spring 2003, Don Lyle replaced Chris Smith as the college's athletic director, a post that Smith had taken over when Behringer retired in 1996. In March 2003, Bruce Ketler was again deployed with the air national guard, this time to Turkey (now known as Türkiye) in conjunction with the Iraq invasion.

One strength of Grove City College throughout its history has been that the vast majority of its courses have been taught by full-time faculty who were deeply committed to providing high-quality instruction, not by adjuncts, graduate students, or professors whose primary interest was their own research and publications.[45] Jerry Combee argued in 1992 that the faculty furnished excellent instruction "while pursuing more significant research and scholarship than ever before."[46] John Moore called the faculty's dedication to the mission of the college and to teaching one of Grove City's greatest assets.[47] The faculty received many significant honors between 1991 and 2003. Spanish professor Cynthia Forrester was one of the 1990–1991 Sears-Roebuck Foundation Teaching Excellence and Campus Leadership award winners. In 1992, Freedoms Foundation at Valley Forge gave John Sparks an honor medal for his article "Increasing Educational Choice." The Society of Automotive Engineers named mechanical engineering professor James Conwell one of the nation's top engineering educators in 1994, and the next year SAE designated Mark Reuber, chair of the mechanical engineering department, an outstanding faculty adviser. Music department chair Ed Arnold won the Pennsylvania Music Educators Association Citation of Excellence Award for 1994–1995. He also was elected a member of the American Bandmasters Association in 1995 and served as the musical director for the seventy-fifth anniversary celebration of the Middle States Association Commission on Higher Education. Art instructor Peter Calaboyias designed a sculpture titled *Tribute* for the 1996 Olympic Games that stands in Centennial Park in Atlanta. In 1996, psychology professor Peter Hill received a Templeton Foundation grant to teach a course on the compatibility of science and religion and French professor Céline Léon was invited to lecture on French philosopher Simone de Beauvoir at a conference in Dublin.[48] In 1998, Reuber was selected to serve on the "relief crew" of the navy's nuclear submarine *USS Pittsburgh*. In 1994, biology professor Fred Brenner received Alpha Phi Omega's National Alumni Service Key Award. In 1998, he was elected president of the forty-five-thousand-member National Association of Academies of Science. The next year, the American Association for the Advancement of Science named Brenner a fellow. In 1998, physics professor Jim Downey was awarded the Meritorious Service Medal for his work as a member of the air force reserve, and he received a National Security Fellowship to study at Harvard University in 2003–2004. In 2000, communication studies professor John Hamilton produced a Cambodian version of Corrie Ten Boom's movie *The Hiding Place*. Doug Browne adjudicated high school choirs in Toronto and New Jersey for the North American Musical Festivals. Psychology professor Kevin Seybold received a $10,000 grant to design a course on science and religion and was chosen to attend the Templeton Oxford Seminars on Science and Technology. In 2001, I was selected as the Pennsylvania Professor of the Year by the Carnegie Foundation for the Advancement of Teaching. That year, religion professor Paul Kemeny won the Intercollegiate Studies Institute's contest for best new course with his "The Search for Christian America." In 2003, political science professor Paul Kengor was named a visiting fellow at the Hoover Institute.

The number of faculty publications remained small between 1991 and 2003 as professors continued to concentrate on providing first-rate classroom instruction and advising and mentoring of students. Faculty books included Tom Rose's *Principles and Policy from a Christian Perspective* (1991), Thomas Cavicchi's *Fundamentals of Electrical Engineering* (1993) and *Digital Signal Processing* (1999), Léon's *Feminist Interpretations of Soren Kierkegaard* (1997), Mark Archibald's *Mechanical Engineering Design* (2000), Charles Dunn's *The Scarlett Thread of Scandal* (2000), Paul Kengor's *Wreath Layer or Policy Player?* (2000), my *The Search for Social Salvation* (2000), Dunn's *Faith, Freedom, and the Future* (2002), and Gillis Harp's *Phillips Brooks and the Path of Liberal Protestantism* (2003). Some faculty, most notably, Brenner, Hill, Seybold, Sparks, religion professors John Currid, Paul Kemeny, and T. David Gordon, electrical engineering professor Alan Christman, and I, wrote numerous journal articles and chapters for edited books. Biology professor Durwood Ray and chemistry professor David Jones led the faculty's scientific research through their cutting-edge work on cancer and DNA sequencing. In the inaugural lecture in Sticht Lecture Hall in HAL on February 7, 2003, Hans Sennholz argued that Grove City faculty needed to publish more books and articles to help raise the college's profile.[49] Spearheaded by Kengor, they did that in the next two decades.

Guest Speakers and Performers

From 1991 to 2003, the college hosted numerous renowned speakers, especially stalwart political conservatives. Several prominent Republican politicians either spoke at commencement or lectured on campus, including Republicans former Pennsylvania Governor Richard Thornburgh, Pennsylvania Senators Rick Santorum and Arlen Specter, Oklahoma Governor Frank Keating, and former attorney general Edwin Meese. Several journalists spoke including *New Republic* editors Morton Kondracke and Fred Barnes, columnist Cal Thomas, feminist critic Midge Decter, and political commentator Dinesh D'Souza.

Religious leaders included author and lecturer Elizabeth Achtemeier; Scott Sunquist, professor of missions at Pittsburgh Theological Seminary; evangelist and Episcopal rector John Guest; Ken Bailey, who spent forty years teaching in Lebanon, Egypt, and

Israel; Presbyterian pastor John Huffman; musician and author Richard Allen Farmer; Walter Kaiser, the president of Gordon-Conwell Theological Seminary; Roberta Hestenes, the chair of World Vision International and president of Eastern College; and evangelist Rebecca Manley Pippert, best known for *Out of the Saltshaker & into the World* (1987).

Other prominent speakers included psychologist and author Kevin Leman; Linda Chavez, director of the US Commission on Civil Rights during the Reagan administration; Lynn Cheney, chair of the National Endowment for the Humanities; author Peter Marshall Jr.; Michael Horowitz, an expert on the worldwide persecution of Christians; Jan Winiecki, an economic adviser to Solidarity; Lee Edwards, the president of Victims of Communism; Eric Harrah, who closed twenty-six abortion clinics he owned after becoming a Christian; Katie Koestner, who discussed date rape; and Karl Rove, George W. Bush's leading political adviser. Leading African Americans speakers were educator Marva Collins; political writer Armstrong Williams; Ward Connerly, chair of the American Civil Rights Institute; Hoover Institute economist Thomas Sowell; George Mason University economist Walter Williams; recurrent Republican candidate Alan Keyes; and Ben Carson, chief of pediatric neurosurgery at Johns Hopkins Hospital. Four experts discussed problems in contemporary higher education: journalist Charles Sykes, author of *Profscam: Professors and the Demise of Higher Education* (1988); Ronald Reagan's policy adviser Martin Anderson, who penned *Impostors in the Temple* (1992); Diane Ravitch, the author of *The Troubled Crusade* (1985); and Joseph Kett, who wrote The *Dictionary of Cultural Literacy* (1993).

On three occasions, Philip Johnson, author of *Darwin on Trial* (1991) explained flaws in evolution and the social and philosophical impact of Darwinism. Astrophysicist Hugh Ross discussed the fine tuning of the earth that made human life possible. Francis Fukuyama lectured on how history reached its culmination in the global triumph of Western democracy. San Diego Padres pitcher Dave Dravecky drew the largest audience of any speaker during these years as three thousand people packed the Arena in 1993 to listen to his account of his courageous comeback from cancer.

The leading guest performers between 1991 and 2003 were world-renowned bass Jerome Himes, the Vienna Boys Choir, Metropolitan Opera star Roberta Peters, Doc Severinsen and His Big Band, the 180-member Kyiv Symphony Orchestra, and Broadway actor Bruce Kuhn, who presented a one-man account of the gospel of Luke.

Campus Life: "There Is Something Exceptional About 'Grovers'"

New forms of campus entertainment emerged during Combee's presidency. The Crimson Ball, a winter formal featuring a buffet dinner and dancing, became popular. Mortar Board's Dessert Theater began in December 1991. The first Karaoke Night drew about nine hundred students in fall 1992. More than fifteen hundred administrators, faculty, and students attended the inaugural Presidential Gala in April 1993, where they listened or danced to twenty-two musical acts consisting of faculty and students—folk groups, pianists, vocalists, instrumentalists, and bands; president Combee performed a tune by The Beatles and a Chuck Berry song. That spring, Student Life and Learning vice president Nancy Paxton held her first etiquette dinner, which, for the next two decades, was a major forum for teaching manners.

In 1991, Ex Nihilo was formed to promote creation science, and a chapter of Students Against Drunk Driving began. In fall 1992, the College Democrats were reconstituted, and a chapter of Kappa Delta Pi, a national education honorary, was established. In fall 1994, one thousand five hundred people attended the three performances of the Tritons' water show featuring the music of Andrew Lloyd Webber. Bon Appétit took over the college's food service in June 1995, and the next May, SGA reported that students were pleased with the quality and variety of the food. In the 1990s, the OB program introduced a stronger spiritual emphasis and OB members worked diligently to make freshmen feel valued and welcome. The organization's chair asserted in 1995 that "God has directed each and every freshman here for a reason" and that OB strove to help them adjust to Grove City College easily and quickly.[50] Some fraternity members decided to test the Combee administration's policies on underage drinking and discovered that they would be strictly enforced; numerous fraternity members were irritated, but most students accepted, and in some cases welcomed, the disciplinary actions.

Several new initiatives, activities, and clubs began in the last years of the 1990s. Commencing in 1996, Reel Talk sponsored several films a year, after which panels of faculty and students appraised the movies and led discussions with viewers. Rape aggression defense classes were first offered in 1997. Springfest, featuring a Hawaiian luau furnished by Bon Appétit, booths operated by student organizations, and performances by college bands, was introduced in April 1997. In September 1997, internet access became available in dormitory rooms, and cable television was offered the next fall. In February 1998, Richard Leo and biology professor Stephen Jenkins formed the Two Books Club to promote dialogue about the relationship between science and religion. In fall 1998, a student chapter of Sigma Xi, the scientific research society, was established. The following year, the chapter received one of the national organization's twelve Certificates of Excellence. Women's Issues Education (WISE) was created to provide a Christian perspective on breast cancer, fitness, nutrition, eating disorders, and depression. Throughout Moore's presidency, Grove City continued to be known as "a date-to-find-your-mate school."

Many students were offended by Dennis Roddy's "demeaning" front-page *Pittsburgh Post-Gazette* article in mid-October 1997 that claimed no one ever had any fun at Grove City College. They objected to Roddy's criticism of their practice of traditional moral standards and stressed that Grovers chose to attend a school whose regulations Roddy mocked. Roddy wrongly assumed that partying and drinking were prevalent at all colleges and poked fun at Grovers for preferring to "crack a book than a beer." Students emphasized that they came to Grove City because they agreed with its Christian values.[51] Attending several homecomings in the late 1990s prompted educator Fred Moon, '50, to declare that "there is something exceptional about 'Grovers.'"[52] The 1998 Middle States evaluation noted that the vast majority of students supported the college's regulations, including its ban on alcohol on campus.[53]

Although the tenor of campus life was very positive during the late 1990s and early 2000s, some students expressed criticisms. Senior Jeremy Mikesell praised the college's academics, infrastructure, and technology and asserted that his engineering and humanities classes had been rewarding. He contended, however, that development office staff pleaded with students to give money without recognizing the underlying problems that made many of them reluctant to give, especially the failure of administrators to treat students as adults and trust them to be responsible.[54] Senior J. H. Huebert disagreed with Mikesell's call for increasing intervls hours, arguing that the limited hours prevented students from being constantly distracted by the presence of the opposite sex, or "sexiled" from their rooms, as they were on most other campuses.[55] A 2001 survey reported that 71 percent of students strongly agreed that Grove City had challenged them to grow academically and that 84 percent would recommend GCC to a friend or sibling.[56]

Like other campuses around the country, Grove City was rocked by the September 11, 2001, attacks by nineteen al-Queda terrorists on the Twin Towers in New York City and the Pentagon, and the hijacked plane that crashed near Shanksville, Pennsylvania. John Moore called the assaults, which killed almost three thousand, an incomprehensible "act of cruelty and malice." Students expressed shock, disbelief, and grief; a prayer service that evening in the chapel was standing room only. History professor Earl Tilford and Charles Dunn insisted that the United States' response must be strong and quick.[57] Some students called for recognizing that most Muslims repudiated the terrorists and extremist actions by fellow Muslims, while others emphasized that God was sovereign and controlled world events.[58] In December, a Crown and Sceptre danceathon raised $9,000 ($16,250 today) for the families of the 9/11 victims.

The college celebrated its 125th anniversary by the publishing of Lee Edwards's *Freedom's College*, sponsoring eight distinguished lecturers throughout 2001, and holding two one-day Vision 2025 conferences in fall 2001 that discussed how Grove City could best address the major social, cultural, and ethical changes likely to occur in the next twenty-five years. Reflecting on these events, John Moore declared, "We are ready to attain national leadership in Christian higher education."[59] The "Faith, Freedom, and the Future" series featured University of Chicago ethicist Jean Bethke Elshtain speaking on "When Faith Meets Politics"; biologist Michael Behe discussing his book *Darwin's Black Box* (1996); George Weigle, a senior fellow at the Ethics and Public Policy Center, lecturing on the demise of communism; Notre Dame historian George Marsden talking about Christian scholarship; James Billington, the librarian of Congress, examining Christianity and history; Princeton philosopher Robert George discoursing on "Freedom, Reason, and the Rule of Law"; and Wheaton history professor Mark Noll assessing "How the Religious Past Frames America's Future."

From 1991 to 2003, hundreds of students and numerous campus organizations participated in various activities to assist community residents, most notably the United Way Day of Caring. Combee listed thirty-seven campus organizations that engaged in community service in 1992–1993, including fraternities, sororities, housing groups, Warriors for Christ, Salt Company, Lamplighters, Young Life, Circle K, College Republicans, Life Advocates, ODK, the Newman Club, Polk Christian Outreach, and the touring choir. These groups worked with an inner-city ministry, assisted the elderly, helped with youth sports, raked leaves, shoveled snow off walks, raised money for charities, packed and distributed food, sponsored indigent children, and cleaned highways.[60] The ninety-member Alpha Omega service fraternity organized blood drives, tutored middle school children, helped with Cub Scout activities and a junior science fair, and worked with the Children's Aid Society. Circle K members organized the first Special Olympics soccer team in Mercer County. Its successor, Helping Hands, promoted drug and alcohol awareness, rang Salvation Army bells before

Christmas, babysat professors' children for free, and played with youth at the YMCA. Steel City Ministries, established in 2002, sent students to work with Hosanna Industries, Urban Impact, and the Pittsburgh Project.

Religious Activities

From 1991 to 2003, Christian organizations flourished, prominent evangelical speakers and Christian bands and artists came to campus, thousands of students served in inner cities, Appalachia, or foreign countries, and numerous students and faculty used The *Collegian*, classrooms, chapel, and other venues to challenge one another to follow Jesus more faithfully. During these years, the chapel program included a variety of services and speakers; students could choose the ones which best suited their interests and needs.[61]

In 1993, Staley lecturer Rebecca Manley Pippert discussed whether believing in Jesus made a difference. In 1994, James Sire, whose book *The Universe Next Door*, was used in HUMA 201, discussed why anyone should believe anything. Tony Campolo visited campus four times during these years, imploring students to seek intimacy with God, care for the poor and oppressed, and strive to understand why many Middle Eastern Muslims despised the United States.[62] Christian artists Michael Kelly Blanchard, Glad, Newsboys, Phil Keaggy, Caedmon's Call (twice), Third Day, Jennifer Knapp, Bebo Norman, and Jars of Clay performed on campus. In 1995, Stonebridge Concerts was created to schedule Christian artists and bands.

Many Christian groups were active. About 150 students participated in the Fellowship of Christian Athletes, meeting together weekly to study scripture, sing, and perform skits. About 125 students attended Campus Crusade for Christ's weekly meetings. InterVarsity Mission Fellowship held missions conferences most years where more than thirty mission organizations were represented. Hundreds of students attended Salt Company's weekly meetings, barn bashes, and coffeehouses. A new group, Warriors for Christ, began in 1991, and throughout the Combee-Runion-Moore years, as many as six hundred students met Thursday evenings in Harbison for worship, prayer, singing, and teaching. Some students argued that interest in spiritual things had significantly increased and that Grovers had become "more outspoken about their faith."[63] The Newman Club held Bible studies and social events for Catholic students (10 to 15 percent of the student body). The Gospel Team, Koinonia, and New Grace went on annual tours to sing, give testimonies, do sketches, and share Christ's love at churches.

To minster to George Junior Republic's five hundred youth ranging in age from nine to nineteen, New Life held weekly large group meetings, group home Bible studies, and kiddie New Life (for younger boys residing in special needs homes) and helped with Sunday morning worship services. Its president, Peter Doerfler, '98, claimed that New Life was probably the college's "most challenging ministry" because of the very different life experiences of Grovers and GJR youth.[64] GJR's program director called the dedication of New Life members "unbelievable"; it was the only group that came every year. GJR's chaplain declared that Grove City students expanded his ministry and were excellent role models.[65]

Under the auspices of Inter-City Outreach (ICO), created in 1988, two hundred or more students annually spent a week or longer during a college break ministering in "the slums, streets, and shattered communities of urban America" and other impoverished places.[66] Students worked in Ashland, Kentucky; Boston; Camden, New Jersey; Cleveland; Nashville; Philadelphia; Raleigh; New Orleans; Pittsburgh; Memphis; Jamaica; the Dominican Republic; and other locales. In 2001, three students thanked God for using "our experiences at The Bowery Mission [in Manhattan] to build friendships, challenge our thinking, and amaze us once again with the power of His love."[67] A group of eighteen students explained how sleeping on the streets while ministering to people experiencing homelessness in Toronto deeply impacted them.[68]

By fall 1992, Red Box missionaries had gone to Guatemala, Nigeria, the Dominican Republic, France, Bolivia, India, Peru, Kenya, Switzerland, Thailand, England, Malawi, Russia, Papua New Guinea, Germany, Belgium, Jamaica, Indonesia, and Liberia. While three to five Red Box missionaries worked in the United States and abroad every summer, numerous other students served with varied mission agencies around the world. Senior Ben Paulus exhorted his classmates to allow "the living and resurrected Christ to burn inside us."[69]

In 2001, about 75 percent of Grovers attended church on a typical Sunday. The most popular churches were the Evangelical Free Fellowship Community Church, Solid Rock Assembly of God, Beloved Disciple Parish, East Main Presbyterian, and Hillcrest Presbyterian Church in America.[70]

Greek Life

The college's fraternities and sororities confronted many challenges from 1991 to 2003. Combee argued that "our disciplinary problems are nearly always Greek-group originated." Their members' alcohol consumption "led many students astray."[71] Because numerous fraternities temporarily lost their charters for violating campus policies, fraternity membership decreased from 30 percent of male students in 1984 to about 20 percent in 1994, while sorority membership declined from 53 percent of female students in 1984 to about 32 percent in 1994. Membership plummeted even more during the next decade as more fraternities and a few sororities were placed on probation.

While many national fraternities and sororities continued to haze pledges during "Hell Week," Grove City's Greeks introduced Greek Unity Week in 1992 to do service projects to aid the college and local community. Sororities continued their traditional "table pounding" in the Arena to introduce their pledges, after which new Greek classes were recognized at a chapel service. Greek Unity Week culminated with a ceremony in the chapel and a dance open to all students.

In 1992, the first annual Greek God and Big Man on Campus contests were held to benefit the American Cancer Society, with male contestants wearing formal attire and bathing suits, answering questions, and displaying various talents. The Greek Games, designed to strengthen bonds between fraternity and sorority members, consisted of swimming races, a soccer kicking competition, an obstacle course, root beer chugging, a Jell-O toss, a hot dog eating contest, an egg drop, a three-legged race, and a powder-puff football game between sororities.

In 1995, Greek life reached a low point as seven fraternities were suspended for various infractions. In November, two hundred members of the college's ten fraternities and eight sororities marched to Crawford. To improve relations between the Greeks and administrators, they proposed that 1) sanctions be levied for a definite period of time appropriate with the violations groups had been committed; 2) the Inter-Fraternity and Pan-Hellenic council presidents be included in disciplinary discussions; 3) groups with suspended charters be permitted to perform community and campus service to expedite their return; and 4) charters be suspended only as a last measure after other forms of discipline were employed.[72] In response, administrators established a policy in February 1996 to hasten fraternities and sororities regaining their charters; suspended groups would hold twelve meetings to discuss various aspects of Greek life, establish a code of conduct, and revise their constitutions accordingly. After completing these three steps, members of suspended fraternities and sororities could participate in Inter-Fraternity and Pan-Hellenic meetings, wear colors, play sports, and appeal for full restatement.[73] Meanwhile, Greeks worked energetically to improve their image on campus by doing service projects and sponsoring social events.

Despite their reduced numbers, sorority women played many significant roles on campus. By one estimate, in 2001, 18 percent of them played a varsity sport; 24 percent volunteered with a campus service organization; 35 percent were officers of a campus organization; and 36 percent belonged to an academic honorary.[74] Speaking for many sorority members, Jill Fitch Slaby, '94, who served as the Pan-Hell president her senior year, maintained that the ABTs helped her grow in her faith.[75]

Speech and Debate

In 1996, after a twenty-year lull, Jess Davis, '98, (who was also the college's first female football play-by-play announcer), with help from two professors, reconstituted the college's speech and debate team, which enjoyed immediate success. Its members competed in seven categories: impromptu speeches for which students had ninety seconds to prepare to give a five-and-a-half-minute speech in response to a prompt; extemporaneous speeches for which they had thirty minutes to prepare a seventeen-minute speech on a current event; poetry and prose interpretations; ten-minute informative, persuasive speeches; after-dinner (humorous) speeches; rhetorical criticism; and Lincoln-Douglas debates, in which students argued for and against a prompt for fifteen minutes. In fall 1997, Grove City placed second at large tournaments at Bloomsburg University and Youngstown State University. The next April, at a twenty-team tournament at Muskingum, Davis finished first in informative speaking and rhetorical criticism, second in after-dinner speaking, and fourth in prose interpretation. That fall, Grove City was second at a YSU tournament, as Rob Perry, '00, placed first in extemporaneous oral interpretation and poetry interpretation and second in prose interpretation, Jason Kline, '00, was first in informative speaking and second in impromptu speaking, and Rebecca Wetzel, '01, was second in extemporaneous speaking. In spring 1999, Jagan Ranjan, '00, placed highly at nationals in Lincoln-Douglas debate. At the Pennsylvania State Individual Events Championship Tournament in February 2000, the Wolverines finished third, as Ranjan was first in extemporaneous speaking, second in Lincoln-Douglas debate, and third in impromptu speaking; Stephen Bond, '02, was first in after-dinner speaking; and Derek Bradley, '03, was second in poetry interpretation. The 2000–2001 team took second at the Pennsylvania state tournament, and the next year, the Wolverines won a nine-team competition at Marietta College.

Theater

Led by directors James Dixon and Betsy Craig, the theater department staged numerous enthralling musicals and plays between 1991 and 2003. Craig directed *Oklahoma* featuring Erich Lascek, '93, and Sue Baker, '93; *The Music Man* with Eric Welchans, '94, as Harold Hill and Danielle Zawodny, '93, as Marian Paroo; *Bye Bye Birdie* with Jonathan Rice as Conrad Birdie; and *Fiddler on the Roof* with Jason Musko, '97, as Tevye and Kiley Perdue, '98, as Hodel. Dixon directed *Guys and Dolls* with J. R. Mitchell, '97, and Musko playing the central characters; *South Pacific* with Perdue playing the lead; and *How to Succeed in Business Without Really Trying* with Chris Jensen, '99, as J. Pierrepont Finch and Perdue as his love interest; *Into the Woods* with Betsy Dupree, '02, and Emily Lorini, '03, playing lead roles; and *Kiss Me, Kate,* starring Lorini. A *The Collegian* reviewer argued that as Finch, Jensen "utilizes many different talents, pulls out all the stops, and creates a character with all the stage presence of Martin Short."[76] Jensen and Dupree also played the leads in *A Midsummer Night's Dream*. Betsy Craig directed *West Side Story* with Chris Graham, '04, playing Tony and Amy Miller, '03, playing Maria. Dixon cast Hans Latta, '05, and Rachel Bovard, '06, as Benedick and Beatrice in *Much Ado About Nothing*, and Derrick Winger, '07, as the Pirate King in *The Pirates of Penzance*. Jeff Sodergren, '92, played Thomas More in *A Man for All Seasons*; Sarah Stitt, '95, had several major roles in the mid-1990s, most notably in *She Stoops to Conquer*; and Allison Conrad, '96, portrayed Helen Keller in *The Miracle Worker*.

Music

Music flourished at Grove City College between 1991 and 2003 as the touring choir, marching band, college orchestra, and stage and jazz bands, led by Erich Lascek and Joe Pisano, '94, respectively, in the mid-1990s, and many student recitals entertained audiences. In addition, several student-organized musical groups were popular on campus and beyond and produced albums.

In spring 1993, the touring choir, directed by Doug Browne, performed twelve concerts in various cities in Ohio and Illinois. Three years later, the choir traveled two thousand miles throughout Virginia, the Carolinas, and Georgia to perform ten shows. In 1998, the choir partnered with the Pittsburgh Concert Chorale in a concert at Heinz Hall. In April 2001, the choir did a California tour, the brainchild of its president senior Ben Spead, performing in the Los Angeles area (including at Robert Schuller's Crystal Cathedral), San Diego, Fresno, and Sacramento to glorify God.[77] In February 2002, the touring choir was chosen to perform with eighteen of the nation's top choral ensembles at the American Choral Directors Association eastern convention in Pittsburgh.

The marching band, directed by Ed Arnold, regularly consisted of two hundred or more members counting instrumentalists, dancers, twirlers, and flagbearers. The band's favorite numbers included "St. Elmo's Fire," "Olympic Fanfare and Theme," and "Music of the Night." The band participated in the Miss America Pageant parade in Atlantic City, New Jersey, in September 1997. In October 2001, the band performed at Disney World and hosted a gala and banquet at Disney's Contemporary Resort, where various Grove City ensembles played. The concerts of the one-hundred- to one-hundred-fifty-member college orchestra, directed by Richard Konzen, which had themes such as "Music Around the World," received rave reviews.

In 1997, music instructor and principal college vocalist Diana Walter conducted an opera workshop for students, which culminated with presenting excerpts of two operas. For many years, college ensembles and individual vocalists performed daily at lunchtime during the first half of December in the Carnegie Christmas Concerts.

The most popular student musical groups during these years included Stinging Rain, a four-man band that released three albums in the early 1990s; Hundred Pines, composed of Dan Petrich, '93, Craig Knepper, '93, and Colleen Denson, '92, which issued an album in 1993; and American Standard, a barbershop quartet that released its first album in spring 2000. Begun by Todd Sproul, '96, in 1994, for a decade, various foursomes performed in churches and chapel and at All-College Sing and other venues.

David Bailey, who sang with Bill Deasy as students from 1985 to 1988, pursued a musical career after college while battling cancer. As part of an acoustic duo with Doug Ebert called Not by Chance, he praised God through song in coffeehouses, colleges (including Grove City numerous times), churches, conferences, sports stadiums, folk venues, and prisons across the country. One reviewer called Bailey, who produced four albums, a happier Gordon Lightfoot.[78] In 2001, Deasy wrote the theme song for "Good Morning America" called "Good Things Are Happening."

WSAJ

In January 1995, WSAJ-FM, which broadcast continuously, boosted its power from two hundred to three thousand watts, enabling it to be heard within a sixty-mile radius. Its programming consisted of classical and sacred music and special religious programs including vespers. A related station, WGCC AM, featured rock, top forty, and contemporary Christian music from 8 a.m. to 2 a.m. It could be heard only on campus. In the early 2000s, WGCC played Christian and secular music including classic rock, jazz, and independent bands.

Student Achievements

Students, especially engineering majors, had numerous impressive accomplishments between 1991 and 2003. An engineering team spearheaded by senior Lynn Caldwell placed first in the US Olympic Design Competition in October 1991 for its diagnostic baseball bat, which analyzed the speed, power, and other aspects of hitters' swings. *ABC Sports* filmed an infomercial about the bat, and it was displayed at the Great Lakes Science Center in Cleveland. Another team of engineers placed second in the 1992 Small Motors Manufacturing Association's national mechanical design contest. At the SAE Super Mileage Competition that year, five GCC engineering majors won sixth place with a vehicle that traversed 665 miles on a gallon of gas. The next two years, Grove City teams took second at this competition. Also in 1992, Jason Biscombe, '93, placed fourth in a national American Society of Mechanical Engineers (ASME) student conference. The following year, Dave Adams, '93, and his teammates captured first prize in the student division of the Firestone Innovators Design Contest for their approach to reducing the shock and discomfort of riding off-road mountain bikes. That same year, five engineering students won a gold medal for their "most unusual" design at the Second International BEAM Robot Olympics in Toronto. Another team earned fourth place in the 1993 ASME Student Mechanism Design Competition, while Grove City and MIT were the two winners of the ASME Solid Waste Management Scholarship. In 1994, five seniors won third place at the SAE Walking Machines Decathlon national convention. In addition, Grove City was one of six colleges that received SAE's Outstanding Student Branch Award based on its special projects, faculty-student interaction, and branch activities. That year, a water turbine designed by a team of engineering majors won a national design competition sponsored by the hydropower industry.

Students had significant achievements in other areas. Senior Karin Hawkins was first runner-up in the Miss Pennsylvania contest in September 1991. The next spring, junior Kristin Wiechmann won first place in the *Pennsylvania CPA Journal* competition. In 1994, senior wide receiver Andy Sems was one of only ten D2 or D3 student athletes to receive a $5,000 NCAA scholarship. In 1997, Heather Busin, '00, became Miss Pennsylvania. J. H. Huebert placed fourth in the 1999 Felix Morley Journalism Competition sponsored by the Institute for Humane Studies; the top three awards went to graduate students. That year, prodded by Charles Dunn, Grove City students applied for a Rhodes Scholarship for the first time. In spring 2000, David Jetter, a mechanical engineering major who was the president of New Life, an ICO leader, and the Senior Man of the Year, became the first Grover to be selected for a postgraduate Fulbright Scholarship. After scoring in the ninety-ninth percentile on the LSAT, Brad Lingo was accepted to every Ivy League law school in spring 2000 and decided to go to Harvard. Dunn used his accomplishment to challenge students to dream big about graduate and professional schools. In spring 2001, Ben Spead, an electrical engineer, the 2001 Senior Man of the Year, and an RA, was selected as one of one of thirteen national ODK Student Leaders of the Year and came close to winning a Rhodes Scholarship. The college's second Fulbright recipient, Nicole Rudolph, '02, a history and French major, taught English in a school near Seoul, Korea. In fall 2002, a five-student Operation Top Management team, led by Kiley Zulauf, '03, earned second place in the Pennsylvania Institute of Certified Public Accountants Business Plan Challenge. Throughout these years, education majors had an almost 100 percent pass rate on the National Teacher Exam and often the highest pass rate among Pennsylvania colleges with at least one hundred students taking the exam.

Other students stand out for their achievements on campus. In 1999, L. J. Gibb became the second African American to win Senior Man of the Year. Gibb was an RA, a member of the Religious Activities Committee and the football and track teams, the chaplain of Alpha Omega, a New Life volunteer, and a leader of two ICO trips. Matthew Divelbiss, '02, is the only person in college history to serve as *The Collegian* editor in chief for three years. Christine Bittler '97, a superb swimmer, won awards for superior achievement in accounting and having the highest CQPA of a sorority member. Karin Hendrickson, '99, held the college records for most steals and assists in basketball and was third in career rebounds; she was also the drum major for the marching band, and her original composition, "Carry the Flame," was the theme song for the 2002 Olympic torch relay. Derek Bradley was the SGA president, a leading actor, and a member of OB, ICO Argentina, and *The Bridge* staff.

Political Conservatism

From 1991 to 2003, Grove City was a bastion of political conservatism. In 1999, Grove City's chapter won the Pennsylvania College Republicans of the Year award. When the television networks prematurely projected around 2 a.m. on November 8 that Republican

George W. Bush had won the 2000 presidential election, one hundred students rushed across the quad, chanting "USA," leaping for joy, and carrying American flags.[79] In 2000, 85 percent of faculty voted for Bush, 9 percent for Democrat Al Gore, and 6 percent for third-party candidates. A 2002 survey found that 33 percent of faculty self-identified as very conservative and 42 percent as somewhat conservative.[80]

Men's Athletics

Men's sports teams had numerous outstanding seasons between 1991 and 2003. Leading the way were the tennis, swimming and diving, track and field, and cross-country squads. The men's tennis team coached by Joe Walter went 152–44 (.780) and won the PAC championship every year. The last six years of coach Jim Longnecker's tenure (1991–1992 to 1996–1997), the swimmers and divers compiled a dazzling 66–7 (.904) record, winning the PAC title all six seasons and finishing in the top forty-five in the nation four of these seasons. The track and field team captured the PAC championship eight times during this period, while the harriers won the PAC all thirteen seasons and finished in the top fifteen in the eastern region every year from 1998 to 2003.

Other teams also had good seasons between 1991 and 2003. The baseball team's best records were 24–13 in 1998 and 19–10 in 2001, and it won two PAC titles. The football team's best record was 9–2 in 1997, and it also claimed two PAC championships. Its star fullback, R. J. Bowers, captured many headlines for his pursuit of the all-time NCAA record for rushing yards between 1997 and 2000. The basketball squad's best records were 16–9 in 1994–1995 and 1998–1999, and 18–9 in 2002–2003. The squad secured one PAC crown and received five ECAC invitations. In 1996, the soccer team finished 16–2 and won the PAC title and the ECAC South championship. The 1995 team reached the semifinals of the ECAC South tournament.

Srinivasan Balaji, '94, from Bangalore, India, led the tennis team to a 44–7 record from 1991 to 1994. The 1992 team went

11–1, beating archrival CMU 9–0. Joe Walters called Balaji "the best player the PAC has ever had." In October 1992, he and senior Paul Crumley made it to the doubles finals of the Rolex D3 championships in Virginia. In 1993, Balaji was the PAC MVP for the third consecutive year as he won the singles and doubles titles. The Wolverines were voted the top D3 tennis team in western Pennsylvania. Balaji finished his career with a 43–4 singles record, surpassing Tim Kirk, '83, who played fourth singles, for most wins. In addition, Balaji won 91 percent of his singles matches, surpassing the record of George Collins, '73, who won 88 percent of his singles matches. Walters credited Balaji with helping GCC's team "reach a level of notoriety" in the East and "play stronger teams."[81]

Led by Matt Woffington, '97, and Chris Kruppa, '95, the number one and number two players, the tennis team went 16–2 in 1995 and 16–3 in 1996, beating perennial powerhouse CMU 5–4. In 1997, Kruppa broke Balaji's record for most wins with fifty-one. With Patrick Donahue, '04, playing first singles, the 2003 squad went 15–2, including vanquishing Allegheny 8–1, Malone 9–0, and Slippery Rock 9–0. Donahue was the PAC MVP as the Wolverines claimed their thirteenth consecutive championship.

At the end of the 1993–1994 season, James Longnecker was the winningest active coach in D3. Jay D'Ambrosio, '94, was a six-time All-American in the 100- and 200-meter backstroke and set five conference records. The 1994 class went 43–9 in their careers. The 1995–1996 team finished 12–0, and the seniors had an even better career record of 46–2. Doug Fullerton, '97, qualified for five events at nationals in 1996 and won All-American honors by placing ninth in the 200 individual medley. A mechanical engineer with a 3.98 QPA, Fullerton held eight varsity records when he graduated and earned NCAA Academic All-American honors.

In spring 1997, Longnecker retired with one of the most spectacular career coaching records in D3 history of 685–177–1 (.794). His three teams—swimming and diving, track and field, and cross-country—had a combined nineteen undefeated seasons and only two losing ones. His 366 wins in swimming and diving were one of the top five totals in all three NCAA divisions; his forty consecutive winning seasons in this sport were thought to be a national record. He coached forty-four All-Americans and won the American College Coaches' Association's Distinguished Coach award in 1987.

Luke Arnholt, '98, played a vital role in Grove City's swimming dominance during the late 1990s by helping the Wolverines achieve a 40–5 overall record and win four PAC titles championships. Arnholt set school records in the 50 and 100 freestyle, and, with fellow swimmers, in five relay events.

The 1992 harriers finished 14–1. Josh Cauvel, '98, won the PAC championship for the second time in 1995 as the cross-country team compiled a 46–4 record. Cauvel triumphed again in 1997, and brothers John, '01, and Tim Sabella, '00, finished fourth and fifth, respectively. The 1998 squad placed sixth at the Mideast Regional, and Tim Sabella was named to the Mideast Regional Team. In 1999, the Wolverines won the ten-team Wooster Invitational, with Tim Sabella finishing second overall. Joining Tim and John Sabella was their sister Angie, '01; all three earned first-team PAC in 1999. The next year, Angie won the PAC championship and set the college women's 10,000 meters record.

The track and field teams won the PAC crown in 1993, 1994, and 1995 and had numerous stellar performers. In 1994, freshman Jim Phibbs went 6–9¾ in the high jump, breaking the school record by almost 4 inches, and earned All-American status. Phibbs won three PAC titles. In 1995, the men's track team had its eleventh undefeated season in the previous thirty-eight years with Josh Cauvel often winning the 5000 and 10,000 meters and Mike Van Grouw, '97, setting college and conference records in the pole vault at 14–6 (which is still second all-time at Grove City). The squad also won the PAC every year from 1999 to 2003. Its top performers during these years were Ryan Mitchell, '99, Scott Sukits, '02, Jeb Schreiber, '03, and Rory Phillips, '04. Mitchell won many 1500- and 5000-meter races and set the college record in the 3000-meter steeplechase (currently third all-time). Sukits also won five PAC titles and still has Grove City's second all-time triple jump (46–4). Schreiber, a hurdler and high jumper, won five individual conference titles.

Phillips, a three-time PAC champion in the javelin, finished tenth in D3 in 2003 and was the national runner-up in 2004. His throw of 215–9¾ is second in college history. Phibbs, Phillips, Sukits, and Schreiber were all selected for the PAC sixtieth anniversary team.

The 1995 soccer team finished 16–2, took the PAC title, and won the ECAC tournament. Center forward Greg Kreutzberg, '97, had twenty-five goals in 1995, the most single-season goals of all-time, and is currently third in career goals. In 1995, he was an NCAA all-region honoree. Future coach Mike Dreves, '97, is fourth in career assists. Goalie Brad Smith, '02, is first in career shutouts and fourth in career saves and wins.

Basketball standouts during these years were Mark Timko, '94, Jim Wherley, '97, and Nate Maurer, who played from 2001 to 2003. In 1993–1994, Timko averaged 26.8 ppg, the third-highest single-season average in college history, and he has the second-highest career average ppg (20.2). His forty-seven points in February 1994 broke Jeff Claypool's single-game scoring record. His senior year, Timko made 53.4 percent of his three-point shots to lead D3. Despite playing only two and half seasons, Timko finished as the college's seventh all-time leading scorer. On February 1, 1997, the basketball team defeated Thiel 77–69 to record its one thousandth victory. Wherley scored 1,162 career points and ranks first in minutes played and third in free throws made and career steals. In 1998–1999, the Wolverines won the PAC title, going 16–8, and earning their fourth ECAC trip in six years. Grove City's field goal percentage defense that year was the best in all NCAA divisions, and its scoring defense was seventh. The 2002–2003 squad went 18–9 and won another PAC title. Sophomore Nate Maurer had two thirty-nine–point games, scored 566 points, the fourth-highest season total in GCC history, and was named second team ECAC Southern Region and first-team All-Great Lakes Region.

Led by David Pifer, '00, the golf team went 21–6 in 1998 and won the PAC in 1999. Nate Miklos, '02, was a three-time PAC first-team member and the medalist at the 2001 PAC golf championship and finished third at the event in 2002. Justin Tulk was the 2003

PAC Player of the Year and the college's first golfer to qualify for nationals.

In 1997, R. J. Bowers, who played five years of minor league baseball in the Houston Astros system, joined the football team. In mid-September, led by halfback Doug Steiner, '98, the fourth-leading rusher in college history, Grove City beat CMU 26–7, its first victory over them since 1986. In October, Grove City upset W&J 31–28, its first defeat of the perennial D3 powerhouse since 1979. The Wolverines then conquered previously unbeaten Waynesburg 42–30, Bluffton 71–21, and Bethany 35–21 and were ranked twenty-sixth in D3. Bowers was the first Wolverine to have two thousand all-purpose yards in a season and was fifth in D3 in all-purpose yards. The team set a college record with 333 total points, which was the second-highest total in D3. The Wolverines had the most rushing yards in a game (586), the most total yards in a game (649), and the most points in a game since 1930 (seventy-one). Steiner received All-America honors from *Don Hansen's Football Gazette* and Hewlett-Packard. After winning its first PAC football title, the Wolverines lost an ECAC contest to the Merchant Marine Academy 25–12.

At the 1998 homecoming game, Bowers gained 304 rushing yards to set single-game college and PAC records. In November, he rushed for his thirtieth touchdown of the season, breaking the D3 record Steiner set the previous year. Bowers ended the season with thirty-four touchdowns and 2,283 yards (becoming only the fourth D3 runner to rush for more than two thousand yards) and had the third-highest average yards rushing per game (228.3) in the history of all three NCAA divisions. The 206 points he scored was surpassed in NCAA history only by Barry Sanders's 234 in 1988; his 2,876 all-purpose yards were the fourth most ever in any NCAA division.

In late September 1999, Bowers set a D3 record by rushing for one hundred or more yards in twenty consecutive games. Through his first three seasons, Bowers averaged 187 yards rushing and 242 all-purpose yards per game. In Grove City's 27–7 triumph over Thiel at homecoming in October 2000, Bowers became D3's all-time leading rusher. In late October, Bowers set the mark for the most rushing yards for all NCAA divisions. He ended his career with 7,353 rushing yards and as the all-time scoring leader in D3 history with ninety-one touchdowns. In addition, he tied the record for most one-hundred-yard rushing games (thirty-four) and two-hundred-yard rushing games (fifteen) in a career. Bowers played in the Blue-Gray Football Classic and the Hula Bowl (becoming only the seventh D3 player to participate in either one). In 2000, he won the Melberger Award, given to the best player in D3, and the D3 Player of the Year; altogether, he set eleven D3 records and eight all-division NCAA records. Bowers's exploits were featured in *USA Today* and on ESPN and brought substantial publicity to Grove City. He played two seasons in the NFL.

Several defensive players shone between 1997 and 2004. Cornerback Brock McCullough, '01, is Grove City's career leader in passes broken up and is tied for fourth in interceptions; he played in the 2000 Aztec Bowl in Merida, Mexico. Defensive end Mark Furgeson, '99, is first in single-season sacks and career fumble recoveries; linebacker Adam Corbett, '02, is third in career tackles; linebacker Casey Creehan is first in single-season tackles. Linebacker Mike Choby, '05, is second in career tackles, first in career tackles for a loss, and third in single-season sacks.

Several baseball players stand out between 1991 and 2003. Steve Shilling, '93, is second all time in career slugging percentage (.695) and third in career on-base percentage. Jim Donnelly, '98, who was first-team PAC in both baseball and football, ranks second of all time in career batting average (.417) and is tied for third in career slugging percentage (.668) and for fifth in home runs. Mike Kashurba, '01, ranks in the top ten in career total bases, RBIs, home runs, runs scored, walks, and stolen bases. Nate Kauffmann, '01, is third in career total bases and home runs, fourth in career RBIs, fifth in career batting average (.393), and sixth in career slugging percentage (.654). In 2001, Kauffmann helped lead the Wolverines to their first PAC championship in seventeen years by hitting .452 and smashing ten home runs. The 2002 team outscored its three opponents 23–3 in PAC tournament games to claim a second title.

The college had an outstanding club volleyball team during much of this period. Led by senior middle hitter Doug Kanouff, the 1992 team was 18–0 during the regular season. The 1994 squad beat Syracuse and Cornell and finished ninth at the national tournament. In 1995, led by captain David Fritz, '95, and outside hitter Andrew Coffin, '98, the team finished 18–0. The 2003 volleyball team, starring Zach Underwood, '07, was undefeated during the regular season.

The men's club lacrosse team, organized in 1992, made it to the National Collegiate Lacrosse League elite eight the next year. A men's rugby club, formed in 1995, won the Allegheny Rugby Union championship in 2000 and 2001. The men's club ice hockey team continued to compete against other colleges.

In 1999, men's water polo became a varsity sport. In September 2000, the press box at Thorn Field was named for Donald "Doc" McMillan, '32. As a student, McMillan excelled in tennis and track. After spending five years as an army physician during World War II, he worked as the school doctor at Mount Lebanon High School. In this capacity, he helped bring several stellar athletes to the college, including Penn-Ohio diving champion Dick Jewell, '67. From 1973 to 1993, he and Jewell worked to recruit athletes.

Women's Athletics

Grove City's women's sports teams, especially the tennis, swimming and diving, volleyball, cross country, and track and field squads, had impressive records between 1991 and 2003. A women's soccer team began playing in fall 1992, and a women's water polo squad started playing in spring 2000.

Coached by Cathy Jacobs and led by number one players Jennifer Mulcahy, '96, Wendy Carlson, '00, Alyssa Bradford, '01, and Allison Atwood, '03, the tennis team won the PAC every year from 1991 to 2002 while compiling a 98–27 record (.784); the Lady Wolverines were 11–2 in 1998 and 12–1 in 1999 (defeating four D2 school decisively). Mulcahy went 33–9 in singles and was a three-time PAC MVP. Bradford was a four-time PAC MVP, claimed PAC titles at first singles and doubles four years, and compiled a 36–2 record in singles and a 38–6 record in doubles. Carlson played two seasons at number two singles and had a career record of 40–7 in singles and 44–3 in doubles. Bradford made it to the final round in number one singles at the 1998 Intercollegiate Tennis Association regional tournament; she was 36–2 in singles and 38–6 in doubles. Atwood won first singles and first doubles at the 2002 PAC tournament and was 34–5 in singles for her career.

The swimming and diving team, also coached by Cathy Jacobs, went 11–1 in 1992–1993, 11–2 the next year, and 11–1 in 1996–1997. Between 1991 and 1999, the team captured the PAC title six times. Hope VandenBerg, '99, won seven events at the 1997 PAC championship. Between 2001 and 2003, Peggy Whitbeck, '04, dominated the PAC and broke numerous varsity and pool records. She finished second in the D3 national tournament in the 200 butterfly and fourth in the 100 butterfly as a freshman in 2001. The next year, she finished fifth in the 100 butterfly and won the 200 butterfly, setting a D3 record and becoming Grove City's first female national champion in any sport. Her junior year, Whitbeck repeated as the national champion in the 200 butterfly and placed third in the 100 butterfly.

Between 1991 and 2003, the volleyball team captured five PAC titles and three ECAC titles. The team's best record was 34–10 in 1995. Her senior year, Lisa Lippincott, '93, was the PAC MVP, seventh in D3 in kills, and a second-team All-American. Jeannie Annan, '96, another PAC MVP, ranks third all-time in both career assists and aces. In September 1998, coach Susan Roberts earned her four hundredth volleyball victory—only thirteen D3 coaches had achieved that milestone. The women won the 2001 ECAC championship by defeating Johns Hopkins, Franklin & Marshall, and Moravian.

The women's cross-country team excelled between 1991 and 2003. Senior Cathy Williams won her second PAC title in 1991. Led by senior Diane Kindel (the PAC MVP and thirteenth at regionals), the 1993 team went 11–1. The Lady Wolverines finished sixth in the NCAA D3 Mideast Regional in 1991, seventh in 1992, and eighth in 1993. In 1994, Caroline Lucheta, '95, placed first at seven multi-school races, set a course record at the PAC championship, and finished forty-third at nationals. Led by freshman Amy Mizzone, the 1995 team finished 44–1, and the 1996 team won three invitationals. She broke Grove City's course record at homecoming by an impressive thirty-eight seconds. Charity Pefferman, '02, was the leading harrier in the late 1990s, setting a course record at the 1998 PAC meet and leading the team to the championship. The women won twelve invitational meets in 1997 and 1998. In 2002, Elisa Pedersen, '06, finished first at the Allegheny Invitational and second at the Case Western Reserve Invitational. That fall, Pedersen was first at the Mideast Regional, as the team placed ninth.

The women's track and field team won the PAC seven times between 1993 and 2003. Its highest place in the ECAC was twenty-first in 1995. Kathy Hair, '92, excelled in the discus (still fourth all-time) and the shot put, Julie Clinefelter, '93, in the 400 and 800 meters, and Nicole Archer '93 in the 1500 and 3000 meters. Versatile Becky Berad, '95, often won the high hurdles, the triple jump, the high jump, and the javelin. Sally Lewis, '04, set school records in the long jump and the triple jump in 2001. At the 2003 PAC championship meet, Lewis won the 100 meters, long jump, and triple jump; Christine Rummel, '05, took the 110-high hurdle and the 400-meter hurdle races and was second in long and triple jumps; and Elisa Pedersen won the steeplechase and the 5000 meters. In 2003, Lewis had the twelfth-best triple jump in D3. Lewis is still the school record holder in the long jump and triple jump, while Rummel is second in the triple jump.

The women's soccer team's best records were in 2000 (14–6, outscoring PAC teams 48–5) and 2002 (13–7–2). The Lady Wolverines won five PAC titles and played in an ECAC tournament and one NCAA tournament, losing in the opening round. The star players between 1991 and 2002 were Abby Anderson, '97, Jody Swauger-Simms, '98, and Meg Tilley, '04. Anderson is Grove City's second leading scorer with forty-nine goals. Swauger-Simms earned ten varsity letters and is sixth all-time in goals scored. In 2002, Tilley led the PAC with twenty-five goals, nine assists, and fifty-nine points and was named to the D3 Great Lakes Region second team.

The best basketball seasons were 1996–1997, when the team finished 17–9, 1997–1998, when the Lady Wolverines were 16–9 and lost in the ECAC semifinals, and 1999–2000, when the squad lost in the finals of the ECAC. Led by Beth Lora, '98, who ended her career with 1,250 points (eighth all-time), the team beat Ursinus 76–63 in overtime to capture the 1997 ECAC title. Kathy Hair is fifth all-time in rebounds and fourth all-time in field goal percentage. Theresa Berg, '93, finished with 1,347 points (fifth all-time).

The softball squad's best record was 20–8 in 1998, when it captured the PAC crown. Its leading players during these years were Cherith Reidenbaker, '97, whose .380 career batting average is the fourth all-time and whose .500 batting average in 1996 is first all-time; Heather Johnson, '00, who had the most hits, doubles, triples, and runs scored in 1998 and is the career leader in stolen bases; and Lynn Hubler, '98, who in 1998 had a sparkling 1.12 ERA, the best in the PAC and the second-best in college history. Hubler's career record is 31–18, and her 1.45 career ERA is the lowest in varsity history.

Led by Laney Black, '97, the women's golf team was undefeated in 1996, its inaugural season, and won the PAC championship. Medalist Megan Wittenwyler, '02, helped the 1998 team triumph at the PAC tournament. The lady golfers also captured PAC titles in 1997, 1999, and 2000. Kristin Costanzo, '03, was named to the first-team PAC in 2001 and 2002. Mary Brown, '05, finished second at the 2002 and 2003 PAC tournaments and led the Lady Wolverines to their sixth title in 2003.

The men and women both captured the PAC all-sports trophy in 1992–1993, 1997–1998, 1998–1999, 2000–2001, and 2001–2002. In 1997–1998, Grove City claimed ten of the nineteen championships; the women won six of the nine titles to take the trophy for the fourth year in a row and the eighth time in nine years. The men also captured the trophy in 1999–2000, while the women claimed the all-sports crown in 2002–2003.

The women's lacrosse club, formed in 1995, was the runner-up in the 1996 Women's Collegiate Lacrosse League. In 2000, the squad beat Western Michigan and Bowling Green on its way to its fifth consecutive national playoff. A women's club rugby team began play in fall 2002.

"A Change Agent"

From November 1990 to July 1992, Charles MacKenzie conducted the first fundraising drive in college history that netted $9.2 million ($21 million today).[82] The three major financial developments during these years were the trustees' decisions to forbid students from accepting federally subsidized Stafford Loans and create the college's own loan program in 1996, to establish a development department in 1998, and to hold the college's first major capital campaign in 1999. Tom Pappalardo, the vice president for development at Allegheny General Hospital in Pittsburgh, was hired to head the development department. The initial $45 million goal of the "Change and Commitment" campaign was increased in May 2000 to $60 million ($111.4 million today). After an eighteen-month "silent phase," the college kicked off the public phase with a dinner at the Duquesne Club in Pittsburgh on October 26, 2000. The drive sought to raise $20 million for scholarships and $40 million to construct the Hall of Arts and Letters and a student union and to enlarge the Pew Fine Arts Center. Trustee Fred Fetterolf, '52, who cochaired the campaign with Dick Jewell, argued that Grove City could become "a change agent" in American culture by providing value-driven leadership. From his student days to the present, he declared, the college had progressed from being a good to an excellent school.[83]

Recognition and Recruitment

During the presidencies of Combee, Runion, and Moore, Grove City's national rankings skyrocketed. The 1992 Templeton Foundation Honor Roll for Free Enterprise Teaching ranked Grove City second in the nation. *The 1992 Guide to the 101 Best Values in Ameri-*

ca's Colleges and Universities included Grove City, declaring that the college's education "is superb in every respect" and its programs in engineering, chemistry, education, mathematics, and religion and philosophy "are among the finest available at any college." In 1993, *Money Magazine* rated Grove City the fourth best value in the Mid-Atlantic region and the thirteenth best value in the nation. *The National Review College Guide* designated Grove City one of the fifty best liberal arts colleges in the nation, and *The Princeton Review* gave Grove City a selectivity score of ninety-one (tied with Johns Hopkins University), one of the highest ratings in the Mid-Atlantic states.[84] In fall 1994, *Money Magazine* ranked GCC as the eleventh best value in the nation and the sixth best value in its highly selective national category, while *US News & World Report* ranked Grove City first among liberal arts colleges in the North as a "best value."

High rankings continued. In 1996, *Money* rated Grove City the twelfth best buy in the nation. That year, *the Princeton Review* designated Grove City as the nation's second most religious school after Brigham Young University and as the country's number six Stone Cold Sober college, based on questions relating to students' use of alcohol and drugs and hours of studying each day and the popularity of the Greek system. In subsequent years, Grove City ranked highly in these categories and in students who prayed regularly and were most nostalgic for Ronald Reagan.

In April 1997, a *USA Today* article proclaimed that Grove City "Puts Its Principles First." Admissions director Jeff Mincey argued that Grove City was a rare Christian college that combined superb academics and a strong spiritual emphasis.[85] In the 2000 *US News* rankings, Grove City was second in best value and fifth among northern liberal arts colleges. Grove City was listed as among the nation's fifty most competitive colleges by Barron's *Profiles of American Colleges* in 2001 and its sixty-four most competitive colleges in 2003. In 2002, Kaplan's chose Grove City as one of its forty-one best values, and *US News* rated Grove City fourth best among northern comprehensive colleges based on its having the highest freshman retention rate, SAT scores, and percentage of students in the top quarter of their high school classes.

His first year, Jerry Combee expanded the budget for recruitment and the college began advertising in national publications and in all prime market high school papers and yearbooks. Direct mailings to prospective students increased from 43,500 to 127,000. The college switched from rolling admissions to a February 15 deadline for regular decision. Combee's changes paid dividends, as the number and geographical distribution of applicants increased significantly. Visitation days for high school seniors and juniors attracted larger numbers of prospective students, and engineering, education, and music held their own open houses. The 1998 Middle States report noted that most colleges would envy Grove City's admissions success. The college had "defined its niche and had been successfully communicating its campus values and ethos."[86]

Applications declined from 2,163 in 1999 to 1,893 in 2000, caused by several factors: the college's reputation for academic rigor had discouraged lower-achieving applicants from applying; the college's website was subpar; the "population drain" in western Pennsylvania reduced prospective students; and college advertising was still inadequate.[87]

Placement and Alumni

In 1993, the Career Development and Placement Office was renamed the Career Services Office and moved from Crawford to Carnegie. That fall, the college held its first graduate and professional schools fair, with forty-four institutions participating. Many companies, including Price Waterhouse and Armstrong World Industries, were eager to hire Grove City graduates.[88] James Thrasher became the CSO director in 1994 and made helping students develop a biblical understanding of vocation a CSO priority. Combee claimed in May 1995 that 83 percent of students applying to medical schools for the fall had been accepted aided by their "solid science foundation," work with physicians, internships, medical mission trips, and high MCAT scores.[89] Thrasher introduced an annual career fair in 1999, which has included as many as 150 businesses and graduate schools each year from the early 2000s to the present. Many recruiters praised the quality of Grove City graduates, especially their preparation and professionalism, and argued that they were superior to students from other institutions they interviewed.[90] Grove City was one of the few small private colleges where all "Big Five" accounting firms recruited on campus.

The *Grove City College Alumni Magazine* was launched in 1991 to improve communication with graduates. In 1999, the states with the most Grove City alumni were Pennsylvania, Ohio, New York, Florida, Virginia, New Jersey, Maryland, and California. The geographical distribution of students and alumni was about to significantly increase.[91]

Trustees

The 1998 Middle States team was impressed by the trustees' knowledge, commitment, and dedication. The board's twenty-nine members, who had backgrounds in business, medicine, finance, law, and education, functioned cohesively as a unit.[92] They established college fees, determined salaries, oversaw the budget, and set major policies. Trustee Don Hayes argued in 1999 that prospective members needed to have at least two of the three attributes the board valued—wisdom, a strong work ethic, and wealth.[93]

In September 1997, the school of science and engineering was named for Albert Hopeman Jr. in appreciation for his forty-four years of service as a Grove City trustee. The next year, Hopeman, who had served as the president of the board of trustees since 1971, died. Like his predecessor, J. Howard Pew, Hopeman constantly emphasized the Christian ideals of freedom and responsibility. Hopeman was deeply involved in the life of the college from major initiatives to daily operations. He spent hundreds of hours conferring with MacKenzie, Combee, and Moore. MacKenzie insisted that Hopeman gave "me new vision when I was weary, courage when I was lonely and under attack," and "insight when I was perplexed."[94] Hopeman's talks at faculty/trustee luncheons each May combined a report on the state of the college with an analysis of trends in American culture and education.

J. Paul Sticht, '39, who had been a trustee since 1968, replaced Hopeman as president of the board. Sticht worked for US Steel and TWA, as a vice president of the Campbell Soup Company and the Federated Department Stores, and as CEO and board chair of RJ Reynolds Nabisco. Under Sticht's leadership, the trustees established a comprehensive committee structure to help the college function more effectively. Prominent economist Walter Williams joined the board in 2003.

Conclusion

In January 2003, John Moore announced that he would retire in June. In his final report to the trustees, the president argued that the college's greatest needs were hiring more professors, devising "the right balance between teaching and scholarship," creating a more diverse student body, generating more alumni support, increasing the endowment, preserving the college's mission, and maintaining its affordability.[95]

Under Moore's leadership, the college bolstered its academic program, Christian identity, and reputation. He oversaw a highly successful capital campaign, arranged an impressive celebration of the college's 125th anniversary, and hired some exceptional faculty including Paul Kengor, Paul Schaeffer, and Paul Kemeny. As president, Moore grew to appreciate the college's valuable role as a Christian institution in a secular society.[96] The college, the trustees declared, had "immeasurably improved" during his tenure.[97] Grove City's "favorable competitive position" in contemporary higher education in terms of its enrollment, finances, programs, staffing, and facilities, the Middle States team argued, would help it maintain "academic quality and institutional integrity."[98] The trustees enlisted Academic Search to direct the quest to find a new president. Incoming board chair David Rathburn, '79, led the search committee, which for the first time included students. After evaluating forty-two applicants, the committee selected a nontraditional candidate, Richard "Dick" Jewell, who was an attorney rather than an educator or pastor. On the other hand, as a Grove City graduate, former president of the alumni association, and college trustee since 1974, Jewell was the consummate insider.[99]

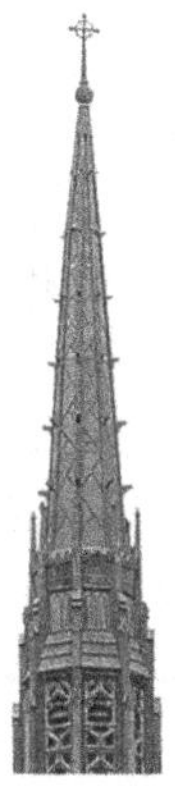

THE PRESIDENCY OF RICHARD G. JEWELL:
A "Revolutionary Institution in Higher Education,"
2003–2014

The years between 2003 and 2014 brought many changes to the college, including a new president, Richard Jewell, '67, and a new board chair, David Rathburn, '79. Together they led the college in devising two five-year strategic plans, undertaking the college's second and third capital campaigns, and constructing several important new buildings, most notably Colonial Hall Apartments and STEM Hall. Jewell created the Center for Vision and Values, raised the college's academic profile, and spearheaded some significant curricular changes. Student Life and Learning implemented a new philosophy of student development, a new initiative strove to increase minority enrollment, departmental curriculum reviews were instituted, and a committee of administrators and faculty revised the general education requirements. Jewell also enlarged the faculty, created three lectureship series, strengthened the college's international emphasis and programs, increased and upgraded the facilities for intramural and club sports, and improved relations with alumni and the town of Grove City.[1] From 2003 to 2011, the college bulletin described Grove City as "authentically Christian, challenging academics, amazing value."

Jewell is among the college's most accomplished students. The 1967 Senior Man of the Year was the swimming and diving team's captain, a Penn-Ohio championship diver, the editor in chief of *The Collegian*, the president of SGA, an RA, and a three-year student assistant for a history professor. Classmate Tom Brown, '68, insisted that Jewell's "disciplined study habits and leadership" provided a great role model for his Kappa Alpha Phi fraternity brothers.[2] After serving in the army for two years, Jewell earned a JD from the University of Michigan Law School and then worked for Navigant Consulting, the nation's largest forensic accounting firm, and participated very actively in Pittsburgh's political and civic affairs. In 1974, Jewell became the youngest trustee in its history; by his estimate, he visited campus about one thousand times between graduating and becoming president thirty-six years later. ODK president Randy Cole, a presidential search committee member, was impressed by Jewell's "friendliness and approachability" and amazing "love and passion for the school."[3]

Jewell's presidency occurred amid numerous challenging domestic and international events. The United States became embroiled in controversial military incursions into Afghanistan and Iraq. The global financial crisis of 2008–2009 caused extensive economic upheaval. Major natural disasters at home including Hurricane Katrina in 2005 and Hurricane Sandy in 2012, and huge earthquakes in Pakistan in 2005, China in 2008, and Haiti in 2010, caused death and destruction. Terrorist attacks in London, Paris, Mumbai, and Boston shocked the world, as did mass shootings in Newtown, Connecticut, and Aurora, Colorado, in 2012. Darfur became a humanitarian crisis. Some hailed the 2005 Kyoto Protocol, designed to reduce the emission of greenhouse gases, as a landmark achievement, while others questioned its effectiveness. Netflix's streaming of movies and television shows changed the entertainment industry, the iPod transformed the way many people listened to music, and Facebook became the world's largest social media platform. Barack Obama was elected the nation's first African American president in 2009, and Navy SEALs killed al-Qaeda leader Osama bin-Laden in 2011. Black Lives Matter emerged as a major political movement.

In November 2003, Jewell was inaugurated as the college's eighth president. Four men spoke at his inaugural ceremony—two of Jewell's close friends, Tyco International CEO Ed Breen, '78, and former Pennsylvania Governor Dick Thornburgh—and his two most important mentors—retired diving coach Jim Longnecker and history professor Robert Neff. Bucking trends of secularization and political correctness in higher education, Grove City, under Jewell's leadership, continued to unabashedly affirm its Christian mission and Western cultural and moral norms that were informed by Judeo-Christian principles.

Jewell faced two primary problems as president—a decline in the number of youths in the region from which Grove City drew students most heavily, which began in 2010, and the replacement of the college's pension system in 2009 with an enhanced defined-benefit plan, which some faculty, who believed it would reduce their retirement income, strongly opposed.[4]

The personable and loquacious president worked diligently to get to know students. Among other activities, Jewell held weekly Gedunk hours to which students brought complaints, concerns, and compliments as they conversed with him.[5] Junior Virginia Larsen encouraged students to talk with the "cool Dr. Jewell" who was committed to helping them remedy problems.[6] Jewell also built relationships by strolling around campus, attending extracurricular events, and hosting students in his home.

In 2005, the trustees adopted a strategic plan to guide the college, which established five-, ten-, and fifteen-year goals. The plan had eight objectives. The first was to equip students to be "leaders and responsible citizens." Residence hall life staff sought to strengthen students' moral character and personal integrity and empower them to lead in all areas of life. Second, the college wanted to enhance its "already excellent academic programs" by enrolling students with high SAT and ACT scores and ensuring that at least 90 percent of graduates had jobs or were attending school within six months of completing their degrees. Third, the college sought to boost its reputation by developing a "a comprehensive brand and marketing program" and achieving high *US News & World Report* rankings. Fourth, the college sought to fortify its Christian environment by repeatedly accentuating its mission and guaranteeing that all faculty and staff supported this mission. The college planned to hire a director of student ministries, help faculty better explain how the biblical worldview undergirded their disciplines, improve the chapel program, and bring more guest speakers to campus to enrich the spiritual climate. Fifth, the college wanted to provide 70 percent of students' unmet financial need, lower the CQPA requirements for aid, and ensure that no student had to borrow more than $20,000 to complete a degree. Sixth, Grove City would evaluate adding master's programs in Austrian economics, public policy, computer science, and physician assistance. Seventh, the college would construct additional "high quality, attractive and functional facilities." Eighth, Grove City would raise enough money to fund its capital, operational, and financial aid needs.[7]

To honor college trustee Ed Breen and his wife Lynn, '78, who donated $5.5 million to the college, the student union was named for them in 2007. This gift completed the Change & Commitment Campaign that began in 1999 and raised $69 million, added by a 55 percent increase in the number of alumni contributors. Campaign chair and trustee Fred Fetterolf contended that the college's fundraising would need to be continuous. Despite this wonderful result, Grove City still trailed many schools that had been soliciting funds much longer and had larger development staffs.[8]

His first year, Jewell hired Jack Freeman, a prominent higher education consultant, to undertake a strategic assessment of the college. Freeman concluded that in recent years, Grove City had "prospered under a dedicated and creative board of trustees and exceptionally able executive leadership." He commended the board's reorganization; the hiring of "strong and experienced" administrators, faculty, and staff; the college's impressive academic programs, student body, and facilities; and Grove City's improving reputation.[9] Freeman lauded the trustees and the president for providing "effective, dynamic leadership." The curriculum served the college's mission and needs very well, and faculty were "committed to integrating Christian principles" into their courses. Freeman noted that Grove City students scored high on standardized achievement tests. He praised the faculty's "exceptional quality," "strong work ethic," and "extraordinary commitment" to the college's mission and students' welfare. Despite their heavy teaching loads, the majority were actively engaged in scholarship. Faculty compensation was "reasonably competitive" with similar institutions, and the lack of tenure appeared not to hinder the college's ability to recruit and retain high-quality professors. The athletic program, which included recreational, intramural, and intercollegiate sports, Freeman maintained, was "extensive, well balanced and focused on health and fitness." The chapel program strongly supported the college's mission and met students' spiritual needs. Grove City worked diligently to prepare students to serve God through their vocational, church, civic, and personal activities. Grove City, Freeman concluded, had "visionary leadership, dedicated faculty and staff, creative administrators, outstanding students, successful alumni, a beautiful campus, ample resources and a welcoming and supportive community."[10]

Freeman offered several recommendations. The college should devise a vision statement; add more women, minorities, and educators to its board; give faculty a greater role in governance and hiring colleagues; conduct reviews of academic departments and programs to compare them with those of similar institutions; lower the faculty/student ratio; hire more support staff; provide a higher percentage of students' unmet financial need; increase the number of minority students, counseling center staff, and development personnel; pursue accreditation in all fields where it was available; involve more alumni in recruiting prospective students; and use technology more effectively.[11] During the next decade, the college implemented many of his recommendations.

Grove City's ten leading competitors, Freeman maintained, included Wheaton, Messiah, Westminster, Calvin, and Penn State. Grove City's comparative advantages, he argued, were its "strong

Christian environment," low cost, scenic campus, first-rate facilities, "commitment to technological innovation," and the "high quality of its students and academic programs." Its comparative disadvantages were its lack of diversity, small library holdings, rural location, and inadequate financial aid.[12]

In 2008, the Middle States Association reaccredited Grove City College. Its team members called the college's self-study "brutally honest." Evaluators commended the board and administrators for giving faculty and staff a larger role in decision-making and for engaging in "spirited exchanges" with the faculty about the college's mission and academic matters.[13]

In 2009, the trustees initiated a second capital drive called "The Third Century Campaign for Grove City College." Fetterolf argued that Grove City was much better prepared for this second capital campaign, especially because larger potential gifts had been identified.[14] The campaign goal was $90 million, and the trustees pledged to provide $18 million. The campaign sought to raise $30 million to augment the student scholarship endowment, $35 million to erect a new Science, Technology, Engineering, and Mathematics Hall, $5 million to construct a Christian activities building, and $5 million to aid both the Center for Vision and Values and the Center for Entrepreneurship. The projected world-class, sixty-three thousand square feet STEM building, Jewell declared, would be "game-changing" for the college.[15]

In 2010, the college hired educational consultant R. Thomas Williamson to produce another assessment and lay the groundwork for its 2011–2016 strategic plan. He concluded that Grove City had "never been stronger or more committed to its mission, vision and values." Campus facilities were in "excellent condition," spiritual life was "vibrant," and the college's constituents felt proud of its traditions and had "faith in its future." One problem Williamson noted was that some prospective students and their parents misunderstood the college's affordability message to mean that "we're the cheapest" and its opposition to federal funding to mean "we're anti-government." Another challenge was that the college was supplying only 40 percent of students' unmet financial need, whereas it had earlier provided 60 percent, which was hampering recruitment, especially as its competitors offered more merit-based aid.[16]

The Student Body

During Jewell's presidency, freshmen had the highest average SAT and ACT scores and highest average high school GPAs in college history, and the student body became more geographically diverse. However, the number of applications dropped from 2,198 to 1,492 (a 32 percent decrease) between 2003 and 2014 fueled by the declining number of youths in the Pennsylvania-New York-Ohio-Maryland region in which Grove City most heavily recruited and by most of its competitors offering high-achieving students deep discounts in tuition, subsidized by other students who paid full tuition. Although Grove City's tuition was substantially lower than most other colleges, the significant increase in its competitors' discounts, coupled with the inability of Grove City students to receive federal financial aid, made attracting outstanding students more difficult. Moreover, despite extensive efforts, the college continued to struggle to enroll a more racially diverse cohort of students.

The 564-member freshman class in fall 2003 had an average SAT of 1270 and a high school GPA of 3.73 GPA; 62 percent of freshmen were in the top tenth of their classes; sixty-seven were valedictorians. Eighty-one percent of them had been involved in church youth groups; 67 percent had been members of the National Honor Society; 47 percent were from Pennsylvania; and 89 percent had interviewed with an admissions counselor on campus. Six percent of freshmen were exclusively homeschooled, but an estimated 40 percent of freshmen had some homeschooling during their K-12 years. In 2005, the average SAT score reached a pinnacle of 1280 as Grove City enrolled seventy-four valedictorians, and freshmen had an average high school GPA of 3.85. The 673-member freshman class in 2006 also had a 1280 average SAT score and included seventy-seven valedictorians and nineteen National Merit Finalists; 63 percent of freshmen came from states other than

Pennsylvania. The 650-member class of 2010 included thirty-nine minority students (6 percent).

The average SAT score of the class of 2011 declined slightly to 1269, and the average high school GPA dipped to 3.72. Fifteen percent of freshmen were exclusively homeschooled, and 21 percent were recruited to play a varsity sport—record highs in both categories. An additional 21 percent graduated from private Christian schools, 23 percent were student council members, 47 percent were active in missions, and 94 percent performed community service. Overall, the 2007–2008 student body, numbering about two thousand five hundred, came from forty-two states, the District of Columbia, and twelve foreign countries. Ninety percent of freshmen usually returned for their sophomore year, the highest retention rate in the nation. Throughout Jewell's tenure, the most popular majors were mechanical and electrical engineering, biology, and elementary education.

In fall 2010, the college hired Lorie Johnson-Osho as its first director of multicultural recruiting and retention. She visited dozens of college fairs and high schools and spoke to numerous organizations in minority communities to recruit students. The college hosted the Pittsburgh Promise Bus Tour, Urban Impact, Higher Achievement, and other minority groups. Johnson-Osho argued that interaction with people from different cultures helped prepared White Grove City students "for life outside the college bubble."[17] While acknowledging that the college was working to increase racial and ethnic diversity, some students complained about the homogeneity of the student body. One maintained that "the biggest outsiders" on campus were Catholics and Democrats.[18]

Facilities

During Jewell's presidency, several major building projects were completed, which enhanced the college's "beautiful, bucolic environment."[19] In 2004, a $2 million renovation converted the former Gedunk into offices for Career Services, physical education faculty, and the SGA. The Student Activities Center was dedicated in May

2004 with a fireworks celebration. The Jewells moved into a new presidential home in fall 2005 that included a large kitchen, study, living room, family room, great room, and five bedrooms. The recreation room in MAP was renovated in 2005; its decor, Ping-Pong table, kitchen, and jukebox made it "the campus hot, new hangout."[20] A new track, synthetic grass football field, and lights were installed in summer 2006, enabling these facilities to be used hundreds of hours per year for varsity practices, club sports, and general recreation. Carnegie Hall, constructed on the lower campus in 1900, had housed a library, auditorium, gymnasium, men's dormitory, and Career Services Office. After a $8 million refurbishment, Carnegie became home in 2008 to the communications/PR office, the alumni relations office, and the college archives. The three largest projects completed during Jewell's tenure were the Colonial Hall Apartments in 2006, which accommodated 208 students; Rathburn Hall, a ministry center, in 2012; and STEM Hall in 2013. Rathburn was named for board president David Rathburn and contains the Morledge Great Room, which honors dean of the chapel Richard Morledge, as well as chapel ministries offices and rooms for meetings, prayer, and events.

Academic Life: Defying the Zeitgeist

Grove City College, wrote senior Matt Sitman in 2003, "is one of the few places in the United States equipping young people to be effective cultural warriors." Undergirding all its academic instruction "is a certain education in character, in Biblical truth, in right and wrong." Consequently, "We are the voices of dissent defying the zeitgeist."[21] Through its core curriculum, courses in every discipline, faculty publications, residence halls programs, religious organizations, and the Christian commitment of administrators, faculty, and students, Grove City College challenged prevailing American cultural norms and offered an alternative vision and morality based on a biblical worldview. That same year, senior Melinda Haring called Grove City "an oasis in the liberal desert." No other college, she asserted, gave "its students four years absolutely saturated in the Western Canon and committed to the pursuit of Truth." "This venerable institution has the audacity," she argued, to embrace the wisdom of ancient political thought, which most other colleges were abandoning. Jewell agreed: Grove City was a "revolutionary institution in higher education."[22] Freeman concluded that most faculty had effectively integrated Christian principles into the curriculum.[23] Survey data from 2006 confirmed his assessment, as students rated the faculty on a five-point scale as successfully doing this at 3.90 in first majors, 4.2 in HUMA courses, 3.77 in other general education courses, and 3.98 in all courses combined.[24]

Several considerations indicate that Grove City fulfilled its lofty goals during the Jewell years. In 2008, students, parents, trustees, administrators, and faculty all rated the college between 4.08 and 4.71 on a five-point scale on achieving its academic development objectives. Eighty-four percent of alumni said that they were well equipped for the workforce or graduate and professional schools. Many claimed that they were better prepared than their peers for graduate school and that it was easier than GCC. The results on Major Field Achievement Tests confirmed the quality of Grove City's academic program.[25] In 2006, for example, the students in biology, business, chemistry, education, English, history, physics, psychology, and sociology all scored at the ninetieth percentile or higher.

Grove City College based its instruction on "a Christian perspective on life," which involved integrating "Christian principles and truths" into courses. New faculty received instruction during their orientation to assist them in faith and learning integration. Every professor was expected to present subject matter from a distinctively biblical perspective.[26] Professors discussed how Christian perspectives informed their teaching and scholarship in various settings—faculty workshops, scholarly conferences, and publications. Faculty forums enabled professors to share and receive feedback on their articles, book proposals, and research projects and to explain how Christian presuppositions informed their teaching, research, and writing. Some faculty served on the boards of organizations committed to fostering the relationship between faith and specific academic disciplines, while others edited or contributed to journals that published faith-based scholarship. Beginning in the early 2010s, the college sponsored off-campus retreats in mid-August to discuss the integration of faith and learning. Several professors complained that some of their colleagues were not subjecting their politically conservative/free-market ideology to a thorough scriptural evaluation.

At the midpoint of Jewell's presidency, the college had 132 full-time professors; excluding physical education faculty, 90 percent of professors held terminal degrees. The college's twenty-three academic departments offered fifty-one degree plans. Departments conducted curricular reviews on a rotating five-year basis. Many faculty began using PowerPoint to enhance their lectures, sabbaticals were introduced in 2004, more money was appropriated to fund faculty and student research and participation in scholarly conferences, the Center for Vision and Values was created in 2004, and a small campus was established in Nantes, France. After the college signed a friendship agreement with the University of Nantes, mechanical engineering professor Mark Reuber and his wife Debbie, a French instructor, took a contingent of twenty-five students, mainly engineering majors, to Nantes every fall semester from 2006 through 2019. Sabbaticals enabled professors to spend a semester researching, writing, and gaining new insight. Four faculty have typically received a sabbatical every year from 2004 until the present.

In 2004, Grove City's education department passed its evaluation with flying colors. The chair of the Pennsylvania Department of Education review committee praised the college's "exemplary" program. Committee members commended the dedication of the department's faculty and staff, the high quality of students, and the close collaboration between certification departments and the education department.[27]

In 2003–2004, only about twenty-five Grovers studied abroad. The Office of International Education, established in 2004, set a three-year goal of tripling that number.[28] Students could have an experience abroad by doing internships, participating in student exchanges offered by six affiliated providers, or going on faculty-led intersession trips. The office set a more ambitious goal in 2007 of sending 250 students per year on long-term trips. By 2008, almost half of students were having some form of international experience; 80 percent of this was short-term, including intersession courses, Inter City Outreach projects, and Red Box mission trips.

In 2004–2005, Grove City changed its method for choosing trustee scholars and doubled the number from twelve to twenty-four. The college required a minimum SAT of 1300, an ACT of 29, and an unweighted high school GPA of 3.75. The selection committee considered students' academic ability, interviews, extracurricular activities, leadership/character/faith, and a four-hundred- to five-hundred-word essay. Trustee scholars had to maintain a 3.60 CQPA to retain their scholarships.

In fall 2005, engineering professor Stacy Birmingham became the college's first female dean when she was appointed to head the Albert A. Hopeman Jr. School of Science and Engineering. Stacy and her husband Bill left tenured positions at the University of Michigan in 2003 to teach at Grove City. In fall 2005, English professor Gloria Stansberry began teaching elementary Japanese, and the next year, the college began to offer courses in Chinese.

In fall 2005, Jewell outlined major proposed changes in academics, student life, facilities, and fundraising designed to make Grove City College "one of America's premier liberal arts, science and engineering colleges, where scholarship combines with Christian principles." These changes accorded with the college's first strategic plan, approved by the board in May. The college instituted writing, speaking, and information literacy intensive courses in the HUMA core and every major. In addition, students were required to take a course in science, faith, and technology and a foundation course in one of the social sciences.[29]

Freeman noted that in 2004 that rules pertaining to intervisitation, the use of alcohol or drugs, curfews, smoking, and quiet hours were quite rigorous and strictly enforced. Most students accepted these rules, but a sizable minority wanted more freedom to manage their own behavior.[30] Jewell asserted that Student Life and Learning would emphasize "personal responsibility." Residence halls would be considered locales of learning rather than "just places to sleep and eat."[31] Under Jean-Noel Thompson, who replaced Nancy Paxton, Student Life and Learning focused less on regulating behavior and more on spiritual, intellectual, and social formation.[32] His successor, Larry Hardesty, continued this approach. Curfews for freshmen ended. More students were added to college committees to provide their perspectives on issues and to hone their leadership skills.

In fall 2004, the Center for Vision and Values was founded, with Lee Wishing, '83, appointed its administrative director. The next year, Paul Kengor became its executive director. The center continued to publish the "Vision & Values" newsletter (created in 1993 to provide "a reasoned defense of traditional education, free competitive enterprise, civil and religious liberty, moral order, and representative government")[33] and introduced a new electronic publication called "Vision & Values, Concise." Guided by Christian principles, think tank contributors analyzed public policy and social issues. The CVV strove to generate op-eds, longer scholarly pieces, and media interviews and sponsored a conference each year. Its April 2005 conference analyzed the War on Poverty. Subsequent ones examined such topics as "The De-Christianization of Europe" in 2007, "Church and State" in 2008, "Faith Freedom and Higher Education" in 2009, and "America: Still the Last Best Hope?" in 2011. In February 2007, the center launched an annual Ronald Reagan Lecture series to highlight the fortieth president's contributions to America and the world. Speakers included the president's son Michael Reagan, a nationally syndicated talk radio host; US Attorney General Edwin P. Meese III; and Department of Education secretary William Bennett. In 2008–2009, the CVV began employing student fellows to assist professors with research and to help market the center. That fall, the CVV introduced an evening dessert program called "Freedom Readers" to educate students about free-market economics.

In 2005, psychology professor Kevin Seybold received a three-year, $15,000 grant from the Metanexus Institute on Religion and Science to facilitate the work of the Grove City College Society for Science, Faith and Technology, an organization created to foster "intellectual, moral, spiritual and social development consistent with a commitment to Christian truth."[34] In fall 2005, the society hosted three discussions of robotics, nanotechnology, restorative medicine, intelligent design theory, what it means to be human, and the religious implications of recent technological advances.

Various departments sponsored special programs. In 2004, the economic faculty held its first annual Austrian Student Scholars Conference, where students from Grove City and other institutions presented papers and distinguished scholars gave lectures. For years, the chemistry department hosted an annual show for local elementary students. The English department held a yearly Christian Writers Conference, bringing noted scholars to discuss Emily Dickinson, C. S. Lewis and the Inklings, and other great authors. Recently retired physics professor Richard Leo developed a lecture in October 2005 impersonating scientist J. Robert Oppenheimer and general Leslie Groves that discussed the Manhattan Project.

In 2005, the college created a faculty-student Ad Hoc Academic Integrity Assessment Committee to promote greater honesty in learning, establish a procedure for dealing with academic dishonesty, and reconsider whether the college should adopt an honor code. Its members worked diligently, committee chair Paul Kemeny explained, to create a culture that valued "academic integrity more seriously."[35]

Other academic developments occurred during Jewell's presidency. To encourage students to arrange internships, Career Services began holding the Internship Fair in fall 2005. The college added a minor in art in 2005–2006, in exercise science in 2006–2007, and in classical studies and classical Christian education in 2011–2012. In fall 2007, the college lowered the CQPA requirement for renewing need-based scholarships from 3.0 to 2.75. Administrators wanted to gradually reduce the CQPA requirement to 2.0. In 2009, Kevin Hoffman, '11, James Van Eerden, '12, and Steven Irwin, '12, created the *Grove City College Journal of Law and Public Policy* to publish articles by faculty, students, and alumni on topics ranging from First Amendment rights to Supreme Court decisions. The journal was one of only six undergraduate publications of this type in the nation. In summer 2011, the college began offering online courses to help lighten students' course loads. In 2012, the college hired archivist Hilary Walczak to organize and oversee its historical documents, and she created a system for housing college memorabilia, legal documents, and news items. The college failed to reach its objective to have 15 percent of the student body studying abroad annually; in 2013–2014, only 2.5 percent were doing so. However, about half of Grove City students had spent some time abroad.[36] In fall 2013, the college added a freshman writing and rhetoric course to the general education curriculum.

A 2013 article in *The Collegian* noted that the college website declares, "Our academics are rigorous" which produces "remarkable outcomes for our students." The author pointed out that Collegeprowler.org had affirmed this claim by rating Grove City 1,392 out of 1,394 on its list of colleges with the most challenging workload.[37] No Grove City program was more demanding than engineering. Only about 50 percent of students who started as engineering majors graduated with an engineering degree. This was in part because the college's program was more challenging than those at most other schools. A core feature of the engineering program was the senior group project, which involved such projects as building a recumbent bicycle and a touring boat.

The quality of the college's programs was attested by the accreditation several of them received from national organizations. In 2013, ABET accredited the college's computer science major. In 2014, the Committee on Accreditation of Allied Health Education Programs approved the college's exercise science major and the programs in accounting, entrepreneurship, finance, international business, management, and marketing received accreditation from the Accreditation Council for Business Schools and Programs.

During Jewell's presidency, many students argued that "the knowledge, wisdom and cultural appreciation" the HUMA courses provided "were invaluable."[38] A whopping 97 percent of students and alumni surveyed in 2008 stated that the HUMA core had increased their admiration of Western civilization.[39] Faculty strove to expose students to varied positions on issues through their lectures and by assigning readings by advocates of different perspectives. Students were not attending a "narrow-minded college," junior Jacob Einwechter argued, "when its Speculative Mind text has readings from Sam Harris, Richard Dawkins and Mary Anne Warren."[40] Meagan Van Til, '15, maintained that Grovers subjected themselves to "endless hours of homework," study marathons, and a "freezing cold trek to class" because a degree from Grove City was worth much more than one from most other colleges and universities. Moreover, Grovers learned "to view life through a critical lens," "ask questions and think for themselves."[41]

The Faculty

The most significant personnel changes during the Jewell years were the resignation of Charles Dunn in 2004, and the retirement of Nancy Paxton in 2004, Joseph Goncz in 2005, and John Sparks, Ed Arnold, and Diane Grundy, '65, in 2013. Dunn, the dean of the Calderwood School of Arts and Letters, left Grove City to become the dean of the Robertson School of Government at Regent University in Virginia Beach. During his six years at Grove City, Dunn encouraged faculty scholarship and mentored students who sought Rhodes, Fulbright, and Marshall scholarships. Paxton retired after twenty-eight years of service in student affairs. She advised numerous organizations and oversaw campus student services. She was highly respected for her vivacious, winsome personality and administrative skills. John Sparks, who chaired the business department from 1990–2003, took Dunn's place and served as a dean until his retirement. Goncz, an electrical engineering professor, taught at Grove City for thirty-six years and was the first dean of the Albert Hopeman Jr. School of Science and Engineering. As the chair of the music department, an administrator, the director of the marching band, and the head of the guest artists series, Arnold contributed substantially to college life. As the director of Buhl Library, Grundy adroitly oversaw its operations and upgraded its services during her forty-four years at the college.

In 2007, Hans Sennholz, the college's most renowned faculty member to that date, died. He helped shape the economic views of thousands of students while teaching at the college from 1956 to 1992. He also influenced the thought of countless economists around the world through his seventeen books and five hundred articles. Alumni remembered Sennholz for "his theatrical delivery" and passionate teaching. Two of his students, George Pearson, '64, and Lawrence Reed, '75, wrote, "At the heart of every Sennholz presentation was a clarion call for personal responsibility, individual liberty and limited government." Jewell called Sennholz "one of our Nation's most articulate, intellectual voices for ordered liberty, limited government and free markets."[42]

Most faculty devoted 90 percent of their time during the academic year to class preparation and instruction, advising students and campus organizations, and mentoring students.[43] Many professors wanted the administration to encourage and reward research more strongly. They asked for reduced teaching loads and more financial support for scholarly activities.[44] The faculty had many noteworthy achievements and received numerous honors during Jewell's tenure. Texas A&M University gave chemistry professor Harold Conder an award for undergraduate mentoring in 2003. Art instructor Peter Calaboyias created sculptures that were erected in Greece, Germany, and throughout Pennsylvania. In 2004, math professor Ralph Carlson developed an algorithm that rapidly identified which documents contained a particular character. That same year, Fred Brenner was reelected the Northeast regional vice president of Beta Beta Beta and cochair of the Forestry and Wildlife section of the American Society for Mining and Reclamation. In 2012, the biology professor was elected president of the Pennsylvania Chapter of the American Fisheries Society. In 2004, history professor Jason Edwards was named a Kentucky Colonel, the state's highest award, for his scholarship and service to the community. That year, physical education professor and track coach Allison Williams received the Black Achievers Award from *Black Opinion Magazine* for her mentoring of athletes.

Warren Throckmorton, a psychology professor who had directed the college's counseling service, created a documentary in 2004 that discussed sexual orientation. Because he argued that homosexuals could change their sexual orientation, the next year, Magellan Health Services, the nation's leading health care provider, dismissed Throckmorton from its advisory board.[45] Protests from conservatives prompted Magellan to reinstate Throckmorton a month later.

Several faculty members had significant achievements in 2005. Business professor Andrew Markley, '82, delivered a series of lectures at the Ryazan State University in Russia in October. That fall, history professor Earl Tilford was asked to analyze the curriculum used at the US Army War College. Electrical engineering professor Frank Duda received the American Society for Engineering Education's global educator award for his work to improve secondary science education in Uganda. Chemistry professor Chuck Kriley was elected to the strategic planning committee of the national science honorary Sigma Xi.

In 2006, music professor Doug Browne served as an adjudicator for North American Music Festivals. William Birmingham, the chair of the computer science department, received the American Radio Relay League's 2006 Instructor of the Year Award for promoting amateur radio. In 2007, the John Templeton Foundation gave psychology professors Kevin Seybold, Joseph Horton, and Gary Welton more than $300,000 to conduct a three-year study on students' attitudes and behaviors. Computer science professor Fred Jenny was elected president of the Association of Small Computer Users in Education in 2007. Dean of Enrollment Services John Inman was chosen as a 2007 Distinguished Member of the Robert Morris University chapter of the National Society of Collegiate Scholars. Throckmorton and dean of the chapel Stan Keehlwetter won alumni achievement awards from their respective colleges. Every summer, biology professor Mark Weber's program sent about twenty premed students to medically and spiritually underserved areas around the world.

Testifying to their effective classroom instruction, Grove City College professors ranked tenth in the nation in 2007 in the "Top Faculty" category of Ratemyprofessors.com. "[This] really speaks to the great job Grove City College professors are doing," declared Jason Rzepka, head of communication for mtvU, which owned Ratemyprofessors.com.[46]

In January 2008, entrepreneurship professor Timothy Mech, sociologist George "Van" Campbell, and Frank Duda taught pastors and strove to alleviate poverty in Chennai, India. Their work led to the founding of Harvest Bridge in 2008, which currently provides leadership training and biblical education for thousands of ministers and missionaries in South Asia, supplies medical care and emergency relief, and supports evangelistic efforts.

To build rapport with students, furnish entertainment, and have fun, numerous professors, assisted by ODK and Mortar Board, participated in Faculty Follies, which consistently drew an audience of eight hundred or more. For many years, faculty also played against students in a basketball blowout.

Allison Williams spent her fall 2009 sabbatical doing research on altitude training with athletes at the United States Olympic Training Center in Colorado Springs. Jennifer Scott served on the editorial board for *Kaleidoscope*, a communications journal, beginning in 2009. Professors Craig Columbus and Tim Mech won the elevator pitch competition at the Babson Symposium for Entrepreneurial Educators in 2009. In 2010, Ed Arnold served on the board of directors of the United Nations Youth Band and was named the Pennsylvania Bandmaster of the Year. That year, DJ Wagner received the Society of Physics Student Chapter Advisor Award, and in 2013, she was elected president of this national organization. In 2011, Connie Nichols was named to the Pennsylvania Governor's Commission on Higher Education. In 2013, she served as Pennsylvania's delegate at the American Association of Teacher Educators conference to help the organization address issues impacting teacher education. Music professor Joseph Pisano, '94, received the 2011 Technology Institute of Music Educators Teacher of the Year Award. The next year, he was awarded membership in the American Bandmasters Association and selected as an Oxford University Press music series editor.

Faculty books increased significantly during Jewell's presidency. Paul Kengor published *God and Ronald Reagan* (2004) and *God and George W. Bush* (2004). His book on Reagan was a *New York Times* bestseller, and he did dozens of radio and television interviews to promote it. Both spiritual biographies ranked among the top five nonfiction bestsellers on Amazon. Other faculty books included mechanical engineering professor Mark Archibald's *Design of Human-Powered and Ultra Efficient Vehicles* (2003); George Van Pelt Campbell's *Everything You Know Seems Wrong* (2004); Fred Brenner's coedited *Wildlife Diseases* (2004); David Ayers's *Investigating Social Problems* (2005); history professor Mark Graham's *News and Frontier Consciousness in the Late Roman Empire* (2006); my *Faith and the Presidency* (2006); religion professor Paul Kemeny's edited book, *Church, State and Public Justice: Five Views* (2007); Kengor's *William P. Clark, Ronald Reagan's Top Hand* (2007); Kengor's *God and Hillary Clinton* (2007); Michael Coulter's edited *Encyclopedia of Catholic Social Thought, Social Science and Social Policy* (2007); Kevin Seybold's *Explorations in Neuroscience, Psychology and Religion* (2008); religion professor Iain Duguid's commentary, *Daniel* (2008); sociologist Steve Jones's *Religious Schooling in America* (2008); Céline Léon's *Kierkegaard on Women, Sexual Difference, and Sexual Relations* (2008); religion professor T. David Gordon's *Why Johnny Can't Preach* (2008); Kengor's *The Crusader: Ronald Reagan and the Fall of Communism* (2009); Kengor's *Dupes* (2010); economist Shawn Ritenour's *Foundations of Economics: A Christian View* (2010); English professor Eric Potter's poetry collection, *Heart Murmur* (2010); Duguid's *Study Commentary on Haggai, Zechariah, Malachi* (2010); Gordon's *Why Johnny Can't Sing Hymns* (2010); Graham's *Ancient Empires* (2011); my *Heaven in the American Imagination* (2011); Paul Schaefer's *The Spiritual Brotherhood: Cambridge Puritans and the Nature of Christian Piety* (2011); Brenner's coedited *Pandemic Influenza Viruses* (2011); Coulter and Throckmorton's *Getting Jefferson Right* (2012); Craig

Columbus and Mark Hendrickson's *God and Man on Wall Street* (2012); Kengor's *The Communist* (2012); Kemeny's edited *Faith, Freedom and Higher Education* (2013), to which numerous faculty contributed; philosophy professor Christopher Yates's *The Poetic Imagination in Heidegger and Schelling* (2013) and his *No Time to Be Lost* (2014); and music professors Paul Munson and Joshua Drake's *Art and Music: A Student's Guide* (2014).

Several professors pioneered scientific research. Working with students, biologist Durwood Ray and chemist David Jones continued to develop cancer treatments. Physics professor Glenn Marsch investigated metabolism, while mechanical engineering professor Erik Anderson studied remora fish, Atlantic right whales, and ocean turbulence. Beginning in 2009, Anderson became a visiting summer investigator at Woods Hole Oceanographic Institution.

In addition, faculty penned dozens of essays for edited volumes and published hundreds of journal and encyclopedia articles and book reviews. Anderson, Seybold, Coulter, Welton, William Birmingham, communications professor Dann Brown, economist Jeff Herbener, psychology professor Kris Homan, and biologist Kevin Shaw led this activity. Between 2003 and 2008 alone, faculty collectively published twenty-one books, forty-five chapters in edited volumes, and 159 articles and made 274 conference presentations.[47] The Faculty Scholarship Workshop, created in 2001, enabled dozens of professors to present their research to their colleagues. Professors also served as keynote and plenary speakers for numerous community and college events and conferences.

Guest Speakers

During Jewell's tenure, the Visiting Scholar Lecture Series, the Pew Memorial Lectures, the J. Paul Sticht Memorial Lectures, and the Hopeman Lectures brought many prestigious scholars and public policy pundits to campus, including Harvard political science professor Harvey Mansfield; Herbert London, president of the Hudson Institute; University of Pennsylvania communications professor David Eisenhower; secretary of Homeland Security Tom Ridge;

chairman of the Joint Chiefs of Staff Mike Mullen; and Associate Supreme Court Justice Clarence Thomas.

A 2004 grant funded bringing four speakers to discuss "The Bible and American Society." In 2009–2010, the Humanities Speakers Series invited speakers including Penn State University historian Philip Jenkins and artist Makoto Fujimura to address topics related to the six HUMA courses. The Evangelical Scholarship Conference lecture series sponsored several speakers on church history subjects.

Additional speakers were Kentucky governor Ernie Fletcher; Ellen Sauerbrey, the US representative to the United Nations Commission on the Status of Women; Ed Breen, who discussed the Tyco scandal; Harvard professor Richard Pipes, who reported on atrocities committed behind the Iron Curtain; Senator Rick Santorum (R-PA), who spoke on immigration reform; Mark Earley, president of Prison Fellowship; Lloyd John Ogilvie, former chaplain of the US Senate; George Marsden, who discussed his biography of Jonathan Edwards; John Perkins, founder of Mendenhall Ministries; Wendy Shalit, author of *Girls Gone Mild* and Dannah Gresh, author of *And the Bride Wore White*, who both discussed modesty and sexual purity; Naomi Schaefer Riley, who talked about her book, *God on the Quad: How Religious Colleges and the Missionary Generation Are Changing America*; Lynn Swann, former Steeler wide receiver and Pennsylvania gubernatorial candidate; Terry Schiavo's brother, Bobby Schindler, who discussed the right to life; George W. Bush's speechwriter Michael Gerson; and Randall Balmer, chair of the religion department at Dartmouth College, who analyzed religion and politics. Other speakers discussed a Christian approach to business, sex slavery, globalization, the war against terrorists, sexual identity and same-sex attraction, and perfectionism. In addition, former cabinet secretary and senator Elizabeth Dole (R-NC), former first lady Laura Bush, and former Florida governor Jeb Bush delivered commencement addresses.

Campus Life: A "Ticket to Serve"

The college bustled with extracurricular activities during the Jewell years. Freeman claimed that Grove City had "a broader and more diverse range" of campus organizations than most other colleges of its size.[48] The average student participated in four extracurricular organizations.[49] The Orientation Board's activities included the Graffiti Dance, a square dance, deans' breakfasts, a freshman talent night, an organizational fair, relay games, and a sunrise service. Freshman and OB members participated in the Grove City Area United Way Day of Caring for the first time in fall 2003. More than two hundred freshmen and seventy-five OB members spent the day painting, cleaning up after vandalism, fixing equipment, and doing other projects. OB also created mentor groups through which upperclassmen and upperclasswomen helped freshmen "learn more about their identity in Christ."[50]

Students expressed their creativity through writing, painting, photography, graphic design, music, and acting. In 2003–2004, students submitted 125 poems, fifteen prose works, eight art works, and sixty-five photographs to *The Echo*, previously called *The Gyre*. In April 2004, the first student Film Fest was held. A year later, a campus television news program was established. In 2008, *The Quad* was founded to promote student discussion. In December 2011, the art department sponsored the largest exhibition in the college's history featuring dozens of works created in classes and independent studies. In 2012, Nate Mancini, '13, cowrote with John Sikma, '13, produced, and directed a feature-length film, *Asleep in a Storm*, starring Sikma and Sam Leuenberger, '13.

In fall 2004, Jewell announced two major projects: a "revolution in student dining" and the construction of apartment-style housing on lower campus. To improve the dining experience, Hicks and MAP dining halls would receive $4 million upgrades, and Hicks would be enlarged. Students extolled the beauty of the Student Activities Center (renamed the Breen Student Center in 2007), which opened in 2004, and liked having the Student Life and Learning offices there.[51]

Many developments occurred in 2005. In April, the college signed a contract with Napster to permit students unlimited music downloads for ten dollars per semester. That fall, the college introduced a card access system for the residence halls. A revision of the college handbook more clearly defined disciplinary procedures and declared that Student Life and Learning sought "to mold students, not scold them." In September, the SGA voted to end a seventy-three-year-old tradition and allow light recreational use on the upper quad. Many students welcomed this change, but others feared it would violate the historic "pledge to keep the campus beautiful."[52] A junior lamented that instead of being noted for "its development of great Christian leaders or high academic requirements, many outsiders know the college only for its strict grass policy."[53] Senior Vivek Thiagarajan was crowned the first-ever homecoming king in October. The Society of Women Engineers sponsored the first annual Mr. Engineering Pageant. Contestants competed in engineering trivia, nerd-wear fashion, business attire, and talent. Grove City's 2005 Relay for Life raised more money for the American Cancer Society than any other college in western Pennsylvania. The next year, 507 students participated in the event, walking laps around the intramural room all night to support the fight against cancer.

The year 2006 was memorable as well. Alpha Beta Tau created an event based on the popular television show *Whose Line Is It Anyway?* A director of student ministries and an apartment life coordinator began their jobs, and intervis hours were extended to Friday from 7 p.m. to midnight, Saturday from 1 p.m. to midnight, and Sunday afternoons in both men's and women's dorms. Meanwhile, Bon Appétit began furnishing meals at the Gedunk at no extra cost to students who had meal plans. Orchesis dance performances filled Ketler Auditorium for three successive nights in December, featuring salsa, tap, hip-hop, lyrical, ballet and swing dance styles.

Student Life and Learning provided training each year for the college's resident directors and its more than eighty resident assistants. RD training focused on emergency responses, student development theory, supervision, the history and mission of GCC, mentoring, and identifying and addressing student needs. RA training discussed the nature of community, vocation, residence programming, drug and alcohol awareness, and mental health issues. All RAs offered at least one spiritual, social, and life skills program each semester. Colonial Hall Apartments staff provided classes and seminars on cooking, budgeting, work-life balance, career planning, spiritual formation, and other topics to prepare students for post-college life.[54] SL&L also instituted Community Living Privilege (CLP) and Excellence in Community Living awards. To maintain their block housing, the twenty-seven sororities, fraternities, and housing groups were required to submit a portfolio showing how they fulfilled the CLP criteria. In dealing with disciplinary problems, Larry Hardesty explained, the SL&L philosophy was to ensure that students learned from their mistakes and changed their behavior. The staff wanted to minister to violators and "bring restoration to the campus community."[55] Meanwhile, Devi Wintrode oversaw the college's discipleship program, all-campus retreat, student ministry groups, and student-led Bible studies, and 150 students had adult mentors from the community. In a typical year, twenty-five ICO trips, half of which were international, served people around the globe. While the trips were still student organized and led, the college provided greater oversight and guidance. Wintrode, Stan Keehlwetter, and OIE director Lois Johnson supplied training in spiritual preparedness, cultural sensitivity, and emergency management.[56]

Long-standing activities continued, and new ones were initiated. By 2007, only eight, including Grove City, of the eighty colleges that once held May Day celebrations still did. To deal with the stress of finals, some students participated in a primal scream at midnight on Sunday during finals. In 2007, a Girls' Nite explored body image through discussions and activities. At a college where "look to your left, look to your right" and "ring by spring" were commonly used phrase, many women were "concerned about their relationship status," prompting Women of Faith to organize an annual Women's Contentment Panel. In 2007, ODK introduced a Paper of the Year Contest, which gave underclassmen an opportunity to win cash prizes for their papers in four different academic areas. One of the most intense sports rivalries on campus during the Jewell years was the annual Tri Rho-AEX game winter football game. In fall 2009, the administration finally permitted students to use the upper quad for recreational activities. In December 2010, The De-Stress Fair, featuring live music, hot drinks, manicures, and massages, was created. It soon also included yoga, flower planting, and furry guests from the Butler Dog Training Association.

In 2011, Jessica Littlejohn founded a gay-straight alliance to promote community among gay students and provide a forum for their interaction with straight people who supported them or were willing to have respectful discussions with them. While the college did not endorse this group, it did not discipline students who openly identified as gay. Hardesty emphasized that Grove City held gay and lesbian students and heterosexual students to the same standard regarding physical intimacy.[57]

In 2011, the Tri-Zeta sorority created Grover Idol, modeled after *American Idol,* to enable students to showcase their musical or comedic talents and to raise money to aid low-income Pittsburgh homeowners. Sororities, fraternities, housing groups, and other campus organizations solicited funds for many other causes. The Relay for Life's annual campaign to benefit the American Cancer Society was the college's highest-grossing fundraiser. In November 2012, the Alpha Beta Tau sorority sponsored Whose Line Is It Anyway? a night of improvisation modeled on the TV show of the same name. Another popular new event during the Jewell years was AEX Live, an evening of music and food, held on the Lincoln lawn.

The college's counseling center played an important role on campus. In 2004–2005, 6 to 7 percent of students used the counseling service, and depression was the major issue. Beginning in fall 2005, the center was staffed by four full-time counselors. By 2013, the center was serving an average of eighty-three students per week; about 30 percent of the class of 2012 used its services sometimes during their four years.[58]

Chris Wetzel, '12, a student at the University of Virginia Law School, argued in 2013 that the college's "rhetoric, administrative priorities and branding" reflected its "political and ideological commitments" more than its "spiritual and scholarly commitments." He claimed that "the College's recent self-representation and academic priorities" had become "increasingly politicized and less Christ-centered." Grove City's "unrelenting emphasis on free markets and individual liberty," he lamented, was "drowning out" its "core Christian principles."[59] About five hundred alumni signed his open letter posted on Facebook.[60] Some faculty shared Wetzel's concern, while others insisted that Grove City's emphasis on political, economic, and social freedom distinguished it from most other Christian colleges.

Sophomore Kayla Peterson maintained that the typical Grove City student strove to get good grades but was also excited to learn. She was religious, sought to grow spiritually, participated in numerous extracurricular activities, and used her "unique talents and interests" to glorify God.[61] The "Top 15 Things to Give Up Before Leaving GCC," provides a good snapshot of campus life during Jewell's presidency. These items included complaining about the college ("How can you complain so furiously about the place that you tried so hard to get into?"); claiming that one's own major is the most difficult ("'rigorous academics' is 1/3 of our slogan"); carping about intervisitation hours; complaining about the weather; "turning Chapel into 'Nap"-el'"; and "throwing your friends in a creek when they get engaged."[62]

Numerous clubs and honoraries enriched campus life. In 2009, the college had fifteen honoraries, eleven service organizations, ten major-related clubs, ten interest groups, ten Christian fellowship organizations, five governance associations, three political societies, and several other clubs. Life Advocates continued to be one of the college's most active student organizations. Its members frequently sponsored a five-week study titled "Making Abortion Unthinkable" and regularly participated in Walk-for-Life Sunday with the Slippery Rock Crisis Pregnancy Center and the annual National March for Life in Washington, DC.[63]

Several new clubs and honoraries began between 2003 and 2014. An affiliate of Prison Fellowship was founded in 2003 by

Kathryn McNulty and Katherine Wray, who had had interned with the organization in Washington, DC. A sign language club was established in 2004 as were chapters of the National Communication Association honorary, Lambda Pi Eta, and Theta Alpha Kappa, a Christian thought honorary. Fencing became an official club the next year. In 2009, Students Excited About Diversity (SEAD) was created to celebrate the societal contributions of different races and cultures. A Middle Eastern Club was established in 2012.

Political organizations were also active. In fall 2003, College Republicans, Democrats, and Libertarians debated the Patriot Act, homosexual marriage, and education policy. In 2005, College Republicans created a website to increase interest in the Republican Party. College Libertarians sponsored many programs, including part of Milton Friedman's documentary series *Free to Choose*.

Speech and Debate

The college's speech and debate team had spectacular success during Jewell's presidency, winning numerous tournaments and placing highly in many others. In 2004, the forensics squad won a fourteen-school tournament, which included West Virginia University. Grove City took the top three places in the persuasive speaking category, with freshman Leah Acker placing first overall. She was also second in extemporaneous speaking, third in informational speaking, and fifth in prose interpretation. Later that year, sophomore Jamie Tucci took first place in persuasive speaking at the Marietta College invitational, while freshman Courtney Winther placed first in extemporaneous speaking. At the 2005 Pennsylvania state tournament, the Wolverines won the small school category, and Tucci was the state champion in persuasive speaking. Tucci claimed first prize in both persuasive and impromptu speaking at a 2006 Geneva College invitational where Sean O'Brien, '07, placed first in after-dinner speaking and second in impromptu speaking. That year, sophomore Renae Smith placed sixth in persuasive speaking at the National Forensic Association tournament.

Despite this impressive record, Grove City decided in 2006 to switch its debating style to be able to compete more effectively with universities. The college changed from Lincoln-Douglas debate, which involved substantial advance research on policy issues, done at larger schools by paid researchers and team coaches, to parliamentary debate, for which participants were given the topic only fifteen minutes before the debate began.[64] When the resolution was announced, debate coach Stephen Jones explained, team members brainstormed to develop ideas. "It is pretty frantic."[65] The team enjoyed instant success using the parliamentary style. At a January 2007 tournament at Berea College, the Wolverines won the first-place sweepstakes award for debate and the second-place award for independent events. At Hillsdale College that same month, Grove City triumphed, with the team of Renae Smith and freshman Justin Olsen earning second place overall. Freshman Luke Juday was named the second-place overall speaker and top novice. In October, Grove City's five debate teams outperformed more than fifty other teams to place first at Berea College's tournament. Grove City also triumphed at a tournament at Carson-Newman College in Tennessee in November.

By spring 2008, Grove City had risen to eleventh in nation in the NPDA, whose 250 members included leading Christian colleges like Wheaton and huge schools like the University of Oregon. That year, the Wolverines won all three tournaments in which they competed, defeating Michigan State, Florida State University, the University of Alabama, and other major universities. By February 2009, led by Juday and Winther, the squad ranked seventh in the nation. During the academic year, the team won seven tournaments. Partners Juday and sophomore Dwayne Batten finished first in six tournaments, compiling a stellar 52–12 season record, and they also claimed numerous individual speaking awards.

After outstanding performances in its first three debates in fall 2009, Grove City was ranked second in parliamentary debate in the country. Over the Christmas break, Juday and junior Dan Hanson represented Grove City at the World Universities Debating Championship in Antalya, Turkey (now Türkiye). In 2009–2010,

Juday and Batten were ranked fifteenth in the country in parliamentary debate, and Juday was named the best speaker at the 2010 national Pi Kappa Delta tournament. The Wolverines continued their winning ways in 2010–2011, capturing first place at several large tournaments led by Batten and Alex Pepper. In January 2011, Batten, Hanson, Pepper, and junior Kirby Gowen participated at the World Universities Debating Championship in Botswana. Grove City finished 2010–2011 ranked fourth in the nation after Batten and Pepper took first place overall at the 2011 Pi Kappa Delta (PKD) national tournament. The 2011–2012 team won tournaments in Indiana, Kentucky, and Ohio. In fall 2012, sophomores Dan Pugh and Allen Scheie captured first place at the National Christian College Federation Association championship, and the team finished in the top ten in an international competition at University of Vienna, which included teams from more than twenty countries. The next spring, the Wolverines won the NCCFA's National Quality Award given to the team that with best winning percentage at the national tournament. The squad also claimed this award in 2014, its fourth victory of the 2013–2014 academic year.

Theater

During the Jewell years, James Dixon and Betsy Craig continued to alternate between directing musicals and plays and staged many well-attended, highly regarded shows. A 2003 *The Collegian* profile hailed Craig, the first woman faculty member in college history to continue teaching after giving birth to a child, for producing outstanding shows, supervising children's theater, and leading travel interims to Europe. "Directing is the greatest creative experience you can have," Craig declared.[66]

During these years, numerous superb actors entertained audiences, most notably Brendan Sandham, '04, Derrick Winger, '07, George Hampe, '10, Rebecca Sherman, '11, Tyler Crumrine, '12, Ethan Mitchell, '15, Jon Warren, '15, and Andy Hickly, '15. Sandham directed several shows, and wrote, directed, and starred in a sixty-minute movie, *Silverwhere*, the most ambitious student film project in college history to that date.[67] Winger was featured in *Much Ado About Nothing, Major Barbara, The Matchmaker, The Pirates of Penzance,* and other productions. George Hampe played the lead in *Crazy for You, Godspell, An Enemy of the People* and *As You Like It*. After graduating from the Yale School of Drama in 2017, Hampe played numerous roles on television, including in *FBI: Most Wanted* (2020), *Law & Order* (2023), and *Up Here* (2023). Rebecca Sherman excelled as Eliza Doolittle in *My Fair Lady* and in principal roles in *An Enemy of the People* and *As You Like It*. Crumrine played major parts in *Carnival!, The Brothers Karamazov,* and *The Mystery of Edwin Drood*. After graduation, he became the founding editor of Plays Inverse Press and received design and dramaturgy credits for productions at the Kennedy Center. Mitchell starred in *Les Misérables, The Tempest,* and *Dancing at Lughnasa*. In 2014, Mitchell and his scene partner Mike Vogel, '15, made it to the final sixteen among more than two hundred contestants at the Irene Ryan Acting Competition, and Mitchell won the competition's voice and speech award. Warren played Jean Valjean in *Les Misérables*. Hickly portrayed Javert in this musical, and he had principal roles in *Red, The Tempest, Measure for Measure,* and several other productions.

The leading playwright during Jewell's tenure was Johnny Sikma, whose show, *Le Gymnopédiste,* was performed in the Little Theater in March 2013. After college, Sikma wrote scripts for several films. The principal student director during this period was Monica Ammirati, '06, who helped direct numerous shows, including *Much Ado About Nothing* and *Glass Stirring*.

The theatrical highlight of the Jewell years was the selection of *La Bête,* directed by Betsy Craig, as one of four student productions from among thousands staged throughout the country, to be performed at the Kennedy Center American College Theater Festival in Washington, DC, in 2009.

Music

Music resounded throughout campus during Jewell's presidency thanks to the marching band, orchestra, touring choir, men's glee club, and several student-led groups and ensembles. In April 2007, the GCC Wind Ensemble performed at the Pennsylvania Music Educators Association (PMEA) conference; it was the only college group of this type to perform. The marching band, directed by Ed Arnold, performed with the River City Brass Band as part of the college's Guest Artist series in March 2008. That October, the band played in a parade at Disney World, while the jazz ensemble played at the Magic Kingdom's Galaxy Palace Theater. In addition to its numerous top-notch concerts on campus each year, in 2013, the college orchestra performed at the PMEA conference for the first time. Arnold conducted the Pennsylvania All-State Band in 2012 and in 2013 was inducted into the Beaver Valley Musician's Hall of Fame. Outstanding instrumentalists during these years included William Keller, '08, Rebecca Smiddy, '09, and Liz Miller, '08. The touring choir continued to delight and inspire thousands during its annual spring tour, while the men's glee club sang in various venues on campus and at All-College Sing. The most successful student band in this period was Aevory Nash, led by vocalist Brian Campbell, '08. During the 2007–2008 Christmas break, the band ministered to thousands through its concerts in eleven major British and European cities. For the next two years, its members entertained audiences in cities throughout the United States.

Greek Life

During Jewell's presidency, Greek life was revitalized, and the mission of many fraternities and sororities became more overtly Christian. The number of Greeks increased from 342 in 2003–2004 to 625 in 2014. Greeks worked diligently to improve their reputation with faculty and students and to contribute more to campus and community life. Jean-Noel Thompson insisted that Grove City's Greeks differed from those at other schools because they strove to "empower one another to serve Christ and give back to the community."[68] In 2005, several changes were made to rejuvenate the Greek system. Rush was limited to two weeks, and Greek Unity Week was renamed Greek Education Period. During this week, sororities and fraternities were permitted to use fifteen hours for pledge activities.

Friction sometimes still occurred between Greeks and independents. In 2006, many Greeks complained that T-shirts declaring, "Stay Independent," which mirrored "Go Greek" T-shirts, were discouraging students from joining Greek organizations. The shirts did not say that it was great to "Be Independent," Greeks protested, but instead admonished students to reject groups that had long helped to keep the college strong. Greeks argued that they actively supported the college's mission in varied ways. They sponsored more events than any other organizations except SGA and raised more money for charitable causes than any other campus groups.[69] Two examples of Greek activism and Christian commitment occurred as the first decade of the twenty-first century ended. The Beta Sigma and Omicron Xi fraternities collaborated with the Pittsburgh-based Open Hands, Healing Hearts organization to rehab houses and provide better care of children. The Pan Sophic fraternity sponsored Greek Aid, a benefit concert that raised money for Red Box missions. Greeks steadily improved their image and increased their numbers. By 2007, 20 percent of students belonged to one of the college's ten fraternities or eight sororities, which were collectively taking pledge classes between 150 and 300 each year.

WSAJ

WSAJ-FM, which had broadcast satellite-delivered classical music for almost a decade, in 2003–2004 added live DJs and six hours of student-created programming daily, including sports, politics, and music. In 2005–2006, the station featured oldies, blues, and contemporary Christian music. The success of WSAJ's large-scale concert in fall 2007 proved that the station's listening audience was "both active and engaged."[70] A significant gift to the station by Dorothy Newman Wilson, '43, enabled its studio to move from Ketler to the TLC in fall 2008. That fall, the WSAJ-FM staff increased from forty to seventy-eight. Remote broadcasts from Breen

Student Union featuring song requests, student discussions, and prize giveaways demonstrated that WSAJ was "vibrant."[71] The next year, student programming composed forty-nine hours of the station's broadcast time. In spring 2011, student DJs broadcast live events on Parent's Weekend. In fall 2013, WSAJ launched a new sports department and broadcast football and basketball games and soccer matches. WSAJ also debuted a community-affairs program involving interviews with community leaders, heads of charitable organizations, and businesspeople.

Student Achievements: "Grovers Try to Excel in Every Area Possible"

During Jewell's presidency, students had major accomplishments in entrepreneurship, economics, the natural sciences, athletics, theater, writing, computer programming, community service, beauty pageants, and education. The Swezey Fund for Scientific Instrumentation and Research, created in 2008, paid twenty students every year to do research with faculty members. That fall, the Hopeman Student Research Seminar Series were established to enable science, engineering, and math students to explain their research projects done on campus and elsewhere. Student scientific endeavors significantly increased. In spring 2010, for example, thirty-six students either presented their research at conferences throughout the country or collaborated with professors on writing articles. In addition, numerous students participated with history professor Mark Graham in archaeological excavations in Tunisia and Italy.

While no Grove City students became Rhodes Scholars, many benefited from applying for the program. Ben Spead, '01, who almost qualified, declared, "While God had different plans for me than Oxford, I am so thankful that I had the experience of preparing for and participating in the Rhodes selection process," which helped "shape my post-graduation academic and career paths."[72] During Jewell's presidency, six seniors were chosen as Fulbright Scholars: Jonathan Bond to study at University College

London School of Public Policy in 2004–2005; Mariah Perrin to teach English in a high school in South Korea in 2005–2006; David Frick to investigate small business accounting at Zhejiang Normal University in China in 2009–2010; Luke Juday to learn about intercollegiate debate and public policy at the University of Botswana in 2010–2011; Jennifer Ferris to study entrepreneurship in Canada in 2011–2012; and Andrew Caffro to work on HIV/AIDS research and public health in India in 2013–2014.

Sophomore Jason Willson placed second in the United States Chess Federation's Pittsburgh Open in March 2004. A Grove City team won three titles at the SIFE (Students in Free Enterprise) USA Regional Competition in April 2005. Alexis Intini, '08, earned three gold medals at a regional Tae Kwon Do tournament in 2005. Two of Amy Good's poems were published in *New Voices and New Visions: Religious Writing from Rising Generations* (2005). In May 2005, five Grovers won the Rookie of the Year Award at the SIFE national competition. Jessica Prol, '05, and Megan Maley, '07, studied public policy's intersection with faith and history as part of the Witherspoon Fellowship in 2005. That year, a team of Grovers finished eighth at an international firefighting robot competition at Hartford. The next spring, a Grove City team placed fifth at the East Central USA computer programming contest. In 2007, Senator Richard Burr (R-NC) presented freshman Andrew McIndoe with the Congressional Award Bronze and Silver Medals, which recognized the achievement, initiative, and service of America's youth.

Four students led by Ruth Dykstra, '07, created Deep Springs International (DSI) to provide safe drinking water in Haiti. With the assistance of professor Timothy Mech and funding from a 2008 Templeton Freedom Award, their nonprofit provided pure drinking water to impoverished Haitians. The month after the devastating January 2010 earthquake in Haiti, students held a "Rebuild Haiti Fundraiser" to help fund Deep Springs International. To date, DSI has assisted two million Haitians.[73]

In 2007, after nationwide testing, the Intercollegiate Studies Institute ranked Grove City College second only to Harvard University in seniors' knowledge of American history and institutions. In 2007, junior Maggie Revilla was selected as Miss Sweetheart Vermont, while the next year, junior Kayla Lynam was chosen as Miss West Virginia. Junior Benjamin Holland became the youngest school board member in Pennsylvania when he was elected to Butler's board in 2008. Seniors Chris Andrew and Greg Kroleski won the 2008 Carnegie Mellon Tepper Venture Challenge for their kit that treated bites from snakes and other venomous reptiles. In fall 2008, junior Jonathon Srour triumphed at a national Irish Step Dancing competition. A team of eight Grovers finished first in the multirider and utility classes at the 2009 American Society of Mechanical Engineers Human Powered Vehicle Challenge East contest. In 2009, Grove City's computer programming teams won the 2009 Carnegie Mellon Invitation, junior Andrew Welton became the first undergraduate to ever present a paper at a leading international conference in late antique studies, and Andrea Phillips, '11, won the paper competition sponsored by the Pennsylvania Sociological Society.

George Hampe qualified to compete at the national Irene Ryan Acting Competition at the Kennedy Center Festival, while Tyler Crumrine was selected as a national alternate for the O'Neill Critics Institute, where students were judged on their critiques of shows presented at the festival. Crumrine also finished second in the Kennedy Center's Undergraduate Theater Writing Competition. By winning a regional stage management competition, LeeAnn Yeckley qualified to participate in the Kennedy Center American College Theater Festival in 2010.

In 2012, senior linebacker Tim Irwin earned a prestigious NCAA postgraduate scholarship. In addition to his accomplishments on the gridiron, the biology major had a 3.93 CQPA and was named a third-team All-American in club lacrosse. The next year, defensive back Chris Gibbs, a biology major with an identical CQPA, who was a summer research fellow at the Mayo Clinic and the fifth man to be both Senior Man of the Year and Sports Man of the Year, also received this scholarship.

Campus organizations and the student body also won awards. In 2005, the college's ODK affiliate received the organization's Circle Recognition Award. In 2006, *Men's Fitness* magazine named Grove City students the seventh fittest cohort in the nation. Meanwhile, the *Princeton Review* rated Grove City number seven on its "Everyone Plays Intramural Sports" list. Students who were interviewed by a television reporter about this distinction stressed that "Grovers try to excel in every area possible in academics, athletics, music, whatever."[74] The college's Mortar Board chapter earned the organization's Silver Torch Award in 2007 for its scholarship, leadership, and service. The college jazz band took first place at the North-Eastern Invitational Jazz Band Competition in 2010. Grove City College's chapter of Kappa Delta Pi, the international education honorary, earned the Achieving Chapter Excellence Award five times during Jewell's presidency for its administrative proficiency and leadership development, and in 2012, it won the "Biggest Impact on Community" award for its service initiative, "Literacy Alive!"

Entertainers

Several guest groups and individuals who entertained the college community during Jewell's presidency stand out. The 165-member Kyiv Symphony Orchestra and Chorus, part of the Christian Music Mission Kiev, performed classics and folk music. The music of the Canadian Brass and Marvin Hamlisch delighted audiences. Melanie (who had been a student at Grove City in 2010–2011), Sofia, Amanda, and Justin von Trapp, the greatgrandchildren of Captain Georg von Trapp, the father of the famous singing family whose story captivated the world in *The Sound of Music*, performed in fall 2011. They also sang "Climb Every Mountain" with the college's touring choir.

Politics

Student polling about presidential candidates continue to display the college's conservative political orientation. In 2004, *The Colle-*

gian featured an article calling for George W. Bush's reelection but did not have one advocating for his Democratic rival, John Kerry. After Bush won, *The Collegian* reported that "the reaction on Grove City's predominantly Republican campus is expectedly happy and relieved."[75] *The Collegian*'s coverage of the 2008 campaign was more balanced, with articles discussing why one student was voting for Democrat Barack Obama, why another was supporting Republican John McCain, and why a third was not voting. That October, 69.4 percent of students said that were voting for McCain and 12.4 percent for Obama, with 13.3 percent undecided.

Religious Activities: "Change the World: Training Found Here"

Sophomore Luke Rumbaugh declared in October 2004, that "we are being trained as light-bearers for the nations—as ambassadors for Christ in all areas."[76] As the number of more deeply committed Christian students increased, religious organizations and activities became even more plentiful and important. Each semester, students had to attend sixteen of about forty-five events, which included speakers, worship services, and choir performances, to fulfill their chapel requirement. Most students supported the chapel program's objective of strengthening their spiritual lives, but a minority disliked mandatory attendance.[77] In 2004, Stan Keehlwetter began working full time as dean of the chapel. In addition to arranging chapel services, he continued to teach HUMA courses and help coach sports teams. During the annual Christian Life Conference, inspiring Christian speakers helped students grow spiritually. Christian Life Conference speakers during the Jewell years included Bible expositor and composer Richard Farmer in 2006, 2009, and 2012 and sociologist and social activist Tony Campolo in 2013. Campolo also spoke to packed chapels in 2006 and 2008 under other auspices. The Red Box program sent four to eight students to mission fields around the world each summer. Freeman was impressed by how deeply Grove City had shaped the spiritual lives of alumni and students.[78] Survey data supported his assessment. In a 2006 survey asking how effectively the college achieved its Christian mission on a five-point scale, seniors rated its success 4.05, alumni 4.31, parents 4.48, trustees 4.94, and faculty 3.76. Results were similar on the question of whether the college promoted spiritual and moral development—students 4.09, parents 4.50, trustees 4.76, administrators 4.50, and faculty 3.80.[79]

In 2009, the board's governance committee members recommended not deleting the word "evangelical" from the college charter because the term, which had been added in 1894, had "served the college well for over a century." When "evangelical" had been adopted, it was synonymous with Protestant, Trinitarian Christianity. At that point, it had no association with the modernist/fundamentalist controversy of the 1920s, the neo-Evangelical movement of the 1940s and 1950s led by Carl Henry and Billy Graham, the religious right of the 1980s, or recent portrayals of evangelicals as Republican "value voters" or megachurch worshippers. They concluded that removing the word from the charter would likely "ignite a spirited discussion" among campus constituencies and produce negative publicity. It would also probably "sow confusion and generate concern among potential students, parents, pastors and others who are familiar with the GCC Brand," thereby hurting recruitment.[80]

The Religious Activities Committee selected spiritually mature Christians as Red Box missionaries. They underwent intensive training before beginning their work. By 2005, eighty-four students had served in forty countries; sixteen had ministered in Latin American countries or the United States and ten in European, seven in Asian, and seven in African nations.

Numerous Christian organizations held meetings that included speakers, Bible study, prayer, worship, and fellowship. The activities of Salt Company and Warriors for Christ continued to attract the most students. Many campus organizations took the gospel into the world. Clowns for Christ, formed in 1984, brought laughter to the college community, local nursing homes, church services, and Outlet Mall customers through its skits. The members of D.R.I.V.E. (Dramas Reaching Inner City through Visual Evangelism) performed Christian skits on the streets of Pittsburgh with messages set to music. Steel City Ministries volunteers tutored children in Pittsburgh and worked with youth at the Pittsburgh Project and Urban Impact. Young Life members met with students at seven area high schools individually and in groups. The one hundred students involved in the New Life ministry sought to glorify God by investing "in the lives of the young men at George Junior Republic through the teaching of God's word, vital relationships and prayer." New Life gained national attention in 2004 when an article in *The Washington Times* highlighted its activities.[81] InterVarsity Christian Fellowship held an annual conference to encourage students to consider missions as a vocation. Helping Hands members painted the local YMCA and Children's Hospital in Pittsburgh, assisted with local blood drives, and worked with Habitat for Humanity, United Way, and the Special Olympics. Streams of Justice, an affiliate of International Justice Mission (IJM), implored students to wage war against human trafficking. In fall 2010, seven campus organization joined forces to increase awareness and stimulate action on behalf of AIDS victims in Uganda. That fall, Project Okello raised funds for an orphanage in Kampala, Uganda. The next year, Project Okello brought numerous artists and musicians to campus to display their works and fund building a water tank in a Ugandan village. In 2010, Koinonia and Gospel Team, two groups that had long led worship services in churches the local area and in other regions during their annual tours, merged to become KGT. In 2012, IJM sponsored an exhibit using statistics and stories from victims to depict human trafficking around the world.

Justin McRoberts came annually for many years and produced a CD titled *Live from Grove City*. Stonebridge Concerts brought several other Christian artists and groups to campus, most notably TobyMac, Audio Adrenaline, Jeremy Camp, Jars of Clay, and Newsboys.

A talk by Scott Hahn, '79, a leading Catholic author and apologist, in 2005 provoked several articles and letters in *The Collegian* discussing his success in making Catholic converts, the Newman Club's growing influence on campus, and critiques of his theology.[82] Newman Club members met weekly to hear speakers, study the Bible, and pray the Rosary together.

During Jewell's presidency, Inter-City Outreach sent thousands of students to help the indigent and victims of natural disasters. In 2006, for example, six teams totaling about two hundred students participated in Hurricane Katrina relief efforts in the Gulf region. Several hundred more worked with varied ministries in Chicago, Pittsburgh, Columbus, Kansas City, and Providence or in Haiti, the Dominican Republic, Belize, Ireland, and Guatemala.

The Collegian editor in chief Emily Kramer declared her senior year, "I came to Grove City College because I believed that it was unique in its mission to educate the whole person," to "prepare students not only to succeed in their personal lives but also to transform their culture and communities."[83] Andrew Patterson asserted in 2012, "I am graduating from a college" that gives seniors "a diploma to influence the worlds of business, government, science and education."[84] Comparing the students of the mid-1960s with those during his presidency, Jewell explained that the faith of his classmates was "evident and important," but they were not "much into witnessing." Most current Grove City students, by contrast, were "strongly committed" to Christ, and actively "living out the gospel."[85]

Women's Athletics

Between 2003 and 2014, women's sports teams had impressive records and produced numerous outstanding athletes. The tennis, cross-country, and soccer squads had the best records. The tennis team, led by number one singles players, Allison Atwood, '04, Kristin McNally, '08, and Tamara Nations, '09, went 115–50, winning the PAC from 2004 to 2011. The team's best seasons were 11–1 in 2004, 13–3 in 2005, and 14–4 in 2010–2011 (the team began playing in the fall and the spring). The Lady Wolverines participated in the NCAA tournament four times. Atwood was 34–5 in singles. Nations won six PAC championships in singles and doubles.

In 2004, junior Elisa Pedersen finished first among D3 runners at the Malone Invitational and won the Allegheny and the Carnegie Mellon invitationals, breaking the varsity record with a time of 18.27 for the 5K. Grove City placed fifth at the Mideast D3 Regional, with Pedersen taking third. She finished sixteenth at nationals, becoming the college's first female cross-country runner to earn All-American honors.

As the 2005 cross-country season began, Grove City women's team had a stellar 246–56–1 (.814) record in its thirty-year history. The women captured the Case Western Reserve Classic that fall, as Pedersen finished first and freshman Kristen Carter third. They outran thirty-four other teams to take second at the Dickinson College invitational, with Pedersen placing third. Grove City beat two teams ranked in the top thirty in the nation at the All-Ohio Invitational in mid-October 2005, as Pedersen placed second in a field of 282. The women won the PAC, with Pedersen finishing first and Carter second. Their teammate Cara Pierce, '07, declared that the runners wanted to win PAC, but their "far higher goals" were achieving team unity and glorifying God.[86] The Lady Wolverines placed fourth at the regional as Pedersen finished fifth. She achieved cross-country All-American status again in 2005 and graduated as the college record holder in the 5K.

In fall 2007, the Lady Wolverines won an invitational at California University of Pennsylvania, with Kristen Carter outrunning all her D3 competitors. Carter won the Lehigh Invitational, helping Grove City place second in the thirty-nine-team event. In 2007, Carter earned NCAA All-American honors by finishing twenty-sixth at nationals, with Julia Seward, '09, joining Carter on the All-Mideast region team.

Carter and Seward ran neck and neck throughout fall 2008. In September, Carter set a college record of 18:22 in the 5K. At the thirty-seven-team Lehigh Invitational in October, Carter and Seward finished fourth and fifth, respectively. Carter placed first at the PAC championship for the third year in a row. She finished second at the 2008 Mideast Regional, as the team captured fifth place, while Seward placed higher—thirty-eighth—at nationals. In

2009, 2010, and 2011, the team finished fourth, fifth, and fifth, respectively, at the Mideast Regional and was twenty-ninth in the nation in 2010. The 2012 Lady Wolverines captured the college's twenty-fifth consecutive PAC title. Sophomore Emily Rabenold won the race, finishing a full minute ahead of the second-place runner. Rabenold also claimed the 2013 PAC title.

The women's soccer team's best records were 16–5–1 in 2003, 14–6–2 in 2004, 16–4–1 in 2007, and 16–4–2 in 2012. The team earned two NCAA bids and four ECAC invitations, making it to the semifinals twice. Meg Tilley led the 2003 and 2004 squads. In 2004, she was named to the College Division Academic All-America first team after breaking the school record in career goals (68), assists (35), and points (171). The history major had a 3.97 grade-point average and was the college's first Marshall Scholar national finalist. During the team's eight-game winning streak in 2004, sophomore goalkeeper Kori Koper surrendered only one goal.

In summer 2007, seven team members and coach Melissa Lamie spent two weeks in South Africa with Ambassadors in Sport, playing several matches, holding soccer clinics, and sharing God's love. Junior Bethany Preston was moved by "seeing people from a different culture passionately worshipping and loving."[87] That fall, freshman midfielder Emily Ostlund earned first-team All-Great Lakes Region honors. Michelle Peck was named the PAC MVP in 2009 after leading Grove City in goals and points. Peck was also All-PAC second team in golf in 2009 and the 2010 Sportswoman of the Year. Hannah Yang, '10, is fifth all-time in career goals. The 2012 squad won the college's first-ever NCAA tournament game, defeating Western Connecticut State 1–0 in overtime before losing to eventual champion Messiah in the second round. In 2013, senior Sarah Cessar became the first Grove City women's soccer player to be named to the first-team all-region twice.

In March 2004, senior Peggy Whitbeck won her third straight national title in the 200 butterfly and finished sixth in the 100 butterfly, giving her eight All-American honors for her career. The swimmers and divers' best records in dual meets were 12–3 in 2008–2009 and 13–1 the following year. From 2010 to 2013, the team finished eleventh, eleventh, tenth, and ninth in the nation. Her exploits at the 2011 meet gave sophomore Angela Palumbo nine total All-America honors. In 2012, Palumbo earned All-American honors in the 50-, 100- and 200-yard freestyles. Palumbo, Kait Riesmeyer '13, Jenna Richert '12, and Jenny Ryan finished tenth in the 200-freestyle relay and sixth in the 400 and 800 free relays, giving them All-American honors in both events. Palumbo finished her career as a twenty-one–time All-American, making her the most-decorated athlete in college history. Riesmeyer garnered seventeen all All-American awards, while Ryan had sixteen. At the 2014 nationals, sophomore Megan Bilko won three All-American honors and set college records in the 500, 1000, and 1650 freestyle events, which she still holds today.

The women's water polo team's best record during these years was 18–8 in 2012. The squad finished first in its division from 2010 through 2013 and earned fifth place in the nation among D3 schools in 2007, 2008, and 2010. In 2008, Kate Stiebler, '10, became the first Lady Wolverine named to the first-team All-Western Division in water polo. In spring 2010, she became the all-time leader in goals scored with 182, while sophomore Chelsea Johnson set a single-season record by scoring seventy-two goals. In 2012, Johnson won her second Collegiate Water Polo Association D3 Player of the Year award; she and senior Andrea Wilson earned first-team All-CWPA honors.

In 2007, the volleyball team defeated Penn State Behrend to give Roberts her five hundredth victory in volleyball at Grove City and to make her the first Grove City coach to capture five hundred victories in one sport. At that point, she had the eleventh-most wins among active NCAA D3 women's volleyball coaches. Roberts had won PAC titles in volleyball, basketball, and softball and had captured nine PAC titles, received seven postseason invitations, and claimed three ECAC championships. Tennis coach Joe Walters praised Roberts's "professionalism, attitude, and family-oriented approach to coaching."[88] Kim Walsh, '07, graduated as the college's all-time assists leader, while middle hitter Natalie Liberati, '08, was the program's all-time leader in kills. Kim Budd, '11, finished her career as second all-time in digs. When Roberts retired in 2013, she had amassed almost nine hundred total wins in three sports without a single assistant coach. She called coaching at Grove City "a privilege, great fun and a great ride."[89]

The women's track and field team won PAC titles in 2004 and 2005, finishing twenty-fourth in the ECAC in 2004 and sixty-seventh in the nation in D3 in 2005. Erin Claxton finished eighth in the 10,000 meters at the 2005 nationals to become the college's first female track and field All-American. At the 2006 PAC championship, Kristen Carter won the 1500 and 5000 meters, Julia Seward captured the 10,000 meters, and Sarah Bray '07 took the javelin. Carter finished sixth in the 1500 and eighth in the 5000 at the ECAC championship that spring. She won three PAC titles in the 1500 meters and two in the 5000. Seward claimed PAC titles in the 5000 and 10,000 meters. In 2008, Carter set conference records in the 1500 and 5000 meters. Sophomore Sara Fisher was named the PAC MVP in 2011 after capturing the 1500, 5000, and 10,000-meter runs. The Lady Wolverines took the 2014 PAC championship by the largest margin of victory since 2005, the last time they won the title.

The women's basketball team's best record was 16–10 in 2004–2005 when the squad received an ECAC invitation. The leading players were Abby Moose, '05 and Christine Slater, '11. Moose finished fifth all-time in scoring with 1,209 points and holds the college record for most three-point shots made. She also helped the United States win a gold medal in Deaflympics women's basketball in 2004. She hoped that her accomplishments would "encourage people not to give up."[90] Christine Slater, '11, is the college's second-highest scorer for women's or men's basketball with 1,643 points; for women's basketball, she ranks second in both career points per game average and rebounds. Her senior year, she earned All-Great Lakes Region and All-ECAC South recognition. Brittany Anderson, '08, earned eleven varsity letters, excelling as a center in basketball, an outside hitter in volleyball, and a thrower in track and field.

The best women golfers during the Jewell years were Mary Brown, '05, Arielle Goyzueta, '12 (who also shined in soccer), and Esther Durling, '15. Brown finished second at the PAC championship in 2005, while Goyzueta placed second in 2009 and 2010 and was the medalist in spring 2011. Durling was the PAC player of the year for women's golf in each of her first three seasons. The women won the PAC championship in 2010–2011, 2011–2012, and 2013–2014.

The softball team had numerous outstanding players. Lauren Pennell, '11, is the program leader in total games played and pitched, career innings pitched, and strikeouts. She is second in career wins, third in career complete games, second in career hits, and third in career total bases. Christine Slater is fifth in career hits and seventh in career runs scored, total bases, and stolen bases. Amy Fisher, '09, is second in career total bases, doubles, and hits, third in RBIs, and fourth in runs scored.

In club sports, the women's lacrosse team had several superb seasons, defeating some D1 squads during the Jewell years. In 2007, the women won their division and defeated Western Michigan in the Women's Collegiate Lacrosse League playoffs before losing to Central Michigan in the second round.

Men's Athletics

The men's teams with the best records from 2003 to 2014 were tennis, cross-country, swimming and diving, track and field, and soccer. The tennis squad won the PAC every year Jewell was president, with its best seasons being 12–3 in 2004, 12–4 in 2005, 10–2 in 2006–2007 (after beginning playing in both fall and spring), and 12–3 in 2010–2011. For the twelve-year period, the team was 113–49 (.697). The Wolverines went 63–1 in the PAC and won first-round NCAA tournament matches in 2011 and 2012. The cross-country squad won the PAC every year from 2003 to 2009. Its top regional places were ninth in 2007 and 2008. The soccer team's best seasons were 13–6–5 in 2005 and 15–6–2 in 2010; both years, the Wolverines reached the ECAC finals. The swimmers and divers captured seven PAC championships during Jewell's tenure. Between 2007–2008 and 2010–2011, the squad was 59–12 (.831). The track and field team won the PAC six times during Jewell's presidency. Its highest finish in the NCAA D3 was thirty-sixth in 2004 and, in the ECAC, was ninth in 2007. The 2009–2010 basketball team was 19–9, won the PAC, and played in the NCAA tournament. The three previous seasons, it earned ECAC bids. The baseball team's best seasons were 2006 (26–13), 2008 (19–18), but it won the PAC and earned an NCAA tournament bid, and 2011 (25–16) when it won the ECAC. The college also had several outstanding club teams and a robust intramural program.

The best tennis players during the Jewell years were Patrick Donahue, '04, Brett Moon, '06, John Moyer, '09, and Peter Riley, '15. Donahue won the PAC first singles championship and its MVP award three years in a row. Moon was 32–4 at first singles in 2004–2005 and received the PAC MVP. Moyer was the PAC MVP in 2008 and 2009, while Riley captured this award in 2012 and 2014. The 2011–2012 team claimed the college's twenty-first consecutive PAC title and won a first-round NCAA match for the second year in a row before saying farewell to Walters, whose forty-year career record was 391–152 (.720).

Steve Brown, '04, Daniel Chittick, '05, Dan Spaulding, '09, Garrett Cichowitz, '10, and Arleigh McRae, '14, led the cross-country team. Brown won the 2003 PAC championship by almost thirty seconds. Spaulding and Chittick helped the Wolverines win several PAC titles. Paced by Cichowitz, the 2008 cross-country team finished ninth at the Mideast Regional Championships. Cichowitz won the PAC championship in 2008, 2009, and 2010. He has the fourth-lowest 8K time in college history and is second all-time in the 3000 meters and the 10,000 meters. McRae, who has the lowest time in the 8K, finished 103rd at nationals in 2013.

In spring 2006, sophomore Caleb Courage became Grove City's first male swimmer to capture a national title when he won the 100 freestyle. Courage also finished third in the fifty freestyle. Courage, senior Ben Haring, and freshmen Drew Snyder and Tim Whitbeck placed second in the 200 freestyle relay to gain All-American distinction, as the team finished thirteenth in the nation. The victory over Bethany in December 2006 was the college's five hundredth all-time win. The Wolverines' fifteen wins that season were the most in college history. Courage won the 100 freestyle again at the 2007 nationals and qualified for the 2008 United States Olympic Trials. Tim Whitbeck won the D3 national championship in 2007 in the 50 freestyle as the team finished ninth. In 2008, the Wolverines crushed eight squads at their own invitational and finished twenty-eighth at nationals. In 2009, the team was sixth in the nation as Courage set a new D3 record in the 100-meter freestyle. Courage concluded his career as a three-time national champion in that event and earned eighteen All-American honors. Tim Whitbeck captured fourteen All-American honors. In fall 2009, the competition swimming pool was named for coach James Longnecker. In 2012–2013, the team's amazing sixty-one consecutive winning season streak finally ended.

At the 2006 PAC championships, Grove City runners, throwers, and jumpers had a total of thirty-seven personal bests as they won the title. Dan Chittick captured the 1500 meters, Chris Andrew took the steeplechase, and Scott Mang triumphed in the pole vault. Excelling throughout the season was Seth Fox, who holds the college 100-meter record at 10.94. In 2007, the team won the PAC title led by senior Andrew Kloes who won the 10,000 meters and junior Josiah Leuenberger who was first in both the 1500- and 5000-meter runs. Leuenberger holds the college record for the 5K. In 2008, the Wolverines captured the PAC crown, led by senior pole vaulter Matt Kulinski (whose 15'¼" vault is the best in college history), senior shot putter Bob Perri (who has the college's third-longest toss), javelin thrower Sean Domer (who also has the third longest throw), and sophomore 1500-meter specialist Derek Kruse. The 2009 team crushed the competition in winning its fifth consecutive PAC championship as senior Darin Miller in the 800, Dan Spaulding in the 10,000, Kruse in the 1500 (who has the second-fastest time in college history), junior Frankie Hourigan in the steeplechase, and junior Matt Six in the discus (the college record holder at 161–4¼) all won their events.

In 2005, sophomore goalkeeper Mike Manahan recorded eleven shutouts as the Wolverines won the PAC. Junior Bob McNees led the conference with eighteen goals and was the PAC Player of the Year. The Wolverines lost to Johns Hopkins in the final of the 2005 ECAC tournament. In 2006, McNees' hat trick against Pitt-Bradford broke Ross Emerson's record for most career goals set in 1957. In 2006, Manahan again had the lowest goals against average in the PAC (0.86). On October 6, 2012, the soccer team, which began playing in 1938, secured its five hundredth all-time win. Its all-time record was 500–331–73 (.600). Goalie Brendan Alfery led the PAC in goals against average (0.69) and save percentage (0.895) in 2013 and has the lowest career goals against average in college history.

The leading basketball players in the Jewell years were Tanner Prosser, '04, Ryan Eller, '05, Shawn Carr, '08, Ryan Gibson, '09, and Andy O'Keefe, '10. Prosser ranks sixth in career points and first in career assists. Eller, Carr, Gibson, and O'Keefe all scored more than one thousand points in their careers; Carr is second in three-point shots made, and Gibson is fourth in assists. O'Keefe is the college's all-time leader in career field goal percentage at 60.8 percent. His senior year, he helped lead the Wolverines to a 19–9 record by shooting 66.8 percent, one of the highest percentages in the nation. O'Keefe became the seventh Grove City men's basketball player to earn Academic All-America honors. Illustrative of the Christian faith and community service of many Grove City athletes, in November 2004, basketball team members conducted a basketball clinic for and had Bible studies with students at Imani Christian Academy in Wilkinsburg. "We are trying to instill the importance of Jesus Christ in their lives," senior Phil Bushre explained.[91]

In fall 2009, Grove City named its baseball field for former athletic director R. Jack Behringer. Several players contributed substantially to Grove City's three best seasons—2006, 2008, and 2011—during the Jewell years. Senior Eric Arneson went 9–0 in 2006 and has the second-highest career winning percentage in college history (.824). Justin Miller, '07, is the career leader in saves.

Brian Moran, '09, has the highest career batting average of.436 and the highest slugging percentage of.730 and stole eleven more bases than any other player. Mike Herringshaw, '10, has the most pitching appearances, second-most innings pitched, and third-most wins. In 2009, catcher Marcus Magister, '11, set the college's single-season record for home tuns and RBIs. He was named to the All-Mideast Region first team and chosen as a third-team All-American by D3Baseball.com. He is first in career RBIs and home runs, second in total bases, third in hits, and fourth in batting average. Scott Moran, '11, is first in career runs scored and fourth in hits.

The football team had only two winning seasons—6–4 in both 2008 and 2012, but it had numerous highlights and some outstanding players. Junior David DiDonato's 719 receiving yards in 2003 were the third most in school history, while senior Mike Titzel had the second-highest punting average in college history that season. Senior linebacker Mike Choby, who was also the SGA president, led the PAC with ninety-two tackles, twenty tackles for a loss, 9.5 sacks (possibly the first time anyone led the conference in all three categories) and earned third-team All-South Region honors. Senior safety Aaron Margo was named a first-team All-American by the American Football Coaches Association in 2005.

In November 2007, sophomore Andrew DiDonato became Grove City's all-time career passing yards leader with 3,023 yards, surpassing the mark set by Jeff Cass (3,006 yards) in 1988. That season, senior center Matt Gregg was selected to play in the annual Aztec Bowl in Chihuahua, Mexico. DiDonato praised coach Chris Smith: "He teaches us to be men of integrity and character." Trainer Kay Emigh argued that Smith's teams should be judged "not by wins and losses, but by the success of his former players in the business, medical, education and coaching world."[92] In 2009, DiDonato led the PAC with 240 pass completions and 2,994 yards of total offense. He finished his career with a school record of 7,509 passing yards and 8,904 yards of total offense. DiDonato grew in his faith at Grove City and dreamed of becoming a college head coach.[93] The next year, senior offensive tackle Pete Polesnak became the fourth Wolverine selected for an All-Star team that played a Mexican squad.

Like the college's basketball players, many football players were committed to serving Christ and the community. For example, members of the 2005 team sang Christmas carols at Orchard Manor and organized a liftathon to raise money for the Make-A-Wish Foundation. Scott Fichter, '07, declared, "Our goals are just to glorify God in the projects we do, and to make a difference in someone's life."[94]

Two golfers standout during the Jewell years. Tyler Fitch, '08, the medalist at the 2005 championship, was the PAC player of the year. Fitch also won medalist honors at the sixteen-team St. Vincent Invitational in April 2007 and tied for the best score at the 2008 PAC championship. Christian Locher, '15, led the Wolverine golfers for four years. In 2012, he had a 77.2 average, finished in the top five in seven tournaments, and captured medalist honors at Grove City's invitational to help the Wolverines win the event.

Grove City excelled in several club sports during Jewell's tenure. About three hundred students typically played annually on club sports teams. The men's club lacrosse team, which joined the US Lacrosse Men's Division Intercollegiate Association in 2005, was very successful. The 2005 and 2006 squads were led by attackman Evan Feinberg, '06, who ranked first in the nation in 2005 with eight points a game. The 2010 team, led by junior goalkeeper Andrew Dymski, whose .75 save percentage was the highest in the country, ranked eighth in the nation. Spearheaded by Dan Caselli, '16, the 2013 team was fifth in the nation, while the 2014 team was fourth.

The college also had an outstanding club volleyball team. The 2003 team was 11–0 in the regular season and finished third in the Eastern Regionals. Led by junior outside hitter Zach Underwood, senior middle hitter Steve Fisher, and junior right-side hitter Matt O'Brien, the 2004 team finished 20–3 and was ranked fifth in the nation. The 2006 squad had a fantastic record of 21–1, won the Penn-Ohio Conference title, and ranked among the top twenty club teams in the nation in D2. The 2008 squad defeated Army, Yale, and Southern Methodist at nationals and finished ninth. In 2009, the Wolverines vanquished the first, fifth and eleventh ranked teams in the nation and finished the season ranked fifth.

The college club rugby team excelled in the 2010s. In 2012 team, led by Casey Lamb, '13, captured the Three Rivers Rugby Championship and was ranked fourth in the nation by the National Small College Rugby Organization. In 2005, the college dropped water polo as a varsity sport because of excessive travel, lack of recruits, and the refocusing of PAC sports. A men's club water polo team was established, which finished fourth in the nation in 2007. The 19–3 college's ultimate Frisbee club team finished second in D3 in 2008–2009. The men's roller hockey club excelled in 2010.

Intramural sports continued to be very popular, and men's football and basketball games often drew hundreds of spectators. Many years almost fifty men's basketball teams competed in five different leagues. *The Princeton Review* ranked Grove City second in the nation in the popularity of intramural sports in 2009, trailing only Notre Dame. There were almost four thousand participants in spring 2008 and more than two thousand participants in fall 2009 (many students played more than one sport each semester). Students competed in men's football, soccer, and Ping-Pong, men's and women Frisbee, volleyball, and badminton, and coed tennis and Quidditch.

Recognition

From 2003 to 2014, Grove City received many accolades. In 2003, *Insight* magazine recognized Grove City as of the "Top 15 Academically Excellent Schools That Refuse to Be Politically Correct," praising its liberal arts core curriculum, academic rigor, and rate of graduate school acceptance. In 2004, *The Princeton Review* included Grove City in its seventy-seven "America's Best Value Colleges." That year, *Business Reform* magazine judged the college's entrepreneurship program one the best Christian programs in the country. In addition, this program as one of two finalists for the United

States Association for Small Business and Entrepreneurship 2005 National Model Undergraduate Entrepreneurship Program Award.

In 2005, *US News & World Report* ranked Grove City number five among northern comprehensive colleges based on it having the highest freshman retention rate (90 percent), highest average SAT score (1280), highest percentage of freshmen in the top quarter of their high school class (89 percent), and lowest acceptance rate (41 percent). That fall, PricewaterhouseCoopers commended Grove City's excellent preparation of accountants.[95] In 2007, *US News & World Report* ranked Grove City College the number one "Best Value" among northern comprehensive colleges for the fifth year in a row. In 2010, the Young America's Foundation named Grove City one of the country's top conservative colleges for the sixth consecutive year. The next year, *Consumers Digest* rated Grove City first in the country in value among all liberal arts colleges. In 2014, TheBestSchools.org ranked Grove City as number two on its list of "20 Best Conservative Colleges in America."

Marketing and Placement

In the early Jewell years, the admissions office increased its placement of ads in college guides and magazines and communicated more electronically with prospective students. The college dealt with the increasing cost and decreasing value of a baccalaureate degree, coupled with the expectation that many students would also need to obtain a graduate or professional degree.96 To help attract and retain students, Grove City strove to supply a greater percentage of students' unmet financial while lowering the CQPA requirement for receiving aid. The recession of 2008–2009 stymied this effort for several years. Many high school guidance counselors recommended Grove City to hardworking, mature students who wanted a Christian college and could handle the rigors of the Grove City curriculum.

In 2011, the college strove to create a new brand to expand its appeal. College promotion materials had long argued that the college was academically rigorous, authentically Christian, and an amazing value. The new marketing campaign used the slogan "freedom for excellence" to summarize the college's culture and mission. A 2012 ad declared: "Freedom to excel. Freedom to explore. Freedom to live your faith.... Freedom to follow God's calling wherever it might lead. At GCC, students from around the world [and] across the nation and the region achieve excellence in all they're called to be." To recruit students, Grove City still relied primarily on high school visits by its admission counselors, visitation days at the college for high school seniors and juniors, alumni interactions with prospective students, and its high ranking in numerous publications.

In fall 2012, the admissions office added a third senior visitation day, a Music Major Day, and an Education Open House. To help reduce "summer melt," admissions held its first Admitted Student Day in March 2014. This two-day event featured panels on internships, careers, campus ministries, and international education, as well as a student organizational fair, Sunday vespers, lunch with academic deans, and a residence hall reception.

During Jewell's tenure, many graduates continued to obtain desirable jobs and fellowships to attend prestigious graduate and professional schools, and *The Princeton Review* consistently ranked the college placement office in the top twenty in the nation. In fall 2003, the CSO created three new events to help students prepare for the annual career fair and find jobs: the Résumé Blitz, a mock career fair, and Mock Interview Day. The CSO also held an Exploring Your Calling program, an annual Camp and Ministry Fair, and Career Services Come to You and Lunch and Learn sessions. To help students determine their best options after graduating, CSO annually sponsored a Health Professions Conference, an Alumni Career Panel Night, and a career fair in which about 140 organizations—including Microsoft, Target, and Teach for America—participated. In 2008, Education Career Services, a CSO satellite program, was created to help the college's 450 education majors secure teaching jobs.

Testifying to the quality of their education and the effectiveness of Career Services, almost every year from 2003 to 2014, 95 percent of graduates obtained jobs or were attending graduate or professional schools within six months after commencement.[97] Recruiters "love Grove City students," senior Diane Kim explained in 2012, because they "are very ethical, very responsible and very professional."[98]

Alumni

Jewell and the development office staff worked vigorously to establish better relations with alumni and cultivate more friends of the college, and their efforts paid off. Fetterolf insisted that Jewell was "tireless in his efforts to connect with alumni and having a very positive effect on fundraising."[99] Jewell used "Moment for Grove City" letters to keep alumni informed about college activities and achievements. The college revamped the *GēDUNK* alumni magazine and sent a monthly email newsletter sent to more than eight thousand alumni and friends. The forty-member Alumni Association Council redoubled its efforts to involve alumni more fully in the life of their alma mater. The council strove to mirror the college's alumni in terms of graduation decade, gender, geography, and professional affiliation. In 2003, the college created Full Circle to solicit donations from alumni. The trustees wanted to help students develop an "Attitude of Gratitude" and donate to the college as alumni.[100] In fall 2005, the college published an alumni directory, and in 2007, the college launched eCommunity to fourteen thousand alumni. Eighty-two percent of the alumni who responded to a 2009 survey had a favorable impression of the college, 92 percent said they would recommend Grove City to prospective students or employers, and 76 percent of them were likely to financially support the college (53 percent of respondents said that they had already done so).[101]

Several alumni achievement winners stand out during Jewell's presidency. Lissa Hilsee, '80, founded and served as the executive director of Philadelphia Cares, a nonprofit that strives to alleviate critical social, educational, and environmental problems in the Philadelphia area. David Jones, '54, served as the director of community medicine at York Hospital in York, Pennsylvania, an associate professor of medicine at the University of Maryland, and vice president of medical affairs for Pennsylvania Blue Shield. His involvement in the college's Christian Service League taught him that he could confidently "live out [his] beliefs in daily life."[102] Nancy Byers Eaton Stedman, '54, who was both the homecoming and May queen, had a long theater career, which included performing on Broadway with Angela Lansbury in *Sweeney Todd* and working with composers Richard Rodgers and Stephen Sondheim in several productions.

Other noteworthy alumni are Victor Kuligin, '86, Andy Sems, Tim Habbershon, '81, Sean Rowe, '97, and Jim Van Eerden, '85. Kuligin taught church history and Christian ethics at Namibia Evangelical Theological Seminary and wrote *Ten Things I Wish Jesus Never Said* (2006). Sems is a highly respected orthopedic surgeon at the Mayo Clinic. Habbershon, an entrepreneur, founded and directs the Institute for Family Enterprising at Babson College. In 2007, Rowe was ordained as the youngest bishop in the Episcopal Church. Van Eerden produced two films in 2010—one about Little League baseball and one about the nation's financial crisis.

Staff

Over the years, Grove City's hundreds of dedicated, hardworking staff have helped the college run smoothly, aided the work of the faculty, and enriched the experience of students. Consider several examples. Betsy Van Hoppe Bentlage emigrated from the Netherlands in 1956 after surviving the Nazi invasion during World War II; she worked for twenty-four years in the Gedunk and mailroom before retiring in 1981. During her forty-five-year career from 1962 to 2007, Carol Magee worked in the bookstore, the mail room, the business office, and security. Nurse Karen Danielson compassionately took care of sick students and faculty in Zerbe from 1987 to 2006. Paul Alessio worked diligently for forty years in maintenance before retiring in 2020. Sherry Decker, beloved by students for her omelets, declared, "You have to put a little love in them to make them special."[103]

Trustees

A thirty-six–member board of trustees governed Grove City College during Jewell's presidency. Organized into eleven standing committees, the trustees were guided by the college charter, the board's bylaws and a "Principles of Governance" booklet. Jack Freeman contended that Grove City's trustees played a "much more active role in the governance and management" than their counterparts at most similar institutions.[104] Board members, who worked in business, manufacturing, education, law, the judiciary, banking, government, and the ministry, ranged significantly in age and experience. Beginning in fall 2003, the trustees conducted half of their meetings on campus and ate lunch with students at least twice a year. "The students are the life of this campus," David Rathburn declared, "and we want them involved."[105]

In 2007, J. Paul Sticht, '39, who served as the board's president from 1997 to 2003, died at age eighty-nine. He worked as an industrial engineer at US Steel, transporting critical military cargo during World War II; as president of Campbell Soup Company International, Federated Department Stores, and R. J. Reynolds; and as the chair of RJR Nabisco. The *Grove City College Alumni Magazine* noted that major newspapers and business magazines used the words "statesman, soft-spoken, courtly, avuncular, successful, approachable and bold" to describe Sticht.[106]

The 2008 Middle States report called the board "a talented, dedicated and generous group of individuals." For forty years, the college was, "according to some Board members, productively managed as if it were a subsidiary business of two long-standing Board chairs." Since 1999, the trustees had taken a "leap in faith" by consulting administrators and faculty on various matters before making decisions. They had given the faculty a large role in hiring new professors and adopted a grievance policy. Evaluators commended the board for following "sound, conservative business practices" and managing the college's resources "exceptionally well."[107]

Conclusion

Jewell claimed that his biggest contributions as president were re-invigorating "the Christian roots of the institution" and tremendously expanding the academic program.[108] The Middle States team praised Jewell's administration for developing "a more 'open' posture in its dealings with faculty, staff and external agencies" while preserving the college's "bedrock principles."[109] During his tenure, the college added thirty-nine professors, reducing the student/faculty ratio from nineteen to one to fourteen to one. The student body became geographically diverse (with students hailing from forty-eight states). Millions of dollars were raised to fund student scholarships. Under Jewell's leadership, the Colonial Hall Apartments, Rathburn Hall, and STEM Hall were built. The president was pleased that fraternity and sorority membership increased from 10 percent of students in 2003 to over 20 percent in 2014 and that the college had more than 140 other affinity groups. Jewell helped lead two highly successful capital campaigns. The college was filled with faculty and students who staunchly supported its historic Christian mission.[110] Finally, he helped improve the college's relationship with the town by meeting frequently with civic leaders, directing the college to contribute $250,000 toward revitalizing the downtown, and purchasing and renovating properties nearby the campus.[111]

Jewell's presidential years were the highlight of his life. They were "first and foremost a partnership" with his "dear wife Dayl" who actively engaged with students, faculty, staff, and alumni. His "talented, loyal" administrative team contributed significantly to the college's advancement.[112] Jewell advised his successor to adhere to the college's "mission, visions and values," collaborate "closely with the trustees," and "trust in the Lord."[113]

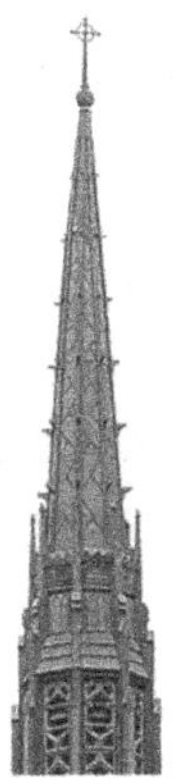

THE PRESIDENCY OF PAUL J. MCNULTY:

"The Pursuit of Excellence for the Glory of Christ,"[1]

2014–2025

After Dick Jewell announced he was retiring in 2013, Paul J. McNulty, '80, who had served on the board of trustees for ten years, decided to apply to be president because he felt called by God to do so, aspired to engage with great ideas, and wanted to help the college "strengthen and clarify its Christian mission and self-identity." McNulty argued that every inch of the college had been claimed for Christ, that everything the college did should be directly associated with being a Christian institution.[2]

McNulty had a distinguished career in public service before coming to Grove City. He had served as the chief counsel and director of legislative operations for the majority leader of the US House of Representatives, the chief counsel for the House Judiciary Committee's Subcommittee on Crime, the US Attorney for the Eastern District of Virginia, and the Deputy Attorney General, the second-highest-ranking official in the Justice Department, where he oversaw more than one hundred thousand employees. McNulty left a flourishing law practice with Baker McKenzie in Washington,

DC, that provided interesting work, worldwide travel, and a high salary to serve as the college's ninth president. Like Jewell, McNulty had an impressive record as a student. He served as a class officer, the social vice president of SGA, a chapel aide, an RA, and a campus tour guide, and had significant roles in several plays. Also like Jewell, McNulty immensely enjoyed the relationships he developed with students through shared meals, Bible studies, and attendance at numerous campus events. Board of trustees president David Rathburn explained that the search committee chose McNulty because of his effective management of complex organizations; his founding and leadership of Faith and Law, a Christian study group on Capitol Hill; his ability to work effectively with Republicans and Democrats; and his service as a Presbyterian elder.[3]

During his eleven-year tenure, McNulty adroitly handled three major problems—the COVID pandemic, a controversy over critical race theory, and the enrollment challenge posed by the diminished number of youths in the areas from which the college primarily drew students. Under McNulty, the college more strongly emphasized its Christ-centered academic program and campus environment.

McNulty delineated four principal goals for his presidency: "strengthening the college's Christian identity, expanding its academic programs, pursuing excellence in the student experience, and building long-term enrollment success."[4] Although Grove City had branded itself as a Christian college throughout its history, McNulty made its Christian heritage and commitment even more front and center. His first board meeting as president, he told the trustees that he wanted a "clearer articulation" of the college's "mission and distinctives."[5] Through the professors who were hired, the students who were admitted, the college's promotional materials, his leadership style and messages to faculty and students, and changes to the curriculum, residence life, and campus activities, McNulty fortified Grove City's Christian reputation and objectives.

McNulty stated that his chief goal was ensuring that "faith, freedom and people matter." He was impressed with spiritual vitality on campus and wanted to enrich and enlarge the life of the Christian mind, foster an environment where faculty, students, and staff cared deeply for each other, and increase the college's worldwide impact.[6] The trustees prayed that he would "stand steadfast in the Providence of God, with the abiding assurance that God's Hand will guide the affairs of the college and inspire his Presidency."[7]

McNulty chose the theme of "For Faith. For Freedom. For the Future" for his inauguration in February 2015. He defined "faith" as Grove City's long-standing devotion to biblical truth. This necessitated championing the virtue of "freedom," which is critically important to enable people to pursue their calling in the Lord unrestrained by the government or other agencies.[8] At McNulty's inauguration, Kenneth Starr, president of Baylor University and a former federal judge, spoke about faith; former US Senator and US Attorney General John Ashcroft discussed freedom; and McNulty talked about the role Grove City could play in the nation's future. McNulty beseeched the college community to "prepare men and women to live according to the highest calling of God as citizens of His Kingdom, through the treasures of wisdom and knowledge, and serve our fellow citizens with uncompromising integrity, exemplary skill and self-sacrificing love."[9]

In 2016, McNulty accentuated the combination of factors that distinguished Grove City from four thousand other educational institutions: its strong Christian identity; intellectually rigorous and values-based curriculum; honest advertising of its price and affordability; political and educational independence; outstanding faculty; graduates' remarkable placement rate; athletic culture and success; and beautiful campus.[10] The college unveiled a new strategic plan in December 2016 to guide it for the next five years, which stressed five fundamental values: faithfulness, excellence, community, stewardship, and independence. The college's new mission statement, adopted in 2017, declared its intention to "develop leaders of the highest proficiency, purpose, and principles ready to advance the common good," equip students to prepare for their God-given callings, and "foster lifelong community engagement." The college promoted its core values through its academic, religious, and residential life programs. The latter program was designed to help students achieve Christ-centered fulfillment through "Living, Learning, Engaging and Thriving."[11]

The 2018 Middle States evaluation team's report accurately summarized Grove City's mission during McNulty's presidency. Evaluators noted that the college "is well-known for its conservative values," expressed by its "commitment to faith and freedom . . . integrated humanities core curriculum, conservative political science and economics departments, Christian behavioral expectations, and institutional independence." Grove City's distinctives included its refusal to accept any federal aid or to offer financial discounts to students. Students paid the full cost unless they received a scholarship from the college. College officials argued that this was a fairer and more transparent approach to institutional finances.[12] About 40 percent of Grove City students graduated debt-free throughout McNulty's tenure.

In fall 2018, the college began describing itself as "Christ centered." McNulty had observed this orientation in a "nascent form" as a student when Charles MacKenzie was president. This focus had grown under MacKenzie's successors and was now fully blossoming. McNulty wanted Grove City to be "the best Christian liberal arts college in the country" whose faculty and students had an excellent "understanding of and passion for the integration of faith and learning."[13] The 2018 Middle States evaluators argued that Grove City was boldly and diligently pursuing this "remarkable mission" during a turbulent period in higher education.[14]

In February 2022, the college unveiled a second five-year strategic plan titled "From Strength to Strength: Timeless Values and Historic Opportunities," which outlined five goals—to "enrich academic excellence," "strengthen community life," "achieve and sustain optimal enrollment," "enhance financial sustainability," and fortify "the college's identity as a distinctive national thought leader and innovative servant of the common good." A strategic planning committee devised this plan to help the college deal with major national trends, including an anticipated decline in students of college age, an increasing demand for affordable education, and the ability to use synchronous learning.[15]

This plan declares that Grove City "strives to be a highly distinctive and comprehensive Christian liberal arts college of extraordinary value," which "equips students to pursue their unique callings through a Christ-centered, academically excellent, and affordable learning and living experience." Committed to transcendent truths, conservative social and political values, and the tenets of free society, the college seeks to develop proficient, purposeful, and principled leaders who will "advance the common good." The plan stresses that Grove City strives to teach and apply biblical truth in every area of college life and to promote Christian formation.[16] To accomplish this latter goal, the college sought to provide "Christ-centered worship" and foster "whole-life discipleship."[17] The college strove to achieve "the highest standards of excellence" in academics, residence life, the arts, and athletics and to do "all to the glory of God." Grove City wanted to create "a dynamic and welcoming campus experience" characterized by rich fellowship, fruitful service, robust hospitality, and deep respect for people as God's image-bearers. The college aimed to manage its resources prudently to maintain its affordability, ensure its sustainability, and enhance the beauty of the campus.[18]

McNulty stressed that from its founding, Grove City had been "nondenominational and welcoming to Christians of all creeds." The college had no "explicit statement of faith" and relied on its rigorous faculty hiring process to ensure that "Christ-centered convictions" guided professors in their teaching, relationships with students, research, and publications.[19] In his numerous chapel addresses, regular faculty devotionals, and hundreds of conversations with faculty, staff, and students, McNulty continually stressed the centrality of biblical faith to the college's mission.

Grove City College has been a "conservative" institution throughout its history, vice president for student recruitment Lee Wishing, '83, explained, which strove to conserve and teach "the best values, ideas and scholarship to the next generation." This included defending major aspects of political conservativism including limited government, laissez-faire economics, and individual liberty.[20]

During McNulty's presidency, five major college figures—Charles MacKenzie, James Longnecker, Nancy Paxton, Dick Morledge, and David Rathburn—went to receive their heavenly reward. David Rathburn called MacKenzie, who died in 2017, one of God's "faithful servants—a principled leader who leaves an indelible mark on our history and the hearts and minds of generations of Grove City College students." McNulty praised "his vision and courage as a leader, his outstanding intellect as a scholar and teacher, and his extraordinary warmth and kindness as a pastor." Religion professor James Bibza credited MacKenzie for the college adopting "a more robust, evangelical perspective."[21] Coach James Longnecker also died in 2017. Without a single assistant coach to help with recruiting or strategy, he compiled a phenomenal 687–177–1 (.795) record in swimming and diving, track and field, and cross-country and mentored many other coaches. Longnecker set a "standard of excellence," athletic director Todd Gibson argued, "that all of our coaches, and athletes strive to achieve." Current swimming coach David Fritz added that countless athletes valued "the lessons they learned from Coach Longnecker outside the pool and the impact it had on their lives."[22]

Nancy Paxton, '54, who had served as the dean of women from 1976 to 1991 and vice president of student affairs from 1991 until 2004, died in 2021. McNulty asserted that "she was a constant source of cheerfulness, kindness and devoted service to the campus community. Now, in the presence of her Savior, she can look to her right and to her left and enjoy fellowship" with "the saints who have gone before her."[23] Dick Morledge, '54, the dean of the chapel from 1984 to 1999 and a trustee from 1995 to 2014, was deeply loved. "No one has ever been more passionate about our college," McNulty declared, and no one had "prayed more for the outpouring of the Lord's grace and goodness on GCC." Board president Ed Breen maintained that Morledge was "among the giants" who built the college's "strong spiritual structure."[24] In 2024, David Rathburn, '79, who had served as a trustee for twenty-eight years and the board president for seventeen, succumbed to his long and courageous battle against cancer. His "transformative impact," Breen insisted, could not "be overstated. He made the trustees' governance more effective "by introducing strategic planning, prioritizing endowment growth, and encouraging more extensive board deliberations on key issues." Few leaders, McNulty added, had displayed such "exceptional intelligence, boundless energy, amazing generosity, consistent respect and heart-felt compassion for others, and unshakable faith in God's grace."[25]

The Student Body

The challenge of generating enough applications to produce high-quality freshmen classes continued during the first half of McNulty's presidency as demographic shifts in the Northeast and Midwest and the rising cost of tuition, room, and board sharply reduced the number of potential students. To address this issue, administrators decided to focus their recruiting efforts from Virginia to Texas, an area which had many residents who shared Grove City's values. They also strove to further accentuate the college's distinctives and strengths and to use alumni and current students more effectively in the recruiting process. Between 2010 and 2024, college enrollment in the United States dropped by 15 percent.[26] Despite this trend, the college's innovative approach and superior quality enabled it to maintain optimal enrollment during the second half of McNulty's presidency.

The freshman class of 2014 had an average SAT score of 1203 and an average high school GPA of 3.73. The top majors for freshmen were biology, mechanical engineering, communication studies, English, and electrical engineering. In 2016, Grove City began sending more admission counselors to college fairs and organizations that targeted high school students who were interested in attending a Christian college or university. The college strove to dispel two misperceptions many prospective students had: that because their cost was higher, other colleges were better than Grove City, and that because these schools were giving students so much financial aid, they valued students more than Grove City did.[27] Applications slowly but steadily increased from 1,530 in 2013, to 1,814 in 2019, to 2,174 in 2022, the highest number since 2003. Many years, almost 90 percent of students who enrolled had previously visited campus. When the 609 incoming freshmen were asked in fall 2022 why they chose Grove City, 96 percent of them said it was because of the college's nationally ranked academic programs in STEM, liberal arts, nursing, and business. In addition, 90 percent liked the college's Christian mission, 90 percent cited the college's "welcoming, supportive and vibrant living and learning experience," and 87 percent were impressed by the outstanding career outcomes of alumni.[28]

The next year's freshman class hailed from twenty-five states, and almost half of freshmen were pursuing degrees in STEM programs. Members of the class of 2028 came from thirty-eight states and five foreign countries. Forty-eight percent of them graduated from public high schools and 27 percent from Christian high schools, while 20 percent had been homeschooled. Mechanical engineering was still the college's most popular major (11 percent of freshmen). The top five reasons why freshmen chose to attend Grove City were its excellent academics, Christian character, conservative values, convivial campus community, and good career outcomes.[29] By 2024, the average freshman SAT score rebounded to 1264. During the McNulty years, the college's four-year graduation rate of 80 percent was far above the national average of 60 percent.[30]

Facilities

The most significant facility enhancements during McNulty's tenure were the purchase of the former United States Investigative Services office building on Lincoln Avenue, the $9 million upgrade to Buhl Library, and the $48 million renovation of Rockwell Hall. The seventy-seven thousand square foot former USIS facility, the largest off-campus acquisition in college history, currently houses operations and the Institute for Faith and Freedom. Sizable donations by alumni led to two buildings being renamed: the Hall of Arts and Letters (HAL) became Staley Hall in appreciation for a $4 million gift by Richard Staley, '62, and Rockwell Hall became Smith Hall in honor of a generous gift from tech entrepreneur William W. Smith Jr., '69, and his wife Dieva Smith. Campus life was further enriched by the installation of high-quality FieldTurf on Thorn Field, turf and lights on the Don Lyle (soccer) Field, refurbished tennis courts, a circle of pavers placed between Thorn Field and Rainbow Bridge, a statue of a wolverine outside the Physical Learning Center, and outdoor pickleball and basketball courts on the lower campus. In addition, MAP café was renovated, and twenty-four-hour markets were added to MAP and Hicks. In 2017, *Reader's Digest* awarded Grove City's *Teaching Window* one of its "14 Most Stunning Stained Glass Windows Around the World." The 2018 Middle States report extolled the "outstanding curb appeal" of the campus's well-maintained facilities.[31]

Academic Life

The college's academic program grew stronger during McNulty's presidency because of the faculty who joined the college; the new programs that were created, most notably, a bachelor's of science degree in nursing and six master's degrees; and several majors and minors that were introduced.

In fall 2014, four minors were added in entrepreneurship: social innovation, social entrepreneurship, social enterprise, and internet entrepreneurship. In 2014, the exercise science program, which began in 2008–2009, received accreditation from the Commission on Accreditation of Allied Health Education Programs. That year, the Social Work Degree Guide ranked Grove City's social work program, which had started only two years earlier and offered only a minor, fourteenth in the nation among Christian colleges granting social work degrees. The program added a bachelor's in social work degree in fall 2017 and was accredited by the Council on Social Work Education in 2020.

In summer 2015, at McNulty's request, Dick Jewell visited ninety-three-year-old Larry Gara at his home to apologize on behalf of the college for Gara's "inappropriate and unfair" discharging in 1963. This public apology, McNulty explained, demonstrated that the college's due process had been improved, which was an important step in lifting the American Association of University Professors' sanction against Grove City that had existed for more than fifty years.[32] After its staff came to campus and talked with administrators and faculty about the college's revised policies, the AAUP removed its censure in September 2016.

In 2016, the college expanded its trustee scholarship program to eight trustee fellows, who each received "full ride" (tuition, room, and board) scholarships and sixteen additional students, who received $8,000 scholarships. The scholarships were renewable for four years if students maintained at least a 3.6 CQPA. Trustee scholars were selected for their leadership skills, community service, maturity, and initiative. The twenty-four students took most of their HUMA courses together. The $8,000 scholarships were increased to half tuition in 2024.

In fall 2016, the Hopeman School began offering new majors in health, molecular biology, and conservation biology. The next fall, the college created new majors in music performance and Christian ministries, while the business management major introduced concentrations in human resources, operations, and entrepreneurship. Minors in writing and creative writing were added in fall 2018. At this point, the college offered sixty-six majors, which included five accredited and certified programs. In fall 2021, Grove City introduced an interdisciplinary design and innovation major. The next fall, the college added a BS in applied science and engineering, a BS in supply chain management, and a BS in computer engineering.

The 2018 Middle States report noted that students made good use of the library, the writing center, and information technology services. Each year, about one hundred students engaged in service-learning projects, and almost two hundred participated in international education programs. Grove City provided ample international and multicultural experiences for students through courses, extracurricular activities, and overseas opportunities.[33] Moreover, hundreds of students participated in travel interims each year.

In 2019, Fitness and Wellness, commonly called Fitwell, was significantly revised. The one-credit required course, renamed Healthful Living, was taught completely online to enable coaches to devote more time to "recruiting, preparing for practices and matches, player development and mentorship."[34]

Using a 2018 Lilly Endowment grant of almost $1 million, a faculty team, led by religion professor Seulgi Byun and Paul Kemeny, the dean of the Calderwood School of Arts and Letters, established the Project on Rural Ministry to facilitate the work of rural church pastors. The five-year project convened three groups of ten pastors serving congregations within 150 miles of Grove City for two conferences and three regional gatherings to help improve their ministry. Pastors also participated in online networking and site visits. After receiving a second grant in 2023, the college established the Center for Rural Ministry to further its work and appointed Charles Cotherman, '06, the executive director. In 2025, the CRM received a $5 million grant to expand its work, which included funding an annual conference, Inter City Outreach mission trips, student summer church internships, and meetings for participating ministers.

In fall 2020, Grove City added a bachelor of science in nursing (BSN) program in conjunction with Butler County Community College. Students took liberal arts and science education classes at GCC their first and fourth years and spent their two middle years at BCCC's Shaffer School of Nursing and Allied Health. Two years later, the Commission for Education in Nursing accredited the program. Director Janey Roach stated that the program aimed to educate health care professionals how to treat patients and their families" in a compassionate, holistic and ethical way."[35]

In 2024, the college's Center for Entrepreneurship + Innovation established E+I Fellows, an initiative that provided paid student interns to organizations and businesses in the Pittsburgh area. That fall, interns were placed with twenty organizations that were positively impacting the region through engaging in social innovation or enhancing economic opportunities but could not afford to hire traditional interns.[36]

In fall 2021, Grove City began offering a master of science in business analytics and created a postbaccalaureate program to enable graduating seniors to earn their teaching certification by taking an additional year of courses. In 2022, Grove City introduced MBA and master of accounting programs. In summer 2024, the Middle States Commission on Higher Education accredited all three business programs. In fall 2025, the college launched a master of arts in economics program to prepare students for careers in market analysis, organizational and institutional design, and public policy as well as for PhD programs.

Throughout his tenure, McNulty made the integration of faith and academics a high priority. He wanted every department to analyze how to teach their courses "in a Christ-centered way."[37] August faculty retreats helped professors think more deeply and collaboratively about how to make their instruction more biblically based, and an assistant dean position was established in the Calderwood School to advance faith and learning efforts. In addition, the college bookstore created a "Life of the Mind" shelf featuring works written by Grove City faculty and guest speakers.

In two 2023 essays titled "Learning for Freedom's Sake," provost Peter Frank argued that Grove City emphasized the "liberating arts"—celebrated books in literature, history, philosophy, and theology, outstanding musical and artist works, and scientific and mathematical achievements—to help enrich students. The college strove to develop "citizens steeped in Christian wisdom" who could promote and protect everyone's freedom. Grove City sought to shape souls by focusing on the good, true, and beautiful embodied in "momentous occasions in history," "perplexing philosophical questions," "stunning literary passages," "exhilarating orchestral harmonies," "the complex structure of atoms," and "the profound truths" of God's word. The liberating arts helped students develop wisdom, courage, and love. Centering the curriculum around Christ helped students better understand him, become more like him, and be light and salt in the world.[38] In his second essay, Frank argued that Christian colleges had a vital role to play in producing graduates who possessed the virtues civil society needed to prosper and flourish.[39]

Several recent studies have demonstrated that political and social conservatives are discriminated against on most campuses. True diversity of thought and expression exists at few colleges. Most surveys find that only 10 to 15 percent of college faculty are conservatives. Several surveys reported in the late 2010s that Republicans composed only 4 percent of historians, 3 percent of sociologists, and 2 percent of literature professors. On many campuses, conservative ideas and traditions "seldom get the sustained, scholarly attention that they deserve."[40] Before Donald Trump's second term, the obstacles to increasing political or ideological diversity at colleges seemed huge.[41] By its Christ-centered approach and politically conservative orientation, Grove City College offers a rare educational alternative. Through its classroom instruction, campus activities, guest speakers, faculty publications, and alumni, Grove City strongly promotes conservative, Christian views. Its faculty, however, expose students to a wide variety of perspectives through assigned readings, lectures, and class discussions. The 2018 Middle States team affirmed that its professors and students had the freedom "to explore facts, focus on primary texts, and consider multiple perspectives in their academic pursuits."[42] Hundreds of students have testified that Grove City has helped them understand and defend the biblical worldview and apply it to their lives.[43]

The Faculty

Faculty achievements and publications both increased during the McNulty years because of more release time and the addition of professors who were more engaged in research and writing. The 2018 Middle States report commended faculty for being well-prepared for their teaching responsibilities and producing "thoughtful and thorough" course syllabi. Evaluators noted that the faculty were not required to engage in scholarly activities, but they received substantial resources to support research projects.[44]

Important faculty additions were Old Testament scholar Seulgi Byun, highly respected church historian Carl Trueman, college provost Peter Frank, '95, music professor Joseph Hasper, and chaplain and senior director of Christian formation Donald Opitz. McNulty called Frank "an innovative leader, accomplished scholar and devoted servant of Christ" who was "very committed to integration of faith and learning in all disciplines."[45]

Many professors had impressive achievements beyond the campus. Business and entrepreneurship professor Timothy Mech served as the president of Harvest Bridge, a mission agency that engaged in evangelism, disaster relief, vocational training, and theological education in Southeast Asia, which he founded in 2008.[46]

In the natural sciences, electrical engineering professor Mike Bright created and hosted the annual BEST Robotics competition beginning in 2010 to enable middle and high school students to build remote-controlled robots to perform designated tasks. In the late 2010s, mechanical engineering professor Erik Anderson supervised students who examined the suction mechanism of remora fish, and he helped construct a better whale tag to enhance the study of the North Atlantic right whale. In 2020, Anderson coauthored a study of blue whales that helped motivate scientists to work to save their lives. In 2023, exercise science professors Philip Prins and Jeffrey Buxton, assisted by several students and alumni, published a study on the impact of low- and high-carbohydrate diets on athletic performance. Fred Brenner retired in 2020 after serving fifty-one years on the faculty, winning numerous awards, writing and editing several books, and publishing dozens of articles, often written with students.

Economics professor Jeffery Herbener received the 2017 Lawrence Fertig Prize for Austrian Economics for his groundbreaking work in Austrian economic theory. Fellow economist Shawn Ritenour was named a Senior Fellow at the Mises Institute, a nonprofit think tank, in 2018. In 2022, political science professor Samuel

Stanton was named an associate editor of the *Global Security Review*. In 2023, Lucian Conway coauthored an article on left-wing authoritarianism in *Frontiers in Psychology*, his 110th scholarly article.

In the fine arts, Joseph Hasper, the author of several hundred published compositions from symphonic orchestra to pep bands, won second place in the American Prize in Composition for his choral music in 2021. In February 2023, ceramics instructor Chris Bauer's art exhibit was featured in Pew. Jeff Tedford, '00, served as the Pennsylvania-Delaware String Teachers Association president from 2019 to 2024 and received the organization's Outstanding Orchestra Director award in 2017 and its Distinguished Service Award in 2024.

In 2019, Paul Kengor collaborated with Robert Orlando to produce a documentary titled *The Divine Plan* based on his 2018 book *A Pope and a President: John Paul II, Ronald Reagan, and the Extraordinary Untold Story of the 20th Century*. In 2022, Kengor was named editor in chief of *American Spectator*, a leading conservative magazine and online site. In fall 2024, a major motion picture based on Kengor's book *The Crusader: Ronald Reagan and the Fall of Communism* was released. Featuring a star-studded cast, *Reagan* depicts the fortieth president's "peaceful crusade to defeat Soviet communism without firing any missiles" and winning of the Cold War.[47] In 2024, Constance Nichols was appointed president of the Pennsylvania Deans' Forum, a group of deans and education department chairs that works to improve teacher education in the state.

Other faculty books during this period included Eric Potter's *Things Not Seen* (2015), Kengor's *Takedown: From Communists to Progressives, How the Left Has Sabotaged Family and Marriage* (2015), Richard Trammell's *Symbolic Logic and Other Forms of Deductive Reasoning* (2016), Kengor's *The Politically Incorrect Guide to Communism* (2017), my *Suffer the Children: How We Can Help Improve the Lives of the World's Impoverished Children* (2017), Kevin Seybold's *Questions in the Psychology of Religion* (2017), Conway's *Complex Simplicity: How Psychology Suggests Atheists Are Wrong About Christianity* (2017), philosophy professor Chris Franklin's *A Minimal Libertarianism: Free Will and the Promise of Reduction* (2018), Kemeny's *The New England Watch and*

Ward Society (2018), Kemeny's and my coedited *The Oxford Handbook of Presbyterianism* (2019), religion professor T. David Gordon's *Promise, Law, Faith: Covenant-Historical Reasoning in Galatians* (2019), Charles Cotherman's coedited *Sent to Flourish: A Guide to Planting and Multiplying Churches* (2019), sociologist David Ayers's *Christian Marriage: A Comprehensive Introduction* (2019), Gillis Harp's *Protestants and American Conservatism: A Short History* (2019), George Van Pelt Campbell's *Invitation to the Torah: A Guide to Reading, Teaching, and Preaching the Pentateuch* (2020), Cotherman's *To Think Christianly: A History of L'Abri, Regent College, and the Christian Study Center Movement* (2020), philosophy professor Ryan West's coauthored *Integrity, Honesty, and Truth Seeking* (2020), Kengor's *The Devil and Karl Marx: Communism's Long March of Death, Deception, and Infiltration* (2020); economics professor Caleb Fuller's *No Free Lunch: Six Economic Lies You've Been Taught and Probably Believe* (2021), Ayers's *After the Revolution: Sex and the Single Evangelical* (2022), Kengor's coauthored *The Devil and Bella Dodd: One Woman's Struggle Against Communism and Her Redemption* (2022), English professor Jeffrey Bilbro's *Reading the Times: A Literary and Theological Inquiry into the News* (2022), Ritenour's *The Economics of Prosperity: Rethinking Economic Growth and Development* (2023), Kengor's *The Worst of Indignities: The Catholic Church on Slavery* (2023), Ayers's *A Student's Guide to Dating, Marriage & Sex* (2023), English professor Joshua Mayo's *Good in Every Thing: Meditations on Shakespeare* (2023), religion professor Christopher Ansberry's *Reading Wisdom and Psalms as Christian Scripture: A Literary, Canonical, and Theological Introduction* (2024), Ansberry's edited *Proverbs: A Discourse Analysis of the Hebrew Bible* (2024), Bilbro's *Words for Conviviality: Media Technologies and Practices of Hope* (2024), Kengor's *The Stigmatists: Their Gifts, Their Revelations, Their Warnings* (2024), Trueman's *To Change All Worlds: Critical Theory from Marx to Marcuse* (2024), Trueman's *The Desecration of Man: How the Rejection of God Degrades Our Humanity* (2025), Fuller's coauthored *Mere Economics: Lessons for and from the Ordinary Business of Life* (2025), Byun's *A Christian's Guide to Trusting the Old Testament* (2025), and history professor Mark Graham's *30 Key Moments in the History of Christianity: Inspiring True Stories from the Early Church Around the*

World (2025). In addition, many faculty wrote chapters for edited works, articles in scholarly journals, and book reviews.

Carl Trueman's *The Rise and Triumph of the Modern Self: Cultural Amnesia, Expressive Individualism, and the Road to Sexual Revolution* (2020) is especially noteworthy. A seminary professor argued that the book was possibly the "most significant analysis and evaluation of Western culture written by a Protestant during the past fifty years," while Rod Dreher called it "without question one of the most important religious books of the decade." In 2022, Trueman published *Strange New World: How Thinkers and Activists Redefined Identity and Sparked the Sexual Revolution*, a shorter, simpler version of this book designed for pastors and Sunday school classes. In 2023, Trueman won the Davenant Institute's first-ever C. S. Lewis Award for Christian Wisdom for his "exemplary public witness as a Protestant scholar."

During the McNulty years, Faculty Follies continued to raise funds for a scholarship, allow students to see professors' lighter side, and build rapport between faculty and students, and often received rave reviews. In addition, in the late 2010s, a team of professors competed against students in Grover Feud to raise money for Young Life. In 2024, two teams of five faculty attempted to guess the most common student responses to survey questions about campus culture in Faculty Feud.

The Center for Vision and Values was renamed the Institute for Faith and Freedom in 2019 to coincide with the college motto "Where Faith and Freedom Matter." The institute increased its activities and outreach during McNulty's tenure through its annual conferences, Reagan lectures, and op-eds posted online and published in many newspapers. The annual conferences featured leading conservative pundits, journalists, and professors. Every year, the institute brought people who played a significant role in the Reagan administration to campus to discuss their work and the fortieth president. In 2024, the college established the Center for Faith and Public Life under the umbrella of the IFF to help "educate a secular culture about the crucial, historical role of Judeo-Christian values in the founding of this nation and its first principles" and to "examine how and why Christians" had "put their faith into action for the common good."[48]

Guest Speakers

The college, IFF, the Chapel Formation Office, and various departments combined to bring several dozen stimulating speakers to campus between 2014 and 2025. Prominent artist and author Makoto Fujimura, distinguished poet and playwright Jeanne Murray Walker, Liberty University English professor Karen Swallow Prior, and nationally renowned graphic novelist and cartoonist Gene Luen Yang all spoke at Christian Writers Conferences. Calvin religion professor James K. A. Smith lectured on "You Are What You Love." Robert Gagnon talked about the Bible and homosexuality. Anglican priest Tish Harrison Warren discussed her award-winning book *Liturgy of the Ordinary: Sacred Practices in Everyday Life* (2019). Catholic theologian and apologist Scott Hahn, '79, returned to campus in 2019 and 2022, the latter occasion to discuss his book *Holy Is His Name: The Transforming Power of God's Holiness in Scripture* (2022). J. Ligon Duncan III, the chancellor of Reformed Theological Seminary; entrepreneur Trudy Cathy White, daughter of Chick-fil-A founder S. Truett Cathy; prolific author Os Guinness; theologian Sinclair Ferguson; and Presbyterian Church of America pastor Kevin DeYoung spoke in the college's Faith for Life series.

Numerous political and social conservatives spoke. Charles Murray discussed his 2012 book *Coming Apart: The State of White America, 1960–2010. The National Review* senior writer David French lectured on religious liberty in 2018 and on political pluralism in 2021. IFF's Reagan lecture series included FOX News's senior political analyst Brit Hume, former Speaker of the House Newt Gingrich, former Wisconsin governor Scott Walker, and former attorney general William Barr. Senator Ben Sasse, R-NB, gave the 2019 commencement address, while Senator Pat Toomey, R-PA, discussed the future of conservatism. Author Matt Walsh detailed the assault on marriage and gender, while Paul Miller discussed his book, *The Religion of American Greatness: What's Wrong with Christian*

Nationalism (2022). Commentator Jonah Goldberg and R. R. Reno, the editor of *First Things* magazine, examined political conservatism.

The speech that generated the most controversy was Vice President Mike Pence's 2017 commencement address. Numerous students were excited that a man respected by many conservatives for his Christian beliefs and political positions was selected, whereas others protested his invitation because they disliked some of his political stances or his association with President Donald Trump. Some students and alumni complained that his invitation appeared to "align the college with the value system of the current administration." Letters to *The Collegian* called Pence's choice "thrilling," "exciting," "an unneeded expense," "just what we need," unforgettable, and deeply disappointing. McNulty "received many appreciative comments as well as thoughtfully stated objections."[49]

Senior Matt Hoekstra complained that recent commencement speakers—Jeb Bush in 2014, Representative Frank Wolf in 2015, and physician Ben Carson in 2016, culminating in Pence—were "all members of the Republican establishment," which sent the message that the only way to be a good Christian was to vote Republican.[50] Fellow senior Joe Setyon countered that most members of the campus community endorsed Pence's stances, including defending the unborn, ensuring religious liberty for Christians, and arguing that homosexual acts are "a sinful affront to Scriptural teaching."[51]

The college's decision in 2024 to appoint Pence a visiting fellow in its new Center for Faith and Public Life provoked more controversy. Paul Kengor argued that 77 percent of the news coverage about Pence's appointment was positive or neutral. While some IFF supporters disagreed with Pence on certain issues or disliked his relationship with Trump, Kengor explained, the former vice president supported Grove City's commitment to its "Judeo-Christian underpinning." Pence praised Grove City College for "helping students grow in their faith and in understanding God's calling for their life through a rigorous education and a faith-based community." It sent out graduates as "beacons of light and truth" into a world "that needs leaders of integrity and principle."[52] Pence taught a course with McNulty in both fall 2024 and spring 2025.

Religious Activities

During McNulty's presidency, thousands of students participated in meetings, retreats, prayer vigils, conferences, and other events sponsored by campus religious groups. Some students continued to oppose requiring chapel attendance. They maintained that chapel services were boring and not worthwhile and that being forced to attend took away the joy of worship and made students less attentive to the speakers. Others countered that mandatory chapel was beneficial because of the stimulating messages students heard and the sense of community the programs created.[53]

McNulty exhorted students to think every day about "the reconciling work of Christ," who came to "redeem us from our sins and liberate all of creation from the curse of the Fall."[54] Supporting the college's spiritual formation mission, Career Services strove to help students realize and pursue God's calling for their lives.[55] Several Christian groups and artists performed between 2014 and 2025 including Newsboys, The Oh Hellos, Jon Foreman (the lead singer of Switchfoot), Johnnyswim, Rend Collective, and Keith & Kristyn Getty.

Polk State School closed in fall 2019, ending students' long-standing ministry there. In fall 2020, the college's numerous women's mentorship groups were combined into one large group called Deeply Rooted, which organized more than 150 upperclasswomen to mentor freshmen. The male counterpart, MENtor Project, had one hundred participants. Every year during McNulty's presidency, hundreds of students went on ICO trips during college breaks to partner with local congregations and parachurch groups to rehabilitate houses, assist homeless shelters and food pantries, lead worship services, and evangelize.

Mirroring the general American religious pattern, the percentage of Grove City students affiliated with mainline denominations declined significantly in the first decade of the twenty-first century, while the percentage connected with interdenominational associations or independent congregations increased substantially. In spring 2021, the religious affiliation of Grovers was 8 percent Baptists, 6 percent Presbyterian Church (USA), 6 percent Presbyterian Church in America; 6 percent Catholic; 25 percent nondenominational, and 45 percent other varied bodies.

Donald Opitz, who began as his work in fall 2020, arranged an impressive lineup for the college's Faith for Life Lecture Series in fall 2021 that included journalist David French, author Andy Crouch, and Cherie Harder, president of the Trinity Forum. Beginning in spring 2022, chapel was switched from Tuesdays and Thursdays to Wednesdays and Fridays and extended from twenty to fifty minutes. The Wednesday services featured speakers, while Friday chapels involved several options. McNulty called the revised chapel structure "an exciting, new and historic chapter." Opitz insisted that chapel speakers "articulated a Christ-centered invitation to the gospel of grace."[56] In fall 2022, Opitz introduced his Fiver program, which entailed faculty leading Bible studies, book discussions, or analyses of religious topics for five weeks during the Friday chapel time slot. Students could instead attend a large group Bible study led by a religion professor or a worship service in Harbison led by chapel staff. About twenty faculty offered Fivers in two waves each semester. By 2025, more than 220 student missionaries had served in fifty-one countries under the auspices of the summer Global Outreach (formerly Red Box) program.

Three testimonials illustrate Grove City's spiritual impact on students. The parents of Natalie Colcombe, '18, praised the college for supporting their daughter by "consistently lifting Christian values and making Jesus bigger than anything in the world."[57] Senior John Kalajian declared, "I was nominally Christian when I arrived at Grove City and boy did God fix that over the past three and a half years."[58] Emily Fox asserted that "the source of my value isn't the earthly standard for success. It is in Jesus and His sacrifice on the cross."[59]

Campus Life: "The Pressure for Excellence Is Almost Palpable Here"

During the McNulty years, campus activities were plentiful, diverse, enriching, and entertaining, although the COVID crisis curtailed them substantially in 2020 and 2021. About half the student body attended the homecoming dance and the Tri Rho Extravaganza each year. Other popular events were the freshman and all-college talent shows, the Monster Mash Halloween dance, AEX Live, the fall Orchesis and synchronized swimming performances, the Big Man on Campus contest, and the biennial Presidential Gala. At the annual Light Up Night, students sang Christmas carols accompanied by the marching band, ate snacks, drank hot chocolate, and heard a gospel message and a recitation of J. M. Lowrie's "Star in the East" preceding the lighting of the star atop Rockwell Hall.

A variety of new events and activities were introduced during McNulty's tenure. In 2015, the SGA hosted its first annual Fall Fest, a carnival with bouncy houses, easy listening music, a dunking booth, and stalls featuring ring tosses, Putt-Putt, and other games. The Pan-Asian Association sponsored a Lunar New Year celebration beginning in the early 2020s. The Lux Mea Film Festival was created in 2021 by communications professor George Bandy to produce films to spotlight "truth and explore what it means to be a human being made in the image of God."[60] Each spring about fifteen very short films were shown at the Guthrie or in Crawford.

Other events grew larger. In April 2016, the art show hosted for several years by Project Eve that displayed art produced only by women was replaced by the Grove City Arts Festival, which filled South lobby of MAP and Old MAP with prints, photographs, sculptures, watercolors, graphite, and mixed media done by both women and men. The next year, the festival included a poetry reading, talks by professors on aesthetics, and student art exhibits throughout campus. The college also hosted two photography contests each year beginning in 2021.

Two major milestones occurred during McNulty's tenure. The 2016 Family Weekend (previously called Parents Weekend) celebrated the one hundredth anniversary of the college's extensive May Day ceremony with its crowning of a queen (which began in 1905) and a king (which began in 2003), elaborate dances to honor the queen, a recognition convocation, numerous athletic contests, and the All-College Sing. The celebration, college archivist Hilary Walczak, '09, argued, was a reminder that "history and tradition matter at Grove City College." To mark the twentieth anniversary of September 11, 2001, the college created a virtual exhibit containing comments, photos, oral history recordings, and firsthand accounts and recollections from Grove City alumni. One of the victims was Ruth E. Ketler, the granddaughter of Weir Ketler.

Each fall, the one hundred members of OB sought to embrace all new students "with a Christ-like love."[61] OB focused on "one of Grove City's defining pillars"—guiding students "to discover and pursue God's calling for their lives."[62] A 2018 survey reported that 92 percent of freshmen were "generally or very satisfied" with the quality of the orientation program.[63]

Several "upgrades" to campus life occurred after 2014. The replacing of Pepsi products with Coke and Sprite in January 2016 caused the campus to buzz with excitement, according to *The Collegian*.[64] Beginning in fall 2019, food trucks came to campus every Friday. At the counseling center, which opened in 2004, professional therapists provided thousands of hours of guidance and seminars on many different topics. In July 2023, the college changed its food service from Bon Appétit to Parkhurst Dining, part of the Eat'n Park Hospitality Group. That fall, a Chick-fil-A restaurant opened in Breen. The construction of the restaurant moved from concept to reality in less than six months. An improvement for independent women was the introduction in fall 2022 of the practice of "squatting," which modeled on male housing groups, enabled women to live near friends for multiple years.[65] In the early 2020s, the main quad was used for many activities and events, including Spikeball, Frisbee, and worship services.

Love, dating, engagement, and marriage were important campus topics. Some students argued that Grovers had the bad habit of either "developing excessively romantic and serious relationships" or avoiding the opposite sex. By not developing male-female friendships, many students placed "unhealthy levels of pressure on new relationships." Meanwhile, the "ring by spring culture" prompted students to rush to engagement.[66] Disputing the "ring by spring" claim, a poll found that only 11 percent of the class of 2018 were married, engaged, or planning to be engaged by graduation.[67] More positively, Krista Heckman, '19, argued that Grove City fostered "a very intentional and genuine community" that impacted students throughout their lives. "The care and effort GCC students pour into their relationships," she maintained, exceeded what students at other colleges experienced.[68]

As in earlier periods, students debated the purpose and value of college rules. Meagan Van Til, '15, beseeched the college "to encourage students to behave in a way which reflected their Christian values" rather "than to enforce a set of rules" which bred "both contempt and resentment."[69] Scott Alford, '15, countered that the college treated students as adults who had the freedom "to make mistakes while providing mostly reasonable rules."[70] Brennan Webb, '20, contended that the college rules about alcohol consumption and intervisitation robbed students of the ability to make their own decisions. The college should focus on teaching students to make good decisions instead of simply following rules.[71] Clark Mummau, '23, responded that it was better to provide "standards for wise living" rather than to expect students to discover them on their own. "As a Christian institution, Grove City College should list rules for students to follow, just as God has given us rules to follow." Director of residence life Jonathan DiBenedetto declared that campus rules helped create an environment that enabled students "to learn how to live wisely" while offering "support and grace to those who make mistakes."[72]

From 2007, when the Stan and Karen Johnson Office of International Education was founded, until fall 2016, 554 Grove City College students studied abroad in forty-four different countries, in addition to the hundreds of students who participated in the Grove City study center in Nantes, France; in fall 2016, fifty Grovers were studying in numerous countries.[73] The OIE's name was changed in 2019 to the Office of Global Programs. Since its inception, 845 Grovers have studied abroad in forty-nine countries. The Nantes program was discontinued in 2021 for financial and staffing reasons.

Molly Wicker, '18, noted in April 2016 that the college had not stated a viewpoint toward LGBTQ student organizations. The two key questions, she argued, were: "At schools where homosexual behavior is forbidden, should gay and lesbian students have to hide part of their identity?" and "Can they be open about their orientation as long as they maintain celibacy like their heterosexual peers?"[74] Wicker exhorted Christians "to love those who struggle with sexual identity issues or homosexual practices."[75] In 2016, an unofficial and short-lived campus group called The Table began providing networking and resources for students who identified "as lesbian, gay, transgender, queer, questioning, intersexual, and asexual."[76] Some students argued that same-sex desires were a form of disordered love and that homosexual relations were sinful.[77]

One area in which Grovers continued to defy the zeitgeist was in their view of abortion. Whereas almost 80 percent of college students in 2024 supported abortion in all cases, 85 percent of Grove City students believed that abortions should be illegal in all circumstances.[78]

"The pressure for excellence," Grace Tarr, '20, declared, "is almost palpable here." Striving for excellence was biblical, but the widespread belief that Grove City students must always do so was very stressful.[79] Meanwhile, communications professor Jennifer Mobley, '99, protested shifting the term "Grovers" from describing hardworking students to overachievers and perfectionists. She insisted that Grove City's campus life was "more complex and nuanced than the stereotypes like 'Groverachievers' and 'Ring by Spring'" suggested.[80]

Several new organizations were created during McNulty's presidency, and many others rendered important service to the campus, community, and world. In spring 2017 the Grove City Investment Society was created to help students learn how to invest money under faculty and alumni supervision. In 2024, Grove City established a chapter of MuKappa, a national collegiate organization that sought to provide Christian community for students who grew up in cross-cultural settings. Brenda McNulty established the Garden Club in conjunction with her creation of a campus vegetable garden behind the president's house. The International Justice Mission and Project Othello raised substantial sums of money to combat human trafficking and fund various African projects.

COVID-19

In March 2020, the COVID-19 epidemic struck, wreaking havoc throughout the world. On March 20, Grove City College closed the campus and sent all students home, obeying an order from Pennsylvania Governor Tom Wolf. The college quickly pivoted to teaching all its classes online and announced that students would not return that semester, and no graduation ceremony would be held. McNulty told students that "they can feel like victims and dwell unendingly on what they've lost. Or, after an understandable season of sadness, they can use this experience to learn how to manage grief and grow in godliness."[81] Unable to spend time together on campus, students used texting, FaceTiming, emailing, and Zoom parties to stay in touch. Searching for jobs and planning weddings were especially difficult.[82]

McNulty aggressively reopened the college in fall 2020, while many colleges decided to continue holding all their classes online. He worried that many students and staff might get sick, and someone might die. The eighteen months from March 2020 to September 2021, he explained, were "ridiculously challenging" and "a daily grind."[83] The college complied with CDC guidelines for mandatory masking and social distancing. Students were encouraged to download a contact tracing app called NOVID that notified them when they had been in contact with another user who had tested positive for COVID-19. To enhance social distancing, dining hall hours were extended and seating was limited.

Signature semester opening events were either canceled or moved outdoors. Every Monday, the college posted a COVID-19 positive test dashboard. Some students complained that the college's mask policy was too restrictive, while others wanted the college to enforce it more stringently.[84] Susannah Barnes stressed that many other colleges had not reopened their doors and argued that Grove City's regulations were relatively mild compared with numerous colleges, which were requiring daily tests and campus-wide quarantines. Grove City was only asking students to wear masks in public and avoid nonessential travel.[85]

Students who tested positive for COVID were required to provide a list of primary contacts—people with whom they had been within six feet of for longer than fifteen minutes. Primary contacts had to be tested for COVID at Zerbe and were sent to a quarantine location on campus or went home for as many as fourteen days. The college had few COVID cases until the first ten days of October. As a result, 340 students were soon in quarantine and self-isolation, leading the college to rent a block of rooms at the nearby Holiday Inn Express, cancel events, increase restrictions, and temporarily ban all group activities including sports practices. Seating for chapel services was capped at 250 attendees, services were broadcast to students in Crawford Hall, and students were required to attend only eight services instead of sixteen.

By November 11, ninety people had tested positive for COVID, and many students chose to leave campus and finish their courses online. The Christmas candlelight service was livestreamed. As the semester ended, McNulty declared that at times his administrative team "felt overwhelmed by the logistics of contact tracing and spread prevention. But the Lord was kind, gracious, and protected the College from unmanageable circumstances and serious illness."[86]

As the spring 2021 semester began, regulations were relaxed somewhat. Now the direct contacts of students in quarantine were required only to stay in their own rooms except when going to class and taking to-go meals from the cafeteria until their primary contact tested negative. Following CDC guidelines, the isolation period was reduced from fourteen to ten days. In mid-February, cases again spiked, straining the college's ability to handle infected and exposed students.[87]

By April, many students and professors had been vaccinated, and *The Collegian* urged hesitant students to set aside their concerns about the newness of the shot or their distrust of the medical profession to establish herd immunity.[88] Between the March break and the end of the semester, the college had few COVID cases. The main causes of stress during 2020–2021 were the cancelation of events, the management of courses from home, and social isolation.[89]

As the 2021 fall semester began, administrators sought to "restore normalcy to campus" and did not mandate that students be vaccinated or wear masks. The college had twenty positive cases the first week of classes, prompting some students to exhort their classmates to "remain vigilant," while others insisted that it was time to return campus life to pre-epidemic patterns.[90] As the fall semester proceeded, COVID cases diminished, and college life resumed its normal rhythm.

Speech and Debate

The record of Grove City College students in speech and debate during McNulty's presidency was outstanding. The college team, coached by professors Jason Edwards, Michael Coulter, and Andrew Harvey, won many tournaments and finished highly at numerous others. Team members, 2015 captain senior Mark Mariani explained, wanted "to engage in public issues critically and thoughtfully, understand how a structured argument can be made and dismantled, and improve their ability to verbally communicate complex arguments."[91]

In 2016, the Wolverines captured their third straight Pi Kappa Delta (PKD) National Comprehensive Speech and Debate Tournament title. The 2017 squad won another national championship at the National Christian College Forensic Invitational (NCCFI), where members competed against the nation's top Christian schools in two formats, both modeled loosely on the British Parliament—National Parliamentary Debate Association (two-person teams) and International Public Debate Association (single individuals). In spring 2018, Grove City triumphed again at the PKD's National Comprehensive Tournament, defeating more than eighty colleges and universities to take the Division I Debate Sweepstakes Championship. In March 2020, the top Christian college and university debating squads traveled to Grove City to compete in the NCCFI tournament. In an amazing performance on their home turf, Grove City claimed national titles in five different categories and earned twice the overall score of the runner-up squad.

In March 2021, Grove City won two more national titles at the PKD national championship and was named the top small school debate team at the NCCFI. The next spring, the Wolverines won the NCCFA's Quality Award, which goes to the team with the best and most consistent results regardless of size or entry types. Edwards explained that "Grove City competes against all comers from fellow liberal arts colleges to Division I research schools, to Ivy League [universities]." With so many "national titles in the last decade, you'd be hard pressed to find a program with better results," Edwards declared.[92] In March 2023, the college team captured yet another PKD national championship. Ginger Schiffmayer and Joshua Xu were crowned the NPDA champions, which Edwards called an "astounding feat" for freshmen competing in the open division.[93] The squad then won four national titles at the National Educational Debate Association's national tournament in Dayton, Ohio. In spring 2024, the Wolverines claimed three national titles at the NCCFI tournament in Nashville, including the Quality Award. In 2025, the team won three more titles at the NEDA National Championship held at Slippery Rock University. This gave Grove City a remarkable twenty-seven national championships, including individual, team, and squad awards, during the McNulty years.

Theater

Despite the retirement in spring 2015 of James Dixon, one of the college's most distinguished directors, and the difficulties the pandemic caused, the theater program maintained its high standards. The mid-April 2015 production of *The Tempest* was Dixon's final show. He departed with a flourish as he not only directed Shakespeare's last play, but he also played the principal role. A writer for *The Collegian* argued that "Prospero's final days on his barren island fittingly allude" to Dixon's "last hurrah" and "his near-flawless execution." The reviewer also praised the performance of three seniors—Jonathan Warren as the forlorn King Alonso, Ethan Mitchell as the mischievous spirit Ariel, who "sprinted, somersaulted and jumped around the set" while delivering his lines, and Andy Hickly as the deformed slave Caliban.[94]

Betsy Craig staged almost all the college's plays and musicals after Dixon retired. John Laurie, '17, played the lead in Craig's production of *Oklahoma* in fall 2015. In the late 2010s, Craig directed Cole Porter's *Anything Goes*, Oliver Goldsmith's *She Stoops to Conquer* ("the most entertaining evening you never thought you'd have," according to *The Collegian*), *The Music Man*, and *Brigadoon* (which, *The Collegian* declared, "delights and thrills").[95] Luke Leone, '18, starred in *The Music Man* and *End of the World with Symposium to Follow*. Craig's 2018 production of *All My Sons* became the third college play to be staged at the Kennedy Center American College Theater Festival. Artist-in-residence Tyler Crumrine, '12, directed the musical *1776* in 2019.

COVID forced the creative Craig to stage *Shakespearacy Theory*, based on classic YouTube shows, through the internet in fall 2020. In mid-March 2021, Craig presented three plays—*A Walk in the Woods*, *Eleemosynary*, and *Art*—during a five-day period with each audience limited to 275. She was the only person doing live theater in the area.[96]

After COVID abated, Craig directed Cole Porter's *Kiss Me, Kate* featuring junior Noah Godfrey and sophomore Katarina Kenlein. Speaking for many actors, Kenlein declared that the theater program gave students an "amazing opportunity to glorify God onstage with the gifts he's given us."[97] *The Collegian* praised Craig's production of *The Sound of Music* and her "stirring rendition" of *Julius Caesar* in 2023.[98] In 2024, Craig and her cast amused audiences with Thorton Wilder's *Our Town*, the fifth time in college history this show had been performed.

Music

The marching band, symphony orchestra, wind ensemble, jazz ensemble, stage band, touring choir, men's glee club, and several other musical groups all strove to exalt God as they entertained audiences and provided memorable experiences for their members. The marching band performed at Disney World during the 2016 fall break, the Collegiate Marching Band Festival in Allentown in 2016 and 2023, and a Pittsburgh Pirates baseball game in 2018.[99]

In May 2017, the chapel choir, touring choir, and music professor Richard Konzen collaborated to perform Duruflé's "Requiem" in Harbison Chapel to celebrate Konzen's retirement. That fall, to commemorate the five hundredth anniversary of the Protestant Reformation, the concert of the eighty-four-member orchestra featured several Reformation-themed pieces. Beginning in 1993, the college held a concerto competition whose winners performed with the orchestra at its spring concert. The twenty-five-member Men's Glee Club sang on campus and at churches and community venues. In April 2018, the orchestra performed various Russian pieces. Its director Jeff Tedford, '00, declared, "Our goal is always to perform music at the highest level, using our gifts to glorify God and bring joy to our audience."[100] The next month, the Grove City College Symphonic Concert Band and Wind Ensemble's pop concert featured music from Broadway and film scores.

In April 2023, the orchestra performed the world premiere of the first AI-generated work that completed Ludwig Beethoven's unfinished *Symphony No. 10*. To celebrate Christmas in 2023, the touring choir, concert choir, and chamber choir, under the direction of Katherine Mueller, collaborated to perform in Harbison Chapel, the Carnegie Concerts, and the Candlelight Christmas services. In February 2024, Grove City won third place in the prestigious American Prize for Orchestral Performance for institutions under ten thousand students. The touring choir was one of only two collegiate choirs selected to perform at the 2024 spring Pennsylvania Music Educators Association state conference. In April 2025, the college orchestra performed the world premiere of music professor Joseph Hasper's *Urban Symphony*.

In January 2015, three acts featuring alumni performed at a benefit concert in Crawford Auditorium: Joel Ansett, '12, The Stairwells (featuring Stephen Horst, '13, Joshua Morken, '13, Peter Christiansen, '15, and Julie Kucks, '14), and the Blue Light Bandits (showcasing Dan DeCristofaro, '13). Christiansen, an electric guitar player, recorded an LP with The Stairwells and released a solo album in 2016. Ansett sang folk and Christian music at the college in fall 2022 as part of his fifteen-stop tour from Denver to New York City.

WSAJ

Beginning in 2008, WSAJ broadcast from a studio in the Technological Learning Center. Under staff director, Darren Morton, between sixty and ninety student DJs worked at the station during the 2010s, and their programming, primarily indie rock, occupied about a quarter of the airtime. The station also played jazz, Americana, classical, folk, and blues music, aired BBC news coverage, and broadcast football, basketball, and soccer contests. Suni Missouri, the station's general manager, noted in 2021 that Grovers were less loyal to WSAJ, which had forty student-run programs, than in earlier decades primarily because they could access the same content on their phones. In March 2022, the Wolverine Broadcast Network, a new streaming service, replaced WSAJ-FM. The station went "all digital to reach a wider listening audience" that was "more likely to tap a screen than turn a dial." WBN aimed to "entertain and engage listeners by uniting excellence, insight, and innovation" in its student talk and music shows, sports broadcasts, and podcasts.[101]

Politics

The Collegian articles, campus organizations, and polls all testified to students' political conservatism. The CVV/IFF's focus on politics, combined with America's increasingly contentious political scene beginning in 2015, made political issues more salient than ever in college history. In a February 2016 poll, most Grovers backed Republican candidates Marco Rubio and Ted Cruz over Donald Trump. Trump had few passionate supporters at Grove City among either students or faculty. Many disliked Trump's policies, personal traits, and lack of political experience.[102]

One student urged Grovers to not vote in the 2016 presidential election, thereby avoiding having to choose "one of two bad options."[103] Another denounced Trump's "fear mongering, xenophobia, racism and misogyny," which brought out Americans' worst traits, and argued that "his wildly shifting policy stances," "frequent insults," and rambling twits demonstrated "a complete lack of impulse control."[104] *The Collegian* noted that many CVV articles had portrayed Trump negatively. An early November 2016 poll found that 52 percent of students planned to vote for Trump, 14 percent for Clinton, and 18 percent for third-party candidates; 16 percent were not going to vote for president.[105] This was a remarkably low percentage for a Republican presidential candidate to receive at Grove City.

Numerous Grovers viewed Trump's first term performance negatively. One was disappointed that his administration had employed numerous unqualified staff, ignored many expectations of the American people, and passed very few pieces of legislation.[106] Another accused Trump's 2019 State of the Union address of using "Orwellian doublespeak" to "mask his shortcomings and lies."[107]

Many students were dissatisfied with both presidential candidates again in 2020.[108] An October poll found that 67 percent of students planned to vote for Trump, 19 percent for Biden, and 14 percent for third-party candidates. This contrasted sharply with national collegiate polls, in which 70 percent of students planned to vote for Biden, 10 percent for Trump, and 20 percent for independent candidates.[109] The College Republicans president urged students to vote for Trump because his administration had implemented much the Republican Party's agenda. The College Democrats president implored Grovers to cast their ballots for Joe Biden who was a moderate, not a tool of the "radical left," and would be a much "more competent and responsible leader" than Trump. Another student called for casting ballots for third-party candidates.[110] In May 2022, Ed Breen clearly articulated the college's guiding political perspective: Grove City College advanced "key conservative principles" rather than supporting particular candidates. "We are far more interested in biblical truth than partisan initiatives."[111]

Although only 46 percent of Grovers supported Trump in the 2024 Republican primaries, 80 percent of them planned to vote for Trump in November compared with a mere 8 percent for Democrat Kamala Harris. However, only 29 percent of students were "very enthusiastic" about their choices; the "overwhelmingly conservative-Republican student body" disliked Trump personally but were voting for him because they believed he would strengthen America's borders and national security, improve the economy, and protect pro-life policies.[112]

Student Achievements

From 2014 to 2025, Grove City students and campus organizations had many significant accomplishments in theater, the natural sciences, the humanities, politics, entrepreneurship, and accounting. Two more students received Fulbright Scholarships, and *The Collegian* captured twenty Student Keystone Media Awards.

In January 2015, Ethan Mitchell and John Laurie finished in the final sixteen of 230 actors in a competition at the Kennedy Center American College Theater Festival. Meanwhile, the college's production of *Red*, directed by Betsy Craig, made it to the final round of shows at the festival. Seniors Emily Bartlow and Tristan Slater won $10,000 on an episode of the Food Network's *Cake Wars* in February 2016.

At the Sigma Xi Undergraduate Research Conference in 2017, juniors Michelle Chu and Ellen Upton won first place for their research on bacteria. Research conducted by students and faculty was featured at the national meeting of the American Association of Physics Teachers in Atlanta that year. In 2022, the college's Society of Physics Students won an Outstanding Chapter Award for the third year in a row. Several senior mechanical engineering majors, assisted by Eric Anderson, designed a high-tech water tank in 2022 that mimics ocean turbulence, and their research was published in the *Journal of Experimental Biology*. In October 2023, freshman electrical engineering major Amanda Lipski, who ranked as the nation's number one pilot, competed as a member of the US team at the FAI World Drone Racing Championships in South Korea. Renee Wright, '24, made presentations at two national American Chemical Society meetings, helping her win two prestigious National Science Foundation summer research projects and gain acceptance into a PhD program in molecular biology at the University of Chicago.

Junior Benjamin Allison received the Founder's Prize at the 2017 Phi Alpha Theta National Paper Competition. In 2023, junior Connor Rodgers and freshman Sophia Cappawanna were elected to town councils in Jim Thorpe and Duncannon, Pennsylvania, respectively. Sophomore John Hatzis won the 2024 National Review Institute's William F. Buckley Jr. Essay Contest on the antidote for the decline in American patriotism. Marley Kropp, '17, earned a Fulbright Scholarship to study in Wales in 2017–2018, while Jessica Mattson, '18 was awarded a Fulbright Fellowship to teach English in Ecuador the next year.

Grove City students won numerous entrepreneurship competitions. The app Benjamin Morasco, '16, designed to help patients navigate hospitals captured first place at the 2014 Perfect Pitch Elevator Pitch Competition at Westminster College, while Elisabeth O'Brien, '16, won the same event the next year for her platform for assisting teens with personal finance. In 2017, Hannah Vaccaro, '18, and Ross Harrington, '19, placed fifth in the e-Fest National Business Plan Competition in Minneapolis for their toilet training aid. The next summer, Vaccaro took first place for this project in a national entrepreneurship contest for colleges with less than five thousand students. That year, Grove City College's Entrepreneurship program won the United States Association for Small Business and Entrepreneurship Model Emerging Program Award, defeating Florida State's $100 million program in the finals of the selection process. In 2021, seniors Cameron Suorsa and Eric Dudgeon received $10,000 for their first-place business design at the Ben Franklin Virtual TechCelerator competition. A six-student team won the Techstars Startup Weekend competition at Duquesne University in February 2024 for their place-based dating app. Sophomore Leyla Zwolinski placed in the top ten at the European Innovation Academy's startup competition in Portugal in summer 2024 as the chief marketing officer for an online tutoring service.

Competing against other schools with less than ten thousand students, *The Collegian* won twenty Student Keystone Press Awards for its news coverage, photographs, and editorials on various topics including its handling of Vice President Mike Pence's 2018 commencement address, the tragic October 2018 Tree of Life Synagogue shooting in Pittsburgh, and the impact of COVID-19 on the college. In both 2021 and 2023, staff writer Isaac Willour, '24, captured a second-place award for his perspectives page essays.

Greek Life

During McNulty's tenure, Greek organizations enjoyed large memberships and became more committed to enhancing the Christian faith of their members and serving the campus and community. In spring 2017, 24 percent of males and 28 percent of females belonged to one of the college's ten fraternities or eight sororities. That fall, about three hundred alumni returned for homecoming to celebrate the one hundredth anniversary of the Tri Zetas, the college's first sorority. Students continued to choose to be Greeks because of the friendships, parties, and community the organizations offered, but their increased spiritual focus also drew members. "The idea that God is at the center of your sorority," declared

Alpha Beta Tau Emma Vetter, '17, "changes the entire dynamic of what most people think sororities are. When you learn to put Christ first in your life, and in your sorority, you are able to see His love grow in others and work in your group."[113]

Women's Athletics

Numerous women's sports teams excelled between 2014 and 2025. The women's cross-country squad won the PAC in 2015 and 2023, led in 2015, by senior Emily Rabenold, who earned All-American honors by finishing twenty-eighth at nationals, and by junior Lydia Bennett, who was 117th at nationals in 2024. The team's best finish at regionals was fourth in 2024. The track and field team captured the indoor and outdoor PAC titles in 2015, 2022, and 2025. Its top place in the outdoor East Coast Athletic Conference championship was ninth in 2024. The tennis team took the PAC title four times during McNulty's presidency and had an overall record of 118–59 (.667). The swimming and diving squad won the PAC crown every year except 2018–2019. Its highest national standing was seventeenth in 2017–2018. The softball team's best record was 26–13 in 2025. The basketball team finished 18–10 in 2017–2018 and 18–12 the next year. The squad received ECAC invitations both years, making it to the semifinals the latter season. In 2019–2020, the Lady Wolverines, led by senior Kate Balcom (the fourth-leading scorer in program history and second team All-Great Lakes Region in 2020) and junior Jess Bowen (second team All-Great Lakes Region in 2021), won a program record twenty-five games, losing only three, and earning an NCAA invitation. The soccer team was superb during the McNulty years, capturing four PAC titles, playing in three ECAC tournaments and four NCAA tournaments and winning a first-round match in 2018 when the Lady Wolverines finished 17–4–1. From 2015 to 2024, the team went 133–55–13 (.707). The water polo squad placed first in the Collegiate Water Polo Association D3 East in 2018. The volleyball squad's best record was 20–11 in 2019. Grove City began playing women's lacrosse in 2022 and enjoyed immediate success, going 14–4 the first season and 15–6 the third season and capturing the PAC crown three times. COVID forced canceling all athletic contests for nearly a year. Because of COVID, all twenty-three college sports teams played in spring semester of 2021.

Mikaela Jenkins, '25, won a gold medal in the 100butterfly at the 2020 Paralympics in Tokyo (held in 2021 because of COVID). Jenkins, whose foot and ankle were amputated when she was eight months old because of proximal femoral focal deficiency, also excelled on the college's swimming and diving team. The biology/health major chose Grove City because of its "solid Christian foundation, stellar STEM program, outstanding swimming and diving program" and "'stunning' campus."[114] "God does everything for a reason," she stated, "and I was born with a disability" to "show His glory."[115]

Numerous other women athletes performed superbly between 2014 and 2025. Her junior year, Lexie Arkwright, '18, led the PAC in scoring average (20.8) and was named to the ECAC D3 South first team. Her junior and senior years, Arkwright was selected for the third-team All-Great Lakes Region. She is first in career steals, second in career free throw percentage (.806), and third in career points with 1,607. Senior Allison Podkul was named to the ECAC D3 second team in 2021–2022. Emil Rabenold won the prestigious Dickinson Long-Short Invite in 2014, finished ninth at the NCAA Mideast regional that fall, and in 2015 became the third runner in PAC history to win the conference cross-country title three consecutive years. Esther Durling, '15, was the PAC medalist in 2014. Lauren Kardos, '26, led the golf team in top finishes in 2023 and 2024. The best tennis players during these years were Caroline McGuire, '15, who was the PAC MVP in 2013 and 2014, and three other number one singles players—Karolina Lagerquist, '16, Maggie Manchester, '19, and Morgan Happe, '21. Softball pitcher Erica Aughton, '17, is second in career complete games, fourth in career innings pitched, and fifth in lowest ERA (2.66). Kelsey Shirey, '15, is first in career hits, triples, total bases, slugging percentage, and batting average (.449), and second in career runs scored, RBIs, and home runs. Janessa Dawson, '23, is second in career batting average (.420) and slugging percentage. In volleyball, Anna DeGraff, '26, is second all-time in single-season hitting efficiency; Kennedy Kerr, '25, is second in career service aces; and Faith Keating, '23 is fifth in career digs.

Several swimmers stand out. Senior Megan Bilko earned All-American honors in 2016 in the 200 butterfly and the 400 IM. She set the college record in the latter event concluded her career as a seven-time All-American. She and Caleb Courage, '09, are the only Grove City swimmers to garner All-America honors in four individual events. In 2017, freshman Anne Shirley Dassow earned All-American distinction by finishing seventh in the 100 butterfly and sixth in the 200 butterfly at nationals. The next year, Darrow became the college's first NCAA D3 title holder since Courage in 2009 when she won the 200 butterfly. This was the eleventh national title for the college swimming programs, and she is one of seventy-seven All-Americans the college's most successful athletic program has produced. Carolyn Eckendorf, '16, is first all-time in three-meter diving and second in one-meter diving, while Kamryn Kerr, '25, holds the college record for one-meter diving and is third all-time in three-meter diving. In water polo, Abby Jank earned first-team All-Collegiate CWPA D3 honors in 2016.

Soccer goalie Trishae Winters, '17, is third in average career goals against (0.87 per match), while Kristi Lathrop, '15, is fourth in goals allowed per match (0.89). They are also first and second in career shutouts, respectively. Goalie Courtney Lisman, '25, is first in career wins with forty-eight, second in career saves, and third in career shutouts. In fall 2017, junior forward Krista Heckman became the first All-American in the twenty-seven-year history of the Grove City women's soccer program when she was chosen for the NCAA D3 third team. She was also named to the All-ECAC first team and the All-Great Lakes Region first team. In 2017, the Lady Wolverines tied the program record with seventeen wins, and the Lady Wolverines defeated the University of Chicago in the opening round of the NCAA tournament. Midfielder Emma Herrmann, '25, finished as the fourth-leading goal scorer in college history despite playing only two seasons. She earned first team All-Region both years.

Several women excelled in track and field. Emma Vezzosi, '23, the most versatile women's performer in this sport in history, holds the college record in the 55 meters, 60 meters, 60-meter hurdles, 200 meters, heptathlon, and pentathlon and is second all-time in the 100 meters, the 100-meter hurdles, and the indoor long jump. Eliza Lowe '16 is the college record holder in the 100- and 400-meter hurdles. Grace Smith '25, who was All-Region in cross-country in 2024, set the college record in the indoor 3000 meters and is second all-time in the indoor mile, the outdoor 1500 meters, and 3000-meter steeplechase. Elly Bruner, '27, is tied for first all-time in the indoor high jump with Katie Baller, '24. Baller also holds the record for the outdoor high jump. Lydia Bennett became a D3 All-American by placing seventh in the indoor mile in 2025, setting a school record. She is the first indoor track and field All-American in college history. In 2025, she finished second in the 1500 meters at the outdoor D3 nationals, becoming the third Grove City track or field athlete to earn second place, setting another college record. Bennett also holds Grove City's record in the outdoor 1500 and 3000 meters and is second all-time in the indoor and outdoor 800 meters

Throughout the McNulty years, numerous women athletes testified that they played for "an audience of One." God, asserted Arkwright, showed "me how to use basketball and anything else I pursue in life as a platform for His glory."[116] Sonja Kiefer, '19, called her water polo team a "Christ-oriented" community that was "driven, disciplined, encouraging, forgiving," and stood together "through thick and thin."[117] The volleyball team built "a Christ-centered team culture," a player maintained, and prayed and worked hard together.[118] Emily Vanderweele, '22, avowed, "We are not swimming for our own glory, but for God's. We find ourselves striving to emulate Him through our attitude and praise to Him in hardships and challenges."[119] "I'm so blessed to have been awarded these incredible titles like All-American, PAC Champion and PAC Track MVP," Lydia Bennett declared, "but none of them compare to the never-fading, ever secure, grace-filled title of 'Christ the King.'"[120] In addition, a sportswriter argued that Melissa Lamie, who had coached soccer, women's basketball, and men's and women's golf, helped her athletes "grow in their relationship with Jesus Christ" and "play to the best of their abilities."[121]

Men's Athletics

Between 2014 and 2025, the men's soccer, baseball, football, lacrosse, swimming and diving, tennis, and track and field teams all had impressive records. The soccer squad went 123–63–22 (.661) and played in five ECAC tournaments, making it to the semifinals in 2015. The 2017 baseball team won the ECAC tournament. From 2019 to 2025, the baseball team went 187–84 (.679) and won the PAC tournament in 2025. From 2018 to 2024, the football team was 55–16 (.775) and triumphed at four consecutive ECAC bowl games. In 2023, the Wolverines captured the PAC with a 10–0 record, won their first-round NCAA playoff game, lost to Cortland State University, the eventual national champion, by one point in the next round, and ended the season ranked tenth in D3. The next year, the team was the PAC cochampion, lost to Johns Hopkins 17–14 in the second round of the tournament, and ranked nineteenth in the final poll. The men's lacrosse program, launched in 2018, has gone 88–43 (.693) despite playing many highly ranked D3 teams. The squad has captured the PAC crown six times and won six NCAA tournament matches. Since 2018–2019, the swimming team has won seven straight PAC titles. The tennis team claimed four PAC championships and won an NCAA first-round match in spring 2021. The track and field team took the PAC outdoor crown in 2015, 2023, 2024, and 2025, and the indoor title in 2025. The Wolverines finished thirteenth in D3 in 2021.

Other men's teams had good seasons. The cross-country team won the PAC in 2017. The harriers finished between thirteenth and nineteenth at regionals six times. The 2015–2016 basketball squad was 18–9, and the 2018–2019 squad went 18–12; both played in the ECAC tournament, with the latter team reaching the semifinals. The 2019–2020 Wolverines finished 21–9, won the PAC title, and beat Wooster 67–62 in the first round of NCAA tournament. The 2015–2016 golf team won the PAC title and finished fortieth in D3. A men's volleyball team, which began competition in 2025, finished second in the PAC during the regular season.

In October 2019, McNulty argued that "Intentional community, excellence and faith-based team culture have been at the heart of a historic chapter in the life of varsity athletics." He added, "We're finally at a point where we have the coaching and character to be consistently successful in every sport."[122] That month, the college named its soccer field for coach Donald Lyle, who directed the soccer program from 1972 to 2005 and won 277 matches.

Seth Loew, '16, led the PAC in scoring in 2015 and was selected for the All-Great Lakes squad three years in a row, including as a first-team member in 2015. Loew holds the college record for most assists and is second all-time in points. Dale Reese, '17, ranks second all-time in assists. The 2017 soccer seniors won fifty-two matches, the highest total of any class in college history. Sam Belitz, '23, led the 2022 soccer team to a 10–0–1 record in the PAC, was named first-team All-Region VII, and finished his career as the fifth-highest scorer in college history. Goalie Luke Greenway, '22, is the program leader in career wins with thirty-one, while goalie Teddy Almeter, '25, has the second-lowest goals against in program history (0.88).

Several male basketball players excelled. Mitch Marmelstein, '15, is the fourth-leading scorer with 1,383 career points. The 2017–2018 squad ranked eighth in the nation in fewest points allowed per game. James Wells, '20, has the most career blocked shots, and scored 1,147 points in three seasons. During the 2019–2020 season, coach Steve Lamie, '85, recorded his three hundredth victory, and Wells was named to the All-Great Lakes third team.

In 2018, freshman Calvin Brouwer won All-American honors by taking tenth place in the 1650-meter freestyle. He holds the college record in the 500-, 1000-, and 1650-meter freestyle. Dane Hoselton, '19, has the fastest school times in the 100 and 200 backstroke. The leading swimmers in the mid-2020s were Caleb

Einolf and Will Sterrett '25. As a junior, Einolf became the 60th male All-American in March 2025 by finishing sixth in the 100 breaststroke and thirteenth in the 100 butterfly. He holds the college record in both these events. Sterrett is a member of two record-setting college relay teams, holds the school record in the 400 IM (individual medley), and is second all-time in the 200 backstroke and 200 IM.

The lacrosse team's three goals are "Be Your Best, Love Deeply and Be Eternally Focused." In spring 2018, sophomore Henry Brannan was named the Ohio River Lacrosse Conference player of the year. His eighty-five points in 2019 is a single-season record. In spring 2021, sophomore Cody Adams and junior Brett Gladstone were named to the United States Intercollegiate Lacrosse Association All-America team as honorable mention. Gladstone finished his career in 2023 with 291 points, the most in program history. Addison Bennett,'24, is the career leader in turnovers caused, Michael La Forte, '23, in assists, and Grant Evans, '23, in ground balls. The team's coach, Alex Jernstedt, coached the Puerto Rican national lacrosse team in 2022 and in 2023 at the Lacrosse World Games, where it earned tenth place. James Petrolle finished his career in 2024 as the college's second two-hundred-point scorer. Junior attack Matt Blythe earned USILA honorable mention in 2024, while senior attack Frankie Hougan was named to the second-team USILA in 2025.

In 2016, football coach Andrew DiDonato, '10, explained that seven leadership traits underlaid the college's football program: "vision, communication, people skills, character, competency, boldness, and a serving heart."[123] In 2017, sophomore Wesley Schools gained 1,266 rushing yards to become the fourth one-thousand-yard rusher in a season in Grove City's history. The 2018 Wolverines went 8–3, including defeating Morrisville State 56–48 in an ECAC postseason game, as Schools rushed for a college record 359 yards. The 2019 team finished 9–2, ending the season with a 41–38 ECAC bowl game victory over Rochester Polytechnical Institute. For the season, Schools was first in D3 in rushing touchdowns (27) and second in rushing yards (1,788). He garnered first-team All-American honors from the American Football Coaches Association (AFCA), finished his career with 5,698 yards, the second-highest total in college history, and is also second in rushing touchdowns.

The college's expectations were high for all its teams, McNulty declared in 2021, but Grove City athletes sought "to honor God first, win or lose."[124] Grove City's 38–0 demolition of Waynesburg in late September 2021 was the football program's five hundredth victory. Cody Gustafson, '21, finished his career with the most receptions, yards, and receiving touchdowns in college history. The AFCA selected Gustafson as a first-team All-American, while the College Sports Information Directors of America named him the 2021 Division III Football Academic All-American of the Year. Gustafson, who earned a 3.93 GPA as a mathematics and finance major, is the first Wolverine to win this award. Quarterback Josh Ernst, '21, concluded his career first in passing yards and touchdown passes and second in passing efficiency. The Wolverines finished 8–3, including a 49–7 throttling of Utica in an ECAC bowl game. As the 2022 football season began, fan enthusiasm soared, fueled by McNulty's leading of a "Hey Baby" sing-along between the third and fourth quarters and the prospects of an outstanding team.[125] The team again finished 8–3 and defeated Fairleigh Dickinson University 31–14 in an ECAC bowl game. Parker Kilgore, '22, finished his career with the most tackles in college history.

"Is This the Year?" *The Collegian* asked as the 2023 football season began.[126] In midseason, the Wolverines beat Carnegie Mellon, ranked fourteenth in D3, 21–14, snapping the Tartans' twenty-game regular-season streak. Grove City finished the season 10–0, won the PAC, and headed to the NCAA tournament. After scoring a final-minute touchdown to defeat Susquehanna 21–20, the Wolverines lost 25–24 to Cortland State University when a thirty-seven-yard field goal attempt narrowly missed as time expired. Running back Clayton Parrish, '23, concluded his career with fifty-four touchdowns (third all-time). The AFCA named offensive guard Vinny LePre, '23, to its All-American second team in 2022 and its first team in 2023.

The 2024 football team continued this stellar play. The Wolverines finished in a three-way tie for first in the PAC. After receiving a first-round bye in the NCAA tournament, Grove City lost 17–14 to Johns Hopkins University. The Wolverines trailed 17–0 with five minutes and twenty-nine seconds remaining but mounted a furious comeback, scoring two touchdowns and driving to the JHU ten-yard line and missing a game-tying field goal with seconds remaining. For the season, Grove City averaged 42.9 points and 444.6 yards of offense per game. The AFCA named junior linebacker Ben Bladel to its All-American second team. He helped Grove City, which allowed only 40.6 yards per game, rank third in D3 in rushing defense. Quarterback Logan Pfeuffer ended his career second in touchdown passes, and third in total passing yards and passing efficiency. Halfback Nico Flati, '24, is third in career rushing yards, while Scott Fraser, '25, ranks second in program history in receptions, receiving yards, and touchdown catches.

In 2016, under first-year coach Matt Royer, the baseball team won the ECAC championship, led by junior Matt Waugaman, who set single-season college records in hits, RBIs, home runs, and total bases, and sophomore pitcher John Bini, who went 9–0. Waugaman was named to the All-Midwest Region third team, is the program's all-time career leader in total bases, and is second in home runs and RBIs. After having the fourth-highest batting average (.473) of all D3 players his sophomore year, catcher Andy Fritz ranked second on the team in batting average (.405), hits, RBIs, total bases, and slugging percentage in 2016 and was selected for the All-Great Lakes Region third team. In 2019, the team finished 28–16 and made it to the ECAC finals. For his career, Bini is first in innings pitched and wins (twenty-seven) and third in complete games and career winning percentage. Third baseman Micah Burke, '20, is second all-time in career hits and fourth in runs scored. The 2021 baseball team, which finished 28–10, had a .325 average and a 3.55 ERA. In 2022, Tate Ostrowski, '23, had the lowest ERA (1.63) of any D3 pitcher in the nation. Ostrowski holds the college record for the highest career winning percentage 26–4 (.866), most strikeouts, and lowest ERA (2.17), is second in wins, and pitched a perfect game. C. J. Saylor, '23, is third in career runs scored and fifth in total bases and RBIs. Pitcher Nick Guidas, '25, is fifth in career wins and second in career strikeouts and has a 2.78 ERA.

Christian Locher, '15, Jordan Alfery, '18, Cole McCook, '19, Ryan Koenig, '19, and Adam Steinmetz, '25, led the golf team. Locher was the medalist at the 2015 Grove City invitational. Alfery had the lowest score in four of the invitationals the team participated in during spring 2016 and was an All-PAC honoree from 2014 to 2017. McCook won five tournaments during his career. He was the medalist at the fall PAC championships in 2016 and 2018 and had the Wolverine's lowest score at the 2016 nationals. Koenig was the co-medalist at the 2017 fall PAC championships and was named to four PAC All-Star teams. Steinmetz, '25, earned first-team All-PAC in fall 2024. The leading tennis players were Peter Riley, '15, and Karsten Lagerquist, '19, who had excellent records at first singles and first doubles.

In fall 2016, senior Dan Christiansen finished third at the forty-two-team cross-country DeSales Invitational and won the PAC championship, becoming Grove City's tenth conference Runner of the Year. Christiansen was fifty-sixth at the 2016 D3 nationals and finished his career with five of the top eight 8K times in program history.

Christiansen, Nick Betz, '17, Ryan Buchalter, '17, Graham Allen, '18, Drew Thibault, '18, and Ryan Budnik, '19, were track standouts in the second half of the 2010s. Christiansen finished first in numerous 3,000-, 5000-, and 10,000-meter races. He set the college record in the 3000 meters and the 10,000 meters and is second all-time in the 5000 meters. Betz is first in program history in the 110-meter hurdles. Allen, who has the second-best time in college history, won many 800-meter races. Buchalter is second all-time in the indoor 400 and third all-time in the outdoor 200 and 400 meters. Thibault holds the college record for the steeplechase and the indoor 3000 meters and is fourth all-time in the indoor 5000 meters, while Budnik is first in the indoor 5000 meters and fourth in the outdoor 5000 meters.

Other men shone in the first half of the 2020s. Seth Ray, '21, is second in the decathlon, third in the high jump, and fourth in the triple jump in college history. Led by shot putter Nick Gustafson, '24, discus thrower Ryan Lenhart, '25, and 400-meter specialist Alex Mitchell, '26, who all won their events, and field MVP Gabe Dunlap, '24, who placed in five events, the men won their sixteenth PAC outdoor title in 2023. The same five men propelled the Wolverines to the PAC title in 2024. Led again by Mitchell and by Nick Petucci, '25, in the triple jump and Michael Chambers, '24, in the pole vault, the Wolverines also captured the 2024 indoor PAC track and field title. Mitchell finished third in the 400 meters at the indoor All-Atlantic Region Track and Field Conference (AARTFC) Championship in March 2024. At the 2025 PAC indoor championship, Mitchell won the 200 meters and the 400 meters in a conference-record time. Dunlap won the javelin, Lenhart captured the discus, and Mitchell triumphed in the 400 meters in a school-record time of 47.37 to help Grove City take the 2025 outdoor championship. Dunlap holds the college record in the decathlon, the heptathlon, and the 60-meter dash. Lenhart is first in the hammer throw and second in the discus.

For the first time since 2005, Grove City won four men's PAC titles in the fall 2023. The college also set a PAC record by placing 104 student athletes on PAC Fall Academic Honor Roll, which required a QPA of 3.6 or higher. In 2023–2024, the Wolverines won both the men's and women's All-Sports trophies for the eighth time since they joined the conference in 1985; it was the first time in eighteen years that a school had swept both trophies.

Grove City's sports teams excelled during the 2025 spring semester. The men's and women's track and field teams won the PAC indoor and outdoor championships. The men's and women's swimming and diving teams, men's and women's lacrosse teams, and the baseball team all won PAC titles. The baseball team set a record for the most wins in a season (thirty-one) as did the women's softball team (twenty-six), which finished second in the PAC. Luke Vittone ended his career as the college's all-time leader in runs scored, hits, and total bases, while Josh Minnich set the career RBI record. The men's lacrosse clobbered Albion 18–3 in the first round of the NCAA tournament before losing to Christopher Newport 16–14 in the second round. Attack Matt Blythe concluded his career ranked second in college history in both points and goals, while attack Zachary Hougan, '25, has the most assists in program history and the third-highest total points. The women's track and field team placed fifth at the AARTFC Championship as Grace Smith and senior Ella Lyle finished first and second in the steeplechase, Lydia Bennett was second in both the 800 and 1500 meters, and college relay teams finished second in the 3200 and fourth in the 1600 meters. The Wolverines captured the men's and women's PAC all-sports trophies in 2024–2025, the first back-to-back sports trophies for both men and women in twenty-five years, giving them nine during McNulty's presidency. Grove City also set a conference record by placing 232 athletes on the PAC Academic Honor Roll during the academic year.

Like their female counterparts, numerous male athletes insisted that their faith played a major role in their accomplishments. "Above all," Jordan McConnell, '21, professed, "we play basketball to honor God, and it is our hope that in watching us play, others will see His love."[127] Soccer starter Blake Baer, '18, declared, "Everything that I am and everything that I do is only because of Him [God] and His grace."[128] "Our goal," athletic director Todd Gibson, '02, asserted, "is to glorify God in all that we do—on the field or court, in the classroom, in the dormitory"—and in the community.[129] All his players sought "to honor each other, the program, and God," declared tennis coach Jeff Buxton.[130] Golfers wanted "to glorify God by the way that we played golf."[131] The football team ended all its practices with prayer to keep players' focus on exalting God. DiDonato declared that the team members strived to "keep faith as their highest priority."[132] In fall 2020, women's volleyball coach Leo Sayles created G.E.A.R.—"Glorifying God together as we Equip Grove City athletes to Affirm their identity in Christ, and to Realize their role as Christ's ambassadors through the platform of sports." G.E.A.R. hosted worship services for athletes, provided resources for spiritual growth, and organized a team chaplains council.

Sayles declared, "We're seeking to bring our best to the Lord."[133] The aim of Grove City's athletic program, Gibson explained, was to help participants "build community through service projects, Bible studies, mission work, and a shared culture that pushes them to compete at the highest level." Coaches challenged players to seek to glorify God "in all that they do—athletically, academically, socially, and spiritually."[134] Team captain Adyen Gutierrez, '24, was very grateful that at Grove City, he could play football, participate in many other extracurricular activities, and develop leadership skills.[135]

The McNulty Athletic Center will be built on the upper campus as part of the college's current capital campaign. Paul and Brenda provided the lead gift for this $5 million project, which is expected to be completed by 2027. "Paul McNulty's legacy includes a renewed focus on varsity athletics and the encouragement of student-athletes to embody excellence and faithfulness and a fierce competitiveness in pursuit of conference championships," Ed Breen declared. It has resulted in numerous PAC championships, "a national ranking for Wolverine football," and "a stronger campus community."[136]

In club sports, the lacrosse team, led by senior Dave Hall, ranked seventh in the nation in the Men's Collegiate Lacrosse Association in spring 2016. In 2019, the club rugby team won its conference, and an ice hockey club team began competition. The 2022 rugby team captured a conference championship. In the early 2020s, three ultimate Frisbee teams made it to the regional finals. The men's club volleyball team had several top-ten finishes at the national championship during its nineteen years of play.

A high percentage of students played one or more sports in Greek or independent leagues as part of the college's intramural program. Basketball, football, ultimate Frisbee, dodgeball, and volleyball were student favorites. Men and women played in separate leagues for most sports, but some were coed.

The CRT Controversy, 2021–2023

In the 2010s, Grove City strove to create a welcoming environment for minority and international students and to enhance the college's diversity. Both the Office of Multicultural Education and Initiatives (OMEI), established in 2012, and Students Excited About Diversity (SEAD) sponsored various events, including trips to historical sites and conferences, documentary films, discussion groups, book studies, and ethnic food festivals, to help minority students (about 5 to 7 percent of Grovers) adapt to the college and students who were part of majority groups better understand and relate to these classmates. SEAD sought to "create an environment where students of all cultural backgrounds are fully known, respected, and encouraged to realize their full God-created potential and God-given identity."[137]

In August 2020, the President's Advisory Council on Diversity was created to enhance the college's efforts to develop a diverse learning community by helping McNulty devise strategic initiatives to better recruit and retain minority students, hire minority employees, and broaden the cultural perspectives of all members of the campus community.[138]

A year later, several factors converged to produce protests about how the college was handling critical racial theory (CRT), creating controversy on campus and capturing national attention. The murder of George Floyd by a Minneapolis policeman in May 2020 evoked protests and riots, intensified disagreement about the Black Lives Matter movement, and fueled a worldwide debate on policing and racial injustice. Seeking to capitalize on the backlash to these developments, some conservative politicians strove to demonize CRT and argued that the more radical proponents of racial justice misunderstood the causes of and solutions for racial discrimination and inequality.[139] Meanwhile, some faculty, students, parents, and campus outsiders accused President McNulty of responding too timidly to the COVID crisis and requiring too many safeguards including masking, quarantining, and prohibiting social gatherings, even though he was following CDC guidelines. Moreover, some of these constituents were upset that McNulty sided with more moderate Republicans rather than Donald Trump and had a long-standing friendship with Mike Pence.

Provoked by outside agitators who had little knowledge of conditions at the college, 475 parents and alumni submitted a petition titled "Save GCC from CRT" to McNulty in mid-November 2021. It warned that "a destructive and profoundly unbiblical worldview"—critical race theory—seemed to be threatening Grove City's "distinctly Christian" "academic and spiritual foundations." CRT, the petition argued, taught that all society "is infected with intrinsic (structural) racism that favors Whites and oppresses Blacks and other minorities." Signers especially complained about inviting Jemar Tisby, an outspoken CRT apologist, to speak in chapel in October 2020; showing a TED Talk by Bryan Stevenson—"a CRT defender"—in chapel that fall; RA training that allegedly advanced CRT by evoking "White privilege and White guilt"; the assigned readings in the studies course EDUC 290; and the Diversity Council's purported promotion of CRT through several book clubs on campus. If their objections were valid, signers asked administrators to state officially that CRT was "unbiblical and inconsistent with the founding principles of the college," stop promoting CRT in RA training and chapel, and disband or at least restructure the Diversity Council. The petition concluded by professing its signers' love for GCC and gratitude for McNulty's leadership "of this fine school."[140] The letter evoked a firestorm of letters, discussion, and articles in Christian and secular publications and online sites and helped prompt the trustees to create a committee to investigate and respond to complaints.

A week later, McNulty insisted that the college rejected critical race theory as "a proper framework" for evaluating contemporary racial issues. College courses and programs discussed racial issues in the context of the biblical worldview to which its administrators and faculty were deeply committed. CRT, McNulty contended, had never been promoted in chapel. Neither Tisby's chapel talk nor Stevenson's TED Talk video had advocated or even mentioned this perspective. McNulty asserted that the OMEI was "fully aligned" with the college's objectives.[141] Many faculty applauded McNulty's rejoinder and thought that the controversy would quietly die.

In early February 2022, however, the board of trustees received an anonymous letter purporting to come from numerous former and current faculty members, which criticized McNulty's response. It alleged that some Grove City faculty were teaching CRT, thereby endangering the college's mission, identity, and financial well-being. The letter argued that CRT clashed with the college's historic Christian values; endorsing it "alienated Grove City College's core constituency" and weakened its ability to compete in the higher education marketplace.

This letter prompted the trustees to create an ad hoc committee to investigate "alleged instances of mission-drift." David Porter, secretary of the board, chaired the committee composed of four other trustees and retired administrator John Sparks. The trustees reaffirmed "GCC's Christ-centered mission and commitment to a free society, traditional values, and the common good" and categorically rejected CRT "as antithetical to GCC's mission and values."[142]

Many professors were upset that the trustees decided to respond to an anonymous missive. In a letter to *The Collegian*, fifty-one of them contended that few faculty supported this protest letter, which was replete with misunderstandings, half-truths, and unsubstantiated statements. Repudiating its claim that the college's institutional processes were broken, they insisted that "respect, integrity and more open communication" had "been hallmarks" of McNulty's administration. Offering a few disputed examples, they argued, did not establish that mission drift had occurred at a college that had hundreds of classes, chapel events, and Student Life and Learning programs each year.[143]

In March 2022, another petition signed by almost two hundred alumni, students, and others exhorted the college "not to inhibit discussions of race and racism on campus and in the classroom." Its signers feared that some faculty might avoid certain topics to prevent being accused of teaching CRT. They called upon the board not to ban faculty from teaching particular theories or perspectives. Natalie Kahler, '94, who initiated the petition, declared, "GCC helped develop my Christian worldview, not by shielding me from conflicting ideas, but by teaching me how to use scripture to discern truth."[144]

In April 2022, the committee issued its report. It affirmed McNulty's leadership and credited him with undertaking various remedial steps identified in the report. Its members insisted that although "CRT is an appropriate subject of academic study and critical analysis, it is antagonistic to basic American principles that GCC values."[145] Committee members concluded that EDUC 290, Cultural Diversity and Advocacy, which had been taught twice to a total of fifteen students, "was ideologically one-sided and effectively promoted pop-CRT."[146] Some faculty objected that the investigators failed to recognize that studies courses were experimental and that the books assigned for this course were meant to stimulate discussion about racial issues, not advocate CRT.

Committee members also concluded that the college's RA training had "promoted CRT-related ideas about race and racism." They failed to acknowledge, however, that the DMEI's one-hour presentation in fall 2021 was the sole discussion of race during the entire two-week RA training program. Committee members asserted without supplying any evidence that some of the OMEI's book selections had "promoted 'woke' concepts." They called for reconstituting and renaming the OMEI to help international and minority students better acclimate to the college and providing programs to stimulate students to "think broadly about race and culture."[147]

The ad hoc committee report asserted that Jemar Tisby's October 2020 chapel presentation had caused the most controversy. In this talk, Tisby, the author of *The Color of Compromise: The Truth About the American Church's Complicity* (2020), had challenged listeners to educate themselves about racial issues, develop friendships with people from different cultural backgrounds, and fight racism.[148] The ad hoc committee report argued that Tisby's current positions on a variety of "racial equity" issues differed substantially from the ones he espoused in 2019, when he was initially invited to speak. In the future, administrators stated, individuals holding similar perspectives would be invited to lecture in an auditorium or teach a class but not to speak in chapel, which appeared "to place the College's stamp of approval on the speaker's message."[149]

Committee members also noted that some viewed the removal of the word "conservative" in the college's revised 2021 vision statement as "a betrayal of the College's historic identity." Critics blamed McNulty for this change, but the board, not the president, had made it. The trustees had deleted the word because of the "shifting meaning of 'conservative' in contemporary American political discourse." Unfortunately, this change had "sown confusion and invited misunderstanding." Committee members emphasized that the college's conservatism transcended "electoral politics and current policy debates." It was based upon traditional Western values and the writings of such authors as Edmund Burke, Alexis de Tocqueville, Russell Kirk, C. S. Lewis, and Ludwig von Mises. The trustees had replaced the word "conservative" with phrases such as "permanent ideas," "traditional values," and the "foundations of a free society," which they thought better expressed the college's commitments than did the term conservative. However, something valuable had apparently been lost by removing the word from the vision statement, and they recommended that Grove City College again be described as a "conservative" institution. Committee members concluded, "Under President McNulty's faithful, steady, and tireless leadership, the state of the College is in many ways healthier than ever. His tenure as president has been a source of joy for each of us."[150] At its May meeting, the board agreed with the committee's recommendation and unanimously reaffirmed its support for McNulty.

Grove City's CRT dispute evoked various responses. Some ultraconservative pundits suggested that the college had become "woke." Other commentators used the events at Grove City to discuss the broader implications of CRT controversy. Writing in *World* magazine, Brad Littlejohn argued that many parents were pressuring Christian college administrators to not allow their children to be exposed to ideas with which they disagreed. However, college students needed to study varied worldviews, which at Christian college would be done in light of a biblical perspective.[151] Debates over CRT, Messiah University history professor John Fea contended, were dividing theologically orthodox evangelicals into a "'Trumpian' wing that sees CRT as antithetical to the gospel, and a 'free inquiry' wing that believes CRT can be utilized as a tool for understanding racial justice."[152] Writing in *The National Review*, Grove City College junior Isaac Willour argued that evaluating alternative perspectives was an important aspect of education and to understand ideas students must read the works of their proponents, not simply criticisms of their writings.[153]

Conservative pundit David French protested that some ultra-conservative activists had fundamentally changed the definition of CRT to encompass many ideas about race, some of which had "nothing to do with CRT." Consequently, many Christians incorrectly thought that numerous "unfamiliar or unpopular arguments," which were "unchristian and poisonous to their souls," were expressions of CRT. He noted that the Southern Baptist Convention had recently adopted a resolution affirming that CRT had some worthwhile purposes.[154] He insisted that CRT could help Christians better understand the world, if it remained "subordinate to scripture."[155] Moreover, distorted views of CRT were hindering Christians from recognizing how persistent and detrimental racism was in American society. The initial Grove City petition made little sense to those who believed that colleges should expose students to competing ideas about race and social justice, he asserted, but it made great sense to those who saw CRT as a threat to Christianity.[156]

In February 2023, college officials reported that all the board committee's recommendations had been implemented. RA training was being closely monitored, the OMEI had been reconstituted and renamed the Imago Dei Center, chapel programming was receiving greater oversight, and all personnel fully supported the college's mission.[157]

McNulty later lamented that the CRT controversy entailed "a certain viciousness and level of inaccuracy that was hard to deal with." He had been attacked on Twitter (now X) for a year for being woke and harming the college.[158] Many faculty believed that this unfortunate "controversy" had been a tempest in a teapot. They were upset that the ad hoc committee's final report ignored their petition. Many professors insisted that no evidence existed that anyone at Grove City College had embraced wokeness; all the issues which the petition and anonymous letter had raised were bogus, fueled by misunderstanding and, in some cases, animosity toward president McNulty. Many faculty believed that the controversy had been instigated by McNulty's critics, who wanted to force him to resign because they despised his COVID policies, detested his political stance, and disliked what they perceived as his tolerant management style.

Recognition

Grove City continued to receive much positive recognition during the McNulty years. Based on educational quality, affordability, and alumni earnings, *Money Magazine* placed Grove City in the top 12 percent of American colleges in 2014. That same year, *Forbes* ranked Grove City as 224th in "America's Top Colleges."

In 2016, its 92 percent retention rate and 79 percent four-year graduation rate contributed to College Raptor naming Grove City its number two "Smartest Choice" college. That same year, the college was placed on PayScale's top-ten list of best value national liberal arts colleges. Acknowledging these accolades, McNulty declared that Grove City challenged "students to grow intellectually and spiritually" and its high expectations produced "well-prepared graduates eager to pursue their life's calling."[159] That year, the college's freshman retention rate (a key indicator of student satisfaction) was 92 percent, 24 percent higher than the national average, while the early career median salary of Grove City graduates was 42 percent higher than the national median.[160]

In 2017, both *The Princeton Review* and *Forbes* recognized Grove City as among the top 10 percent of the nation's four-year institutions. Grove City was ranked 120th in the 2019 *US News's Best Colleges* guide and fifty-second in best undergraduate teaching because of its strong emphasis on classroom instruction. That year, *The Princeton Review* rated Grove City eleventh on its list of top twenty-five best schools for internships. In 2021, Grove City was ranked forty-fifth in *Forbes*'s national liberal arts colleges and universities category. The financial website SmartAsset named Grove City one of the ten best-value colleges in Pennsylvania based on starting salary, tuition, expenses, and other factors for 2021–2022.

Grove City's shift to awarding more than half of its degrees in STEM fields led *US News & World Report* to reclassify it from a liberal arts college to a northern regional college in 2022, where it captured the number five ranking.[161] The next year, the magazine ranked Grove City its best value among colleges in states from Maryland to Maine, and fourth overall based on academic quality and graduate outcomes. In 2024, *The Princeton Review* noted that students strongly valued Grove City's "outstanding academics, interesting professors, Christian community, high quality campus life," and "focus on student flourishing." The guide added that Grove City "provides a Christ-centered, non-sectarian environment in which students and faculty 'create a vibrant and uplifting community that encourages one another to live to the fullest in a Christ-like manner.'"[162] The *US News & World Report* ranked Grove City fourth for value, overall quality, and undergraduate teaching in Regional Colleges North on its 2025 list of best colleges.

Recruiting students presented a challenge during McNulty's presidency. In September 2014, he introduced Project Wolverine to assess innovative ways to reach potential students and address the college's 41 percent decline in applications from 1992 to 2013. The president attributed this decrease to three factors: the economic downturn in 2008–2009, the college's limited financial aid, and the smaller number of high school graduates in Pennsylvania, eastern Ohio, and New York. The substantial discounts given to many students at colleges with high price tags made them more attractive than Grove City, which had a lower sticker price but gave much less financial aid. The decline in applications led to an increase in the acceptance rate from 44 percent in 2005 to 81 percent in 2013 and a decline in average SAT scores from the upper to the lower 1200s. Project Wolverine's goals were to increase applications to two thousand and to lower the acceptance rate to 50 percent.[163]

The COVID epidemic prevented employing some of its standard recruiting tools, but the college restored them all by 2022. They included Made to Order Mondays, Admitted Student Day, and Spring Preview Day, which could entail a class visit, a coach meeting, a financial aid discussion, an admissions interview, a group campus tour, lunch, and a reception with McNulty. Admitted Student Day enabled youth to further evaluate whether they wanted to attend Grove City and to celebrate their acceptance with their future classmates. Spring Preview Day's major interest fair, college planning session, campus tour, and lunch provided high school students and their families an overview of Grove City.

Placement

Grove City's placement record during the McNulty years was strong. The annual career fair attracted representatives from between 140 and 170 companies and graduate schools. At annual internship fairs, fifty student interns shared their experiences. Six months after graduation, 97 percent of the class of 2015 was employed or attending a graduate or professional school, well above the national average of 60 percent. This outcome continued through 2024.[164]

Finances

The four-year capital campaign that began in 2011 called "Grove City Matters" raised a record $95 million, 105 percent of the original goal, to construct new buildings, renovate several older ones, and provide scholarships. More than $37 million was used to establish 130 new scholarships. The largest gifts were $7 million from an anonymous donor, $4.5 million from the Richard King Mellon

Foundation for STEM Hall, and $3 million for the Christian activities building from David and Jayne Rathburn, '79. McNulty argued that these gifts would help prepare students "to be exemplary citizens through an extraordinary education impacting heads, hearts and hands."[165] Campaign funds were provided by Grove City's "powerful alumni base and the legion of friends of the College who have aligned themselves with its historical mission of providing a rich academic tradition at an amazing value in a community of Christian learners."[166]

During McNulty's tenure, the amount of money raised through the annual Wolverine Challenge in November, which primarily funded merit scholarships, skyrocketed from $600,000 given by eight hundred donors in 2016 to $2.93 million in 2024 supplied by 2,058 donors. In fall 2020, 66 percent of students were receiving need- or merit-based financial aid. For the 2024–2025 academic year, the college gave need- and merit-based aid to 74 percent of students, awarding about $11.7 million, an average of $7,611 per student.

In 2023, college officials announced a new capital campaign called "Impact 150" to coincide with the celebration of Grove City's 150th anniversary. The $185 million campaign consists of three phases, all of which seek to increase the scholarship endowment. The first phase seeks to raise $90 million by 2026 to also retrofit Rockwell Hall (renamed Smith Hall of Science and Technology in fall 2025) and build a new field house on the upper campus for the college's six hundred student athletes that includes more training spaces and locker rooms and a film study space and varsity weight room. In addition, a $3 million gift from Bill Stewart, '63, led the college to name the new baseball field for him. Phase two, expected to begin in 2026, aims to raise $43 million to renovate residence halls and Crawford Auditorium. Phase three will provide $32 million to renovate residence halls and augment the scholarship endowment.[167]

A record $70 million gift from the estate of David Rathburn in 2024 increased the college's endowment to almost $300 million. The goal of Isaac and Weir Ketler and Alexander Ormond was finally being realized. The generosity of Grove City's donors, McNulty declared, facilitated the college's efforts to develop outstanding Christian leaders.[168]

The Alumni

The stories of alumni who returned to campus to speak, Rachel Smith, '19, asserted, were always "inspiring, informative, and insightful."[169] The Alumni and College Relations staff and student members of the Crimson and White Society worked to connect current students with alumni through various means including holding an annual Thank a Donor Day. Their work was supplemented by the Alumni Council, consisting of fifty-eight members representing the nearly thirty thousand Grove City College alumni throughout the world. "Alumni engagement," Ed Breen effused in 2022, "has never been more energetic and encouraging."[170] In 2024, the college's annual Distinguished Service Award was renamed for David Rathburn.

Alumni achievement abounded. Faith Whiteley McCoy, '64, served as a clandestine service staff officer for the Central Intelligence Agency for thirty-three years. Christine Keener, '97, worked as ALCOA's vice president of operations for Europe and North America. Since 2022, she has served as the COO of the North American region of Barrick, a leading gold and copper producer. Troy Demmer, '11, and Jake Loosararian, '13, founded Gecko Robotics, a company that designs robots to perform safety inspections for industrial facilities, leading Demmer to be chosen as one of *Forbes*'s "30 Under 30" young stars in the energy field. Jacob Sims, '10, has worked in a variety of management positions for International Justice Mission, including directing its work in Cambodia and helping lead its labor trafficking initiative and its battle against transnational crime and human trafficking. J. D. Larsen, '96, is the CFO of the company that produced the multi-season hit TV series *The Chosen* about the life of Jesus. In 2018, trustee David Porter was appointed to the Third Circuit Court of Appeals, becoming the highest-ranking judge in school history. Sean Rowe, '97, began a nine-year term in 2024 as the presiding bishop of the Episcopal Church, the denomination's highest office. Richard Staley, '62, a generous benefactor of the college, founded Flavor House to create and manufacture quality savory flavors and the Staley Equipment Company to provide materials for ports, waterways, recycling, construction, demolition, and forestry. In September 2024, the college's school of business was named for Howard Winklevoss, '65, in recognition of his $4 million gift. Winklevoss is a distinguished business technology entrepreneur, a former professor at the Wharton School of the University of Pennsylvania, the author of several books, and the founder of several ventures including Winklevoss Consultants, which assists 125 major corporations, and Winklevoss Technologies, which develops software for the actuarial consulting community. Winklevoss declared. "This gift is a way to give back to an institution that has given me so much."[171]

The Trustees

In October 2020, Ed Breen succeeded David Rathburn as the chair of the board of trustees. Reflecting on his long service, Rathburn declared, "I am grateful that God brought me to the college, and I have worked hard to repay as much of that blessing as I possibly could."[172] Breen majored in business and economics at Grove City. After serving as the vice president of sales and then the CEO and chair of General Instrument Corp, he oversaw its merger with Motorola Inc. He became the executive vice president of Motorola and then its president and CEO. In 2002, Breen was appointed the CEO of Tyco International. In 2015, he became the CEO of DuPont and is currently the company's executive chairman. "I was very well-prepared by Grove City," Breen testified.[173]

Conclusion

McNulty's eleven-year tenure at Grove City, Breen maintained, had generated "great forward momentum." His "innovative, energetic, and winsome style has truly been transformative." Under

McNulty's leadership, applications reached a twenty-year high; the endowment tripled; fundraising records were set; academic offerings were expanded (most notably, the establishment of schools of nursing and business and seven master's degree programs); innovative initiatives on rural ministry and faith and public life were launched; discipleship opportunities for students increased; varsity athletics programs reached "new heights of success and national recognition"; and several new buildings were constructed or renovated.[174]

McNulty called leading Grove City College his "most professionally fulfilling experience." He added that "Shepherding our tremendous flock of Grovers is the best part of this job, and, frankly, the hardest to give up." McNulty declared that "The Lord has richly blessed us with increased enrollment, historic financial strength, many exciting new programs, projects, and opportunities, and an exceptionally strong Christ-centered community. Most importantly, we have strengthened our resolve to advance Christian education while remaining committed to the enduring and conservative principles undergirding Western Civilization. Enhancing our Christian foundation has been the number one priority."[175]

McNulty's quest to make the college more authentically Christian initially provoked pushback from some alumni who feared that he was trying to transform the institution into a Bible college. This resistance largely dissipated as these alumni realized that Grove City could be authentically Christian and still highly respected. McNulty believed that he had helped clarify Grove City's mission, enrich the student experience, beautify the campus, strengthen the academic program, fortify Grove City's scholarly reputation, improve the sports teams and culture, and motivate the faculty and students to pursue excellence. He wanted to be remembered as "a man who loved God and students."[176]

Probably speaking for every Grove City president, McNulty explained that the job was very physically demanding, filled with activities from morning to night every day. He had very little free time and often felt isolated. Making changes was very difficult because tradition was so strong at Grove City. Nevertheless, the extent to which faculty and students embraced his relational approach, the innovative programs he created thrived, his vision for the college was accepted, and the college's financial resources increased all exceeded his expectations.[177]

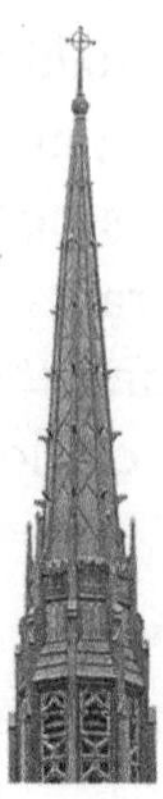

EPILOGUE

Throughout its history, Grove City has been an institution where Jesus Christ is proclaimed and glorified and students are prepared to serve the risen King in all areas of life. Through its academic, student life, and religious programs, Grove City College has sought to prepare well-educated, committed Christians who serve God and people compassionately, joyfully, courageously, and diligently through the professions, the business world, the arts, the church, and voluntary organizations. Grove City's history demonstrates that colleges can stop going down the road to secularization and restore their Christian mission while maintaining high academic standards.[1]

In advertising Grove City's presidential search in October 2024, board of trustees president Edward Breen, '78, maintained that its "rigorous academics, Christian orthodoxy, and independent spirit are a distinctive and attractive combination in American higher education."[2] Kristen Waggoner, the CEO and president of the Alliance Defending Freedom, argued that Grove City is one of the nation's "preeminent institutions preparing the next generation to boldly contend for truth" and "the liberties enshrined in the US Constitution" in "law, policy, and the public square." As Grove City celebrates its 150th anniversary, it continues to provide "a Christ-centered, academically excellent, and affordable education." Committed to defending conservative values and the foundations of a free society, Grove City College seeks to develops "leaders of the highest proficiency, purpose, and principles ready to advance the common good."[3]

In March 2025, Brad Lingo was named the college's tenth president. Lingo graduated summa cum laude from Grove City in 2000 as a business-economics major where he served as the executive vice president of SGA, led Bible studies at George Junior Republic with New Life, and participated in an Intercity Outreach trip to Chicago. Lingo graduated with honors in 2003 from Harvard Law School, where he was an executive editor of the *Harvard Journal of Law and Public Policy*. Lingo then worked as a law clerk for Morris Arnold, a judge on the US Court of Appeals for the Eighth Circuit, as a litigator at the Washington, DC, firm of Gibson Dunn, and as a partner in the trial and global disputes practice of King & Spalding. In 2019, he began teaching at Regent University Law School and became its dean in 2022. Lingo's college experience profoundly impacted his "heart, mind and soul."[4] He declared, "I found professors who believed in me and friends who encouraged me in my faith, and I experienced the joy of working hard to pursue excellence in a Christian community." Lingo wants students to continue to receive "the Christian, conservative, academically excellent, affordable education that profoundly shaped" him.

Paul McNulty is confident that Lingo has "the faith, character and remarkable ability" to lead "the college to new heights in advancing our vital mission." Breen lauds Lingo "vibrant commitment to Christian orthodoxy, tight alignment with the college's conservative vision and character, extraordinary professional experience and sophistication, and keen understanding of higher education and the challenges and opportunities facing Grove City College."[5] David Porter, '88, the secretary of the board of trustees, contends that Lingo's professional and academic experience equip him to faithfully lead Grove City's quest to be a "Christ-centered, conservative, and independent" institution. Regent University professor Erin Morrow Hawley praises Lingo's "commitment to defending constitutional principles, strengthening academic excellence, and equipping Christian students to faithfully live out their callings."[6]

The future of higher education is very challenging, especially for Christian colleges. Colleges and universities face rising costs, a potential reduction in federal funding, frequent claims that a college degree is not worth the money spent to obtain it, declining numbers of students of traditional college age, and the difficulty of offering liberal arts majors in an age that prioritizes STEM programs and practical career preparation. Christian colleges confront the additional challenge of lower numbers of prospective Christian students. Various surveys report that less than 10 percent of Gen Z (individuals born between 1997 and 2012) are White evangelicals, historically the principal market for Christian colleges.[7] About 42 percent of Gen Z members identify as nonreligious.[8] Only 26 percent of children under eighteen go to religious services once a week, and only 40 percent of them receive any kind of religious education, in large part because two-thirds of their parents are millennials (those born between 1981 and 1996) who either view religion as obsolete or have little interest in it.[9] Sociologist John Hawthorne argues that many Christian colleges today are driven by fear about demographics, funding, possible public relations crises, the pressures caused by culture wars, and mission drift.[10] Fear of being contaminated by the secular world or capitulating to its values has led many evangelical colleges and primary and secondary schools to avoid the world as much as possible.

Throughout its history, Grove City has taken a different approach. Driven by its mission to be light and salt, to fulfill the Bible's cultural mandate, and to promote the common good, Grove City has long prepared its graduates to serve people and glorify God through their vocations, families, and churches. Hawthorne maintains that Christian institutions that properly understand their role in higher education, clearly articulate their mission, and organize their constituencies and programs to support their mission can serve as models of how "people of faith engage the broader culture."[11] Grove City has done this effectively for most of its history. Many members of Gen Z are experiencing anxiety about the future, a sense of isolation, and a loss of trust. Colleges that help them not simply obtain a degree and job but gain fulfillment through a combination of a robust faith, rewarding vocation, and reliable character will always be attractive destinations.[12] Grove City's trustees, administrators, and faculty have for 150 years sought to make Christ preeminent in every area of the college's life and throughout the world. They have striven to equip students use their talents and education to promote God's kingdom on earth, do everything "the name of the Lord Jesus" (Colossians 3:17, NIV), develop the riches of nature, and help people experience the goodness of God's creation.

Dick Jewell argues that the current cultural climate provides a great market for Grove City. Its unique "pedagogy, history, and values" enable the college to effectively educate students, whether they attended public or private high schools or were homeschooled.[13] McNulty maintains that Grove City College's greatest strengths are its "interesting, principled history"; dedicated and talented faculty and staff who have an impressive work ethic, strong character, and genuine faith; outstanding board chairs; "loyal and passionate alumni"; and astute financial practices. With an endowment currently approaching $300 million, first-class facilities, and a very successful capital campaign, the future of Grove City College is bright indeed.[14]

Lingo writes that J. Howard Pew reportedly gave the same talk every year at Grove City College. Pew said, "This school should encourage and inculcate in the minds and hearts of the students an abiding faith in God and country, a love for freedom, a respect for truth, an acceptance of personal responsibility, and a desire to contribute to the betterment of the human race." "When Mr. Pew spoke those words," Lingo declares, "he must have realized how much a school like Grove City was needed in our country. But even he could not have foreseen how much it is needed in America today. There's never been a more important time for a school like ours. Grove City's singular combination of faith and freedom makes it a beacon of light and a bastion of hope for our country's future."[15] Lingo maintains that after its 1984 Supreme Court's decision, Grove City "chose faith and freedom over federal funds and decided to operate without the benefit of federal taxpayer dollars.

Forgoing federal largesse imposed financial discipline and forced the college to control costs, find alternative sources of funding, and avoid the administrative bloat that plagues many universities. It was the hardest, and best, decision ever made at Grove City."[16]

Lingo, like many other administrators, faculty, staff, students, and alumni throughout its history, wants Grove City to become nation's "premier Christian college."[17] May it soon receive this distinction as it continues to faithfully serve the Lord.

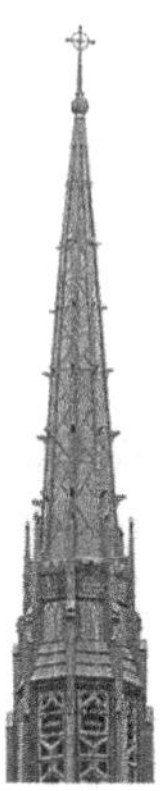

TEN GROVER GREATS

During its first 150 years, Grove City has had many outstanding administrators, professors, and students who have contributed substantially to the college's mission on campus and in the world. Here are ten prominent examples of hundreds of individuals who could be profiled.

One of the college's greatest athletes was Levi Lamb, who attended Grove City from 1909 to 1911 and served as the freshman class president. At six feet and six inches, Lamb towered over his competitors as he led the Grove City football, basketball, and track and field teams. For example, in a 75–17 thrashing of Carnegie Tech in March 1911 in basketball, Lamb scored thirty points. He finished his collegiate career at Penn State, where he excelled as a tackle on the university's undefeated 1912 football team, a wrestler who lost only two matches in four years, and a discus thrower. Penn State's first three-sport letterwinner joined the US army in August 1917 and fought at Château-Thierry, France, in June and July 1918. The second lieutenant was killed on July 18, 1918, the first day of the offensive stage of the Second Battle of the Marne, while leading his unit during the Battle of Soissons. A scholarship is named for him at Penn State.[1]

Herbert Harmon earned a bachelor of law at Hobart College in 1893 and a BS at Cornell University in 1895. After teaching at St. John's Military Academy in Wisconsin from 1895 to 1898 and

California Normal School from 1898 to 1906, he served a professor of physics and mechanical and civil engineering at Grove City from 1906 to 1946. Harmon coached highly successful football and baseball teams from 1906–1915, conducted pioneering research in radio technology and broadcasting, and created the college's radio station, one of the first in the nation. The 1916 *Ouija* lauded Harmon for producing championship teams in two sports and asserted that everyone he coached respected him. He motivated players to "work hard and do their best."[2] Harmon devised a radio-phone unit, which won first prize in a national contest for its efficient operation. His work helped lay the groundwork for later advances in and the commercialization of radio. Harmon also operated a weather station on campus from 1907 to 1942 and sent daily reports to the US Weather Bureau. During World War I, Harmon assisted the radio division of the Bureau of Standards in Washington, DC. Weir Ketler extolled Harmon as "a remarkable teacher" who was admired for his "unusual patience, persistence, and energy."[3] He and his wife Flora Friedline Harmon, who was named Pennsylvania's Mother of the Year in 1950, had nine children, most of whom had distinguished careers in science or education.

As a student at Grove City College, Alva John Calderwood, 1896, excelled in the classroom, on the gridiron as a halfback, and on the diamond as a pitcher. After graduating, he immediately began teaching at the college. He left briefly to earn a second BA at Harvard in 1899 and did graduate work at Harvard and Yale. He married Leonara Neal in 1900, and one their children, Helen Francis, wed J. Stanley Harker, Grove City's fourth president. Calderwood taught several subjects, but his specialty was Latin. He served as the dean of the college for thirty-five years and was a faculty member for fifty-three years, the longest tenure in Grove City history. In addition to his responsibilities as dean, he handled alumni relations work for many years. A student declared, "I never talk" to Alva Calderwood "without being enriched by a new idea or some new outlook on life." He is "rich in wisdom, humor, and common sense." Students who spent time with him with consider it among the best moments of the semester.[4] Calderwood retired in

June 1949 and died six months later. The trustee minutes claimed that the dean knew more alumni personally than any other person; he was always thoroughly prepared as a teacher; the college had "suffered an irreparable loss."[5] The building that served as the college's principal classroom for liberal arts students from 1958 to 2003 bore his name at the request of the alumni. When Calderwood Hall was dedicated in 1958, a tribute in the program, expressing the alumni's affection, declared "he was far more than a teacher and administrator. He was our friend. He had an uncanny memory for names."[6] At this ceremony, one alumna argued that for three decades, Calderwood served as "the balance wheel" between Weir Ketler and the powerful board of trustees and the faculty on one side and the students and community on the other.[7] The Grove City School of Arts and Letters was named for Calderwood in 2002.

After earning degrees at the University of Cincinnati and Eastman Business College, Rea Gillespie Walters, who went by R. G., taught at Grove City from 1918 until his death in 1952, except for three years in the late 1920s. He chaired the business department and served as both the college's supervisor of teacher training and placement director. Walters was a national leader in the fields of sales and retailing. He was an outstanding teacher, a prolific scholar, and a frequent speaker at community, civic, and educational events and conferences. Walters received numerous accolades and awards for his advising of campus organizations and civic offices. His books include *Fundamentals of Selling* (1937), *The Community Survey* (1942), and *Retail Merchandising* (1943), which were used in many college business courses. *The Collegian* editor in chief stated in 1949 that Walters "can't be rated high enough by those lucky to have had him in class."[8] He played numerous roles at Grace Methodist Church, held many civic offices, and for thirty years educated hundreds of business and commercial students and helped countless graduates find jobs.

Creig Hoyt taught chemistry at Grove City College from 1913 to 1950 (except for one year when he was finishing his doctorate) and served as the academic dean from 1950 to 1957. As a student, he was an intercollegiate debater, a band leader, a baseball player, and an active member of the Webster literary society. The devout Christian was an elder and longtime Sunday school teacher at First Presbyterian Church. Widely considered an inspiring teacher, Hoyt helped train more than four hundred chemistry students. For many years, he served as the adviser to the Epsilon Pi fraternity and as the chair of the college's publications committee.[9] Hoyt made several important discoveries in industrial chemistry and was an expert in ground and surface water problems and the secondary recovery of petroleum. J. Howard Pew maintained that many industrial leaders valued Hoyt's advice, while J. Stanley Harker argued when he died that "America has lost a great man of science, [and] Grove City has lost one of her most loyal sons and greatest teachers."[10] Hoyt was also very active in the Grove City's educational, civic, religious, and social life. Grove City's engineering building, which opened in fall 1966, is named after him.

In 1939, George Carpenter left Grove City College to prepare to fight the Germans. He served with the Royal Air Force in Great Britain, where he flew with the American Eagle squadron. In September 1942, Carpenter transferred to the 4th Fighter Group, 335th Squadron of the US Army Air Corps. He was named the commanding officer of this squadron in February 1944 and by mid-April 1944 he had flown 143 missions and 257 combat hours in Spitfires, P-47s, and P-51s. Carpenter destroyed 13.84 enemy aircraft and earned the title of "double ace." On April 18, his plane was shot down near Berlin. After parachuting to the ground, Carpenter was captured and spent more than a year as a POW in Stalag Luft III and Moosburg near Munich before being liberated in May 1945. Altogether, he flew more than two thousand missions in Europe. Major Carpenter received numerous medals including the Air Medal, the World War II Victory Medal, and the Distinguished Flying Cross. The citation for this last award praised "the skillful and zealous manner" in which Carpenter searched for and destroyed enemies and "his devotion to duty and courage." After the war ended, Carpenter worked for a while in the lumber business, but he returned to Grove City College, lived with his British wife in married student housing, and earned a chemistry degree in 1952.

He graduated from Kirksville College of Osteopathy in Missouri in 1956 and practiced medicine in Paris, Tennessee, until his death in 2005.[11]

African American Brad Scott, '69, a graduate of Clairton High School near Pittsburgh, came to Grove City College in large part because his guidance counselor told him that the institution was "interested in capable, competent minority students" and that attending the college would help him to succeed in a largely White world. "She was absolutely right," Scott declared. "My parents taught us," he explained, "to speak up with dignity, grace, honor, and clarity about who we were." The French education major became one of the college's most distinguished students, serving as the president of SGA and the touring choir, vice president of the theater honorary, and a member of the Inter-Fraternity Council, the chapel choir, and the men's glee club. He also had major roles in several theater productions and was a featured musical soloist. As SGA president, he helped inspire students to improve the campus and community and to grow as thinkers and activists. "We thought we could make the world a better place," he explained. "At times we were very successful," while other times "we felt we were hitting our heads against a brick wall." The charismatic SGA president worked diligently to enrich students' chapel experience, provide a study day, and make other constructive changes.[12] His words and actions displayed his Christian commitment. The 1969 Senior Man of the Year insisted that his experience at Grove City prepared him to engage in a world where he often was the only person of color. Scott had an impressive career as an educator and community leader. Scott earned a PhD at the University of Texas in educational administration, penned numerous books, articles, and reports, and fought tirelessly to increase educational opportunities for all students regardless of their race, gender or national origin.[13] He received numerous accolades and awards, including a Grove City College Alumni Achievement Award in 2018.

Jeff Claypool, '69, was an All-State honorable mention high school basketball player in Ohio. He was recruited by Westminster coach Buzz Riddle, who boasted that Westminster had beaten Grove

City forty years in a row, but after spending time with Grove City's coach Cliff Wettig, Claypool applied to the school, from which his father, an engineer, had graduated in 1940. Because Claypool's grades were mediocre, he was initially not accepted, but Harker overrode this decision. Claypool set out to prove the director of admissions wrong as he prepared to be a high school history teacher and coach. He soon decided, however, that he wanted to work in human resources, changed his major to psychology, and made the dean's list numerous semesters. Nevertheless, the basketball court was where he most excelled. Many of Claypool's basketball exploits are discussed in the chapter on the Harker years, so just as few of his highlights are mentioned here. His senior year, Claypool led the Wolverines to a 19–5 record, averaging 29.8 ppg, sixth highest in the nation. He ended his career with 2,234 points, the second-highest total in western Pennsylvania history. The Associated Press and United Press International both named him an honorable mention small college All-American in 1967 and 1969. He was selected as the Western Pennsylvania Player of the Year his junior and senior years. Claypool was also a superb team leader who constantly stimulated his teammates to play their best. After graduating, Claypool was drafted by the NBA's Baltimore Bullets and almost made the team. Claypool instead went on to serve as a vice president of human resources for both Bridgestone/Firestone and Sealy Inc. Claypool has been very active in his community and church, serving on the board of United Way, the Chamber of Commerce, the Randolph County Economic Development Corporation, and Industries of the Blind. He currently volunteers with the outreach ministry of First Presbyterian Church in Greensboro, North Carolina, to aid the area's unemployed and underemployed.

At Grove City College, Lee Kessler, '68, shone on the stage and at speech and debate tournaments, and she went on to an impressive career as an actor, screenwriter, playwright, and director. Kessler began college as a chemistry major, but her rewarding experience as a freshman as Hedda Gabler in Henrik Ibsen's play of the same name prompted her to change her major to speech and theater to pursue what she loved. Kessler starred in every play that William Teufel directed during her four years at Grove City. She was also the student director for *The Fantasticks* and *The Good Woman of Setzuan*. In April 1967, Kessler won the Pennsylvania state championship in women's oratory for her favorite speech, "The Uncommon Man." Kessler also placed in National Interstate Oratory Finals at Wayne State University in May 1967. She praised Teufel for training her in the Stanislavsky technique of acting and boosting her self-confidence, which equipped her to thrive in a master's program in theater at the University of Wisconsin and led her to believe that "I could go to Hollywood and make a go of it." Teufel demanded excellence and continually challenged Kessler to do her best in theater, speech, and debate. She appreciates the self-discipline she learned at Grove City through her classes, residence life, and extracurricular activities, the understanding she gained of the foundational principles of government and the US Constitution, and the grounding she received in Judeo-Christian values. These all contributed to her belief that a "girl from a small Christian college" could succeed at Wisconsin and in Hollywood. Like many aspiring actors, she went to Hollywood with no connections or contacts, but she joined a repertoire company and procured "a wonderful agent" who helped her get the role of Margaret Truman in the 1976 television movie *Collison Course: Truman vs. MacArthur*. Kessler developed a reputation for being easy to work with, which led to dozens of more roles including in the 1977 miniseries, *Roots*. Kessler also played a major guest role in an episode of *Barney Miller* and recurring characters on *Matlock*, *L.A. Law*, and *Hill Street Blues*. Kessler has enjoyed success as a director (especially for A. R. Gurney Jr.'s *Who Killed Richard Corey?* 1976), screenwriter, and playwright, most notably for her 1976 play *Anais Nin: The Paris Years*, in which she also played the principal role in New York and on tour for eight years. During the last two decades, Kessler has written a series of *White King* suspense novels, which revolve around the war against terrorists. In 2008, Kessler was inducted into the Dazzling Daughters of the American Revolution, a prestigious group of 130 first ladies, writers, artists, and social activists that includes Susan

B. Anthony, Clara Barton, and Eleanor Roosevelt.[14] She received a Grove City College Alumni Achievement Award in 1994.

Paul Cameron, '73, who starred in cross-country and track at Grove City College, grew up in a blue-collar family from New Castle, Pennsylvania. He was the first person from his extended family to attend college. Cameron was reared in a Christian and Missionary Alliance Church, and his faith became stronger at college through his coursework (especially with religion professor Andrew Hoffecker), involvement in the Fellowship of Christian Athletes, friendships with classmates, and attendance of services at Tower Presbyterian Church. When Jim Longnecker, who coached both sports at Grove City, recruited him, he declared that Cameron is "a picture runner, very dedicated to the sport" who could become "best runner in the history of Grove City" and "the best small college competitor in Western PA, second only to Pitt's Jerry Ritchey."[15] Longnecker's words were prophetic. During his career, Cameron went 38–3 in dual cross-country meets and won almost every mile and two-mile track race. Cameron led the college's first cross-country team to go to nationals in 1972. He earned All-American honors in cross-country in 1972 and 1973 by placing seventeenth and twenty-third, respectively, at the NCAA College Division Championships. Cameron holds Grove City's record for the one mile (4.16) and two mile (9:31.4). Grove City, he declared, "opened doors I never thought possible." His education provided "a great foundation for life." After graduating, Cameron completed thirteen marathons, including the Boston Marathon, and earned an MA in Counseling and Student Services at Indiana University of Pennsylvania. Cameron then spent thirty-five years working at Stevens College of Technology (named for abolitionist Thaddeus Stevens) in Lancaster, Pennsylvania, which educates many disadvantaged students. Cameron worked in a variety of capacities, most notably as the vice president of student services and as the athletic director and is now a vice president emeritus. For seven years, he coached the cross-country and track and field teams. Under Cameron's leadership, the cross-country team dramatically improved, and he and his 1996 squad were inducted into the

Thaddeus Stevens Sports Hall of Fame in 2012. Cameron served for four years on the board of Teen Challenge (now Adult and Teen Challenge), a Christian ministry to adults and youth who are struggling with addiction and other issues. Cameron was inducted into the Lawrence County Hall of Fame in 2024.[16]

Appendix

James Dixon's Top Actors, 1976–2015

1. George Hampe as Orlando in *As You Like It* (fall 2008) and as Jesus in *Godspell* (fall 2009)
2. Doug Baker as Valere in *La Bête* (spring 2008)
3. Ethan Mitchell as Ariel in *The Tempest* (spring 2015) and as Thenardier in *Les Misérables* (fall 2013)
4. Andy Hickley as Caliban in *The Tempest* (spring 2015), Javert in *Les Misérables* (fall 2013), and the Duke in *Measure for Measure* (spring 2013)
5. Derrick Winger as the Pirate King in *The Pirates of Penzance* (spring 2006), John Wintergreen in *Of Thee I Sing*, and Horace Vandergelder in *The Matchmaker*
6. Betsy Dupree as the Witch in *Into the Woods* (fall 1999) and Hermia in *A Midsummer Night's Dream* (spring 1999)
7. Chris Jensen as Lysander in *A Midsummer Night's Dream* (spring 1999) and J. Pierrepont Finch in *How to Succeed in Business Without Really Trying* (fall 1997)
8. Kiley Perdue as Rosemary Pilkington in *How to Succeed in Business Without Really Trying* and Ensign Nellie Forbush in *South Pacific* (fall 1996)
9. Tammie McKenzie as Lady Macbeth in *Macbeth* (spring 1980), Maria in *The Sound of Music* (Crossroads Theatre Co., summer 1981), and Aldonza/Dulcinea in *Man of La Mancha* (Crossroads, summer 1980)
10. Jesse Aukman and Megan Krimmel as musical and comedy teams in *Crazy for You* (fall 2007) and *The Matchmaker* (spring 2007)
11. Sam Leuenberger as Fyodor Pavlovich Karamazov in *The Brothers Karamazov* (spring 2011) and Lucio in *Measure for Measure* (spring 2013)
12. Jon Warren as Jean Valjean in *Les Misérables* (fall 2013)

James Dixon's Top Ten Shows, 1976–2015

1. *Waiting for Godot* (spring 1977). My first production at the Pew Fine Arts Center. The cast consisted of Lou Kilgore, Jim Weldon, Bill Kennedy, and Paul McNulty. McNulty played the part of Lucky, a has-been philosopher enslaved to a rough master and is silent the entire play except for a four-page monologue without any punctuation consisting of nonstop philosophical/theological babble.
2. *The Tempest* (spring 2015). My final production at GCC. Having taught Shakespeare for thirty-nine years, I finished my career with his final play in which Shakespeare wrote himself as the character of Prospero, a magician who gives up his magic at the end of the play—just as Shakespeare gives up his magic at the end of the play.
3. *Les Misérables* (fall 2013). A superb cast for the final musical of my career.
4. *The Brothers Karamazov* (spring 2011). An excellent cast with an excellent stage adaptation of this literary classic
5. *As You Like It* (fall 2008). Amanda Griswold and George Hampe were superb as the leads, Rosalind and Orlando
6. *Much Ado About Nothing* (spring 2005). Rachel Bovard and Hans Latta were outstanding as the leads, Beatrice and Benedick
7. *Into the Woods* (fall 1999). A fun romp in the woods.
8. *A Midsummer Night's Dream* (spring 1999). An equally fun frolic in the forest, with Betsy Dupree and Chris Jensen leading a good cast
9. *Murder in the Cathedral* (spring 1989). T. S. Eliot's classic play, staged in Harbison Chapel, which I directed and in which I played the part of Thomas Becket.
10. *Man of La Mancha* (Crossroads, summer 1980). I codirected with Bill Kennedy and played the part of Don Quixote, opposite Tammie Mackenzie as Aldonza.

Doug Browne's Top Five Vocalists, 1981–2014

1. Matthew Boice, '83, was an outstanding Pittsburgh-area high school choral director, as well as a tenor soloist, a church choir director, and a longtime member of the Mendelssohn Choir of Pittsburgh.
2. Emily Lorini, '03, has had an impressive opera career in Germany.
3. Jonathan Mark Sallade, '02, a lead member of the American Standard quartet, is the pastor at Calvary Orthodox Presbyterian Church in Glenside, Pennsylvania.
4. Becki Toth, '96, is a professional singer, actor, director, and teacher in Pittsburgh.
5. Emily Peterson Merow, '14, teaches voice and piano lessons and prepares people for auditions in eastern Pennsylvania while also singing with the Saltworks Performing Arts.

All five were superb soloists for either the touring choir or chapel choir. Lorini, Toth, and Merow also played leads in college musicals.

Grove City College's Greatest Instrumentalists Since 1976, as Submitted by Richard Konzen, Jeff Tedford, Joseph Pisano, and Ed Arnold

Richard Konzen's top four choices are organ majors Jeremy Roberts, Brian Gurley, '06, and Derek Stauff, '03, and violinist Jagan Ranjan, '00. Roberts directed the music program at First Presbyterian Church in Asheville, North Carolina, and then at Plymouth First Congregational Church in Lincoln, Nebraska. Gurley earned a PhD in choral conducting at the University of Wisconsin and is currently the cathedral musician at St. Paul's Cathedral in Pittsburgh. Stauff completed an MA and PhD at Indiana University and teaches music at Hillsdale College. Ranjan, who was the concertmaster for four years at Grove City, is a federal judge in the Western District of Pennsylvania and plays in a community orchestra.

Jeff Tedford's top five selections are Karin Hendrickson, '99, Jay Loose, '95, John Seybert, '95, Jeff Judd, '85, and Joe Pisano, '94. Hendrickson, a pianist, earned music degrees at the Peabody Conservatory and the Royal Academy of Music in London and has worked with the Concertgebouworkest Young in the Netherlands, the Royal Conservatoire of Scotland, and the Royal Welsh College of Music and Drama. Loose, who played the trumpet in several ensembles at Grove City, is the master chief musician with the US navy. Seybert, who played the saxophone at Grove City, earned his PhD at Indiana University and is currently the performing arts coordinator and band director at Upper St. Clair High School in a Pittsburgh suburb. He has toured internationally with Chuck Mangione. Judd, who played string base in college, founded a violin store in Williamsport, Pennsylvania, that supplies instruments to thousands of students. Pisano, who played trumpet and served as a student conductor at Grove City, taught at the college from 1995 to 2018.

Joe Pisano also included Hendrickson and Loose on his list, as well as organist Ed Moore, '91; Jeff Tedford, a violin and voice double major and student conductor; and Travis Weller '95. Weller received his PhD in music education at Kent State University and teaches music at Messiah University. He has received numerous J. W. Pepper Editor's Choice and Bandworld Top 100 nominations, and his compositions for bands have been performed by dozens of groups.

Ed Arnold added Donald Kephart, '78, a member of the marching band and concert band, who served as the director of bands and music department chair at Geneva College; Tad Greig, '83, who played in the marching, concert, and jazz bands at Grove City, was the director of bands and chair of music department at Westminster College; and Amanda Schlegel, '98, who was a member of the concert and marching bands and the orchestra. She teaches music at the University of South Carolina, does clinics at universities around the nation, and publishes extensively in scholarly journals.

The Great Debaters, 2008–2025, Compiled by Jason Edward, Michael Coulter, and Andrew Harvey

Since 2008, the Grove City College debate team has captured thirty-seven national championships in various forms of forensic competition. The following are the ten greatest debaters, all of whom served as team captains.

1. Dan Pugh, '14, won three national championships with three different partners in three different leagues (Novice Nationals, NCCFA, and Phi Kappa Delta) and was a member of the 2011 NCCFI Quality Award–winning team. Pugh's use of humor demonstrated his intelligence and mastery of topics and acted as catnip for judges.
2. Mark Mariani, '15, captured the PKD National Championship and helped win the NCCFI Quality Award. None was more confident in knowing how to win a round or more determined to do so.
3. Carolyn Hartwick, '19, scored three national championships (PKD Novice, NCCFI Division II, and NCCFI IPDA JV). Her no-nonsense approach generated both love and fear in her teammates and led to victories.
4. Drew Brackbill, '16, won his national championships in the 2015 PKD tournament and as part of the NCCFI Quality Award. The debate team's formula for success has long been to "Speak Better and Know More," and the college has always had at least one person on the team like Brackbill with a seemingly encyclopedic knowledge of current events and politics.
5. Christopher Ostertag, '20, demanded excellence from the team and unleashed verbal jujitsu on his opponents. Ostertag dominated the National Christian College Debate Invitational by earning four different national championships there throughout his college career.

6. Joshua Xu, '26. Arguably, Grove City's greatest single accomplishment in debate is having two freshmen win the 2023 PKD varsity championship of PKD, the world's largest forensic tournament. Xu did that with Ginger Schiffmayer and contributed later that year to the college's first overall national championship in the National Educational Debate Association. He followed these up with another national championship in 2024 in the NCCFI.
7. Zack Voell, '17, expected no quarter and gave none to friend and foe alike. His second-to-none work ethic helped him and his partner Josiah Vehrs take gold at the NCCFI in 2015 and the team to win the NCCFI Quality Award by the highest margin ever.
8. The Anastasi brothers excelled at displaying Christian kindness to teammates and eloquence in competition. Sebastian won the NCCFI top JV speaker in 2020, while his younger brother Benjamin was named the top NCCFI Varsity Speaker in 2024. They helped Grove City take home the NCCFI Quality Award both of those years.
9. Kelsey Winther was named the top speaker at NCCFI in 2008, helping catapult the college's team into national prominence. Additionally, her family, who ran a high school debate league in Modesto, California, created a pipeline of talent to the college, which fostered the squad's initial success in the twenty-first century.
10. Justus Carnley, '24, specialized in the National Educational Debate League's Crossfire format, helping the team capture its first NEDA National Championship in 2023. The next year, Carnley won all his regular season matches, leading him to being named a NEDA All-American/NEDA Hall of Famer.

The one Grove City debater who did not win a national championship is nevertheless the greatest of them all. Luke Juday launched Grove City into forensic prominence in the twenty-first century and established the rigor and commitment that characterizes student-run practices. A multi-year captain, Juday created a standard of excellence that guided other debaters. Juday also secured the college's greatest debate-related achievement by receiving a Fulbright Scholarship to study debate in South Africa.

Endnotes

Preface

1 See Scott Amon, "We Were Founded When?" February 26, 2021, 5. (Every article without attribution in this book is in *The Collegian*); L. John Van Til, *The Soul of Grove City College* (Grove City, PA: Pine Grove Publishing, 2015).

2 William Ramsay, *The Making of the University* (London, 1915), 13. A School Amid the Pines: Isaac Ketler Fulfills His Dream, 1876–1913

1 By 1900, most states had made school compulsory through eighth grade.

2 Dwight Guthrie, "Academies and Female Seminaries," in William Wilson McKinney, ed., *The Presbyterian Valley* (Pittsburgh: Davis and Warde, 1958), 204.

3 Weir C. Ketler, *An Adventure in Education: 75 Years of Grove City College (1876–1951)* (New York: Newcomen Society, 1953), 10.

4 Weir C. Ketler, "Grove City College in the Last Fifty Years," *Commencement Week and Semi-Centennial Exercises of Grove City College*, June 13–16, 1926, 20.

5 *Catalogue of Pine Grove Normal Academy, 1878–1879*, 10.

6 "Pine Grove Normal Academy Educational Leaflet" (c. 1877), cited by David Dayton, *'Mid the Pines: A History of Grove City College* (Grove City, PA: Grove City College Alumni Association, 1971), 50.

7 *1878–1879 Catalogue*, 12, 14; quotations in that order.

8 *1878–1879 Catalogue*, 22.

9 Ketler, *Adventure in Education*, 12.

10 "Mrs. Isaac Ketler," April 17, 1940, 8; "A Tribute," April 24, 1940, 3.

11 *1878–1879 Catalogue* 16, 18.

12 *Catalogue of the Pine Grove Normal Academy, 1880–1881*, 29.

13 *Pine Grove Normal Academy Charter*, Charter of Incorporation, March 19, 1879, Appendix A.

14 *Catalogue of the Pine Grove Normal Academy, 1879–1880*, 28–29.

15 *1880–1881 Catalogue*, 37.

16 *Catalogue of the Pine Grove Normal Academy, 1881–1882*, 29.

17 *Catalogue of the Pine Grove Normal Academy, 1882–1883*, 37.

18 *1882–1883 Catalogue*, 40; *Catalogue of the Pine Grove Normal Academy, 1884–1885*, 37; quotations in that order.

19 *1880–1881 Catalogue*, 37–38.

20 Grove City College, *A Historical Sketch with Charter and By-laws* (1886), 11–12. Subsequent college publications reiterate this point.

21 *Historical Sketch*, 6, 11.

22 John Ray, *A History of Western Pennsylvania* (Athens, PA: Riverside Press, 1941), 318.

23 *Catalogue of Grove City College, 1884–1885*, 30.

24 *1884–1885 Catalogue*, 29, 31 (first quotation), 32–33 (second quotation).
25 *Catalogue of Grove City College, 1886–87*, 37.
26 *Catalogue of Grove City College, 1888–1889*, 42–43 (first and second quotations), 44 (third quotation).
27 *Catalogue of Grove City College, 1891–1892*, 37, 38 (quotation).
28 *1890–1891 Catalog*, 20.
29 Ketler, *Adventure in Education*, 18.
30 "J. N. Pew: A Biographical Sketch," *Our Sun* (Philadelphia: Sun Oil Company, 1961), 11–12.
31 Ketler, *Adventure in Education*, 21.
32 February 1891, 17.
33 March 1891.
34 *1891–1892 Catalogue*, 30–31. Rowell was killed in action during the Spanish-American War in 1898.
35 *1891–1892 Catalogue*, 8.
36 Dayton, *'Mid the Pines*, 78.
37 *Catalogue of Grove City College, 1892–1893*, 35.
38 "Editorial," December 1893, 9; "Local Department," 19.
39 Isaac Ketler, "A Sure Foundation," Baccalaureate Sermon, June 17, 1894, 1–7. Cf. Ketler, "Strength Not Gained by Wrong Doing," December 1893, 2–8.
40 E.g., Isaac Ketler, "Trial of the Bible," June 1891, 57–65.
41 *Catalogue of Grove City College, 1893–1894*, 5.
42 *Catalogue of Grove City College, 1894–1895*, 4.
43 Ketler, *Adventure in Education*, 19.
44 Dayton, *'Mid the Pines*, 44.
45 George Marsden, *The Soul of the American University* (New York: Oxford University Press, 1997), 156–59.
46 Isaac Ketler, "The Problem of Life," *Homiletic Review* 27 (1894), 130.
47 *1884–1885 Catalogue*, 21; *Catalogue of Grove City College, 1895–1896*, 10. On Dana and LeConte, see Ronald Numbers, *The Creationists: From Scientific Creation to Intelligent Design* (Cambridge, MA: Harvard University Press, 2006).
48 Dayton, *'Mid the Pines*, 56.
49 *1895–1896 Catalog*, 53.
50 *Catalog of Grove City College, 1896–1897*, 54.
51 Dayton, *'Mid the Pines*, 76.
52 Isaac Ketler, *An Historical Sketch with Charter and By-Laws* (1895), 3.
53 Minutes of the Board of Trustees [hereinafter Trustee Minutes], II, 11, 13, 14. All trustee minutes, presidents' reports, and letters not otherwise identified are in the Grove City College Archives [hereinafter Archives].
54 *1896–1897 Catalogue*, 56.

55 Borden Bowne to Isaac Ketler, May 16, 1908, Box: Ketler Correspondence Collection, Folder: Letters—Dr. Borden P. Bowne & Mrs. Kate Bowne.
56 These words are on a Harbison Chapel stained-glass window depicting Isaac Ketler, Joseph Newton Pew, and Samuel Harbison at a board of trustees meeting.
57 "The Worth of a College," January 1901, 8.
58 *Grove City College Bulletin*, January 1906, 77.
59 *Grove City College Bulletin*, September 1905, 3.
60 *Catalogue of Grove City College, 1904–1905*, 70.
61 *Catalogue of Grove City College*, 1912–1913, 57.
62 Isaac Ketler to Ralph Harbison, December 6, 1909, as cited by Dayton, *'Mid the Pines*, 72.
63 Herman Rodgers, "Interesting Highlights in the History of Grove City College," February 19, 1936, 2.
64 "The Music Department," February 17, 1917, 1.
65 *Catalogue of Grove City College, 1902–1903*, 66.
66 *1902–1903 Catalogue*, 46.
67 *Grove City College Bulletin*, September 1905, 3.
68 *Grove City College Bulletin*, June 1905, 6.
69 Isaac Ketler to Charles Killie, Paotingfu, China, January 16, 1909, as cited by Dayton, *'Mid the Pines*, 78.
70 Hans Sennholz, *The First Eighty Years of Grove City College* (Grove City, PA: American Book Distributors, 1993), 19, 21, 22.
71 *Grove City College Bulletin*, September 1905, 32–33.
72 See Isaac Ketler to J. N. Pew, Pittsburgh, October 14, 1904, as cited by Dayton, *'Mid the Pines*, 76.
73 *Grove City College Alumni Quarterly*, August 1911, 2.
74 *Catalog of Grove City College, 1900–1901*, 40.
75 *Grove City College Bulletin*, June 1905, 57.
76 June 1903, 198.
77 *Catalogue of Grove City College, 1911–1912*, 57.
78 Dayton, *'Mid the Pines*, 74.
79 *Grove City College Bulletin*, May 1906, 9.
80 *1911–1912 Catalogue*, 59.
81 *Catalogue of Grove City College, 1912–1913*, 58.
82 "Surprising Facts," April 17, 1934, 3.
83 "Educator Was Great Star," March 31, 1949, 3.
84 Don Thompson, "Sport Chatter," April 11, 1932, 3.
85 The others were pitcher Mal Eason, '00, who went 36–73 with a 3.43 ERA; outfielder Spike Shannon, who attended Grove City intermittently from 1896 to 1904, played with three MLB teams and had a career average of .259 in 694 games; and catchers Sam Brown, '01, and William Riddle "Doc" Marshall, who attended Grove City in 1904, and centerfielder Charlie Jones, '01, who all played sporadically in MLB between 1901 and 1909.
86 "College Glee Club," October 1911, 18; "Y.M.C.A.," ibid., 26.

87 "Keep Off the Grass," January 1912, 17; "Step in Progress," May 1912, 14.
88 February 1901, 45.
89 Isaac Ketler, "Joseph Newton Pew in Memoriam," October 14, 1912, 2, 3 (first quotation), 10 (second and third quotations), 13 (fourth quotation).
90 Isaac Ketler to John Bowman, New York City, August 13, 1907, cited by Dayton, *'Mid the Pines*, 68–69.
91 Isaac Ketler to The College Board of the Presbyterian Church in the United States of America, February 9, 1910; Ketler Correspondence Collection.
92 *Ninety-Fourth Annual Report of the Board of Education of the Presbyterian Church in the United States of America* (Philadelphia: Board of Education of the Presbyterian Church of the United States of America, 1913), 15.
93 William McEwan, *In Memoriam: Joseph Newton Pew and Isaac Conrad Ketler* (1917), 25 (first and quotations), 10 (third quotations).
94 McEwan, *In Memoriam*, 28–29 (first quotation), 36 (second quotation).
95 1914 *Ouija*, 3–4; quotation from 4.
96 W. M. Ramsay, *An Estimate of the Educational Work of Dr. Isaac Ketler* (London: Hodder and Stoughton, 1915), 22–23.
97 Ketler, *Adventure in Education*, 14, 19; quotations in that order.
98 Alva Calderwood, "Dedication Address," *Grove City College Bulletin*, September 1932, 8.
99 Isaac Ketler, "Address before the YMCA in Butler, PA, November 1888," Ketler Papers.
100 Ketler, "Problem of Life," 132.
101 *Catalogue of Grove City College, 1912–1913*, 37.
102 P. C. Kemeny, "The Ecumenical Evangelicalism of Isaac Ketler," *Journal of Presbyterian History* 102 (Spring/Summer 2024), 32. Kemeny's article helped shape my analysis of Ketler.
103 Ramsay, *Educational Work*, 25.
104 Dayton, *'Mid the Pines*, 81.

Alexander Ormond, Weir Ketler, and World War I, 1913–1920

1 Marietta Dietrich, "The History of Grove City College," MA thesis, University of Pittsburgh, 1933, 71.
2 "Dr. McEwan's Address," January 22, 1916, 3.
3 Trustee Minutes, October 10, 1913, 55.
4 *Grove City College Alumni Bulletin* (November 1913), 16 (first two quotations), 3 (third quotation) 12 (fourth, fifth, and sixth quotations), 4.
5 In 1915, however, the college's financial problems prompted the trustees to dismiss six professors, which saved Grove City $6,765

without negatively affecting the "high standard" of the college instruction (Trustee Minutes, July 3, 1915, 89).

6 *Grove City College Friends and Alumni Monthly*, December 1914.

7 Grove City College *Alumni Bulletin*, November 1913, 10.

8 *Catalogue of Grove City College, 1915–16*, 141–42.

9 *1915–1916 Catalogue*, 16, 71, 39.

10 Letter to the editor [hereinafter letter], November 27, 1915, 2.

11 *Greenville Angus Record*, March 13, 1914, 1; ibid., March 24, 1914, 1.

12 "The European War," December 5, 1914, 2.

13 *Alumni Monthly*, September 1914, 4.

14 *Alumni Monthly*, November 1914, 4.

15 *Alumni Monthly*, November 1914, 2–3.

16 "The New Paper," October 10, 1914, 2.

17 "Great Success in Bible Study," March 13, 1915, 2.

18 "Report of the Colleges," February 20, 1915, 2. A high percentage of students at other church-related schools surveyed also claimed to be Christians, but so did 95 percent of those attending at Penn State, whereas only 50 percent of students at Johns Hopkins and Penn professed to be Christians.

19 "Grove City Alumni Win Honors," May 8, 1915, 1.

20 "Grove City Defeats Geneva," April 10, 1915, 1.

21 "Successful Play," March 13, 1915, 5.

22 "The Third Degree," April 10, 1915, 3.

23 "Arabian Night," June 19, 1915, 2.

24 "Ice Proves Treacherous," March 6, 1915, 1.

25 "Narrow Escape," May 15, 1915, 2.

26 "Trip Ends in Accident," February 26, 1916, 1.

27 "With the Racquet," April 17, 1915, 1. See also "Girls' Tournament," May 22, 1915, 1.

28 "Students Serenade Dr. Ormond," May 1, 1915, 1.

29 "Campus Sing," April 17, 1915, 2.

30 "First Campus Sing," May 1, 1915, 1.

31 "Ouija Proves a Success," June 19, 1915, 5.

32 S. E. O. "The Honor System and Good Government," February 1914, 10.

33 "Student Government," May 22, 1915, 2.

34 "Plan for Student Government," May 15, 1915, 1.

35 "Self-Government Plan Defeated," June 5, 1915, 2.

36 "The Honor System," March 4, 1916, 3–4.

37 "An Honor System?" February 2, 1916, 1.

38 "President Ormond's Speech," October 2, 1915, 1.

39 "Former Stars Are Missing," October 7, 1916, 3.

40 "Grove City Defeats Invincible Allegheny," November 27, 1915, 1.

41 "President Ketler's Speech," March 4, 1916, 4.

42 "Dr. Ormond's Memory Honored," January 22, 1916, 1.

43 "Faculty Resolution," January 22, 1916, 3.

44 Trustee Minutes, January 18, 1916, 98. See the testimony of several of Ormond's classmates and students in the *Princeton Alumni Weekly*, as reprinted in *The Collegian*, February 6, 1916, 2–4.
45 "A True Steward of Faith," September 16, 1983, 4.
46 "Our New President," June 17, 1916, 1.
47 *Catalogue of Grove City College, 1916–1917*, 20, 6–8
48 President's Report to the Board of Trustees [hereinafter President's Report], June 1916, 3.
49 Trustee Minutes, January 18, 1916, 97.
50 Trustees Minutes, January 16, 1917, 121.
51 "Y.M.C.A. Made Part of the College," October 21, 1916, 5.
52 "Young Woman's Christian Association," September 30, 1916, 5.
53 "Y.M.C.A.," October 7, 1916, 4.
54 "An Appeal," January 29, 1916, 3.
55 "Dr. Naysmith Will Speak," February 19, 1916, 2; "Peace Movement Discussed," February 26, 1916, 1.
56 "Smoking Under the Ban," February 5, 1916, 1.
57 "On Hazing," October 14, 1916, 2.
58 "Initiation," September 30, 1916, 3.
59 "GCC Official Yells," October 7, 1916, 5.
60 "Hallowe'en Party," November 4, 1916, 1; "Left-Handed Party," October 21, 1916, 1, 4.
61 "Gymnasium Exhibition," April 1, 1916, 1.
62 March 1904.
63 "Mass Meetings," October 21, 1916, 3.
64 "Editorial," February 5, 1916, 2.
65 "Use the Gymnasium," November 4, 1916, 3.
66 "President Ketler's Speech," February 19, 1916, 2.
67 "Plan Proposed," February 19, 1916, 3.
68 "Ideals of Our College," October 14, 1916, 1.
69 "President Ketler's Speech," March 4, 1916, 4.
70 "Teams Chosen," February 12, 1916, 1; "Grove City Debaters Win," March 11, 1916, 1.
71 1916 *Ouija*, 61.
72 Trustee Minutes, January 16, 1917, 114.
73 "Military Training," January 6, 1917, 1.
74 "Physical Preparedness Against War," January 6, 1917, 3.
75 Trustee Minutes, January 16, 1917, 130.
76 "Military Training," April 21, 1917, 1.
77 "College Red Cross Organized," April 21, 1917, 2.
78 "Grand Concert Attracts Large Crowd," March 4, 1916, 1.
79 Minutes of the Faculty [hereinafter Faculty Minutes], March 6, 1917.
80 "Message from President Wilson," April 28, 1917, 1.
81 Trustee Minutes, January 16, 1917, 129, 132–33; President's Report, June 13, 1917, 1.

82 "Students Walk Out," October 30, 1917, 1; "Men Are Reinstated," November 3, 1917, 1.
83 "Interesting Campus Incident," October 29, 1941, 1. Another student stunt was bringing a cow to Carnegie Auditorium every year on Halloween eve.
84 E.g. "Faculty Attendance," October 13, 1916, 2.
85 President's Report, January 10, 1918, 1, 3.
86 Trustee Minutes, January 16, 1917, 130.
87 President's Report, June 13, 1917, 3.
88 "Music Department," February 17, 1917, 5.
89 "Poehlmann to Be Soloist," April 22, 1916, 1.
90 Dayton, *'Mid the Pines*, 106.
91 President's Report, June 11, 1918, 1, 6–7, 3–4; quotation from 6.
92 *Catalogue of Grove City College, 1918–19*, 91.
93 President's Report, January 21, 1919, 1, 3.
94 President's Report, June 10, 1919, 2.
95 Isabelle Blyholder, "The Girls," April 21, 1919, 2.
96 1919 *Ouija*, 34.
97 President's Report, January 21, 1919, 7.
98 President's Report, June 15, 1920; Schedule A: The Minimum and Efficient College, 4.
99 Tentative Report to the Trustees of the Committee on Plan and Program, 1920.
100 *New Castle News*, April 27, 1920. Determining which college made the first radio broadcast, historian Jennifer Waits argues, is very difficult, but Grove City College has a legitimate claim to being the pioneer. "Grove City College Radio: A Century 'on Air,'" GCC, https://www.gcc.edu/Home/Staff-Directory/Staff-Detail/grove-city-college-radio-a-century-on-air.

Devising and Implementing the Master Plan, 1921–1940

1 "Forty-Fourth Year Opens with Record Enrollment," October 8, 1923, 1.
2 President's Report, June 14, 1921, 2.
3 *Catalogue of Grove City College, 1920–1921*, 131.
4 President's Report, June 14, 1921, 4.
5 January 31, 1921, 6.
6 1922 *Ouija*, 4.
7 *Catalogue of Grove City College, 1922–1923*, 24 (quotation), 19.
8 Faculty Minutes, December 4, 1923.
9 Faculty Minutes, April 1, 1924; ibid., April 29, 1924.
10 President's Report, January 16, 1923, 7; ibid., June 13, 1923, 2.
11 *Grove City College Bulletin*, May 1923 Catalogue Supplement, 3–4.
12 "American Education Week," November 19, 1923, 2, 6.
13 "Join Some Activity," October 3, 1921, 2.
14 "Doris Dow Wins Contest," March 9, 1925, 2.
15 Trustee Minutes, June 5, 1924, 1.

16 1925 *Ouija*, 216.
17 President's Report, January 1925, 3.
18 President's Report, June 10, 1926, 6.
19 Don Thompson, "Sport Chatter," November 4, 1931, 2.
20 "Best Record," December 14, 1931, 7.
21 Faculty Minutes, April 6, 1926.
22 Frederick Rudolph, *The American College and University: A History* (New York: Knopf, 1962), 176–77.
23 President's Report, June 1928, 9–10.
24 President's Report, June 1928, 4; ibid., January 10, 1928, 2, 4; quotations in that order. In 1926–1927, Grove City replaced its trimester system with two semesters, a schedule it still follows.
25 *Catalogue of Grove City College, 1928–1929*, 18.
26 *1928–1929 Catalogue*, 40–45, 79; President's Report, June 11, 1929, 7.
27 *Catalogue of Grove City College, 1926–1927*, 29.
28 Freshman Rules Card, c. 1929, Archives.
29 President's Report, January 21, 1924.
30 "Tribunal Gives Sentences," November 19, 1930, 1.
31 Becky Koller and Marion Frack, "1926—Long Ago," October 30, 1946, 2.
32 "Ineligibility List," November 14, 1927, 3.
33 "Upperclassmen Declare War on Insubordinate Frosh," November 12, 1930, 1; "Appeal Is Made," ibid.; quotations in that order.
34 "What Is College?" October 1, 1930, 4.
35 "Poverty Day," October 15, 1930, 1, 7.
36 *Campus and Dormitory Customs and Standards Observed by Women Students of Grove City College*, c. 1929, Archives.
37 President's Report, December 1929, 1.
38 "Calamity," December 3, 1930, 4.
39 *Catalogue of Grove City College, 1931–1932*, 102, 104.
40 President's Report, January 1932, 11.
41 President's Report, June 1935, 10.
42 Faculty Minutes, October 24, 1939.
43 President's Report, January 1938, 12, 14; President's Report, June 1938, 8.
44 "P.S.E.A. Convention," October 12, 1932, 1.
45 J. B., "Why Professors Go Gray," October 20, 1930, 6.
46 President's Report, June 1939, 3–4.
47 President's Report, January 1935, 2.
48 "College Expansion Program Started," October 15, 1930, 5.
49 "Dedicatory Services," February 11, 1931, 7.
50 "Laying the Cornerstone," February 11, 1931, 4.
51 "Our Progress," October 7, 1931, 4 (all quotations); "Dedication Will Be Milestone," ibid., 1.
52 *Dedication Exercises of Harbison Chapel, The Hall of Science, [and] Frances St. Leger Babcock Memorial Organ*, October 8, 1931, 14.

53 Laura Hamilton, "MAP in Memorium [sic]," November 13, 2020, 5.
54 E.g., *Catalogue of Grove City College, 1935–1936*, 14, 16; quotations in that order.
55 "Oxford Convention," October 12, 1930, 1, 6; "Oxford Fellowship," October 12, 1932, 2.
56 "Y.M.C.A. Holds Conference Here," December 7, 1932, 1.
57 "Y.W.C.A.," October 21, 1931, 4.
58 "YMCA Conference a Huge Success," December 14, 1938, 1.
59 1938 *Ouija*, 132.
60 "Dr. Vale Leads Chapel Services," February 16, 1938, 1. On the other hand, Bob Kresge, '41, asked J. Stanley Harker in a June 28, 1958, letter if Grove City was "a Christian college in fact as well as in name? My experiences on campus from 1937 to 1941 gave me sizable doubts." Grove City College "did not make me soul-conscious." He gained little from the required Bible courses. He wanted to donate to "soul-serving agencies. Does Grove City College qualify?"
61 President's Report, December 14, 1936.
62 President's Report, June 1937, 12.
63 Trustee Minutes, June 14, 1938, 1.
64 "Easter," March 25, 1931, 4.
65 Paul Merkle, "Prayer Week," February 12, 1936, 2.
66 "Look and Live," May 3, 1939, 2; "The Cross and Crown," November 30, 1938, 1 (quotations).
67 "Cross and Crown," October 26, 1938, 6; ibid., November 16, 1938, 1 (quotation).
68 "So Different," February 28, 1940, 2.
69 President's Report, January 1932, 8.
70 "Shakespeare Discusses School Problems," March 21, 1934, 1.
71 "Sunday Chapel," December 14, 1938, 4.
72 "Courtesy in Daily Chapel," April 19, 1939, 4.
73 "One Advantage," March 6, 1940, 2.
74 E.g., "Students Take Chapel Roll of Faculty," October 31, 1934, 1–2.
75 See Neil Steinberg, *If At All Possible, Involve a Cow: The Book of College Pranks* (New York: St. Martin Press, 1992).
76 "Laissez Faire," October 30, 1935, 2.
77 "School Spirit," October 12, 1938, 4.
78 "Allegheny Visits Campus," October 26, 1938, 1, 6.
79 "Grovers Teach Vandals a Lesson," November 15, 1939, 2. A column in *The Collegian* titled "After Hours" detailed some of the Grover shenanigans in the late 1930s.
80 President's Report, June 1932, 7.
81 "Coach Amos Speaks," December 7, 1932, 1.
82 "Football Banquet Held," December 11, 1934, 1.
83 "President Ketler Attends Three Conventions," January 24, 1934, 1.
84 Don Thompson, "Sport Chatter," April 4, 1932, 3.

85 W. J. Elwood, "Chatter," November 6, 1935, 2.
86 Charles Bryan McHugh, "Today's Guest Writer," December 11, 1935, 4.
87 "Subsidized Sports?" March 25, 1936, 4.
88 President's Report, January 1932, 5; ibid., June 1932, 5, 6.
89 President's Report, June 1933, 2.
90 "Great Year of Intramural Sports," April 11, 1934, 3.
91 J. Floyd McClymonds, "Down the Sport Trail," *GC Herald-Reporter*, reprinted in *The Collegian*, November 3, 1937, 4.
92 "Should Grove City College Have Subsidized Athletics?" March 2, 1938, 3.
93 "Football Banquet Held," December 11, 1934, 1; "Vern Smith Voted Most Valuable Player," December 14, 1934, 1.
94 1932 *Ouija*, 239.
95 President's Report, January 18, 1927, 10.
96 "Honorary Baseball, Hockey Teams Chosen," January 14, 1931, 1.
97 "Posture Contest," February 11, 1931, 1.
98 President's Report, January 1934, 3.
99 "Anniversary Broadcast," April 27, 1938, 1, 6.
100 "Station WSAJ," November 17, 1937, 4.
101 "Our Forensics," February 16, 1925, 2.
102 1933 *Ouija*, 179.
103 "Who's Who in Grove City," January 8, 1935, 1–2; "Who's Who," April 3, 1935, 1.
104 Don Bashline, "Pet Campus Gripes," October 26, 1938, 4.
105 "Bingham Climaxes Musical Career," May 13, 1939, 4.
106 "Ad Absurdum," November 21, 1932, 2. See also "In a Rut," ibid.
107 "Are You Educated?" December 7, 1932, 2.
108 E.g., "Let's Waken Up," October 26, 1932, 1; "Lack of Student Patriotism," October 17, 1934, 1; Paul Smith, "Cheer Leading," January 22, 1936, 2; "Grover Spirit," February 17, 1937, 2; "Boost GCC," February 23, 1938, 4.
109 "Student Council Co-operation," October 3, 1934, 2.
110 "Chapel," April 27, 1938, 4.
111 "Use of Social Room," February 6, 1939, 4.
112 "Strictly Stag," February 22, 1939, 1.
113 "A Farewell," May 26, 1937, 6.
114 E.g., "Walk on Walks," March 29, 1939, 4.
115 "Student Assistants," October 13, 1937, 1.
116 "Dear Mr. Editor," October 20, 1937, 4.
117 "Assistants, Concluded," October 27, 1937, 4.
118 "Both Sides," February 8, 1938, 2.
119 "Honor System," February 22, 1939, 4.
120 "High Ranking is Given to College Commerce Dept.," December 16, 1936, 5.
121 "Pride Cometh Before a Spring," February 16, 1938, 4.
122 "Congratulations, Grove City," April 26, 1939, 4.

123 "Webster Minstrel Show," May 19, 1939, 1.
124 "Ouija Review Hailed as Epic," November 29, 1939, 1. This fee was not instituted until the late 1950s.
125 "In Retrospection," May 19, 1939, 4.
126 "For What?" November 3, 1937, 4. See also "A Bigger Navy," March 1, 1937, 4.
127 Bob Van Vleck, "Van Views the News," March 22, 1939, 6; "Arms Embargo," November 1, 1939, 4; "Civilization," November 8, 1939, 1–2; "Should the Arms Embargo Be Repealed?" September 27, 1939, 4–5; "Poll on Embargo Repeal," October 4, 1939, 1. In a survey, 219 students opposed repealing the arms embargo, while 215 supported it.
128 "Let Us Be Defenders," January 10, 1940, 2.
129 "Our Last Editorial," January 19, 1938, 4.
130 "New Collegian Staff," January 24, 1940, 1.
131 Judy Bernard, "Vox Pop," March 6, 1940, 2.
132 October 23, 1935, 4.
133 "Frosh Swing Out," October 12, 1938, 1.
134 "Freshmen Initiated," September 30, 1931, 8.
135 "Just a Frosh," January 30, 1930, 7.
136 "Freshmen Rules Enforced," November 9, 1932, 1.
137 "Student Council Urges Freshman Co-Operation," October 17, 1934, 1.
138 "Council Show White Feather," October 31, 1934, 2.
139 Jane Poffinberger, "Freshman Writes Impression," September 23, 1936, 5.
140 "To the Freshmen," September 29, 1937, 4.
141 "'Snap' Tribunal Held," October 5, 1938, 1.
142 "To the Freshmen," September 27, 1939, 4.
143 "Tribunal No Snap for Bad Freshmen," October 4, 1939, 1.
144 "Hell Week Tribulations," March 15, 1939, 1, 6.
145 "Sorority Rushing," December 6, 1939, 1.
146 "March of Time," March 5, 1941, 3.
147 "College Band," October 18, 1939, 4.
148 "Hoover Wins by Landslide," October 2, 1932, 1.
149 "Collegian Poll," October 14, 1936, 4.
150 "Landon Leads," October 28, 1936, 1.
151 "Willkie Favored 4–1," October 23, 1940, 1, 8.
152 J. Howard Pew, "The Fallacy of Economic Planning by Government," remarks at Princeton Theological Seminary, January 24, 1939. See also Pew, "Which Road to Take?" Institute of Public Affairs, July 12, 1935, Washington, DC; Pew, "What the Future Holds for the American System of Free Enterprise," an address to the 44th Congress of American Industry, December 6, 1939.
153 Lee Edwards, *Freedom's College: The History of Grove City College* (Washington, D.C.: Regnery, 2000), 179 (quotation), 180.
154 "Racial Discussions," December 14, 1931, 1.

155 "Something New and Different," March 6, 1940, 2.
156 *Grove City Reporter-Herald,* June 12, 1931.
157 "College Rating High," January 18, 1932, 1.
158 "G.C.C. Alumni Active in Law and Medicine," February 15, 1932, 2.
159 President's Report, June 1940, 11.

The Challenge of World War II, a Building Program, and the End of the Weir Ketler Presidency, 1941–1956

1 President's Report, December 8, 1947, 13 (quotation); ibid., December 13, 1948, 16.
2 J. Howard Pew, talk to GCC alumni, June 1932, Archives.
3 Edwards, *Freedom's College,* 114; John Brubaker, *Higher Education in Transition: History of American Colleges and Universities* (New York: Routledge, 2017), 230. See also Diane Ravitch, *The Troubled Crusade: American Education, 1945–1980* (New York: Basic Books, 1983), 15–17.
4 Remarks by J. Howard Pew at a Grove City College alumni luncheon, June 5, 1948, Archives.
5 Brubaker, *Higher Education,* 232.
6 Edwards, *Freedom's College,* 118.
7 Quoted in George Roche, "The Corruption of Education," *Imprimis* 20, no. 10 (October 1991), https://imprimis.hillsdale.edu/the-corruption-of-education-failing-colleges-political-correctness-and-federal-funding/.
8 President's Report, June 6, 1947, 8.
9 President's Report, June 5, 1953, 12.
10 E.g., Jack Kennedy, "God Bless America," September 25, 1940, 8; "The Middle Class," January 8, 1941, 2.
11 E.g. "All Shall Make a Sacrifice," April 1, 1941, 1.
12 "Bundles for Britain," January 8, 1941; "Prayers for Peace," November 26, 1941, 2.
13 President's Report, June 9, 1942, 1.
14 Nicholas Peterson, "If You Ask an Old Man to Reminisce," April 29, 2000, 2.
15 Mary Love, "December 7, 1941," *Wolf Pack,* 1942, 38.
16 "Dr. Ketler's Chapel Message," December 10, 1941, 1; "Reactions to the Outbreak of War," ibid., 2.
17 "Ketler Urges Students to Study," September 23, 1942, 1.
18 *Grove City College Bulletin,* January 23, 1942, 4.
19 "No Time to Lag," November 18, 1942, 2.
20 "Army Reserve to Leave," February 10, 1943, 1.
21 "Navy Program Is in Operation," *Grove City College Bulletin,* April 1942, 1; Faculty Minutes, December 15, 1942.
22 President's Report, December 14, 1942. On the Civilian Pilot Training Program, see Jane Gardiner Birch, *They Flew Proud* (2007).
23 Sennholz, *First Eighty Years,* 50.
24 President's Report, December 6, 1943, 3.

25 "Navy Shows Liking for College," April 7, 1943. See also: "Air Corps Impressions," March 17, 1943, 1.
26 "Our Attitude in War," March 25, 1942, 2.
27 "Should We Have Peace?" December 2, 1942, 2.
28 Edwards, *Freedom's College*, 181–82.
29 J. Howard Pew to Weir Ketler, June 23, 1944, J. Howard Pew Papers, Hagley Museum and Library, Wilmington, Delaware.
30 "Smith Sees Heavy Action," December 9, 1942, 1, 3.
31 "Alumni Write Vivid Letters," February 24, 1943, 1.
32 "Carry On," May 5, 1945, 2; *Grove City Bulletin*, May 1945, 1.
33 President's Report, December 11, 1944, 1.
34 "Sunday Night Thought," February 8, 1945, 2.
35 "Good Bye," April 12, 1945, 2; "Servicemen Give Impressions," April 12, 1945, 2.
36 "Truman's VE Day Address," May 10, 1945, 1.
37 President's Report, May 18, 1945, 1, 3, 5, 7–9, 12–13; quotation from 3.
38 "U.S. Navy Awards College Plaque," October 30, 1947, 1.
39 President's Report, December 17, 1945, 14.
40 President's Report, December 16, 1946, 15.
41 President's Report, June 14, 1946, 1, 3 (quotation), 4.
42 President's Report, December 8, 1947; Calvin Lee, *The Campus Scene, 1900–1970* (New York: David McKay, 1970), 77.
43 Trustee Minutes, June 3, 1955, 504.
44 The college accepted 325 of nine hundred applicants for fall 1947 freshman class. See President's Report, June 6, 1947, 5.
45 "A Few Pointers," October 30, 1940, 2.
46 "Dean Says Students Lack Originality," November 13, 1940, 3.
47 President's Report, December 16, 1946, 2.
48 January 20, 1949, 1.
49 "'Ten Percenters' Reach Land of Promise," October 19, 1949, 1.
50 President's Report, December 14, 1949, 9.
51 Gene Jordan, "Hi Freshmen!" November 2, 1955, 2.
52 President's Report, June 3, 1949, 7.
53 E.g., "Toujours Gai," March 11, 1948, 2.
54 Trustee Minutes, December 8, 1947, 369.
55 "New Gymnasium Is Second Heaven," April 28, 1949, 3.
56 President's Report, June 3, 1949, 10.
57 Trustee Minutes, June 3, 1949, 404.
58 *Grove City College Bulletin*, December 1953, 1.
59 An Evaluation Report, submitted by the Commission on Higher Institutions, Middle States Association of College and Secondary Schools, February 1957, 6.
60 Marsden, *Soul*, 394–98, 412–16.
61 *Grove City College Bulletin*, April 1950, 6.
62 "Humbert Leaves G.C. Impressed," March 10, 1949, 2.
63 "BeJabers," February 15, 1950, 2.

64 "Spiritual Emphasis Week Well Received," February 22, 1950, 1,
65 Ray Felz, "Puppy Love," February 26, 1948.
66 E.g., "George Junior Republic," October 21, 1942, 3.
67 Trustee Minutes, June 3, 1949, 394.
68 President's Report, June 8, 1951, 2.
69 Weir Ketler, "A Greeting," October 4, 1945, 1.
70 John McMillan, letter, November 7, 2003, 2.
71 "A Tribute," November 13, 1940, 2.
72 "Easter," March 16, 1951, 2.
73 "The World Can Start Over Again," May 9, 1951, 2.
74 Nelson Craig, "A College Student Views the News," January 18, 1955, 2.
75 Dave Prince, "Spiritual Emphasis," February 21, 1954, 2.
76 Marsden, *Soul*, 3.
77 "Chapel Courtesy," October 28, 1942, 2.
78 "Warning Wasn't Enough," May 2, 1946, 2, 5. Cf. "How Do You Behave?" October 9, 1946, 2.
79 "Collegian in the Middle," December 10, 1951, 2.
80 "Seventy Times Seven," October 12, 1954, 2 (quotations); "Let's Change Seats," May 13, 1954, 2.
81 "Co-Ed School?" November 9, 1954, 2.
82 E.g., "Faculty Interest in Chapel Service," April 22, 1942, 2.
83 President's Report, December 8, 1947, 9.
84 President's Report, June 6, 1947, 11.
85 Trustee Minutes, June 4, 1954, 484; Trustee Minutes, June 3, 1955, 505.
86 "Student-Faculty Day," May 21, 1941, 1 (quotation); "Faculty and Students Vie for Honors," May 28, 1941, 1.
87 "Play Day," May 10, 1945, 1.
88 "Two Profs Tie for First Place Honors," February 27, 1952, 1.
89 "Most Dating Girl Will Receive Prize," March 6, 1947, 1.
90 E.g., "Attempted Raid on Girls Dorm Fails," May 28, 1955, 1.
91 "Diet Tables," October 30, 1940, 1.
92 February 15, 1950, 1.
93 October 29, 1941, 1.
94 "Skits and Sketches," February 19, 1941, 2.
95 E.g., "Editorially Speaking," March 12, 1952, 2; "GCC Spirit on Way Back," ibid., October 12, 1954, 1.
96 "School Spirit," October 7, 1942, 1.
97 "Booster Club," October 1, 1941, 1.
98 "Editorially Speaking," May 12, 1943, 2.
99 "Honor System Introduced," February 15, 1945, 1; "Honor System," ibid., 2. See also "Success Depends on Student Body," March 22, 1945, 1.
100 "What Value Honesty?" December 11, 1946, 2.
101 "You're on Your Honor," May 2, 1956, 2.
102 Merle Porter, "Food Pinch," May 25, 1946, 1.

103 "Editorially Speaking," April 11, 1946, 2, 5.
104 Bill Weil, "Tepee Talk," February 24, 1949, 2.
105 "Check Communism," May 2, 1951, 1, 4.
106 "Students Back Crusade," October 11, 1950, 1.
107 "Frosh Rules Enumerated," October 7, 1948, 1.
108 "Frosh Comply with Traditions Crackdown," October 7, 1949, 1.
109 "The Foolegian," April 1, 1945, 1.
110 E.g., Sunny Colwell, May 9, 1946, 2.
111 "They Deserve Credit," November 13, 1946, 2.
112 Faculty Minutes, June 5, 1952.
113 Lee, *Campus Scene*, 86.
114 "Letter to ROTC," October 12, 1954, 3.
115 "Grover Beat," October 13, 1951, 2.
116 "Let's Be Realistic," November 2, 1951, 2.
117 "Time Magazine Analyzes Modern American Youth," November 17, 1951, 4.
118 "Disillusioned with Co-Eds?" January 19, 1952, 1.
119 E.g., "Editorially Speaking," March 26, 1952, 2; Jonathan Ladd, letter, April 23, 1952, 2.
120 E.g., "WGB Gripes Poll," March 11, 1953, 1; "WGB List," ibid., March 25, 1953, 6.
121 "Activities Fund Petitions," March 16, 1954, 1.
122 Thomas Ream, letter, November 23, 1954, 3 (quotation), 6.
123 "Thanksgiving," November 23, 1954, 2.
124 "In Retrospect," January 15, 1941, 2; "Power of the Press," April 7, 1949, 2: "Knock on Wood," October 23, 1954, 2.
125 Gus Welty, "Grover Best," December 10, 1951, 2.
126 "Gone But Not Forgotten," May 28, 1955, 2.
127 "Appreciation," December 18, 1940, 2.
128 "Crushing Attack of the Grove City Debating Squad," January 17, 1951, 1.
129 President's Report, June 3, 1949, 5.
130 Trustee Minutes, June 9, 1950.
131 "Talk by Noted Athlete Well Received," October 29, 1941, 1.
132 "March of Time," March 5, 1941, 3.
133 "Fraternity Programs," March 4, 1942, 2. See also "Editorial," April 22, 1953, 2.
134 "Flattery Turns to Jeers," March 18, 1948, 1.
135 "Hell Week," April 12, 1945, 2.
136 "Friends to the End," March 16, 1955, 2.
137 "Fraternities Rush; Sororities Crush," March 8, 1950, 1.
138 March 22, 1950, 1.
139 "Frats Abandon Fate to Power of Administration," May 13, 1948, 1, 3 (quotation).
140 December 10, 1948, 1.
141 "Pan Hell Meet," February 25, 1951, 1.
142 "Hell Week Gets New Treatment," February 27, 1952, 1.

143 There were 106 fraternity bids in 1952, 136 in 1954, and 126 in 1955, 108 sorority bids in 1955, and a combined 245 Greek bids in 1956.
144 "Football Over the Years," October 20, 1951, 3.
145 Dan Angeloni, "Sports Staccatos," May 19, 1949, 3.
146 President's Report, December 7, 1951, 13.
147 "Education or Athletes?" October 26, 1954, 2. Cf. Gus Welty, "Sink or Swim—or Subsidize," November 15, 1950, 3; "What's Wrong with Our Team?" November 17, 1951, 3.
148 "Placement Record Best in Twelve Years," October 1941, 4.
149 "Teachers Placed," September 20, 1942, 1.
150 "Hoyt Speaks," October 12, 1954, 3.
151 *Grove City College Bulletin*, September 1932, 10.
152 J. Howard Pew, remarks upon the retirement of Weir C. Ketler, June 9, 1956, GCC Archives.
153 Trustee Minutes, June 7, 1957, 532.
154 Trustee Minutes, June 7, 1957, 532 (all quotations), 533.
155 "Ketler Submits Resignation," February 22, 1956, 4.
156 "College Mourns Death of Dr. Weir C. Ketler," January 22, 1988, 1.
157 Trustee Minutes, January 27, 1956, 509–10.
158 Pew, retirement of Weir C. Ketler, 5.

The Harker Years: Strengthening the Academic Program and a Drift Toward Secularization, 1956–1971

1 1923 *Ouija*, 41.
2 Lee Edwards, *Freedom's College: The History of Grove City* (Washington, D.C.: Regnery Publishing Company, 2000), 132.
3 "Harkers Arouse New Spirit," October 3, 1956, 1.
4 Rose Imig, "Ever Heard of School Spirit?" October 3, 1956, 2 (first and third quotations); Imig, "A Most Auspicious Occasion," November 7, 1956, 2, 3 (second and fourth quotations).
5 President's Report to the Board of Trustees, November 8, 1956, 4–13.
6 Rich Weinstein, "Have You Met?" December 8, 1959, 3.
7 A Self-Evaluation Submitted to the Commission on the Higher Education, Middle States Association of Colleges and Secondary Schools, December 1959, 7.
8 President's Report, October 30, 1961, 3.
9 President's Report, June 7, 1963; President's Report, June 5, 1964, 3.
10 J. Stanley Harker [hereinafter JSH] to Herbert Brockway, May 14, 1968, GCC Archives (all letters).
11 President's Report, October 30, 1961, 4.
12 Wayne Gregg, "Unique Negro Problem," October 29, 1969, 3.
13 "Middle States Submits Evaluation," May 13, 1970, 1.
14 "New Girl's Dorm," May 19, 1971, 6.

15 "An Evaluation Report, Submitted by the Commission on Higher Institutions, Middle States Association of College and Secondary Schools," February 1957, 4 (quotation), 5–7, 16, 22–24, 42.
16 See Bob Luckock, "Economics and Life," March 29, 1960, 2.
17 President's Report, November 2, 1959, 10; "Course Offerings," *Alumni News*, March 1958, 4.
18 Grove City College, A Self-Evaluation Report Submitted to the Commission on Higher Education of the Middle States Association of Colleges and Secondary Schools, December 1959, 36, 49, 65, 66; quotations in that order.
19 Confidential Report for Grove City College of an Evaluation Conducted by The Middle States Association of College and Secondary Schools, February 21–24, 1960, 1.
20 JSH to Chandler McMillan, February 10, 1961.
21 JSH to Mrs. George Stafford, April 27, 1960.
22 Trustee Minutes, June 1960, 578.
23 JSH to Chandler McMillan, February 10, 1961.
24 Stephen Taaffe, "Firing Larry Gara," Grove City College, Due Process, and Institutional Autonomy," in Roger Geisler, ed., *Shaping the American Faculty* (New York: Routledge, 2017), 113.
25 Taaffe, "Larry Gara," 123.
26 "Campus Controversy Crystallized," March 23, 1962, 2.
27 See Taaffe, "Larry Gara," 127.
28 Larry Gara, "Surviving Attacks on Academic Freedom," *Academe Magazine*, September-October 2017, https://www.aaup.org/article/surviving-attacks-academic-freedom.
29 Taaffe, "Larry Gara,"114.
30 Gara claimed that Pew ordered Harker to fire him, that the college hired two detectives to investigate him, and that Harker told false stories to discredit him. Gara argued that "the AAUP's thorough investigation revealed no wrongdoing or incompetent teaching on my part" (Gara, letter to the editor, *The Collegian*, May 19, 1961, 2). Taaffe confirms these points and discusses the detectives' activities ("Larry Gara," 120–21).
31 Trustee Minutes, June 8, 1962, 601a.
32 JSH to Howard Warner, September 16, 1963.
33 Taaffe, "Larry Gara," 127.
34 JSH to Scott McCormick Jr., April 8, 1963.
35 JSH to William Benjamin Pratt, October 31, 1963.
36 Taaffe, "Larry Gara," 17.
37 JSH to William Benjamin Pratt, October 31, 1963.
38 Trustee Minutes, November 24, 1964, 3.
39 Report of the Instruction Committee to the Board of Trustee, June 4, 1965.
40 "Academic Freedom," November 5, 1957, 2.
41 Ann Lewis, "Intellectual Freedom," February 17, 1961, 2.
42 Daryl Dean, letter, December 1, 1961, 2.

43 Judy Shaffer, "Once There Was an Individual," February 14, 1964, 2; Lyle Bainbridge, "Incompetent Professors," May 8, 1964, 2; Bainbridge, letter, May 15, 1964, 2. Cf. Grace Ferguson, letter, November 4, 1966, 2; "Editorial," March 10, 1967, 2.
44 Richard Jewell, "The Long Road," January 6, 1967, 2.
45 JSH to Harold Dodds, November 2, 1965.
46 Dodds to Albert Hopeman, November 11, 1965.
47 Tate DeWeese, "New Student Role," February 23, 1968, 2.
48 "Dissatisfaction with the Calendar," May 17, 1968, 3.
49 "Student Government Discusses 5-Day Week," April 23, 1969, 3.
50 Georgetta Smick, "Five-Day Week," October 29, 1969, 2.
51 "AAC Drops Investigation," March 4, 1970, 3.
52 Report to the Faculty, Administration Trustees of Grove City College by an Evaluation Team Representing the Committee on Higher Education of the Middle States Association, November 1970, 32.
53 1970 Middle States Report, 33.
54 Alan Mesches, "Middle States Survey," April 15, 1970, 1.
55 Grove City College Report to the Middle States Association, September 1, 1970, 35–36.
56 Becky Beinlich, "GCC Grad Tells Keys to Her Success," May 2, 1992, 5.
57 "Bull Session," May 19, 1971, 4.
58 "Dialogue with a Dean," February 24, 1967, 2.
59 JSH to Anita Gritzmacher, October 20, 1966.
60 "Dialogue," 2.
61 Scott, phone interview with the author, July 8, 2024.
62 Christian Smith, *Soul Searching: The Religious and Spiritual Lives of American Teenagers* (New York: Oxford University Press, 2005). Smith delineated its main principles as God created, structured, and watches over the world; God expects people to be good, considerate, and just; the primary purpose of life is to achieve happiness and develop positive self-esteem; and people connect with God principally to help them solve problems.
63 JSH to Thruston Morton, August 2, 1960.
64 "Nixon Takes Election," November 11, 1960, 1, 3.
65 JSH to Leonard Read, September 29, 1964.
66 JSH to M. J. French, July 22, 1963.
67 Dayton, *'Mid the Pines*, 28.
68 Doug Anderson, "Choice '68 Results," May 2, 1968, 5.
69 *The Collegian* editor in chief Lori Bolz defended bringing Welch to campus. In contrast to the college's numerous more liberal speakers, Welch would argue for reducing government intervention in political, economic, and social life, increasing individual responsibility, stopping the spread of communism ("Hear Robert Wetch," March 11, 1970, 2).

70 Marilyn Wolfe, "Feminist's Talk," February 24, 1971, 6; "Ti-Grace Disappoints Audience," February 24, 1971, 2.
71 "Baird Reviews Abortion," May 5, 1971, 2.
72 Marilyn Wolfe, "Bill Baird Stresses Need for Legal Abortion," May 5, 1971, 3.
73 J. Aubele, letter, May 12, 1971, 3.
74 Mesches, "Balance Speakers Program," October 29, 1969, 2.
75 JSH to Peter Firth, August 18, 1959.
76 JSH to Karl Hess, editor, *World*, June 30, 1962.
77 JSH to K. P. A. Taylor, October 17, 1962.
78 JSH to Herbert Brockway, May 14, 1968.
79 Trustee Minutes, November 5, 1962, 624.
80 "The President Speaks," February 17, 1959, 4.
81 "Northway Mall," April 22, 1966, 1–2.
82 "The College Student and His Future," May 17, 1968, 6, 9. See also "Placement Program," April 22, 1966, 6, 8.
83 "Placement Program Recap," May 17, 1968, 6.
84 The YMCA disbanded in 1958 and the YMCA in 1962. Most other religious groups that met during these years—the Newman Club, the Wesley Fellowship, the Canterbury Club (Episcopal), the College Fellowship (Presbyterian), and the Lutheran Student Association—had dwindling attendance after 1964, and by 1970 only the Newman Club was still meeting.
85 Marianne Grace, "Morning Chapel," November 11, 1958, 2, 4.
86 "Christ in Christmas," December 10, 1957, 2.
87 Ellen Egbert, "George Junior," October 28, 1960, 2.
88 JSH to Fred Foy, October 7, 1960.
89 James Allen Nash, letter, March 22, 1960, 2.
90 Carl Hull, "Religion in Life Week in Retrospect," February 24, 1961, 3, 6 (quotation).
91 JSH to Lloyd Brown, November 1, 1961.
92 David McCalmont, "Religion on Campus," October 11, 1963, 3.
93 Michael Worman, "The Easy Way Out," November 22, 1963, 2.
94 Anonymous, letter, November 2, 1962, 2.
95 "Chapel Facts and Figures," May 3, 1963, 4.
96 Dick Connors, letter, March 15, 1963, 3.
97 Robert Dent, letter, March 15, 1963, 2: Cf. Peter Monsma, "Required Chapel Defended," October 25, 1968, 1–2.
98 David George, "On Compulsory Chapel," November 20, 1964, 3, 7.
99 Richard Conolly, letter, May 7, 1965, 2.
100 Jud Dolphin, letter, February 10, 1967, 2.
101 JSH to Charles M. Adams, September 20, 1965 (quotation); JSH to John Arthur Visser, September 18, 1965.
102 JSH to Carl Henry, February 28, 1967.
103 JSH, "The Small College Speaks Up," December 8, 1967, 4, 9.
104 "Group Acts to Change Chapel," February 19, 1969, 1.

105 Bill Jarrell, letter, February 19, 1969, 2.
106 Brad Scott, "Lazy Religion Requires Change," February 19, 1969, 3.
107 Mesches, "Chapel Not to Be Abolished," February 26, 1969, 2.
108 Scott, "What About Chapel?" March 1, 1969, 3, 7.
109 "Chapel Survey Reveals Student Dissatisfaction," April 30, 1969, 3.
110 Scott to JSH, May 20, 1969.
111 Trustee Minutes, June 5, 1970, 2.
112 E.g., Mesches, "Welcome Reverend Heinsohn," November 5, 1969, 2.
113 Mesches, "Rev. Heinsohn Please Stay," May 13, 1970, 2.
114 1970 Middle States Report, 13.
115 Trustee Minutes, November 9, 1970, 4.
116 Wayne Gregg, "Rose Enjoys Freedom, Feeling of Achievement," March 10, 1971, 5.
117 Letters, November 11, 1970, 2; December 2, 1970, 2.
118 "Guest to Speak Tonight," May 19, 1971, 1.
119 Bob Scott, July 16, 2024, email.
120 Daryl Davis, July 16, 2024, email.
121 Ralph Pontier, July 16, 2024, email.
122 "Religion Grows on Campus," January 13, 1971, 2; "Christian Groups Present Diverse Programs," January 13, 1971, 3; Tom McWhertor, "Involved Christians Reach Out," April 30, 1971, 9.
123 "Harkers Arouse New Spirit," 1.
124 John Werren, "In Retrospect," May 15, 1957, 2.
125 "Our Principles of Honor," May 1, 1957, 1.
126 E.g., "Can We Do It?" March 8, 1960, 2.
127 "Second Monthly Wash," March 29, 1960, 2.
128 Letter, March 15, 1963, 2.
129 "Honor System Poll," September 20, 1963, 2–3.
130 "Greek Co-Eds Adopt Honor Code," November 9, 1963, 1.
131 "Honor System," February 14, 1964, 2; "Vote on Honor System Approaching," ibid., 1.
132 Clarence Carson, "The Honor System and the American System," February 21, 1964, 1.
133 "Honor System Defeated," March 6, 1964, 1.
134 Anonymous, letter, May 15, 1958, 2.
135 Jim White, letter, March 10, 1961, 3.
136 Pat Kurzewski, "Discontent of G.C.C.," May 5, 1959, 2; "Escape from Reality," ibid., 4.
137 "Editorial," December 14, 1962, 2.
138 JSH to Charles G. Benham, March 8, 1963.
139 E.g., Mary Troup, letter, March 23, 1962, 2.
140 "College Concern Over the Cuba Issues," October 26, 1962, 2.
141 "Students Mourn President," December 6, 1963, 1.
142 Al Doerr, letter, March 25, 1966, 2.
143 "Editorial," October 23, 1964, 2.

144 "Editorial," April 22, 1966, 2.
145 John Reitinger to JSH, December 30, 1966.
146 "Devoted to Seniors," May 19, 1959, 2.
147 "Editorial," October 25, 1963, 2.
148 "Evaluation of a Tradition," January 6, 1967, 6.
149 Bill Rundorff, "Five-Day Party," May 7, 1969, 2.
150 Lori Bolz, "OB Improves Program," September 30, 1970, 2.
151 "Thoughts on Orientation—1967," March 10, 1967, 2.
152 Evan Adair, "Expectations of a Freshman," October 11, 1968, 3.
153 "Editorial," January 19, 1968, 2.
154 "Poll Results Revealed," September 30, 1966, 1.
155 Letter, November 1, 1968, 2.
156 L. Wayne Fox, Grove City College News, May 28, 1968. A representative letter is that of Jack Boelens, a pastor in Orchard Park, New York, to JSH, May 21, 1968.
157 Dave Kelly, "Kelly's Column," WIIC TV, May 27, 1968.
158 Peggy Matzie, "Curfews," February 26, 1969, 3.
159 "Poll on Women's Rules," May 16, 1969, 4.
160 "JUDO Board Urges Thought, Cooperation," December 9, 1970, 10.
161 1970 Middle States Report, 23.
162 Dick Jewell and John Sparks, "Teach-In on Vietnam Question," November 19, 1965, 2.
163 "Editors Consider Viet Nam," April 22, 1966, 7.
164 "Opinions of Vietnam," September 29, 1967, 2–3.
165 "Profs Speak Out on Vietnam," December 1, 1967, 3.
166 Jim Brown, "Grove City Honors Fallen Hero," *Warren Tribune Chronicle*, October 1968.
167 Paul Pavlick, "Moratorium Day," October 22, 1969, 6.
168 Mesches, "Violence Still Lingers," May 13, 1970, 2; Rick Wolfe, letter, ibid.
169 "Group Surveys 'GCC Normalcy,'" November 4, 1970, 4.
170 "Committee of 13," November 8, 1968, 1.
171 Larry Griswold, "Where the Action Is," September 28, 1968, 2.
172 Trustee Minutes, June 6, 1969, 1.
173 Tate DeWeese, "Character Reference from the Devil," October 4, 1968, 3.
174 "Editorial," December 7, 1962, 2.
175 "Editorial," February 11, 1966, 2.
176 Bill Nutt, "Editorial," December 9, 1966, 2. Cf. Donald Steighner, "Games Grovers Play," February 10, 1967, 2.
177 "Kring Comments on Students," March 4, 1970, 2.
178 "Middle States Submits Evaluation," May 13, 1970, 1.
179 "Student, Faculty Expression Lacks Board Representation," April 30, 1971, 4.
180 Rob Macomber, "Open House Boosts Student Interaction," March 3, 1971, 2.
181 "On Co-ed Dining," November 17, 1967, 2.

182 "Dean Smith Attended Drug Conference," May 6, 1970, 3.
183 Steighner, "Please Don't Smoke the Grass," November 3, 1967, 2.
184 "On the Use of Drugs," November 3, 1967, 3.
185 E.g., Evan Adair, "Nationwide, Campuswide Drug Problem Discussed," November 5, 1969, 3; Mesches, "Drug Problem Strikes Middle Class Suburbs," March 4, 1970, 2.
186 "Organizations Need Willing Leaders, Active Participants," May 12, 1971, 2.
187 "Random Middle States Survey Analyzed," April 15, 1970, 1.
188 "Mrs. Puffin," November 3, 1967, 1.
189 Neil Bittenbender, "Talent Show," April 22, 1966, 1.
190 "Mary, Mary,'" April 28, 1967, 1.
191 Letter to Harker, April 24, 1964, 2.
192 "In This Corner," May 22, 1957, 4.
193 JSH to Al Abrams, *Pittsburgh Post-Gazette* sportswriter, May 29, 1961.
194 "Athletic Recruiting Demands Much Effort from Crimson Coaches," April 10, 1964, 5.
195 "1964–65 Banner Year," October 8, 1965, 8.
196 Lyle Mook, "Sports Corner," September 24, 1965, 6.
197 "Cagers Crush Titans," December 10, 1965, 4.
198 JSH to Donald Schmidt, September 26, 1966.
199 "Swimmers Prep for Rough Sailing," February 10, 1967, 6.
200 JSH to George Towle, November 24, 1967.
201 "Zeigler's Performance Unexcelled," December 8, 1967, 5.
202 Dave Simpson, "Basketball Practice," November 10, 1967, 3.
203 "A Champion Determines Life," February 23, 1968, 3.
204 Dave Simpson, "Sportsman of the Year," May 17, 1968, 7.
205 Trustee Minutes, June 7, 1968, 2.
206 Paul Pavlick, "Longnecker's Success," October 8, 1969, 4.
207 John Kelly, "Time Out," March 19, 1969, 4.
208 "GCC Booters Win," November 5, 1969, 5.
209 "Grades, Finances Hamper Recruiting," March 4, 1970, 4.
210 Wayne Bissell, "Coach's Philosophy," March 24, 1971, 6.
211 "Broadcast Celebrates 50 Years," April 22, 1970, 4.
212 Letter, May 6, 1970, 2.
213 "National Fraternities?" March 23, 1962, 2.
214 April 21, 1959, 2.
215 "Criticism of Policy," April 5, 1960, 2.
216 JSH to Ralph Leighty, March 18, 1961.
217 "Editorial Opinion," April 10, 1964, 2.
218 Gary Brook, "Give Us a Break," March 5, 1969, 2.
219 John Frankel, letter, March 25, 1966, 2.
220 James Hanushek, letter, January 13, 1967, 2.
221 Nancy Jaques, "A Scar Marring Campus," May 16, 1969, 5.
222 Letter, November 22, 1968, 6.
223 Wayne Gregg, "Fraternities Need Change," March 11, 1970, 1, 4.

224 "IF Ignores Power," March 31, 1971, 2.
225 Dick Conners, Adels president, letter, March 6, 1964, 2; anonymous, letter, March 13, 1964, 2,4; John Venneman, '69, letter, February 10, 1967, 2.
226 "Frats Must Enlarge Scope," December 9, 1970, 2.
227 JSH to Kenneth Hanushek, January 11, 1969.
228 Dave Thayer, "ROTC Change Possible," March 26, 1969, 2.
229 "Smokey Enjoys Grove City," November 12, 1969, 4.
230 "Harker's Dedication Brings Vast Improvements," May 12, 1971, 2.; see also "Harker Retires After 15 Years of Service," April 30, 1971, 7.
231 Dayton, *'Mid the Pines*, 239.
232 "A Tribute to President and Mrs. Harker upon Their Retirement from Grove City College," May 24, 1971, GCC Archives.
233 "Board Names MacKenzie to Top College Post," April 21, 1971, 1 (quotation); Trustee Minutes, April 16, 1971, 4.
234 *Grove City Reporter-Herald*, June 15, 1971, 11.
235 Trustee Minutes, June 4, 1971, 117.
236 Taaffe, "Larry Gara," 121. See also Frederick S. Kring, *One Day in the Life of Dean Fred: Autobiography or Legend* (New Wilmington, PA: Globe Printing, 1988), 39.
237 J. Howard Pew, "Remarks on Parents' Day," May 1, 1971.

The Presidency of Charles S. MacKenzie: Reversing Course and Restoring the Mission, 1971–1991

1 See William Ringenberg, *The Christian College: A History of Protestant Higher Education in America* (Grand Rapids: Christian University Press, 1984); George Marsden and Bradley Longfield, eds., *The Secularization of the Academy* (New York: Oxford University Press, 1992); George Marsden, *The Soul of the American University* (New York: Oxford University Press, 1994); James *Burtchaell, The Dying of the Light: The Disengagement of Colleges and Universities from Their Christian Churches* (Grand Rapids: Eerdmans, 1998).
2 Trustee Minutes, April 16, 1971, 1, 2 (quotation).
3 "The Grove City College Oral History Project: The Reminiscences of Charles S. MacKenzie," interviewed by Joel Gardner, 2000, [hereinafter "Oral History"], 2, Archives.
4 "Oral History," 12, 13 (first and second quotations); Charles S. MacKenzie, "Reminiscences of the Hopeman-MacKenzie Era at Grove City College (1971–1991)" (1992), 5 (third quotation), Archives. Ironically, as the board's president from 1930 to 1971, Pew had presided over the college's drift toward secularization.
5 See George Marsden, *The Outrageous Idea of Christian Scholarship* (New York: Oxford University Press, 1997); Arthur *Holmes, The Idea of a Christian College* (Grand Rapids: Eerdmans, 1999); Douglas Jacobsen and Rhonda Jacobsen, *Scholarship and Christian Faith: Enlarging the Conversation* (New York: Oxford University Press, 2004).

6 George Marsden, "The Soul of the American University," in Marsden and Longfield, eds. *Secularization of the Academy*, 5.
7 Marsden, *Soul*, 340. See also Merrimon Cuninggim, *The College Seeks Religion* (New Haven, CT: Yale University Press, 1948), 250.
8 Marsden *Soul*, 22.
9 *Burtchaell, Dying of the Light, 823–29;* James Arthur, *Faith and Secularization in Religious Colleges and Universities* (New York: Routledge, 2006); 134 (quotation).
10 Robert Wood Lynn, "The Survival of Recognizably Protestant Colleges: Reflections on Old-Line Protestantism, 1950–1990," in *Secularization of the Academy*, ed. Marsden and Longfield, 173–74 (quotation 173).
11 Merrimon Cuninggim, *The Protestant Stake in Higher Education* (Washington, D.C.: Council of Protestant Colleges and Universities 1961), 10–12, 17 quotation).
12 Marsden, *Soul*, 415. See also Christopher Jencks and David Riesman, *The Academic Revolution* (Chicago: University of Chicago Press, 1968), 327, 332.
13 Richard Hutcheson Jr., "Are Church-Related Colleges also Christian Colleges?" *Christian Century* 105 (1988), 839.
14 Marsden, *Soul*, 430 (quotation); Douglas Sloan, *Mainline Protestantism and Twentieth-Century American Higher Education* (Philadelphia: Westminster Press, 1994).
15 Jencks and Riesman, *Academic Revolution*, 322.
16 Larry Lyon, Michael Beaty, and Stephanie Mixon, "Making Sense of a 'Religious' University: Faculty Adaptations and Opinions at Brigham Young, Baylor, Notre Dame, and Boston College," *Review of Religious Research* 43 (2002), 332.
17 Marsden, *Soul*, 33.
18 See, for example, Marsden, "The Decade Ahead in Scholarship," *Religion and American Culture* 3 (Winter 1993), 9–15.
19 Perry Glanzer, "Why We Should Discard "the Integration of Faith and Learning": Rearticulating the Mission of the Christian Scholar," *Journal of Education and Christian Belief* 12, no. 1 (2008), 41.
20 Ken Badley, "The Faith/Learning Integration Movement in Christian Higher Education: Slogan or Substance?" *Journal of Research on Christian Education* 3, no. 1 (1994), 31.
21 Badley, *"Clarifying 'Faith-Learning Integration': Essentially Contested Concepts and the Concept-Conception Distinction," Journal of Education and Christian Belief 13 no. 1 (*2009), 11.
22 Beers and Beers, "Integration of Faith and Learning," 68–69.
23 Bradley *Longfield and George Marsden, "Presbyterian Colleges in Twentieth-Century America," in The Pluralistic Vision: Presbyterians and Mainstream Protestant Education and Leadership, ed. Milton Coalter, John Mulder, and Louis Weeks (Louisville: Westminster John Knox Press, 1991), 239.*

24 "'Concerned Christian' Opposes 'Secular Route,'" March 14, 1972, 2.
25 Gary Smith, letter, November 16, 1971, 2, 4.
26 MacKenzie, "Reminiscences," 4.
27 President's Report on the State of the College [hereinafter President's Report], November 15, 1971, 1, Archives
28 "MacKenzie Enthusiastic, Goals Stress Excellence," September 28, 1971, 1. Cf. "MacKenzie Calls for 'New Vision,'" September 19, 1972, 4.
29 President's Report, November 1972, 1 (first quotation); ibid., November 15, 1971, 1 (remainder of the quotations).
30 President's Report November 1972, 1, Archives.
31 President's Report, May 18, 1973, 2, Archives.
32 MacKenzie, "Reminiscences," 12, 6; quotations in that order.
33 MacKenzie, "Reminiscences," 37.
34 MacKenzie, "Reminiscences," 6, 11 (quotation).
35 MacKenzie, "Reminiscences," 15 (quotation), 16; "Oral History," 59–60.
36 Charles MacKenzie, "Is GCC Fulfilling Its Role as a Liberal Arts College?" February 15, 1972, 4.
37 "Curriculum Revision," February 29, 1972, 1.
38 President's Report, May 1974, 4 (first two quotations), 10 (last two quotations).
39 "Oral History," 60–67; quotation from 67.
40 "New Curriculum Merits Support," February 12, 1973, 2.
41 Ken Heffner, "Christian Alternative to Humanism," September 25, 1973, 5; George Yates, "Christ-Believers Should Unite," May 2, 1974, 3.
42 "Oral History," 117.
43 President's Report, May 1974, 2 (first and third quotations), 9 (second and fourth quotations).
44 President's Report, May 1978, 1.
45 President's Report, November 1979, 1 (first three quotations), Appendix A (remainder of quotations).
46 MacKenzie, "Crawford's Corner," April 30, 1982, 3.
47 Floyd Getz, letter, April 30, 1982, 3.
48 President's Report, May 1986, 13.
49 "The Purpose and Identity of Grove City College," Appendix 4, President's Report, November 15, 1988, Archives.
50 MacKenzie to R. Heath Larry, April 18, 1989, Archives.
51 President's Report, May 1990, 6.
52 Report to the Trustees, Administration, Faculty, Students of Grove City College . . . by an Evaluation Team representing the Commission on Higher Education of the Middle States Association of Colleges and Schools (April 1990), 9, 56, 18, 45; quotations in that order.
53 Marsden, *Soul*, 33.

54 "A Statement of the Association of Presbyterian Colleges and Universities," March 25, 1990, 2, 5, 6.
55 "G.C.C. 60th Out of 60?" October 26, 1979, 1.
56 "College Finances," November 13, 1973, 1.
57 "Admission Policies," December 13, 1973, 6.
58 "Disagree in Love," September 19, 1980, 2.
59 "Ketler, Thorn Honored," October 17, 1975, 1.
60 "As We See It," January 23, 1976, 2; Paton, letter, February 6, 1976, 5.
61 Letter, October 12, 1971, 2.
62 Sue Soloman, "Academic Environment," December 5, 1972, 4.
63 "Five-Day Week," December 7, 1971, 2.
64 "Is GCC Fulfilling Its Role?" February 15, 1972, 4.
65 Greg Chronister, "Academic Evaluation," April 10, 1972, 6.
66 "Upperclassmen Felt Programmed for College," February 15, 1972, 7.
67 "In Loco Parentis Overused," May 5, 1972, 2.
68 E.g., Patricia Cofiell, letter, May 5, 1972, 2, 8.
69 "Communication Gap," April 10, 1972, 1.
70 E.g., "Faculty Profile," February 22, 1972, 5.
71 "Bull Session Examines Gripes," December 13, 1971, 7.
72 "Faculty Attitude Justifies Optimism," January 18, 1972, 1.
73 "AAC Launches Faculty Evaluation," September 25, 1973, 1.
74 Robb Jones, "Core Curriculum," October 24, 1972, 1; "Faculty, Students Endorse Core," February 13, 1973, 3 (quotations in that order).
75 "Faculty, Students Endorse Core," 3.
76 "Core Curriculum Proposal," April 18, 1972, 7.
77 "Academics and the Christian Perspective," December 13, 1973, 6
78 MacKenzie, "Sounding Board," February 12, 1974, 2.
79 Dave Voltz, "Groesbeck Aims for a Wide Spectrum," March 5, 1974, 2.
80 Ken Warren, "Why I Am Resigning," March 26, 1974, 2.
81 MacKenzie's comment, March 26, 1974, 2.
82 Linda Petruzzl, "Keystone Objectives," October 3, 1974, 4.
83 "Key Courses Rated," September 3, 1976, 1.
84 William Snyder, "Buhl Library," September 17, 1976, 2.
85 "Book Circulation," October 14, 1977, 1.
86 "As We See It," October 8, 1976, 4.
87 Gordon Gamble, "Pass-Fail Gym," February 4, 1977, 3; "Academic Inconsistency," April 15, 1983, 2.
88 "Saturday Classes," February 4, 1977, 5.
89 "As We See It," April 22, 1977, 4.
90 "Survey and Commentary," April 11, 1980, 6.
91 "Middle States Evaluation: Part One," September 26, 1980, 5.
92 "Middle States Evaluation: Part Three," October 11, 1980, 3.
93 "Middle States Evaluation: Part One," 5.

94 "Middle States Evaluation: Part Two," October 3, 1980, 4.
95 "Middle States Evaluation: Part Five," October 24, 1980, 5.
96 "Crawford's Corner," April 30, 1982, 2.
97 "1984 in 1985?" October 25, 1985, 2. Cf. Lisa Lesklw, "Grover Syndrome," December 5, 1986, 2.
98 Hopeman, trustee-faculty luncheon, May 15, 1987.
99 "Leadership in Academic Ranks," *Grove City College Alumni News*, March 1988, 1.
100 Janice Zinsner, "New Curriculum Changes," January 26, 1990, 1.
101 Hopeman, trustee-faculty luncheon, May 14, 1988.
102 "College Lauded in Accreditation Report," September 7, 1990, 3.
103 Charles MacKenzie, "Reminiscences," 35.
104 Brian Leftow, email to the author, July 29, 2024.
105 "Chapel Convocation," January 30, 1976, 1.
106 For a fuller description of the case, see Hugh Davis Graham, "The Storm Over Grove City College: Civil Rights Regulation, Higher Education, and the Reagan Administration," *History of Education Quarterly* 39 (1998), 407–29 and Edwards, *Freedom's College*, 195–226.
107 As quoted by Edwards, *Freedom's College*, 196.
108 MacKenzie, notes on Grove City College's opposition to the HEW compliance form, circa 1980, Archives.
109 MacKenzie, "Will Government Secularize Christian Colleges?" April 1978, Archives
110 Julie Furber, "Government Intrusion—Will It Ever Stop?" September 29, 1978, 1.
111 Hopeman to David Lascell, September 4, 1979, David Lascell Papers, Rochester, New York.
112 Hopeman, trustee-faculty luncheon, May 18, 1979.
113 Hopeman, trustee-faculty luncheon, May 18, 1984.
114 David Moss, "Cameo," April 28, 1979, 2.
115 Tom Michaelian, "GCC v. HEW," April 28, 1979, 3.
116 "Update: G.C.C. v. HEW," November 16, 1979, 1.
117 Decision of the United States District Court—Western District of PA—March 10, 1980, in *Grove City v. Patricia R. Harris*, 17; "GCC Wins 'Landmark Decision' Over HEW," March 14, 1980, 3.
118 "Education: Sundae Punch," *TIME*, March 24, 1980, https://time.com/archive/6855765/education-sundae-punch/.
119 "Looters Must Learn," February 6, 1981, 2.
120 "HEW Update," April 18, 1980, 1.
121 William Miller, "A Little School Against the Big Bureaucracy," *Reader's Digest*, August 1980, 3.
122 "Education Official Defends Reversal of Anti-Bias Rule," *St. Louis Globe-Democrat*, May 20, 1982.
123 Petition for a Writ of Certiorari to the United States Court of Appeals for the Third Circuit, *Grove City College v. T. H. Bell*, November 9, 1982, 5. See also Cheryl Fields, "Even Colleges That

Get Only Indirect Aid Must Obey U.S. Bias Laws," *Chronicle of Higher Education*, September 1, 1982, 1.
124 Garet Romeo, "GCC Vows to Appeal Ruling," September 10, 1982, 1.
125 Curtis Sitomer, "College Asks High Court to Halt Government Meddling," *Christian Science Monitor*, January 28, 1983.
126 Kathy Gardner, "Civil Rights," September 9, 1983, 1.
127 Brief for the Petitioners, *Grove City College v. T. H. Bell*, June 7, 1983, 7, 12.
128 Transcript of Oral Argument, November 29, 1983, *Grove City College v. T.H. Bell*, 3. See also MacKenzie, "Why Grove City College Won't Take the Pledge," *Wall Street Journal*, December 14, 1983.
129 "Students, Administration Stand United," December 9, 1983, 4.
130 *Grove City College v. Terrel Bell, Secretary of Education*, in *The United States Law Week*, February 28, 1984, Supreme Court Opinions, 7.
131 "President Testifies in D.C.," September 20, 1985, 1.
132 "A Letter from the President," March 25, 1988, 1.
133 "Forty Years Ago, Supreme Court Case Changed GCC Forever," GCC, February 26, 2024.
134 Email to the author.
135 "Open House, Chapel Get Board Approval," November 9, 1971, 1.
136 "Is GCC Fulfilling Its Role?" February 15, 1972, 4.
137 "Chapel Argument," February 29, 1972, 6.
138 "Administration Evades Issue of Required Religion," May 16, 1972, 2.
139 Trisha Cofiell, "College Restrictions," September 25, 1973, 5.
140 Sally Gupton. "Dudley Leaves," September 18, 1973, 1.
141 Michael Jensen, "Religion Editor Speaks Out," September 18, 1981, 4.
142 Rue Hayes, "One Further Point," October 30, 1973, 5; Peiffer, "Godly Faith," May 2, 1981, 2.
143 Reed Davis, "Man Does Not Live by Bread Alone," December 4, 1973, 5; Jenny Korn, "New Vision of Christianity," February 12, 1974, 3; Pete de Blecourt, "Morality Must Reign," May 2, 1981, 2.
144 Ken Heffner, "About Community," April 2, 1974, 9; Yates, "Christ-Believers Should Unite," 3.
145 Leftow, "Christian Gentleman," May 2, 1974, 4.
146 Email to the author.
147 Leftow, "Retrospect," January 31, 1974, 5.
148 Email to the author.
149 "As We See It," February 27, 1975, 4.
150 "WSAJ Accuses Collegian of Perpetuating Distrust," March 13, 1975, 3.
151 See, for example, "Coalition According to Daryl," September 21, 1979, 2.
152 Chip Mander, "George Junior," November 14, 1972, 4–5.
153 "Easter," March 21, 1980, 3.

154 Lori Truxal, "Pannell's Visit," October 11, 1980, 9.
155 "Morledge Appointed," September 7, 1984, 1.
156 Jenni Moser, "Faith and Life Week," September 14, 1984, 1.
157 Courtney Smith, "Class of '75 Survey," October 11, 1980, 9.
158 MacKenzie, "Down with Information Screens," October 19, 1971, 2.
159 "Student Government President Surveys Year," September 21, 1971, 1.
160 Email to the author, July 29, 2024.
161 Ken Roos, letter, February 22, 1980, 2.
162 Mander, "As We See It," September 18, 1973, 4; Robb Jones, "Collegian's Role," September 17, 1974, 4.
163 "Let's Win One," December 7, 1984, 2.
164 "False Witness," May 16, 1972, 5.
165 "Glad You Asked," September 25, 1973, 2.
166 "As We See It," October 2, 1973, 4.
167 "Ottaviano Reviews Year," May 23, 1972, 4.
168 "Women's Rules Stifle Growth," February 29, 1972, 2.
169 "Grove City Builds Girls," April 2, 1973, 2.
170 Editorial, October 11, 1973, 6.
171 "We're Adults," February 28, 1973, 2.
172 Letter, October 22, 1974, 2.
173 "A Cynical View," November 6, 1973, 5.
174 "Catalog Raises Questions About College Philosophy," September 25, 1973, 4.
175 "Telling It Like It Is," October 30, 1973, 4.
176 Mander interview with MacKenzie, October 11, 1973, 8, 10 (quotations).
177 "Salute to the Gedunk," November 13, 1973, 4.
178 Greg Chronister, "Juniors Speak Out," January 31, 1974, 1.
179 "SGA Progress," January 31, 1974, 2.
180 "Student Controversies," April 9, 1974, 4.
181 "Co-Ed Dining Policy," November 22, 1971, 1.
182 February 12, 1974, 2.
183 "Lower Drinking Age," October 10, 1972, 2.
184 Rob Macomber, letter, October 10, 1972, 2.
185 "Balanced Ratio," February 28, 1974, 4.
186 "Frosh Hours," February 28, 1974, 1.
187 Terry Lyons, "New Discipline Committee," September 17, 1974, 1.
188 "Crimson Regulations," September 17, 1974, 2.
189 Don Dotterer, "Community Campus Relationship," November 12, 1974, 3.
190 "AWS-MGB Survey," May 9, 1975, 3; "SGA Survey," October 17, 1975, 3.
191 "Happiness Is GCC," January 30, 1975, 6.
192 Courtney Smith, "Class of '75 Survey," October 11, 1980, 9.
193 "Regulations for Off-Campus," September 28, 1971, 2.
194 Mike Bucci, "Off-Campus Housing," December 10, 1976, 8.

195 "As We See It," February 25, 1977, 4.
196 Sam Mullin, "Eulogy of Sorts," December 8, 1978, 5.
197 "Middle States Questionnaire Results," May 4, 1979, 2.
198 "Bursting the Bubble," October 20, 1979, 2.
199 Ann Brody and Diana Marks, "Students Get a Chance to Express Views," October 12, 1979, 1.
200 "Crawford's Corner," October 12, 1979, 3.
201 "Middle States Evaluation: Part Two," 4.
202 Griff Surowka, "Off-Campus Surveyed," September 25, 1981, 3.
203 Michael Jensen, "Off-Campus Conflict," October 2, 1981, 2.
204 Griff Surowka, "Off-Campus Conflict," October 9, 1981, 1.
205 "Crawford's Corner," April 23, 1982, 2.
206 Lori Dodge, "The Bridge," April 30, 1982, 4.
207 "Crawford Responds," October 12, 1984, 3.
208 "Intervis Question," November 30, 1984, 3.
209 "Head Resident Releases Research," May 3, 1985, 3.
210 "Unity Rally," March 14, 1986, 1; "Statement of Goals and Concerns," ibid., 2.
211 1986 *Bridge*, 123.
212 "Change Requires Effort," September 28, 1971, 2.
213 Letter, September 28, 1971, 2.
214 "Supreme Court Invades Moral Realm," March 27, 1973, 2.
215 Letter, April 10, 1973, 2.
216 "He Knew Us Before All Time," October 23, 1973, 2.
217 Sally Gupton, "Adoption," October 23, 1973, 3.
218 E.g. Michael Coulter, "Life Advocates Respond," September 18, 1989, 2.
219 "An Insecure Left," March 20, 1981, 2.
220 "Vote for the Wimp," October 23, 1987, 4.
221 Lee Miller, "GCC Students Choose," November 4, 1988, 1.
222 Letters, November 16, 1971, 2, 4.
223 Letter, October 12, 1984, 2.
224 Peter Johnson, letter, November 2, 1971, 2; Jim Steadman, letter, November 9, 1971, 2; Bill Calder, letter, February 17, 1978, 2; Dave Durham, "Pledging?" ibid., 4.
225 Bob Montgomery and Tim Jamison, letter, March 12, 1982, 3. Cf. Michael Montanile, letter, ibid.
226 "A Defense," October 5, 1984, 2.
227 Leftow, "Silly Season," March 5, 1974, 5. Cf. Jenni Moser, "Pledging," October 14, 1983, 2–3.
228 Henry Pearce, "Leftow Misses the Point," March 26, 1974, 3.
229 Jim Ambrose, "Pledging," February 15, 1972, 5. See also three letters, April 25, 1972, 3–4.
230 Paula Wray and Robb Jones, "Greek Pledging Revised," February 28, 1974, 1, 3.
231 Dave Huffman, "Fraternities," October 20, 1979, 5.

232 Mike Kelly, "Housing Group or Frat?" February 13, 1987, 2, 7; Monte Moser, Gary Martini, and Niles Laughner, letters, February 20, 1987, 2–3.
233 Bruce Damasio, "Swimmers Finish Well," December 13, 1973, 8.
234 Bruce McClymonds, "Of Cabbages and Kings," November 5, 1976, 7.
235 Ida Alleman, "They Call Her the Best," December 10, 1982, 5.
236 Alleman, "Basketball Phenomenon," February 11, 1983, 4.
237 Editorial, April 27, 1973, 8.
238 "Sporting Chants," February 28, 1974, 8.
239 "MacKenzie Shares Impressions," September 28, 1971, 4.
240 Dave Longstreet, "Trustees Encouraged by Visit," October 31, 1972, 1.
241 Mark Ketterer, "Presidential Paternalism," December 13, 1973, 5.
242 Danette Dean, "Furber Reflects," December 7, 1979, 5.
243 Chris Klicka, "Who Really Cares?" October 23, 1981, 2.
244 "President Celebrates Fifteenth Year," December 5, 1986, 5.
245 L. John Van Til, "'Mid the Pines," December 13, 1973, 2.
246 MacKenzie, "J. Howard Pew," in *An Uncommon Man—J. Howard Pew* (Grove City, PA: Grove City College, 1982), 49.
247 Greg Chronister, "John Howard Pew," December 7, 1971, 4.
248 "Chapel Focuses on Pew," January 29, 1982, 5; *The Collegian* does not clarify which speakers used which terms.
249 Albert Hopeman, Jr., trustee-faculty luncheon, June 1972, Archives.
250 "Combee Named Sixth Grove City College President," Grove City College News release, April 17, 1991.
251 Kelly Erickson, "Professors Salute MacKenzie," April 26, 1991, 6.
252 MacKenzie, "Reminiscences," 35.
253 Jewell, interview by Joel Gardner, July 14, 1999, Grove City College Oral History Project.

Jerry Combee, Garth Runion, and John Moore: "We Are Ready to Attain National Leadership in Christian Higher Education," 1991–2003

1 President's Report, May 1992, 2.
2 President's Report, November 1992, 2.
3 "Nothing More. . . Nothing Less," September 13, 1991, 6.
4 "Rise with Me to This Challenge," May 2, 1992, 1.
5 "Combee's Opening Speech," September 10, 1993, 4.
6 Executive Committee meeting of the Board of Trustees, September 23, 1991, 1.
7 Executive Committee meeting, November 19, 1993, 39–40.
8 Phone interview with John Moore, March 14, 2025.
9 1997 *The Bridge*, 2.
10 Matt Summers, "GCC Stands Strong," April 25, 1997, 1–2.
11 1997 *The Bridge*, 195.

12 Trustee Minutes, May 16, 1997, 1.
13 Report to the Faculty, Administration, Trustees, Students of Grove City College by an Evaluation Team Representing the Commission on Higher Education of Middle States Association of Colleges and Universities, April 1998, 4, 23, 24 (quotation).
14 Interview with Moore.
15 1998 Middle States Report, 4 (quotations), 6.
16 Lynzi Godlove, "Class of 2002 Speaks," October 23, 1998, 3.
17 1998 Middle States Report, 31.
18 Matthew Divelbiss, "Breaking Ground," September 29, 2000, 4; Meghan Price, "HAL Christened into the Kingdom," January 31, 2003, 1; quotations in that order.
19 Jenn Kunn, "Faculty Voice Praise," January 31, 2003, 7.
20 Grove City College Middle States 1990 Self-Study, 37.
21 Janice Zinsner, "Curriculum Changes," January 26, 1990, 1.
22 President's Report, May 1992, 22.
23 President's Report, November 1992, 8.
24 "GCC Silences the Critics," September 11, 1992, 2.
25 President's Report, May 1992, 11.
26 "Computers for All," *Allied News*, September 14, 1994.
27 President's Report, May 1995, 10.
28 Matthew Summers, "Student Concerns," April 26, 1996, 3.
29 "Board Does Away with Saturdays," December 10, 1999, 1.
30 Cited in the Grove City College Periodic Review Report, May 2003, 49.
31 1998 Middle States Report, 1 (first and second quotations), 8, 11 (third quotation).
32 E.g., Colleen Keating, "Seat on the Fence," October 8, 1999, 3; Angela Moore, letter, February 8, 2002, 3 (quotation).
33 Adrian Monza, "Attendance Policy," March 16, 2001, 3.
34 "Common Beliefs," November 15, 1996, 4.
35 "Running the Gauntlet," May 3, 2003, 5.
36 1998 Middle States Report, 22. The 1998 self-study reported that most faculty wanted to be more involved in the college's decision-making processes and desired better communication among faculty, administrators, and trustees (95).
37 Meghan Price, "Morledge Set to Retire," October 15, 1999, 4.
38 Megan Evans, "Morledge Will Be Missed," October 15, 1999, 14.
39 Leigh Anne Metz, "Dr. Stanley Keehlwetter," February 23, 2001, 6.
40 Email to the author, March 24, 2022.
41 "Nothing Less Than the Best," May 4, 1996, 8.
42 "Mr. R. Jack Behringer," *Alumni News*, Spring/Summer 1996, 21.
43 "Coach Walters Bids Farewell," May 2, 1998, 1–2.
44 "Dr. Ross A. Foster," April 29, 2000, 4.
45 See, for example, Martin Anderson, "What! Me Teach?" *Wall Street Journal*, September 8, 1992, A16,
46 President's Report, November 1992, 3.

47 Interview with Moore.
48 Megan Opdyke, "GCC Prof Gains World-wide Recognition," April 29, 1995, 12.
49 Lorraine Krall, "Sennholz Inaugurates Lecture Hall," February 7, 2003, 3.
50 "OB Hits the Road," September 8, 1995, 5.
51 Lisa Fabian, "Misrepresentations of the College," October 31, 1997, 3.
52 Fred Moon, letter, September 1, 2000, 3.
53 1998 Middle States Report, 18. On the other hand, 54 percent of students surveyed for the 1998 Self Study said that college policies were too strict, rigid, restrictive, and punitive, 65.
54 "Suggestions of a Departing Senior," April 27, 2001, 3. Cf. Michael Foust, "Freedom at Grove City College?" April 26, 2002, 2.
55 "Praising the Administration," May 5, 2001, 2.
56 "SGA Student Survey," December 7, 2001, 5.
57 Megan Standish, "Day of Infamy," September 14, 2001, 1 (quotation), 6.
58 Sean Ammirati, letter, September 21, 2001, 3; Nicholas Turner, '05, letter, September 28, 2001, 3.
59 Mathew Divelbiss, "Making History," November 3, 2000, 1, 6 (quotation).
60 President's Report, May 1993.
61 *Catalog of Grove City College, 2000–2001*, 21.
62 Rebecca Coffin and David Coleman, "Students Mull Challenges Posed by Campolo," September 18, 1998, 4.
63 Jennifer Gouker, "Warriors Continue to Grow," October 2, 1992, 1.
64 Valerie Frey, "New Life," February 16, 1996, 5.
65 Kristie Morgan, "New Life," October 11, 2002, 4.
66 Catrin Hughes, "GCC Students to Reach Out," March 1994, 1.
67 Anne Hartman, Bethany Dean, and Katy Marshall, "ICO Trip," April 27, 2001, 7.
68 Martha Cohen, "Homeless in Toronto," May 5, 2001, 17.
69 "May We Burn," May 2, 2003, 13.
70 Valerie Sands, "Spiritual Haven," September 14, 2001, 5.
71 President's Report, May 1992, 39.
72 Amy Clingensmith, "Strength in Unity," December 1, 1995, 1–2.
73 Matt Summers, "Returning to Brotherhood," February 16, 1996, 4.
74 Jillian Brosius, "It's All Greek to Me," November 9, 2001, 8.
75 Jill Slaby, letter, October 4, 2002, 2.
76 Noah Huss, "Musical Says Successfully 'I Can!'" December 5, 1997, 8.
77 Stephen Bond, "California, Here We Come!" March 16, 2001, 6.
78 "Cancer Survivor to Perform," November 2, 2001, 1, 4.
79 Jacob Smith, "Running the Quad," November 3, 2000, 3.
80 Matt Scheff, "Professors Break the Mold," October 4, 2002, 4.
81 Jim Allen, "Bal's 40–4 Mark," April 30, 1994, 16.

82 "$7 Million Campaign," July 30, 1992, Executive Committee Report, September 21, 1992, 11.
83 Matthew Divelbiss, "Making History," November 3, 2000, 1, 6 (quotation).
84 See "No Longer the 'Best Kept Secret,'" *Grove City College Alumni Magazine*, Spring/Summer 1993, 7.
85 Lindsay Oram, "GCC Gets Deserved Recognition," April 11, 1997, 1–2.
86 1998 Middle States Report, 16.
87 President's Report, May 2000, 10–11.
88 Karin Hawkins, "High Marks," November 8, 1991, 1.
89 President's Report, May 1995, 15.
90 President's Report, May 1998, 1.
91 Alumni Relations Office, November 19, 1999.
92 1998 Middle States Report, 23.
93 Trustee Minutes, November 19, 1999, 3.
94 MacKenzie, "Reminiscences," 42.
95 Trustee Minutes, May 16, 2003, 1–2.
96 Interview with Moore.
97 Trustee Minutes, May 16, 2003, Appendix D.
98 1998 Middle States Report, 34.
99 Rachel Leonard, "Dr. Moore Is Retiring," January 31, 2003, 1.

The Presidency of Richard G. Jewell: A "Revolutionary Institution in Higher Education," 2003–2014

1 Phone interview with Richard Jewell, March 20, 2025.
2 Zoe Sandvig, "Dr. Jewell Then and Now," October 17, 2003, 8.
3 Brandon Carper, "Meet the New Boss," August 29, 2003, 4, 1 (quotation).
4 Interview with Jewell.
5 Interview with Jewell.
6 Virginia Larsen, "Wednesday Afternoons with Dr. Jewell," October 14, 2005, 13.
7 Leah Acker, Strategic Plan Released,", September 9, 2005, 1. The 2011–2016 strategic plan included these same eight goals and added a ninth: devise a "marketing program to support the strategies and mission of the college." It retained the vision statement from the 2005–2010 plan: "To be one of America's premier liberal arts, science and engineering colleges, where scholarship combines with Christian principles."
8 Trustee Minutes, November 14, 2003, 3.
9 Jack Freeman, "Grove City College: A Strategic Assessment," May 5, 2004, 3.
10 Freeman, "Strategic Assessment," 4 (first and second quotations), 5, 36 (third quotation), 6 (fourth quotation), 65 (fifth quotation).
11 Freeman, "Strategic Assessment," 28, 3–4, 31, 5–6, 8, 42, 49.
12 Freeman, "Strategic Assessment," 9.

13 Team Report to Faculty, Administrators, Trustees and Students of Grove City College by an Evaluation Team Representing the Middle States Commission on Higher Education, April 2008, 6.
14 President's Report, May 15, 2009, 6.
15 Mariah Syre, "$4 Million Gift," February 1, 2013, 1.
16 R. Thomas Williamson, Grove City College Framework for Strategic Planning, 1 (first quotation), 4 (second quotation), 6 (third quotation), 7, 9.
17 Josh Evans, "Steps Toward Diversity," January 31, 2014, 3.
18 Lauren Schade, "White Like Me," March 11, 2005, 12.
19 2008 Middle States Report, 4.
20 Acker, "Retro Hangout," October 7, 2005, 16.
21 Matt Sitman, "Defying the Zeitgeist," August 29, 2003, 2.
22 Melinda Haring, "An Oasis in a Liberal Desert," September 5, 2003, 2.
23 Freeman, "Strategic Assessment," 33–34.
24 Grove City College Comprehensive Self Study Prepared for the Commission on Higher Education of the Association of Colleges and Schools, April 2008, 10.
25 2008 Comprehensive Self Study, 9–10, 70, 86.
26 Grove City College Periodic Review Report, May 2003, 15.
27 Barbara Scheffler, "Educators Get Good Grades," March 19, 2004, 1.
28 Marie Tyler, "Study Abroad," October 1, 2004, 1.
29 Acker, "Jewell Details Change, Commitment," September 2, 2005, 1 (quotation), 5.
30 Freeman, "Strategic Assessment," 43–44.
31 Acker, "Jewell Details," 1.
32 Sharon Fuhrey, "VP Brings New Life," September 3, 2004, 1.
33 President's Report, May 1993.
34 Amanda Muetzel "Grant Connects Faith and Science," April 15, 2005, 5.
35 Nicky Lipartito, "Integrity Discussions," December 7, 2007, 5.
36 Kristie Eshelman, "Grove City College: Chile Style," September 7, 2012, 1.
37 Timothy Lagoy, "Rigorous Academics' No Joke," December 6, 2013, 2.
38 Ryan Biese, "'Pesky' HUMAs Have a Purpose," November 9, 2007, 13.
39 2008 Self Study, 97.
40 Jake Einwechter, "Before You Criticize," September 28, 2012, 11.
41 Meagan VanTil, "Are We All Masochists?" February 7, 2014, 9.
42 "Losing a Legend," August 31, 2007, 7.
43 2008 Middle State Report, 17.
44 2008 Self Study, 64.
45 Sarah Fuhrey, "College Counselor Snubbed," March 11, 2005, 1.
46 Nicky Lipartito, "Students Rate Professors," November 2, 2007, 1.
47 2008 Self Study, 61.

48 Freeman, "Strategic Assessment," 44.
49 2008 Middle States Report, 16.
50 Megan Smith, "Mentor Groups," September 19, 2003, 10.
51 Megan Kincaid, "Students React to the SAC," September 24, 2004, 5.
52 "SGA Votes to Open Quad," September 23, 2005, 1; statement of SGA president Matt George.
53 Ryan Rutt, letter, December 9, 2005, 17.
54 Megan Kincaid, "Apartments Announced," December 9, 2005, 1, 4.
55 Trustee Minutes, November 21, 2008, 5.
56 President's Report, May 2011, 29.
57 Anna Tracey, "Gay-Straight Alliance," January 28, 2011, 1.
58 Trustee Minutes, November 19, 2004, 4; Trustee Minutes, May 2013, 38.
59 Louis Petolicchio, "Alumni Letter Provokes Debate," November 15, 2013, 1.
60 Email from Chris Wetzel, March 22, 2025.
61 "No Longer an Insult," March 21, 2014, 10. See also Jenne Mante, "Turn It Off, Groverachievers," February 21, 2014, 3.
62 Paige Polesnak, "Why It's Good to Be a Grover," September 24, 2010, 10.
63 Allison Postma, "Life Advocates Speak," October 8, 2004, 12.
64 Marie Tyler, "Speech and Debate Team Alters Competition Style," December 8, 2006, 6.
65 Laura Levai, "Speech and Debate Team Wins," February 2, 2007, 1, 2 (quotation).
66 Zoe Sandvig, "Prof File: Betsy Craig," December 12, 2003, 8.
67 Megan Stehle, "Entertaining Old and Young," March 26, 2004, 9.
68 Natalie Bradley, "Greek Life Grows," February 11, 2005, 1.
69 Letter, February 3, 2006, 18.
70 President's Report, November 2007, 12.
71 President's Report, May 2008, 17.
72 Ben Spead, "Walking the Road to Rhodes," October 5, 2007, 5.
73 Deep Springs International, https://deepspringsinternational.org/.
74 Hannah Abbott, "Students and Faculty React," October 6, 2006, 4.
75 Neil Manzullo, "Bush Victorious," November 5, 2004, 1.
76 "Change the World," October 8, 2004, 18.
77 Freeman, "Strategic Assessment," 46.
78 Freeman, "Strategic Assessment," 34.
79 2008 Self Study, 9–10.
80 May 15, 2009, Memorandum in President's Report, May 2009, 6–8; quotation from 8.
81 George Archibald, "George Jr. Gets Results," *The Washington Times*, in *The Collegian*, October 8, 2004, 4.
82 E.g., Christopher Lee, "Hahn Confuses the Issues," April 30, 2005, 23–24.
83 "Are We Walking the Talk?" September 2, 2011, 11.

84 "Diploma: A Ticket to Serve," May 5, 2012, 14.
85 Jewell, "Presidential Farewell," May 3, 2014, 12.
86 Darin Miller, "PAC Championships Galore," November 4, 2005, 20.
87 Mallory Skarupa, "Universal Game, Uniting Force," September 14, 2007, 16.
88 Zach Fletcher, "Roberts Wins 500th Game," October 8, 2004, 23.
89 Ian Mikrut, "Roberts to Retire After 29 Seasons," October 4, 2013, 16.
90 Oak Moser, "Hearing Impairment Is No Obstacle for Moose," March 19, 2004, 16.
91 Derek Long, "ICO on the Hardcourt," January 30, 2004, 16.
92 Chris Rich, "Football Coach Sets Career Record," October 16, 2009, 17.
93 Alexandra Omicioli, "DiDonato Connects Faith, Football," November 13, 2009, 16.
94 Josh Hoey, "Football Finds Holiday Spirit," February 17, 2006, 14.
95 *Pittsburgh Business Times*, October 7, 2005.
96 GCC Academic Program Committee Spring 2004 Report, Trustee Minutes.
97 Soren Kreider, "94 Percent of Grads Find a Job," February 24, 2012, 1.
98 Josh Evans, "On the Hunt," October 5, 2012, 1.
99 Trustee Minutes, May 19, 2006, 4.
100 Trustee Minutes, May 13, 2005, 4.
101 President's Report, November 2009.
102 Barbara Scheffler, "College Honors Three Alumni," October 17, 2003, 11.
103 Stephanie Pitman, "Sherry: Breakfast of Champions," December 7, 2012, 1.
104 Freeman, "Strategic Assessment," 29.
105 Sarah Fuhrey, "Chairman Eager to Engage Students," September 12, 2003, 7.
106 "J. Paul Sticht Directs Board," *Grove City College Alumni Magazine*, Winter 1999, 5–6.
107 2008 Middle States Report, 9 (first quotation), 10 (second and third quotations), 7 (fourth quotation).
108 Breanna Renkin, "President Reflects," October 8, 2013, 6.
109 2008 Middle States Report, 11.
110 Interview with Jewell.
111 "Grove City Is Remarkable," *Allied News*, July 30, 2014, A-4.
112 Note to the author, April 22, 2025.
113 Josh Evans, "Jewell to Retire," September 6, 2013, 1–2.

The Presidency of Paul J. McNulty "The Pursuit of Excellence for the Glory of Christ," 2014–2025

1 Recognition Convocation, April 23, 2025.
2 Phone interview with the author, January 15, 2025.

3 "Alumnus Paul J. McNulty '80 Named College's Ninth President," GCC, May 16, 2014, https://www.gcc.edu/Home/Campus-Calendar/Event/alumnus-paul-j-mcnulty-named-colleges-ninth-president.
4 Email to the author, June 24, 2025.
5 President's Report, November 14, 2014.
6 Scott Alford, "D.C. to GCC," September 7, 2014, 1, 3; quotation from 3.
7 Grove City Board of Trustees, "A Resolution of Prayer for Paul J. McNulty," September 2014, Trustee Minutes, Appendix A.
8 Grayson Quay, "Freedom's Future," February 20, 2015, 1.
9 "McNulty Memo," February 20, 2015, 9.
10 "McNulty Memo." September 30, 2016, 11.
11 "Vision, Mission & Values," https://www.gcc.edu/Home/Our-Story/Faith-Freedom/Vision-Mission-Values.
12 The Evaluation Team Representing the Middle States Commission on Higher Education, Team Report to the Commission on Higher Education, April 2018.
13 "McNulty Memo," August 31, 2018, 2.
14 Team Report, 9.
15 David Zimmermann, "New Strategic Plan," February 4, 2022, 1.
16 "Vision, Mission & Values."
17 "Faith and Purpose," https://www.gcc.edu/Home/Faith-Purpose.
18 "Vision, Mission & Values."
19 Clark Mummau, "Grove City Welcomes All," September 2, 2022, 7.
20 Laura Hamilton, "When Did We Get Conservative?" April 23, 2021, 5.
21 Joe Seyton, "Remembering MacKenzie," February 3, 2017, 1 (McNulty and Rathburn quotations), 2 (Bibza quotation).
22 Aly Kruger, "One Last Lap," September 22, 2017, 1.
23 "Beloved Alumna Passes Away," February 26, 2021, 1.
24 David Zimmermann, "Morledge Leaves Behind Legacy," September 30, 2022, 1.
25 "Remembering Rathburn," February 9, 2024, 1.
26 Melanie Hanson, "College Enrollment & Student Demographic Statistics," EducationData.org, December 21, 2024, https://educationdata.org/college-enrollment-statistics.
27 Caleb Harshberger, "Apps Are Up," April 28, 2017, 1.
28 Violet Whitmore, "Class of 2026," August 26, 2022, 5.
29 Emily Fox, "Freshmen Finish First Week," August 30, 2024, 3, 6.
30 Lyss Welding, "College Graduation Rates," BestColleges, March 4, 2024, https://www.bestcolleges.com/research/college-graduation-rates/.
31 Team Report, 20.
32 Molly Wicker, "College Makes Amends," October 31, 2015, 1.
33 Team Report, 10.

34 Connor Schlosser, "Farewell to Fitwell," August 30, 2019, 1, 6 (Jeff Buxton quotation).
35 "Nursing Program," October 29, 2021, 3.
36 "E+I Fellows Program," August 29, 2024, GCC, https://www.gcc.edu/Home/Staff-Directory/Staff-Detail/area-nonprofits-startups-to-benefit-from-ei-fellows-program.
37 James Sutherland, "Looking for a Mix," September 7, 2018, 1.
38 Peter Frank, "Learning for Freedom's Sake, Part 1: The Liberal (Liberating) Arts," The Institute for Faith and Freedom, January 11, 2023, https://www.faithandfreedom.com/learning-for-freedoms-sake-part-1-the-liberal-liberating-arts-at-grove-city-college/.
39 Frank, "Learning for Freedom's Sake, Part 2: 'Freedom From' vs. 'Freedom To,'" The Institute for Faith and Freedom, January 23, 2023, https://www.faithandfreedom.com/learning-for-freedoms-sake-pt-2-freedom-from-vs-freedom-to/.
40 Jennifer Schuessler, "Should a 'Diverse' Campus Mean More Conservatives?" *The New York Times*, September 14, 2024, https://www.nytimes.com/2024/09/14/arts/viewpoint-diversity-universities-conservatives.html?. See also Michael Roth, "The Opening of the Liberal Mind," *The Wall Street Journal*, May 11, 2017; John Shields and Joshua Dunn, *Passing on the Right: Conservative Professors in the Progressive University* (New York: Oxford University Press, 2016); Virginia Foxx, "The Left's Thought Police Are Destroying America's Colleges," *The Washington Examiner*, September 25, 2023, https://www.washingtonexaminer.com/opinion/beltway-confidential/2743184/the-lefts-thought-police-are-destroying-americas-colleges/; Neil Gross, *Why Are Professors Liberal and Why Do Conservatives Care?* (Cambridge, MA: Harvard University Press, 2013); Jonathan Haidt and Greg Lukianoff, *The Coddling of the American Mind* (New York: Penguin Press, 2018).
41 Jon Shields, "The Disappearing Conservative Professor," *National Affairs*, Fall 2018, https://nationalaffairs.com/publications/detail/the-disappearing-conservative-professor.
42 Team Report, 7.
43 E.g., Emma Vetter, "Grove City Alums Reminisce," October 3, 2014, 5; Zimmermann, "New Strategic Plan," 2; Noel Elvin, "Seniors Reflect," April 29, 2022, 6.
44 Team Report, 9.
45 Paige Fay, "Frank-ly Speaking," January 30, 2021, 1, 2 (quotation).
46 Liesl McClintock, "Bridge of Faith," March 27, 2015, 4.
47 Kengor, as quoted in Dom Puglisi, "Kengor's Reagan," August 40, 2024, 8. See also "Perseverance Pays Off for Professor Behind 'Reagan' Biopic," GCC, July 10, 2024, https://www.gcc.edu/Home/News-Archive/News-Article/perseverance-pays-off-for-professor-behind-reagan-biopic.
48 IFF newsletter, May 11, 2024.

49 Molly Wicker, "Grovers React to Pence Announcement," April 7, 2017; 1: Joe Setyon, "Veep to Address Class of 2017"; quotations in that order.
50 "Politics Over Christ," April 7, 2017, 9.
51 "In Defense of Pence," April 7, 2017, 9.
52 IFF newsletter, May 1, 2024.
53 E.g., Meagan VanTil, "Mandatory Chapel," September 19, 2014, 10.
54 "McNulty Memo," December 7, 2018, 2.
55 James Sutherland, "Find Your Calling," September 21, 2018, 1.
56 Sarah Soltis and Noel Elvin, "Fall Chapel in Review," January 28, 2022, 5. See also Mummau, "Chapel Changes," February 4, 2022, 9.
57 "Parents' Perspective," GCC, November 25, 2017, https://blogs.gcc.edu/insider/2017/11/25/parents-perspective-grove-city-college-ivy-league-university/.
58 "Advice," December 5, 2020, 7.
59 "Defining Your Worth," September 15, 2023, 2.
60 Noel Elvin, "Missed the Oscars?" April 30, 2021, 1.
61 "First Week," September 2, 2022, 6.
62 Emily Fox, "Reflections on Calling," September 13, 2024, 2.
63 Team Report, 13.
64 Rio Arias, "GCC Dumps Pepsi," January 29, 2016, 4.
65 Emma Whiteford, "Squatters," September 2, 2022, 5.
66 Eleanor Lynn, "Grove City's Dating Culture," February 11, 2022, 8–9.
67 "Ring by Spring," September 15, 2017, 4.
68 "What Do You Advise?" GCC, April 24, 2017, https://blogs.gcc.edu/insider/2017/04/24/what-do-you-advise/.
69 "College Rules," February 13, 2015, 9.
70 "Freedom's College," February 13, 2015, 9.
71 "Grove City Rules," February 7, 2020, 8.
72 "Rules Are Good for Community," February 7, 2020, 8.
73 Justine Simon, "Around the World," October 7, 2016, 3.
74 "LGBTQ Challenge Colleges," April 8, 2016, 1.
75 "Christian Response to LGBT," April 15, 2016, 1.
76 Kelleigh Huber, "The Table," March 24, 2017, 4.
77 Mason Bennet, "Love Is Not Love," March 22, 2024, 8; Abigail Kengor, "Hate the Sin, Love the Sinner," May 5, 2024, 9.
78 Violet Whitmore, "Pro-life View," April 12, 2024, 1.
79 "Character Under Pressure," April 12, 2019, 2.
80 "Faculty Spotlight: Dr. Mobley," GCC, October 2, 2017, https://blogs.gcc.edu/insider/2017/10/02/faculty-spotlight-dr-mobley/.
81 "Campus Stays Closed," April 3, 2020, 2.
82 Fiona Lacey, "Together Apart," April 18, 2020, 2.
83 McNulty interview.
84 "A Method to the Mask-ness," August 28, 2020, 1.
85 Susannah Barnes, "Protect the Grove," September 4, 2020, 8.

86 Shelbi Henkle, "Pandemic Semester in Review," December 5, 2020, 6.
87 "Three Weeks in," February 12, 2021, 3.
88 Liona Fay, "To Vax or Not to Vax," April 9, 2021, 5.
89 David Zimmermann, "2020 Hurt Mental Health," April 30, 2021, 3.
90 Annalese Aderholt, "College Seeks to Return to Normal," September 3, 2021, 1 (first quotation); David Zimmermann, "Embracing the New Normal," ibid., 2 (second quotation); Ben Seevers, "Don't Panic," ibid., 8.
91 Huber, "Debate Team Finishes Strong," December 5, 2014, 2.
92 Nick Grasso, "Debate Team," December 2, 2022, 2.
93 "College Debate Team Captures National Championship," GCC, March 20, 2023, https://www.gcc.edu/Home/News-Archive/News-Article/college-debate-team-captures-national-championship.
94 Julian Anderson, "Swan Song," April 27, 2015, 4.
95 Jonathan Fisher, "An Entertaining Evening," March 14, 2017, 6; "Brigadoon," December 7, 2018, 1.
96 "Miracle on Stage," March 19, 2021, 7.
97 Emily Fox, "Fall Musical," November 4, 2022, 1.
98 Mia Gallagher, "Cast Slays on Stage," March 2024, 1.
99 Michelle Jeffries, "Great Day for Band," May 4, 2018, 5.
100 Ayden Gutierrez, "Concert Features Aria/Concerto Winners," February 11, 2022, 5.
101 Haley Steele, "WBN Goes Digital," March 11, 2022, 1.
102 Joshua Delk, "Grove City and Donald Trump," September 7, 2017, 1–2; Huber, "Palin Endorses Trump," February 5, 2016, 3; Gary Scott Smith, "Why the Devil Are Evangelicals Backing Trump?" *Newsweek*, January 13, 2016; Tucker Sigourney, "Life for a Pro-Lifer," April 8, 2016, 10.
103 Grant Wishard, "One Chance to Reject Trump," September 9, 2016, 9.
104 "Colin Combs, "Could Clinton Turn Texas Blue?" September 16, 2016, 10.
105 Molly Wicker, "Down with the Donald," November 4, 2016, 1.
106 Rio Arias, "President Falls Short," February 9, 2018, 10. See also "Character Counts," February 2, 2018, 6.
107 Joshua Sikora, "Trump's Best Falls Flat," February 15, 2019, 2.
108 David Zimmermann, and Anna DiStefano, "Two Sides, Little Moderation," October 2, 2020, 1, 5; Chris Murphy, "It's No Debate," ibid., 9.
109 "Is Anyone Surprised?" October 30, 2020, 1.
110 Aaron Riggleman, "Give Him Another Chance," October 30, 2020, 10; Rebekah Scharfenkamp, "He Deserves a Promotion," ibid., 11; Benjamin Seevers, "Vote Third," ibid., 10.
111 Isaac Willour, "Board Chair Discusses CRT," April 29, 2022, 3.
112 "Trump Is GCC Pick," October 25, 2024, 1, 3.

113 Breanna Renkin, "Alpha, Beta, Gamma, Who?" November 6, 2015, 1.
114 "Incoming Freshman Swimmer Is Paralympics Contender," GCC, August 12, 2021, https://www.gcc.edu/Home/Student-Alumni-Stories-template/Student-Detail/incoming-freshman-swimmer-is-paralympics-contender.
115 Emma Whiteford, "Glorifying God Through Her Disability," October 29, 2021, 4.
116 Mallory Trumball, "Lexie Arkwright," March 23, 2018, 12.
117 Lily Riale, "Water Polo Victorious," March 23, 2018, 11.
118 Emily Rupczewski, "Volleyball Plays for an 'Audience of One,'" October 4, 2019, 16.
119 "Just Keep Swimming," November 6, 2020, 12.
120 Mia Gallagher, "Top of the PAC," March 21, 2025, 12.
121 Moriah Williamson, "Melissa Lamie," September 11, 2015, 11.
122 "McNulty Memo," October 4, 2019, 5.
123 Tim Hanna, "Behind the Scenes," September 16, 2016, 12.
124 "McNulty Memo," September 3, 2021, 3.
125 Ayden Gutierrez, "We Want Willie," September 2, 2022, 3.
126 September 1, 2023, 12.
127 "COVID Can't Kill Culture," December 5, 2020, 8.
128 Adam Young, "Blake Baer," October 27, 2017, 12.
129 "Wolverine Den," September 7, 2018, 12.
130 Ethan Paszko, "Looking Strong," April 15, 2016, 11. As of this date, the tennis team had won the PAC 25 consecutive years and had an all-time overall record of 629–310 (.670).
131 Emily Rupczewski, "Fall Sports Scratched," September 4, 2020, 11.
132 Ayden Gutierrez, "Aren't for the Boys," September 18, 2020, 12.
133 Emma Rossi, "Tradition of Excellence," September 30, 2022, 15 (quotation), 16.
134 "Wolverines, Together," GCC, June 15, 2022, https://www.gcc.edu/Home/News-Archive/News-Article/wolverines-together-see-a-year-of-success-in-sports.
135 Adyen Gutierrez, "Opportunities Abound," September 1, 2023, 2.
136 "Grove City College Center Will Bear Retiring President's Name," *Business Journal*, May 9, 2025, https://businessjournaldaily.com/grove-city-college-center-will-bear-retiring-presidents-name/.
137 Anna DiStefano, "Finding Community," September 6, 2019, 4.
138 David Zimmermann, "Task Force to Address Diversity," August 28, 2020, 1, 3.
139 Adam Harris, "The GOP's 'Critical Race Theory' Obsession," *The Atlantic*, October 7, 2021, https://www.theatlantic.com/politics/archive/2021/05/gops-critical-race-theory-fixation-explained/618828/.
140 "Save GCC from CRT," Petitions.com, November 10, 2021, https://www.petitions.net/save_gcc_from_crt.

141 Paul McNulty, "A Response to the CRT Petition," GCC, November 18, 2021, https://www.gcc.edu/Home/Our-Story/Leadership-Teams/Office-of-the-President/A-Response-to-the-CRT-Petition.
142 "Statement from the Grove City College Board of Trustees," GCC, February 16, 2022, https://www.gcc.edu/Home/Our-Story/Leadership-Teams/Office-of-the-President/A-Response-to-the-CRT-Petition.
143 "Faculty Address Letter Claims," February 18, 2022, 9.
144 Nick Grasso, "Another CRT Petition," March 18, 2022, 1.
145 Report and Recommendation of the Special Committee, Grove City College Board of Trustees, April 13, 2022, 5, https://www.gcc.edu/Portals/0/Special-Committee-Report-and-Recommendation_0422.pdf.
146 Report and Recommendation, 9.
147 Report and Recommendation, 11.
148 David Zimmermann, "Tisby Talks Colors of Compromise," October 23, 2020, 1.
149 Report and Recommendation, 12.
150 Report and Recommendation, 13–14, 16; first four quotations from 13, fifth from 14, sixth from 16.
151 Brad Littlejohn, "Are Universities Really the Enemy?" *WORLD*, February 14, 2022, https://wng.org/opinions/are-universities-really-the-enemy-1644583570.
152 Kathryn Post, "Grove City College Caught in Crossfire of Evangelical CRT Battles," March 11, 2022, https://religionnews.com/2022/03/11/faculty-students-alumni-push-back-after-grove-city-college-rejects-critical-race-theory/. This article provides the best background on the controversy at Grove City.
153 Isaac Willour, "Grove City College's Supposed 'Wokeness,'" *National Review*, January 14, 2022, https://www.nationalreview.com/2022/01/grove-city-colleges-supposed-wokeness/.
154 "On Critical Race Theory and Intersectionality," SBC, June 1, 2019, https://www.sbc.net/resource-library/resolutions/on-critical-race-theory-and-intersectionality/.
155 David French, "How the Fight Over Critical Race Theory Became a Religious War," The Dispatch, April 10, 2022, https://thedispatch.com/newsletter/frenchpress/how-the-fight-over-critical-race/.
156 French, "Religious War."
157 "CRT Report Recommendations," February 23, 2023, 1.
158 Phone interview.
159 Molly Wicker, "Grove City Tops Rankings Lists," September 9, 2016, 2.
160 Wicker, "Wall St. Journal Ignores GCC," October 7, 2016, 2.
161 Adyen Gutierrez, "Liberal Arts Live On," November 11, 2022, 1.
162 "Princeton Review Recognizes GCC," GCC, August 27, 2024, https://www.gcc.edu/Home/News-Archive/News-Article/princeton-review-recognizes-gcc-in-best-colleges-guide.

163 Emily Bartlow, "Project Wolverine," September 18, 2014, 1.
164 Wicker, "2015 Graduates Get Jobs," January 29, 2016, 1.
165 Wicker, "College Raised $95 Mil.," September 4, 2015, 1.
166 "Grove City College Campaign Raises $95 Million, Surpasses Goal," GCC, August 21, 2015, https://www.gcc.edu/Home/Staff-Directory/Staff-Detail/grove-city-college-campaign-raises-95-million-surpasses-goal.
167 "College Fundraising Shatters Record, Builds Momentum," GCC, July 30, 2024, https://www.gcc.edu/Home/Academics/Faculty-Directory/Faculty-Detail/college-fundraising-shatters-record-builds-momentum.
168 "Honor Roll of Giving, 2023–2024," *GēDUNK Magazine*, December 2024, 36.
169 Rachel Smith, "10 Reasons I Am Grateful to Be a Grover," GCC, December 14, 2017, https://blogs.gcc.edu/insider/2017/12/14/10-reasons-grateful-grover/.
170 "Holiday Greeting from Ed Breen '78," GCC, December 8, 2022, https://www.gcc.edu/Home/Our-Story/Leadership-Teams/Board-of-Trustees/Greeting-from-the-Board-Chairman.
171 "School of Business to Bear Winklevoss Name," GCC, September 17, 2024, https://www.gcc.edu/Home/News-Archive/News-Article/school-of-business-to-bear-winklevoss-name.
172 David Zimmermann, "Rathburn Distinguished," October 2, 2020, 3.
173 Nick Douglas, "Grove City Roots Took Him to the Top," May 1, 2004, 4.
174 "President McNulty Announces Retirement Plan," GCC, August 6, 2024, https://www.gcc.edu/Home/News-Archive/News-Article/president-mcnulty-announces-retirement-plan.
175 "Retirement Plan"; John Wisley, *Religious Freedom: A Conservative Primer* (Grand Rapids: Eerdmans, 2025) is a good overview of the conservative political tradition, with an emphasis on limited government, constitutional safeguards, and traditional moral norms, which Grove City staunchly supports.
176 Phone interview.
177 Phone interview.

Epilogue

1 See Richard Hughes and William Adrian, *Models for Christian Higher Education* (Grand Rapids: Eerdmans, 1997), which provides case studies of fourteen colleges and universities that are first-rate academic institutions and have strong religious commitments.
2 "Committee Established, Firm Hired to Find New President," GCC, October 3, 2024, https://www.gcc.edu/Home/Staff-Directory/Staff-Detail/committee-established-firm-hired-to-find-new-president.

3 “Introducing the Next President of Grove City College,” GCC, https://www.gcc.edu/Introducing-the-Next-President-of-Grove-City-College#:~:text=Grove%20City%20College%20has%20announced,00%20as%20its%2010th%20president.
4 Emma Rossi, “New President Picked,” March 21, 2025, 1.
5 Megan Swift, ‘Grove City College Names Its 10th President,” *Trib Live*, March 17, 2025, https://triblive.com/local/regional/grove-city-college-names-its-10th-president/#:~:text=Bradley%20J.,the%202024%2D25%20academic%20year.
6 “Next President.”
7 “Interview with the Author—John W. Hawthorne,” EerdWord, February 13, 2025, https://eerdword.com/author-interview-john-hawthorne/.
8 Ryan Burge, as cited in Jessica Grose, “The Share of Religious Americans Will Continue to Decline,” *The New York Times*, March 12, 2025, https://www.nytimes.com/2025/03/12/opinion/decline-religion-america.html. See also Ryan Burge, *The Nones: Where They Came From, Who They Are, and Where They Are Going* (Philadelphia: Fortress Press, 2021); Bunge, *The American Religious Landscape: Facts, Trends, and the Future* (New York: Oxford University Press, 2025).
9 Grose, “The Share of Religious Americans.” The quotation is from Christian Smith, author of *Why Religion Went Obsolete: The Demise of Traditional Faith in America* (New York: Oxford University Press, 2025).
10 John Hawthorne, The *Fearless Christian University* (Grand Rapids: Eerdmans, 2025).
11 Excerpt from chapter one at https://www.amazon.com/-/es/Fearless-Christian-University-John-Hawthorne/dp/0802884563.
12 “Interview with the Author—John W. Hawthorne.”
13 Telephone interview with the author, March 20, 2025.
14 Telephone interview with the author, January 15, 2025.
15 Email to the author, May 13, 2025.
16 Brad Lingo, “The Cost of Independence,” *WORLD*, May 5, 2025, https://wng.org/opinions/the-cost-of-independence-1745549651.
17 Rossi, “New President,” 6.

Appendix

1 “Alumni Notes,” April 10, 1915, 3; “Penn State All-Sports Museum, Nittany Lion Club to hold Levi Lamb Day on July 18,” PennState, July 18, 2018, https://www.psu.edu/news/athletics/story/penn-state-all-sports-museum-nittany-lion-club-hold-levi-lamb-day-july-18; “Levi Lamb Fund,” PennState, https://gopsusports.com/levi-lamb-fund.
2 1916 *Ouija*, 71; 1915 *Ouija* 70 (quotation).
3 Supplement to the President’s Report of June 14, 1946, 18.

4 Donn Drake, "Keeping in Step," September 25, 1947, 3.
5 Trustee Minutes, June 9, 1950, 418.
6 Dedication of Calderwood Hall program, October 26, 1958.
7 Ruth Harker Mills, "Alva John Calderwood," at Calderwood Hall dedication, October 26, 1958.
8 Bill Weil, "Tepee Talk," May 12, 1949, 2.
9 "Three Professors to Retire," March 27, 1957, 1–2.
10 J. Stanley Harker, "Tribute to Our Dean," May 15, 1957, 2.
11 Judy Etzel, "Oil City Aces," Oil Region Libraries, November 5, 2021, https://oilregionlibraries.org/oil-city-aces/; "George C. Carpenter," American Air Museum in Britain, https://www.americanairmuseum.com/archive/person/george-c-carpenter; "George Junior Carpenter," Hall of Valor, https://valor.militarytimes.com/recipient/recipient-359708/; Hilary Walczak, November 2022 GeMail.
12 See "The Work Must Continue," May 16, 1969, 2.
13 All other quotations are from an interview with the author, July 8, 2024.
14 Much of the information and the quotation are from an interview with the author on June 24, 2024.
15 Pete Mollica, *New Castle News*, 1969.
16 Much of the information in this profile comes from a July 18, 2024 interview.